JOINING THE CLUB

July 6, 2001

For Tzvi,

With appreciation from
Congregation B'nai Jacob
on the occasion of your speaking
in the Summer Series.

Fondly,

Dan Oren

JOINING THE CLUB

A History of Jews and Yale

Second Edition

Dan A. Oren

Yale University Press

New Haven and London

Published with assistance from the Mary Cady Tew Memorial Fund.

Set in Garamond and Stone Sans types by The Composing Room of Michigan, Inc. Printed in the United States of America.

Library of Congress Cataloging-in-Publication Data

Oren, Dan A., 1958–
    Joining the club : a history of Jews and Yale / Dan A. Oren. — 2nd ed.
        p.   cm.
    Includes bibliographical references and index.
    ISBN 0-300-08468-4 (cloth : alk. paper)
        1. Yale University—Students—History.   2. Jewish college students—
    Connecticut—New Haven—History.   3. Jewish college teachers— Connecti-
    cut—New Haven—History.   4. Discrimination in education— Connecticut—
    New Haven.   5. Jews—Education—Connecticut—New Haven—History.
    6. Jews—United States—Intellectual life.   I. Title.
    LD6343 .O74 2001
    378.1'9829'924—dc21   00-049542

The paper in this book meets the guidelines for permanence and durability of the Committee on Production Guidelines for Book Longevity of the Council on Library Resources.

10 9 8 7 6 5 4 3 2 1

In memory of A. Bartlett Giamatti

There are hundreds of stories and plots of the strange old days in New Haven for you, . . . in books in the city and Yale libraries. When the Wanderlust sends you in fancy to Paris or India, take a yet longer voyage in that terra incognita, New Haven!

H. Sinclair Lewis, "Editor's Table," The Yale Literary Magazine 71 (April 1906):288

Contents

Illustrations follow page 230

Illustrations

*Manuscripts and Archives, Yale University Library

A New Preface

Fifteen years after delivering the first edition of this book to Yale University Press, I submit this text as the University prepares for its Tercentennial. It is a struggle to attain the necessary goals of professional objectivity and detachment concerning the past two decades while writing about an institution that is one's own and in some cases about people whom I consider friends. It is a more daunting challenge to revise a history text that through its own writing inadvertently may have become part of the recent narrative as well. Equally problematic is the unavoidable dependence on fallible human impressions and oral history, each of which entails the risk of perpetuating the intrinsic distortions that time creates in people's perceptions of the past. Recollections are usually based on truth but are sometimes expressed in fantasy. In trying to address these problems, I have attempted whenever possible to present oral history that has been confirmed by other oral or, if possible, written sources. Where that is impossible, I hope that discretion has served fairly.

With a number of emendations and additions, the core material in this edition still stands as previously written. Where new data offer a critical nuance to a scene, in particular those depicting Morris Cohen and Corbey Court, I have revised the text and notes. With twenty years of hindsight it now becomes possible to consider more thoroughly the watershed events of 1980 and their outcomes that bring us to the present day.

Because this examination is a review of only selected parts of an institution, I ask the reader to appreciate that "Yale" is used as a many-faceted, shorthand expression in the text. In its full sense, "Yale" is a collection of buildings, individuals, groups, and traditions. In concrete terms, Yale includes dormitories, offices, residential colleges, halls, libraries, tombs, laboratories, auditoriums, gymnasiums, and tennis courts. In human terms, Yale includes students, counselors, professors, deans, administrators, coaches, cooks, laboratory technicians, plumbers, alumni, and Corporation fellows. In organizational terms, Yale includes departments, schools, boards, committees, teams, societies, and clubs. In spiritual terms, Yale includes patterns of behavior and thought that are seemingly (though sometimes not actually) ancient. I hope that the reader will understand that my use of the term often refers imprecisely to the parts and not to the whole. Yet the reader should also appreciate that each of Yale's parts has been inextricably bound up with the whole.

Some readers will consequently notice the absence of discussion of certain topics here. One such subject is the history of the staff of Yale (e.g., dining hall, physical plant, and office personnel). Though modern Yale can function only imperfectly in the absence of its blue- and white-collar employees, I have concentrated my research on the activities and careers of those members of the Yale community who have been most central to its educational mission: its students and its faculty. Other readers will expect more discussion regarding the influence of other universities upon Yale's growth. There is no question that national trends impact at Yale, and whenever the university fell sufficiently beyond the standard deviations of the nation's leading universities, Yale was bound to find its way to the norm. But the timing and actions that determined when Yale would lead and when it would follow are Yale's own particular thread in the broad tapestry of life. As part of the University Tercentennial, Yale University Press is releasing Gaddis Smith's new history of *Yale in the Twentieth Century.* It will provide critically important context with which to read this account.

One limitation of this work, as with other historical works, is the improper emphasis that is placed on events that may have seemed trivial at the time they occurred. In the context of this writing, which examines not just overt prejudice but also the more subtle attitudes of insensitivity, I hope the reader will be led to appreciate that what may have been insignificant events to some were vital matters to others.

Yet another difficulty was in defining a Jew. As a simple premise, I started with Sartre's concept of a Jew as someone whom others consider to be a Jew. This rule is neither firm nor all-inclusive, and the exceptions and problems inherent in it should be noticed. Under most circumstances, I considered the children of two "Jews" to be a Jew. I did not classify a child of a Jew and a non-Jew as a "Jew" unless he or she identified himself or herself as one, or unless I had evidence that contemporary college or university administrators considered him or her to be one. Because of the imprecise definition of a "Jew," the informal nature of Yale's past limits on Jews, and the different methods of determining the number of Jews at Yale, statistics mentioned may not always agree with one another or with other sources. Far more significant than the precise values of listed numbers are the general trends that changes in the numbers indicate.

Much of history is a tale of broad forces that sweep through time. An equally critical part is a story of human relationships that wrestle with each other and with those forces. I wish to emphasize that this text is not a history of Jews *at* Yale, though that is certainly part of its story. It is consciously a history of Jews *and* Yale. It was titled and remains *Joining The Club* to emphasize that it is a study of a societal relationship and ultimately a study of human relationships, many successful and some failed.

In addressing questions of prejudice, elitism, and the mission of a College and a University, the story of Jews and Yale is in some ways unique, but in more ways it is a focal point to consider broader questions that many groups and many institutions have faced. And a story that challenges us to confront the human tendency to judge too quickly that at times confounds us all.

The reader should note that, unless specified otherwise, whenever a parenthetical reference is made to the award of a degree—for example, Moses Simons (B.A. 1809)—that reference is to a Yale diploma.

Acknowledgments

Olive Schreiner's "The Hunter—The Story of an African Farm," tells of an unreachable great wild bird of "Truth" that sails in the blue. Once one has glimpsed the bird, he never rests again in its pursuit. Had I appreciated how difficult the quest would be, I might never have begun my search for the interrelated history of Jews and Yale. Like Schreiner's hunter, I have not completed my journey, but I do not doubt that the research may have brought me closer to "Truth." Fortunately, the effort has provided its own reward.

Several before me have traveled portions of the route that I took, each cutting away the steps that I climbed. Others lent their experience to help further the path. The bibliography lists the many whom I interviewed and with whom I corresponded in this research. Their assistance was crucial in the preparation of this work, and meeting and getting to know many of them made history come alive and made this work most enjoyable.

On a personal basis, I must first recognize the women in my life: my wife Jeanette Kuvin Oren, daughters Sarah and Amalyah, sister

Daphna, and my mother Rebeka. All made this updated edition possible in the giving ways that make them who they are.

Too many who first helped make this book possible have passed from the scene in the fifteen years since initial publication. My father, Gideon, wisely insisted I start typing this text on a Model III Radio Shack personal computer, before I or almost anyone had a clue of what word processors could do. Rabbi Richard J. Israel allowed me to build on the extensive historical detective work that he had begun. William and Miriam Horowitz took me under their wings and shared their affection and eternal youth. Professor Arthur J. Viseltear offered his storehouse of medical history with his characteristic decency and wisdom and was stripped of life far too soon. University Presidents Kingman Brewster, Jr., and A. Bartlett Giamatti graciously permitted me to interview them at length and in candor. Mr. Giamatti's generous encouragement beyond that point will always be a source of strength for me.

Archivists are unsung heroes of researchers. I remain particularly appreciative of the assistance of Judith A. Schiff, Patricia Bodak Stark, Gloria Locke, and William R. Massa, Jr. at the Sterling Memorial Library, who helped me so often to find my way through the voluminous Yale collections.

In addition, I thank the following people for their assistance at different points in the writing: Candace Bryce, Scott B. Cantor, Carl Carlson, Richard Claman, Julie H. Gale, Susan Hauser, Edith Hurwitz, James H. Hutson, Joanne Lipman, Rabbi Herbert G. Panitch, Lenny I. Picker, Jonathan D. Sarna, Ida Cohen Selavan, Judah Shechter, Bruce Stark, Harold Wechsler, John S. Whitehead, John A. Wilkinson, and Fannie Zelcer. Manuscript editors Michael Joyce and Ali Peterson were immensely helpful as well. I am also thankful for the supportive friendship of my classmates in the Morse College Class of 1979.

That this book appeared in the first place and now, in the second place, is especially due to the counsel of Charles Grench, former Executive Editor of Yale University Press. He and Abraham J. Peck of the American Jewish Archives stuck with this manuscript during the time when the text and its author were still immature, and saw it to publication when both had grown. Donald J. Cohen, currently the Sterling Professor of Child Psychiatry, played a central role in encouraging this updated edition. I am similarly appreciative of John Ryden and Tina Weiner, Director and Associate Director of Yale University Press, respectively, for their energetic institutional support. I wish to record my appreciation for the substantial support of this academic aspect of the University's Tercentennial celebration by Linda Koch Lorimer and Richard Levin, respectively the Vice President/Secretary and President of Yale today.

I owe a special debt to those who first taught me to appreciate the paradox that the more one knows, the more one knows how much more there is to be known. A Yale College course that Lloyd Gartner taught during the U.S. Bicentennial and my sophomore year was the stimulus for my first inquiry into the topic of this book. The late Sydney Ahlstrom, Rollin G. Osterweis, and Rabbi Arthur A. Chiel all provided invaluable further guidance. The personal kindness of Rabbis Arnold Jacob Wolf and James Ponet provided critical perspective and understanding.

Most especially in this context, I recall the late George Pierson, Larned Professor Emeritus of History and Historian of Yale University, and his painstaking efforts in reviewing early drafts of the first edition. For me to claim that we agreed on the interpretation of every issue that we discussed would be unfair to Mr. Pierson. Yet there is no doubt that if I made any progress in this search for "Truth," much of that progress was a result of his thoughtful criticism and his unwavering support. By virtue of birthright, upbringing, career, and conviction, he embodied three hundred years of Yale in so many ways. Because of who and what Mr. Pierson was, therefore, I had the privilege of learning not just from a teacher, but in some ways from the persona of Yale itself. That, too, is a part of this story. I am grateful for the many bits of good fortune that contributed to the completion of this work, but I am forever grateful to Providence for permitting me to have learned from and to have learned with George Pierson.

Introduction

The inaugural charter of Connecticut's "Collegiate School" assigned a
dual character to the education and the mission of the tiny Congregational seminary. By right of the Connecticut General Assembly's 1701
"Act for Liberty to Erect a Collegiate School," the college was to be an
institution "wherein Youth may be instructed in the Arts and Sciences
who through the blessing of Almighty God may be fitted for Publick
employment both in Church and Civil State."[1] In time the college
changed its name to Yale, expanded to become a university, and grew
to become one of the most prestigious educational enterprises in the
United States. In time it became a secular institution, but many of its
graduates continued to follow the pathways that the college's founders
had envisioned. George Pierson, university historian, noted the success of Yale graduates in his 1979 review of the institution's history:

> Second (at times only) to Harvard, it has seen more of its graduates earn
> public responsibility than any other college or university, produced more
> men of character and achievement, qualified more alumni for inclusion in
> *The Dictionary of American Biography* and *Who's Who in America,* and con-
> tributed to the leadership of the Protestant churches and the direction of

today's major philanthropic foundations. Seven per cent of all the major diplomatic officers of the United States since 1789 have been educated in New Haven; and each year since our national beginnings four senators (on the average) and eleven representatives in Congress have been sons of Yale.[2]

Beyond the realms mandated by charter, Yale became the top producer of executive talent for the business suites of the nation. In terms of academic leadership, Yale's various schools produced a disproportionate share of the nation's professors and university presidents.[3]

Over the same centuries, American Jews, descendants of the ancient Israelites commemorated by the Hebrew words on the Yale Seal (see appendix 1), grew in numbers to 3 percent of the American people, and achieved a status in American society far above the level indicated by their share of the population. By the 1970s, Jews at Yale University represented a substantial share of the university community and occupied a social position comparable to that of Jews in the society at large. For many years, however, the social status of Jews at Yale lagged behind the status of Jews on the American intellectual scene and behind their position at some of the other elite national institutions of higher education. In contradistinction to other ethnic and minority groups, Jews became an issue at Yale (and elsewhere) in the twentieth century because so many of them achieved intellectual success before they received social approval. In contrast to many other minorities, the cultural baggage of the Jews included a proclivity for learning. In the Yale setting, the gap between the intellectual achievement of Jews and their social acceptance was bound to generate tension. It was this conflict that often created a second-class status that, for a time, was apparent to most Jews who came in contact with the institution's ivy-covered walls.

Gradually, as Yale asserted the primacy of its scholastic goals over its social goals, this conflict was resolved. Though the process took years to implement, it crystallized in a 1948 report to the Yale president by William Clyde DeVane, dean of Yale College, who stated:

> The activities of our students—athletic, social, managerial, and commercial—are so attractive that they all but overwhelm the intellectual aspects of a college education at Yale. This is not surprising, perhaps, since Yale is a fairly faithful reflection of American life. There may be professors at Yale who live in ivory towers, but very few students inhabit those dim and quiet heights. But it surely is not enough for Yale to *reflect* the life of America. Our graduates must be critics and leaders, or else we are not justified as a university. What I want for Yale College is an intellectual eminence as great as her athletic or her social or her eminence in activities of all sorts. . . . I would have Yale turn out more leaders of the intellectual life of our country. For the

man of action we unquestionably provide a superb training—none better. For the man of intellectual achievement I am afraid that we are surpassed by Harvard, Columbia, and Chicago, in that order. . . .

The rewards which American society offers to brains are meagre. We have only to look about us to see that men of stupidity and grossness have a far better chance to obtain financial rewards than wiser and more modest men. There are, moreover, in our country very few devices for non-material rewards. In this, Yale is a perfect reflection of the country: the honors which the undergraduates bestow—and those are the ones which the undergraduates value—all seem to go to the athletes and the managers of affairs. . . . In any case, it should not be the function of Yale to reflect American life but to lead it. "If gold rust, what will iron do?"[4]

Though Dean DeVane did not direct this statement toward Jews, the issues that he raised are relevant to the story of the Jews at Yale in the first half of the twentieth century. How the university would perceive DeVane's questions as raising legitimate problems is largely the continuation of this same story. This essay will attempt to present the historical relationship of Jews and Yale—the institution that George Pierson has called "a tradition, a company of scholars, a society of friends."[5]

Part One **1701–1878**

Chapter 1 The Beginnings

The year was 1701. Scattered throughout the land, some one hundred Sephardic Jews (of Spanish or Portuguese ancestry) resided among a total population of one hundred thousand in the British Colonies of America. By 1750, Ashkenazi Jews (of Central or East European ancestry) were joining their co-religionists in the colonies on the order of a few dozen every year. A large proportion of these Ashkenazi Jews migrated from Europe via England. A few were farmers or cattlemen; others were craftsmen or merchants engaged in the triangular trade of rum, molasses, and slaves that fueled colonial development. The developing colonies generally granted Jewish immigrants civil, but not political, rights: In order to vote or hold political office, one had to be a member of the local established church.[1]

Ironically, Connecticut, one of the most "Hebraeophilic" of the colonies, was also one of the strictest in curtailing religious dissenters. Because Connecticut's Puritan founders saw themselves as successors to the ancient Hebrews, the early law of the colony was called the "Mosaic Code," and the early law of New Haven Colony (separate from Connecticut until 1662) was entitled "Moses his judicials." De-

spite the Puritans' past exposure to religious persecution, the first Puritan settlers were an intolerant group who desired religious liberty for themselves but
not for others. There was no "state" church, but until 1791 every Connecticut
resident was taxed to support the Congregational Church. Leniency began
with the "Certificate Law" of 1791, which excused any Christian who could give
evidence of supporting a non-Congregational church from paying the assessment. Then, when the new Connecticut Constitution was established in 1818,
all Christian churches were placed on an equal footing. The state laws, however, did not permit organization of any non-Christian religious society; nor
did they grant rights of residence to non-Christians. Quickly forgotten, the law
prohibiting non-Christians from possessing residential rights was not stricken
from the state constitution until 1965.[2]

Congregational Protestantism was at the core of tiny Yale College during its
first decades. To ensure the college's religious character, its trustees voted in
1722 to require the faculty to accept the tenets of Congregationalism before
taking office. Assent was indicated by recital of the ecclesiastical oath called the
"Saybrook Platform" (See appendix 1). Thomas Clap, defender of orthodox
Congregational Christianity and president of Yale (1740–66), emphasized that
knowledge of the arts and sciences was "comparatively worth but little" without religious understanding to support it. At the same time that Harvard College moved toward nonsectarianism, Clap moved Yale toward orthodoxy. In
1753 he led the Yale Corporation to require that its faculty, in addition to the
previous prescriptions, acquiesce to the stricter Westminster Catechism of
Faith and simultaneously renounce any contrary principles. The Corporation
further reserved the right to interrogate any faculty member suspected of deviation from the true faith and subject him to possible dismissal. Four years later
Yale established the first college church in America.[3]

The religious opinions of students were permitted to deviate more than those
of their teachers. No test of faith was asked of incoming students, and Protestants of all sorts were welcomed. In his 1766 history of the college, Clap wrote
of Yale's conditional enthusiasm toward students with non-Congregational religious beliefs: "It is not inconsistent with the general Design of the Founders,
and is agreeable to our own Inclinations, to admit Protestants of all Denominations to send their Children to receive the Advantage of an Education in this
College: Provided that while they are here, they conform to all the Laws and Orders of it."[4] When Episcopalians threatened to protest the legitimacy of the Yale
corporate charter, Clap thwarted the challenge to Yale's monopoly on Connecticut higher education by granting them the right to attend their own

church's Sunday services. Catholic and Jewish students would likely have been completely unwelcome in Clap's day. If Catholics represented the machinations of the Pope, the Jews represented even worse. Christian theology was predicated on the belief that the Israelites had gone astray and were condemned to suffer eternally for their sins. One of the major theology texts used at Yale taught that Jews, along with "Heathens" and "Mahumetans," were the "open foes" of the church: "The Jews deny the Trinity, and the coming of the Messiah, and interpret carnally, what is spoken of Christs Kingdome in the Prophets spiritually." Only conversion, the theologians believed, could save a Jew from his presumed fate.[5]

The religious climate of the college changed little during the tenure of Clap's successor, President (Pro Tempore) Naphtali Daggett (1766–77). Socially, however, Yale changed substantially. Daggett, an ardent champion of democracy at a time of national democratic fervor, abandoned the customary practice of ranking students in Yale classes according to their fathers' social positions. First rankings had gone to the sons of prominent citizens in church and state. Progeny of less illustrious college-educated men were placed in an intermediate position. Trailing the rosters were the sons of farmers, merchants, and artisans. Reacting to student dissatisfaction with the system, in 1767 Daggett began to list students by the more acceptable alphabetical ordering.[6]

THE FIRST KNOWN JEW AT YALE

Historians have commonly thought that the first Jews attended Yale during the Daggett administration. But, though the Pinto brothers—Abraham, Solomon, and William—were half Jewish, it seems that they were not Jews at all. Abraham, Solomon (B.A. 1777), and William (B.A. 1777) Pinto had all been born and raised in New Haven. Their paternal grandparents, Abraham and Sarah Pinto, are known to have been Jewish and to have been living in Stamford, Connecticut, in 1725. Jacob Pinto, the second son of Abraham and Sarah, was settled in New Haven by 1755. If he had not accepted the Christian faith before then, Jacob Pinto likely did so upon his arrival in the city, where he attached himself to the First Ecclesiastical Society, and in 1755 married Thankfull Peck of New Haven. Along with one in six American Jews who married before 1840, Pinto married outside his original faith. Both Thankfull and her sister Abigail, who married Jacob following Thankfull's death, were buried in the crypt of the Center Church on the New Haven Green. There is no evidence that any of the three sons of Jacob and Thankfull ever had any affiliation with Judaism.[7]

Under the administration of Ezra Stiles (1778–95), the college grew from what the historian Brooks Mather Kelley has called a "narrowly sectarian institution" into a center of learning where knowledge could be pursued for its own sake. A beacon of liberalism and tolerance in a bigoted and closed-minded era, Stiles was the guiding spirit of Connecticut's first antislavery society. He also displayed the rare ability to separate his attitudes toward a person from his attitudes toward that person's beliefs: "It has been a principle with me . . . to work and live in a decent, civil, and respectful communication with all; although in some of our sentiments in philosophy, religion, and politics, of diametrically opposite opinions. Hence, I can freely live, and converse in civil friendships, with Jews, Romanists, and all the sects of Protestants, and even with the Deists." Christians benefited from his tolerance when he modified the faculty oath of office so that almost any believing Christian could assent to the required wording. Though Stiles regretted that Aaron Lopez, a Jewish merchant from Newport, Rhode Island, never accepted the Christian faith, Stiles remained able to call Lopez "my intimate Friend." A deep fellowship between the inquisitive Stiles and Rabbi Haim Carigal, whom Stiles had met in Newport, stimulated Stiles's emphasis on Hebrew language study as part of the college curriculum.[8]

Following the death of Stiles in 1795, Yale came to be led by Timothy Dwight, a disciplinarian who hoped to return religious feeling and morality to a campus that had become racked with rowdiness and violence. The Dwight years were ones of growth for Yale, both in its physical facilities and in the size of its faculty. Dwight's most precedent-setting faculty appointment, perhaps, was that of Benjamin Silliman, who became professor of chemistry and natural history in 1802. Silliman spent his first two years as a professor studying chemistry and medicine, since he had never studied the subjects before. Silliman's subsequent excellence in teaching and his successful development of science at Yale were factors that established the wisdom of his appointment.

Dwight had chosen Silliman for two reasons. First, he feared pure scientists who studied only for the sake of study and saw science as an end in itself rather than as a means of demonstrating the glory of God's creations. Just as troubling to Dwight was the lack of American-born men properly trained in the sciences; he hesitated to depend upon a foreigner to help mold Yale. The stranger was to be feared, since "a foreigner, with his peculiar habits and prejudices, would not feel and act in union with us, and that however able he might be in point of science, he would not understand our college system, and might therefore not act in harmony with his colleagues."[9] The first priority in selecting a professor, then, was not scholarship but compatibility with the peculiarly American college system as practiced at Yale, where experience outside the classroom was considered as integral to learning as that inside. The spirit and learning evoked by a corps of young men constructively spending all of their time together were the essence of the American collegiate vision. Only an American, it was thought, would be able to appreciate such a philosophy. Consequently, at Yale, immigrants were not to be looked to as a source of professors for the college students.

Dwight's desire for uniformity among his faculty notwithstanding, it was during his administration that the first bona fide Jewish student is known to have attended and have been graduated from Yale. Little is known of Moses Simons (B.A. 1809). His grandfather was Isaac Simons, member of the Duke's Place Synagogue in London. His father, also called Moses Simons, was born in London and in 1783 was earning a living as a shopkeeper in Savannah, Georgia. From Jacksonboro, South Carolina, Simons (father) sent his son north to study at Yale in 1805. Simons (son) eventually studied law and practiced in New York City between 1816 and 1821. His obscure life ended in London in 1822.[10]

STATESMAN OF THE LOST CAUSE

The fact that seventeen years separated Moses Simons from Judah P. Benjamin, the next known Jew to have attended Yale, is not surprising. Even had Yale not had a Congregational character and not required semi-daily chapel services, few Jews would likely have attended Yale; prior to the 1840s America's Jews made up less than one-tenth of one percent of the population. (See appendix 2.) Nineteenth-century Yale students were permitted to be excused to attend Sabbath services at the local church of their choosing.[11] Since there was no Jewish community in New Haven as yet, excuse from Congregational service would not have been an option for any Jewish boy at Yale.

Judah P. Benjamin was born to English emigrants who, contrary to the American dream, found rags, not riches, in America. His father, Philip Benjamin, was active in Jewish life in Charleston, South Carolina, and, as a member of the Corresponding Committee of Charleston's "Reformed Society of Israelites," was active in the development of the first attempt at Reform Judaism in the United States. Outside of his education at the Fayetteville Academy and Charleston's St. Michael's Alley, young Benjamin received a basic training in the Hebrew language. A "confirmation" ceremony took place at age thirteen, and in 1825, at age fourteen, the boy was packed off (along with his Hebrew Psalter) to become the youngest member of the Yale class of 1829.[12]

Benjamin had a distinguished freshman and sophomore year record, each semester earning the highest marks in the class. During his first and fourth semesters his 3.3 average was the absolute highest in the class, and during his second and third semesters his 3.0 average was tied for highest in the class. To honor this scholastic excellence, college president Jeremiah Day presented him with a personally inscribed "Berkleian prize book." Socially he was just as successful. Tutor Simeon North reported that Benjamin had a "pleasing manner," that he was popular among the students, and that his scholastic attainment allowed him to be "regarded by his mates as an ornament to the class."[13] Interested in forensics, freshman Benjamin joined Brothers in Unity—one of Yale's two great debating clubs—during a year when the topics of discussion included "Ought Missouri to have been admitted into the Union with the privilege of holding slaves?" "Ought the United States take immediate measures for the manumission of the slaves of our Country?" and "Is it probable that our country will continue under its present form of government for a century?" At the onset of his sophomore year, he was "Hon[orably] dismissed" from the Brothers in Unity so that he could take a membership in the Southerner-dominated Calliopean society, where pro-slavery views were, doubtless, more popular. At the end of that sophomore year, however, in September 1827, Benjamin suddenly disappeared from the campus, leaving unpaid bills behind.[14]

The question of why Benjamin left Yale has long been a minor mystery. Speculations have been traded by gossipmongers, but few substantive theories have been offered. The detailed faculty record makes no mention of his having been expelled. Benjamin was likely being partially honest later in life when he attributed his departure from Yale to his father's financial difficulties. There is no doubt that his parents were in poor straits and that Benjamin did not have the money to continue with college after his sophomore year. However, what Benjamin apparently obscured was that he left Yale in brilliant notoriety, as well as brilliant poverty. He may have allowed himself to be caught up in the violence that was commonplace in his era at Yale. According to his "patron" and Yale tutor, Simeon North, Benjamin, who was prone to carry out collegiate pranks, "left College . . . without the knowledge or the permission of his friends & instructors—in a manner which justly exposed him to sensure [sic]." Whether he rang the college bells at midnight or left a cow in the president's house or indulged in some form of undergraduate skullduggery is unknown. In any case, he left with the admiration of his tutor and his classmates intact. His method of leaving was disruptive, but his fellow students cared enough for him that when they discovered that he was penniless and stranded in northern New York, they raised a collection to assist his return home to South Carolina. Nevertheless, the faculty may not have been so favorably disposed to the young boy. In January 1828 Benjamin felt compelled to write to President Day and apologize for his rude actions. Benjamin also thanked the president for the college's financial assistance in his time of hardship.[15]

Though he married a Catholic, Benjamin was the most prominent nineteenth-century American Jew. His election as United States senator in 1852 was the first ever achieved by a Jew. During a brief period as secretary of war for the Confederacy, Benjamin was subjected to many anti-Semitic attacks, inspired by military disasters that befell the South. Nevertheless, President Jefferson Davis retained his trust in Benjamin and appointed him secretary of state. (His work in that position won him the nicknames of the "Brains of the Confederacy" and "Statesman of the Lost Cause.") Following the war Benjamin escaped to England, where he had an even more distinguished career as a lawyer. Though Benjamin took no interest in Jewish affairs, he never denied his religious origin or converted to Christianity.[16] To the extent that one may fairly judge Benjamin by his noninvolvement with Judaism as an adult, it is likely that his religion was not a part of his school interests. In any case, Benjamin's religious background seems to have been completely irrelevant to his successes and failures at Yale.

FOUNDATION OF THE NEW HAVEN
JEWISH COMMUNITY

Many Jews from outside New Haven followed the southern-born Moses Simons and Judah P. Benjamin to Yale. Yet, for a century, the experience of Jews at Yale would be closely tied to the New Haven Jewish community, which itself had been slow to develop. Ezra Stiles noted the first Jews in the city in his *Itineraries* of September 13, 1772: "This summer past a family of Jews settled here, the first real Jews . . . that settled in New Haven. . . . This is the first Jewish worship in New Haven, A.D. 1772. . . . These Jews indeed worship in the Jewish manner; but they are not enough to constitute & become a synagogue."[17] Not until the 1840s, when a number of Jews, particularly from Bavaria, would come to the city, would an actual community form.

These Bavarian Jews were part of the first mass migration of Jews to the

United States. Spurred by a slump in European trade in 1836, they and many other Germans left a land that humiliated Jews financially and emotionally with discriminatory taxes and restrictions. In Bavaria the oppression extended to limiting the number of Jewish marriage contracts in order to restrain the growth of the Jewish population. Following suppression of the 1848 German revolution, many more German nationals grew disillusioned enough to depart for America; some 5 percent of them were Jewish. Along with the Germans came many Jews from the Austrian Empire who were not of German origin but spoke German and followed German cultural patterns.[18] This immigration peaked between 1850 and 1855, years of American prosperity and German depression. Between 1840 and 1860, the Jewish population in America jumped from fifteen thousand to one hundred fifty thousand, while the total population doubled. (See appendix 2.)

Most of the German immigrants found the land they had sought, and they began to establish homes and farms in America's back country. But the Jewish immigrants, who had been prohibited from owning land in the Old World, were unaccustomed to working the soil and consequently settled in the large cities along major trade routes. Few entered the traditional professions of that day: law, medicine, and the clergy. While many Jews brought ample training in crafts and trades to their new country, few chose those careers either. Instead, they saw the lucrative options available in peddling goods to the many settlers outside the large cities: they began to sell products made by others. Often the peddlers traveled the countryside for five days each week, returning home to restock and to celebrate the Sabbath. Those who advanced beyond the peddling stage became shopkeepers and merchants. Many of the great department stores of the twentieth century developed from stores founded by these immigrant Jewish peddlers.

Opposition to immigrants of most ethnicities was bitter in this era. The reasons for such hatred were varied. Protestant prejudice was aimed mostly at poor and uneducated Catholics, who were thought to be both displacing "native" Americans from jobs and weakening the religious fiber of America with their "Popery." That many of the immigrants became Jackson Democrats did not endear them to their established neighbors either. As more Americans met real Jews, biblical stereotypes of the Jew faded, and the medieval depiction of the Jew as an aggressive businessman reasserted itself. Nonetheless, because they were still relatively invisible in society in the mid-nineteenth century, German Jews seem not to have been the victims of significant discrimination. Some Jews, like some individual Catholics, rose to the top echelons of society.[19]

Blacks and Indians remained the sorriest victims of American indifference. In contrast to later generations of Jewish immigrants, the German Jews, arriving as part of a larger mass migration, at first considered themselves and were considered by other Germans to be a component of the German ethnic group. This intra-ethnic acceptance helped them to be accepted into society at large.

Religious intolerance (as opposed to racism) was the strongest prejudice that the Jewish immigrants to New Haven encountered after settling there in 1840. In 1843, when Connecticut law was amended to permit Jews the same rights to form religious societies as Christians enjoyed, fifteen Jewish families established Congregation Mishkan Israel—the first synagogue in Connecticut, the second in New England, and the fourteenth in the nation. New Haven's local newspaper, *The Columbian Register,* reported the event with dismay:

> Whilst we have been busy converting the Jews in other lands, they have out-flanked us here, and effected a footing in the very centre of our own fortress.—Strange as it may sound, it is nevertheless true, that a Jewish Synagogue had been established in this city—and their place of worship . . . was dedicated on Friday afternoon. Yale College divinity deserves a court-martial for bad generalship.[20]

For Jews who would attend Yale, this news was significant. They would have co-religionists in town. From 1843 onward, both New Haven and Yale would have to deal with Jews on a continuing basis and vice versa.

From this early New Haven Jewish community came the first known Jew to teach at Yale: Sigmund Waterman, instructor in German from 1844 to 1847. He was also the first Jewish doctor to graduate from Yale, receiving his M.D. in 1848. Waterman had emigrated from Bavaria to New Haven in 1841 and established himself as a merchant. Together with his brother Leopold, the first president of Congregation Mishkan Israel, Waterman helped lead New Haven Jewry. A chance meeting with a Yale professor led to his employment as a German instructor, and he became one of several local immigrants who were given faculty titles and hired directly by the students to tutor on a fee-for-service basis.[21] The German language, Waterman's specialty, was necessary for students of the new sciences that men like Benjamin Silliman had brought to America. The hiring of a Jew did not compromise the college's religious policies, since the centrality of faith that had once guided the college had already been tempered by the advance of modernity. In keeping with the growing tolerance, perhaps in an attempt to forestall the foundation of Episcopally oriented Washington (later Trinity) College or in an attempt to attract the interests of a broad-minded donor, the once-mandatory oath of religious faith had already been dropped by the Yale Corporation in 1823. While Waterman was teaching German, he became interested in medicine and began to study in the medical department of the college.[22] Within a year of his employment, Waterman brought his Jewish interests to bear upon Yale, arranging for the first lecture by a rabbi before a Yale audience. On December 19, 1845, at a talk attended by the mayor of New Haven and several of the college professors, Rabbi Samuel M. Isaacs, editor of the *Jewish Messenger,* spoke "On the Present Condition and the Future Spiritual and Temporal Hopes of the Jews." Following his graduation Waterman settled in New York, where he was well regarded as a professor of medicine and as one of the early presidents of B'nai B'rith, the national Jewish fraternal service organization.[23]

Shortly after Waterman received his degree in 1848, Henry Jacob Labatt, the next known Jew to study at Yale, entered with the college class of 1852, though he was not graduated with his class. Labatt identified himself with other Jewish students at Yale, as evidenced by a letter that he wrote to Philadelphia's Rabbi Isaac Leeser in 1849. Labatt hoped to peddle some of Leeser's books to some of the "theological & Hebrew students" on the campus. A student at Yale in an era when the college faculty was struggling to protect the religious atmosphere of the college, Labatt left Yale before his graduation, but there is no evidence that his leaving was anything but voluntary or cordial. As long as a nonbelieving student did not try to sway other students from their commitment to Protestantism, the Yale faculty did not take punitive action. When the University of Louisiana granted Labatt a law degree in 1865, Yale reciprocated by granting him an honorary master's degree. Two decades later, Labatt asked for a more substantial attachment to Yale College and his former classmates. The college dutifully added his name to their roster of 1852 graduates.[24]

TIME OF EQUALITY, SEEDS OF DIVISION

The discrimination against Jews that would later infest social life at Yale was apparently nonexistent through the 1870s. *The Yale Literary Magazine,* the major campus publication of the era, recognized the open atmosphere in 1857: "It matters not what one *has* been or *has* done, before he entered College. His standing here is gained by what he *does,* and what he *is,* in College."[25] Social acceptance was not yet predicated upon a person's religion. The acceptance Jews found in society at large was matched by their comfortable position at Yale. With the continuation of German Jewish migration, Jews came to be regularly represented among the undergraduates in Yale's liberal arts "College" or its more technically oriented "Sheffield Scientific School." These Jews, like American Jews in general, constituted too small a group to be noticed. They had occuped a middle-class position for many years and offered no target for jealousy because of either their numbers or their achievements.[26]

Those Jewish students who chose extracurricular involvement were full participants in college life. Siegwart Spier (B.A. 1866), for example, had emigrated alone to the United States from Rotenburg, Germany, at the age of thirteen. He entered Yale College at age eighteen, became a member of the Brothers in Unity debating society and the freshman Gamma Nu fraternity, and won election to Phi Beta Kappa. His greatest extracurricular involvement was with the singing groups that were already a popular institution at the college. Spier directed the Beethoven Society and was responsible for bringing some of Yale's disparate class glee clubs together to form the University Glee Club.[27]

Not every Yale student, however, was a socialite. Through the eyes of Lewis Ehrich (B.A. 1869), the seeds of the social difficulties that would sprout decades later are visible. Ehrich's vision is apparent in the pages of his college diary— the earliest known journal of an American Jewish college student.[28] Ehrich was not representative of every Jew at Yale, but a substantial number of Yale Jews would later hold educational values similar to Ehrich's—values at odds with prevailing undergraduate sentiment—resulting in cultural conflict.

An American-born product of New Haven, Ehrich was filled with pride for his country and his religion. When Washington's Birthday was observed at Yale with the cancellation of classes but without any celebration or formal ceremony, Ehrich lamented the death of American patriotism. Christian Yale encouraged Ehrich's Jewish identity by excusing him from Sunday prayers on the condition that he attend Saturday service at a local synagogue—which Ehrich did, except when he had too much school work. Attendance at the quotidian college chapel was mandatory, though it was much less a religious service than an opportunity to bring the college together once a day. Ehrich observed major Jewish holidays, though sometimes in rebellious ways. On the fast day of Yom Kippur he attended synagogue and then at lunchtime went "to Hoadley's and partook of a good dinner." In an era when American Reform Judaism was taking shape through a modernization of synagogue worship and a removal of theological and lifestyle differences between Jews and Christians, Ehrich's defiant behavior was typical. Ehrich's religious philosophies were radical, but his religious identity was strong. In the wake of General Ulysses S. Grant's Civil War expulsion of Jewish traders from the front lines (later rescinded by President Lincoln), Ehrich, like many other Jews, had no confidence in the only man to implement overt anti-Jewish feeling into national policy: "As a Jew I cannot re-spect Grant. My nation is too dear to me, to allow me to respect one who in-jured it."[29] Ehrich could not, therefore, support Grant's 1868 presidential bid.

Harmless in Ehrich's own day, but ominous for the future record of Jews and Yale, were Ehrich's attitudes toward Yale organizational life. As a freshman he participated as a member of the Linonia debating society and as secretary of the freshman fraternity Kappa Sigma Epsilon. Because he lived in New Haven with his aunt and uncle, most of Ehrich's social activities revolved around the New Haven Jewish community. At the time it was not unusual for Christian or Jew-ish college students to socialize and meet young women within the framework of their local religious community. When Ehrich and two friends—Morris Goodhart (LL.B. 1867) and Nathan C. Myers—wrote to a national Jewish pe-riodical in 1866 to suggest the creation of a nationwide fraternity of "Israelitish" young people to promote the welfare of young Jewish men in America, there was no issue of undemocratic religious bias. Jews were able to join Christian fraternities if they were interested. If they wanted a society with Jewish over-tones, they were free to form their own. At a time when campus life was open, a Jewish fraternity was no issue. In later decades, however, when prejudicial feelings erupted among the Yale undergraduates, the need for Jews and Chris-tians to have their own separatist communities would leave campus prestige forbidden for Jews.[30]

Also ominous was Ehrich's scholarly interest. The steady growth of secret se-nior societies and the emergent emphasis upon intercollegiate athletics that be-gan with the 1852 Harvard-Yale rowing race and the formation of the Yale Navy in 1853 were just beginning to sap the college of its respect for intellect. Regard-ing Tap Day—that fateful time when the senior societies designated their suc-cessor members from the junior class—Ehrich wrote of his disappointment that Skull and Bones, the most prestigious of the secret societies, did not ap-plaud scholarly merit. Of equal significance was his lack of interest in the secret societies: "As for myself, if an election to Skull & Bones were offered to me in one hand, a set of Waverly novels or any other good books in the other, I should choose the latter ten times."[31] In later decades the differences between the ed-ucational values that prevailed among Jewish students and among their class-mates would compound racial prejudices and suffocate the hitherto open at-mosphere on the campus.

If one were arbitrarily to designate one year as the end of the "ancient his-tory" of the Jew at Yale, 1878 would be a good candidate. Through that year scholarly achievement continued to be a hallmark of the Jewish students in the college.[32] Few in number, the Jewish boys were an accepted part of the campus community. The presence of students of all leading religious denominations and the permission that Yale granted for all students to attend the Sabbath religious services of their choice were sources of pride to the college faculty.[33] Perhaps the best sign of acceptance of Jews by Yale was the warm reception given to Louis Hood (B.A. 1878, M.L. 1881, D.C.L. 1882), a Prussian emigrant, for a speech presented in 1878 before a distinguished college audience in Battell Chapel. Entitled "The Ancient and Modern Jew," this survey of Jewish history brought Hood the college's DeForest Prize, conferring upon him the dual honor of delivering the address at commencement ceremonies and of seeing the address published in *The Yale Literary Magazine*. Hood had been a member of the Linonia and 'OL Philologoi societies and the Kappa Sigma Epsilon freshman fraternity. The DeForest Prize was a unique honor, however. Lyman Bagg, Yale commentator, had written in 1871 of how the DeForest Prize had once been coveted: "There is no other college award over which there is such a general excitement. . . . it is the very highest of the literary honors, and, as these are thought more of than any others, it may be called the highest honor of the whole college course."[34] An eyewitness to the speech competition in Battell Chapel took note of the meaning that Hood's award had for Jews:

> The intense interest of the cultured audience during its delivery and the prolonged applause at its close was the true indication of the opinion of the judges, who for the first time in the history of Yale College awarded the medal to a Jewish student; more than that, it was their first opportunity, for it is the first instance in which one of our faith succeeded in being permitted, through merit, to compete for the prize. . . . Our people take a natural pride in one who during his four year's sojourn in our midst has so studiously applied himself to his work, and yet found time to commingle with his people freely, as to gain a fine education and win the proudest honor in the gift of the college.[35]

In the last glimmering moments of an era that respected learning, that gave social reward more for merit than privilege, Louis Hood had succeeded. At the moment of his individual success, however, the manner of the Jewish community at large was being called into question.

Part Two **1878–1941**

Chapter 2 Increasing Biases:
Undergraduate Life until the
First World War

The 1870s inaugurated a change in the view of American Jewry held by the general populace. By the end of the decade, when Jews began to be publicly excluded from upper-class social circles, it became evident that the bounds of prejudice in American society were expanding. The Seligman incident of 1877, when the fashionable Grand Union Hotel at Saratoga Springs denied a room to banker Joseph Seligman, was the harbinger of a darker era for American Jewry. Some exclusion had occurred before, but, wrote Stephen Birmingham in *"Our Crowd,"* "by overlooking it, [the Jews] had tried to rise above it. Now . . . it was out in the open and a fact of life: certain areas of America were closed to Jews."[1] These discriminatory practices stemmed in part from a prejudicial reaction to the rapid economic rise of German Jews in America. In mercantile affairs, wrote historian John Higham, Jews had become visible everywhere:

> Not only were most Jews more or less uncultivated, but there is consider-
> able evidence that many were loud, ostentatious, and pushing. . . . The
> Jew became identified as the quintessential parvenu—glittering with con-

spicuous and vulgar jewelry, lacking table manners, attracting attention by clam-
orous behavior, and always forcing his way into society that was above him.[2]

Biased Americans added their new impression of the Jew to their collection of
wanton stereotypes.

At Yale in 1878, undergraduate social prejudice was focused on the Catholics
and Jews. Following the death of Pope Pius IX that year, the newly founded
Yale News reported that "The Pope has rolled off the LOG! To heaven with the
Pope!" One week later, in a further comment on the late pontiff, the *News* directed its petty biases simultaneously against Jews and Catholics: "The Pope's
wealth is said to amount to $24,000,000, which is mostly in the hands of the
Rothschilds at Paris." Barely one month later the student editors returned to
Jew-baiting and discussed the "Old Clothes men" (many of whom were Jewish)
who would buy the clothes of affluent Yale students in need of urgent cash and
then resell them for profit. The resentment that students who mismanaged
their money might have directed at themselves was turned toward these entre-
preneurs:

> From the rag-a-muffin and guttersprites that daily greet us with "give me penny," to
> the obsequious proprietess of the most high-toned students boarding house, there is
> a kind of human vermin in New Haven, that have no other purpose in life than to
> fleece the unwary student. Their motto in business is "Receive much, give nothing."
> . . . It is of the outsiders and intruders we would speak; those men who roam about
> the building, interrupt our studies, and pick up such spare articles as may come in
> their way. . . . Banana pedlars, furniture menders, and especially that cheekiest and
> most contemptibly familiar Jew picture framer, Levi. If someone would kick that
> man down four flights of stairs and off the campus, he would confer an inestimable
> favor upon the college community. But these sink into insignificance when we come
> to the "old clo'" men, those vultures that hover around the fence patiently awaiting
> until some poor devil has squandered his allowance, and is willing to sacrifice a good
> suit of clothes for a collar or two; the bow-legged, flat-nosed Bierbaum, the hand-
> some Herberger, and chief among ten thousand, "Ike," "Mr. Hartenstein of the
> Yales," a humbug that has imposed more upon the good-will of Yale men, than any
> other fraud in existence. . . . Once we were comparatively free from these scourges,
> . . . but that time is gone, perhaps never to return. . . . One other "special" yet re-
> mains, a remarkable creature, a dangerous beast that rarely quits his lair; but from its
> murky recess comes the little game of the spider and the fly. Engel! the rapacious
> usurer, who is willing to accommodate gentlemen, leaving personal property as se-
> curity, for the slight consideration of ten per cent per month.[3]

In New Haven the stereotype of the aggressive Jewish businessman thrived.

Because of the tendency of establishment Americans "to think of all Jews in terms of the immigrant and to think of all non-Jews in terms of the highest standards of gentility and Christian virtue," immigrant East European Jews provided new timber for maintaining the structure of the Jewish stereotype. During the reign of Czar Alexander II of Russia many Russian Jews had hoped to win equal rights as citizens, but, following Alexander's assassination by revolutionary terrorists, a wave of government-inspired anti-Jewish pogroms spread across the country. Mired in poverty, their hopes for religious and political equality shaken, half a million East European Jews began a migration to the "new country" of America.[4] The United States offered the last great opportunity for advancement—an attractive promise for a people long subjugated. That in America in one generation an immigrant could pull himself up by his bootstraps and escape centuries of inferiority tempted East European Jewry far more than the distant dream of Palestine. With a high birthrate and immigration rate, the Jews in America skyrocketed from a population of two hundred eighty thousand in 1880 to over four million by 1925, in a period when the overall United States population only doubled. (See appendix 2.) The first East European Jewish families arrived in New Haven in 1882; over the next forty years, the number of Jews in New Haven increased more than twentyfold.[5]

Of all the ethnic groups migrating to the United States at the opening of the twentieth century, only Southern Italians and Poles brought less capital with them to America than the Jews. The great majority of Jews arrived penniless, dirt poor. They had one relative economic advantage, however: Of those Jews with previous occupational experience, a higher percentage were "skilled workers" compared with other ethnics with previous job experience. Physical appearances worked to their disadvantage. In their East European trappings, the new wave of Jewry presented an alien appearance to most Americans. Enough of them achieved financial success quickly enough, however, to inherit the parvenu status from their German Jewish co-religionists.[6]

Throughout the 1880s and 1890s, petty prejudices grew while racial theories were elaborated. Voices of intellectual leaders like Charles W. Eliot, who advocated what later would be called cultural pluralism, began to be muffled by the nationwide growth of racist sentiment. Anti-Jewish feeling infiltrated the nation's social corridors, though Jews were certainly not the only victims of the intricate doctrines of bigotry: "The racist found equally his enemies all the colored peoples, the Latins, and the Slavs. If the Jews were often the first to draw fire, that was because local circumstances sometimes made them the most prominent targets."[7] The rise in prejudices exhibited toward Jews at Yale coincided with a change in the character of Yale that made Jews more visible targets on the campus.

The process of this change at Yale was gradual and reflected a change in American character in general, as academic effort came to be placed well below the pedestal of an all-absorbing, extracurricular life of sport and snobbery.[8] Throughout the country, learning and good grades had become unfashionable while social status dominated student energies. By 1860 the extracurricular had come to dominate student life at Yale. The 1870s saw the demise of Phi Beta Kappa and the complementary rise in the importance of sports on campus—thus betraying the underlying materialism that gripped the country.[9] From then until the University of Michigan's 1901 national championship, great football was synonymous with Yale. E. Digby Baltzell described these years at Yale by recalling that

> The snobbish mass mores of the campuses of the Gilded Age were nowhere more binding than at New Haven. In the nineties, Yale became the first football factory and led the national trend toward anti-intellectualism and social snobishness. . . . By the turn of the century, "We toil not, neither do we agitate, but we play football" became the campus slogan.

In Edwin E. Slosson's analysis of *Great American Universities* of this era, he wrote that "the professional spirit prevails in Yale athletics, and the amateur spirit prevails in Yale scholarship."[10]

In such an environment, there was little place for an intellectual attitude or a concern for study. Academics were at times almost incidental to the real Yale education. Harvard's George Santayana noticed in 1892 that the Yale creed produced men with defined characters rather than men of intelligence:

> The solution of the greatest problems is not sought, it is regarded as already discovered. The work of education is to instill these revealed principles and to form habits congruous with them. Everything is arranged to produce a certain type of man. . . . The essential object of the institution is . . . to educate rather than to instruct, to be a mother of men rather than a school of doctors.[11]

In 1903 a Yale faculty committee reported on the widespread disdain for learning:

> Scholarship has apparently declined throughout the country; certainly at Yale. . . . In fact, in late years the scholar has become almost taboo. . . . An impression is very strong and prevalent that the athlete is working for Yale, the student for himself. To be a high stand man is now a disadvantage rather than otherwise.[12]

The committee noted that of nine valedictorians after 1893, none had been elected to a senior society, though in the thirty-four prior classes some twenty-six valedictorians had been elected. The college class of 1904 recorded that it had "more gentlemen and fewer scholars than any other class in the memory of man." Respect for the mind had been quashed by the glorification of athletic prowess and social achievement.[13]

Cheating and the use of purchased papers were widespread among the elite students, and the "menial labor" of writing papers was left to the "'grinds,' 'fruits,' 'meatballs,' and 'black men' of minority ethnic origins and a public school education." Enthusiastic intellectuals were not considered in the same category as grade-grubbers, but, recalled Henry Seidel Canby (Ph.B. 1899, Ph.D. 1905), they were equally despised:

> The second generation from the East of Europe was beginning to come to college: Polish Jews with anemic faces on which were set dirty spectacles, soft-eyed Italians too alien to mix with an Anglo-Saxon community, seam-faced Armenian boys, and now and then a Chinese. These, except the last, were all in college to learn how to live in America. Their mien was apologetic; you could see them watching with envious curiosity the courteous indifference of the superior race; they took little part in discussions and asked for no credit. Yet often their more flexible minds could be felt playing round and round the confident Anglo-Saxons, admiring, skeptical, puzzled, and sometimes contemptuous. Occasionally there would be a revelation of intellect or a hint of the future, when some Chinese boy, caught off his guard, and forgetting the convention of the classroom, which was to answer a question and sit down, would give a precis of the entire lesson, and perhaps the previous one and the next, which only a French intellectual could have equalled. Or some Russian Jewish exile, asked to comment on an Ibsen play, and losing control of his guarded intellect, would expound a social philosophy that made the class squirm as if a blast of fire had scorched the seats of their comfortable pants.[14]

The social codes and the racist thinking did not tolerate academic nonconformists.

THE ARRIVAL OF WEALTH

The campus mores that had once encouraged intellectual activity were a casualty of America's Gilded Age. Wealth became so important and concentrated in the hands of so few, wrote E. Digby Baltzell, that "it is no wonder that the production of pig iron rather than poetry, and the quest for status rather than salvation, now took hold of the minds of even the most patrician descendants of

Puritan divines."[15] As wealth and its attendant status translated themselves into national power by the 1890s, college and university boards of trustees came into the hands of businessmen. The character of American educational institutions changed, perhaps beyond their control. When wealthy businessmen sent their children to colleges like Yale, the presence of a wealthy class (bearing a disproportionate influence on their fellow students) became an enduring element. In an attempt to preserve the boundaries between the upper class and those who aspired to it, wrote Robert Wiebe, the collegiate experience became primarily social in character:

> In the battles for social positions between the beleaguered old families and the nouveaux riches, both increasingly sought advantage beyond their cities, usually through marriage. Intermarriage tended to draw separate aristocracies into a single group; and in order to demarcate this national upper class new modes of identification such as a common educational experience in an exclusive boarding school and then in one of a select set of Eastern colleges assumed far greater importance.[16]

Accommodating the exclusive spirit of such institutions as the nation's first country club (founded 1882), the Groton School (founded 1884), and the Social Register (founded 1887), by the 1890s, Yale, and colleges like Yale, became links in a national chain of associations that defined America's social elite.[17]

Because admissions were still open, Yale was by no means exclusively a playground for the rich. Any "qualified" male was able to enter without having to face prejudicial barriers. The college and scientific school had long attempted to keep tuition at modest levels, within the reach of most Americans,[18] and generous financial aid policies permitted academically talented poor boys to attend. Yet the rise of the wealthy class in the 1880s and 1890s threatened to end Yale's century-old tradition of social opportunity and openness to all, regardless of background.

The threat grew during the 1890s as the college greatly increased its size, soaring from 832 students in 1890 to 1,190 students in 1900. More dormitories were built, but there remained far more students than could be housed on campus. Private dormitories for the wealthier undergraduates opened and soon began to dominate social life. Hutchinson, nicknamed "The Hutch," was the most famous of these buildings where well-to-do prep school students grouped to improve their chances of election to membership in the sophomore societies and junior fraternities. In 1905 *The Yale Alumni Weekly* worried that the three older fraternities had taken three-fourths of their members "from the 'swell' dormitories of College Street, and that about two-thirds of those men as Freshmen

had roomed in the high-priced dormitories of York Street." The senior societies, too, selected their members partially on the basis of money and the social
status that it bought.[19] Money had emerged as a major factor in helping one
achieve social success at Yale.

SUCCESS AT YALE

A key element that motivated the Yale students' actions was the striving for
"success." But this success did not concern itself with the classroom. Historian
of the University George Pierson explained that many students had come to
New Haven

> to learn not from books but from each other—not how to be scholars but how to
> succeed. Success was really their goal, not Veritas. What they were surely preparing
> for in their competitions was the struggle of making a living. . . . [The] undergradu-
> ates knew that, provided they first learned the rules of the game, they were destined
> for great prizes, sure to make fortunes, and bound for the managing posts in soci-
> ety.[20]

The college traditions became sacred laws unto themselves. Success was defined
in terms of those regulations:

> Euclid would be forgotten. The Greek and Latin, too. But the College trained you to
> work. It made you a man and fitted you for public trust. Yale was the mother of col-
> leges and outstanding citizens. Yale made you succeed in life and in your success re-
> mained the best part of you.[21]

By the turn of the century the markers of success were well defined. From each
class of two hundred, a chosen few were permitted to enter the two sophomore,
several junior, or three leading secret senior societies of Wolf's Head, Scroll and
Key, and Skull and Bones. The latter organization was *the* pinnacle of student-
recognized success at Yale. Together, the three senior societies honored 15 percent of each class.[22] The Sheffield Scientific School had a parallel social system
for its undergraduates.

The secret societies claimed to be protectors of the Yale democratic system.
By rewarding talent of all sorts, they attempted to reward contribution to Yale.
Yet, behind their democratic veils lay the defects in the supposed Yale openness.
Sinclair Lewis (B.A. 1907), commenting in 1906 on the "Unknown Under-
graduates" who deserved more recognition, suggested that some of the factors
that restrained often-deserved honors to some students were beyond the con-

trol of those individuals: "Why are these men unknown? Partly because you do not look for them, to your own disadvantage; and partly because they are kept down by lack of money, or racial influences, or interest in some line which is not popular." Yet another part of the defect lay in the limited number of spaces at the top of the pyramid:

> Outsiders asked how so exclusive a system could be reconciled with Yale's democracy. The answer was not too hard. Yale stood for equality of opportunity, not equality of reward. . . . The trouble with this defense was that there were too few senior societies to reward all the men of merit or achievement. Also troublesome was the fact that the societies were secretive while Yale life was open. . . . Some good men always carried away scars. And the finality and exclusiveness of the choosing created and would continue to create a faint and enduring fault line in the Yale brotherhood.

In themselves, the senior societies had no power outside the fraternal network. By tapping only the student who participated in the "right" activities or moved in the "right" social circles, however, they exerted a tremendous force over undergraduate life. Recognizing the top athletes, sport managers, newspaper and magazine chairmen, dramatic and musical leaders as the big men on the campus, the societies earned for themselves an awesome, almost fearful, respect.[23]

The influence of secret society alumni in American academe, business, and government was (and remains) substantial. At Yale that influence was stupendous. Of thirty-four consecutive elected alumni fellows of the Yale Corporation from 1872 to 1936, seventeen were "Bones Men" and seven belonged to Keys. The university treasurers for forty-three of the forty-eight years between 1862 and 1910 were Bones Men. University Secretaries from 1869 through 1921 were Bones Men, as were 80 percent of the professors teaching in the university between 1865 and 1916. The university presidency had been occupied by a member of Skull and Bones, Scroll and Key, or Wolf's Head for seventy-six of the one hundred seven years between 1886 and 1993.[24]

Small wonder, then, that life at Yale revolved around the period of selection known as Tap Day. Ernest Earnest described the moment of truth for the students in his *Academic Procession:*

> On that fatal afternoon in May juniors gathered tensely . . . near the Yale fence. As the clock struck five, men issued from the society buildings and moved about among the white-faced juniors. Each of the chosen felt a slap on the shoulder and heard the words, "Go to your room." Those others who had hoped for the honor were broken men.[25]

What determined success was whom one knew and the group with which one associated. Owen Johnson, in his classic novel *Stover at Yale*, emphasized this point as he described an older student advising freshman Dink Stover: "You came from a school that doesn't send many fellows here. You haven't the fellows ahead pulling for you the way other crowds have. I don't want you to make any mistakes. Remember you're going to be watched from now on."[26] Success was based on connections, Stover learned from his mentor: "You may think the world begins outside of college. It doesn't; it begins right here. You want to make the friends that will help you along here and outside. Don't lose sight of your opportunities and be careful how you choose."[27] The old-boy network had become everything to the Yale student. His concerns were with "making it," whether that meant being chosen for the football team, the *Yale Daily News*, the Prom committee, or a society. Social success at Yale helped to assure one's success in the outside world.

THE 1890s

The combination of a rigid definition of the national elite on the basis of membership in the right clubs and societies, the invasion of Yale by the wealthy, and the increasing racial theorizing combined to disenfranchise the Yale Jew socially in the 1890s. For the wealthy undergraduate whose parents vacationed at summer resorts that excluded Jews, or belonged to social clubs that had begun to exclude Jews in the 1880s, it was natural to feel prejudice against the Jew in New Haven.

In 1884 an observer in New Haven had no sense of Jews being the victims of any prejudice. Noting that some of Yale's Jewish students of the time had "distinguished themselves in the class-room, others in the social world, and the rest in nothing particular," the writer believed that success was still predominantly a matter of an individual's efforts.[28]

But prejudice was working its way into Yale. As early as 1890 the junior members of the elite campus fraternity of Delta Kappa Epsilon, in an initiation play for the fraternity's sophomores, put on trial not just the habits of some local and specific annoying Jews, but of the entire people. In a play entitled "Shylock: The Sarcastic Sheeny, or the Manoeuvering Merchant of Verdant Venice," DKE member J. R. Herod played the part of "Shylock—A State street pawnbroker, combining at one and the same time all the thrifty motives and tendencies of his race."[29]

Hidden behind closed doors, vocal expression of social prejudices was limited, so that some Jewish students had no difficulty freely admitting their ancestry in public. Lafayette B. Mendel (B.A. 1891), for example, recorded that his blood was German and that Mendelssohn the musician was his relative. Classmate and valedictorian Nathan Glicksman recorded in his classbook section on race and ancestry that he could trace "his descent to the exodus from Egypt 1491, B.C.," and that he claimed German, Italian, and Polish blood. Eugene Isaac Meyer (B.A. 1895), future publisher of *The Washington Post,* chose to minimize his pedigree, however, and traced "his ancestry to Noah, via William the Conqueror and Columbus."[30]

But social opportunities were no longer as open to Jews as they had once been. By the last decade of the nineteenth century, sectarianism had become so firmly implanted in the fraternity life at Yale that three Jewish students—Louis Samter Levy (B.A. 1898), Frederic Manfred Werner (B.A. 1898), and Henry Mark Fisher (B.A. 1897)—proposed an idea that was both novel to Yale and original in the nation. It was not surprising that Yale, setter of the nation's undergraduate social trends in the 1890s, was the source of the nation's first non-sectarian fraternity: Pi Lambda Phi. In March 1895 the three students had concluded that the current Yale fraternities were functioning less as rewards for campus achievements and contributions than as private clubs for the maintenance of students from upper class socioeconomic backgrounds. They were also aware that religious and racial exclusiveness were sometimes a part of the fraternity bonds. Valuing the principles of democracy that so many on the Yale campus pledged fealty to but ignored in practice, Levy, Werner, and Fisher founded the Alpha chapter of Pi Lambda Phi. In one of their first "rush letters," they explained their dissatisfactions:

> In the early part of this year a number of students at Yale met to consider a college fraternity on lines broader and more liberal than those employed at the present time.
>
> It appeared feasible to found such a fraternity, having for its cardinal principles non-sectarianism and the recognition of men on the basis of ability above all consideration.

Purely Jewish student organizations were not the answer either: "There have been at times other fraternities founded by sects not included in the existing fraternities. These naturally have served as counter-irritants, rather than as remedies." The young men hoped that their members would exhibit the best qualities of human nature: "The fraternity seeks no members save those seeking it. And only the best of those men who are progressive, industrious, and non-prejudiced, can seek it successfully." Pi Lambda Phi enjoyed an initial success, which might have been what led founder Henry Fisher to record in his classbook that "Yale is the best college on earth." Soon after, chapters were established at Columbia University, The University of Pennsylvania, City College of New York, Cornell, Massachusetts Institute of Technology, and Harvard.[31]

After 1898, however, the Alpha chapter at Yale ceased to exist, and the other chapters also quickly succumbed. The fraternity's original records are unavailable, so only speculation can be offered to interpret the demise.[32] What seems probable, however, is that the upstart, nonconformist fraternity was anathema to much of the Yale community. Members of the secret societies from that era were industrious people, but they were generally not progressive and many were prejudiced. The idea of tapping members of a fraternity whose ideals ran counter to prevailing undergraduate sentiment would have been ludicrous. A member of a nonsectarian fraternity would therefore have been "queered" for associating with the wrong type of students. For Yale students of all religions that dreamt of membership in a secret society, joining a non-sectarian organization that professed to reward talent more than privilege would have destroyed any chances of their dream becoming reality. Yale had successfully produced and exported the football and social status interests that swept the nation, but in the 1890s, when privilege laughed at merit, the Yale production of nonsectarianism became unmarketable both on the national scene and at home.

THE CLASSROOM SETTING

In contrast to the social world, in the classroom racial or religious bias was not a factor. Occasionally there might have been a break in proper behavior, some unmistakable faux pas. But the standards of a faculty of gentlemen demanded that, even if barriers existed in the social world, the classroom should be a place of fairness and civility. When the choice of a black law student to participate in an 1892 prize debate prompted the withdrawal of a white debater, the black received the support of nearly everyone connected with the law school.[33] Other occasional lapses in courteous classroom behavior were, in general, not tolerated by university and college administrators.[34]

A rare example of anti-Jewish sentiment in the classroom of this era was the so-called British-Israel movement, as disseminated by Charles A. L. Totten, professor of military science and tactics from 1889 to 1892. The British-Israel racial theories claimed that the Anglo-Saxon peoples were the racially pure and superior descendants of the ten lost tribes of ancient Israel. At Yale, where Totten was detailed by the War Department (as part of the conditions for Yale's receiving Connecticut land grant monies through 1893), Totten appealed to the martial interests of undergraduates and packed them into his army training course. During Totten's last year at Yale, seven out of ten Yale College and Sheffield Scientific School seniors registered for the course. Totten used the opportunity occasionally to inject his racial theories and his predictions for upcoming apocalypse into the Yale curriculum. One might suspect, though, that students may have attended the course as much to laugh at the man as to learn from him. To the religiously skeptical late nineteenth-century Yale students, a man who could take exegesis to the unprecedented level of using Mother Goose rhymes like "Jack and Jill," "Little Boy Blue," "Dickery Dickery Dock," "Mother Hubbard," and "Little Jack Horner" to prove his theories must have provided an hour of rollicking variety to spice the otherwise dull recitations of the standard curriculum. Totten left Yale after three years to pursue his philosophies independently on a full-time basis.[35]

BACKGROUND OF THE JEWISH STUDENTS

On the historical stage, the Jewish "players" tended to fit one of three patterns in pre-First World War Yale. A handful were the affluent and largely nonreligious children of German Jews who had risen to great levels of economic achievement. They came to Yale for the same reasons as many of the wealthy gentile students (some of whom had been their friends in the nation's better preparatory schools). Reconstructing a childhood memory, Waldo Frank (B.A.-M.A. 1911), son of a wealthy lawyer, recalled his older brother's words that dissuaded him from an education at Heidelberg and instead sent him to Yale:

> "You're an American, aren't you? You've got to get trained to live in America. You're not a European. You're remote enough as it is from your country." . . .
>
> "All right," I said at last, "I'll go to Harvard." . . .
>
> "No!" brother Joseph said again. "Harvard would be almost as bad for you as Heidelberg. Harvard is full of anarchists and aesthetes. They're 'above' America, which is even worse than to be out of it. . . . I want you to go to a college which believes in America, not just New England, and loves America. Which models citizens to be and to act American. What about Yale? Have you ever thought of Yale? The good Yale man puts poets in their place. Believes in success."

A second group were middle-class German Reform Jews (often from the midwest). Finally came the East European Jews.[36] Raised in orthodox homes, usually impoverished, they generally lived at home or with relatives during college. The public high school mythology that held that America's great universities were temples of learning attracted the East Europeans to "worship" at Yale.

From a geographical standpoint, the state that supplied the largest number of Jewish students (according to 1911–18 figures) was Connecticut. Half of the in-state Jewish Yale students came from New Haven. Connecticut was followed by New York, Ohio, and Illinois, in descending order. As the number of East European Jews in America came to dwarf the number of German Jews and as the number of East European Jews in Connecticut grew, the number and proportion of East European Jewish students at Yale similarly increased. The college class that entered in 1915 had a record 25 percent of its Jewish students being Russian or Polish emigrants, a record 78 percent of its Jewish boys as sons of Polish or Russian-born fathers. A near record 82 percent were public high school graduates.[37] (See appendix 6.)

The personal attitudes of Yale Jews toward their religion and their co-religionists were always mixed. A Jewish observer in 1884 recorded the variances among some of the first group of Jews to attend Yale College simultaneously:

> There are some who enter with a fixed determination to become as little identified with anything Jewish as possible. They avoid our people, never visit the temple (though not infrequent church-goers) and abjure everything that tends in the least to associate their names with the descendants of Abraham. How these insignificant cubs are regarded by their Jewish fellow-students can as well be imagined as described. Another class is that which devotes itself almost entirely to the circle of its Hebrew acquaintance. Its favor is courted by many of our Mosaic daughters with an eagerness quite astonishing. There are also intermediate classes who in a greater or less degree lean toward one or the other of these extremes.[38]

The writer was well aware that generalizations might be made about Jews but considered that any claim that the generalizations had universal applicability would have been false.

The most prevalent, and perhaps the most accurate, stereotype of early twentieth century Jews regarded the East Europeans from the Jewish "ghetto" environment. The largest single group of ghetto Jews at Yale came from the slums that stood just a few blocks from the campus.

> It was a depressing region, but it was accepted on the whole with few complaints. The recurring holidays gave [its inhabitants] the opportunity to brighten up their

homes frequently. Squalid and fallen into disrepair as many of the dwellings were, [the] living quarters answered [people's] needs. . . . Large families, often of eight members augmented by a childless aunt, . . . occupied small flats in congested tenements. Between rows of such buildings were alleys and streets that were poorly paved if at all. Within the tenement houses were long halls, feebly lighted, with mouldy walls, separating the quarters rented by the families on one of the three or four stories. Bannisters along the broken stairways offered some protection against accidents. The walls and ceilings were poorly patched; and a fire escape served as sleeping quarters for the Rubin children during the hot summer nights. During the winter, the windows were frosted in the largely unheated, crowded rooms.[39]

From a physical standpoint, the Jewish ghettos in America were not unique, but in terms of industriousness and intellectual activity, the Jewish slum neighborhoods had few rivals. Respect for scholarship had been an integral part of Jewish culture for centuries. In Europe the study of Talmud (commentary on religious law)—not for the purpose of achieving any particular goal but wisdom, often for its own sake—was the accepted norm of Jewish life, and the reputation of a Jewish community rested on the talents of its greatest scholars.[40] In America the thirst for knowledge continued in the Jewish ghettos, including the one in New Haven:

> The East-European Jews who came to live in the Oak Street area brought with them an intimate knowledge of the Hebrew Bible. While some of the more learned had studied in the various *Yeshivas* [religious academies] . . . , even the less educated among them had such schooling as their community *Cheders* [religious elementary schools] afforded them and they knew the content of the Bible, were able to read Biblical Hebrew with considerable comprehension, could even quote and select from its pages significant passages as occasions called for. . . . In many instances the Jews of the Ghetto had placed the Aramaic Targum [translation] of Onkelos, portions of the Talmud, and the Commentaries of Rashi on the shelves or in the book cases in their homes.[41]

The Atlantic passage had taken away some of the desire for religious understanding, for religion had to compete with the enterprise and excitement of American life. But though the religious drive would falter, the searing passion for a better understanding of one's world remained.

At the core of life, recalled Louis Sachs (B.A. 1914, LL.B. 1917), were parents who taught their children that education was to be prized:

> [They] were a remarkable lot. These small shopkeepers, tailors, and butchers and shoemakers . . . opened up at seven in the morning and with their wives and children

they worked until twelve o'clock at night. And for what purpose? To provide for the *kinder*, for the kids and their education, naturally for the boys a college education. They dared even dream about Yale for their children.

Education was seen as the basis of personal fulfillment and economic advancement. Sach's day began with morning classes, a five-block walk from campus to the Jewish neighborhood for lunch at home, and more classes in the afternoon. He would then deliver his route of 425 Yiddish newspapers, which provided him with pocket money throughout his years of high school, college, and law school. Then followed work at the family store, dinner, and study at the Yale Library for a few hours—in a place where he was certain to find the quiet that was absent at home. On a less busy evening he would take a break by going to the nearby Globe Theater on Chapel Street. Having returned to do the store's bookkeeping and his remaining studies, Sachs would end his day by two or three A.M.[42]

In addition to the cultural respect for scholarship, the dependence by many Jewish students upon Yale for financial aid motivated strong academic efforts. In the 1910s annual tuition was approximately one hundred fifty dollars, a figure out of reach for most ghetto Jews. As in Sachs's case, with financial aid often reducing tuition by as much as 90 percent, many impoverished Jewish students felt that they "had to work like the devil to maintain [their] scholarship standing." The additional awareness of the financial sacrifice that a boy's family was making to send him to Yale often motivated him further to study and make good the investment in terms that his parents could appreciate.[43]

Consequently, there was bound to be a conflict of ideals. The intellectual way of the "people of the book" was not the "Yale way" for the majority of students. Not that only Jews were studious or were thinkers. Many Christians were, too, but the stereotypical ones were not. In 1914 J. Carlisle Peet, urging diversification of opinion and personality among the cliques on the campus, wrote in *The Yale Literary Magazine*, "We are most of us Anglo-Saxons, and those who are not naturally follow the general custom."[44] But the tradition of scholarship and the tuition investment directed many Jewish boys away from the prevailing pattern of academic indifference. When Russian-born undergraduate Samuel Rosenbaum (Ph.B. 1907) and his brother Harris (Ph.B. 1908) organized the Rosenbaum tutoring school to pay their way through Yale, they gained the attention of undergraduates in the college and the scientific school. A cartoon in the *1908 Sheffield Scientific Classbook* humorously, and perhaps jealously, assigned Harris the words, "I von't help you, but I'll tutor you."[45]

Such coaching helped Yale undergraduates handle potentially unpleasant moments at recitations and examinations, but often the Yale students were not genuinely interested in the studies for which they crammed. Some, no doubt, resented the Jewish students' devotion to learning:

> "Just what does our type take from here to the nation?" said Stover; and then he was surprised that he had asked the question that was vital. . . .
>
> "First, a pretty fine type of gentleman, with good, clear honest standards; second, a spirit of ambition and a determination not to be beaten; third, the belief in democracy."
>
> "All of which means," said Regan, "that we are simply schools for character."
>
> "Well, why not?" said Pike. "Isn't that a pretty big thing?"[46]

To many a Jewish student, such a concept of college was incomprehensible. For someone like Waldo Frank, an atypical Yale Jew in that he had spent a year after high school at a private preparatory school in Switzerland, extracurricular activities were a full part of his collegiate experience, but academics always came first. In three sentences, Frank summed up a decision that many a Jewish boy made: "I was a fair tennis player (shrewd rather than brilliant) and resolved to go out for the team. But afternoons devoted to tennis, I learned, would prevent taking on the history of Europe, a course that sounded good. I chose the course."[47] By the First World War it was as if the majority of boys were coming to Yale for social enlightenment and the Jewish students were coming to learn truth.

The typical Yale student thought of New Haven (and its Jews) as existing in a universe different from their own. Sinclair Lewis, who as an undergraduate was already concerned about the less glamorous side of American life, penned an editorial in *The Yale Literary Magazine* of 1906 in which he chastised the students in William B. Bailey's popular "American Social Conditions" course for their narrow outlook on New Haven:

> How many of [them] think that only New York has slums? Do they know of the strange region of Oak Street, of its Saturday night when the Jewish Sabbath is just over? Have they ever seen it in the morning when huge rats frisk boldly down the sidewalks, and the shops are opening for a new day?[48]

Typical of the reaction of one sphere of life to another was the shock expressed by the Christian students when one Jewish boy showed up for class during the first week of school in 1910 wearing shorts—a most ungentlemanly action. But rather than an open display of antipathy between townies and on-campus students, indifference prevailed.[49]

Ironically, one outlet on the campus for developing friendships was in the old Dwight Hall, a YMCA adjunct. Many nonresident students, Jews and Italians in particular, would go there to find a place for study between classes. Generally apart from the mainstream of college life, they became studying partners and a close social group.[50]

Despite the Elis' often looking at New Haven as a different world, the local New Haven boys loved their Yale. As early as 1882 a Jewish Yale student proudly reported to the rest of American Jewry of the Yale Junior Promenade, "the grand event of the season . . . , which surpassed any affairs of its character ever given before in this city."[51] An appreciation of the regard for Yale may be grasped from an article written by Joseph S. Alderman (Ph.B. 1915) on the "Yale Life of the New Haven Student." The sentiment he exhibited toward Yale was as strong as anything shared by other students of the era. Alderman, a stereotypical Jewish student of this time, had been born in Russia in 1894, attended the New Haven High School, and lived at home throughout his Yale course. His Sheffield Scientific School classmates voted him "Most Scholarly" and *The Yale Sheffield Monthly* editors recorded that "his writing has been superior to that of any man in Sheff—possibly in Yale—that we know of."[52] Though his own perspective was that of a Sheffield student, he could have been writing about Yale College just as easily. Though he was a Jew, his depiction had validity for non-Jews as well:

The New Haven youngster is brought up to regard Yale as distinctly his own. Beneath the atmosphere of romanticism with which he views the torchlight processions, the fantastic reunion garbs and the football crowds, is a vaguely exultant feeling that all these form a necessary component of the city in which he lives, that they are a definite, indestructible part of the "City of Elms," as much so, indeed, as East Rock or the Depot.

Already before the arrival of his teens, the flutterings of patriotism begin to assail him. A Yale victory is an occasion for public rejoicing; a defeat, a signal for gloom and lamentation. I remember distinctly how, some ten and eleven years ago, we gathered along George Street, my comrades, and I, and all the youngsters of the neighborhood, and waited on the nerve-tingling November Saturday until the crowds returned from the Field. And then how we cheered those of *our* side, the ones whose autos came whizzing past with the blue banner conspicuously placed; and how we hissed, and booed, and hooted those who sped past with the hateful crimson or orange! Who of us would have dared that day to wear a red or saffron tie? We shudder to think of what might have happened.[53]

Alderman's brother Abraham later vividly recalled the excitement of a spring Derby Day when Yale defeated the Harvard crew and returned to downtown New Haven for a torchlight parade that won the attention of the boys of the Jewish ghetto. Joseph Alderman wrote that the passage of New Haven boys into high school strengthened their bonds with the nearby university:

> The University began to lose that atmosphere of impersonality, of glorified remoteness, with which our youthful fancy regarded it. It grew in definiteness, in concreteness; it became a kind of older brother. A brief, premature introduction was gained for us at the annual college entrance examinations, when we climbed, with more or less trepidation, to the upper floor of Winchester, and gazed through the window upon the Grove Street Cemetery below, seeking to find therein inspiration for the inexplicable reasons why our third line of Dido's plaint had seven feet instead of six. How startlingly those periods of trial came back to us, with all their semi-pathetic, semi-ludicrous yearnings and aspirations, when we mounted the same stairs some years later to draw endless views and projections in the very rooms where Vergil erstwhile racked us!"[54]

During the halcyon years before limited admissions became a reality, many a Jewish boy assumed that hard work in high school and, if he was lucky, liberal financial assistance from the university would help make Yale a reality.

> The first days of college proved a disappointment to us. In the main, we found our life at Yale quite analogous to the life in high school, and the disillusionment was great, in consequence. We had, chiefly, the same associates, the same daily habitudes. . . . Sister Ruth still found no time so congenial to her interpretation of Beethoven as when we were travailing with the ideas for our next composition. . . . Nor could we find refuge when we seized our papers and our thoughts and betook ourselves indignantly to Byers Hall, there to seek that tranquility our soul hungered for. The ubiquitous gentlemen of the piano were there to distort our thoughts with their lopsided ragtime or to crush them entirely under the heavy weight of Rachmaninoff's "Prelude," played with the utmost *fortissimo*.
>
> We found ourselves . . . more constrained in our actions, less able to participate freely in the University functions than the dormitory student. The evening whereon we had confidently expected to attend a smoker in Byers Hall proved to be that very one which Cousin Edith had selected for her engagement party. . . . And then, that evening on which we had vowed that neither heaven nor earth would keep us from seeing the basket-ball game to which we had looked expectantly forward, the sudden arrival of Uncle Albert and Aunt Hannah, with the children, demonstrated to us how futile our vows when we lived amid the uncertainties of home life.
>
> Our slightest aberration is soon disseminated throughout the neighborhood. Like

Fame, *viret in eundo,* it waxes in strength as it passes along. "Oh dear, yes!" cries charming Mrs. Sampson from across the way to another neighbor, "Milly was walking down Temple Street from work last evening, and who do you think she seen? Well, there was a band of students going into one of them swell cafes—*Ratkiller,* they call it, or something like that—and you know," here she lowers her voice as she pronounces the name of the awful culprit, "well, he was among them. Ain't it just perfectly scandalous?" . . . We tremble, as we think what horrible diagnoses as to our mental equipment might be circulated throughout the neighborhood were Mrs. Sampson, or Millie . . . to see us decked in the costumes of Rush night!

And yet, after all, though we live at a longer radius from the center of Yale, though we must accept the supervision, the circumscribed life and the intimacy of the family roof for that independence, that freedom of movement and action, that better understanding of his fellow-men of the out-of-town dormitory student, we find ourselves as definite a part of Yale as he does. We exult as much as the others in being sons of our *alma mater.* If we live somewhat aloof from her now, if we have to dwell away from that center where her heart beats fastest, we are nevertheless her oldest sons; we have grown up to her from our infancy. To us, as to all of our college associates, she is a noble part of that grand trio, "for God, for country and for Yale."[55]

Often, however, the "out-of-town" dormitory students did not consider the townie students to be a significant part of their Yale.

ORGANIZATIONAL LIFE

Thorough evaluation of the Jewish students' places in the social scene of the pre-World War I years is difficult to achieve. Since their lives were often centered at home, it was difficult for them to play an active role in the university social life. Townie Jews did not usually feel that they were victims of discrimination. Any inequalities that did exist were considered a normal part of the order of life. Few thought of complaining, because, compared to the Poland and Russia that they or their parents had left, they were already living in a state of relative equality. In most campus organizations, there was space for Jewish students who were willing to work hard enough to join them. Someone like Eugene Lehman (B.A. 1902) could look back on his undergraduate days and have recollections so positive that they were almost saccharine:

I am mighty proud of the old college and what she did for me. . . . Despite that fact that I landed on the campus in my Sophomore year when friendships are already pretty well formed, and that I arrived there totally unknown, coming from a small western town and having only $5.00 in my pocket, I had plenty of fun, formed worthwhile friendships, learned a great deal about my own in-born powers and weaknesses, and much about how to live happily and harmoniously as a member of a democratic community. So that now the very name of Yale on a banner or elsewhere has come to bear a meaning to me not dissimilar to that which the flag bears to a patriot—the inspiration to try a little harder to be loyal to its ideals because Yale has a right to expect such loyalty from her sons.[56]

Not everyone, of course, was satisfied. Robert Moses (B.A. 1909), for example, who had little special interest in Jews or Judaism, embarked on a quixotic campaign to make the myth of Yale democracy a reality. He called for election of class officers on the basis of merit, not fraternity membership, and he insisted that some form of special recognition be given for scholastic achievement. Others were content to ignore social distinctions and join the less prestigious student clubs on the campus. Many joined the campus debating society and the orchestra. Stanleigh P. Friedman (B.A. 1905), composer of the "Down the Field" football song that became a staple of Eli music, was elected president of the university orchestra. Some invested their social efforts in New Haven organizations.[57]

Of the inner attitudes of Yale students, recollections of Jewish and non-Jewish alumni from this era ranged from descriptions of Yale as a perfect institution where everyone was *always* treated equally regardless of background to descriptions of Yale as a stifling center where the odd fellow who arrived without a prejudiced mind might wonder what was wrong with him.[58]

How, then, should we reconcile seemingly reliable but sometimes strikingly disparate recollections? The best resolution may be to appreciate that Yale College had approximately three hundred students per class in the years before the First World War. The Sheffield Scientific School, considered by rival Yale College to be of an inferior academic and social status, had some four hundred per class. With over two thousand undergraduates at Yale, there was room for greatly divergent attitudes and policies. Whether gates were seen as open, half-open, or closed depended on the particular cliques that managed the gates. When a specific group was fair-minded it would be open to all, and when a specific group was committed to prejudice it would exclude.[59]

Sport merits special attention, because on a day-to-day basis it dominated the extra-curriculum.[60] At Yale, where the extra-curriculum dominated the curriculum, sport therefore dominated all. There were exceptions to the rule, but it is universal opinion that the Jewish students (even those whose financial position allowed them the time to compete) were generally uninterested in the sports deity to the extent that it was worshiped at Yale.[61] As in academics, there

was a cultural conflict. Already in 1875, *The New Era,* an American Jewish periodical, went on record as opposing the embryonic sports complex in America's
colleges. The newspaper's particular plaint regarded crew racing. As a means of
physical exercise, the editors thought that crew racing was worthy of encouragement, but limits on the activity were necessary:

> Like every other pleasure, its pursuit may be carried to excess, and to excess it will be
> carried, if it be permitted to occupy, either in thought or in practice, the hours that
> properly belong to other occupations. . . . If the students of a college be told by their
> president, that the victorious crew have done more to make their college known than
> all the men of worth and learning that have emerged from its halls, what wonder can
> it be, if these students attach more importance to the exercise of rowing than to the
> furnishing of the chambers of the mind?[62]

Because the majority of the Jewish students came to Yale to learn, their excluding themselves from sports in the pre-First World War era was, in effect, a dou-
ble-edged sword. As sport dominated social life, those who were uninvolved
with sport removed themselves from a large chunk of the Yale social scene.
Those who did not "go out" for a team thus generated for themselves a handicap that existed off of the playing field.

More often than not, Jewish students who were athletes flocked to sports
that stressed individual rather than team effort. (Robert Moses, of German-
Jewish parents, but having minimal Jewish consciousness, was the most visible
of these young men. As a swimmer and young machinator he championed the
cause of minor sports at Yale.) There were a number of possible reasons for the
Jewish predilection toward individual sports. Jewish students may have been
attracted to wrestling by Coach "Izzy" Winters, or to boxing by Coach "Mosey"
King. Football and crew may have been too traditional, old-line American, in
the way that baseball was proverbially dominated by the Irish, so that Jewish
boys kept their distance. The subject remains to be explored more fully.[63]

FRATERNITIES AND SECRET SOCIETIES

The badge of bigotry that Yale earned for a time was displayed most prominently in the fraternities and secret senior societies, the undergraduate institutions most important to Elis.

In the fraternities, prejudice existed alongside indifference. As noted previously, by the 1890s Yale's Christian fraternities tended to restrict the presence of
Jews. These informal limits were likely intended to help the fraternities main-

tain their superficially Christian character. In the era under consideration, there were yet no Jewish fraternities on campus, and nonsectarian Pi Lambda Phi had not succeeded in its first incarnation. The annual junior fraternity elections in Yale College therefore resulted, between 1900 and 1916, in the entrance of over 40 percent (i.e., two thousand) of the non-Jewish students and 5 percent (i.e., nine) of the Jews. Proportions of this sort were common nationwide.[64] Scions of American Jewry's wealthiest financiers were among the fraternity members of this time: Robert Lehman (B.A. 1913), for example, in Delta Kappa Epsilon and Joseph L. Seligman (B.A. 1908) in Psi Upsilon. Another factor, however, was more important than money, self-exclusion, or social indifference in accounting for the differing proportions of Jewish and non-Jewish members of the Yale fraternities: When it came to offering "hold-offs" (the nighttime knock on the door that led to the eagerly anticipated invitation to join the fellowship), recalled Beta Theta Pi member Ralph H. Gabriel (B.A. 1913), Jews were often rejected *only* for possessing the label "Jew."[65]

At the top of the Yale social pyramid, "the distinction most coveted by the undergraduates and respected by their elders"[66] was barred to Jews. No Jew reached the top; few had even come close. How much this exclusion was a matter of generally accepted philosophy, as opposed to specifically implemented policy, cannot be said, but the undergraduates were aware that the Jewish presence at Yale was increasing. Of the college class of 1909, for example, less than 3 percent were Jews; the class of 1915 had a Jewish enrollment of almost 8 percent. At a time when resorts publicly advertised their racial and religiously biased prohibitions, the leading Eis were not about to show kindness to a group of social pariahs. An example of the local expression of the nationwide attitude was the unanimous 1911 vote by members of the class of 1912 Elihu Club (the newest senior society on the campus of that year) on the motion "That Jews should be denied recognition at Yale." The vote evidenced the underlying prejudice of some of the most elite on the campus.[67] Since the policy was directed outside of Elihu—to all the circles and organizations where Elihu Club members had influence—when it was implemented, it severely widened the range of the prejudice at the highest ranks of the undergraduate campus.

Chapter 3 The Limitation of Numbers: Undergraduate Admissions between the World Wars

From the beginning of the twentieth century, admissions had been a sensitive issue at Yale. Because American society had placed a low premium on formal education, the public high school curriculum through much of the nation, particularly in the west, was directed toward "life adjustment," rather than intellectual development and college preparation. Yale College's admissions policies, which demanded Latin as a prerequisite, did not mesh well, therefore, with the nation's public school systems, and these policies effectively limited the number of non-eastern public school graduates entering the college. For example, of three thousand students admitted to Yale College between 1901 and 1910, only seventy-five came directly from midwestern high schools. Many a non-eastern student who hoped to attend Yale therefore would enroll for at least one year of study at one of the eastern preparatory schools to provide himself with an intellectual and social preparation for the college.[1]

Frustrated by the difficulty of sending their sons to Yale, western alumni called on the university to accept high school certificates for admission, instead of demanding entrance exams in numerous specific subjects, many of which the average western high school student had never encountered. Dean Frederick Sheetz Jones of Yale College thought the idea preposterous and forcefully told the alumni in 1911 that "we are not going to have any certificate system, even if the Western Association of Yale Clubs tells us to. That is flat."[2] Jones infuriated those alumni at a time when Yale was genuinely interested in obtaining more high school boys. The university was well aware that it was difficult to claim to be a democracy when it accepted a higher percentage of students from private prep schools than any other college except Princeton. Following Harvard's lead, Yale College and the Sheffield Scientific School tried to open their admissions and make their own policies similar to those elsewhere. A major reason for Yale's joining the College Entrance Examination Board (CEEB) in the first decade of the century, suggested educational historian Harold Wechsler, was its desire to attract students from throughout the country to the university.[3] In 1916 Yale's undergraduate schools became full-fledged members of the CEEB. Though Yale admissions policies liberalized, alumni, whose donations kept Yale running, remained dissatisfied. Their recurrent complaints were of Yale's need to improve relations with the public schools. The Latin language requirement for admission to the college was a great obstacle to improving those relations. The complaints were effective. As part of a 1919 reorganization of the university, the degree of Bachelor of Philosophy was transferred from the scientific school to the college as a program for non-Latinists, the B.S. was reserved for the scientific school, and the B.A. was awarded by the college to those students who satisfied Yale's Latin requirements. When the university established a common undergraduate admissions board in 1920, admissions procedures were further relaxed to permit an alternative form of entrance to Yale known as Plan B, in which students who did not wish to struggle with the fifteen exams previously required could be judged on the basis of four exams and their secondary school grade record.[4]

ENTRANCE OF JEWISH STUDENTS

It was a natural consequence of the new procedures that Jewish students in New Haven (and in New York, Boston, and Philadelphia, where similar changes were occurring) would take advantage of the opportunities afforded by Yale's attempts to broaden itself. The Jews' desire for college was tied to their traditional educational values and to the growth of social mobility as a function of degree of formal education. In a manner then unequaled in American history, a substantial number of one immigrant group achieved in one generation a marked representation at the top American universities. Jewish migration had been characterized by the travel of entire families. Consequently, the percentage of children among Jewish immigrants to America at the turn of the century was double the average of all immigrant groups. Once these children entered high school, they tended to enroll in college preparatory courses and to complete their degrees. Unlike American Catholics of the nineteenth century, who built their own elaborate educational system integrating religion into academics through the collegiate level, Jews preferred to take advantage of the high quality of education available at the surrounding public and private institutions. President James Rowland Angell (1921–37) himself recognized that neither most Jewish students "nor their families [would] . . . be likely to look upon a Jewish university as satisfactorily meeting their requirements, unless it were notably more liberally endowed, staffed and equipped than other existing institutions." As long as college admissions were open, there was little need to form Jewish institutions.[5]

The shift toward restrictive admissions was part of a national trend toward restriction. Henry Ford was actively propagating the "Protocols of the Elders of Zion" conspiracy, accusing American Jews of participating in a plot to dominate the world by weakening American morals. The receptive nation was simultaneously debating the necessity for and the character of restrictive immigration laws, particularly the Immigration Act of 1921, which had restricted annual immigration of a group to 3 percent of the number of that nationality residing in the United States in 1910. At the college level, the presence of Jews had also aroused concern. By 1918 Jewish enrollment at the City College of New York had increased to almost 80 percent and the city university had become stigmatized as "the Jewish University of America." New York University's Jewish enrollment was then approaching the 50 percent level, and Columbia was working its way down from 40 percent. A collegiate song from the 1910s reflected the attitudes of those who feared that Jews would destroy the prestige of the nation's great universities:

Oh. Harvard's run by millionaires,
And Yale is run by booze,
Cornell is run by farmers' sons,
Columbia's run by Jews,
So give a cheer for Baxter Street,
Another one for Pell,
And when the little sheenies die,
Their souls will go to hell.[6]

To avoid receiving the "Jewish institution" epithet, eastern colleges began to consider the merits of Jewish quotas. And discussions at one college provoked similar considerations at others, for none wanted to become a dumping ground for unwanted Jews.

Yale, with its urban location, readily attracted Jewish applicants. Family Yale traditions were not the primary reason that Yale was desirable to so many of this era's Jewish applicants. They were often immigrants or children of immigrants, and their goals were to improve their lot by a degree, more than to enter America's social elite. But Yale, as an eminent symbol of learning and a preeminent citadel of success, offered Connecticut Jews the same alternative to Harvard that it had for centuries offered Connecticut non-Jews. In the first two decades of the twentieth century, Yale's Jewish enrollment grew rapidly. The number of New Haven Jews in Yale College jumped from three in the class of 1911 to twenty-seven in the class of 1926. The number of Hartford, Connecticut, Jews in Yale College climbed from one to eight over this same period. (See apppendixes 6 and 7.) Yale's proximity to New York, the hub of American Jewry, also had a magnetic effect in attracting Jews to New Haven. (In 1927 Jews made up 13 percent of the combined populations of Connecticut, Massachusetts, New York, and Rhode Island, as compared with less than 2 percent of the population in the remainder of the United States.) If they were of the "right type," announced University Secretary Anson Phelps Stokes in 1915, Yale welcomed them. Indeed, as late as that year, Secretary Stokes considered the presence of Jews at Yale as an asset: They showed themselves capable of "the highest scholarship"; their differing backgrounds and points of view were essential to the life and thought of a "democratic American university"; and their presence attracted gifts to Yale in the area of Semitic studies—an important field for a university to cover, Stokes thought. For other Yale administrators, however, too many Jews ended up being of the "wrong type," lacking the manners, the upbringing, the social styles that would allow them to blend invisibly into the Yale body. In May 1918 Dean Jones of the college privately noted the growing problem at a meeting of the Association of New England Deans:

> I think we shall have to change our view, in regard to the Jewish element. We should do something to improve them. They are getting there rapidly. If we do not educate them, they will overrun us. We have got to change our policies and get them into shape. A few years ago every single scholarship of any value was won by a Jew. I took it up with the Committee and said that we could not allow that to go on. We must put a ban on the Jews. We decided not to give them any scholarships but to extend aid to them in the way of tuition.[7]

When Jews began to win a substantial portion of the scholarship awards, the nonsectarian terms under which Yale had previously awarded them were abandoned. Prejudice would prevail. Hand in hand with the university's decision to institute a "Limitation of Numbers" to control the unmanageable flood of students streaming through Yale's newly opened waterways of admission came the decision to limit the presence of Jewish students.

Definitive action was first called for in the fall of 1921, when the 866 men beginning the common freshman year of the college and scientific school were the largest class to enter Yale up to this time. This mammoth group, George Pierson has described, came near to bursting Yale at its seams. Classrooms overflowed, dormitories were oversubscribed, and discipline verged on collapsing.[8] Yale felt itself under pressure to do some introspection and house cleaning. Near the beginning of the semester, therefore, on October 18, 1921, the undergraduate board of admissions voted to refer the "question of a possible limitation" of numbers to the University Council—an institutional policy advisory board. The following month Robert Corwin, chairman of admissions, brought the idea before the council, which delegated President Angell to chair a committee to investigate the proposal. Also appointed to the committee were Dean Jones; Russell H. Chittenden, director of the Sheffield Scientific School; Roswell P. Angier, dean of freshmen; and Wilbur L. Cross, dean of the Yale Graduate School.[9] Beyond forming a committee, no immediate actions were taken.

After a dinner conversation with President Angell in January 1922, Director Chittenden sent the president statistics that the scientist had been collecting for over a decade. The figures detailed the increasing number of "Hebrews" enrolled in the scientific school. Through the 1910s there had been about a 5 percent Jewish enrollment, but by 1921 this level had reached 8 percent.[10] (See appendix 4.) In April 1922, Alfred K. Merritt, college registrar, alerted the chairman of admissions, the college dean, and the university president to the news that the representation of the "chosen race," as Merritt put it, in Yale College had risen from 2 percent in 1901 to 7.5 percent in 1921.[11] Of the Yale College class of 1925—freshmen that year—over 13 percent were Jewish. By far the greatest percentage and number of Jews to matriculate in undergraduate Yale were represented in that year's freshmen. (See appendix 5.)

ASSESSING THE PROBLEM

Discussion of the Jewish question began in the offices of Robert Nelson Corwin. When the Yale Corporation created in 1920 a University Admissions

Board for a common freshman year for the scientific school and the college, Corwin, chairman of Yale athletics, became chairman of the new board. Until his retirement in 1933, Corwin—captain of Yale's 1886 championship football team, alumnus of Skull and Bones—would be the most influential administrator in determining the type of applicant that would enter Yale.

His May 3, 1922, letter to the college's Dean Frederick Jones formally set in motion the study of a quota on Jewish enrollment at Yale:

> The Corporation's Committee on Educational Policy has asked me to report at an early date on the number and status of students of Jewish origin now in the Undergraduate Schools and to discuss with them the advisability or necessity of concerting [*sic*] measures for limiting the number of those of this race or religion to be admitted to the college.
>
> The restrictive measures enforced or to be enforced at other colleges which draw from the same sources as we make the serious consideration of this question imperative. . . .
>
> (1) Does your experience lead you to believe that it is desirable, for reasons purely scholastic in the larger sense, to limit the number of Jewish students admitted to Yale?
>
> (2) If so, what measures do you suggest for accomplishing this end?
>
> (3) Do you regard the present proportion of Jewish students as too great when the interests of the whole undergraduate body are taken into consideration?[12]

Dean Jones, also a Skull and Bones man, replied with grave dismay regarding the position of Jewish students within the college:

> While many of these Hebrew boys are fine students, I think the general effect on the scholastic standing is bad. Some men say that they are not disposed to compete with Jews for first honors; they do not care to be a minority in a group of men of higher scholarship record, most of whom are Jews. It is also cited that the recent vote that the [varsity sport letter] "Y" is preferable to Phi Beta Kappa is indicative of a change of feeling which may be attributed in part to the feeling that the Jew is properly the "greasy grind" and that other students may hesitate to join the group.[13]

Jones in no uncertain terms stated his own academic priorities. In answering the question of whether it was the college's job to train scholars or to educate citizens, "Dean Jones had bet serenely on the citizen, and been frankly uninterested in the bright student."[14]

At Corwin's request, Roswell Angier, a psychologist and the dean of freshmen, also examined the Jew at Yale. Angier found that the Jewish students did well academically, averaging 73.2 as opposed to the class average of 70. It followed that a low ratio of Jewish students (5 percent) had been dropped for poor academic performance. The grade differences may have been statistically significant, but they were small. Jewish students averaged 11.3 points better in intelligence than the class average of 50. Jews numbered seven of the nineteen freshmen suspected of cheating in the previous two years, but only one of the five actually found guilty was Jewish. Nevertheless, Angier, too, favored a restrictive admissions policy. He conceded that in terms of scholarship and intelligence Jewish students led the class, but their personal characteristics made them markedly inferior:

> On the whole . . . many of them are personally and socially unacceptable. They're very likely eager for all sorts of scholarship aid, even though in some cases they are not in dire need of it, and I feel that they are more or less in the nature of a foreign body in the class organism. They contribute very little to class life. So far as conduct is concerned . . . they give very little trouble.[15]

The best solution, thought the dean of freshmen, would be a limit on the number of foreign bodies at Yale.

Robert Corwin summarized his analysis of the situation in his "Memorandum on the Problems Arising from the Increase in the Enrollment of Students of Jewish Birth in the University." The continuing increase in Jewish enrollment and recent actions to limit Jewish enrollment at Columbia, Princeton, Dartmouth, and Harvard forced Yale, Corwin said, to take action. Otherwise, the four major problems that Jews represented for Yale would not change. First was the possibility of Jews overrunning the university:

> The character of the Pre-Medical course in the Sheffield Scientific School is well known, even outside of the college. This course has become almost exclusively Jewish with unfortunate results for the Scientific School as a whole. Similar infiltration of other courses seems not improbable. Byers Memorial Hall serves as a college ghetto except on Sunday. Dwight Hall has not yet departed quite so far from the plans of its founders.

Second, Corwin claimed, the presence of Jewish students created tension between Yale and the New Haven Jewish community:

> The Bureau of Appointments reports that local Jews demand assistance and assume in general the attitude that Yale owes an education to every poor boy of this locality who can maintain a satisfactory record. Those who have been refused scholarships usually maintain that they have been discriminated against and not infrequently threaten retaliating measures.

In fact, Jewish students had been subjected to bias in scholarship awards, but this was irrelevant to Corwin's point. He resented local Jews protesting the bias. Third, Corwin noted that all of the undergraduate deans felt that Jews were disproportionately represented among the violators of the Honor Code. Finally, the Jewish boys, "perhaps not wholly from preference," tended to form groups by themselves, separate from the rest of the class.[16]

Rather than try to resolve the situations that had arisen, Corwin thought preventive measures were necessary to contain the source of the problems:

> The opinion is general in the Faculty that the proportion of those in college whose racial elements are such as not to permit of assimilation has been exceeded and that the most noticeable representatives among those regarded as undesirable are the Jewish boys, especially those of local origin. . . . It seems necessary that we should take some action.[17]

On May 12, 1922, Corwin brought these issues before the Yale Corporation Committee on Educational Policy and asked for further direction:

> Does the Corporation desire a restriction of numbers by the exclusion of low class Jews and their like so that the total quota of this type of student shall not [exceed] 6% or 8% or 10%?
>
> Does the Corporation desire to have the matter discussed in the three Undergraduate Faculties or by the Board of Admissions?
>
> Does the Corporation desire to state the general terms of restriction or should it prefer to instruct or empower the Board of Admissions to exercise such powers of restriction as expediency and experience shall dictate?[18]

After considerable discussion the committee returned the matter to Corwin's hands for further investigation. They directed that "the Committee on Admissions be asked to advise if admissions to the Freshman Class other than those established by scholastic examinations be desirable and if so what limitation should be and what form they should take."[19] The Corporation thought the issue of too much gravity to be treated lightly; it wanted to think very carefully before modifying an ancient standard.

To further matters, President Angell, who served as an intermediary between the Corporation and the rest of Yale, instructed Corwin to investigate disciplinary cases involving Jewish students. Reporting to the president, Corwin noted that the Jewish students conflicted with Yale expectations, not in their discipline, but in their ethics:

> Boys of this race conform in general to the routine regulations of college. Most of them live at home and are therefore rarely involved in any campus disturbance or like

breaches of discipline. All administrative officers, however, agree that the students of this race are in most frequent conflict with the honor system where this obtains and that the ethical code of a large proportion of the individuals of this race differs from that of the average student especially in matters of student honor and financial honesty.

But failure to observe the Yale Honor Code was not a Jewish problem alone. Whatever good qualities the character of the Yale man included, probity in academics and willingness to report dishonesty were lacking in enough Elis of all faiths that the honor system proved a failure and cheating was a component of the Yale educational fabric in the 1920s and 1930s. But on this occasion, Jews were on trial. Corwin urged President Angell to return to the Yale Corporation and press for a new policy toward Jews: "There seems to be no question that the University as a whole has about all of this race that it can well handle, that the number of applicants for admission is increasing and seems likely to increase still further. Many feel that the saturation point has already been passed."[20] This conclusion set the tone for Yale policies: The undergraduate schools did not want any more Jews than they already had.

FIASCO AT HARVARD

The question that would trouble the Yale administration was how best to accomplish such a goal. Yale, which prided itself on a fine public image and lived under a self-created legend of being a democratic institution, greatly feared falling victim to the same ugly publicity that Harvard had brought upon itself. Yale had often looked to her elder sister in Cambridge for guidance, so the events at Harvard in 1922 were followed closely in New Haven. In Cambridge, President A. Lawrence Lowell of Harvard (who had been a vice-president of the Immigration Restriction League) was urging the adoption of a quota system to solve what he saw as Harvard's Jewish problem. Between 1900 and 1922 the proportion of Jewish students at Harvard College had tripled, rising from 7 percent to 21.5 percent.[21] Through the carelessness of the Harvard publicity manager, word of the impending Jewish quota was allowed to leak out. Falsification of character and psychological tests, the manager implied, might also be options for limiting the proportion of Jews.[22] Once the news became public President Lowell, a firm believer in the justice of a ceiling on Jewish admissions, steadfastly defended his proposals, and a public relations nightmare ensued.

Julian Morgenstern, acting president of Hebrew Union College, outlined what he perceived to be the facts in the case of Harvard:

Recently . . . a steadily growing number of Jewish students from Boston's "East Side" have matriculated; immigrants, who live not in the Harvard dormitories but in their own Boston homes, with their families, and for the most part speak English with an accent, and persist in reading the Yiddish papers. They overrun the campus and crowd the library and class-rooms, and even presume to take the best seats there. Frequently they are noisy and assertive. They have little interest in athletics and other intercollegiate activities. They think only of what they can get out of the University and not of what they can contribute to it. They have little or no appreciation of the life of an American university and threaten seriously to undermine its peculiar standards and institutions. In short, so the argument goes, they are foreigners and not Americans, and their presence in numbers sufficient to exert a positive influence is threatening to America and Americanism.[23]

To end this threat to the Harvard spirit, argued some, Jewish quotas were a necessity:

There is a . . . a tradition, a flavor, that hangs about an historic institution like Harvard. A Harvard man can be recognized, wherever he goes, as a Harvard man, in no way to be confused with a Yale man, a Princeton man or any other of the multitudinous academic breeds. This peculiar flavor is a thing of unique value. It is what men send their sons to attain, rather than any mere form of scholarly equipment. And those who are responsible for the conduct of the institution owe it to themselves and to the alumni and to everyone else revering the name of Harvard to maintain the conditions under which this flavor may be imparted.

It is not to be denied that the flavor is most easily imparted to men of the old New England stock. Others take it effectively only when they are well immersed in social groupings of the original character. They must therefore be present in relatively small numbers; to change the metaphor, they must not increase beyond the saturation point. . . . Better one true Jewish Harvard man than ten mere Jewish scholars.[24]

The justification that Harvard officials offered for quotas ironically stated that a limitation on the number of Jews would best serve to eliminate anti-Semitism. President Lowell explained the concept in a June 1922 letter to a Harvard graduate:

The anti-Semitic feeling among the students is increasing, and it grows in proportion to the increase in the number of Jews. If every college in the country would take a limited proportion of Jews I suspect we should go a long way toward eliminating race feeling among the students, and, as these students passed out into the world, eliminating it in the community. This question is with us. We cannot solve it by forgetting or ignoring it. If we do nothing about the matter the prejudice is likely to increase.[25]

The identical argument would later appear within Yale circles.

For the American Jewish world, Harvard and quotas became the *cause célèbre* of 1922. Many Jewish intellectuals felt betrayed by Harvard, which they had considered to be a national institution. An editorial in *The American Hebrew*, the most widely circulated Anglo-Jewish journal, bewailed the situation: "Harvard's new policy of "limitation" is leading it to the outskirts of Avernus, the lake in Campania, whose sulphurous and mephitic vapors kill all birds who happen to inhale them. It was regarded by the ancients as the entrance to Hades."[26] Students in Cambridge and elsewhere were offended that Harvard required an applicant to state his color, religious preference, father's birthplace, and whether or not he or his father had ever changed their names.

Some editorial writers realized that private institutions, in those days before massive amounts of federal aid, had the right to refuse admission to whomever they chose. Consequently, they urged the nation to abandon its hope in private universities and instead to support state and city institutions of higher learning as the new repositories of American democracy.[27] Others, like Ralph P. Boas, urged the private universities to examine the negative consequences of quota systems:

> Character, personality, . . . eligibility to social circles, conformity to discipline and to accepted thoughts and usages—these [have] formally become the important criteria of admission. . . . It is needless to say that such a conception of educational eligibility would exclude a large proportion of Jewish students, all negroes, and most members of other immigrant groups. . . . Under a policy of exclusion of certain racial groups, of preferring the development of social qualities to active scholastic competition, the colleges are bound to lose more than they will gain.[28]

Decades would pass before institutions like Harvard and Yale would be able to reconcile themselves with such a conclusion.

The intensity of the scandal at Harvard increased when the American Federation of Labor entered the fray, passing a resolution to investigate Harvard's plans to restrict admissions on racial and religious grounds. The AFL's executive council was instructed to take action to prevent the contemplated discrimination.[29] On a state level, Governor Cox of Massachusetts appointed a legislative committee to investigate the charge that Harvard discriminated against Jews and was violating a state law assuring equal opportunity in Massachusetts colleges.[30]

In the wake of vociferous criticism from both outside and inside his university, President Lowell was forced to retract publicly his proposed quota system. He passed the issue over to a faculty committee whose members included Jews and non-Jews. In February 1923 the committee came out as unanimously opposing any racial discrimination in admissions. Two months later the report was approved by the Harvard Board of Overseers and released to a jubilant press. *The American Hebrew* predicted that the Harvard action would carry influence far beyond Cambridge, for it had proved that by avoiding the *numerus clausus* adopted by some European nations, "the United States is not aligned with slimy Rumania, with darkest Russia, [and] with barbarian Hungary."[31] Contrary to the magazine's prognostication, however, the strongest influence of the Harvard affair was not in preaching justice, but in teaching the nation's private colleges to keep their admissions policies away from the eyes of the press. Each generation's public would receive the pronouncements that it expected to hear, but with admissions procedures shielded from public view, the goals of each generation of administrators could efficiently be implemented.

OPTIONS FOR LIMITATIONS

To prevent a reaction like the one Harvard had experienced, Yale administrators treated the admissions problems gingerly. With utmost secrecy and caution Yale considered various methods of limiting Jewish enrollment. Dean Jones suggested insistence on passage of an English examination as an absolute requirement for admission and called for putting "a very definite limit, and a rather low one, on the amount of beneficiary aid that we grant to Jewish students."[32] Dean Angier suggested several methods of selection. One proposal was to require all applicants from within a fifty-mile radius of New Haven to have a personal interview with the chairman of the Board of Admissions. Another option was for Yale to undertake a more careful selection of those students admitted "on trial." Extreme care in the award of scholarships would also serve the purpose, Angier thought.[33]

Based on his correspondences with the deans, Corwin offered the Yale Corporation Committee on Educational Policy a "Memorandum on Jewish Problem" that detailed four methods for limiting the number of Jews:

   a. Restriction of the number admitted to the Freshman class, if not to a definite figure,—800, 850, 900,—at least to a point which would make a selection necessary and logical among those satisfying the scholastic requirements.

   b. Restriction of the number of Jews admitted to something below 10% of the total number if possible, by refusing transfers and by eliminating through . . . examination those who would presumably remain an alien element in our student body. . . .

    c. The restriction of scholarship grants.

    d. Psychological tests and personal inspection of local candidates.[34]

Following the Corporation's initial delay on May 12, 1922, Corwin reconsidered his proposals and settled on a three-point program that he urged President Angell to present to the Corporation at its May 26 meeting. The first method to limit Jews would be a general limitation on the number of freshmen to be admitted, which would force Yale to develop a selection procedure to choose among applicants who might otherwise be qualified on the basis of scholarship alone:

> This proposal is based upon the assumption . . . that there are several characteristics other than scholarship essential to success in college,—manliness, uprightness, cleanliness, native refinement, etc., which are, it would appear, lacking in a large proportion of the representatives of this race whose parents have but recently immigrated from eastern and southern Europe.

The second proposal, patterned after most of the leading prep schools, was to admit frankly that there would be a Jewish quota and limit admissions to some arbitrary percentage close to the proportion of Jews in the national population. Corwin suggested 6 percent. (At this time Jews in New Haven made up over 12 percent of the population, in Connecticut over 5 percent, and nationally over 3 percent.) The third proposal was to restrict the number of scholarships granted to Jewish students to a level commensurate with the Jewish proportion of the undergraduate body:

> There is, I believe, a feeling on the part of those who have studied the scholarship problem in college that that class which has felt the financial and social readjustment most is the solid middle class, composed in large part of people of education and refinement. The purchasing value of the salaries in this class has been so reduced as to, in many cases, place a college education out of their reach unless assistance is given, but the sons of such families are usually too self-respecting to ask such assistance. Many feel that the sons of this class are more deserving of our aid than those of recent immigrants and that our obligations are greater toward them.[35]

Any, or all, of these proposals, Corwin felt, would help Yale to face its future squarely.

With only one month of serious discussion behind it, the Corporation was reluctant to take action. President Angell remarked in a June letter to President

Harry Garfield of Williams College, "Some of our people have been getting a little nervous, but we have as yet taken no action of any kind." Yale was plainly all too aware of the controversies that could result from a misstep in handling the admissions problem. Angell recognized that "our Harvard friends have been passing through a rather unpleasant experience as a result of their discussion of methods of discouraging Hebrew patronage."[36] For the moment, Yale thought it best not to risk its honor with hasty action.

In light of the Corporation's hesitation, Dean Jones reexamined the Jewish question. By fall of 1922 he prepared a detailed study of the Yale College classes of 1911 through 1926. Hand-printing elaborate tables for each class, Jones identified the name, home residence, birthplace, father's birthplace, extracurricular activities, secondary school background, and future plans of each Jewish student that he knew of or could identify from class records. Most were products of the New Haven High School. The largest group of students had Russian-born parents; those with American-born parents made up the next largest group. Jones examined their financial position as well. They made up 25 percent of the scholarship and loan applicants to Yale College, though they received only 15 percent of the scholarship grants. The economic figures for the university as a whole were similar. Jones also counted the changing numbers of Jews, determining that "the Jewish element . . . nearly doubled" in the college between 1911 and 1926. Whereas the classes of 1911 through 1914 averaged 5.5 percent Jewish, those of 1923 through 1926 averaged 10.2 percent Jewish. The grades of the Jewish students were slightly higher than average, he found. The grade distribution was:

	A	B	C	D & E
Jews	5%	30%	45%	20%
All Students	7%	20%	43%	30%

Jones noted that 16 percent of Yale's Jews were elected to Phi Beta Kappa and that Jewish students won more than their share of academic prizes. Seventy-seven percent of Jewish students of the era were successfully graduated. This figure was comparable to the general average. Jones's final assessment of Yale's Jewish problem was most revealing. Even for a dean who disliked Jews, there were two sides to the issue. The social side encouraged restriction, the academic encouraged openness:

> The Jew, with ten and two-tenths per cent of the college enrollment, does not at present constitute an acute evil, but if the percentage increases during the next four college generations at the same rate as the last four, it will become a serious problem.

The best Jewish students have not the ability of the best students in the college, but despite the handicaps of poverty and working their way, the Jews make better average records than their Gentile fellows. They are ambitious and industrious and dinstinctly worth educating.[37]

Yale, Jones felt, could live with its present Jewish enrollment. Since Yale was partly an intellectual enterprise, the Jewish presence was an asset, so long as its growth could be restrained.

LIMITATION OF NUMBERS

Restraint would come in 1923, when the university decided to slay two Goliaths—the overcrowding and the Jewish question—with one stone. By publicly confronting the growing postwar housing shortage, Yale opportunistically could implement a discriminatory policy and avoid arousing public wrath. The public was well aware that the unity that had once bound the Yale student to his classmate had been strained by the numbers that had entered Yale's open door. People understood that to preserve the special character of Yale, enrollment would have to be limited. President Angell consequently would present to the Corporation a "Limitation of Numbers" program that would be acceptable to the public palate. "Limitations of Numbers" would mean many things at Yale. In particular, it served as a code word for restriction of Jews. Limitation would apply to raw numbers and especially to a "raw" race.

The new admissions criteria grew out of the Committee on Limitation of Numbers that President Angell had begun to lead in 1921. The committee was dormant until October of 1922, when President Angell solicited his deans on the question of whether it was necessary for the committee to meet. Dean Wilbur Cross of the graduate school saw "no good reason" to cause the committee to meet. Dean Jones of the college replied that there was "no immediate necessity" for a meeting. Yale College was not quite to the point of overflow, but, Jones believed, such a meeting would be required eventually. Dean Angier was the most concerned. The large number of freshmen that were pressing him as dean of freshmen led him to think that a meeting would be valuable. Instituting a limit on numbers, thought Angier, also "might give some ground for tackling the race question." Since action was being contemplated, the chairman of admissions, Robert Corwin, was brought on to the committee.[38]

Corwin apparently was quick to start to work on the numbers problem. To begin the investigation, Yale asked other universities to share their solutions to the problems of too many students and too many Jews. However, they responded cautiously, if at all: "It is difficult to get frank statements from the officials of other universities as to the means used in applying the requirements for admission with a view to limiting numbers, more especially the limitation as applied to those of the Hebrew race." Harvard remained sunk in a quagmire of indecision following its embarrassing encounter with public opinion and had taken only one action toward limitation: adoption of an application blank that left no doubt as to the candidate's race. The dean of Columbia College reported success in lowering Jewish enrollment from about 40 to 20 percent, mostly through psychological testing. "Most Jews," he informed Yale, "especially those of the more objectionable type, have not had the home experiences which enable them to pass these tests as successfully as the average native American boy." Princeton limited its Jewish enrollment through two means. First and perhaps foremost, the intensely unpleasant social environment for Jews at its college served to dissuade them from applying. Second, personal interviews with all "doubtful candidates" also served to exclude undesirables. At Amherst, Dartmouth, and Williams Colleges, Corwin reported, there was no pressing Jewish problem because few Jews lived in the cities in which these colleges were established: "Such limitation or repression as is exercised is effected by insisting upon residence in the college dormitories."[39]

The Yale committee recommended that a limit of approximately eight hundred freshmen be set. Only then could the Jewish problem be tackled, since "the fixing of a maximum number of Freshmen admitted seems a necessary basis for any restrictions which have to do with character rather than with scholarship." Representatives of several races with "undesirable characteristics" attended Yale. The most numerous were the New Haven Jewish students, the townies whose interests at Yale were often more academic than social.

> The serious phase of the problem here as at Harvard is the local Jew, who lives at home, knows nothing of dormitory associations, sees nothing of Chapel or Commons, and graduates into the world as naked of all the attributes of refinement and honor as when born into it. His wits have probably been sharpened but he has not gained wisdom, at least not the kind expected of college men.
>
> The question arises as to whether this type of man should be graduated upon the basis of his class room experiences only.

If Yale wished to stress the development of learning it had that option; if it wished to stress participation in extracurricular activities that route was open as well. But if it was to be an ethically mature institution, it then had an obligation to ensure that extracurricular pathways to success were as free of prejudice as those in the classroom. In this matter, Yale standards of educational polity failed. While the Jew was condemned by Yale administrators for avoiding the extracurricular associations, the extracurricular organizations were permitted to exercise their racio-religiously exclusive policies.

The committee recommended that finances also figure into the limitation of numbers equation. By discriminating against Jewish applicants in the awarding of financial aid, as Frederick S. Jones had done since his deanship had commended in 1909, Yale had already forced a higher percentage of Jews to devote their spare time to earning their way through college than otherwise would have occurred. The few chances that they had of participating in campus social life were further diminished.[40] Financial aid policies that discriminated against middle class students in favor of poor students consequently were suspect in the committee's report:

> There seems to be an inclination among alumni associations to choose as the recipi-
> ent of the various Yale Alumni Scholarships the corner newsboy or the son of the
> janitor of their building or a boy similarly circumstanced in the evident belief that
> the boy who is in the most distressing financial circumstances must be the most
> needy intellectually. The recipients are in quite a number of cases Jewish boys.[41]

In Dean Jones's opinion, the best Yale student (of any faith) was a rich Yale student. Answering an alumnus who complained of decadence at Yale in 1914, Jones wrote:

> My experience is that the sons of the wealthy parents are the best material we get here
> at Yale. This may sound undemocratic and you may think I have been inoculated
> with the social and financial germ, but it isn't true. I am simply doing justice to these
> young men who are the best type of Yale men we have.[42]

The "Limitation" committee thought that financial pressure would be an appropriate way to restrict the number of members of the uncouth and unwanted races at Yale:

> The number of scholarships allotted to this unassimilable element should be strictly
> limited upon the understanding that they are not so good an educational risk as the
> sons of the cultured, salaried class of native stock who hesitate to ask for aid but
> whose children will not reach college without such aid.[43]

More than the Yale purse, thought the committee, would have to be tightened, however. The decision-making process itself would have to be refined.

Race, alone, would not be the decision-making factor for admission. Any candidate who satisfied all of the requirements of admission with regard to examinations and secondary school recommendations would be accepted to Yale regardless of race. The prejudicial sorting would take place at the level of the marginal applicants, the "doubtful candidates." They would have to compete in a character test against other such students:

> All those who have shown even slight deficiencies in any of the subjects of study should appear before the Board of Admissions and be admitted or excluded upon the basis of visible evidence of educability, it being understood that the Corporation and Faculty believe that the alien and unwashed element in college should be reduced rather than increased.[44]

This method of selection became the core of the Limitation on Numbers policy. The committee's report was quickly sent on to the Yale Corporation, which on February 10, 1923, voted to restrict the size of each entering freshman class to 850.[45] With character of applicants to be judged by men of deep biases, discrimination against Jews would be a cornerstone of Yale undergraduate admissions for the next four decades.

Throughout the years of the Angell administration the number of Jews at Yale, as well as their demands on the university, would be closely monitored. The first formal count, Robert Corwin explained to President Angell, was "for the purpose of determining the Jewish representation in our domestic melting pot." Counted in February 1924 were the first freshmen who had entered under the new limitation of numbers policy:

> 115 members (or about 13%) of the students enrolled in the Freshman Class (total 854) are of the self-styled chosen race. Of these Jewish boys, forty-two live in New Haven and fifteen more come from nearby towns. These figures you will note do not indicate any radical change.
>
> Our census is based to some extent upon the surname. This test of race is not as accurate as that employed by Jephthah at the passages of the Jordan, but the count is, I think, approximately correct.[46]

In its first incarnation, the new policy failed to stem the flow of Jews to Yale. To counteract this failure, President Angell, exercising his wry sense of humor, could only suggest that "perhaps what we really need is a rejuvenation of the house of the Philistines."[47]

Without resorting to Philistines, the board of admissions slightly modified its standards over the following years to fine-tune the limitation on enrollment. Without specifically discriminating against Jews, the board adopted policies that would, seemingly impartially, discriminate against population groups that were largely, but not wholly, Jewish. In June 1924 the board accepted the second of Corwin's proposals from his "Memorandum on Jewish Problem" and voted to refuse admission to transfer students "from this general district (New Haven, Hartford, Bridgeport) who have attended schools which regularly prepare for the admission examinations."[48] Since nearly 75 percent of Yale's Jewish students from this era were products of the high schools of these three cities, the denial of transfer privileges would affect their entrance rate through this portal of Yale.[49] To assure that Limitation on Numbers would not exclude applicants with family ties to Yale, the board voted in 1925 that "limitation on numbers shall not operate to exclude any son of a Yale graduate who has satisfied all the requirements for admission." Among Yale, Harvard, and Princeton, Yale was the first to institutionalize admissions policies favoring alumni children.[50] This favoritism was to work against any relative newcomers to the campus, Jews prominently among them. The proportion of "legacies" (alumni sons) rose from 13.7 percent in the class of 1927 to 21.4 percent in the class of 1931. By the Depression class of 1936, when Yale was even more dependent upon alumni contributions, the enrollment of legacies would be 29.6 percent.[51] In 1926 the board adopted the last of Corwin's "Jewish Problem" recommendations from 1922 and voted to require that applicants sit for the new "scholastic aptitude test," developed by the College Entrance Examination Board.[52] Since a leading expert on the use of intelligence tests had concluded in 1923 (on the basis of poor data) that the average Jew was less intelligent than the average non-Jew, and since Columbia College had used similar tests to reduce Jewish enrollment, the aptitude tests were expected to weigh more heavily against Jewish examinees than against non-Jews.[53]

At all times a concern of Yale administrators was to prevent a public cry of outrage. When the Limitations committee was first meeting in 1922, a notation was made that "it would give us better publicity if we should speak of *selection* and of the rigid enforcement of high standards rather than of the limitation of numbers." In 1922 the term "limitation" had been linked to Harvard's proposal to restrict Jews.[54] By 1923, when the furor had already waned, Yale no longer felt constrained to announce publicly a Limitation on Numbers while it privately carried out its racial objectives. In 1930, when President Angell suggested that Yale require more detailed personal information from its applicants—in the style of the Harvard application—Corwin showed strong interest in not arousing public fears. He explained that by requiring an applicant to submit his full name, his father's birthplace, his mother's maiden name, and the comments of principals and headmasters, Yale was rarely left in doubt concerning the ethnic classification of an applicant. With no real need for prying further, Corwin concluded, "it seemed best, therefore, for the present at least, not to alarm our public by asking questions which might seem to indicate a sudden anti-Semitic attitude."[55] When the class of 1934 was enrolled in 1930 with Jews representing 8.2 percent of the class, the smallest proportion in nine years, Corwin proudly announced the result to President Angell:

> I trust you will be favorably impressed with the figures for the Class of 1934. In this connection it might be stated that the result shown, whether desirable or not, was attained without hue and cry and without any attempt on the part of those chiefly affected to prove that Yale had organized a pogrom.[56]

It had taken some time to succeed, but a limit on Jewish enrollment had been achieved.

STUDENT SENTIMENT

Many of the college students supported the administration's attempts to preserve the Yale of the past. When Harvard announced in 1926 that it would place much weight on "character, personality, and promise" in its admissions decisions, as well as require applicants to submit their photographs, the editors of the *Yale Daily News* applauded Harvard's actions and jumped on the bandwagon. They called for similar refinement of admissions at Yale, fearing that "Yale will soon reach the sorry state where her sons will be mere brain specimens, where Yale graduates will find no room for what children of theirs are not abnormal." Representing one major school of undergraduate thought, the *News* editors worried that Yale's need to restrict the size of its classes would result in admissions by academic criteria only. The editors insisted that "Yale must institute an Ellis Island with immigration laws more prohibitive than those of the United States government." Were Yale not to do so, the time would soon arrive when

> potential captains of industry must absent themselves from the groves of academe and take up their unpurposeful studies elsewhere, while the intelligentsia of the approaching renaissance Americanize even such an isolated province as Yale in a merciless competition for seats in the University. If this era is admitted, Yale will no longer be a heterogeneous group of average citizens, but will be essentially a brain plant.[57]

For many years, though, Yale had not been a school for "average citizens." The question was which elite it would draw its population from.

The editors called for Yale to establish a personnel bureau "to study the character, personality, promise and background of men who wish to enter the University." It was obvious, they felt, "that Yale would be justified even with her ideal of 'service to the nation' in sloughing off the unkempt at the same time she drops the unlettered." The *News* went so far as suggesting that Yale "might go [Harvard] one better and require applicants to submit photographs of their fathers also."[58] Though no mention was made of Jews, it is clear that if this opinion had become policy, its effects would have been felt the most by that "unkempt" racial group.

Jewish students suspected that bias was a factor in admissions, but, lacking firm evidence to justify complaints, few challenged the natural order. In 1931 Eugene V. Rostow (B.A. 1933), writing in the undergraduate publication *Harkness Hoot,* reported that Clarence W. Mendell (dean of Yale College 1926–37) had told him that he had not observed any anti-Jewish discrimination in the course of his work on the undergraduate admissions committee. Further attempts to separate fact from fiction in Yale admissions left Rostow stymied:

> In spite of the number of suggestive incidents and no lack of faculty suspicion, the Board of Admissions impresses the observer, like the excellent Scholarship Committee, as being above callous prejudices. Here as elsewhere, the investigator is puzzled by the mass of reliable rumour and unprovable fact. This unavoidable situation, (for few people are capable of admitting anti-Semitism openly) clouds the entire question.[59]

To preserve the confidentiality of applicants, the admissions process had to be closed to inquiring eyes. A hidden process also allowed the "callous prejudices" of some faculty and administrators to be withheld from public and student scrutiny.

ALUMNI OPINIONS

The economic situation at Yale, as at many private universities, in the twentieth century required the institution to depend on the good will of its graduates for financial support. And because few things in life were free, the university was required at least to consider, if not honor, the thinking of its alumni. With regard to Jews, expressed alumni sentiment tended to favor the idea of strict limitations. One alumnus, on the faculty of the Swarthmore Preparatory School, in 1927 wrote to a Yale alumni fund-raiser to share his concern at the changing population at Yale:

I try to induce a number of boys to go to Yale from here. At present they will not consider going, saying there are too many Jews. What is the use of raising money for Yale
if it is to be filled with "Yids"?

This year two boys [are going to Yale] from here, one is a Jew, or in other words
50% Jewish contingent going from this school, which probably represents the proportion from all schools all over the country. . . .

Make it a purely selective admission by interview and school record and Yale will
again have a student body like in the old days.[60]

The letter of protest was passed along to Thomas W. Farnam, associate treasurer and comptroller of the university. Writing to the fund-raiser, a 1909 Yale
College graduate, Farnam indicated that the feelings of Yale administrators coincided with those of the Swarthmore Prep teacher:

It will interest you to know that we are making every effort to remedy the condition
that [the letter-writer] fears. You will realize that conditions have changed since you
graduated, and that there are boys that come through the Connecticut high schools
that have sufficient scholarship and recommendations as to character, that we cannot
refuse to accept. However, the fact that we have limited our Freshman Year . . . and
that we have a very large excess of applications, gives our Board of Admissions an opportunity to make selections, and when they do make their choices they are just as
interested as [your correspondent] is in keeping out the undesirable element.

We handle our scholarship funds in the same way. Those applying far exceed the
number available, and here again we are able to stem the flow to some extent.[61]

The processes employed were not watertight, but they restrained enough Jews
to keep the Jewish population down.

Some of the most influential alumni were those who sat on the Yale Corporation. As a group, the Corporation refused to countenance strict Jewish quotas. Rather, some of its members encouraged admissions officers to employ
more subtle biases to achieve the same end. One noteworthy instance occurred
in 1929, when *The Hartford Courant* published the names of all the Connecticut residents accepted to enter the Yale class of 1933. Francis Parsons (B.A. 1893,
LL.B. 1897), fellow of the Yale Corporation, became incensed that roughly 20
percent of these names appeared to be Jewish. Having underlined every Jewish
name that he could identify, Parsons sent off the article with a note of protest
to Admissions Chairman Corwin. Corwin's response outlined the admissions
officers' attitudes, the need for subtle means of prejudice, and the difficulties
that would be involved with imposing an outright Jewish quota:

The publicity impressed me quite as unfavorably as it did you and your associates. I had in fact discussed this matter with one of the deans rather fully and with some feeling earlier in the day. The list as published reads like some of the "begat" portions of the Old Testament and might easily be mistaken for a recent roll call at the Wailing Wall. . . .

As a matter of fact, the Jewish representation in our Undergraduate Schools has not as yet run to embarrassing proportions, though I should not put on black if it were less. No accurate count has been made of the Jewish representation in the present Freshman class, but it will not be far from ten per cent,—a little under, I think and hope. . . .

This racial problem is never wholly absent from the minds of the Board of Admissions. . . . It would be easily possible to limit the number or proportion of Jews admitted, if those associated with you in higher authority approve and will stand by whatever the immediate consequences. . . . Harvard ran into rough weather by attempting to justify her proposed action publicly before putting it into force. She is now, however, sawing wood and saying not a word. Those now being excluded under her present silent process expect us to take up the slack which she is paying out. . . .

Certain phases of this intricate problem reach beyond the competence of the Board of Admissions and arise in some measure from the fact that so great a proportion of our Jewish representatives are of local origin. . . . Some of our prominent local Jews hold key positions, politically and financially, and it is I suspect feared that questions of taxation and like matters might become troublesome if any possible excuse or occasion were given. If, however, the matter were handled without publicity and firmly, any agitation would probably exhaust itself largely in threats and innuendos.

Whereas Harvard was using one silent "saw," Yale was employing a combination of inaudible surgical knives. Not without the encouragement, Corwin noted, of some elements of the Jewish community itself. He considered these elements to be "the more intelligent and influential members of the race" who frequently expressed a preference for some limitation on Jewish enrollment and preferred to send their sons to universities that practiced such limitation.[62]

Within two weeks of Corwin's letter to Parsons, the entire Corporation acknowledged its satisfaction with the work of the admissions committee. The Corporation formally resolved to express "appreciation of the effective manner in which the Board of Admissions has dealt with its difficult task and especially to commend the action of the Board of Admissions in reducing the number in the entering class."[63] The high proportion of Connecticut Jews entering Yale was not enough to suppress the Corporation's pleasure with the overall trend in Yale admissions.

LIMITATION OF NUMBERS IN THE GRADUATE AND PROFESSIONAL SCHOOLS

With the exception of the school of medicine (see chapter 7), anti-Jewish bias does not seem to have been a significant component of admissions policies in the various graduate and professional schools of the university. Since their missions were more academically oriented than the mission of the college and since their leaders generally upheld those missions, racial, religious, and social factors were generally not permitted to interfere with academic criteria for entrance. Shortly after Yale commenced its freshman year Limitation on Numbers program in 1923, President Angell asked each of his deans (except for those of the freshman year and the medical school—the two schools where limitations had already begun) to consider whether the limitations were necessary for their own sections of Yale. At the time, none found limits urgently needed. Within two years the Limitation on Numbers was extended to cover each of Yale's schools. Available evidence, however, does not suggest that there were any particular anti-Jewish biases outside of the undergraduate and medical schools. The fact that few academic positions were open to Jews put a damper on the number of Jewish applicants to graduate-level schools; this factor was likely far more significant in keeping down the numbers of Jewish graduate students than any actions of admissions officers. In 1927 Dean Wilbur Cross of the graduate school reported that "the Hebrew element in the Graduate School" had been as high as 9 percent in past years, but by that year it had fallen to 4 percent. It does not seem that the decrease was a result of anything but normal variation.[64]

THE 1930s

Although Yale fared better than other universities during the Depression years, financial concerns prompted President Angell to suggest in 1932 that the Limitation on Numbers at the levels of both freshman and transfer admissions be relaxed in order to increase tuition revenue. His deans reminded him that if the limits were raised, Yale might be forced to accept many of the Jews for whom the limits had been created. Chairman of Admissions Robert Corwin posed several objections to the idea, among them the unwelcome publicity that Yale might garner if it hoped to enlarge its class without accepting more Jews: "You will, of course, see some of the racial problems involved if it should become known that we propose to increase the size of the Freshman class."[65] Charles Warren, dean of the Sheffield Scientific School, was concerned that accepting more transfer students might bring in more undesirable Jews and might actually eliminate the financial advantage Yale hoped to gain:

> For the last two or three years at least the great majority of these [transfer] applications have been from young gentlemen of Hebrew persuasion who are anxious to come here for the purpose of preparing for medical work. In my opinion there are very few of these who are really desirable students, and among those who appear to be fairly desirable, there are almost none who do not apply for substantial scholarship aid.[66]

President Angell insisted, nevertheless, that the need for income demanded an increase in enrollment. He promised Corwin that he was "not insensitive to your solicitude on racial grounds," but allowed that finances had to come first in decision-making.[67] By May 1932 the Yale Corporation accepted Angell's recommendation and voted to increase the size of the freshman class slightly. Revenues would be gained by admitting more students, especially those with the ability to pay their own way.[68] The number eventually accepted to the class of 1936 was 959, over 200 of them on provisional terms—without the financial aid they had requested. Many of this latter group were Jewish, but Corwin remained confident that the Jewish proportion would be maintained: "The racial quota among the provisionally accepted applicants is somewhat larger than is usual or desirable. I trust that it will be reduced by the conditions imposed in the letters sent to those requesting aid."[69] On this occasion, poorer applicants had been the primary victims of Yale policies. Since many of this group were Jewish, Jews suffered disproportionately in the admissions scheme. The final Jewish proportion of that class, 11.7 percent, would remain within previous bounds. (See appendix 3.)

The retirement of Robert Corwin in 1933 did not change Yale admissions policies. The application form was, however, soon modified to include birthplace of students' mothers along with the previously collected data. Alan Valentine, successor to Corwin, concisely explained the need for the additional information: "This knowledge will give us a more accurate check as to the race of the applicant."[70]

PRESIDENT ANGELL

Life provides each generation with the opportunity to prove its mettle, and the 1920s were a time of testing at Yale. Leading the university and sometimes prodding Yale College toward modernity was the man whom the Yale Corporation elected as president on February 19, 1921, James Rowland Angell. His administration transformed Yale into as great a university as Yale had long been as a college. His commitment to intellectual concerns reminded the institution of its central purpose as a stimulant to inquiry and a protector of learning. Harkness family money founded residential colleges, and donations from the estate of lawyer John W. Sterling were used to rebuild Yale physically and to expand intellectually as never before. Angell's leadership was not without challenge, however. Angell was the first non-Yale graduate in 175 years to assume the Yale presidency. Angell simply had no previous Yale connection, a serious disadvantage. He also did not interact well with the faculty, many of whom distrusted the "foreign" president: "Try as he might—and try as his friends in the Corporation might—within the sacred precincts of the old College Angell remained a stranger. Between him and the old guard there was a barrier and it did not melt away." For his part, Angell was dissatisfied with the college leadership and distrusted their intellectual motivations. Angell encountered resistance in his attempts to eliminate some of the childish aspects of the college, improve the quality of the faculty, and gain some control over an institution with a long tradition of faculty dominance.[71] Unlike many newcomers to Yale, Angell would succeed in changing it. But he would never succeed in becoming a welcome part of it.[72] Perhaps his failure to gain personal acceptance among his Yale peers prevented him from acting forcefully to restrain prejudice. A cynical sense of humor had to suffice. Though he was far less prejudiced than his colleagues within the Yale administration or his contemporaries at other northeastern universities, his subtle encouragement of bias and his sometimes complacent attitude toward racial and religious prejudice allowed the growth of a fearful attitude toward Jews that would affect admissions policies at Yale for forty years.

The logical Angell did not condemn Jews in the same harsh tones used by Chairman of Admissions Corwin, but his actions had similar effects. When Milton Winternitz, dean of Yale's medical school, asked Angell to write a letter of recommendation for the dean's son Thomas to attend preparatory school, the president sent a letter of qualified praise: "Dr. Winternitz is a Jew. His wife was not. This boy has in his physique the Jewish traits. . . . So far as I know, the lad has not traits at all that are in any wise a source of anxiety."[73] On another occasion, Angell was willing to waive his racial feelings in support of one boy's application for admission to Yale College:

> I have known [the applicant's father] for some years and have every reason to think [the father] a man of the highest quality. I think his ancestry is Polish and so far as I recall, not Jewish. In any case, I hope the boy may encounter no obstacles in his plan to come to us, as the family enjoys a position in Philadelphia which would represent some real values to us in our alumni body.[74]

In a world dominated by power and money, influence could sometimes run thicker than blood.

When a private inquiry concerning discrimination against Jewish applicants reached his office, Angell replied with an honesty that spoke only half the truth: "We have no definite policy which involves our accepting or rejecting any specific number, or percentage, of Jewish students."[75] The Yale admissions system did not invoke a *numerus clausus,* so Angell was not dishonest. A formal quota was abjured, but informal policies of prejudice were accepted as routine.

On a broader scale, Angell allowed his deputies to perform the "dirty work" of sifting out applicants of unwanted backgrounds, but he was fully supportive of their anti-Jewish goals. In 1934, for example, taking cognizance of a national trend to reward applicants having distinguished secondary school achievements by reducing entrance requirements, Angell suggested that Admissions Chairman Valentine institute a policy of accepting applicants in the upper fifth of their school classes to Yale without examination. The opportunity could be offered, Angell suggested, only in areas where high Jewish populations would not force the university to accept students that it did not want: "To avoid a possible influx of undesirable racial groups, it might be necessary to limit the privilege to schools not in metropolitan centers, at least not in the eastern centers."[76] In public, the president strongly criticized the fiery ranting of "Radio Priest" Father Charles Coughlin. In private, however, Angell's black humor encouraged the racist attitudes that thrived at Yale, as we learn from his response to Robert Corwin's final report on Jewish enrollment, written shortly before Corwin's retirement. Corwin reported in the classes of 1926 through 1936 a Jewish enrollment ranging from 8.2 percent to 13.3 percent, with an average of 10.9 percent. In the last seven of those classes, over one-third of Yale's Jews had come from the New Haven, Hartford, and Bridgeport, Connecticut areas.[77] Angell could only chide Corwin on the results:

> I am extremely [interested] in the Hebraic record which you are kind enough to send me. The oscillations from year to year are rather larger than I would have expected.

In any case, the material is very informing and it seems quite clear that, if we could
have an Armenian massacre confined to the New Haven district, with occasional in-
cursions into Bridgeport and Hartford, we might protect our Nordic stock almost
completely.[78]

This was New Haven, not Heidelberg, but in retrospect, considering the storm
brewing in Europe, Angell's reference to the earliest example of modern geno-
cide loses its humorous tone and appears more a tragic comment on the American intelligentsia.

The Limitation of Numbers plan implemented at Yale in 1923 became a part
of a process that engulfed the Northeast and the nation. Nevertheless, sociologist Stephen Steinberg has noted that limits on Jewish enrollment at the elite
eastern colleges in the 1920s "did not constitute a major obstacle to Jewish aspirations."[79] Jews were not completely "excluded," and the most qualified could
always find admission at the colleges of their choice. The marginal students had
the bitter experience of knowing that they were unfairly denied admission; still,
most who sought a college education could find one, even if it required attendance at a less prestigious institution than they preferred.

The real problem, of course, was not a "Jewish problem" but an "institutional problem." At Yale it was a "Yale problem." When the great college in
New Haven turned against more than a century of admissions policies that
were open to all scholastically qualified, college-age males, Yale took up the
mantle of righteous duplicity and gave sanction to insidious bigotry.[80]

Chapter 4 Mixed Messages: Undergraduate Life between the World Wars

The First World War, like an efficient catalytic convertor, had a rapid and profound effect on American Jewry. Entering the conflict with the impurities of immigrant status, those Jews who fought for America in the war felt cleansed of the alien fetters they had once borne. With gusto they returned home to convey to their families and friends a powerful sense of belonging. One manifestation of that sense of belonging was their zeal for the public school system. Since education was the prime route for the acculturation of youth, many young Jews flocked to the colleges and reached for the opportunity to become fully Americanized.

American attitudes had not, however, been so "liberated" by the great folly in Europe. Instead, the vicious fear of the foreigner, a concept exported from Europe, stimulated the nascent racism in the American character. The outbreak of war triggered an upsurge of xenophobia, primarily directed against German-Americans, and the spread of racism. Oscar Handlin described the sounding of the nativist alarm in the 1910s:

Three enormously popular books by an anthropologist, a eugenist, and a historian revealed to hundreds of thousands of horrified Nordics how their great race had been contaminated by contact with lesser breeds, dwarfed in stature, twisted in mentality, and ruthless in pursuits of their own self-interest.[1]

The anthropologist was Madison Grant (B.A. 1889), member of New York City's social elite. His widely read book, *The Passing of the Great Race,* warned that racial intermarriage led to propagation of the lesser races. Grant pleaded for racial consciousness and pride to stop the "hybrids" that reduced proud races to the lowest common denominator of an interracial marriage. Grant's words found receptive ears. By 1920 the anti-Catholicism that had sprouted in 1914 ripened to direct itself against immigrants from Ireland, Italy, and Poland. The Sacco-Vanzetti case perpetuated the racist belief that all Italians were anarchists. Writing in a national magazine, a New Haven social worker lamented that immigrants "surround our city in colonies like a Roman wall." Deteriorating, immigrant-filled slums bordered elegant buildings of colleges like Yale. Old-stock Anglo-Saxon Americans felt besieged.[2]

Jews, too, were caught up in the wave of prejudice. Anti-Semitism spread from elite resorts and clubs to the common man. The growing anti-Jewish feeling had already become so strong in the Chicago of 1913 that a local Jewish fraternal organization, the B'nai B'rith, founded the Anti-Defamation League. When Henry Ford launched his anti-Jewish campaign in the *Dearborn Independent* of May 22, 1920, he found a public eager to believe the distortions that he supplied. The Ku Klux Klan chose this time to add Jews to their list of "enemies of America." At the peak of Klan activity in Connecticut, in 1924, "Konclaves" staged around the state attracted thousands of supporters.[3]

What the racist resented as much as anything about the Jew was his success at becoming an American. Whereas nineteenth-century German-origin Jews had prospered greatly, the same was just beginning to happen to Jews of East European origin. With colleges serving as a mark of both social achievement and education in America, the educational institutions became a major locus of Jewish-Christian interaction and a source of bitterness for the racist:

> Of all our immigrant groups, [the Jew] is at once the most self-assured and the most eager to get the benefit of all the Anglo-Saxon has to offer him. No other group flocks to our colleges with the same pathetic thirst for learning. The Russian Jew has an hereditary respect for culture, and he seems also to have a certain intensity which . . . translates itself into an ambition and a persistence which we Anglo-Saxons hate. It defeats us at our own game. It not only wins scholarships and prizes in the schools and universities; it solves problems, and achieves intellectual or financial success be-

fore social adjustments have been made—while the voice is still uncouth, the accent strong, and the sense of tact and social relationship still in the stage of a push-cart peddler. The very rapidity with which the Jew adjusts himself to the primary conditions of life in America is his chief handicap. The very fact that he appreciates the opportunities of America is a cause of prejudice; he sends his children to college a generation or two sooner than other stocks, and as a result there are in fact more dirty Jews and tactless Jews in college than dirty and tactless Italians, Armenians, or Slovaks.[4]

The failure of other minorities to succeed by American standards mitigated resentment toward their presence on the campuses. The great academic success of Jews was, in that era, their social downfall.

Though the ritual of Judaism had come to mean little on a daily basis to most Jewish students, they did not want to dismiss their heritage completely. Instead, they wanted to be both genuine Americans and genuine Jews. This obstinate straddling of religious and social positions enraged the entrenched bigot. The more that Jews held on to a Jewish identity, thought the biased, the more American would be debased:

Anglo-Saxon Americans have small interest in the "melting-pot" except as a phrase. They do not want to be fused with other races, traditions, and cultures. If they talk of the melting-pot they mean by it a process in which the differences of the immigrant races will be carried away like scum, leaving only the pure ore of their own traits . . . They consider the American a completed product, perfection already attained, and they resent any racial or cultural group which comes among them and persists in believing that it has something worthy of its own.[5]

So grew a powerful pressure to conform. To begin to be accepted by the dominant group required the "minorities" not just to remove from their bodies the coats of unfamiliar colors, but also to embrace the governing sacred ideals.

In its own microcosmic way, Yale mirrored the society about it. In his sentimental novel *Who Took the Gold Away,* John Leggett (B.A. 1942) captured the social pressure that existed in the lull between the world wars:

Yale was a goldfish bowl in which we fluked about, earnestly unfurling our aspirations. The telling marks on a man were his prep school, his dress and what he did with his leisure. Grace, detachment, not seeming to care and, above all, being with acceptable companions—these were prizes.

This piscine trope governed Yale life. It was not important what one was, as long as one was like all the other fish in the bowl. Anyone with the slightest bit of social awareness knew how important it was to fit the accepted mode, and to do so in almost every aspect of existence. If everyone "heeled" the *News* or the *Lit*, only a "terrible goon" would not follow the trend. If everyone went out for a sport or a team managership, only an "unenlightened oaf" would stay in the library to study. If everyone found religious practices absurd, a "true believer" was suspect. If everyone from a preparatory school was marked with class, then a public school student was a barbarian. If the out-of-towner bore the stamp of breeding, a townie carried the stench of the gutter. The natural spirit of a university, the encouragement of divergent thought, had not yet been accepted in terms of encouraging independent styles in the college.[6]

The Yale social system of the era was a castelike collection of cliques. On the simplest of levels, there were "insiders" and "outsiders." Altogether 25 to 30 percent of the students were of an "underprivileged" status. Meanwhile, those who "belonged" controlled the centers of student authority and prestige, dominating life on the campus. The fraternities, the societies, the major publications were all the domain of the well-bred. On the campus the major factor that divided students socially was preparatory school versus public school background, and it was the prep-school ethos that dominated.

> In so wide-open a race the man who entered from Andover or one of the other large preparatory schools, with a wide acquaintanceship in his own and preceding Classes, had an obvious head start. Certain not to be overlooked in the Sophomore fraternity elections, he enjoyed an almost prohibitive advantage for nomination to one of the important managership competitions. Preparatory-school background also gave some small advantage in the later election of officers for the *News* and the *Record*, the Glee Club and Dramat, while means and social polish seemed very nearly prerequisite for election to one or two of the Senior societies.

In this atmosphere of extreme class-consciousness, there was little interaction between social classes.[7]

What fundamental force operated to define the Yale social system? This tantalizing question is difficult to answer simply. . . . Was this force an electromagnetic energy, whereby like repulsed like and opposites attracted? Hardly. The regularity with which students of a similar background sought each other's company made some of New Haven's clothes-dealers expert at predicting society elections months in advance. Yale students, on the whole, did not come to Yale to learn from the examples of other social classes. Unlike electromagnetic force, undergraduate opposites stayed far apart. . . . Was the force a "strong nuclear" force, as essential for holding Yale together as it is for preserving the structure of an atom? Perhaps. Without its intermeshing cliques and its chain reactions propelling freshman neophytes to sophomore heelers to junior managers to senior powerhouses, Yale would not have been Yale. Yet programs of advancement do not require a caste system for validity. . . . Was the force a "weak interaction"—like the almost imperceptible decay of a proton into neutron, positron, and neutrino—acting silently, but creating real divisions? To some extent. There were no formalities of final division that acted prior to the ritual of Tap Day, but undergraduate practice, stealing softly like a spider through the night, did erect gossamer walls between the students. . . . Or was the force a weighty "gravity" that kept Yale students entrenched in their positions? Most likely. Yale's Brahmins, for all practical purposes, spoke only to Brahmins. The social exclusivity that they had learned at home was naturally carried on at Yale. The idea of associating with an Untouchable was in gross violation of custom. If Brahmins did not maintain the tradition of superiority, then the bounds that defined the elite would have been blurred.

Aside from school background, the major factor that defined the elite was financial. Fed by wealth, Yale symbolized wealth. A 1926 report on its thirty million dollars worth of property holdings claimed that Yale was America's wealthiest institution of learning.[8] In the heady era before the Great Depression, for colleges across the nation, conspicuous consumption by the rich was common. Yale seniors, the only students permitted to have cars at college, indulged their fantasies. Stories would circulate of thousands of dollars lost in one evening's crap game.

> Hip flasks and coonskin coats, football weekends and reckless driving, wild drinking and dances close to brawls: such became the caricature of the postwar generation, its passport photograph.
> By no means everyone participated.[9]

One had to have financial backing both to afford the good life and to be accepted by those experiencing the *joie de vivre*. Those of moderate means, the middle-class students, might not have been able to fritter away fortunes but, if they were ambitious, found Yale life open to them. Students identified as poor, students who had to perform a "low-class" job such as waiting on tables, however, landed in an almost inescapable social dungeon. The rare student who was dependent on part-time earnings and exceptional at something (football, especially) might win the admiration of the elite and be admitted to their ranks. The less sensational poor student found himself unable to escape his caste. The student who was so poor that all his nonacademic time had to go toward a job never participated in social life at all. Not that they did not want to, one poor student recalled: "I'd ask myself, 'How can these guys go out for the *Yale Daily News,* work hard on the *News,* and still come prepared for class?' I knew it was because they didn't have to work. It got me depressed." A wealthier Jewish student such as L. Richard Gimbel (B.A. 1920, son of "Gimbel Brother" Ellis Gimbel), for example, found the time to become business manager of the *Yale Record,* the campus humor magazine. Describing those whose wallets were not so endowed, another wealthier student said of the poorest of his classmates, "They really never got a chance to go to Yale."[10]

Yet another aspersion that could be cast upon the Yale student's status was to be labeled "townie." This designation deposited a student at the base of the Yale pyramid. As E. Digby Baltzell described in *The Protestant Establishment,* Jewish students, in particular, were affected: "There were . . . a few rich and socially ambitious Jews at Yale, where the majority of the others were 'townies' from New Haven who were accepted in order to accommodate the local community and were no problem socially simply because, as it were, they did not count."[11] In one of life's painful ironies, Yale's sympathy toward New Haven applicants, motivated by political considerations and exhibited by a generous quota of local students admitted, created a large group of third-class citizens of the undergraduate republic. Numerous parents jumped at the opportunity to send their sons to Yale. Yet often they only jumped half-way. Not that they did not want their sons to have a full collegiate experience, but money at home was tight. A few dollars could easily be saved and a boy could help with work at home if he did not live in the dormitories. College-level learning was the necessity; collegiate socializing, for many, was an unaffordable luxury. Many a townie (10 percent of the undergraduates) therefore attended but half of Yale.[12]

Some attempts had been made to integrate townies into campus life. For instance, as part of "Big Brother"–type volunteer programs in the 1910s, students like Howard Malcolm Baldrige (B.A. 1918), destined for Skull and Bones, would take local children to visit the dormitories on Yale's Old Campus. There the Elis might teach the youngsters to throw a football or read a story to them—so acculturating the greenhorns to American ways. Abraham Alderman, who grew up in New Haven, warmly remembered how in winter the Yale students would bring him and his friends inside the dormitories, which were heated to a comfortable degree rarely found in the ghetto. And Max Lerner (B.A. 1923) recalled a "get acquainted" program for townie freshmen that Dwight Hall, the campus YMCA, sponsored in the fall of his freshman year of 1919. Each off-campus freshman was assigned a junior or senior student adviser. This upperclassman—for Lerner it was Thornton Wilder (B.A. 1920)—was to show the neophyte the ropes of Yale. If all went according to plan, the freshman and the upperclassman were to meet occasionally during the school year. Unfortunately, as with many an advisory system in many a situation in many an institution, this program for freshman townies failed. Cultural gaps sometimes proved too wide to bridge.[13]

Many townies recalled that, living at home, they felt that they did not belong to Yale. This alienation of the New Haven student represented a marked change from what had prevailed prior to the First World War. Whereas a Joseph Alderman (Ph.B. 1915) had once proudly laid claim to being as much a son of Eli as anyone (see chapter 2), townies of the 1920s and 1930s often felt like strangers in a strange land. They calmly took the invisible role: "We kept our distance, and never felt discriminated against, since we didn't push our way in."[14] Whatever crowd they belonged to in high school, they stayed with. Only their crowds were headed not for Skull and Bones, but for oblivion. A few tried to escape the high school gang, but to do so often meant fighting one's way into a circle that was quite happy the way it already was. Remembered Max Lerner: "We were kept out of everything. Not in any formal way, but in how we were treated." Born in Russia, Lerner had moved with his family to the United States when he was a four-year-old. At age ten, he arrived in New Haven. Four years of achievement at New Haven's Hillhouse High School had won him a crucial four-year scholarship from Yale, without which he could not have afforded the college. Yet college was in many ways a painful experience. He tried hard to be an Eli, but could not find acceptance among the polished crowd. Naively hoping that appearances could overcome all prejudices, he saved his money to buy a raccoon coat and hip flask like all the local elite, but found these nostrums insufficient to save him from himself: "I didn't look right or sound right. I didn't know how to behave. . . . I lacked social graces." He made many efforts to be with non-Jews and win their friendships: "It was clear that I was reaching out. They knew it." In non-townie circles, he received little acceptance. It was as if those New Haven boys who had come to Yale from a high school were ritually unclean for certain aspects of Yale life.[15]

Nevertheless, townie student life was not devoid of social intercourse. Friendships between New Haven Jews and Italians, who shared immigrant family experiences, were sometimes carried over to the campus. In Dwight and Byers halls, centers for townie life on the campus, many of the local Jewish and Italian students congregated during spare daytime hours. Figuratively hidden away from the Yale limelight, Dwight and Byers were integral parts of Yale for many of the townie undergraduates. The old Dwight Hall stood ground on the college's Old Campus from 1885 to 1926. Headquarters for the Yale University Christian Association, the building offered the local college boys a convenient place for socializing—for conversation or a game of cards. The dorms were not theirs, but in Dwight they could be separate and unequal.[16] Byers Hall filled the same need for the Sheffield Scientific School students. There the boys could lock up their books and lunches in the morning, and briefly relax in lounge chairs and read newspapers later in the day. After old Dwight was razed in 1926, Byers served both the college and the scientific school as the sole outpost to New Haven students.[17]

CATHOLIC STUDENTS

Looking at the position of Catholics and other "minorities" adds further insight into the Yale caste system in the interwar period. Historically, Catholics in America had been less inclined than Jews to send their children to institutions like Yale. Part of the reason was the lower regard that Catholics had often had for advanced education. American Catholics heard the message from the pulpit: Do not educate your children beyond their proper station in life. But the nature of higher education also entered in. When a Catholic youth was considering college, bishops and priests of the nineteenth century warned of the dangers lurking in non-Catholic institutions.[18] Catholics, therefore, tended to avoid Protestant campuses, preferring instead their own learning centers such as Fordham, Holy Cross, Georgetown, and the Catholic University of America. Prior to the Second World War there were more Catholics than Jews at Yale, but whereas the percentage of Jews attending Yale was greater than their national representation, that of Catholics was just below their national level.[19]

With regard to campus life, Yale behavior was not consistent in reflecting the prevailing anti-Catholic sentiment on the national scene. In 1922 a placement director found that while 67 percent of job offers in one locale specified that Jews were not wanted, 30 percent also excluded Catholics. The pronouncements of the Ku Klux Klan were as anti-Catholic as they were antiblack. But at the college entrance level, nationally, Catholics faced few significant restrictions as Catholics.[20] Nor is there evidence of a quota system having limited Catholic enrollment, in particular, at Yale. Catholic Yale students enjoyed a greater degree of social success than any other group of non-Protestants or any nonwhites. Many Catholics were varsity athletes and many belonged to the senior societies and junior fraternities. Historian Marcia Graham Synnott, using the rosters of the Yale Catholic Club, found at least token representation of

Catholics in the fraternities and senior societies in 1927.[21] The same non-Jewish alumni who remembered discrimination against Jews in fraternity elections were unable to remember any discrimination against Catholics. Indeed, the presence of Father T. Lawrason Riggs (B.A. 1910), a likable Keys man who served as Catholic chaplain at Yale from 1922 to 1943, maintaining close associations with the seniors in Scroll and Key all the while, helped Catholics find a welcome place among the highest echelons of Yale society.[22] That is not to say that Yale Catholics always felt comfortable. Father Riggs occasionally challenged the criticisms of Catholicism offered in some of the undergraduate religion courses, and anti-Catholic innuendos occasionally appeared in Yale undergraduate publications. Professor Henri Peyre recalled that "in not a few cases, old fashioned authorities (including chaplains) were more fearful of Catholics, than of Jews. Among the students, the Catholics occasionally converted Protestant students: the Jews, seldom, if at all." The small degree of anti-Catholic feeling on campus, however, was easily overcome by those who tried. Though some Catholics were among the Untouchables at Yale, their religious background generally did not interfere with their full acceptance in Yale organizational life.[23]

BLACK STUDENTS

Prior to the 1920s, blacks were most evident at Yale as workers—porters, janitors, and fraternity caretakers—but there were few black students at the university, primarily because few applied for admission. In 1910 W. E. B. DuBois had found no evidence of discrimination against blacks in the Yale admissions process. As early as 1926 President Angell expressed pride in Yale's having avoided the Princetonian tradition of systematically excluding blacks, even though this tolerance might have discouraged racially conscious Southerners from attending Yale.[24] In 1931 Dean of Admissions Corwin firmly stated that "there has never been any negro question here, nor has the necessity been felt for adopting a policy of determining our acceptance of negroes or our treatment of them." At the same time President Angell asserted that he was unaware of discrimination against blacks at Yale, nor had he heard any complaints of such. There was, nevertheless, at least an undercurrent of antiblack feeling at Yale. Yale's few black students tended to occupy a lower status than their fellow white students.[25] Maynard Mack (B.A. 1932, Ph.D. 1936, instructor in English, 1937–40), fellow of Yale's Davenport College, recalled that in the late 1930s Master Emerson Tuttle of Davenport had asked him to serve as adviser to a black student. Though little was said, Mack understood that he was being asked because the master knew that Mack was open-minded, whereas an older faculty member might have hesitated to advise a black.[26] The advisee, undoubtedly, ended up with a competent mentor as a result of this discrimination: Mack *was* a man of fairness and he eventually became one of Yale's finest professors of English. Nevertheless, the student might easily have asked himself why his classmates were being advised by older faculty while he was receiving the guidance of a junior man. The experience of other blacks at Yale awaits further study.

ASIAN-AMERICAN STUDENTS

Yet another area that calls for further understanding is the position of Asian and Asian-American students at the university, especially given Yale's well-known China connection via its Yale-in-China Association. The university proudly claimed to have educated Yung Wing (B.A. 1854)—the first Chinese person to obtain a degree from a Western university. Retrospective accounts of his undergraduate career make no mention of any social difficulties that this devout Protestant—who was admitted to the Church of Christ at Yale in 1851—might have had. Describing Yale in the First World War era, Lee Tsu-fa (B.A. 1919) explained that the ten to fifteen Chinese students at Yale were no different from their classmates except for their interest in Chinese issues. Forming their own Chinese association, Tsu-fa's Chinese classmates, however, were apparently not intimate with their non-Chinese classmates. The experiences of other generations of Chinese students, and those of other Asian-Americans, have not yet been well documented.[27]

POSITION OF THE JEWISH STUDENTS

In the 1920s and 1930s the majority of Jewish students at Yale were of a humble economic background and a public school education. Most of them, therefore, were among the campus's lower class, along with many a Protestant and Catholic. Some of the Jews, mostly of a prep school background, most of them descendants of German emigrants, were among the campus upper class. But this separation was not along religious lines, and the question remains: Was there, in fact, a division along religious lines as well?

The answer depends on whom one listens to. A national survey (circa 1927) revealed that Yale was among eighteen American universities where Jewish students perceived a "pronounced anti-Jewish feeling on the part of their fellow students."[28] Many Yale students "knew" from the grapevine that a Jew would have to be unusually outstanding to gain election to a respected campus organization. Nonetheless, some Jewish alumni from this period did not see their religion as affecting their Yale opportunities whatsoever. Perhaps the crucial distinction to understand was as follows: Even a minimal affiliation with other Jewish students threatened to tie a student into a low class. Only the student who chose virtually no affiliation with a Jewish group or activity had a chance to join the elite. It was important to be seen in the right crowd, but Jews tended to belong to the wrong crowds. A Jew in the right crowd, however, sometimes had a chance for full acceptance. Some Jewish students of this era therefore changed their surnames or hid their Jewish origins in order to facilitate their integration. "Being" Jewish meant little to these students, and they preferred not to be known as having ties to lower castes. Others were proud of their religious past, but were afraid of being seen as "different." Irving Drabkin (B.A. 1941) explained the sentiment: "We walked on eggshells [and] tried to conform. Because the more you conformed, the less you stood out."[29] The interwar social system was strong enough and flexible enough that Jews had a choice: They could cast off their background and achieve full equality with non-Jews, or else they could suffer discrimination for overly much association with Jews.

A crucial question is whether this segregation, which by all accounts *was* real at times, was generated by the Jewish students themselves, or whether it was imposed by their fellow students. Historian John Higham, looking at the problem nationally of Jewish versus non-Jewish social splits, saw discrimination arising from a circular process, since "the more desperately the Jews sought to escape from confinement and move up the social ladder, the more panic-stricken others became at the possibility of being 'invaded.'"[30] As Jews tried to move up, they were (as we saw in chapter 2 in the Elihu Club vote of 1911) often restrained. The problem was reciprocal, however. As discrimination and rumors of discrimination grew, Jewish students withdrew from the competitions. Fred Hirschhorn (B.A. 1942) thought the situation a form or reactive self-exclusion: "The chips on their shoulders became blocks."[31] Whether the group was Mory's or the Dramat, many Jewish students would ask themselves: Why become part of a group that does not want us? Why create unnecessary frustration? Why not succeed where doors were clearly open—as they were inside the classroom?[32]

If we recall that student organizations of this era were still run by hundreds of students, and that there were fair-minded individuals among the crowds, it again becomes reasonable to conclude that both the open-minded and closed-minded pictures of Yale students have an element of truth. J. Richardson Dilworth (B.A. 1938), a Bones man, recalled an effective caste system's existing during his undergraduate days, but he vigorously denied knowledge of religion ever having been considered in choosing friends or campus leaders.[33] The picture painted by Carlos "Tammany" Stoddard, Jr. (B.A. 1926), powerful campus manipulator and influential chairman of the *Yale Daily News*, confirms this view of interwar campus life. From a 1982 perspective, Stoddard did not recall ever having thought about Jews, having had much to do with Jews, or ever having considered religion in judging a fellow student. He did not recall if many Jews had tried out for his paper but believed that it would have been "awfully embarrassing" for him and for his *News* Board not to have elected a "heeler" who had done well in competition just because he was Jewish. There was, however, another side to the nondiscrimination, Stoddard recalled:

> Lest I make it seem all too innocent, if a boy looked handsome . . . it wouldn't have crossed [my] mind to think about religion. But if he fit a caricature of the Jew, I would have been very conscious of it. I wouldn't have opposed him or been unkind to him, but I would have been very conscious of him.[34]

So was built a gossamer wall. The Jew who might have heeled the *News* may have sensed that he was not wanted in the way that others were. He would therefore feel discriminated against, because he had not been discriminated for. Many Jewish students wanted to "succeed," but not in a place where they were not wanted. Segregation of Jews therefore arose from within as well as from without.

When the editors of the 1926 *News* (the team that succeeded Stoddard in office) declared that "Yale must institute an Ellis Island with immigration laws more prohibitive than those of the United States government" (see chapter 3), Jewish readers must have shuddered. The new quota laws had stemmed the flow of Jews from East Europe to America. One can imagine the Jewish (and Italian) students asking themselves, why even desire to try out for a student organization led by people who really do not like our presence at Yale, let alone on their newspaper? Though Stoddard's *News* Board might have been above thinking in racial or religious terms, it is hard to imagine that Stoddard's successors were similarly high-minded. Most Jews, sensing that they were unwanted or "diswanted," therefore contented themselves with living within the areas of the campus where they would be welcomed under the clauses of a "gentleman's agreement."

Discrimination was such a routine part of undergraduate life in those years that few Jews or gentiles thought to challenge it. On at least one occasion a cross-burning inspired fears among ethnic minorities, but at Yale most of the prejudices that minorities encountered were subtle and sugar-coated, rather than overt or violent. Most Jewish students appreciated that on a campus where discrimination occurred for so many trivial reasons, where social status was so important, where cliques were so reluctant to mix, the Jewish social problem (without minimizing it) was part of a larger problem of widespread discrimination. Jewish students recognized that they were better off at Yale and in America than they would have been in virtually any other country. When Jewish students of the 1930s turned the pages of their newspapers, they read of the restriction of the rights of German Jewry. The frightening biases abroad were of far greater concern to them than the petty prejudices they were suffering from at Yale. Rather than wrangle over the inherent evils of a caste system or mount a challenge to Yale society, Jewish students chose to acquiesce and take their assigned places in the system. Complacency therefore ruled the kingdom of campus life.[35]

One province in the kingdom was the Elizabethan Club—a social organization that exemplified the notion that the "gentleman's agreement" was often one of limitation rather than one of exclusion. Prior to the Second World War the club was known for not accepting Jews. In fact, however, it had had a token Jewish presence throughout the preceding decades. Louis S. Weiss (B.A. 1915) may have been its first Jewish member. The 1921 membership roster lists his name and that of possibly one other Jewish student among its four hundred fifty names. Geoffrey Hellman (B.A. 1928), cousin to the Seligman banking family, was on the club's Board of Governors during his senior year. Ervin Seltzer (B.A. 1930), member of the Jewish Pi Lambda Phi fraternity, was also a member of the "Lizzie." In the 1930s, both Eugene V. Rostow and his younger brother Walter W. Rostow were elected to the organization. Other Jewish students, however, were not so fortunate. Richard Ellman (B.A. 1939), who would become the world's leading authority on James Joyce and a professor at Oxford, was said to have tried in vain for admission to the select group. Charles Feidelson (B.A. 1938), class valedictorian and later a Yale professor, was put up for election but disqualified, presumably because of anti-Jewish feeling. Whether this in fact was the reason or not, what operated was not blanket anti-Jewish prejudice, but inconsistent prejudice. The consequences of the prejudices exhibited in the "Lizzie" were more than social. This campus watering hole, where students and professors would drink tea together, and make "polite conversation," served as the chief center for aesthetic criticism on the campus of the 1930s. Indeed, many of the critical changes that would take place in the teaching and conduct of the Yale School of Fine Arts and the Yale English department in the 1940s were first discussed within the "Lizzie."[36] Therefore, Jews who had hoped to share in the intellectual social life of the campus often found themselves left high and dry.

The reasons used to justify anti-Jewish feeling, when it existed, were simple in theory, but many in number. The stock explanation was that Jewish students were clannish and therefore not worthy of inviting into dominant cliques. As noted earlier, the claim of Jewish self-segregation was only a half truth. Jews kept themselves out no more than they were kept out. For that matter, the wealthy prep school boys also tended to be clannish—yet for them it was acceptable. A second reason given was that Jews had poorer manners than gentiles. Considering that many of the Jewish students were products of a slum environment, this may have been true to some extent. Third, the Jewish students were said to have lower standards of ethics than other students. There is no evidence, however, that any racial or religious group at Yale had a monopoly on morality. Fourth, there was the interest that Jewish students tended to show in their studies. This was no idle canard. The Jewish boys did, to some extent, have academic objectives in attending Yale. Many genuinely enjoyed learning as much as their classmates might have enjoyed singing or football. Some students, like Samuel Kushlan (B.S. 1932, M.D. 1935), acutely aware of the restrictive medical school admissions policies toward Jews, gave up sport or social competitions to seek the outstanding academic record required for professional school entrance.[37] Not a few, however, finding their social development restrained by the undergraduate caste system, turned to intellectual pursuits to sublimate their energies. When some gentiles found that a sizable number of Jews were ignoring the (discriminatory) organizational and athletic competitions at the heart of extracurricular Yale, they further resented the Jews. The greatest cause of anti-Jewish feeling, though, was the Yale students' traditional acceptance of stereotypes. The logic was the same that Harvard medical professor Richard C. Cabot had offered in 1931 to describe his care of a patient who happened to be Jewish:

> As I sit in my chair . . . , Abraham Cohen, of Salem Street, approaches, and sits down to tell me the tale of his sufferings; the chances are ten to one that I shall look out of my eyes and see, *not* Abraham Cohen, but *a Jew;* not the sharp, clear outlines of this

unique sufferer, but the vague, misty composite photograph of all the hundreds of Jews who in the past ten years have shuffled up to me with bent back and deprecating eyes, and taken their seats upon this same stool to tell their story. I see a Jew,—a nervous, complaining, whimpering Jew,—with his beard upon his chest and the inevitable dirty black frock-coat flapping about his knees. I do not see *this* man at all. I merge him in the hazy background of the average Jew.

I look behind, beyond, through this actual flesh-and-blood man, to my own habitual mental image of what I expect to see. Perhaps if I am a little less blind than usual to-day, I may hear what he says instead of what I expect him to say. . . .

[He] was no more real than the thousands of others whom I have seen and forgotten,—forgotten because I never saw *them,* but only their ghostly outline, their generic type, the racial background out of which they emerged.[38]

The tradition of judging people for what they appeared to be, rather than for what they were, defined what territories were acceptable and unacceptable for Jews to inhabit.

Some Jewish students were plainly relieved to be excluded from some elite circles. Abraham Alderman (B.A. 1923) remembered one occasion when Professor George H. Nettleton of the English department invited Alderman and six of his classmates to the professor's fashionable Prospect Street home. From the moment that Alderman entered the house, he was awed by its elegance. As a child of the ghetto, Alderman was certain that he was paddling in unfamiliar waters. The dinner that began the evening created further discomforts. On the one hand, the meal was graced by a formality that he was unaccustomed to. On the other hand, the food itself was unfamiliar. Did it contain pork or shellfish? Was something being served that his religious tradition would have barred? Alderman did not know—and did not want to embarrass himself or his host by asking. Only when the group adjourned to Nettleton's study for a discussion of life and literature did Alderman regain his bearings and feel more at ease. He was greatly relieved to receive no further invitations of a similar nature. To the extent that Alderman's experience is representative, it leads us to appreciate that, despite the fact that some Jews (and other ethnics) were kept out of upper-class circles, a good number did not have the background to make them feel at ease among the upper class—and they knew it. For students who to some degree observed Jewish dietary laws, eating with non-Jews required an extra vigilance that sometimes made for uneasiness. Some parts of the elite were closed to or restrictive toward Jews, but not all of the Jews always wished to take part.[39]

ORGANIZATIONAL LIFE

When Dean Jones carried out his detailed evaluation of Yale's Jewish students in 1922, he noted that many belonged to the Society for the Study of Socialism. Musical organizations, particularly the orchestra, as well as debate teams had many Jewish members. Jones knew of many Jews who had gone out for the football and basketball teams, and of a smaller number who had tried out for swimming and baseball. He noted that, for whatever reason, few made the university teams. Jones's conclusion—that "the Jew in Yale College is as active in extra-curriculum activities as he is encouraged to be"[40]—seems valid in light of the record. Where Jewish students felt welcome they entered. Where they sensed they were in unfriendly territory, or in an unexplored land with no map to guide them and no trail to follow, they stayed away.

The accepted dichotomous way of Yale life may be understood better by looking, once again, at the position of sports on the campus. In the period under discussion, no longer was the real Yale religion monotheistic; sport had become but one deity among many. But if sport was now less exalted at Yale, athletic endeavor had also become less alien to Yale Jews.

The swiftest vehicle for East European boys traveling from the classroom to the gymnasium was the golden orb of basketball. The sport of urban America was the sport of many an American Jew in the early decades of the twentieth century. Too cramped for baseball, too hemmed in for football, too densely occupied for tennis, the American ghetto long provided a fine training camp for basketball. As early as 1904, basketball had become the sport that was teaching New York Russian Jews the joys of athletics. Two years later, New Haven East European Jewish high school boys who were interested in basketball founded the Atlas Club. Guided by Christian students from Yale Divinity School, ironically, they regularly met for practice drills at the Edwin Bancroft Foot Boys' Club on Chapel Street.[41]

Despite the fact that most of the Jewish basketball players, immigrants or first-generation Americans, were raised in Orthodox homes, Friday nights were usually chosen to schedule basketball games and the dances that followed. Though this violated Orthodox Sabbath observance, the boys held the events on Friday nights since that evening drew the largest crowds and therefore was the most profitable. Club members took their basketball as a form of a mission. Joseph Weiner (Ph.B. 1916), an Atlas member who later became the first Jew on Yale's varsity basketball team, recalled that the club played in cities where a Jewish athlete had never before been seen: "We looked upon ourselves not simply

as another team of players but also as a group of goodwill representatives on behalf of the Jewish community. We were shattering the stereotype of the *nebbich*
Jew." No longer, Weiner felt, would people have to pity the helpless Jew. As if to
emphasize the point, in 1922 the Atlas Club, boasting some one hundred members—many of whom were Yale students or alumni—played the Yale varsity
team in an exhibition match and won 42–22. That game, a benefit for the Jewish Relief Fund, drew a crowd of three thousand, the largest attendance at any
New Haven basketball game until that time.[42]

Though Weiner was part of a league championship Yale team in 1914–15, his
presence did not immediately assure a place on the Yale team for Jews that
would follow him.[43] Suspicions ran high that Jews were kept off the team
through the following years. Matters came to a head in 1922 (the year of the Atlas Club victory), when Yale's varsity basketball team and entire competitive
athletic program fell into a slump, becoming a butt of ridicule. For some of the
alumni, Yale's performance was too much of a disgrace to the university. In response, a self-appointed alumni committee, led by George Trevor (B.A. 1915),
prepared a scathing report that attacked Yale's management of athletics. Critical enough to gain the attention of the national press, the report stated that "the
athletic situation is so befuddled and mishandled that it seems nothing short of
a complete remolding of the system of control, finance, and coaching will serve
to remedy it." It charged that the coaches consistently kept out Jewish athletes,
therefore hurting team performance, especially in basketball: That year Yale
had finished last in its basketball league. The committee, which had no Jewish
members, was displeased with Yale's connivance at explaining the team's performance: "The excuse for the miserable season was lack of material, yet the
committee has learned that capable men were cut off the squad without handling a ball. Jewish candidates say they were discriminated against. No Jew
made the squad." The charge was equivalent to a modern-day charge of exclusion of blacks from a basketball team. With Jews like Nat Holman of the
Celtics then among the nation's best basketball players, a team that excluded
Jews destined itself for mediocrity. Trevor's group proposed a new outlook on
athletics at Yale: "Less alibis for defeats, . . . eliminate all snobbish intolerance,
and accept a broader vision of our athletic future." Drastic action was called
for.[44]

Officially, Yale treated the report with derision. In the lead article of *The
New Haven Evening Register* of June 17, 1922, entitled "Exposé of Yale's System
of Athletics Proves Only Subject of Great Ridicule," Yale athletic officials labeled it a part of a personal vengeance campaign by a Yale parent whose son had

not attained the first base position on the university baseball team.[45] Yale deemed the report inaccurate because it had not been made by an authorized Yale committee. President Angell defended the financial management of Yale athletics, but skirted the issue of anti-Semitism:

> The other charges are not of a character to lend themselves to discussion at this time. I would like to say, however, that the members of the Athletic Board of Control are open and fair-minded men. Athletics constitutes one of the greatest responsibilities of the present university, which holds a conviction that our athletics are a part of the desirable life of the institution. We are going to treat them as we would treat other branches of our life and activity.[46]

Platitudes aside, Yale did take notice of the report's recommendations and proceeded with a substantial reorganization of its athletic program.

For basketball the results were quickly apparent. At the insistence of Joseph Fogarty, the new basketball coach, players were selected whether they were "black or white, Jew or Gentile, so long as [they could] play basketball."[47] Fogarty built his team around two Jewish players, leading the *Register* to report that

> because Fogarty had the guts to pick the best players at Yale and impart his sound knowledge of the game he has given the Blue its first basketball winner in a decade. Yale has obviously found the Jewish undergraduate a credit both as an athlete and a scholar.[48]

The *Register* was elated that in one year Yale had come from the bottom of the intercollegiate race to capture the basketball title. Just after the victorious season, President Angell congratulated the team captain and expressed Yale's pride in the team and its sportsmanship, saying, "Few championships have been more thoroughly deserved."[49] The following year, 1924, when Yale again won the Eastern Collegiate League basketball title, a Jewish student, Sam Pite (B.S. 1924), was team captain. For Yale basketball, "the Jewish issue" became a memory.[50]

The remainder of the sports record is mixed. Listings in the annual classbooks indicate that Jews did participate in sports, and some excelled. Arthur Loeb captained the 1936 track squad and Dick Marcus led the 1938 baseball team. Yet all was not fully open.[51] Heywood Broun and George Britt noted in 1931 that for Jews the Yale sports scene was comparable to that at Harvard and Princeton: "Discrimination is somewhat subtle and under cover, . . . yet [perceived by Jews as] real and punishing." As student prejudices shifted, so did the boundaries of discrimination. For one generation of Elis, the crew was a forbidden zone for Jews; for another, crew was a meritocracy.[52] As for football—that Yale-influenced and authentically American sport—there was an occasional Jewish player on the interwar teams. In general, though, Dean Jones's depiction of Yale opportunities also held for sport. Where Jews were welcomed, they entered. Where they were unwanted, they stayed out. Both the welcome and the coldness were consistently inconsistent.

FRATERNITIES

The circular dilemma of exclusion breeding seclusion breeding exclusion shrouded fraternity life during the years between the world wars, as the fraternities continued to act as sieves for the senior societies. The Sheffield Scientific School societies provided rooms for a campus tight on housing. The Yale College frat houses provided the daily meals that were otherwise unavailable on the campus. Ever since the closing of the University Commons in 1842, college men who did not enter the junior fraternities had had to find nourishment in the boarding houses, restaurants, lunch counters, diners, and drugstores nearby.[53] It was not a difficult task, but an inconvenient one. The fraternities therefore served as a center for social life and simultaneously provided some of the practical amenities that Yale proper lacked. While serving as a sieve for the "right kind," they also fostered attachment between members. John Leggett recalled this closeness in *Who Took the Gold Away:*

> These are the guys we'll be eating and drinking with for the next three years and I suppose they'll be our friends for the rest of our lives. We'll be working with them in some office, playing golf with them on Sundays, marrying their sisters, borrowing their political opinions. It's pretty goddam intimate when you come to think about it.[54]

In general, the old-American Yale fraternity men were not ready to be friends with the Jews around them, not ready to play golf with them, not ready to borrow their political opinions, and certainly not willing to marry their sisters. There was hardly reason for them, therefore, to take in Jews.

Yet, exclusion was not universal. Alexander Lowenthal (B.A. 1920) recalled that classmates such as Henry Luce and Thornton Wilder remained friends of his for life: "We ate together, went to football games together, rushed to daily chapel together and generally socialized in each other's dormitory rooms." Where the barriers went up, Lowenthal recalled, was for organizations and functions that involved dating and socializing with women. Friendships were held in abeyance when it came to fraternities, New York debut parties, and weekend jaunts to women's colleges.[55] No public declaration of Christian faith was required for one to be tapped for a fraternity. A Jew could "pass," and some did. Theodore Zunder (B.A. 1923), descendant of a prominent New Haven German-Jewish family, was elected in 1921 to the university fraternity of Alpha Chi Rho, whose normal policy required that its members be Christian. Later in the 1920s, recalled Irving Krall (B.A. 1930), when a non-Jewish friend of his was invited to join Alpha Chi Rho and tried to have Krall elected to the fraternity along with him, the fraternity leaders refused to bend their religiously restrictive rules. Samuel Kushlan recalled being offered membership in two Sheffield fraternities because he was an athlete and because his "crowd" was Christian. As far as he knew, those who offered him the membership had no inkling of his Jewish background. The opportunity to join the elite crowd, though, did not appeal to him: "I had no interest in joining, since if they knew I was Jewish, they wouldn't have wanted me."[56]

Kushlan's conviction was not based just on the atmosphere of suspicion that was a part of many an immigrant's home (especially those of East European Jews who had been victims of anti-Jewish feeling in the Old World). The bias *was* real. Sometimes excluded because of religious and racist bias, sometimes excluded because of chapter tradition, sometimes kept out by what Kingman Brewster termed a "subliminal anti-Semitism," known Jews, with few exceptions, did not enter the fraternities between the world wars.[57] At the City College of New York, the Alpha Delta Phi fraternity chapter had been suspended by its national parent in 1913 for having too large a Jewish proportion. At approximately the same time the Yale fraternities (perhaps influenced by the secret societies) began to tighten their informal traditions that had kept Jewish membership at a minimum. In practice this meant routinely excluding Jewish boys from the parties at which prospective fraternity members were screened. Not every fraternity member approved of the traditions that excluded Jews, yet, remembered Vernon Lippard (B.S. 1926), "nobody had the guts to change," the prevailing patterns. Conformance and congeniality were the watchwords at Yale.[58]

The national record of admission of Jews into fraternities had in fact presaged what would happen at Yale in the 1910s and 1920s. Before the nineteenth century was over, many Jewish students in New York City had become sensitive to exclusion from collegiate fraternities that "did not exclude Jews under their constitution, but simply did not invite Jews into membership." Consequently, about 1898, Jewish students from the Jewish Theological Seminary, City College of New York, and New York University gathered to form Zeta Beta Tau. With the initials ZBT, taken from the Hebrew transliteration of Isaiah 1:27 (*"Zion Be-mishpat Tippadeh"* — "Justice shall redeem Zion"), the group was established to afford a pleasant social experience for Jewish collegiate males. ZBT was a definite reaction to the perceived exclusion, as indicated by its goal of demonstrating

> to those outside the fraternity, to the world at large, the best of which Jewish young manhood is capable. In no greater way can Jewish young men serve the cause of Judaism; for the best is good, and in the demonstration of their best, they strike the most powerful blow at anti-Semitism on their college campuses.

Respect was not won easily, however. From the founding of the national Interfraternity Conference in 1909 through 1915, no Jewish fraternity was let into its ranks. Discrimination continued as a national pattern long enough that by 1936, there were thirty-six different Jewish Greek-letter fraternities.[59]

The Yale administration was no more enthusiastic about the formation of Jewish fraternities than the national conference was. The first attempt to form such a fraternity at Yale came in December 1916, when law student David Cohn (LL.B. 1917) asked the university Committee on the Protection of the Yale Name for permission to establish a local branch of Zeta Beta Tau. The committee was a small group, consisting of John W. Bristol, university counsel; Russell H. Chittenden, director of the Sheffield Scientific School; George P. Day, university treasurer; Frederick S. Jones, dean of Yale College; and Anson P. Stokes, secretary of the university. The committee's vote (Dean Jones was absent from that day's discussion) was, unusual for its day, a refusal to countenance religiously or racially exclusive organizing: "Voted, that in the opinion of the Committee it is inadvisable to allow the formation at the University of any Greek letter fraternity based on religious or racial qualifications."[60] The committee likely hoped that its action would discourage racial and religious separatism on the Yale campus. It was not, however, able to legislate unbiased attitudes among the fraternities that already existed on campus. The following October, the fraternity issue once again came before the committee. On that occasion Abraham S. Weissman (B.A. 1918) entered a request to establish a chapter of the Jewish Sigma Alpha Mu fraternity as a "University" fraternity, by which classification it would draw students from throughout Yale's schools. (Most of Yale's fraternities, in contrast, drew their members from only one of Yale's subdivisions). Again, the committee moved to halt the separatist effort: "Voted, that in the opinion of the Committee the establishment of new chapters of University fraternities at Yale at this time is undesirable."[61] In this manner, for a number of years, Yale placed its fraternally minded Jewish students in a double bind. Most of them could not have joined a Christian fraternity at Yale. And the traditional Yale outlet for solving a shortage of fraternity or society spaces, the process of forming a new club to compete with the established organizations, was officially denied to them.

Several Jewish students, nevertheless, were determined to enjoy the fruits of fraternity life, whether or not the Christian fraternities excluded them, whether or not Yale gave them official recognition. The first Jewish fraternities to be organized at Yale were Pi Lambda Phi (1917) and Sigma Alpha Mu (1917). The former was a reincarnation of the first "nonsectarian" collegiate fraternity in the nation, which, however, had failed to achieve its 1895 founders' hopes of true nonsectarianism. Across the nation, few non-Jews had chosen to join a fraternity that was "non-sectarian" by constitution, but Jewish by membership. The reborn Yale chapter became an entirely Jewish group. Reacting somewhat bitterly to being excluded from gentile parties, members of the new Pi Lambda Phi countered with parties that were exclusively for Jews. Sigma Alpha Mu took shape in the same year, despite the Yale committee's refusal to recognize it officially. When Sigma Alpha Mu again requested recognition in 1920, the committee again voted that it could not "extend recognition to the so-called University society of Sigma Alpha Mu." "Pi Lam" and SAM fraternities were quickly joined by Tau Epsilon Phi (1918), Phi Alpha (1920), Zeta Beta Tau (1920), and Alpha Mu Sigma (1922). Yale officials were aware that some Jewish fraternities existed without their approval, but, having already denied them permission to exist, the administrators tacitly chose to ignore their presence.

Following a number of years of avoidance of the issue and continued social stalemate, the university eventually gave in to the Jewish students' fraternal demand. In 1923 the petition of the Pi Lambda Phi fraternity chapter at Yale for official recognition apparently went as high as the level of the University Council. Dean Jones of the college was consequently instructed to investigate the status of the unapproved fraternities. Pi Lam was recorded as having been organized as a nonsectarian fraternity, though it was entirely Jewish in composition. It was reported that its members were of good character and scholarship and, in a pungent aside, that its financial affairs were "well managed (as is not surprising)." By 1923 university administrators had come to realize the limitations of their powers in influencing undergraduate behavior. Then, too, Yale depended upon the fraternities to supply some of the physical facilities that Yale lacked. For the moment, if the Christian fraternities obstinately continued to insist on limiting their Jewish memberships, and if the Jewish students were determined to react with equal degrees of exclusiveness, Yale administrators had few ethical options. They might have taken the Solomonic action of closing down the entire fraternal enterprise; they chose instead the less disruptive course of accepting the divisive situation. To the extent that Yale administrators had powers of introspection, they may also have appreciated that it was unrealistic to expect less prejudice from undergraduates than they were willing to permit in themselves. That the policy of official nonrecognition was reversed was best symbolized in October 1923, when Dean Jones wrote a cordial letter to the Yale Zeta Beta Tau chapter that had been snubbed six years before. On this occasion Dean Jones formally invited ZBT to establish itself with the university authorities.[62]

The Jewish fraternities, no less than their Christian counterparts, were caught up in competitions for status. Within the Jewish fraternities, four criteria denoted eliteness: prep school background, Yale-educated relatives, origins from outside the northeast, and American-born parents. Not being of northeastern background was also an asset to Jews in areas outside of the fraternities. Charles Feidelson (B.A. 1938) recalled his freshman adviser, Associate Professor of English Roswell Ham, telling him that he would "do alright here," since Southern-born Jews were well regarded at Yale. Being an atypical Jew made one a more respectable Jew. Zeta Beta Tau, the most aristocratic of the Jewish fraternities, primarily consisted of wealthier German-origin Jews, who practiced on their East European classmates a discrimination strikingly similar to that shown by Yale Christians toward Jews as a whole. As an example that the Jewish fraternities could be just as "evil, wicked, and snobbish" as their Christian counterparts, recalled Rollin Osterweis (B.A. 1930 and a former president of Zeta Beta Tau), on one occasion the president of Beta Theta Pi was asked by one of his members to invite Louis Rappaport (B.A. 1930), a prominent swimmer on campus, to join his organization. The Beta Theta Pi president knew that his fraternity would not want a Jewish member, so he asked Osterweis if ZBT would accept the young man. Osterweis was doubtful, but put the East European student's name up for election. Like many others of his background, Rappaport was refused membership in the German Jewish fraternity. Pi Lambda Phi was, like ZBT, a predominantly German Jewish enclave; Sigma Alpha Mu, Tau Epsilon Phi, and Phi Alpha were dominated by East European Jews. Historian John Whitehead, in his brief study of Jewish fraternities at Yale, concluded that the Jewish students tended to care less about the differentiations created by Yale than about the distinctions they made among themselves. Whereas the average Yale College student considered the Sheffield students to be an inferior breed of slouches, the Jewish fraternities nearly always crossed school boundaries. Whitehead also concluded that the Jewish fraternities were not founded by rejected relatives ("legacies") of former Yale fraternity members, but by new Jewish blood at Yale. Indeed, several of the Jewish "legacies" never joined the Jewish houses, since they were hoping that the Christian organizations would honor their family tradition.[63]

Dominated by a prep school–Anglo-Saxon ethos, Yale was "fairly enlightened . . . up to a point." There was no harsh prejudice toward Jews, yet the "gentleman's agreement" prevailed. Jews were not wanted among the elite, but it was as much a matter of Jews not subscribing to the prep school–WASP ethos as it was a strict bias. Indeed, the Jew willing to accept fully the dominant mores could sometimes find a place among the elite.

One of the best examples of the integration permitted those who accepted those mores was the experience of John M. Schiff (B.A. 1925). His grandfather Jacob Schiff had been the leading Jewish philanthropist in America. His father, Mortimer L. Schiff, was a partner in the investment banking firm of Kuhn, Loeb & Company. John Schiff was a product of the Taft School, then a major feeder school for Yale. At the college he was assistant business manager of the *Record* for one year, manager of the varsity swim team another year, and a member of Beta Theta Pi—a usually Christian fraternity. In consonance with his successful pattern of integration, Schiff's first marriage was to Edith Baker, of a prominent Episcopalian background. As Schiff recalled some sixty years later, his religion had not overtly affected his Yale experience. His Yale friends had, mostly, come from the Taft School and he tended to follow their pursuits. The philosophy that governed his Yale was, "If others did it, you did it, too." So there was no question of his joining a Jewish fraternity. His Taft friends were joining Beta Theta Pi, so he would join it as well.[64]

A parallel, yet somewhat more revealing tale was told by Fred Hirschhorn, Jr. (B.A. 1942). Hirschhorn, also of wealthy German Jewish parentage, was more conscious of his Jewish identity. As he described it, "I have always felt a Jewish identity, but not a difference." For him, the Yale atmosphere with regard to Jews was "a Garden of Eden" compared to what he had experienced elsewhere. Educated at Exeter, Hirschhorn had allowed his physical prowess as an athlete to carry him through his secondary school years. There, he had been a fraternity member and found integration quite easy. After being rejected by Yale because of mediocre College Board examination scores, Hirschhorn entered Wesleyan College, where the "harsh, ungentlemanly" anti-Jewishness that greeted him was unlike anything he would experience at Yale. Fitting well into the Wesleyan social milieu, Hirschhorn received offers from Delta Kappa Epsilon and Delta Tau Delta, the two most "sophisticated" fraternities on that campus. To make sure that he was not entering under any false pretenses, Hirschhorn informed the DKE president that he was a Jew:

> The fraternity president got scared. He dropped his jaw and said, "Some of my best friends are Jewish. . . ." Then he explained to me that the national fraternity had rules which could not be broken. The same thing happened at Delta Tau Delta.

A Wesleyan dean explained to Hirschhorn that there had been a slip in the protocol: "In order to save embarrassment, I asterisk each Jewish student, so the fraternities will know who is and isn't Jewish." In Hirschhorn's case, the dean had missed his mark. Frustrated by the Wesleyan system, Hirschhorn reapplied to Yale. This time he was accepted.

In the relative paradise called Yale, Hirshhorn thrived. He avoided most of the other Jewish students at Yale, because "They weren't my type." Most of the Christian friends that he made seemed genuinely surprised at meeting a Jew who did not fit the picture of a Jew that they carried in their minds. Informing Yale fraternity members of his Wesleyan experience, Hirschhorn found that the rush committees would not oppose his election because of his Jewish background. He then joined the Yale chapter of the same Delta Kappa Epsilon fraternity that had rejected him at Wesleyan. Members told him that he was the first Jew to belong to the Yale DKE chapter. Hirschhorn played football on the university teams for four years and also became a manager of the *Record* and the polo team. Though he attributed his non-election to a senior society to religious discrimination (an assertion impossible to verify or contradict), Tap Day was the only occasion when he was denied something at Yale that he felt he merited.[65]

SENIOR SOCIETIES

Long a strength and a bane of Yale, the senior societies maintained their great influence on the college spirit in the Yale of the interwar period. Powerful forces for the betterment of their members, the societies were forums for the presentation of autobiographical sketches for commentary and criticism, intellectual debates, faculty talks, clandestine ritual, and deep fellowship. Some societies were avenues for influential alumni to attempt to sway undergraduate opinion. The societies were tremendously important to Yale undergraduates with a family tradition of society membership. In some cases alumni parents lived out their own unfulfilled college fantasies by encouraging their sons to work for a society membership.[66]

Just as family traditions limited the entrance of Jews into Yale in the first place, family traditions helped keep Jews out of Yale's societies. As we have seen, Jews specifically were excluded from Yale senior societies during the 1910s, a period of tremendous expansion of undergraduate enrollments. Family tradition was an important factor in determining society admission. Thus, even given a mood of tolerance, or even with acceptance of the "right kind" of Jew in the rare cases when it occurred in the 1920s and 1930s, there was little room for Jewish entrance into established societies. Patterns of discrimination were often passed on by inheritance. What little room was available, though, was kept away from Jews. In his 1922 report on the position of Jews at Yale, Dean Jones had noted that, as a general rule, Jews were not elected to the senior societies.[67]

The public school/private school social barriers at Yale also operated in the societies. A preparatory school background was a tremendous asset to society membership. Of sixty senior society entrants in 1928, for example, only two had come to Yale directly from a public school.[68]

The only known Jew from this era to be tapped for membership was Albert Hessberg II (B.A. 1938). Hessberg had little contact with the Jewish community at Yale and felt that Judaism had had little influence over his personal behavior or his Yale experience. Nevertheless, he did pass through as a Jew. Co-captain of the freshman football squad, later outstanding in track, but best known as the star halfback of the Yale football team, Hessberg was tapped in 1937 for Skull and Bones—the pinnacle of undergraduate social success. This action by the Bones men (who were permitted to tap their successors without alumni interference) sent shock waves through the Yale community—ripples not of anger, but of amazement. For Bones members themselves, there was hardly an issue. They saw themselves as tapping members on merit (by their definition), and Hessberg was qualified. Within the tomb, reportedly, he was treated just like anyone else.[69]

EUGENE VICTOR ROSTOW

Eugene Victor Rostow (B.A. 1933, LL.B. 1937), though never a member of a senior society, was the prime example that it was not even an absolute necessity that a Jew be wealthy, of a prep school education, or of German background to succeed as a Yale undergraduate. Rostow, who later would serve as an undersecretary of state for President Johnson, spend two terms as dean of the Yale Law School, become the first Jewish college master at Yale, serve briefly as President Reagan's Arms Control and Disarmament chief, and break a number of social barriers to Jews at Yale, was quite an achieving undergraduate as well. Though he had none of the usual prerequisites for success, no manacles held him down to an inferior position. Educated at New Haven High School, the currency of his social background was as worthless as any townie's. As a Russian Jew, his chances for status within the Jewish community were far from assured. Coming from a poor family, he lacked the finances to live on-campus. Three factors, however, worked in his favor. First, he had been awarded one of the eight New Haven High School Scholarships that Yale presented to graduates of the local high school, and this commitment by Yale to town-gown relations enabled him to attend Yale in the first place. Second, an additional scholarship that he was awarded after his freshman year enabled him to live on-campus. And that, he said, "made all the difference in the world," for then, theoretically, he could fully participate in Yale social life, which he chose to do. His third advantage was just as valuable: a formidable intellect, matched by a written eloquence. This ambitious and talented undergraduate won numerous prizes, swam for the water polo team, wrote for *The Yale Literary Magazine,* belonged to the Elizabethan Club and the Alpha Delta Phi fraternity, and became an editor of the stirring campus publication *Harkness Hoot.* His dominant concern was egalitarianism, and for years he preached the need for justice for all. Though the Russian aspect of his background was more conspicuous than the Jewish, Rostow did not completely ignore Jewish issues. His article "The Jew's Position— The Unveiling of an Ancient Prejudice. An Account of Its Persistence in Circles of Highest Academic Freedom. An Analysis of its Effect upon the Jew in the University," which decried admissions quotas in the United States and openly implied that Yale was discriminating against Jewish faculty, was something of a groundbreaker on the New Haven scene. The national press had previously discussed anti-Jewish feeling in universities; Rostow brought the matter home. While some Yale Jews quaked in their boots as a result of campus bigotry and resigned themselves to second class citizenship, Rostow, characteristically, took Yale to task for its hypocrisy. He was away from Branford College, site of Tap Day (courtesy of a good friend of his who was opposed to the secret life of the societies), but rumors had circulated that Skull and Bones or another prestigious society would have tapped him. When he was graduated in 1933 he was awarded the Alpheus Henry Snow Prize "for the Senior in Yale College, who, through the combination of intellectual achievement, fine character, and personality, shall be adjudged by the faculty to have done most for Yale by inspiring in his classmates an admiration and love for the best traditions in scholarship." For all practical purposes, Rostow had done it all.[70]

THE EMERGING UNIVERSITY

Though complacency governed the campus, it was an enlightened despot that tolerated dissent in a few corners of its territory. Doubtless, few realized that the pockets of dissent would later foment an intellectual revolution. In hindsight, it seems that the vanguard of the profound changes in the Yale of the early 1960s (see chapter 9) was the undergraduate of the 1920s and 1930s. At the time, the Yale social system—based more on breeding than on merit—was as strong as ever. In general, people flocked to be with their own kind: some by choice, some because of no other choice. Yet, beneath the surface, the forces that would later permit Jews, Catholics, blacks, public school graduates, poor students, and all at the bottom of the pyramid to claim Yale, once again, to be as much their own as anyone else's, were almost imperceptibly gathering force. The university spirit was slowly invading the college.

Under President Angell one thousand flowers were blooming in one thousand places across the university. Most noticeable was the growth of the professional schools, rapidly taking their places among the nation's best. Undergraduates were beginning to learn that the hidden meaning of university was diversity:

> Formerly all Yale had believed; now many were openly skeptical. On that campus where tradition had always governed, and conformity and enthusiasm gone hand in hand, now almost everything ancient was suspect, and authorities existed only to be challenged. As the sun of the hero-athletes set, the stars of a wider firmament came into view. Now acting, singing, writing, painting took on a new dignity and excitement, and students themselves were receiving unwonted respect. Standards were going up irresistibly, and an able minority had made the discovery that scholarship could be creative and exciting.

The impetus making it legitimate for students to pursue divergent interests and encouraging them to value scholarship came straight from the top. President Angell was anxious to make the stimulation of the intellect the prime goal of Yale. Character alone would not be enough for Yale students: "The central business of a university college, he felt sure, was scholarship; the finding and the making of intelligence." Now the majority still did not agree with this "foreign" president, the first outsider to lead Yale since colonial times. The college faculty, in particular, were unenthusiastic about his governance, and the students, for the most part, were too caught up in their own world to pay him much attention. The road leading to acceptance of the Angellic view of a university college would be a long and twisted one. Yet some students were already embarking on that journey.[71]

Marcus Rothkowitz (ex-college class of 1925), better known later in life as the painter Mark Rothko, was among the first and most caustic of the rebels. Sharing an attic in the Jewish section of New Haven, Rothkowitz worked his way through his freshman and sophomore years as a waiter and a laundry employee. Involved in politics (with a strong leaning to the left), content to receive B's and Gentleman C's for grades, Rothkowitz spent most of his time devouring books. Before he decided that the scholastic life was not for him (he dropped out at the end of his sophomore year), Rothkowitz set out to devour Yale. Aided by two friends, he became the first editor of *The Yale Saturday Evening Pest*—a "morosely critical" underground newspaper that flayed conventional campus attitudes. Taking as its pithy axiom, "The Beginning of Doubt is the Beginning of Wisdom," the *Pest* sprang into the Yale vocabulary in February 1923. The preamble to the first number foreshadowed the challenges that would issue forth from the *Pest:*

> We believe
>
> That in this age of smugness and self-satisfaction destructive criticism is at least as useful, if not more so, than constructive criticism.
>
> That Yale is preparing men, not to live, but to make a living.
>
> That the life of the average undergraduate consists chiefly of our contemporary— *The Saturday Evening Post.*
>
> That athletics hold a more prominent place at Yale than education, which is endured as a necessary evil.

Such an introduction did not win the *Pest* many friends on the campus. The *Pest*'s depictions of Yale life were, to a large extent, fair representations of reality. Yet this was not the *Pest*'s problem. The problem was that "destructive criticism" was not part of the Yale tradition. When Rothkowitz left Yale at spring semester's end in 1923, the *Pest* died unlamented.[72]

The protagonists of the old college way survived the first attack but in the next battle found a more challenging and respected opponent, the *Harkness Hoot,* which at the beginning of the 1930s arose from the spiritual morass of *The Yale Literary Magazine.* The *Hoot* sent forth a clarion call across the slumbering campus. George Pierson described the event: "A subtle shift in Yale's prestige system took place. And there emerged in the foreground a brilliant co- terie of iconoclasts, loud in speech, brutal in analysis, enthusiastically uninhib- ited in their attack on the old tribal gods." Not only did men like Maynard Mack (non-Jewish) and Eugene Rostow (Jewish) rant, but the readers began to listen and the *Hoot* received raves. Head-on, the *Hoot* tackled football and the sports complex that overshadowed Yale and universities all over. If Yale did not stress education as the chief point of college, argued the *Hoot,* it would share blame for the contempt that most of the country had for scholarship. By im- plication, the *Hoot* editors were calling for a new definition of the elite, one based on merit rather than breeding, on brains rather than brawn.[73]

The 1930s also saw the first genuine, collegewide effort to break down the class lines that separated the undergraduates. Edward Harkness (B.A. 1897), with money from Standard Oil, donated eleven million dollars to Harvard and sixteen million dollars to Yale for the development of residential colleges. Pat- terned after those of Oxford and Cambridge, Yale's residential colleges were in- stituted in a deliberate attempt to restore to the large college a feeling of com- munity and to break down social walls between undergraduates. As the university historian explained, it had bothered Harkness that some men he knew, liked, and considered "average men" like himself had not been selected for the fraternities and societies, and were consequently excluded from what he felt were rewarding and constructive experiences.[74]

Creation of the colleges was intended as a major step in the slow process of desegregation. From the start, the planners assumed that all Yale upperclass- man would participate, including the isolated students of Sheff, the poor, and the commuter crowd. In 1920–21, 38 percent of the undergraduates lived off- campus; because of the colleges, the proportion who lived off-campus declined to 13 percent by 1940. The incorporation of townie stronghold Byers Hall into Silliman College by 1940 symbolized the planners' hope for absorption of the outsiders and the homebound into the life of the majority. Political considera- tions complemented altruism in the decision to include townies in the college plans. Since ten percent of the undergraduates lived at home, any indication by Yale of further alienating local students stood to upset local officials and evoke demands for the university to pay previously unlevied taxes. The planners therefore stressed residential college membership (even for nonresidents) and provision of inexpensive rooms. Harkness committed himself to endowing a support fund for the impoverished as well. The "bursary system" he funded provided well-paying jobs in the colleges, enabling poor students to earn their board and sit down in the same dining room as the wealthy.[75]

The college masters, honored faculty appointed to reside within the quadrangles and coordinate their activities, desired some degree of diversity within the students of each college. Pierson recalled that the masters "disliked the prospect of athletic or fraternity or preparatory school cliques. Also it was plain that the bursary students had to be and the religious groups ought to be pretty evenly distributed." Rather than establishing rigid quotas, the masters set up a committee to adjudicate rival claims between students' preferences for a particular college and the masters' desires for social planning. Respecting masterial preferences, the allocation committee dutifully carried out the tedious task of dividing the poorer students among the colleges and fighting the tendency of members of a single fraternity to apply to live within the same set of buildings. That is not, however, to say that Yale was intent on breaking down all walls. Fraternity members were permitted dining hall contracts that allowed them to eat eleven meals per week outside of their colleges. In terms of residence, instructions given to those on the rooming committees were explicit: Unless students specifically requested otherwise, never mix Jew and Christian, Protestant and Catholic, prep school and public school student, or well-off and scholarship student. Even when mixing Jewish students, the rooming committees were "warned never to put a Gimbel or a Fleischmann or an Altschul with the son of a New Haven Jewish tailor."[76]

Development of the residential colleges struck a blow at the security of the Yale fraternities, which had already been under fire since the late 1920s. In a 1928 warning to the brotherhoods, Dean Clarence W. Mendell of the college notified the chairman of the university's Interfraternity Council that the Yale faculty would no longer tolerate continuation of the fraternity system as it was. It was evident to Mendell that the fraternities were drawing students with poor academic records and excluding many public high school students. Angriest about selection methods that chose men on the basis of pre-college affiliation rather than merit, dragged out the painful election process, and resulted in public displays that were embarrassing to the university, Mendell drew his executive sword. Declaring that the fraternities would soon have to justify their place at Yale, Mendell threatened that the faculty would act if the fraternities did not.[77]

Neither pointed sword nor pointed words, however, were sufficient weapons to suppress the fraternal verve. An economic gallows was required. Ironically,

the framework of the gallows had been constructed by the fraternities themselves. In the 1920s, with the physical expansion of the university and the building of the magnificent Harkness Memorial Residential Quadrangle and Sterling Memorial Library, the fraternities found their land needed for university
growth. With the confident, expansive mood of that era to support them, the
organization replaced their cloistered tombs with luxurious buildings, each
saddled with a hefty mortgage. In the Depression-ridden 1930s, the mortgages
alone would have caused many a fraternity hardship. Yale provided the noose.
The first residential colleges opened in September 1933, and students were
quickly attracted to the elegant, college-provided facilities. The fraternities
could not compete with the double onslaught of opulent college accommodations and mandatory ten-meal-per-week dining requirements for college residents. The Jewish fraternities were among the first to fall. For their members,
they had served as a "separate but equal" social system, providing the companionship that many Jews could not find among their classmates. After 1933, at
least in theory, the need for companionship was met by the colleges "together
and equal" social system. A belated display of tolerance by Christian fraternities, many of which began to abandon their religiously restrictive or exclusive
practices, did not stave off disaster. Some, like Psi Upsilon (later called the
Fence Club), were forced to give up their national affiliation. Others went
completely bankrupt. By the Second World War, the long list of Yale fraternities had been considerably shortened.[78]

There was one last force of moderation also at work in this era, one far
greater than anything in New Haven. Racism as a politically acceptable theory
was beginning to die. In 1923, when Lewis Gannett decried racial and religious
discrimination, his was but a still, small voice lost in the cacophony of societal
debate:

> It shocks us, but if we exclude the non-Anglo-Saxon stocks we must expect them to
> establish their own institutions. They formed them after, not before, we began dis-
> criminating. The choice is not so much one for Jews as for Anglo-Saxons. We are
> forcing the Jew to choose between assimilation with complete loss of group identity,
> and the establishment of entirely independent cultural institutions—and we are
> shoving more and more toward the latter choice. Either of these solutions is a defeat
> for our ideal of America.[79]

In the 1930s many took up the theme that anti-Semitism threatened American
democracy and freedom. No better evidence was available than the growing
cancer in Germany. Slowly there came a turn, Oscar Handlin noted:

Americans ceased to believe in race, the hate movements began to disintegrate, and discrimination increasingly took on the aspect of an anachronistic survival from the past rather than a valid pattern for the future. . . .

By 1940, it was difficult to find a serious, reputable American exponent of the racist views once so widely held.[80]

Discrimination practices against Jews and blacks still continued, but the theories behind the practices were losing credit. The voices that would combat discrimination had not yet emerged with rousing clarity, but those that had once favored it were now silent.

As in any era, the experiences of Jews at Yale in the interwar period were not homogeneous. For some, the four undergraduate years were "by no means ghettoizing," as Eugene Rostow recalled.[81] Yale was what students like him made of it. Others felt so insecure about the acceptability of being a Yale Jew that they "walked on eggshells." For four years they avoided approaching the social ladder—where they were convinced they were unwanted. Yale was what they did not make of it. And then for others it was a place of trial—a place where they were embittered by the stinging defeats of attempts to break the gentleman's barriers. Anti-Jewish discrimination was real, but inconsistent. A Jew who avoided the lower class campus groups or avoided other Jews sometimes found a place among the elite.

As for the elite, they were of at least two sorts. There were the benevolently naive youth portrayed by Thomas Bergin (B.A. 1925) in his memoir of college days: "They were quite simply, unaware of the existence of the lower orders. . . . They didn't scorn my sort; they simply felt we had nothing much to offer."[82] Often this form of discrimination was unconscious, as John S. Ellsworth (B.A. 1929, M.A. 1946, Ph.D. 1947) recalled: "We didn't know we were discriminating against Jews. But we were terrible!"[83] There was another type of elite Yale student as well: the kind that excluded Jews from fraternities and social organizations just for being Jewish, the kind that excluded lower class students just for their background, the kind who discriminated less on the basis of personal character than on stereotypical images. These, too, were prominent on the campus. And, as Rollin Osterweis pointed out, some Jews were just as narrow-minded as their Christian counterparts.

An expert actuary would be required to calculate the relative importance of the risk factors governing the status of Jews at Yale before the Second World War. It is clear that being a townie, of public school education, of an overly academic bent, from a relatively poor home were all serious handicaps to social success for any Yale student. Since Yale cultivated snobbery, students reached for mechanisms to set themselves above the rabble. Jewishness was sometimes invoked as a mechanism for the distinction. Therefore, being a Jew was an added risk factor affecting an Eli's social status. It was not the only distinction, nor was it the most important distinction in between the world wars. But the vicious snobbery that separated the mass of Yale students, while bringing small groups together, based itself on many devices. It would take the flowering of the college system and a war of tragic proportions to teach newer and less prejudiced bases for making social distinctions.

Chapter 5 Religious Spirit

Although religious motivations led to the founding of Yale, the nature and place of religion at the college and university, from almost the first, have been insecure. Largely this result reflected the uncertain and changing attitudes toward religion in the greater American society. In the 1700s, the chief threat to the nature of religion at Yale was the competition that Episcopalian and evangelical ministers offered the Congregational establishment. When Congregationalism lost its position as the official Connecticut state religion in 1818, Yale widened its horizons, becoming a Protestant-oriented rather than specifically Congregational body. To preserve, in some manner, the religious mission of Yale's founders, a separate theological department (eventually to become the Yale Divinity School) was organized in 1822. Within the college proper, however, student apathy toward religion had grown so strong by the 1850s that the college faculty, concerned about the disintegrating religious environment, felt compelled to expel one student for leading some twenty others to become "free thinkers."[1]

President Timothy Dwight (1886–99), grandson of the previous President Dwight, may have let go a few teachers because of their unsatisfactory religious views; however, Yale was not spared from the onslaught of Darwinism which led to skepticism toward religious beliefs throughout the United States in the nineteenth century. In 1892 the last required theology course, "Evidences of Christianity," was dropped from the curriculum. Seven years later Arthur Twining Hadley, the first layman to lead Yale, was appointed as university president. During his administration Yale committed itself to nonsectarianism. In 1905, in yet another step toward secularization, the Yale Corporation successor fellows (who had always been a group of ministers) chose the first non-minister to fill the space left by the retirement of one of their number. What had been a group dominated by Protestant ministers was becoming a group dominated by Protestant businessmen. In 1906, applying for a grant from the Carnegie Foundation, Yale went on record as committing itself to religious neutrality within the classroom. The Yale Corporation then authorized President Hadley to certify "that no denominational test is imposed in the choice of trustees, officers, or teachers, or in the admission of students, nor are distinctly denominational tenets or doctrines taught to the students of Yale University."[2] Near the end of Hadley's term, the Corporation reaffirmed its 1906 vote when it requested Anson Phelps Stokes, university secretary, to ensure that the name of Yale University not appear in any list of Congregational colleges, "as the University is an entirely undenominational institution."[3]

It was no small irony that in the latter part of the nineteenth century Yale was one of the stronger forces in New Haven for the encouragement of Jewish youth in the principles and practices of their own religion. Daily attendance at the university's Battell Chapel was a firm requirement for the college undergraduates, but the Sunday service was a different matter. If a student of any faith wished to attend his own local house of worship, Yale made that option available. Some Jewish collegiates chose to follow the majority of their classmates and remain on the campus for the Congregational Sunday service. Enough, however, chose the permitted alternative, and they became a noticeable component of the Jewish congregants of New Haven. Frustrated by the lack of interest that New Haven Jewish children showed in their religion, one author recorded in 1882 the surprising religious role that Yale played in the New Haven Jewish community:

> The Friday evening services are . . . well attended in this city. There is a Yale College law that compels all students to attend divine service at least once a week, which necessarily results in a large attendance each Friday evening, and it is no unusual sight to see many Jewish students with invited friends forming a most conspicuous part of the audience. . . .

Why think of it. The Jewish young men at college are obliged to attend divine service by the faculty of a college which is most conspicuous for its Christian tendencies. But even they recognize the fact that it is proper for man to receive religious instruction in some form at least once a week.[4]

Later, usurping the name of Christianity for their own bureaucratic ends, some mid-twentieth century Yale administrators would justify their unwillingness to accommodate the religious practices of traditionally minded Jewish students (see chapter 11). In the late nineteenth century, however, the encouragement of Judaism was considered a valid form of inculcating the religious feeling that the college leadership hoped would develop in all of its students.

FOUR FAILED CLUBS

Following the arrival at Yale of traditionally minded East European Jews, the college began to rein in its previous encouragement. Attendance at weekly Jewish services remained an acceptable alternative to Sunday chapel. Any traditional Jewish practice that interfered with the college routine, however, was expected to yield its position. For many of the traditional Jewish boys, the first conflict came before college, for the undergraduate entrance examinations were often administered only on Saturdays. The scenario was simple: Jewish Sabbath or no Jewish Sabbath, if Jewish boys wanted to attend Yale, they had to write the exam on Saturday. Once in the college, Jewish students, like the rest of their classmates, were expected to write on Saturdays. For those students who wished to miss classes on major religious holidays, Yale was reluctantly accommodating. Louis Sachs (B.A. 1914) remembered approaching Dean Jones of the college for an assurance that Sachs's scholarship would not be canceled because of his absence from classes on the Jewish High Holy Days. Jones's response was intimidatingly unhelpful:, "Young man, we don't run a Jewish institution here, nor a Mohammedan institution, nor a Buddhist institution. This is a Christian institution and you'll take your chances. It's entirely up to you."[5] Actually, the remark to Sachs was probably more reflective of Jones's naturally gruff style than of his intentions. George Pierson, writing of this college dean who was nicknamed "Tyrannosaurus Superbus," described a typical encounter with the awesome dean: "At first you were scared stiff. Then you recognized the essential warmth of the man. The bark was much worse than the bite. He would scare you first, then punish you, then help you. . . . Dean Jones loved to threaten unmentioned terrors."[6] Indeed, when a distraught Sachs left Jones's presence, the dean's assistant (Thomas Tully, later to become mayor of New Haven) approached Sachs and promised to solve any problems that might arise. Sachs's scholarship was left unharmed, and other students who missed classes for the High Holy Days in this era were not subjected to penalties.[7]

At a time when religion was moving from its historically dominant position to a new defensive place, from a position of security to insecurity, the university favorably viewed the activities of its religiously minded organizations. Most prominent was Dwight Hall, the campus YMCA. When Jewish-oriented religious organizations would form, they, too, would receive university encouragement. The most promising of these was the Yale Hebraic Club. Founded about 1907 at the instigation of Charles Foster Kent, a Christian who was Woolsey Professor of Biblical Literature, and Eugene H. Lehman (B.A. 1902), a graduate student in Jewish literature, its purposes were

  1. To arouse a deeper and more intelligent interest in the study of Hebraic History, Literature, Religion, and Ideals.
  2. To promote a better understanding of the historical relationship between Judaism and Christianity.
  3. To develop a *truer* appreciation of the Jewish heritage from the past and the opportunities offered to the race in the present and future.
  4. To obtain a deeper and more sympathetic insight into certain vital social problems of the age.

This club organized a small library and sponsored a number of lectures. Eugene Lehman felt sufficiently confident of its merit to attempt raising financial support for it among Hew Haven Jewry. Most promising was its membership. Of the seventy-five men listed on the one extant membership roster, forty-eight were Yale College students, four were Sheff students, and the rest studied in the law, medical, divinity, or graduate schools. It had a good mix of religions as well. Though the divinity school members in it were all Christian and the law students predominantly Jewish, the undergraduate listing was made up of roughly equal numbers of Jews and non-Jews. Jewish students must have found the organization especially satisfying. Elliot E. Cohen, student at Yale a decade later, for example, recalled how he was influenced by Yale's recognition of Judaic learning:

> As an undergraduate, it meant a great deal to me to realize that respect for Hebraic learning was a tradition that harked back to the early beginnings of the College and I am not likely to forget how much I owe to the teaching of men like [Charles C.] Torrey, [Charles F.] Kent, [Albert T.] Clay and others who so splendidly carried that tradition forward.

A glance at the list of dues-paying members also reveals that some of the Christian "insiders" on the campus must have found the study of Hebraica promising as well. Many of the Christian members were active in Dwight Hall. A number of the non-Jews later joined secret societies. Names like Robert A. Taft (the future president's son who in 1939 became a U.S. senator) and T. A. D. Jones (the "knight of the backfield" who later became a Yale football coach) are but examples of the real potential that the Hebraic Club had for integrating Judaism into the dominant Christian life. That William E. Hendricks (B.A. 1908), one of the few blacks to attend Yale at this time, was also a member is evidence of the club's diversity of membership. But the grand endeavor collapsed when its leader, Eugene Lehman, received his master's degree and left Yale in 1909.[8]

The demise of the Hebraic Club left a vacuum for some of the Jewish students. No longer was there an outlet on the campus for the intellectual consideration of issues pertaining to their religion. In the early 1910s some of them made an effort to fill this gap and organize a new forum for their religion. What shape it would take was up for discussion. Norman Winestine (B.A. 1914) recalled that the Jewish students, sensitive to religious discrimination in some quarters of campus life, and also well aware of charges of self-segregation, wanted a group that would not attract much attention. After days of simmering debate, a large group of Jewish students met at Temple Mishkan Israel, a few blocks from the campus, to confront the issue. The house of Yale Jews was divided. Some wanted a group, while others, led by Robert Lehman (B.A. 1913) and his cousin Arthur Lehman Goodhart (B.A. 1912), who was later to achieve prominence as a scholar at Oxford, were opposed. Lehman and Goodhart, who served as managing editors of the *Yale Daily News* and *The Yale Literary Magazine*, respectively, had successfully integrated into the Yale social scene and feared a separatist Jewish organization. Others present, believing that college was the time to break the restrictive bonds of the past, similarly wished to submerge their Jewish identities: "Can't we be freed of Jewish problems?" one student asked. "Can't we have four years of happiness?"[9]

The solution that emerged from this meeting was to form, in the spring of 1912, a group called Kadimah, translated from Hebrew as the "Forward" association. Kadimah was to be an intellectual, pro-Zionist society based off the campus. Away from Yale, so the logic ran, it would not threaten to be publicly divisive. Founded by Charles Cohen (B.A. 1914), Kadimah had one known guest lecturer, Rabbi Judah L. Magnes, a leader of New York Jewry and the man who would become chancellor and president of Jerusalem's Hebrew University.

Speaking in New Haven on "The University Man and Judaism," Magnes urged the creation of Jewish societies as a reaction to racist feeling that was excluding Jews from Christian societies. If there was no alternative to exclusion, Magnes felt, campus Jews would lose all pride in their Judaism. Later meetings of Kadimah were less stimulating and less controversial as the group concentrated on studying the Hebrew author Ahad Ha'am. The writer did not, however, prove stimulating enough to sustain Kadimah for long. Not long after its founding, Kadimah dissolved.[10]

The most significant Jewish group at Yale in this era was to be the Menorah Society, a chapter of the Intercollegiate Menorah Association—a national body that dedicated itself to "knowledge and service, which may be regarded as the very cornerstones of Jewish idealism."[11] Menorah had its origins at Harvard in 1906 when sixteen Jewish students organized a society "for the study of Hebraic learning and ideals." Shepherded by Henry Hurwitz, the society grew in 1913 into a national organization to promote the academic study of Jewish culture in American universities. According to writer Alfred Jospe, Hurwitz "aimed to liberate the Jewish college student from the feeling that his Judaism diminished his American identity."[12] When Norman Winestine at Yale read of the national organization's existence he wrote to Hurwitz and asked how to go about starting a chapter in New Haven. Promised financial backing by national Menorah president Hurwitz, Winestine approached President Arthur T. Hadley and University Secretary Anson Phelps Stokes for their support. Stokes and Hadley were equally and extremely enthusiastic. The Yale president speculated that the society might lead to "a renaissance of Hebrew culture." Both men hoped that an inspirational group such as Menorah might help Yale develop as a center for Judaic scholarship. In short order the Yale chapter was hastily organized in 1913, and Eugene Lehman (now returned to the college as an instructor in Jewish literature) was elected its president.[13]

From the start, the German Jewish students shunned Menorah. The Hebraic Club had been oriented to increase Judeo-Christian understanding, so some of their predecessors had joined that group. Menorah, however, was geared to study Jewish culture. Many of the German Jewish students, anxious not to lose their position among the dominant groups at Yale, would have no part of the organization. It was no matter to them that there were Christian religious organizations on campus. Many of them had come to Yale to forget their differences, and Menorah was not about to stop them. In addition, the prejudices of upper class German Jews against lower class East Europeans, likely, would have prevented the former from joining a Jewish organization that was dominated by the latter.[14]

In an era of growth of both Catholic and Jewish religious activity at Yale, the local Menorah chapter grew despite the split. The society was officially opened to all schools of the university at an organizational meeting on November 5, 1913. Its student leaders came from the college, the scientific school, and the law school. Secretary Stokes, Dean Jones of the college, Director Russell H. Chittenden of Sheffield Scientific School, English professor William Lyon Phelps, and former United States president and professor of law William Howard Taft all sent letters of support. At that opening meeting student leader Charles Cohen, Henry Hurwitz, and Benjamin W. Bacon, acting Yale pastor, all spoke. President Hadley was the featured speaker at the inaugural meeting of the 1914–15 academic year. Other fortnightly sessions heard addresses by the popular Yale English professor Johnny Berdan, Yale German professor Arthur H. Palmer, philosopher Horace Kallen, educator George A. Kohut, Rabbi Hyman G. Enelow, Rabbi Mordecai M. Kaplan, Rabbi Louis Mann, Rabbi Stephen S. Wise, and former president William H. Taft. The lecture topics of the first year were quiet revealing. Enelow spoke, for example, on "Some Common Errors about Judaism." Rabbi Wise spoke on "What's Wrong with the Jew?" and Rabbi Kaplan took as his topic "The Problem of Judaism."[15] Even those students on the campus who were most interested in their religion were uncertain about Judaism's place in twentieth-century America. The questioning attracted sufficient interest for Menorah to claim a membership of between fifty and one hundred in the years before the United States entered the world war. In 1917 Benjamin Levinson (B.A. 1917, LL.B. 1920) reported that the Yale chapter, though perhaps coercive, was a great success: "The Menorah Society has greatly revolutionized Jewish student life on the campus, and the Jewish students feel themselves on the defensive if they do not belong to the Menorah. The entire student body gives the Menorah its co-operation."[16] The society's most famous member was Elliot E. Cohen (B.A. 1918), son of a Mobile, Alabama, dry goods merchant, who became secretary of the society during his junior year and winner of the society's prize for outstanding writing. His essay on "The Promise of the American Synagogue" won the Intercollegiate Menorah Medal for being the best collegiate writing in the nation on a Jewish topic. As a senior, Cohen was Menorah president. In 1945 he would become the founding editor of *Commentary* magazine.[17]

What Menorah did not achieve was the bringing of Christians and Jews together. Anson Phelps Stokes, the university secretary, had called upon the society in 1915 to consider as part of its mission the task of interesting Christian students, as well as Jewish ones, in matters of Jewish culture.[18] Given the growing prejudice of the 1910s, perhaps this was an impossible dream. Social class may also have been a factor. If the German Jewish boys resisted supporting an organization dominated by East Europeans, how much less could upper class Christians be expected to socialize with lower class Jews. But neither did Menorah attract lower or middle class Christians.

The Yale Menorah Society, despite its impressive beginnings, followed a national pattern, joining its Hebraic Club and Kadimah predecessors in oblivion. It, too, proved unable to withstand two onslaughts of the late 1910s that would strike Menorah societies throughout the nation in the 1920s. The first challenge was a product of its environment. As we saw in chapter 4, the growing exclusivism of the Christian fraternities at Yale in the 1910s led to the formation of Jewish fraternities, beginning in 1917. For on-campus Jewish students who were sensitive to accusations of self-segregation (as most Yale Jews of that era were), the idea of belonging to two Jewish associations would have been discomfiting. Menorah's intellectual bent may also have discouraged the Jewish fraternity men, who like many Yale fraternity men were not always the most avid supporters of intellectual pursuits. The second cause of Menorah's decline was its own doing, when, under the national leadership of Henry Hurwitz, Menorah refused to become involved in politics. In its first years the Yale Menorah Society had been of a Zionist bent. The Zionist tendencies of the Jewish students only increased in 1917, with the worldwide rise in nationalistic feeling, and with Jews witnessing the Turks' harassment of Palestinian Jews and the British government's publication of the Balfour Declaration, which placed Britain on record as favoring the establishment of a Jewish state in Palestine. Because of the controversial political nature of Zionism, Hurwitz discouraged his chapters from embracing the topic. With the Jewish fraternities sapping Menorah of one source of its membership, and Zionism eliminating those for whom religion had become a political cause, the Menorah membership dropped to a paltry dozen students.[19]

Whereas the university, like the national Menorah Association, was happy to promote religion, political partisanship was another matter entirely. To circumvent the restriction on Zionism as a Menorah activity, a group of Yale students approached the university in 1919 for recognition of the "Yale Zionist Society." Steering its normal course of disassociating Yale from political causes,

the university Committee on the Protection of the Yale Name rejected the title
that the new group had chosen for itself:

> Voted that, although the Committee . . . raises no objection to the meeting together
> of students in the University interested in the Zionist cause, it thinks it inadvisable,
> in view of the fact that a Yale Branch of the Menorah Society has already been estab-
> lished for the study of Jewish ideals and Jewish problems, to give official recognition
> to the Zionist movement, or to take sides in the Zionist controversy, which might be
> implied by formally authorizing the use of the Yale name in connection with the
> title of a society of Yale students.

With Zionism barred from the Menorah agenda by its own national leadership,
the option that Yale offered was not viable. The immediate fate of the Yale
Zionist Society is unknown. By 1920, nevertheless, it seems that aside from the
Jewish fraternities, all Jewish religious and political activity on the Yale campus
was dead.[20]

THE END OF MANDATORY CHAPEL

The chief remaining element of Christianity in collegiate life at Yale as of 1920
remained the required chapel services. Mandatory daily and Sunday chapel had
long been a requirement in the college, but increasingly secular undergraduate
sympathies had turned the daily service into something of a circus. Decades
earlier, the daughter of President Jeremiah Day (in office from 1817 to 1846) and
a few of her friends presented an exaggerated description of chapel disguised as
the president's advice to the students:

> Rush up the aisles in a crowd and find your seats with the greatest possible noise, . . .
> in your seat assume a horizontal position . . . go to sleep . . . whisper with your
> neighbors. . . . In short do anything rather than listen to the reading. That is de-
> signed to divert the faculty and give you a chance to enjoy yourselves. . . . Crack
> jokes with your right and left hand neighbors . . . notify everyone of your presence
> who is within reach of your hands and feet . . . keep up a brisk circulation of peanuts.
> It is a very good plan to bring in a bat which can be let loose if things seem to be get-
> ting dull.[21]

During the twentieth-century years of daily services, only student waiters and
those boys living over one mile from the campus were entirely excused from the
obligation. Many of the local Jewish townies, therefore, were required to attend
the sessions. One prominent New York minister had defended the requirement

by arguing that "compulsory chapel is the only way by which you can keep the Catholic and the Jew out of Yale." Whether it was an effective deterrent or not, those Jewish students who enrolled at Yale found chapel no more bothersome than did their Protestant classmates. Like their Christian neighbors, the majority of Jewish boys voted in senior year opinion polls for continuation of the requirement. The rationale behind some of the Jewish votes was exactly the same as that of the Christians: As a religious session, daily chapel was almost valueless, but, if they as seniors had had to go through it, it was only fair that younger classes should also be compelled to suffer the same punishment. For other Jewish students, the novel experience was a valuable form of foreign language and comparative religion education, providing an introduction to the unknown New Testament and the Greek language. Looking at the service like visiting anthropologists, these Jewish students felt they were being educated, not proselytized. In the rare case of a Jewish student who found the daily chapel too onerous, an excuse would be granted if he was willing to certify that he followed the traditional Jewish ritual of donning phylacteries for daily morning prayers. On one occasion, when a Jewish student merely wanted to protest the chapel requirement, without adopting a traditional Jewish alternative, Dean Jones, in his inimitable way, encouraged the boy to transfer to Harvard, where chapel had not been a requirement since the nineteenth century.[22]

The end of mandatory chapel at Yale, though, had next to nothing to do with Yale's Jews. Rather, it was a result of one of the finest examples in Yale history of the adroit manipulation of the college by the leadership of the *Yale Daily News*. With the drive of Managing Editor Arthur "Squidge" Lord counteracting the complacency of the mid-1920s, the 1926 *News* Board decided that it ought to have a purpose, a cause to campaign for. The board selected compulsory chapel as its target. The collegiates' behavior, thought the board, was disrespectful: a circus atmosphere still competed with the Christian doxology.[23] One visitor to the chapel recorded his appraisal of the shenanigans in 1925:

> At my request we went to Chapel in the morning and I never laughed so much as during that ten minutes. Very few people stood up for hymns or prayer, no one sang except a few members of the choir and funniest of all was that openly many fellows were reading the New York Times and funny papers during the entire service. They had scholarship fellows come around to the pews and marked if present or absent. As soon as one gave his name, if he were near the rear, he casually walked out and when the preacher started to say the Benediction, there was a rush for the door and when he said the final Amen, the place was almost deserted.[24]

The *News* Board was aided by the growth in the number of college students. When it became impossible to squeeze the entire body of students into Battell Chapel, forcing Yale to divide the college up into groups that would attend the service separately, the *News* was given an opening round of ammunition for its battle. Plainly, in addition to the mockery of religion, the secular aim of bringing the whole college together once a day also had failed. The *News,* impartially presenting both sides of the issue of mandatory chapel on its front page, and decisively supporting optional chapel on its editorial page, stirred up an avalanche of opinion where once there has been complete lack of interest. The faculty and administration were consequently forced to abolish all mandatory chapel requirements, and a ritual that had endured for two hundred twenty-four years so became a memory.[25]

Ending the required chapel was no panacea for the malaise in religious activity at Yale. Though the congregation's behavior improved, as of 1929 the choirboys continued to sit behind the reredos during services and, thinking themselves unseen, read newspapers in between their melodies. Through the following decades, religion, regardless of denominational label, earned little respect from either the majority of students or the Yale faculty. A course labeled "religion" would have been sure to discourage student enrollment. Perhaps in much the same way that "believers" once exercised prejudices against nonbelievers, the "nonbelieving" student majority of the twentieth century was suspicious of students who seemed sincere about their religious beliefs.[26]

REVEREND SIDNEY LOVETT

Reacting to the end of compulsory chapel, the university established the position of university chaplain in 1930. In concert with this office grew a permanent Jewish religious presence on the Yale campus. When Reverend Sidney Lovett (B.A. 1913) assumed the position in 1932, the chaplaincy began to take on its full dimensions in Yale life. An almost legendary figure, Lovett was said to have embodied "all that Yale stands for and wants to be." Working to promote all segments of religious life at Yale, Lovett showed an early concern for presenting the Jewish viewpoint to the university community. To achieve this goal he invited the first rabbi to deliver a sermon at university worship in Battell Chapel. The man he invited to speak in April 1934 was Louis Mann (Ph.D. 1920), former rabbi of New Haven's Congregation Mishkan Israel, former national director of the Hillel Foundations of the B'nai B'rith, and current rabbi of Chicago's prestigious Congregation Sinai.[27] Two years later Lovett planned to invite another rabbi, Baltimore's Morris Lazaron—one of the pillars of the National Council of Christians and Jews. This time, though, Lovett thought it best to solicit President Angell's advice. Choosing a Sunday very near to exam time, when student attendance was likely to be low, Lovett thought the rabbi's presence might spark an increase in the regular attendance and might bring "our . . . Jewish friends within and without the University" to Battell.[28] Angell replied that he would be quite pleased to have a rabbi preach again—as long as speaking in a Christian church would not offend the rabbi and as long as Lovett did not make a habit of such invitations:

> Unless you fear that bringing Rabbi Lazaron in on May 23rd, when he would almost certainly have a small student audience, would be likely to ruffle any sensibilities he might naturally have to coming to speak in a Christian church, I should be personally entirely glad to have you make the experiment. I heard very little unfavorable comment the last time that a Rabbi spoke in our pulpit. I think the public attitude would be far more definitely determined by the quality of his performance than by the fact that he was a Hebrew. If you can get evidence of a kind which you personally would regard as entirely trustworthy about the impressiveness of his preaching, I should not be shy of the experiment. I should not wish to do it very often, for we still have a considerable body of somewhat unimaginative conservatives from which criticism flows with extraordinary ease.[29]

The invitation of a rabbi to preach at a university chapel service subsequently became an annual occurrence.

In his pastoral duties, Lovett found a number of Jewish students who desired counseling. He provided such advice as he could and enlisted the aid of local rabbis when necessary. Lovett's greatest assistance was to come from Isaac Rabinowitz (Ph.D. 1932). As a graduate student in Semitics, Rabinowitz had developed a sense that university attitudes made Jewish students feel as if they were at Yale on sufferance. He saw a great amount of religious self-hatred among the Jewish students and a "good deal of incipient student Marranism." He consequently felt that a Jewish counselorship at Yale might help them feel more comfortable, since "if the Jewish students knew that the University countenanced this kind of counselorship, there would be that much less pressure on them to hide their Jewishness."[30] Rabinowitz was the catalyst for an innovation.[31] With the support of his teacher associate professor of history Erwin Goodenough, Dean Clarence Mendell of Yale College, and Rabbi Edgar Siskin of Temple Mishkan Israel, Rabinowitz approached Lovett about engaging the services of a counselor for Jewish students to parallel those already available to

Protestants and Catholics. Lovett's response was favorable, as he believed that each of the three faiths comprising Yale's pluralistic society needed its own representative. The Protestant ministry at Yale was already strong, the Catholic ministry was growing, but there was nothing yet for the Jewish boys. With the blessing of both Lovett and President Angell, Rabinowitz approached Judge Solomon Elsner (LL.B. 1905) of Hartford in the hope that he would form an alumni committee to sponsor the counselorship. Elsner agreed to aid the project on the condition that the Union of American Hebrew Congregations, on whose lay leadership board he served, would lend its name to the program. The Union had no desire to enter the college field but for practical reasons was unable to reject Judge Elsner's suggestion, accepting it on the condition that Elsner raise the needed funds. Rabinowitz was appointed the first counselor and began his work with the 1933 fall term. From Yale's viewpoint, the office of the counselorship was under the jurisdiction of the university chaplain, although its financial support came from outside Yale.[32]

Achievements did not come easily to the counselorship. The office that Yale provided in Lawrance Hall on the Old Campus of the university, open on weekday afternoons, suffered from its location in an inferior spot in a campus basement. Charlotte Horton, secretary to Chaplain Lovett, recalled that the office "was a dreary old place. I don't know how they managed." Because the office faced an open bathroom, it was logistically difficult for Rabinowitz to hire a secretary. If one were to judge by the quality of the allocated space, the university's recognition of the counselorship was meager, at best. Some of Rabinowitz's activities consisted of encouraging the independent pursuit of Judaic studies and directing Jewish students interested in charitable work to some of the organized Christian groups. To indicate his presence on campus Rabinowitz left notes at students' doorsteps. Several Jewish students reacted angrily to this practice and told Rabinowitz that they had no interest in him because they had come to Yale to escape their Judaism. Rabinowitz, with varying success, usually tried to pursue the matter and invited the student to meet him and intellectually discuss the meaning of Judaism.[33] Local congregations cooperated to welcome students who were interested in their religious services. Jewish students altogether avoided on-campus social activities, however, as they were considered "segregating."[34] They continued to fear that a close identification with Judaism would be a stigma on their attempts to participate in "nonsectarian" campus activities. Gradually, as the office of the Jewish counselor became an institution and not an innovation, the Jewish students began to accept the idea of the campus counselorship. By the end of the 1934 spring terms, a

"Jewish Club" had been formed to study matters of Jewish interest and pursue improved Jewish-Christian relations.[35]

Rabinowitz, who left New Haven that summer, was succeeded by Irving Goleman, a graduate student in English. Among the undergraduates in the Jewish Club during his year were Charles Feidelson (B.A. 1938) of Birmingham, Alabama, and Felix Zweig (B.A. 1938) of Fort Wayne, Indiana. Both had attended high schools, and represented the more diverse group of students that was beginning to attend Yale as part of its attempts to broaden itself in the 1930s by the establishment of nationwide regional scholarships. (Feidelson would later become the first Jew appointed to the Yale English department faculty, and Zweig would be among the first Jews in the Yale engineering department. From 1962 through 1966 Zweig was dean of the Yale School of Engineering.) Goleman provided counseling, and the club sponsored monthly meetings, lectures, and discussion groups. President Angell himself, much to the delight of club members, took time to spend an evening with the Jewish Club to discuss problems facing American universities.[36] Another guest speaker to address the club that year was the eminent Rabbi David de Sola Pool.[37] When Goleman's progress on his dissertation slowed and the economic pressures of the Depression worsened, Goleman left Yale in the spring of 1935 for a full-time position in California. Rabbi Edgar Siskin then turned west, inviting his Hebrew Union College classmate of 1929 Rabbi Maurice Zigmond of Denver to come to New Haven for graduate study in anthropology. Siskin suggested that Zigmond pay for his learning by serving as the Yale Jewish counselor. Zigmond accepted the opportunity, despite the initial concerns of Rabinowitz and Goleman that Zigmond's being a rabbi and not a layman might hinder his relationships with students.[38]

Though warmly received by Chaplain Lovett's office, Zigmond was made to feel very removed from the central authorities of the university. Zigmond recalled that when he initially presented himself to university officials in the Woodbridge Hall administration building, one senior administrator rebuffed him by asking: "Who ever gave you the right to call yourself 'Counselor to Jewish Students at Yale'? We don't need you!"[39] Rabbi Siskin, recalling some of the administrators from this era, felt that "when they greeted Jews who had the effrontery to attach the Yale label to themselves, they held clothespins to their noses."[40] If not for the benevolence of a few men like Sidney Lovett, Zigmond might have despaired early on.

But he persevered, and soon after his arrival the Jewish students expressed interest in establishing a more formal Jewish organization, one that would give status and credibility to Jews, "to show that Jews weren't all bests." Led by Arthur Berliss (B.A. 1936), Sam Weintraub, Jr. (B.S. 1936), an Exeter graduate from Denver, and others, some of the former Jewish Club members began to meet occasionally in the university's Kohut Judaica library, then housed in Lawrance Hall. (For more on the Kohut collection, see appendix 9.) Calling themselves the "Kohut Forum," the group that replaced the Jewish Club was founded in January 1936. The forum had a student cabinet and officers, but no membership roll or dues. Leaders of the group in its first years included Herbert Salzman (B.A. 1938, a New Yorker who was graduated from the Reali School in Haifa, Palestine), Eugene Meyer, 3d (B.A. 1937, son of the Jewish *Washington Post* publisher and a Lutheran mother)—a Zeta Psi member who, finding meaning in his Jewish background in light of Nazi actions in Germany, became a Kohut Forum president—and Herbert A. Friedman (B.A. 1938, later to be the outstanding leader of the United Jewish Appeal, a national fund-raising body), who served as secretary. The group irregularly brought speakers from within and without Yale, sponsored mixers and other social events at Congregation Mishkan Israel, held discussion groups, and worked on interfaith projects.[41]

Like his predecessors, Zigmond had a part-time schedule at Yale, but his office became the focal point of Yale Jewish life.[42] In the late 1930s he became the first Jewish counselor to be included on Freshman Conference outings. From that time onward, at the annual religious retreat prior to the start of school, freshman would be signaled early on that Judaism was at least a recognized interest within the university religious hierarchy. Reverend Lovett's office went far to provide this recognition, for which Zigmond was thankful. He expressed this feeling in his 1940 annual report: "Reverend Lovett continues his unfailing interest in all phases of the Jewish program. No problem of major importance is considered without consultation with him. Indeed, our activities are, in a real sense, a part of his own."[43] When another Jewish counselor, Rabbi Joseph Gumbiner, arrived at Yale in 1949, again it was Lovett who would make Gumbiner feel a welcome and integral part of the Yale religious ministry.[44]

The Young Men's Christian Association, under the leadership of E. Fay Campbell (General Secretary 1925–42), opened its Dwight Hall campus building to Kohut use. To twentieth-century Yale Catholics and Jews alike, the campus Protestant ministry always did its best to make its facilities available. Apparently the most active Protestants at Yale were also the kindest to their religiously inclined neighbors, perhaps because the Protestant religionists were also a minority on the campus and may have identified themselves more with the followers of other faiths than with their nonreligious co-religionists.[45]

Zigmond's work was also greatly aided by his warm relations with the New Haven Jewish community.[46] Since many of Yale's Jews were still local boys, the community was willing to give the Kohut Forum ample organizational backing. The students responded by becoming involved with Jewish youth groups in the city, by serving as group leaders at the nearby Jewish Community Center, and especially by assisting the fund-raising drive of the New Haven United Jewish Appeal. Although New Haven's Jewish community, like most in America, was split along denominational lines, communal service agencies crossed those lines. Members of the Kohut Forum Board became campus solicitors and succeeded in adding a fair share to the campaign total.

By the end of the 1930s, sponsorship of the Yale Jewish counselorship became difficult. Judge Elsner found himself unable to raise the small budget and initially made up the deficit from his own pocket. To survive the crisis it became necessary to lower Zigmond's salary. To bail himself out, Elsner then hoped to persuade the Union of American Hebrew Congregations (UAHC) to assume financial control of the project, as he felt that it ought to remain under Reform control. Elsner's desires notwithstanding, both Rabbi George Zepin, UAHC director, and Rabbi Gustave Falk, UAHC northeast regional director, thought it best to release the Union from its Yale responsibility, still the only activity of its kind under the Union's auspices. Zigmond, for his part, was interested in bringing the B'nai B'rith Hillel organization into New England. Hillel, an arm of the Jewish fraternal service organization, was not tied to a religious wing of Judaism and therefore had a broad base of support. It had begun as a campus counselorship at the University of Illinois, Champaign-Urbana, in 1923. In 1924 the counselorship received national B'nai B'rith sponsorship. In time Hillel Foundations became the nuclei of Jewish communities on many American college campuses. Although Judge Elsner resisted the change, it soon became clear that without Hillel the Yale office would die for lack of financial support, as Elsner could not pay for it alone. In contrast, Zigmond was close to New Haven's B'nai B'rith leaders, who were enthusiastic about the possibility of bringing a Hillel to Yale. In July 1941, just prior to a parallel action at Harvard, the B'nai B'rith Hillel Foundation at Yale was established and officially declared to be the fifty-sixth unit in the national Hillel organization. As far as the students were concerned, the only real change was in the name. As before, no Jewish religious services were yet conducted on campus, since most students and religious officials still felt that the students should go out into the local community for such functions. A less substantial change, though, had occurred during the Kohut Forum's last year of existence: Yale remodeled the Lawrance Hall basement and walled off the conspicuous bathroom.[47] In large ways and small, Hillel was ready for the future. When the United States entered the Second World War and Yale began to experience the jarring changes brought about by the war the Jewish presence on the campus would be legitimate and secure.

Chapter 6 The Faculty

Though Yale's restrictive policies vis-à-vis the hiring of a faculty never achieved the notoriety of its discriminatory admissions policies, the history of Jewish faculty at Yale is an issue of far greater significance, because of its impact on the Jewish students at Yale. Within the ranks of the faculty were the inspiring examples for the students, giants who were timeless heroes, not just for those who planned academic careers, but for those entering the so-called real world as well. The greatest giants of all were the members of the gentleman's club known as the Yale College faculty. Its membership did not all think the same way and their loyalties sometimes conflicted, but, for the first half of the twentieth century, it was a club whose door was closed firmly to the spiritual "foreigners" that President Timothy Dwight (the elder) had once feared. As "guardians of a way of life, not just a system of classrooms and laboratories," the professors considered a homogeneous group essential.[1] By remaining exclusive, they presented to Jews, as other faculties did elsewhere, a bitter irony. If any part of Yale (save perhaps the library) was perceived by the public as the seat of intellect at the university, it was the faculty. Yet at Yale, and at university after university,

Jews saw that intellect alone was not the ticket to success. Thus was engendered a crisis of conscience for the American Jew. In Russia the Jew's dream of academic achievement had been thwarted by exclusion from the universities. In Prussia he had been barred from teaching religious subjects and the humanities.[2] Only in continental Europe had his intellect allowed him to rise to the heights of intellectual prestige without regard to his religious origin. And in the United States he was taught that the intellect and drive that had allowed him to move from peddler to storekeeper to businessman to professional would not earn him legitimacy and respect. Across the country the difficulties that faced Jewish faculty of the 1910s through the 1940s taught those lower on the ladder that the more one identified as a Jew, the less were his chances of going up that ladder. Yale, mother of colleges, possessor of one of the most respected college faculties in the nation, a leader in American intellectual thought, was a prime promoter of this concept. By closing itself off to Jews—on an absolute basis at the upper ranks of the college faculty and on a less absolute basis in the faculties of the graduate and professional schools—Yale created a legacy of inhospitability that took years to expunge.

The impacts of such policies was not lost on the Jewish boys who attended Yale. Some, for reasons of religious background alone, saw all hope of a career in academe, particularly the humanities, vanish in the absence of opportunity. Others, consciously or unconsciously, decided to submerge their Jewish identity and hope their sacrifice would be accepted, or better yet forgotten. For many Jewish young men, who had long been taught to seek knowledge, the strength they planned to gain from entering the crucible of assimilation would be worth the cost of avoiding their pasts.

EARLY TWENTIETH-CENTURY TEACHERS

For some Jewish faculty members, the university's social situation required maintaining a delicate balance between being a Jew and being an Eli. The record of Lafayette B. Mendel (B.A. 1891, Ph.D. 1894), the first Jew to receive a regular appointment at Yale, was symbolic of the acceptance of Jews on the faculty. By its success it represented the open minded attitude toward intellect that prevailed in the United States before the rise of rampant anti-Jewish feeling in the 1910s. By its social failure it represented the personal barrier that even the most eminent of Jewish scholars found difficult to break.

Lafayette Benedict Mendel, son of a Delhi, New York, merchant, first arrived at Yale in 1887 as a young boy of fifteen. He received undergraduate honors in political science, history, and law and simultaneously earned membership in the honorary academic fraternity of Phi Beta Kappa. At nineteen years, five months of age, Mendel was the youngest graduate of his class. In only three more years, he had received his Yale doctorate in physiological chemistry. Working under the tutelage of Russell Chittenden, who in 1898 would begin a twenty-four-year term as director of Yale's Sheffield Scientific School, Mendel became well known in Yale scientific circles.[3] His exponential ascent up the academic ladder began with his appointment in 1894 as an instructor on the scientific school faculty, where he began to develop an honored scientific reputation. In *Science at the Bedside* A. McGehee Harvey described Mendel's most important contributions:

> With Chittenden, Mendel became one of the founders of the science of nutrition. . . . In collaboration with Thomas Burr Osborne of the Connecticut Agricultural Experiment Station, Mendel made the fundamental discovery that some proteins were nutritionally inadequate since they lacked amino acids that could be synthesized by the body. These he christened "essential amino acids." As early as 1910 he found an important growth factor . . . later known as vitamin B. Three years later he discovered that a serious eye disease, xerophthalmia, developed in rats lacking . . . vitamin A.[4]

In 1896 his appointment to the scientific school was extended to include the graduate school; the following year he was promoted to assistant professor in both schools. Then in 1903 he was appointed full professor of physiological chemistry—a phenomenal achievement for a thirty-one-year-old. In promoting Mendel, the university made him one of the first high-ranking Jewish professors in the country. When Mendel was at his peak, wrote Harvey, no other physiological chemist had so great an impact upon the medical profession. When the department of physiological chemistry was partly absorbed by the medical school in 1920, Mendel's appointment was extended yet again to make him a full professor on the scientific, graduate, and medical faculties. That same year he was also appointment chairman of the department of physiological sciences—a post he would hold until his death. Finally, capping an illustrious career, Mendel was appointed Sterling Professor of Physiological Chemistry in 1921. His appointment as Sterling professor was significant in that the brand-new Sterling-endowed chairs were Yale's most prestigious faculty title, reserved for professors who truly represented the finest in scholarship. Of the twenty professors to be designated Sterling professor in the decade following their inception in 1920, only two were selected before Mendel. Of the twenty, Mendel was the only Jew.[5]

What of Mendel's Jewish affiliations? As an undergraduate he apparently affiliated himself with Congregation Mishkan Israel (the local Reform synagogue) and became a Sunday School teacher there. As a member of the faculty, Mendel appeared a retiring, shy, and private man.[6] Like the idealized product of the *Haskalah*, the Jewish Enlightenment, Mendel was a Jew at home and an ordinary man on the street. In public he never tried to indicate that he was a Jew. Mendel told one friend that "he didn't object to being a Jew, but he never wore it on his coat."[7] On the Sabbath, however, he identified himself as a Jew, continuing his long-standing association with Congregation Mishkan Israel. Edgar Siskin, rabbi of the congregation, recalled that Mendel attended Friday evening services regularly: "A genial man of dignity, always impeccably dressed, he would come up with his wife when the service was over and invariably compliment me on the sermon no matter how mediocre an effort it had been. He was a generous man."[8] The respect of the national scientific community therefore was matched by the local Jewish community's personal respect for this quiet man.

Russell Chittenden, Mendel's mentor, also considered Mendel to be a great scientist, teacher, and human being, and Mendel's rapid advancement at Yale was undoubtedly due in no small part to Chittenden's support. But in the rest of the Yale community there are hints of a different reaction. Mendel was never accepted socially by the "insiders" among the faculty.[9] When, in 1918, for example, President Hadley was evaluating professors recommended to serve on a committee to select a site for a library, he realized that some faculty disliked working with Jews. Hadley thought, therefore, that someone besides Mendel might better serve the committee, acknowledging that "while everybody likes him, the fact of his race has kept him in some measure apart from the life of this place." Mendel had not been able to play down his Jewishness sufficiently to meet the social standards of the Yale faculty. Hadley, though not a vigorous leader for Yale, was an opponent of racial discrimination and finally chose Mendel to serve on this committee and several others at Yale.[10]

Mendel's role on the undergraduate admissions committee remains one of the great unsolved mysteries of Yale in the 1920s.[11] It is not known if he was aware of the extent of prejudices among the Yale administrators. The recorded discussion of specifically anti-Jewish admissions procedures was confined to the Committee on Limitations of Numbers, of which Mendel was not a member. It is possible, therefore, that any anti-Jewish admissions policies were first "sanitized," and then presented to the board of admissions in completely impartial terms. Since most of the biases at this time were applied either at the level of financial aid allocations or in the personal interview, it is also possible that Mendel was unaware of the actions of his colleagues. Again, Mendel may have been completely cognizant of the implications of all the Board of Admissions' decisions. Our only clue to Mendel's role is contained in Robert Nelson Corwin's 1932 report of Mendel's retirement from the Board of Admissions:

> Lafayette B. Mendel withdrew from the Board of Admissions at the end of [1930–31]. After serving for many years as a member of the Committee on Admissions of the Sheffield Scientific School, he became one of the representatives of that school on the Board of Admissions when this was established by the Corporation in January 1920. Through his constant interest in the work of the Board and his wise counsel, especially during the formative period of the new Board, he has rendered great service to the University.[12]

Whether Mendel was one of "the more intelligent and influential" Jews who, Corwin had once noted, preferred a limit on Jewish enrollment, whether he acted as a moderating influence on the racist prejudices in admissions, or whether he went along with Yale's limitation and tried to "play the Yale game" of conforming remains a mystery.[13]

His attitudes toward his accomplishments at Yale and his acceptance at Yale are also unknown. The sixtieth birthday gift—a portrait of Mendel by John Quincy Adams—that four hundred of his students and associates presented him in 1932 must have been encouraging. But all that can be said with certainty is that on December 9, 1935, after a long illness, Lafayette B. Mendel died of "organic heart weakness." His funeral service, at which Rabbi Siskin officiated, took place in Battell Chapel and everyone of consequence among the Yale administration and the Yale science faculty attended.[14]

Although no Jew held a senior position on the faculty of Yale College prior to the Second World War, there is no evidence that anti-Jewish feeling played any significant role in that absence prior to the First World War. Indeed, Anson Phelps Stokes, secretary of the university, spoke before the Yale Menorah Society in 1915 and urged its members to use their intellectual talents for scholarly careers, rather than for the professional careers of law and medicine, which he felt were the choices of many Jewish students. His words were not the words of a man who favored a religio-racially restrictive college faculty.[15]

The encouragement that the university offered Eugene H. Lehman (B.A.

1902, M.A. 1909) indicates that had fate treatment him more kindly, he might in time have achieved a senior position on the Yale faculty. During his graduate school years, with the backing of President Hadley and Charles F. Kent, Woolsey Professor of Biblical Literature, Lehman solicited various "Hebrew philanthropists" for support of the Yale Semitics department. President Hadley took his cues on when to approach potential Jewish donors from Lehman. Pleased with Lehman's scholastic efforts, Hadley also suggested that Lehman might earn a permanent position if he could complete the writing of a Yale-caliber doctoral thesis.[16]

Neither the fund-raising nor the thesis-writing, however, would succeed. The first blow to Lehman was the refusal of philanthropist Jacob H. Schiff to do "anything of importance" for Yale. Schiff was doubtless unable to predict that his own grandson (John M. Schiff) would be a Yale undergraduate only twelve years later. From Schiff, hopeful fundraiser Lehman turned to Adolf Lewisohn, another prominent New York Jewish philanthropist. Lewisohn offered a token contribution of three thousand dollars as a beginning for the endowment of a chair in Jewish history and literature. It was not enough to support even an instructor, yet Lehman and Hadley persevered. Full of doomed confidence, Lehman promised Hadley in 1909 that more would soon follow:

> My personal faith in the readiness of the Jewish people to help materially any movement that tends to promote the study of their history and religion was strong enough to keep me at this line of work during several discouraging years immediately after graduation, and to induce me to refuse other more lucrative opportunities when the possibility of carrying out my plans at Yale was presented to me.[17]

But the money did not come forth.

To provide limited support to the man on whom it had placed its hopes for Judaic studies, Yale appointed Lehman as a part-time instructor in Jewish literature in 1910. Through 1913 he taught a survey course on the "History and Literature of the Jewish People" for interested students in the college and graduate school. To supplement his income he commuted to New York City to serve as principal at the religious school operated by Rabbi Stephen S. Wise's Free Synagogue. Failure again struck when Lehman's religious attitudes proved at odds with those of others in the synagogue and he was fired from his post. He then entered the field of secular education, which allowed him to sustain a living but prevented him from devoting sufficient time to intensive scholarly study. This sealed his fate. Even without adequate endowment for the teaching of Judaica in the college, President Hadley continued to encourage Lehman to complete his thesis and take full-time employment at Yale. But Lehman could not afford the necessary time for the project. Writer's block may also have caused him to tarry. The thesis was never written, and the man who might have been the first Jewish professor and the first professor of Jewish studies in Yale College left the New Haven scene forever.[18]

The prejudices that spread through America during the First World War did not spare the Yale faculty. Once those feelings became entrenched in New Haven, the encouragement that Eugene Lehman had received would not be matched for other Jewish faculty. A noteworthy example was Max Mandell, instructor in Russian from 1907 through 1924. Mandell had been preceded in that position by another Jew: Meyer Wolodarsky (Ph.B. 1894, Ph.D. 1899), who held the post in the college between 1899 and 1902. When Mandell arrived at Yale in 1907, he made himself available as a tutor in the Russian language. With the backing of William Lyon Phelps, professor of English literature, Mandell, who had published an English translation of Chekhov's *The Cherry Orchard*, was given the instructorship. Phelps took such a liking to Mandell that he invited this Russian teacher to his home on several occasions. A dedicated worker who was not a practicing Jew, Mandell only paused from his work to relax on Sunday afternoons. To support his family (the instructorship was but a part-time position) he spent much of his time at his podiatry practice on Orange Street. For many years he commuted to New York City three times a week for graduate work at Columbia University, eventually completing all of his doctoral requirements except for publication of his dissertation. He also translated *The Plays of Ivan Turgenev,* for which Phelps wrote the introduction to the published volume, and Mandell's translation of "A Month in the Country" was used on the stages of London and New York for many years.[19]

Trouble began for Mandell in 1922 when President Angell happened to meet him and discover that, after teaching at Yale for fifteen years, Mandell was still serving as an instructor. Hoping to introduce rigorous tenure policies to Yale, Angell found it necessary to act. Thinking it best that Mandell either be placed on the academic ladder or else be released, Angell engaged in a sparring match by mail with Dean Jones to settle the instructor's fate. Angell tried to prevail upon the college faculty to accept Mandell; Jones led in the other direction. A major factor working against Mandell was that Yale then had no department of Russian: Therefore the field did not have a respected place at Yale. But for Jones, the essence of the problem was that "Mr. Mandell's Russian is distinctly Yiddish Russian, although he may be able to teach the pure Russian."[20] Though Mandell's excellence in teaching and his devotion to his students were unquestioned, Jones felt that if Yale was interested in developing a department of Russian, it would have been better to "secure somebody who has a somewhat different background from that possessed by Mr. Mandell."[21] Accepting the limits of his presidential authority, Angell agreed with Jones to allow Mandell to continue in his current position under a limited contract. At the end of the 1923–24 school year Dean Jones thanked Mandell for his "loyalty" and his "conscientious work with our Yale students," and terminated his position. Having cut off its Jewish "nose" to spite its prejudiced "face," Yale would go without Russian instruction for two decades.[22]

THE NATIONAL SCENE

Given the fact that in the early years of the century, few Jews aspired to academic careers, the relative absence of Jews on college faculties was not seen as unusual. By 1930, attitudes had changed. Jews, generally immigrants themselves or children of European emigrants, looked back to Europe and saw that the "promised land" of America had not lived up to its promise. Writing in *The Reflex,* a magazine whose one self-proclaimed goal was "to report and interpret the realities of modern life," S. M. Melamed lashed out in 1927 at the absence of Jews on American university faculties:

> With a very few exceptions, the Jewish university professor in America is nonexistent. . . . Europe is surely not a haven for the Jew, yet, with the exception of Hungary and Russia, every university in Europe has a number of Jewish professors. . . . In Germany, the Jewish population is only one-half of one percent of the total population, yet the proportion of Jewish professors in German universities is three per cent of the teaching staff. . . . In the Vienna university, where the beating of Jewish students by the Teutonic classmates has become a national sport, there are probably more Jewish professors than in all the American universities combined.[23]

Melamed's statistics are not wholly reliable, but his choler paints a poignant picture of the frustration that beset those Jews who sought academic careers in the America of the 1920s. For black Americans, the restrictions were even more severe. Of 330 blacks with Ph.D.'s in the United States of 1940, none taught at a white-dominated university. There were several reasons for the difference in faculty hiring practices between Europe and America. Most important was that the Central European universities' hiring policies were generally based on academic merit alone, in contrast to practices in the United States. Since race, personality, and compatibility were not considered important factors, faculty prejudices against Jews or Jewish personalities were not permitted to play a great role.[24]

For American Jews the exclusion from faculties was far more problematic than undergraduate admissions biases. If a Jewish boy did not make a quota at Harvard, Princeton, or Columbia, for example, he might legitimately suspect that he was being discriminated against. But he would realize that if he was determined to have an excellent (though less prestigious) education, other institutions (most notably the public universities) were available. Or, if a Jewish boy was rejected by Yale—where the outstanding applicants were accepted and the marginal ones rejected in favor of marginal non-Jews—he might have been able to console himself with the knowledge that he had some control over his own destiny, for had he only studied a bit harder in "that one course," perhaps he might have been admitted. Exclusion from faculties was a far different matter, leaving fewer honorable alternatives and fewer ways of retaining self-esteem short of disavowing one's ethnic background. Especially in the humanities the aspiring Jewish academic knew that no matter how prolific a writer, how dynamic a teacher, how sparkling a person one was, one could have no control over one's fate. It was like being returned to the ghetto all over again: only this time walled out, not in.

YALE COLLEGE

The most insular of all of the Yale faculties was that of Yale College proper. As of 1929, neither a Jew nor a known Catholic had ever achieved a full professorship in the college. Not until after the end of the Second World War would a Jew be granted tenure. (See appendix 8.) Jewish students were occasionally warned by their professors not to waste their time in graduate school, since academic careers were not open to them.[25] Such warnings took their toll, wrote Eugene V. Rostow in the *Harkness Hoot:*

> The bald fact remains, in spite of all official disclaimers, that there is not one Jew on the faculty of Yale College, and only a few, of great repute, scattered through the Scientific, Graduate and Professional Schools.
>
> The younger men on the faculty recognize the situation, and confess themselves powerless. Apparently, nothing can be done, and even the most liberal dare not be sanguine. Yale College is closed to the Jewish teacher, the Graduate Schools only recently and hesitantly opened.
>
> But more important than flagrant incidents of a definite character is the effect on the Jewish student of the knowledge that he is accepted only as a dilettante, a dabbler

in learning, that his academic ambitions can never be realized. This condition needs no formal expression; it is tacitly understood, a galling "gentleman's agreement" of bitterness and betrayal.[26]

It remained for Yale's law school to provide Rostow the open door that he was looking for.

Nowhere at Yale were the barriers more evident than in the English department, the most prestigious center of influence on the campus. Writing of that department as it existed in the 1920s, Pierson noted that "English ruled heaven and earth in Yale College, and for a student generation English attracted more than half of each class into its major." The English faculty, like the history and sociology faculties, was largely the province of Yale alumni. Outsiders who joined these faculties without a Yale background were generally considered unrespectable until long after they had arrived and had proven themselves. In English, particular disrespect was saved for Jews. Morris Sweetkind, the top student in the class of 1920 of the Sheffield Scientific School, recalled Albert Stanburrough Cook, professor of the English language and literature, trying at an admission interview to dissuade him from continuing his application for graduate studies in English. Not that Sweetkind's scientific background was insufficient; the Yale Graduate School could not bring itself to reject one of Yale's very best students who desired further learning. Rather, Cook saw no future for Sweetkind, a Jew, in English. After he had enrolled in the department, Sweetkind became convinced that Cook's words had been serious when Tucker Brooke, professor of English, sounded the death knell to the hopeful scholar: "Look, Sweetkind. You're a good student, but we've never had a Jew. Don't apply [to teach here]. It's just a waste of time."[27] Max Lerner (B.A. 1923) was similarly shocked by Robert Dudley French, assistant professor of English, whose good relationship with Lerner permitted the teacher to be candid. Lerner's expressed hope of becoming a professor of English was met with a friendly rebuttal by French: "Max, you can't do this. You can't teach literature. You have no chance of getting a position at any good college. You're a Jew."[28] The most popular rationalization for the attitude that Jews had no place in the Yale English department was the conviction that Jews lacked the cultural and religious background necessary for teaching English literature, much of which derived its meaning from the New Testament. When applied nationwide, this defense made English departments notorious for their discriminatory policies.[29] Sweetkind recalled a great argument that he once had with William Lyon Phelps, Lampson Professor of English (the same man who had befriended Max

Mandell), over whether a Jew could capably teach Robert Browning's "Easter Day" poem.[30] Chief advocate within the Yale department of the concept of native Jewish incapability was Chauncey Brewster Tinker, Sterling Professor of English Literature and Yale's "Dr. Johnson." Pierson has written that Tinker

> would not allow appointments of Jews to teach English literature on the ground, as he insisted, of cultural incompatibility. . . . He did not genuinely believe that a Jew could be understanding of the English literary tradition. . . . He was a high-church Episcopalian himself—and his position was taken on religious-cultural or on cultural grounds.[31]

Ignorant of the New Testament, Jews were incapable of teaching English, thought Tinker, and therefore unworthy of being hired.[32] Others, looking back on this era, saw the biases more bluntly. According to Richard Sewall, then a graduate student and instructor in the department, "The English department in the 1930s was frankly anti-Semitic." Sewall insisted, though, that there was no malice behind the anti-Jewish feeling of the era: "We look back on those days with shock. We were in an age of innocence. We didn't know what we were doing."[33] The prejudices were ingrained so deeply that biases often successfully masqueraded in the guise of detached objectivity.

Especially ironic was the fact that many of Yale's best students of English were Jewish. Elliot E. Cohen (B.A. 1918) won the John Addison Porter Fellowship to finance two years of graduate study in English at Yale. But the lack of opportunity for Jews on English faculties led him to turn his interests elsewhere.[34] Of the five New Haven boys to receive honors in English in 1922, three were Jews: Abraham Alderman, Max Lerner, and Theodore Zunder. Zunder (B.A. 1923), one of the more successful students of his era, won a coveted fellowship to attend the Yale Graduate School and received his Ph.D. in 1927. For employment, however, he had to look elsewhere. He became an instructor at Brown University and Hunter College each for a year; then he settled for a permanent position on the Brooklyn College faculty of the City University of New York. Several of the other Jewish graduate students left the Yale English program with master's degrees, not the doctorates needed to provide them the credentials for teaching elsewhere. Learning the unusual difficulties that a Jew faced in English, they often gave up their educational plans in the middle of their graduate course.[35]

Rarely did the students complain. Sidney Hook, professor emeritus of philosophy at New York University and witness to similar prejudices at Columbia

University, analyzed the submissive attitude of the Jewish students denied a
faculty position in this era:

> In retrospect and in the present climate of opinion, it may be difficult to explain the
> absence of moral indignation on the part of the Jewish students [in] those days when
> they were passed over for others who "belonged." This discrimination was some-
> thing we took for granted like consciousness of the fact that we had to be "twice as
> good" as any non-Jewish competitor to have the ghost of a chance of even being con-
> sidered for a desirable post. Although many of us lived in the universalist socialist
> dream of a secular classless society in which cultural differences would either be can-
> celled out or in which we would enjoy the same moral status of all other ethnic
> groups, we felt that in the meantime we were outside the Establishment. We had no
> desire to push our way in socially; it was really love of our subject matter and the
> hope of living with it in a whole-hearted dedicated way that moved us. In those days
> the academy was the last place one would look forward to or prepare for, if one
> wanted to make money.

When the day of reckoning came, and money finally had to be earned, some of
the most capable, like Zunder, would join a creditable but less illustrious faculty, while others left academe altogether.[36]

MORRIS R. COHEN AND THE
PHILOSOPHY DEPARTMENT

In departments outside English, the Yale record varied. Philosophy was a special case, for it was the first in Yale College to consider Jews for appointment,
and, in turn, eminent Jewish faculty were attracted to it. Lewis Feuer has noted
that philosophy held a unique attraction for the American Jewish student. It
was a discipline that proved inviting to those scholars who needed a field of
learning to balance the loss of orthodox religion in their lives.[37] But discrimination was present in this segment of academe as well. At Harvard, for example, the only two Jews allowed to stay on permanently in this era were paid
through gifts of Jewish philanthropists. When the Harvard philosophy department recommended its Jewish graduate students for appointments elsewhere,
it described its students as "by no means offensive," or "with none of the faults
which are sometimes expected in such cases."[38] For philosophers, as for other
academics, a Jew was often offensive until proven decent.

Morris R. Cohen, a product of the Harvard department of philosophy, was
a case in point. Earning a B.S. in 1900 from the City College of New York and

a Harvard Ph.D. in 1906, Cohen became the first Russian-born Jew to achieve prominence as an American philosopher. In 1929–30 he was brought to Yale as visiting professor of philosophy and he taught a course in the graduate school. The following academic year he returned for the spring semester and co-taught the Yale College "Modern Idealism" course with Wilmon Sheldon, professor of philosophy. Except for a five-week stint as a visiting professor in Spring 1940, Cohen's Yale association ended in the spring of 1931. Why he did not stay on at Yale is a matter of speculation. Filmer Northrop, an associate professor of philosophy when Cohen was first at Yale, suggested that Cohen's short stay was due to the Yale Corporation's disdain for philosophy. In an era when the theme "Philosophy is Rubbish" dominated the Corporation, argued Northrop, the university made little support available for Cohen. Charles Bakewell, chairman of the philosophy department and intimate friend of Cohen's, therefore urged Cohen not to think about Yale, since Bakewell doubted that the Corporation would provide the philosophy department the slot for the full professorship that Cohen deserved.[39] This hypothesis, however, does not appear valid in light of the appointment in 1931 of Wilbur Marshall Urban (B.A. Princeton 1895) as professor of philosophy. The following year Northrop himself was promoted to the rank of full professor.

Cohen's personality likely worked against him. Richard Sewall recalled that when Cohen was being considered for a faculty appointment, English professor William Lyon Phelps went to meet Cohen and took a strong dislike to him. Phelps (who had once vigorously argued the case for retaining Russian instructor Max Mandell) reported back to the faculty that Cohen was "Jewish and no gentleman. We don't need him." This character assessment may have been fatal to Cohen's appointment. In his day Cohen was widely considered one of the greats. But his personality could be difficult. Indeed, as a teacher who practiced a harsh Socratic style, he could be cruel and exhibited "browbeating, sarcasm, and absence of simple courtesy" that led him to "hurt too many others in what was for him a form of theater."[40] Whether this style was an expression of bitterness that grew out of finding his great intellect unwelcome on the permanent faculty of America's great universities, or whether it stemmed from earlier psychological trauma, or whether it was an innate part of his temperament is beyond the scope of this discussion. Being a Jew and a bully were not synonymous, but a Jew who was a bully had two separate and real handicaps to consideration for a Yale faculty appointment. Had his human decency equalled his intellect, it is not unreasonable to wonder if his Judaism would have been less of a handicap to a permanent appointment at Yale.

From Cohen's own perspective, it seems likely that he, too, would have been uncomfortable with a permanent position on the Yale faculty of the 1930s. Writing to Felix Frankfurter in 1936, Cohen could not reconcile himself to Yale's contradictory efforts to be a liberal arts institution, open to all philosophies and people, and to maintain its racial and religious heritage:

There is a certain duplicity about liberalism which shocks intellectually conscientious people. . . . this is the case with our Universities. They claim to stand for universal truth, but in the end they do not want to get away from certain sectarian and partisan commitments. I have no objection to Yale University insisting that it is a white, Protestant organization and acting accordingly [as it used to in regard to compulsory chapel]; but it should make some effort at consistency.[41]

To admit non-Protestants and nonwhites in the name of universality, while in the name of tradition denying them full acceptance in university life, smacked of callous exploitation. Cohen's own unwillingness to accept Yale's attempt to have its cake and eat it may have made him as unwanted in some faculty circles as he was dissatisfied with those circles.

Yale's refusal to place Jews on its college faculty hurt the status of some of its departments. Discussing the problems in assembling a good science faculty in the 1930s and 1940s, historian Brooks M. Kelley blamed the rivalry between the faculties of the Sheffield Scientific School and Yale College. Yet he found another, more significant reason:

Perhaps even more damaging was the fact that the science departments did not take advantage of the great influx of talented Jews fleeing Hitler's Germany. The same attitude prevailed in most parts of the university until after World War II. In only a few fields was there any willingness to tolerate Jews on even a temporary basis. . . . Where this attitude was not present—as at Princeton or Columbia—science blossomed. At Yale . . . it prevented the university from seizing a great opportunity.[42]

President Angell was superficially concerned about the plight of the German refugees (30 percent of those who arrived in America were non-Jews) but was reluctant to commit scarce university funds to provide them employment. The prevailing sentiment among the Yale faculty was one of indifference. In the prewar and war years, Yale had hired on at least a temporary basis Gustave Cohen (1941–43), Ernst Cassirer (1941–44), Erik H. Erikson (1936–39), Max Forster (1934–36), Hajo Holborn (1934–69), Friedrich Kessler (1935–38), Karl Loewenstein (1934–36), Fredrick Redlich (1942–72), and Arnold Wolfers (1933–57). But even this impressive list of scholars—not all of whom were Jewish—overstates Yale's acceptance. Cohen was brought to Yale solely on the basis of funds provided for that purpose by the New School for Social Research. The initial appointments of Forster, Holborn, Kessler, and Loewenstein were funded, not by Yale revenues, but through the coffers of the New York "Emergency Committee in Aid of Displaced German Scholars." The reluctance of Yale to hire refugees was as much a reflection of anti-Jewish feeling as a sign that the attitude of distrust of the foreigner that had been endemic to President Timothy Dwight (the elder) a century earlier (see chapter 1) was still thriving in the twentieth century. Writing in 1941 about Einar Hille, the Erastus L. DeForest Professor of Mathematics at Yale, Dean Charles H. Warren of the scientific school explained that foreigners were still considered unsuitable for some positions of authority in a university:

> No foreigner should be chairman of a department where undergraduate work is involved. . . . One of the criticisms of these foreign importations is that they are not suited to undergraduate work or do not wish to do it. Hence they take the most desirable positions away from our American product.

Hille, who had been born in the United States but educated at the University of Stockholm, had been branded an outsider. Only on the graduate faculty of Alvin Johnson's New School for Social Research, founded in 1933 as the University in Exile, were refugee scholars truly welcome. At Yale, the campus community preferred to concentrate on helping faculty wives and children from Oxford University to find new homes in America.[43]

HARRY SHULMAN AND THE
YALE LAW DEANSHIP

In sharp contrast to the exclusiveness of the college faculty was the law school. The outstanding example of Louis Brandeis's service on the United States Supreme Court from 1916 to 1939 encouraged the acceptance of Jews on many law faculties nationwide. The open-mindedness of deans Thomas W. Swan (1916–27), Robert M. Hutchins (1927–29), and Charles E. Clark (1929–39) set the pattern for a long tradition of meritocracy at the law school. Dean Swan gave one of the earliest Yale Law School Jewish appointments to Leon Tulin (B.A. 1922, LL.B. 1925), assistant professor of law from 1926 until his death in 1929. Tulin occasionally brought small groups of Jewish undergraduates together to listen to men like Chaim Weizmann (later to be the first president of Israel), Julian Mack (the Chicago judge who was Harvard's first Jewish overseer), and Tulin's father-in-law, Stephen S. Wise (American Jewish leader and rabbi).[44] When in 1931 Judge Jerome Frank of New York (a Jew who was uncomfortable with his ethnic background) wrote to Dean Clark and asked for "a list of uncircumcised neophytes" to join a discussion group, Clark returned to him a list of twenty-three, six of whom were Jews: "Those who have the figure (1) after their name are of Hebrew extraction, although in each case I am glad to recommend them as very fine."[45] Heywood Broun and George Britt, in their book *Christians Only*, noted that in the Yale Law School of the 1930s, as at the most famous of the nation's law schools, all admitted students were treated fairly. Because academic merit was a major factor for any position on the *Yale Law Journal*, often half of the *Journal* men were Jewish. There was similar lack of prejudice at the level of faculty hiring. Abe Fortas (LL.B. 1933), the future Supreme Court justice, was an assistant professor of law from 1936 to 1938.[46]

Yet even the lack of implemented prejudices among the law faculty could not fully protect the law school from the anti-Jewish feeling of the nation, of Yale alumni, and of Yale administrators. The case of Harry Shulman exemplified this. Shulman, a Russian-born graduate of Brown University and Harvard Law School, joined the Yale law faculty in 1930, following service as a clerk to Justice Brandeis. His "unabashed" identification as a Jew had little adverse effect upon his popularity within the law school. According to Rabbi Siskin, Shulman was "one of the best liked teachers in the law school. Anybody could come to his office to speak with him. He had the reputation of never ending an interview with a student; the student had to make the break and leave."[47] Shulman fell victim to anti-Jewish feeling in 1939, when the retirement of Charles Clark as law school dean set a search for a successor. The faculty was overwhelmingly inclined to support Shulman, at thirty-six a full professor. Legal scholars and prestigious lawyers from across the country also saw him as the ideal man. Judge Learned Hand wrote that "my choice remains Harry Shulman." He was the first choice of law professors Karl Llewellyn and Edmund M. Morgan. Wrote the latter: "None [of the other candidates] is superior . . . to Harry Shulman." Shulman's only substantial handicap was his Jewishness in a time of rising anti-Semitism in the nation.[48]

The national atmosphere of 1939 saw the United States edging closer to the brink of war. The demagogic Father Charles E. Coughlin had fanned the fires of prejudice with his anti-Jewish, anti-Communist campaign, in which he defended Nazi anti-Jewish actions as a means to halt Communism. Upper class resentment toward Roosevelt's New Deal also stimulated racist feelings, as a contemporary verse slurring Franklin and Eleanor Roosevelt attested:

You kiss the negroes,
I'll kiss the Jews,
We'll stay in the White House,
As long as we choose.[49]

Oscar S. Cox, assistant counsel in the U.S. Treasury Department, pointed out in regard to Shulman's candidacy that "the *fact* is that many people have" racial prejudices and that this might make his life as dean difficult, yet Cox thought him to be the "best bet" for the job. Professor Frank R. Strong of the Ohio State Law School said of Shulman that "I am sure that his Jewish origin would carry no weight against him in any circles whose judgment is worthy of considera- tion." But Yale would place great weight on the opinions of prejudiced circles. One Yale law graduate wrote that "any dean has a tough enough road to plough without having to contend with racial prejudices," and when university presi- dent Charles Seymour traveled to Washington to solicit the opinions of leading Washington legal experts, he came away with the same impression. In a memo to himself after a November 1939 meeting with Justice William O. Douglas (who that year had left his Sterling law professorship at Yale for a seat on the Supreme Court), Seymour wrote:

> Douglas regarded Shulman as an admirable candidate and one who from the per- sonal and intellectual point of view was equal to [the other two candidates] men- tioned. The racial problem however could not be forgotten. In view of this fact he did not place Shulman on a par with either [of the others]. . . . I gathered that Doug- las would regard Shulman as a wise appointment provided the University was willing to take the widespread and unfair criticism which would certainly result throughout the country and especially among our Yale College alumni.

Seymour admitted to himself that he might have gotten a wrong impression of Douglas's views on the "racial problem," but for the purposes of this discussion, the crucial result of their conversation was not what Douglas thought, but what the Yale president concluded from their discussion. For a president whose tenure was characterized by "hesitancy, timidity, and conservatism in the poli- cies pursued," to have appointed Shulman as dean would have been unthink- able in an emotionally charged limelight. Shulman was the clear favorite, but his Jewish background *alone* held him back. In February 1940, President Sey- mour formally asked the Yale Corporation to appoint Ashbel Green Gulliver (B.A. 1919, LL.B. 1922, Garver Professor of Law and acting dean of the law school) to a five-year term as dean. Unable to bring himself to explain the Jew- ish factor in Shulman's non-election, Seymour explained to Shulman "that one factor that has bulked very much in my own mind has been the importance of your scholarly work and the necessity of making it possible for you to push this forward under the most favorable conditions." As a consolation, apparently given with genuinely good intentions, later that year Seymour designated Shulman to be a holder of one of Yale's coveted Sterling professorships.[51]

THE GRADUATE CLUB

Paralleling the exclusivity of the undergraduate world within Yale and the social world outside of Yale was that within the club ranks of the faculty. The most prominent and broadly based association to attract Yale faculty was the Graduate Club of New Haven. In the first decades of the twentieth century it played a central role in the club life of Yale. Although never an official component of the university, the association was intimately associated with Yale. During the six decades between 1894 and 1954, Yale professors were club presidents for thirty-six years. From 1901 through 1938 some 40 percent of the officers came from the ranks of the Yale faculty, administrators, and corporation fellows. A similar proportion of the board of governors had the same background. Nearly half of this club's admissions committee were from this group. Sixty percent of the members of the entertainment committee were drawn from these ranks as well. Because there was substantial turnover from year to year in committee, board of governors, and officer membership, an extremely wide range of Yale-employed people took leadership positions within the club. They ranged from deans and department chairmen to instructors and tutors. In educational background, the members had an even greater Yale connection. In the period between 1901 and 1938, approximately 75 percent of the members had received their first (not to mention any other) college or university degree from Yale. Among the members of the club's admissions committee, the proportion claiming their first degree at Yale was nearly 85 percent.[52]

The Graduate Club had its origins in the club ethos of Yale when a number of undergraduates of the Yale College class of 1889 drifted together during their senior year for talk on any subject they fancied, with a tendency toward politics and government. Wilbur L. Cross (club president from 1923 to 1925) recorded the organization's growth:

> They became known among their less intellectual classmates on the outside as "Deep Thinkers"—a name, which, disregardful of the satire lurking in the title, they adopted, doubtless with pride in being thus set off as the intelligentsia of the student body. . . . Some of the "Deep Thinkers" remained on in the Law School, where they

formed a much larger group under the guiding hand of [William Pope Aiken, B.A. 1853]. Several men of the class of 1890 in Yale College, who came over into the Law School, were taken in, and men also from the Divinity and Graduate Schools. By 1890–1891, the "Deep Thinkers" had taken shape as a club.[53]

When they realized that there were a number of older graduates in the city who desired to join a good social club, the group decided to expand. In March 1894 they chose the name for themselves of "The Graduate Club" and numbered their resident membership at 133. Among that group were two Jews: assistant in physiological chemistry Lafayette B. Mendel and local physician Max Mailhouse (Ph.B. 1876, M.D. 1878, lecturer in neurology 1900–07). The club was limited to degree-holders only, as the membership wanted a refuge from the "principal public resorts" of Mory's, Heublein's, and Traeger's—all dominated by undergraduates.[54] By 1895 the club had 242 resident members and had become so large that it felt it necessary to purchase property at 77 Elm Street. Aided by a twenty-year mortgage loan from Yale, in 1902 the Graduate Club enlarged the Whitney Blake House, an old white frame colonial building adjacent to the Yale campus.[55] The club considered itself so tied to the nearby university that when it published its 1901 directory, the Yale coat of arms with the *Urim V'Thummim* and *Lux Et Veritas* was placed in the middle of their own symbol. The Yale arms remained at the center of the insignia for decades to come.[56]

Life at the Graduate Club in the first years of the century was a gentlemanly one. David L. Daggett recorded his blissful memories:

In the golden years before World War I, club life was never more pleasant. . . . Dues and charges were low: an Orange Blossom (gin and orange juice) was served to members at the price of two for a quarter. . . . During this happy era, the Dutch Treat table stood in the far end of the Great Hall, and at 4 p.m. on weekdays it was supplied with an urn of tea, a decanter of rum, cheese and crackers. There would gather well known figures . . . and other members discussing and debating topics of endless variety. In the later afternoon, many businessmen and professional men . . . found time to drop in at the Club frequently for a cocktail and a chat, then strolled home. . . . If one entered the Club in the evening, he often found a group enjoying a Welsh rabbit and a bottle of beer before going home to bed.[57]

It was at the Graduate Club that men like Clarence W. Mendell, professor of Latin, and George E. Woodbine and Charles Seymour, professors of history, could gather when they wanted a somewhat diverse company for playing cards, drinking tea or rum, and partaking of a leisurely meal.

The club was nominally diverse, but there were limits to its eclecticism, as it was a private club and not a public institution. As a prerequisite, candidates had to possess a college or university degree. The next requirement was that the candidate's name be proposed in writing by a club member. The proposal, which had to be posted in the club for two weeks, needed to state the prospective member's name, resident, college, class, degree, occupation, and any other "necessary facts." The parallel sets of data for the proposer and someone who would second the proposal also had to be posted for the fortnight. Finally the name had to come before the club's eight-member committee on admissions. The procedures were simple: "Two negative ballots shall be sufficient to exclude; one negative ballot shall be sufficient to defer consideration of a candidate's name for one regular meeting, but said postponement shall occur but once. No candidate shall be elected by less than four affirmative ballots."[58] Since New Haven Jews tended to be poor, the lower proportion of Jews among the resident-members of the club as compared to their proportion among the city population is hardly surprising. For the year 1901, when Mendel and Mailhouse made up nearly one percent of the resident membership and Jews represented less than 5 percent of the entire New Haven population, economic factors alone can be invoked to explain the gap. In 1906 Harry Washington Asher (Yale class of 1879) was added to the roster, and in 1919 Isaac Wolfe (Yale class of 1887). By the 1910s a new factor besides economics was operating, though. The Jewish membership in the club still remained below one percent, despite the Jewish proportion in New Haven being greater than 12 percent. Many Jews likely lacked the social refinement to meet the standards of the average club member. No doubt the vast majority of New Haven Jews (particularly of East European origin) lacked the time or money to spend in the parlors of Elm Street and, therefore, had no interest in the association. Certainly only a small proportion of the Jewish community then was made up of college or university graduates. But these explanations do not give the entire picture.

That picture is suggested by the interaction between the Yale president and the admissions committees of the club. When the name of Fred Adler, member of a local factory-owning family, was proposed in 1918, President Hadley became a staunch advocate of Adler's election to the club:

> I have known Mr. Adler a long time, and like him exceedingly. I like to talk with him, and I like to work with him. The only objection that it seems to me could possibly be suggested against him is based on the ground of his race. I should regard the election of Mr. Adler to the Club as having this positive advantage: it would show that we

chose a man on the basis of his personal qualities, and not on the basis of prejudice or convention.

I do not know how the members of the Club in general feel about this matter; but I am inclined to think that if they knew Mr. Adler as well as I do they would share my views.[59]

Despite Hadley's recommendation, Adler did not become a club member. And two years later, biased politics directly affected a Yale Jewish faculty member. Milton Charles Winternitz had recently been appointed dean of the medical school. Winternitz, whose achievements at Yale were nothing short of outstanding and whose personality was among the most complex of anyone at Yale (see chapter 7), made quite a name for himself in New Haven. A man who could be aggressive and combative, Winternitz was kind to people he liked and behaved in gentlemanly fashion among the faculty and administrators on the university's main campus.[60] In November 1920 his name was proposed for membership. At the initial meeting of the admissions committee he apparently was not elected. Either he received one negative vote, or he failed to receive four affirmative votes. Again, President Hadley saw the issue as being a reflection of anti-Jewish feeling. To combat it he swiftly drafted a letter directed personally to Frederick Bliss Luquiens, professor of Spanish and chairman of the admissions committee:

I have seen something of [Winternitz] socially as well as professionally, having had him at my house at dinner. He is most interesting in his conversation and considerate in his manner. But it is not primarily on this ground that I am urging careful consideration of [Dr.] Winternitz's name. I am urging him because he is Dean of the Yale Medical School, and as Dean should naturally be invited to become a member of the Club, unless there is stronger objection to him than that which is based on the fear that the Hebrew element in the Club may become too large. In his position as Dean, Winternitz will need to hold a number of conferences for which the Graduate Club is the natural place, partly because most of the men will be Graduate Club members, and partly because the Graduate Club is regarded by the public, and rightly so regarded, as the natural place for the discussion of Yale affairs by intelligent graduates. While our Club is not nominally connected with Yale more than with any other college, it is actually connected with it a great deal, and a belief that the Club allowed itself to ignore the interests of Yale in a serious matter would greatly imperil its prosperity.

This, of course, does not mean that the Club ought to elect a man on account of his relations to Yale if they feel that he will be objectionable to his fellow members, but I think it does make it very unfortunate that it should adopt a policy of race discrimination, which it has not always practiced, at a time when it will exceptionally [affect] the Yale Medical School and create an unusual necessity for public discussion of the Committee's action.[61]

Luquiens decided to share the letter with the committee, all eight of whom were Yale graduates, and Winternitz's nomination was approved. Hadley was never forced to back up his thinly veiled threats of disclosure. But for the next thirty years no other Jew would be permitted to join the Graduate Club.[62]

EDWARD SAPIR

In the 1930s the club's policy exploded into a scandal in the case of Edward Sapir. Sapir's appointment to the faculty was a product of President Angell's attempts to make his own mark at Yale. Since as a newcomer and an outsider to the Yale scene, Angell lacked the personal and political strength to influence many areas of decision making, he concentrated some of his efforts on raising the standards of Yale research by bringing in brilliant scholars to the Graduate School faculty.[63] Sapir, an anthropologist who had studied under Franz Boas at Columbia, had become known for developing the idea that culture has an impact upon personality and also argued the notion that every language has a specific frame of reference toward the universe. His collaboration with Harry Stack Sullivan and Harold D. Lasswell in New Haven would later influence the entry of psychoanalysis into the social sciences.[64] Angell, expanding Yale's social science horizons, brought in this intellectual giant as Sterling Professor of Anthropology and Linguistics. Intellectuals from all over were subsequently attracted to his Yale "Seminar on the Impact of Culture on Personality."[65]

But Sapir's brilliance, charisma, decency, and personal warmth were not enough to win him social acceptance, and this made his New Haven experience an often bitter one. At issue were Sapir's identity and status as a Jew. Sapir had been born in Germany to a cantor and had been raised by his mother in a traditional Jewish home. Like many other Jewish anthropologists of his day, he drifted away from his religious tradition and had little contact with Jewish life. But during the years of the Nazi rise to power, Sapir's interest in Jewish matters was awakened. He began to study the ancient rabbinic writings of the Talmud and involved himself in the field of Judaic studies. In conversation he began to discuss his Talmud studies and expound on how profoundly Judaism had influenced his life. Sapir helped organize the Conference on Jewish Relations, a national committee of eminent Jewish scholars interested in the scientific evaluation of social trends affecting Jews. Two men who had been somewhat alienated from Yale became the founders. Morris R. Cohen was its first president and Sapir its first vice-president. In 1939 the Conference inaugurated the journal *Jewish Social Studies* with the intent of creating a better understanding of the position of Jews in the modern world. *Jewish Social Studies* was a reaction to the events in Germany that indicated that modernity was being "achieved at the cost of a war of extermination against the Jews." The East and Central European centers of learning were being systematically destroyed, and men like Cohen, Sapir, Hans Kohn, and Salo W. Baron felt that American Jewry must pick up the slack.[66]

Although it was the Nazi rise to power that had aroused Sapir's interest in Jewish affairs, it took a personal confrontation with an exclusive social world to make him aware that prejudices were as much a part of his Yale life as they had been a part of his earlier years. This occurred when the Graduate Club, the center of faculty social life, denied him membership. Some explained that the club was merely trying to preserve its Jewish proportion.[67] In truth, however, the four Jews (Mailhouse, Mendel, Winternitz, and Wolfe) among its 569 resident members in 1930 made up the lowest Jewish proportion in the thirty-six years of the club's existence. Sapir's candidacy had been brought to a halt by one member's campaign of prejudice in the context of an unwritten club law that excluded Jews and all undesirable minorities from admission.[68]

Occurring one year after Sapir's 1931 arrival in New Haven, the Graduate Club rejection sent shock waves through the university. "Liberal opinion on the campus was stunned," wrote Rabbi Siskin, for "how could a Sterling professor be blackballed?" A searching debate broke out among the members of the admissions committee. Ralph Henry Gabriel (B.A. 1913, M.A. 1915, Ph.D. 1919), professor of history and member of the club's board of governors at the time, recalled that amidst the "hullaballoo," Dean Edgar Furniss strongly protested the treatment of Sapir's candidacy. A few club members resigned on principle.[69] Several faculty members expressed their dismay by avoiding the club's premises for many years thereafter. What action President Angell may have taken is unknown. To Jews in New Haven and at Yale, the event confirmed their underlying suspicions: Although the Yale and New Haven establishment might treat Jews with the utmost respect on a personal basis, on a social basis the Jew would be ostracized. Sapir himself was particularly hurt by the social exclusion. At the University of Chicago, where he had previously taught, the enlightened atmosphere of the campus presided over by Robert M. Hutchins had allowed him to flourish. When he accepted the offer to come to

Yale, he wrote to President Angell that he hoped for more of the same: "May I take this opportunity of saying that . . . everything looks bright to [my wife and me] and that we are looking forward to our participation in the University life of New Haven?"[70] His bitter disappointment was that at the Yale he found, he would have difficulty in gaining personal acceptance. Rabbi Siskin recalled that Sapir would communicate his surprise and disappointment:

> He would speak to me in smiling disbelief of the social pecking order which he discerned among the faculty, of the fripperies and trivialities with which he had little patience. The caste distinction between professors struck him as *kinderspiel*, unbecoming a community of scholars. The social emphasis on the campus cast Sapir in the role of parvenu, outsider. He felt strange [and] lonely in the Yale community.[71]

In conversation with Harry Stack Sullivan, Sapir expressed his hopes of leaving the anti-Semitic climate that he had found at Yale.[72] In a gesture of good will Franklin Edgerton, the distinguished professor of Sanskrit, persuaded the less popular Faculty Club to admit Sapir (who became its first Jewish member). But Sapir had been pained: He never set foot in that club.[73]

When Edgar Furniss became provost of the university in 1937 his social science empire was divided up into the four duchies of anthropology, economics, government and international relations, and sociology, and Sapir was given the chairmanship of anthropology.[74] In the year before declining health would force him to give up the chairmanship, he was able to consolidate his position and continue strengthening Yale's stature as a center for anthropology and linguistics. In February 1939, he died.[75]

Controversy again ensued in the wake of Sapir's passing from the Yale scene, over the question of who would succeed the great man. The general thought was that George Peter Murdock would be the natural successor to Sapir. Murdock was a former social science major and graduate student of the influential Albert Keller; by then he was associate professor of ethnology and the anthropology department's only former Yale undergraduate (B.A. 1919, Ph.D. 1925). Extremely industrious, Murdock had done field work under Sapir in British Columbia with the Haida Indians. The rub was that "his standing and experience as an anthropologist could in no way be compared with those of Leslie Spier." Spier, a widely respected researcher on Indian tribes and also an associate professor, received the support of virtually every graduate student in the department. They thought his selection would be the best way to further the work and spirit of Sapir. Some days of tension ensued, "punctuated by some memorable name-calling encounters between the circulators of [a] petition and Murdock."[76] Nevertheless, Murdock was soon appointed. In retrospect, it seems that race and religion were not involved in Spier's rejection. Personality was the dominant issue. One student recalled that Spier "went around campus trying to show he was a westerner and anti-academic."[77] Siskin remembered him in similar terms: "A smallish man with a bristling mustache, he smoked a pipe and sported a ten gallon hat amid the New Haven winter snows. He seemed to want to be taken for an ol' cow hand."[78] That Yale of the 1930s (or any decade) would have been prepared to give the responsibility of department chairmanship to someone whose very style challenged the security and traditions of old is unlikely. By the end of the year Spier was gone.

RETROSPECTIVE

Anti-Jewish feeling at the faculty level acted not just against "unwashed elements" in the Jewish community but against men as personally respected as Mendel, Sapir, and Shulman. Even the best of Jews found difficulty in being tolerated among Gentile society. The door to the senior ranks of the graduate and professional school faculties was half-open; to the college it was shut. (See appendix 8.) The reluctance to hire Jews and the social exclusion of those who maintained their religious affiliations gave credence to the sorrow expressed by Melamed in 1927 that the Jewish scholar had to submerge his identity to be accepted in academe:

> Only a few Jewish scholars have succeeded in conquering a place for themselves in American academic life. Those who, after a long, bitter struggle, managed to do so, lost their ethnic personality. The American university has forced them to become ex-Jews. I do not know of one great Jewish scholar in this country—with the exception of Felix Frankfurter—who takes an active interest in Jewish life. Since the Jew is not admitted to the professional sanctuary, those who manage to squeeze in cannot remain Jews.[79]

In the sense that there arose a social milieu whose fabric strongly favored the rise of the "non-Jewish Jew" Melamed accurately captured the American university atmosphere during these years. The only kind of victory a Jewish academic achieved was culturally Pyrrhic.

And such pressures, which occasionally crossed the boundary between the subtle and the obvious, most definitely obtained at Yale—where the university atmosphere was polarized by the collegiate tradition. Henri Peyre, who as chairman of the Yale French (later Romance languages) department from 1939 through 1964 was responsible for bringing several Jews to the Yale faculty, re-called that, in general, "by toning down their differences," Jews might have had an easier time in obtaining Yale faculty appointments. Nor did these pressures to conform apply just to Jews. When Peyre arrived in New Haven as an assistant professor of French in 1928, other faculty members recommended that he call himself a Huguenot and emphasize this aspect of his background to others, since the claim of being a Huguenot would bring him more prestige in socially conscious Yale. So Peyre "played the game" and played up his "Huguenot" status, despite his ardent atheism and despite his preference to call himself a descendant of French Protestants. (At this time, recalled Peyre, the term "Huguenot" was rarely used in France.)[80] In the ranks of the faculty, success at Yale, especially in the college, had as much, or more, to do with others' expectation about social class, religion, race, and sex as it did with intellectual ability.

Chapter 7 The School
of Medicine

The attraction that medicine holds for Jews is legendary. Indeed, in the Jewish tradition the greatest thinker since the Bible's Moses was Rabbi Moses Ben Maimon (Maimonides), a physician. This outstanding twelfth-century scholar of Jewish law also wrote several medical treatises.[1] Jews accorded respect to physicians because a physician was seen as doing God's work by healing and caring. The action of caring for the sick was given such high priority in Jewish law that one of the most important commandments (outside of the Ten Commandments) was the requirement to visit the ill.[2] Rabbinical tradition placed a high premium on human life: according to Maimonides, "He who has saved one life from destruction is considered to have saved the whole world." When this injunction was combined with the post-Biblical Jewish respect for intellect and proclivity for learning, the ancient art and growing science of medicine readily lured Jews. That university laboratories had been closed to Jewish students in medieval Europe perhaps made the field even more attractive.[3]

Thus, it was perfectly natural that if Jews lived in New Haven, they would be interested in studying at the Yale School of Medicine. And with increasing numbers of Jews in New Haven and its environs, many would want to study medicine at Yale. Given time, it was also only natural to expect that a number would want to become professors there as well. How the Yale School of Medicine would respond to these phenomena in the years before World War Two is the issue to be considered here.

In many ways that response was intimately linked to the persona of Milton Charles Winternitz, dean of the medical school from 1920 to 1935. Though others also played important roles, Winternitz was the man who raised the Yale School of Medicine from a dismal second class institution to one of the finest schools in the nation. He would also become almost a caricature of the American Jew striving to become part of gentile society. Renewing the age-old tradition of apostate Jews becoming among the most vocal in denouncing Jewish practices, Winternitz rejected Jews, Judaism, and Jewish associations in his drive for achievement. In so doing he presented the New Haven and Yale Jewish communities with stunning evidence that the key to rising in the Yale establishment lay in becoming the "ex-Jew" to which S. M. Melamed had referred. (See chapter 6.) And in the process, he earned for himself and Yale a great deal of resentment from the local Jewish community.[4] One cannot blame Yale for appointing Winternitz. He was an undeniably superb choice, someone who would upgrade the study, practice, and teaching of medicine at Yale. Yet throughout the university no other Jew rose as high or had as much influence as Winternitz. Thus, to young Jews trying to leave the lower ranks of immigrant life, Milton Winternitz became evidence of the price of admission. Of course, Winternitz was not alone in promoting Jewish entrance ceilings and in his strong reluctance to hire Jews as senior faculty, and those factors will be considered in their place. But first, it is best to turn to the very beginnings of the "Medical Institution of Yale College."

FOUNDING PRINCIPLES

Three years after it was chartered in 1810, the school of medicine opened in the fall of 1813. The delay had been caused by the difficulty in finding a suitable professor to guide the students. Though Dartmouth's Nathan Smith was willing to move south, he was considered an infidel—and therefore rejected by President Timothy Dwight (the elder). Fortunately for Yale, Smith suddenly renounced his past ways. No longer, he wrote to a friend, would he be a heretic: "My earnest prayer now is to live to undo all the evil I have done by expressing my doubts as to the truth of Divine Revelation, and to render to Society all the good my talents and powers will permit me to do."[5] Because the medical school, like the college, required chapel attendance, it was important to have a religiously minded faculty. When the religious regulations proved unenforceable among the medical men, the requirements were dropped. For the school's first sixteen years its pillar was Nathan Smith, professor of the theory and practice of physic, surgery, and obstetrics. With his death, a promising light dimmed. The remaining years of the nineteenth century at the medical school were, at best, forgettable. They were decades of accusations of body-snatching, of mediocre and in-bred teachers of little scholastic standing, tenuous finances, and a weak curriculum. From time to time unsuccessful attempts were made to raise admissions standards and lengthen the curriculum. In 1829 such an effort would be followed by a dramatic drop in enrollment: When Yale pushed its standards ahead of the nation's other medical schools, the students merely shifted elsewhere. To survive, the school reversed its course. The state medical society also resisted the advancement of scientific learning. In 1879 a written entrance examination and graded in-course examinations were instituted, and again enrollment plummeted. Finances were in such straits that in 1875 the college treasurer took charge of all medical funds.[6] Despite significant changes at the Sheffield Scientific School in the nineteenth century—curricular alterations that would set a pattern for a revolutionary change in American medicine—the medical school failed to catch wind of the intellectual ferment.[7]

The inadequacy of medical education at Yale was embarrassingly brought to the fore in 1906 by Harvey Cushing (B.A. 1891), when he rejected an offer to return to the city of his alma mater. The great neurosurgeon was extremely critical of the lack of a year-round program and of mature students at Yale. His greatest complaints focused on the medical school's inadequate relations with the New Haven Hospital. Cushing's comments were echoed in Abraham Flexner's 1910 report for the Carnegie Foundation for the Advancement of Teaching. Flexner stated that of the medical schools in New England, only those of Harvard and Yale were worth developing. The strength that Yale Medicine had, Flexner implied, was the solid university of which it was a part, but the medical school required much development. The laboratories were poorly staffed. Instruction was routine and was below the level that could be expected by students with the two years of previous college education that Yale hoped to attract. The connection with the hospital was too limited, and the hospital, which was poorly organized, had too few beds.[8] The small population of New Haven also worked against the development of a fine teaching hospital. Flexner's report was no paper tiger. As a result of its devastating criticisms and parallel critiques made by the American Medical Association, half of the medical schools in the nation would close and the remainder would be forced to reorganize.[9]

To his credit, Anson Phelps Stokes, the energetic secretary of the university, refused to allow the end of the teaching of physicians in New Haven. At moments when President Hadley was ready to allow Yale to withdraw gracefully from medical education, Stokes's zeal prevailed. The dawn of progress began when George Blumer, the John Slade Ely Professor of the Theory and Practice of Medicine, was elected dean of the School of Medicine in 1910. By 1913 an agreement was signed between the university and the General Hospital Society of Connecticut that formalized the affiliation between the school and the New Haven Hospital. That agreement came about largely as a result of the efforts of Colonel Isaac Ullman, a local Jew who was not a Yale graduate. One of the most dedicated proponents of good relations between town and gown, Ullman—corset manufacturer, Republican "boss" of New Haven, president of the New Haven Chamber of Commerce, co-founder of the New Haven "Community Chest," and chairman of the New Haven Hospital Board—declared in 1910 that

> The interests of the city and those of the university are in a measure inseparable. . . . The university brings fame to our city and income to our people. And, upon the other hand, the city gives to the university freedom from taxes and protection of its property. By working together in harmony, the interests of each can be enhanced, and from such cooperation there is bound to grow results which will be of mutual benefit.[10]

The close cooperation between Ullman and the hospital likely dispensed with the need to build a separate Jewish hospital in New Haven, unlike many other cities with substantial Jewish populations. The construction in 1917 of the Anthony N. Brady Memorial Laboratory adjacent to the hospital gave the school its first "modern" facilities. A good hospital affiliation and a fine research building, however, did not solve the problem of the school's faculty, which consisted mostly of local physicians who volunteered their time. Professor Blumer remedied this as well. He made the two crucial appointments—Charles-Edward Amory Winslow as Anna M. R. Lauder Professor of Public Health in 1915 and Milton Charles Winternitz as professor of pathology and bacteriology in 1917.[11] For Winternitz, who had been told by William Henry Welch (B.A. 1870) in Baltimore that he should not plan to stay permanently at Johns Hopkins but instead should make a name for himself and go elsewhere, the Yale offer was a godsend. His only other offers had been from Peking, China, and from Albany Medical College. During World War One, Winternitz's powerful force, together with that of his colleague Frank Underhill, ran the Yale Chemical Warfare Unit—the country's center for the study of the medical aspects of chemical warfare. Later, Winternitz and his co-workers would make major discoveries delineating the pathophysiology of atherosclerosis.[12]

A NEW CAPTAIN ON BOARD SHIP

In 1920, the same year that Lafayette B. Mendel's appointment was extended to the medical school, President Hadley named Winternitz as its dean. Winternitz thereby became one of the first Jews in the nation to hold a major position of academic leadership. The position, however, was not exactly an illustrious one. *The Yale Scientific Magazine* would later use nautical imagery to recall the floundering state of affairs in 1920:

> When Dr. Winternitz was asked to step up and take command of the vessel he was not an object of envy. More interest was being manifested in the lifeboats than in the engine room or wheelhouse. . . . A cartoon is still extant which pictures the situation. It shows the School as a rowboat, with two members of the crew pulling at the oars in opposite directions, and a third about to leap overboard. Surrounding the boat are submarines, labeled Faculty, University, Hospital, and Community, merrily firing torpedoes at the School and at one another.[13]

The school's standing was so wretched that in selecting its class of fifty it had but sixty-eight applicants to choose from, "of whom five might be considered desirable." If improvement saw its dawn under Blumer, its light blazed brightly under Winternitz. In fifteen years as dean he took the mediocre school and shaped it into excellence. As dean, he quadrupled the medical school's endowment, secured a building fund, and reorganized its faculty and educational system. He earned the praise of the critical Flexner, who called him "one of the most energetic, keen, and able administrators that I encountered in the whole course of my dealings with medical schools."[14] William Welch is reputed to have stated that he knew of nothing in education so remarkable as the transformation of the Yale School of Medicine "from the old type into a modern school."[15] Coinciding with Winternitz's term was the great Sterling bequest that allowed the erection in 1924 of the Sterling Hall of Medicine. Thus the school's clinical departments could be located next to the New Haven Hospital wards.[16] In 1929 the Institute of Human Relations was established contiguous with the Sterling building. There, Winternitz hoped, medical and social scientific efforts would occur in conjunction to improve the lot of humanity. Winternitz was also able to convince the Rockefeller Foundation's General Education Board to provide the grants enabling the inauguration of full-time appointments in clinical departments.[17] Winternitz was inexhaustible and made it a point to get to know everyone of importance in the business and academic world in order to obtain the sums necessary to support his school. While growing up in Baltimore he had sold health insurance to the local poor; he claimed to have learned his techniques from this experience. As he would tell his associate Harry Zimmerman: "You must never beg for money. You must convince your prospective donor that it's an honor for him to have you take his money."[18] Convince he did. When he retired from the deanship in 1935 President Angell would accord him a stirring tribute:

> Dr. Winternitz' achievement has few parallels in American educational history. When he took charge, the School of Medicine faced the most disheartening prospects. . . .
> Into this situation was injected the dynamic personality of the new Dean. He brought a dauntless spirit which could not be discouraged, extraordinary imagination, sound ideals, and a capacity for endless hard work. His enthusiasm was contagious, and . . . the result is a medical school everywhere recognized among the leaders in the United States. . . .
> The University is under deep and lasting obligation to Dr. Winternitz, and the School of Medicine will always stand as a monument to the wise and devoted service which he rendered at a critical point.

Winternitz brought about such an improvement in the school that in 1933 Harvey Cushing consented to return to Yale as Sterling Professor of Neurology, after Harvard no longer wished to retain him on its salary.[19]

What kind of person could move mountains and turn an insignificant blotmark in American education into the most progressive of medical schools? The characterizations of him are vivid and quite consistent:

> He was a genius, a great teacher—one of the best ever.
> He was a bastard and power-hungry.
> [Just over five feet tall,] he had the typical Napoleon complex that goes with short stature.
> He had virtually everybody scared of him (including faculty).
> He was at times brutal and sadistic and could massacre students.
> Students revered him and feared him and loved him and hated him.

He was everywhere at all times. . . . He was involved. . . . He was on the wards, in the offices, in the labs.

He ruled [the Yale School of Medicine] with an iron hand.

There was something electrifying about him. . . . He carried with him a sense of greatness.

He was a leader.

He was a real character.[20]

In a prudently anonymous article in *The Yale Scientific Magazine* in 1932, the author carefully dissected Winternitz's intricate character:

His personality is like a thermometer, fluid and full of seeming contradictions, in its indications. It is highly sensitive to external and internal contradictions. There are long periods when it is at a low mark, followed by a flare-up of brilliance; brusqueness and graciousness; a biting tongue and an ingratiating manner; humbleness and pride; intellectualism and emotionalism; despair and gayety. . . . Everyone who has been in contact with him knows that here is a definite personality, one that is thoroughly liked or disliked but is never colorless. Winternitz is the Worcestershire sauce in an academic bill of fare which otherwise often enough would be flat and uninteresting.[21]

Dean Winternitz's famous course was "Pathology"—the major staple of the second year, a time when every student learned just what a medical education was all about:

Each class period he'd pick one student and call that student down to the front of the room. He'd hand the student a heart [, for example,] and attack the student with an incessant stream of questions: What is this? What does it do? How do you know that? What color is it? Why does it have that color? Can it have a different color? Why is it shaped like that? Why did it develop that way?

Many of the questions were unanswerable.[22]

If the unfortunate student was unable to answer Winternitz's barrage, he would then be castigated in front of his classmates. If Yale-educated doctors were to be "real men," the dean would see to it. Once a student responded that the particular organ the dean had handed him was, in his opinion, normal—it had no evident pathology. Winternitz replied, "You think it's normal? Are you normal?" So began a tirade of vicious and personal insults directed at the young man.[23] Max Taffel (M.D. 1931) recalled that: "Several students suffered greatly under this kind of teaching. They almost didn't know their names by the end of a class period." Others, reportedly, were reduced to tears. God help the Yale doctor-to-be who dared arrive late for pathology. The wrath of the dean would make insignificant any punishment the student had ever previously received.[24]

The radical nature of his teaching method, however, made him a great (if terrifying) teacher. No matter how much the students resented his style, they felt they were learning a tremendous amount:

> Winternitz's teaching taught the students to develop a critical and independent habit of thought. He taught the students to accept nothing just because someone had told it to them. . . . Winternitz was keen on picking you apart . . . , compelling you to defend every statement you made. It wasn't really a course in pathology, but in how to think in medical terms. . . . We didn't learn pathology, but we came out with an excitement and inquisitiveness about medicine. He taught that an ordinary person with open eyes could learn a lot.[25]

"Winter," as he was affectionately called, had a similar impact upon the faculty. He conducted weekly clinical-pathological correlation conferences (CPCs) that attracted all the senior medical faculty and many of the community physicians along with the students:

> People would stand in the lobby outside the auditorium to listen through the open doors because it was always full inside. He ran the [conferences] just like his classes. He would challenge the department chairman (from whose department the case originated) and force the chairman to defend his views.[26]

Playing to a full house, Winter ran a one-man show for fifteen years.

In step with the mercurial aspects of his overall personality noted above, the Jewish component of Winternitz was no less complex. His son William reported that Winter had not wanted anything to do with his Judaism.[27] His son Thomas denied any knowledge of his father ever having been a Jew.[28] His daughter Mary Cheever reported that Winter did not like being Jewish or the personality characteristics that he attributed to Jews.[29] Some who knew him as a teacher in his earlier years and later as co-faculty members, such as Harry Zimmerman (M.D. 1927) and Alfred Gilman (B.S. 1928, Ph.D. 1931), saw him express and act on strong prejudices against Jews.[30] In contrast, some students who knew him from the end of his deanship, such as Samuel Yochelson (Ph.D. 1930, M.D. 1936), David Dolowitz (M.D. 1937), and Alan Rozen (B.A. 1933, M.D. 1937) felt that he acted protectively towards them.[31]

The data are not available to explain what childhood trauma, adolescent revelation, or adult experience could have elicited the anti-Jewish strain that some, but not all, saw in Winternitz. Certainly, he was not rebelling against religious principles that his parents imposed. As he described to Abraham Flexner, "My father [, a Czechoslovakian-born physician], was not religious and cared little about the ceremonials, so they were not practiced."[32] Winternitz was not an academic who would reject Jews and Judaism in the process of trying to reconcile tradition with modernity, for modernity was the environment he grew up in.

In his youth in Baltimore, he first developed a fascination for the upper ranks of society, which he formed a strong desire to become part of. Winternitz looked at his America and saw that to have power, one couldn't be a Jew. A Jew, he thought, was uncouth until proven otherwise. (In recommending a Jewish student for a hospital residency, he once wrote, "Mr. Thalheimer is as his name indicates, a Hebrew, but of a very fine type.") Since Judaism was to him a badge of shame, Winternitz would never publicly admit that he was a Jew.[33] He hoped to transcend the burdensome heritage of his ancestors and rise to the highest levels of American society. In the words of one of his daughters: "Father had a fantasy of being a gentile, and he admired the accoutrements of wealthy gentile life."[34] As a young teacher at the Johns Hopkins Medical School in 1913, he married the woman of his dreams, Dr. Helen Watson—daughter of Alexander Graham Bell's assistant Thomas A. Watson.[35] After her death, Winternitz tried to improve his social position by marrying the widow of Stephen Whitney. But the move brought him notoriety, as expressed by the *Waterbury Herald* in its headline announcing the marriage:

DEAN WINTERNITZ QUIETLY MARRIES PAULINE WHITNEY
MEDICAL HEAD CRASHES SOCIETY BY WEDDING SMART SET LEADER[36]

A man of "passionately transferred loyalties," *Time* magazine described him with the Freudian term of "ante-Semite"—the person born a Jew who comes to think ill of Jews.[37]

The first place he encountered overt anti-Semitism directed toward him, he would tell one son, was in New Haven. When, as a new pathology professor, Winternitz tried to purchase a home in the august neighborhood along Prospect Street the local residents tried to prevent the sale, to keep the Jewish population out of their neighborhood. Eventually, though, Winternitz, who possessed both the sting of a serpent and the charm of a kitten, succeeded in buying a resident at 210 Prospect.[38] He would find it humorous that, despite his aversion to Judaism and things Jewish, his racial background would make his finding a home difficult. It is doubtful he ever knew of the hesitancy the Graduate Club had in admitting him. (See chapter 6.) The admissions committee members were sworn to secrecy concerning their deliberations, and his eventual admission made the whole issue moot, in any case.

When he arrived in 1917, Winternitz became the first full-time Jewish professor at the Yale School of Medicine. That the only previous Jew to teach medicine had been Max Mailhouse (Ph.B. 1876, M.D. 1878, lecturer in neurology 1900–07, clinical professor of neurology 1907–20) may be seen as evidence, not of discrimination, but rather of the lack of Jews in New Haven who had studied medical sciences at a postgraduate level. (Clinical professorships, as distinct from regular professorships, have generally been honorary titles given to part-time faculty who earn their keep in private practices.)

The medical school atmosphere at the turn of the century (as in the college at the same time) must have been relatively free, since Jewish medical students regularly joked about their Hebraic origins in their classbooks. For example, when the only Jew among the thirty-seven members of the medical class of 1897, Maximilian Laurence Loeb, gave his ancestry he revealed that "his ancestry extends all over the world. His blood then has been proved to [be] French and German, a little Japanese, much Hebrew and now and then a corpuscle of American."[39] In the class of 1905 (with two Jews among the twenty-two seniors) one Jew stated that his ancestry dated "back to and is lost among the bull rushes."[40] The classbooks show that over the years Jewish students would occasionally serve as class officers and might join the medical secret societies of Delta Kappa Iota, Alpha Kappa Kappa, and Skull and Scepter. When the Jewish proportion reached 18 percent (5 of 28) in the class of 1910, there was one Jewish member in each of the three societies.[41] If at this time there were anti-Jewish feelings in the medical school they probably did not play a significant role.

In the medical school, unlike the college, the student societies never adopted absolutely exclusive policies. The Christian-dominated medical associations (which drew from all classes) had few Jewish members, but this happened because people tended to select for their own types, rather than because of anti-Jewish prejudice. David Dolowitz (M.D. 1937) recalled that he had been invited to join one of the established groups but turned down the offer because he did not want to be a "court Jew." The atmosphere was free enough, however, that he was able to take his meals with his friends in the nonsectarian club and simultaneously join Phi Delta Epsilon, the Jewish medical fraternity whose Yale chapter had been established in 1926. PDE's activities consisted of meals (provided as an alternative to the inadequate dining facilities in and around the medical campus) and a few social events per year. Again, in contrast to the college scene, relations among the medical students remained pleasant, and Jewish students did not feel as if they were second-class citizens. In the absence of racially and religiously restrictive senior societies, the medical student community remained relatively free of the divisive feelings of the undergraduate world.[42]

ADMISSIONS UNDER WINTERNITZ

From its earliest days, Yale School of Medicine had preserved the virtual monopoly that males had long enjoyed in medicine. As a professional school—the only medical school in Connecticut until the 1970s—it was an important conduit for young people to advance from societal consumers to societal producers. By banning women from its ranks, it played its part in limiting bright women's career options. With World War I reducing the supply of applicants, during the war years Yale and twelve other medical schools began a slow move toward the equal treatment of women and men, and in 1916 women were first permitted to represent up to 5 percent of the medical class. In those days when a male high school graduate could still enter the Yale medical track, a woman had to be a college graduate. Not until 1924 would women be admitted on the same terms as men. For much of the next four decades, however, the number of women admitted to medical school would be limited.[43]

Regarding discrimination against Jews in medical admissions, it is especially important to understand that the motivations of the discriminators and the means of discrimination in the professional school were somewhat different from those obtaining in Yale College. As previously described, specifically anti-Jewish feelings were at the core of the Limitation of Numbers policy in the college. Just as important was the desire by collegiate officials to protect the homogeneous nature of the studentry. The college method of implementation was a complex and subtle means of producing a "balanced" class. In contrast, the method in Yale medicine was a system of stark quotas. And at Yale, as at many northeastern medical schools, the motivation for bias was the desire to preserve the monopoly that the white Anglo-Saxon Protestant male held in medicine. In 1934 William G. Turnbull, superintendent of the Philadelphia General Hospital, summarized the concept: "Right or wrong there is a feeling among Christian physicians and I believe the Medical Schools, that the Jewish race is gradually attempting to dominate the profession."[44] As long as the belief prevailed in America that the best doctor was someone of the same ethnic background as the patient, then any ethnic group that was overrepresented in medical schools represented a commercial threat to others. Consequently, John J. Mullowney, president of Meharry Medical College (an institution for black students), would explain in 1936 that, paradoxically, the black medical students were in a far better situation than their Jewish counterparts who also suffered discrimination:

> As a friend of the Negro youth and education . . . and being of an Irish sympathetic nature I have tried to comfort the Negro youth in medicine by pointing out to him that however nasty his problems are, that in certain aspects at least the Jewish . . . youth is faced with more serious problems. . . . While it may be true that there are too many white physicians and possibly too many Hebrew physicians . . . it is *not true* of the Negro medical student.[45]

Enough Jewish physicians in east coast metropolitan areas subscribed to this philosophy in 1936 so that Jacob A. Goldberg, a sociologist, would later record: "It is the common complaint of Jewish doctors that an organized effort should be made to restrict the number of Jewish students in medical schools."[46] To preserve the economic balance, discrimination was seen as a necessity. William Pepper, dean of the University of Pennsylvania Medical School, explained that many factors were included in the balance: "It is natural that Medical Schools do not want to admit too many of any particular kind of students. They do not want to admit too many local students or colored students or women or Jews, etc."[47] In 1935 the secretary of the Association of American Medical Colleges noted that "the Italians are flocking into medicine at an alarmingly rapid rate."[48] Italians were discriminated against under quotas broadly directed against Catholics or specifically against Italians. Because there were so many more Jewish medical applicants than any other recognized subgroup, the discrimination that Jews experienced was quantitatively the largest. Nevertheless, the discrimination that other recognized "minorities" experienced was every bit as real.

The first impact that Milton Charles Winternitz had on admissions was to make Yale a desirable medical school. The pool of applicants rapidly climbed from a meager sixty-eight in 1920 to a respectable five hundred by the 1930s. Of the latter number, far too many were fully "qualified" for admission. When the Yale Limitation of Numbers policy was adopted for the common freshman year in 1923, a limitation was also seen as necessary for the medical school. Fifty students per year were to be admitted.[49] Although the documentation remains lacking, since the admissions files from the 1920s are not complete, it seems that the restrictive admissions policy coincided with the introduction of the racial and religious quotas. Fragmentary data from medical school classbooks from 1900 through 1910 indicate a rise in the Jewish enrollment in the medical school over that period. It is likely that the further rise in Jewish enrollment that the

college saw in the 1910s was paralleled in the medical school. If Dean Winternitz was in contact with his counterparts in New York City he must have been
aware that at Columbia Jewish enrollment began to be limited in 1918 to near
20 percent and that at Cornell the Jewish enrollment in medical school would
begin a drop from 14 percent in 1920 to under 5 percent by 1940.[50] By the 1930s
a 10 percent Jewish quota was common at many American medical schools.
Led by Dean Winternitz, Yale would do the same.[51]

A student's contact with the dean began with the admission interview, since
Winternitz insisted for many years on personally reviewing everyone who
hoped to enter his school. One critic described that experience:

> The interview is more than a casual one, for it occupies from one-half to two hours.
> This procedure does not rest, however, on any deep-seated interest in human beings
> as such. The attitude is more that of an experimenter and analyst who enjoys for its
> own sake the process of dissection.[52]

Winternitz was often arbitrary in deciding whom to admit. One applicant was
accepted because he caught a book that the dean had thrown at the surprised
interviewee. Indeed, those who stood up to his abuse were often admitted precisely for their courage. Others would claim wealth or personal connections
and Winter would open the doors.[53] It was common knowledge that money
and the power it carried impressed this ambitious leader:

> Himself a person who has had to create his opportunities, Dr. Winternitz likes par-
> ticularly those who have been highly favored by circumstance. The struggling, cir-
> cumscribed lad usually finds small favor with him. This is another seeming contra-
> diction, for he likes to extol the virtues of poverty and struggle in which he does not
> believe.[54]

Jewish applicants, in particular, were confronted with attacks on their background. One doctor recalled his own interview with the dean:

> *Winternitz:* You came from [City College of New York]. There are mainly Jewish
> boys at CCNY. You know that not too many CCNY boys get into Yale.
> *Applicant;* Why don't they?
> *Winternitz:* They're so ambitious and grabbing.

This physician, who was accepted and did attend Yale, was afraid to say more.
He might have had pride in his college and his race, but to defend them would
have risked rejection, he thought.[55] One Jewish student with an Italian surname prided himself on making it through four years of medical school without allowing Dean Winternitz to learn of his religious background. The fear of

Winternitz's having one more reason to terrify him (just being a student was already satisfactory) was enough to make the student into a "closet" Jew.[56]

One technique that Winternitz used to intimidate his students was to rename them as he called on them: "He had a strange quirk. He would pick on a student named Kelley, for example, and say, 'Now Goodman, what do you think of this?' Then he would turn to Goodman and say, 'Now Kelley what do you think?' " Though Winternitz would eventually pull a surname switch on almost every student in the class, Jews were singled out more often. Goldbergs and Bernsteins were quite susceptible to becoming McCarthys and Bronsons.[58]

To ease the tremendous job of handling admissions alone, by 1930 Winternitz created an admissions committee, which he made sure to keep under a tight personal rein.[59] According to his associate Harry Zimmerman (B.S. 1924, M.D. 1927, admissions committee member 1930–42), Winternitz's instructions to the committee were explicit: Never admit more than five Jews, take only two Italian Catholics, and take no blacks at all. Confidential forms for the assessment of applicants by undergraduate faculties did not ask for race or religion, but some letters of recommendation gratuitously added this information. To facilitate selection, the dean instructed his secretary to use whatever sources she had available and mark an "H" (for Hebrew) on Jewish students' applications and a "C" on Catholics' applications. Women, Zimmerman believed, were not discriminated against on the basis of sex at this time.[60]

In the mid-1930s, the Jewish admissions problem flared from a chronic to an acute state after an American Medical Association report called for a reduction in the nation's total medical enrollment. Most of the subsequent cuts were achieved by reducing the Jewish proportion at the east coast medical schools. New York ethnics were particular victims in that they were caught between the geographic quotas of New York's private medical schools and the out-of-state discriminatory policies of most of the nation's state-supported institutions. Writer Lawrence Bloomgarden explained the irony: "A native of Texas has an even chance of getting into a medical school when he applies. His medical schools prefer Texans. A New Yorker, however, has only one chance in four of being accepted. . . . His medical schools also seem to prefer Texans."[61] To understand fully the dimensions of the issue, Rabbi Morris S. Lazaron, influential leader of the National Council of Christians and Jews, wrote to almost every medical school dean in the nation in 1934 and solicited a confidential analysis. The responses were as varied as the personal prejudices of the deans. Many asserted that Jewish students were academically superior and personally inferior to their classmates. Some deans saw no difference between the average Jewish and non-Jewish medical students. Still others saw the average Jewish medical student as more desirable than his non-Jewish classmate. A. R. Larrain, acting dean of the Chicago Medical School, thought the limitation of Jewish enroll-ment to be a far less significant issue than other, more pressing, dilemmas: "From a social and political point of view we have far greater problems to con-tend with in the immediate future, such as the procreation and education of the biologically unassimilable races such as the Negro and the Asiatic."[62] Rabbi Lazaron's files do not record if Dean Winternitz responded to the survey.

The Yale medical records, fortunately, are quite explicit. When James L. Mc-Conaughy, president of Wesleyan University, sent his school's Jewish pre-med-ical students a letter advising them of the difficulties that they would face in gaining admission to medical school, Bernard Postal, managing editor of the Seven Arts Feature Syndicate, wrote to Dean Winternitz for clarification. Ap-parently choosing not to embarrass himself publicly by admitting a prejudicial policy, Winternitz prepared a response but never sent it. In that statement were explicit details concerning the quota mentality that dominated the admissions process:

> From 50 to 60 percent of the applicants for admission to the Yale University School of Medicine each year are Hebrews. . . . These applicants are given the same consid-eration as all others. . . . The number of Hebrews admitted to the School . . . has never been more than 10 percent of the total number of students admitted.
>
> Although the limitation upon Hebrews is no more arbitrary than for students of other religious faith, . . . it would be unwise in any event to permit the student body to include an unduly large proportion of any racial or religious group. About 5 per-cent of the population in this country is Jewish; hence the proportion of Jewish to non-Jewish physicians ought to be somewhere around this figure. On the same basis, the number of candidates admitted from Catholic institutions to the Yale University School of Medicine is not over 10 percent of the total enrollment of the School.
>
> The Yale University School of Medicine is national, not local, in its character. It is endeavoring to adjust itself to the conditions of the country as a whole in respect to the kind of physicians needed in practice. Therefore it cannot afford to specialize in the training of any one type of specialists or any one racial or religious group, but must endeavor to maintain a balance representative of the population which is to be served.[63]

"Balance" did not include women or blacks, but it was a convenient rational-ization for preventing the professional rise of ambitious and competent Catholics and Jews.

THE FALL OF WINTERNITZ

In its Autumn 1932 edition, *The Yale Scientific Magazine* acknowledged the tremendous personal impact that the spirited dean had on Yale: "No one would deny that the personality of Winternitz has strongly colored every event in the history of the School since he became Dean. His has been a vital, dominating force, and the work he has accomplished in a few years would constitute a full life history for many a good man."[64] Almost no one could conceive that the captain of the ship of Yale medicine might soon lose his commission. For those who might imagine such a thing, the penalties were severe:

> As for the bridge . . . there is no doubt about the control it exercises over the ship. The ship has headway, too, and there is not much play in the wheel. The . . . brig is definitely going somewhere. . . . The charthouse is full of maps. Naturally, there are those who do not like the course or the destination. On such matters it is rather hard to have unanimity of opinion, and that is why captains so rarely ask for a vote from passengers and crew. . . . A few malcontents from time to time resent this and foment minor mutinies in the forecastle, but these have dissipated themselves. One and all are quite aware who the skipper is, and so far no one has asked him for his job. It is such a long leap from the bridge to the briny waves.[65]

Yet a captain who does not sufficiently honor his crew risks waking one day and finding himself without sailors to serve him. The dean's eccentricities grew too much for the men he had hired. His arbitrariness antagonized them.[66] His single-handed grip on the school's budget and policies left them feeling resentful.[67] His revolutionary concepts of tying medicine into the social sciences were only begrudgingly accepted.[68] It could only be a matter of time before the ship's captain, himself, would be confined below deck.

The moment of reckoning approached in the fall semester of 1934, which marked the beginning of Winternitz's fifteenth year as dean. By then the captain was well aware that a mutiny was brewing. In a few months of political intrigue, while a plot to oust him was being fashioned, Winternitz secretly engaged in defensive maneuvers of his own. In confidential correspondence with President Angell and in a personal appearance before the Yale Corporation Committee on Educational Policy, Winternitz tried to change the university traditions that honored faculty opinion in the appointment of school deans. Despite President Angell's thinking Winternitz the best man for the job, Winternitz's moves were unsuccessful. The faculty, waiting until he left town to attend the funeral of his father-in-law, in a palace coup, recommended that Stanhope Bayne-Jones (B.A. 1910), a Skull and Bones alumnus, succeed Winternitz.[69]

THE LATE 1930s

Anti-Jewish action as part of medical school policies continued in the era that Bayne-Jones served as dean. Quotas remained an active ingredient in the admissions recipe at most American medical schools. The principal victims continued to be Jews, but Catholics, Italians, blacks, and women were also affected. At Yale there continued a "rigid quota system, denied in words but applied in fact." At least one admissions committee record from this era indicates that applicants to the Yale School of Medicine were grouped under one of three categories, "Women," "Americans," and "Hebrews."[70]

Jewish faculty members were well aware of the discriminatory quotas. According to Mrs. Edna White, wife of the late biochemist Abraham White (assistant professor of physiological chemistry 1937–43, associate professor 1943–48), her husband had been continually frustrated by the discriminatory policies of the admissions committee. As a member of that body for some five years before the Second World War, Abraham White, a Jew, became completely disillusioned by the committee's practice of categorizing applicants during the Bayne-Jones years as Jews, Catholics, blacks, women, and "none of the above." The committee would often ask if a candidate's name had been changed, hoping, it was said, to determine if someone's background was being covered up. The members, however, did not look at dividing applicants into racial, religious, and sexual groups as being discriminatory. Through their actions, the proportion of each group that would most benefit society as physicians was carefully regulated. White was so shocked by the Panglossian confidence of the committee that he once told his wife, "It's extraordinary how anyone in a university of this caliber could be so unaware that discrimination was occurring." White finally resigned from the committee in despair caused by his inability to modify admissions policies. Louis S. Goodman, assistant professor of pharmacology and toxicology in the later 1930s, recalled how he learned of the explicit quotas:

> On one occasion about 1940, I was sent a student application to review. . . . The thick document had on the face sheet a handwritten summary of [Dean Bayne-Jones's] review & conclusion. . . . The [dean's] note said in effect: The applicant has the oily skin & thick lips characteristic of his race. . . . Credentials are excellent. Hold for consideration in his group.
>
> "Group" meant the pool of Jewish applicants.

The oily-skinned student entered Yale and went on to a successful career in academic medicine.[71]

Other evidence of the continuing discrimination came from a note contained in the May 1938 correspondence between Dean Bayne-Jones, President Charles Seymour, and 1909 Sheffield Scientific School graduate David T. Weinerman, regarding his son's failure to be accepted by the medical school. The internal note, of uncertain authorship, is definite in its statement of policy:

> Edwin R. Weinerman, [Class of] 1938, Pierson College, [resident of] Hartford, Conn. . . . Applied in December for admission to the Medical School but was declined, as he did not measure up to the limited number of Jewish boys who could be taken. . . . He was advised to try for Harvard, Columbia, Pennsylvania, but has had no success. . . . He was considered again in February, but again turned down by the Dean, who felt that there was no sense in prolonging the agony, and that he just did not—intellectually, personally, etc.—measure up to the others in the group.[72]

Whether the young man would have been accepted on a universal scale of admission is debatable. His record, though respectable, was not spectacular. But such questions are hypothetical, for this student was evaluated on a scale with different standards. It would be Georgetown University, a Catholic institution, whose medical school would find a place for this applicant.[73]

In his 1938–39 year-end report, Dean Bayne-Jones testified as to the exact status of Jews in Yale medical admissions. Of 505 applications, 226, or about 45 percent, were from Jewish students. Although 26 percent of non-Jews were accepted, only 3 percent of the Jewish applicants received a favorable answer. The final Jewish proportion of the incoming class thereby remained at the 10 percent level. In a time of crisis in Europe, of thirty-four European Jewish medical students who applied for advanced standing at Yale because of an inability to continue their education in their home countries, none were accepted.[74]

MEDICAL FACULTY

Prospects for Jewish faculty were also poor. A conscious policy of the 1930s was to keep German refugees away from Yale. The open-minded C.-E. A. Winslow, chairman of the department of public health, on at least one occasion proposed the appointment of such a refugee: industrial hygienist Ludwig Teleky. But Winslow alone could not buck the faculty trend. American-born or -raised Jews had dim prospects as well. The unwritten rule was that a Jewish teacher should not hope for promotion beyond the rank of associate professor. Only the most extraordinary of persons could be Jewish and a full professor simultaneously. The three Jews to hold full professorships at the Yale School of Medicine between 1900 and 1950 confirmed the maxim that a Jew had to be twice as good to succeed: Eugen Kahn (Sterling Professor of Psychiatry and Mental Hygiene 1930–46), one of the great psychiatrists of his day; Lafayette B. Mendel (Sterling Professor of Physiological Chemistry 1921–35), the nutrition expert; and Winternitz (Anthony N. Brady Professor of Pathology 1925–50).[75] Anything short of such excellence was unacceptable.

Kahn's appointment revealed how Yale, in its slow, conservative way, had liberalized its attitudes concerning faculty appointments, at least in the graduate and professional schools. A century earlier, rather than having Yale import a foreigner, President Dwight had commissioned Benjamin Silliman to become a scientist. By 1929 an alien, if sufficiently outstanding, might occupy a professional school position of authority. President Angell, speaking to the Yale Corporation's educational policy committee some thirteen days before the nation would know the economically shattering meaning of what was later called "Black Thursday"

> commented upon the necessity of calling upon foreigners to fill the positions. . . .
> Obviously if Americans were at hand to fill the posts, foreigners would not be called;
> but in the circumstances, in view of the absolute lack of qualified Americans, [Angell] believed that the policy was practicable and sagacious. In the case of Dr. Kahn,
> he had reached the conclusion . . . that the vital necessity was to secure a man of personality and clinical experience, and that the linguistic factor was of secondary importance. He believed that the chance of Dr. Kahn's making a distinguished success
> was great.[76]

In contrast to the college, where Angell considered himself a weakling at bringing in faculty, in the graduate and professional schools, where he felt he could make his mark, Angell insisted that Yale attract the best. Kahn's nonanalytic approach to psychiatry made him almost unique in America.

In the case of Jewish faculty who were excellent, though not outstanding, suspicions ran high that Yale would not be the place to give a senior appointment. Yale was in no wise unique in having such an attitude toward senior Jewish medical professors. Melamed, in his piece "The Academic Boycott," noted that "out of the four or five thousand Jewish physicians in New York City there is not one who holds the position of a full-fledged professor in any of the medical schools attached to a university."[77] That in 1927 Yale could point to both Mendel and Winternitz was a sign of relative tolerance. But, inside and outside the medical school, the concern remained. Could a Jew be less brilliant than a

Mendel or a Winternitz and still become a full professor? For non-Jews it was possible. Suspicion of anti-Jewish hiring practices grew so strong that, in 1931, T. Swann Harding used the pages of *The Atlantic Monthly* in an emotional diatribe to accuse Yale, the University of Chicago, and the United States of mistreating the late U.S. Public Health Services physician Joseph Goldberger. As Harding saw it, Goldberger (a Hungarian immigrant who discovered the etiology, therapy for, and means to prevent pellagra, a widespread disease in the southern states) had suffered from five handicaps preventing his success in American academe. He was a Jew; he possessed an M.D. and not the "scientific" Ph.D.; he studied a problem (pellagra) that leading scientists (including Mendel) had considered already solved; he challenged America's false sense of security by disclosing that thousands of Americans were habitually underfed; and he was a man of unswerving ethics. Harding charged that Yale was specifically guilty of denying Goldberger a position because he lacked a Ph.D. Mendel, Harding implied, was guilty of forcing Goldberger to keep his conflicting scientific opinions to himself.[78] When the provocative article came to Agnell's attention, the startled president, who knew nothing of Goldberger, commenced an investigation of the matter. Writing to Winternitz, Mendel, and Frank P. Underhill, professor of pharmacology and toxicology, the president pleaded for enlightenment. As Angell had envisioned things, it was "nonsense" that Yale would refuse a qualified man a professorship because he had only a medical degree. Mendel and Underhill completely denied the charges on which Yale had been indicted. Mendel wrote:

> Until I read the article in the *Atlantic* I had never heard even the slightest rumor that Dr. Goldberger had ever been under consideration for any sort of a permanent post at Yale; nor did he ever, during all the years of our acquaintance, express to me any desire to become affiliated with Yale or give any intimation of the existence of a situation such as the writer in the *Atlantic* has presented.

Professor Underhill agreed with Mendel. As for the "somewhat veiled insinuations" against the physiological chemist, Mendel was equally firm: "The statement of Harding that out of deference to me Dr. Goldberger refused to make certain pronouncements is bunk. . . . I am confident that Goldberger himself would not have countenanced it."[79] Although there is no frank evidence that anti-Jewish feeling kept Goldberger out of Yale, Angell had asked the wrong people for advice. In fact, Goldberger had been one of the candidates considered by the medical school in 1914 to fill the newly designated Anna M. R. Lauder Professorship of Public Health, which was eventually awarded to the outstanding scholar C.-E. A. Winslow. The evaluation of Goldberger from that occasion in the Yale medical files asserts that Goldberger was "a Hebrew, although not of the objectionable kind."[80] Thus, there may have been at least a sliver of truth to Harding's charges.

The advancement of Jewish graduate students and junior faculty, too, was often stunted. Some limitations grew out of endowments given for non-Jews only; other limitations were embedded in tradition. One physician, who found himself fixed at the level of associate professor, remarked that "anti-Semitism played a role through force of habit. . . . All else being equal, a Jew would be the one not to be promoted."[81] Louis Weinstein (B.S. 1928, M.S. 1930, Ph.D. 1931) recalled that after seven years as a research fellow and instructor in bacteriology and immunology, he approached Dean Bayne-Jones for advice regarding his career plans. It was 1939 and Weinstein had possessed a doctorate for eight years; perhaps, he thought, it was time for him to be promoted to assistant professor. Bayne-Jones suggested to Weinstein that his prospects for further advancement at Yale were poor. Weinstein asked for an explanation. The dean's straightforward response was that Weinstein was a Jew and the Yale School of Medicine could hire only so many Jews.[82]

METAMORPHOSIS

Because Jews were most interested in medicine among the groups that admissions officers evaluated, Jews were most greatly affected by quotas. Such limitations, though widespread, were not universal in America. At the University of North Carolina, for example, President Frank Graham forced his medical school dean to resign because of a 10 percent Jewish quota that the latter had established. Graham thought the quota to be antithetical to the university spirit.[83] Neither James Rowland Angell (1920–37) nor Charles Seymour (1937–50) was an equally strong moral force. Many of the Yale medical faculty were thought to be fair-minded, but they often acquiesced to the prejudices of others.[84] The support that Milton Winternitz gave to the status quo legitimized the unfair biases. That he could "out-gentile" the gentiles, force his way into New Haven's highest social circles, and brutally throw Jewish students and faculty into an abyss of insecurity regarding their religion was testimony that a Jewish academic could be as disappointingly human as his fellow Christian professors. Of even greater irony was the historical fact that the strengthening of Yale medicine in the twentieth century was largely due to the efforts of three Jews: Abraham Flexner, Isaac Ullman, and Milton Winternitz. Nevertheless, in their generation, their co-religionists could not reap the benefits of any sympathy from the Yale medical community.

On the eve of the Second World War Jews were excluded in parts of Yale College. In the graduate school they were isolated. In the medical school they were limited. Unlike some Yale College students of the late twenties and thirties, who felt the world was theirs to challenge, the Yale faculties found it difficult to confront their own stereotypes of race, religion, and sex. For change to occur would require the decline of that generation of faculty and the rise of a new generation of teachers. The new generation, many of whom would fight in the world war, would see the previously unthinkable consequence of not restraining man's capacity for inhumanity to man. Prejudice would continue, but it would no longer be fashionable. Tradition and complacency would continue, but they would no longer be acceptable barriers to what was perceived as needed change. Like a monarch butterfly wrapped in its chrysalis, the university would find that forces from within and without would no longer permit it to remain a caterpillar in time and thought. To the metamorphosis at Yale, the story now turns.

Part Three **1941–1980**

Chapter 8 Evolving Meritocracy: Undergraduate Life after the Second World War

The Second World War was a watershed for Jews throughout the world. In Europe two of every three Jews perished in the Holocaust. In the Soviet Union, a dormant interest by Jews in Judaism was suddenly revived. In Palestine, the Jewish community pressed the British for creation of a Jewish state. In the United States, too, the position of Jews shifted dramatically.[1] Sociologist E. Digby Baltzell described the tremendous impact that the war had in remolding American democracy:

> [It was] the most leveling and homogenizing war in our history. Meritocracy was firmly in the saddle, particularly in the rapidly expanding army and navy corps, where twenty-twenty vision was far more important than family connections. . . . Actuality, in many instances, shattered stereotypes throughout the various theaters of war.[2]

Both Jews and non-Jews gradually ceased viewing Jews as a race. The idea of Jews belonging to a religious group and a "people" remained, but the disastrous consequences of the Nazi menace motivated removal of the racial edge from the concept of peoplehood. The embryonic civil rights movement that grew out of the war also helped to redefine race. More and more, as Americans examined their own racial attitudes, "white" versus "black" were the important variables. Also, as Jewish students came to be the grandchildren, rather than the children, of immigrants, and accepted the styles and interests of the dominant American society, the differences that had separated them from non-Jews lessened. Increasingly, American Jews seemed a subset of American whites.

Manifestations of the rapidly spreading liberalization quickly appeared at Yale as, characteristically, Yale turned its campus over to the American war effort. Though the administration of President Charles Seymour (1937–50) often lacked imagination, its war record was commendable. Students were drafted, the younger faculty members entered the armed forces, and the older ones often served the State Department or joined the Office of Strategic Services—predecessor to the C.I.A. American soldiers placed at Yale for training were adopted by the university as its own sons, and, as of 1942, Yale operated an accelerated three-year educational program of three semesters per year. Democratized by "average" American soldiers, the residential colleges lost some of their elegance. The dining halls switched from waiter service to cafeteria lines. All but two of the residential colleges were taken over by the military at one point or another. As military people and veterans abandoned the practice of wearing jackets and ties, visible distinctions between students began to decline. A tremendous momentary increase in the proportion of Yale undergraduates who were products of the nation's public high schools—the heart of American democracy—augmented the decline of the old caste system at Yale. The relatively small number of nonmilitary undergraduates made homogeneous cliques harder to form, and the national emergency helped diverse students develop common bonds, so that numerous friendships blossomed across former religious and racial barriers.[3]

Like an old elm tree, Yale swayed with the winds blowing across the campus. But even if it had been a more renitent institution, the university would still have been drastically affected by the energetic postwar wave of American egalitarianism. One indication of an evolving meritocracy was the reorganization of undergraduate education that moved preparation for the Bachelor of Science degree into the domain of the college faculty and left the Sheffield Scientific School name a forlorn Ozymandias. No longer, reasoned Charles H. Warren of Sheff, would the study of science automatically place one in a subordinate social class.[4] Silliman and Timothy Dwight colleges, proximal to the campus science buildings, would for many years suffer from the dismal reputation of attracting "engineering" types, but their students, at least, did not suffer from the worse social stigma of being "Sheff" students. Sheff students had long been condemned to be Sheffs, but after the reorganization, a scientist could (if he was sufficiently broad-minded) also be a collegian. The beginnings of real egalitarianism at Yale, therefore, did not toll the end of distinctions; rather, they inspired the rise of merit as a way to define distinctions.

The Serviceman's Readjustment Act of 1944 (popularly called the "G.I. Bill of Rights") imposed, in effect, a meritocracy upon the nation and upon Yale. Substituting for a rich father, the United States guaranteed an education and job training for all military personnel who had served a minimum of ninety days in the armed forces. The Veterans Administration contributed toward students' tuition expenses, meanwhile providing the students with monthly subsidies. Hordes of eager students suddenly became able to afford a Yale education. The veterans' interest in education had surprised educators nationally. Sociologist Willard Walker of Columbia University was typical in his thought in 1944 when he predicted that the veterans would be indifferent to education. Few government or university officials anticipated the deluge of applicants. At Yale, rapid troop demobilization flooded the university with veterans' money before the Seymour administration could prepare, and the G.I. Bill brought in more sorts of people than Yale had ever seen before. It would then have been un-American, unthinkable to invoke a Limitation of Numbers policy, restricting the number of those who had risked their lives for their nation. So many students enrolled in Yale after the war that Quonset huts and barracks had to be erected for dormitories, while parts of the university's Payne Whitney Gymnasium were converted to accommodate nocturnal use.[5]

Nor was the character of the veteran student the same as that of the typical prewar student. Having spent some years risking their lives for democracy, the ex-soldiers were older, more mature, more vocationally oriented, and less interested in the games of college life than previous generations of students had been. They were also often unwilling to tolerate at Yale the discrimination that they had fought against abroad. Many were idealists. Some joined liberal or leftist organizations; others protested against bias of any kind. Many participated in the widespread informal and formal discussion groups that emerged to consider discrimination. Most shared an uncommon enthusiasm for learning and reminded their university of its prime purpose: educating students. One observer wrote that the "student veterans . . . virtually created an academic golden age on the campus, and only their excessively large numbers and brief stay prevented them from fully doing so." The national picture was the same. A *Fortune* magazine survey called the national college class of 1949, with more than two of every three members a war veteran, the best, most mature, most responsible, and most self-disciplined group of college students in American history. By any standard, it was a formidable group.[6]

For Jews the most significant impact that the veterans had at Yale was in opening up the social pyramid controlled by the secret societies, the arbiters for undergraduate prestige. The veterans broke down society restrictions by race and religion (sometimes meeting great resistance on the part of elder society alumni). Scroll and Key historian A. Bartlett Giamatti recorded one observer's 1952 comments on the changing social scene:

> The base of membership in the fraternities and in Senior Societies . . . has been consciously broadened. A variety of factors have caused this. . . . The veterans . . . elevated and dignified Yale in many ways. It was the skepticism of these veterans which first permitted the early, organized mockery of the senior societies and caused several of the societies to reassess themselves. . . . Juniors are still tapped on many of the quaint criteria of the past, but each year a number are also tapped for more mature reasons.[7]

In the freshman year, lists of prom officers, which had once been devoid of Jews, began to include Jewish names in more than token numbers.[8] At the social summit, Skull and Bones, a society that tended to tap "offices" and not individuals, affirmed that social doors at Yale were opening, this most dramatically in 1949 when it offered memberships to two Jews and an African-American. The Jews were Thomas H. Guinzburg, managing editor of the William F. Buckley, Jr.–led Yale Daily News, and Victor H. Frank, Jr., head of the undergraduate athletic association. The tapping of Levi Jackson was even more significant. That academic year the Yale football team had chosen Jackson, the first black ever on the team, to be its captain, and there was widespread speculation on campus as to whether Bones would continue its tradition of tapping the football captain. Jackson was offered a space in the society, and a barrier was broken. He chose, though, to be with friends in Berzelius (an old Sheffield society that had become incorporated into the college). This was not without cost in Berzelius. Some of the society's alumni reportedly severed their association with Berzelius amidst the controversy. Years later Jackson would joke that, "if my name had been reversed, I never would have made it."[9] But the tapping of two Jews belies Jackson's remark. Early Jews in societies included Anthony Astrachan (B.A. 1952) in Elihu Club and the first Jew to be chairman of the Yale Daily News, Calvin Trillin (B.A. 1957), in Scroll and Key. Trillin's cousin Lance Liebman (B.A. 1962), a National Merit Scholar who was later News chairman and winner of the college's Snow prize for outstanding scholarship and character, was tapped for Elihu Club in 1961.[10] Future U.S. vice presidential candidate Joseph I. Lieberman (B.A. 1964, LL. B. 1967) followed Liebman as *News* chair and Elihu Club member two years later.

In contrast, Wolf's Head was not ready to elect a Jew until 1957: Larry Bensky, managing editor of the *News*. By unanimous vote, the fifteen seniors that year chose to tap Bensky. Unfortunately Wolf's Head's system of election, involving review of prospective members by an alumni committee, proved a bone of contention. The alumni, arguing that Wolf's Head had never previously allowed a Jew to join its group, rejected Bensky. According to Henry Chauncey, Jr. (B.A. 1957), this edict was unacceptable for his group of seniors. Within the tomb these privileged members of the "Silent Generation" spoke up. They had never considered Bensky's Judaism a factor in their decision to elect him: In the students' minds, the alumni committee's complaint was irrelevant. If the old society alums blocked the tapping, the seniors threatened, their group would resign en masse. Faced with an embarrassing ultimatum, the alumni backed down and Bensky was tapped. He chose, however, to accept an offer made to him by Berzelius. Lewis Lehrman (B.A. 1960), unsuccessful candidate in 1982 for the governorship of New York, became the first Jew to join Wolf's Head. Following Lehrman by two years, Eli Newberger (B.A. 1962), undergraduate president of the Hillel Foundation at Yale (who turned down the presidency of the Yale Band to lead Hillel) also joined Wolf's Head. Newberger had hesitated before accepting the Hillel mantle, for fear of being labeled as "too Jewish." His being tapped indicated that "success" still required subscribing to the dominant mores, but that the mores no longer required suppression of one's ethnic identity.[11]

If, in addition to the specific incidents, we examine the general characteristics of the societies, the postwar change is also evident. In 1942, when 25 percent of Yale freshmen were public school graduates, only 6 percent of the society men were of such background. In one decade the gap would narrow so that while 35 percent of freshmen were public school graduates, fully 25 percent of the society men were public school products. A review of the 1956 society elections showed that private school graduates still dominated the rosters, but public school graduates held a secure place. With the exception of Manuscript (founded in 1952), 70 percent of society positions were occupied by fraternity men, but each society had a fair number of students receiving financial aid from the university. Some of the societies could boast a few scholars in their ranks, though Book and Snake (which had become a senior society in 1933) drew its class of 1957 membership entirely from the academic bottom half of the Yale class.[12]

As important to Yale as the rise in proportion of public school and scholarship men was the proliferation of secret societies. Keeping pace with the enlarging undergraduate population, the creation of new societies worked to perpetuate the status of the society system, while preventing it from becoming too elite to be noticed. To the college societies of Bones, Keys, Wolf's Head, and Elihu were added Berzelius and Book and Snake from the scientific school in 1933 and Saint Elmo in 1962. The new society of Manuscript joined several more "underground" societies that emerged in the 1950s. These especially clandestine fellowships chose not to build ostentatious tombs but instead took chambers in various New Haven buildings. Among them were Desmos, Gamma Tau, Ring and Cradle, Spade and Grave, and Sword and Gate. If there were incidents of racial or religious bias in the postwar societies, they did not earn more attention than has been noted above.[13]

IN THE LAW SCHOOL

The postwar era also began to make more room for Jews in the law school social life. In 1946 Arlene Hadley, registrar of the school, had set aside one entryway in the Sterling Law Building to house Jewish undergraduates. Law students did not appreciate the segregation any more than the undergraduates would, as shall be described later. Social divisions in the law school were narrowed, however, after the Second World War, as evidenced by Corbey Court, a prominent law school eating club. Founded in 1887 as a senior law society, later opening itself to all law school academic classes, this chapter of the national Phi Delta Phi legal fraternity had a Jew and an Asian among its earliest members. From the turn of the century until after the Second World War, however, relatively few Jews were permitted membership. Social rank and wealth were more critical barriers than religious identity, however. This was particularly significant since, as J. Richardson Dilworth later recalled, "Getting into Corbey Court was damned important." Corbey Court provided the meals that the Law School then could not offer its students. Prior to the war it had provided a club atmosphere to men like Gerald Ford, Potter Stewart, Cyrus Vance, Najeeb Halaby, and Dilworth. After the war Corbey welcomed a significantly greater number of Jewish members. Jewish members from this era included Robert Morgenthau, Jr. (LL.B. 1948), Frederick Nathan (LL.B. 1948), and William Lee Frost (LL.B. 1951). Morgenthau was the son of Henry Morgenthau, Jr., former secretary of the treasury, and would one day become a New York City district attorney in his own right. Nathan was a descendant of an old, prominent Sephardic family from New York City. Symbolic of the era, Frost has been president of the Harvard Hillel as an undergraduate. In the early 1950s, Corbey Court, in a deliberate effort to minimize its elitist nature, opened itself up to all interested third-year students.[14]

SEGREGATION

Religious discrimination after the Second World War was propagated in part by small acts of Yale administrators. Norman S. Buck (1938–54), dean of Freshman Year, acquired a reputation in some circles of being unsympathetic toward Jewish students, particularly because of his rooming policy, which continued to segregate Jewish students. Though he was no more prejudiced than his predecessors, his attitudes had become anachronistic. The impact of his policies was portrayed by Anthony Astrachan (B.A. 1952):

> I never wanted to stop being Jewish, but at Yale I quickly wanted not to be stereotyped as Jewish. . . . I was innocent enough to be surprised that my being Jewish played a part in my travels through the caste system. The first surprise came at the start of freshman year with the discovery that if you did not request specific roommates, the Yale of 1948 automatically put four Jewish strangers together. This concern for our comfort discomfited us by telling us we were all outsiders. I had been an outsider before—but only for such understandable reasons as being good at school and bad at punchball.
>
> We laughed at this and other examples of genteel anti-Semitism—some of us in total innocence, some because we had already experienced worse, all of us because we knew by instinct or osmosis that some things you just don't talk about at Yale.[15]

But now, even at a college for gentlemen, where propriety made an accusation of anti-Jewishness a social sin, there were limits beyond which discrimination was not tolerable to those being discriminated against. Before the war Yale Jews had, in general, timidly accepted inferior status. After the war, year by year, they would challenge that status. And the university, year by year, began to listen. When it became clear that Jewish boys were being placed not only in the same rooms but also in the same entryways, the Jewish students protested. In 1948, on their behalf, Rabbi Samuel Sandmel of Hillel approached University Chaplain Sidney Lovett for support. With Lovett's blessing, Sandmel confronted Dean Buck over the issue. The Jewish freshmen, Sandmel explained, did not appreciate being placed in a "ghetto." Buck's response, as Sandmel remembered it, was forthright and revealing: "I want to say to you two things. [First, hearing] this from you, it will change immediately. Second, from time to time these Jewish things have come up and no one has come to me about them. I thought the Jewish students would like [rooming together.]"[16] Thereafter Jews were no longer segregated in rooming assignments, and black freshmen were integrated into the rooms of white students. (In the latter case, for several years the freshman office would first write to prospective roommates to be sure that such an arrangement was satisfactory to the white boys.)[17] Buck's words to Sandmel reveal much about the prejudices of Yale administrators, the timidity of Yale Jews, and the character of Yale. Buck's thought that the Jewish students would enjoy segregated rooming was not as disingenuous as it might sound to a suspicious ear. For if his attitudes were as ingrained as some have claimed them to be, then he may have readily latched on to the stereotype of Jews as always being self-segregating and therefore assumed that Yale's Jews had no desire to be part of the campus "mainstream." Thus, he might have (incorrectly) believed that Jews at Yale would have been happier in isolation. He could not have been further from the truth. Yale Jews, by and large, were anxious to be part of the larger social life. The insight that may be gained from Buck's comment that no one had complained is that Yale Jews had previously been too insecure to challenge campus gentlemen's agreements. They were now beginning to demand that the gentlemen of Yale act like true gentlemen and ban discrimination from their midst. Finally, Buck's words hinted at a greater problem at Yale. Partly because of Yale's long-standing educational conservatism, partly because of the frosty "old school" men who administered Yale, warmth, understanding, and compassion were not always readily found in parts of Yale leadership. Dean Buck, like Dean Jones a generation earlier, typified the gruff Yale administrator. Yale, which bred the ultimate in self-reliant men, aloof and disinterested, was simply not a place for an individual to feel comfortable in appealing a perceived injustice. Even if, as in Buck's case, the outside appearance was a façade for an inner warmth, an individual insecure about his place at Yale would have to breach a sturdy wall in order to arrive at the underlying character.[18]

"DUSTY BUCKS"

After the veterans passed through, some of the fresh air turned stale. The "Silent Generation" that followed the veterans set about to reimpose the prep school ethos on Yale culture. There was little renewed sense of religious discrimination, but Jews, then predominantly of a public school education, were aware that they came from a different cultural and social background than the influential undergraduates at Yale. There was discomfort among Jews, but the motivation for the discomfort was only minimally based on religion. By 1951 the color of one's shoes was the key to whether one "belonged" at Yale. Those who wore "Dusty Bucks"—the white shoes "specially treated to look ever so slightly worn and ever so slightly dirty [, providing] the air of insouciance that Ivy Leaguers are supposed to enjoy"—were generally of the proper families and the proper preparatory schools. *Time* noted their weekend dress to be "almost like a uniform" consisting of "button-down shirt, striped tie and Brooks Bros. suit." A parody of Yale snobbery portrayed the situation:

> Now as far as shoes at Yale are concerned, there are only two primary colors: black and white. Everybody has brown shoes, so they count for nothing, but a real index is obtained by noticing whether a man happens to be wearing shoes that are black or white.
>
> Suppose they are black. Dismiss the man. Forget him. He will never get you anywhere. . . . *men who wear black shoes at Yale University will never be worth a tinker's dam.* . . .
>
> On the other hand, suppose the shoes are white. . . . Ah, my friend, that man will go far. . . .
>
> Now as a last possibility, suppose the shoes are white all right, but not the same as those described above. . . . Cross to the other side of York Street. This man, God help him, has neither the background for "right whites" (as the term is) nor (realizing this) the common decency to wear blacks. In the Eli caste system, he is something akin to untouchable.

Henry Chauncey recalled that many of the undergraduates "were terribly conscious of social status." He remembered the graphic example of an impoverished student (who happened to be Jewish, though this was not an issue) forced to wear white T-shirts as his outershirts because of his financial straits. The student was consequently subjected to "horrible ridicule" from some of the wealthier students. Though the young man made sure to keep his T-shirts spotlessly neat and clean, he was the victim of the social snobbery that began to re-enter the Yale of the 1950s.[19]

What made the post-Second World War situation different was the more genuine meritocracy imposed by the veterans and the condemnation of racial discrimination aroused by the war. Anti-Jewish actions were no longer simply ungentlemanly; they had become, in most circles, unacceptable. Racist attitudes had not completely died among the students. Occasionally a Jew might be unwanted as someone's roommate for religio-racial reasons, but by the 1950s such incidents were well outside of behavioral norms.[20]

The postwar fraternity issue at Yale, as elsewhere, did not involve religious concerns. On the national stage, fraternal religious prejudice was in the last gasps of its existence. Just after the war, Phi Mu Delta had forced its chapter at the University of New Hampshire to remove a Jew from its roster. In 1947 the president of the National Inter-Fraternity Council echoed prejudiced sentiments when he upbraided foes of segregation and promised to "fight to the last ounce of my strength to defend the right—the democratic right—of any man or group of men to form a fraternity . . . of blacks for blacks, of whites for whites, of Jews for Jews, of Gentiles for Gentiles, of Catholics for Catholics, of Protestants for Protestants." In the center of New Haven there were few such desires. Attitudes at Yale were more consistent with the 1949 student-led initiative of the National Inter-Fraternity Conference, which called for an end to racial, religious, and national barriers among its constituent members. Religion was no longer a Yale fraternal problem. Financial survival was. The brotherhoods saw themselves as *personae non gratae* in the university community and they were anxious to attract new pledges. In the case of at least one Yale fraternity, however, the honoring of a national fraternal requirement barring blacks from membership kept it free of blacks as late as 1959. Significantly, the *Yale Daily News,* an opponent of prejudice in that era, came out with an editorial decrying the vestiges of prejudice in the campus fraternities. When the university administration, slowly becoming attuned to civil-rights concerns in the late 1950s, got wind of the remaining bias being practiced, it threatened to crack down on local fraternities that continued with their biased practices. Even if nondiscrimination meant violating restrictive national fraternity rules, by the early 1960s, Yale asserted that local autonomy in this matter would be required. In that decade the Yale frats remained the territory predominantly of the wealthiest students at the college. Some offered scholarships to attract less well-off students, but there were few of them. The organizations' precarious financial situations prevented further aid. In the face of bankruptcy, almost all who could support the economic health of the frats were welcome.[21]

The departure of the veterans left the residential colleges in danger of losing their democratic character. With masterial preferences shaping the quadrangles, each college was acquiring a unique character of student. Under the influence of biologist Daniel Merriman, Davenport was the preppy college, replete with hockey and squash players. The football players converged on Calhoun, while, for complex reasons of architecture, convenience, street noise, and wealth, Pierson and Saybrook joined Calhoun and Davenport as the "in" colleges of the mid-1950s. Those colleges that became concentrations of social power attracted the wealthiest students and therefore produced the richest alumni contributors. Timothy Dwight, Davenport, and Calhoun, in particular, developed vast financial resources. Trumbull College, once known for its abundance of bursary students, remained a social wasteland.[22]

PRESIDENT GRISWOLD

Perhaps the most important factor besides the veterans in the "de-class-ification" or "re-class-ification" of postwar Yale, however, was A. Whitney Griswold (B.A. 1929, Ph.D. 1933, university president 1950–63). When the Yale Corporation offered him the presidency, they told him that they did not want a fund-raiser, but someone with ideas for change. Griswold took their charge seriously. This remarkable man of compassion, good humor, and insight prodded the campus to value talent and integrity more than social class, religion, and race. Whereas Hadley threatened, Angell acquiesced, and Seymour colluded, Griswold would act. Already as an assistant professor (circa 1940) Griswold had risen to fight discrimination at the ever-popular Mory's Association. As Carlos P. Stoddard, Jr., recalled, at one meeting of the Mory's admissions committee he and Griswold were facing each other when the committee chairman announced the application of two students possessing obviously Jewish names. Ready to discard the applications routinely, the chairman announced, "I don't suppose you want to take these [students]." Griswold and Stoddard caught each other's eyes and, in a meaningful split-second, communicated a provocative move with one silent thought. Raising their arms to bask in a moment of playful glory, the two saluted in Nazi fashion, barking in rapid unison, "*Heil Hitler.*" The Jewish applicants were enrolled. From that moment, reported Stoddard, anti-Jewish discrimination, per se, was gone from Mory's.[23]

As the university president, Griswold rapidly earned for himself a reputation as the "conscience" of American higher education. He applied his standards to Jews at a 1953 dinner for Louis Rabinowitz, a major contributor to Judaic study at Yale. (See appendix 9.) At the meal Griswold declared that, "A respect for the rights of others . . . is in keeping with the true fundamental purposes of the founders of the university."[24] By later standards, his words were tame, yet their significance was in his subsequent actions to back them up. In 1954 he was asked to chair an Association of American Universities committee that prepared a report on "The Rights and Responsibilities of Universities and their Faculties." Though labeling communism as a philosophy that did not belong in the psyche of an American university professor, the committee "asserted that university faculties must be guaranteed freedom of expression." Griswold demanded that members of a university community learn to respect rather than sneer at differences between themselves. In 1957, in recognition of his humane spirit, the Jewish Theological Seminary of America awarded Griswold its Universal Brotherhood Medal at the same time it gave a similar honor to Eleanor Roosevelt.[25]

In the undergraduate world Griswold worked against the class structure developing in the residential colleges. Under pressure from his new dean of admissions, Arthur Howe, Jr. (B.A. 1947), who reportedly argued that "if I'm going to admit a class that is national in character, [the different student groups] shouldn't live in little enclaves by themselves," Griswold forced the democratization of the colleges. The system of allowing a great degree of personal choice in application for college assignment was dropped. Beginning in 1954–55 with the class of 1958, a child or sibling of an alumnus could choose the same college that his relative had belonged to, but the remaining students were assigned in a manner intended to achieve as "balanced" sets of students as possible.[26]

Finally, in behind-the-scenes whispering, Griswold began to play the role of Jeremiah, threatening the secret societies with divinely wrought doom if they did not further change their character. Though a Wolf's Head man himself, Griswold had grown disenchanted with the overly exclusive associations:

> I don't see anything wrong in recognizing talent and ability and outstanding character. . . . On the contrary, I am all for it, and believe that it is our failing to do so, out of a misunderstanding of the true meaning of democracy, that has got our whole educational system into so much trouble. Indeed it is precisely because I feel the senior societies fail to recognize such talent, ability and character in such large measure that I am critical of them. They also fail, because of their extreme secretiveness, to reveal to the Yale public their true purposes and basic standards of selection. Since these are unknown, their selection must and does seem capricious, especially when so much talent is overlooked in the process.[27]

Even though it was expressed privately, this was strong language for a Yale president. In Griswold's eyes, the increasingly tolerant societies were still missing outstanding Yalies in their election process. (Wolf's Head was not the only society never to have taken a Jew as of 1957, when Griswold wrote the above letter.) Griswold called for membership in a senior society finally to be the recognition for outstanding contribution to Yale life and the recognition of quality that society members had imagined it to be. Previous Yale presidents had tended to view the university and its components only in terms of excellence: Griswold saw the university as standing for fairness as well.

Throughout the 1960s Yale grew to stand for democracy, as well as for excellence and fairness. The central change was the flowering of the residential college system, which had been instituted in the 1930s precisely to democratize Yale. In large part this flowering was inspired by a 1962 faculty report on the Yale freshman year. (See chapter 9.) One of the major recommendations of the report was to integrate freshmen into the colleges. Previously they had participated in an entirely separate social program and were forbidden to join non-freshman organizations until late in the school year. All of their meals, too, were together in the Commons dining hall. Beginning in the fall of 1962, Yale freshmen were given a residential college identification that bound them to Yale College forever. No matter what kismet had operated to assign the student to his particular college, he was no longer destined to consider himself only "Class of ———," he would always carry the label of being a "Sillimander" or a "Morsel" or a "Saybrugian." Another result of the 1962 report was the appointment of a dean in each college. These junior faculty and administrators acted as strong forces to unify the colleges. Unlike the masters, whose roles in the colleges were somewhat nebulous, the deans were hired to know every student and to supervise counseling in their college. In the late 1960s credit-earning seminars were instituted, giving each college its own academic responsibility. Thus the colleges became more than conveniences for the students. Embedded with democratic spirit, the colleges, loci of social, athletic, and intellectual life, became meaningful to the students.[28]

Thomas Bergin, master of Timothy Dwight College through 1968, recalled the growth of residential college feeling:

> The plebeian class now had an opportunity to enjoy a richer social life. . . . If you couldn't heel the *News,* you could very easily win a place on the college paper's editorial staff. . . . Most significant of all, if [DKE] or Fence passed you by, you need feel no concern; after all, Calhoun or Branford or T.D. provided all the amenities and a tolerably good facsimile of the camaraderie that traditionally was to be found only in the fraternities. . . .
>
> [The] fact the elite and the hoi polloi lived under the same roof, ate their meals together in the same hall and . . . cultivated a loyalty to the same college, blunted resentments and created bonds stronger than those of the old commitments.[29]

Symbolic of the changing centers of Yale social life, recalled John A. Wilkinson, Ezra Stiles College's first dean, was an occasion when the social chairman of the Zeta Psi fraternity called Wilkinson and asked for assistance in becoming the social chairman of Stiles College. In the colleges, where prestigious social committee chairmanships and college council chairmanships were given to those who earned the positions by working the hardest for the college, rich and poor, Jew and Gentile, black and white, all took their turn at leading Yale.[30]

With the colleges at the center of Yale life, fraternities found themselves to be no match for the college social life. During the political turmoil of the late 1960s, students found themselves facing profound moral issues that the socially oriented fraternities were not geared to confront. It was difficult to make meaningful plans and engage in public demonstrations when students were organized in divisive fraternal groups. The open residential colleges provided more appropriate forums for gaining widespread support. Finances continued to play a major role in the fraternities' decline. Property taxes increased greatly over the 1960s, and the fraternities were forced to continue raising their dues. In 1969 the *Yale Banner* wrote that "today, when a student can get a good sound system for $300, a second-hand car for $400, and a spring vacation to Puerto Rico for about $200, it is hard to justify spending a comparable amount to join a fraternity." Increasing use of illicit drugs by students of that generation also decreased the consumption of alcohol, on which fraternal bars thrived. The exposure of illegal fraternity hazing rites in 1967 generated much negative publicity on the campus. The fraternity spirit certainly ran counter to that of a democratic institution, but by 1969 fraternities were such an insignificant pockmark on Yale life that the *Banner* would call them a "benign irrelevancy." The contemporary attitude, wrote the *Banner,* was, "Who cares enough about the frats to even bother to attack them?"[31]

The entry of freshmen into the campus social system shifted the center of campus power downward by a degree. Juniors became the leaders of most of the campus organizations. Seniors concentrated on more metaphysical matters than campus politics, or devoted time to planning for their after-college lives. With some of the power base for seniors gone, the senior societies, too, became less influential. It became less and less easy for senior society cliques to direct an ever-enlarging college. The elites would continue, but they no longer could dominate those who were not yet part of the elite. Except for Skull and Bones, Scroll and Key, and Wolf's Head, the others—fifteen other "above ground" and "underground" societies—became co-educational entities fifteen years after women were admitted to the college in 1969. The secrecy of some of the societies also decreased as they came to hold lectures and social functions (that were open by invitation) within their halls.[32]

The postwar social story of Yale was a fifty-year tale of opening closed institutions and rebuilding a meritocracy open to anyone with the talent and inner drive to succeed. The tapping of a Jewish Second World War veteran, Edwin Wolff, as a Whiffenpoof in 1948 heralded this passage. Mory's waiter Davey Parker later told him he was the first Jew to be part of Yale's premier singing group, but the Whiffs themselves made nothing of the passage. Acceptance of religious and racial and sexual minorities was not universal, but the change brought about by the Second World War had been so thorough that Hillel's Rabbi Joseph Gumbiner found himself able to write in 1950 "that it was at least conceivable that one could be Jewish and not lose caste in the university environment."[33] Over the following decade, theory increasingly became reality. Nowhere was the trend toward openness more visible than in Yale College admission policies. The catharsis of racial, religious, and sexually discriminatory practices continues this narrative.

Chapter 9 Undergraduate Admissions

In its original "Australopithecine" days, Yale College had been open to any unmarried young male who was sufficiently knowledgeable and financially able to pay his way. A numerically unlimited admissions policy that lasted over two centuries eventually brought Jews and Catholics in among the Protestant majority. Married students, too, found a foothold in the college. As the college acquired capital, varying amounts of financial aid became available. By the 1920s, with popular demand threatening to harm the quality of a Yale education, admissions at Yale moved into its "Neanderthal" period. As the Limitation of Numbers plan was introduced, various schemes and criteria were established to control the rising numbers of students and to freeze the growth of the Jewish representation among the students. Refinements restricting the number of transfer students and protecting the prospects of alumni children moved the Yale of the 1930s into a "Cro-Magnon" era. Similar in style and process to the previous years, but increasingly experienced and sophisticated, the tenure of Arthur Howe as chairman of admissions (1953–64) was the harbinger of an end to an anomalous period of Yale history when admissions policy served as an instrument of religious and racial prejudice. This chapter records the evolution of the "Homo sapiens sapiens" admissions policies that were anticipated by Edward S. Noyes, first implemented by his successor Arthur Howe, Jr., and expanded and brought to public attention by R. Inslee Clark, Jr., Howe's successor, and the impact of these policies on Jewish students.

Conflicting trends of development had begun to operate in the Cro-Magnon days. A progressive trend grew out of the realization that the pressures of a Depression economy and an aggressive and well-advertised scholarship plan conducted by Harvard in the 1930s had captured many of Yale's most desirable applicants from across the country. Many of the finest students that in previous decades might have been educated in New Haven chose the more attractive offers from Cambridge. Family and prep school traditions kept the Yale educational furnace well-stocked, but some of the worthiest sources of energy were clearly being diverted to the north. Students of the 1930s and early 1940s were also more interested in learning than their predecessors had been. Edward Noyes, chairman of the Board of Admissions, recognized this phenomenon when, during the first week of the Second World War, he wrote a memorandum to President Seymour that considered the future of admissions policies:

> My own experience with applicants for Yale has convinced me that most of these boys have chosen Yale . . . because of our academic reputation. There is, of course, a considerable backlog of candidates influenced at least in part by family tradition, but many of these . . . would go elsewhere if they did not feel sure that Yale standards are at least as high as those of any other institution. . . . If the conviction expressed above is correct, it follows that a lowering of our undergraduate standards would before long be followed by a decrease both in the number and in the calibre of boys who want to come to Yale.[1]

The chairman was quite correct in assuming that many students applied to Yale only because they felt that it was a first-rate institution. So arose an attempt, albeit limited, to change the popular image of Yale as a rich man's college. A 1941 handbook for Yale alumni instructed recruiters on how to counter this impression:

> The real cost of four years at Yale is exaggerated. Nothing is known of the enormous sums expended each for the aid of the student body. It is generally assumed that, even with a scholarship, the poor boy entering Yale will be handicapped socially unless he happens to be an athletic star. He is assumed to have no chance to compete successfully with the graduates of Eastern preparatory schools for anything except

scholastic honors. . . . [Such] false notions can be dispelled by proper promotional methods. [Superior intellect is essential, but] Yale will polish rough exteriors.[2]

This promotion, however, was written for the eyes and the wallets of alumni only. Yale was not ready to approach the public directly with its desires to attract new applicants. And, as we have seen, the myths of the Yale caste system, if not always correct to the letter, were often based on truth. But, by the 1940s, some at Yale had begun to believe that a closed society was wrong. Yale administrators, too, were beginning to believe that the growing image of Yale as a closed community was costing the college some of the students it most wanted to attract.

Jews, however, were not among that number. Frankly anti-Jewish bias remained one cornerstone of Yale admissions. The hateful language that permeated the correspondence of deans Corwin and Jones in the 1920s and 1930s was gone, replaced by a more insidious feeling. This was a necessary stand, so the argument went, because if Yale were to accept only the very best students available, "they would all" be Jewish boys from New York City. Despite a Yale experience, it was claimed, the Jewish students remained provincial. Therefore, to further Yale's understandable goals of becoming a national institution, preference was shown for applicants from distant states with much smaller Jewish populations than New York.[3] Yet this logic was flawed. The assertion of permanent provinciality was a cruel way of blaming the victim for his suffering. Even though some Jewish undergraduates kept themselves apart from the masses (as did every other clique at Yale) a large proportion were kept out, remaining provincial perforce. Whereas Yale administrators of the 1960s would maintain a posture that racial and religious discrimination in student organizations was intolerable, in the 1940s social organizations were permitted to operate freely. The second flaw in the logic involved an incorrect syllogism. In explicit terms the argument was: Yale Jews remain provincial, therefore students from states with fewer Jews should be accepted. This argument tied together two separate issues. Provinciality involved an undergraduate social problem. Desiring a national constituency evidenced Yale's cosmopolitan interests. To use the second goal as a means of solving the first problem—thus justifying limitations on Jewish enrollment—ignored direct means of preventing undergraduate prejudices and evidenced the underlying bias of admissions officers searching for rationalizations for their policies.

In the 1940s Jews became increasingly suspicious of the silent quota operating at Yale.[4] Leonard Shiman (B.A. 1924) complained directly to his former history professor President Charles Seymour. Writing in 1944, Shiman noted that although Laurence Tighe, university treasurer, had "jocularly remarked that almost any draft exempt student with the proper educational background could secure admission to the Freshman class" during the tense war years, several highly qualified Jewish boys that Shiman knew had been refused admission. Suspecting a hitherto unappreciated and carefully masked quota, Shiman asked the university president for an explanation. As a loyal alumnus, Shiman felt betrayed. He had always told others that Yale did not discriminate against Jews in admissions and that any claim to the contrary was "idle gossip and unfair innuendo."[5]

The presidential response was candid and lengthy. Seymour began by denying that Yale excluded any racial or religious group, but he insisted that it was "a definite policy to maintain a balanced undergraduate population in so far as this can be achieved without detriment to the average quality of the student body." If necessary, Seymour continued, the policy might "involve some temporary restriction on the numbers selected from one or another of the nation's population groups in order to prevent distortion of the balanced character of the student body." In defense of restrictive policies, Seymour noted that many "of my Jewish friends have told me that it is because of this balance that they want their boys to come to Yale." Echoing President Lowell of Harvard, Seymour justified quotas as a method of preventing "prejudice against any minority or racial group." He concluded, therefore, that because "the percentage of applicants from Jewish homes was larger than ever before," Yale had "decided to stand by its policy of selective admission and to preserve as in past years the balanced character of the Freshman Class."[6] The president then dispatched copies of his discussion to Provost Edgar Furniss, Secretary Carl Lohmann, Treasurer Laurence Tighe, Dean Norman S. Buck of Freshman Year, and Chairman Edward S. Noyes of the Board of Admissions. Noyes praised Seymour's letter and called it "a very fine statement of our Board's policy."[7]

Seymour's logic operated to make the victim of social discrimination a double victim: The perceived need to restrict a group implied a social deficiency of that group, thereby encouraging social discrimination. The vicious circle of increased minority presence increasing prejudice ran in two directions. Limiting minority presence implied a valid reason for prejudice.

Internal memos from the university archives reveal that Shiman had good cause for questioning policy. The discrepancy between Treasurer Tighe's offhanded remark and the difficulty Jewish students faced in undergraduate admissions was more substantial during the Second World Ward than at any

other time in Yale history. The wartime draft had withdrawn a greater proportion of non-Jewish students from college than Jewish students, who were on
the average younger. Consequently, wrote Chairman Noyes in 1944, restrictive
changes had been made:

> For any or all of a number of reasons, Jewish boys apparently finish secondary school
> at an earlier age than Gentiles. It may be that they mature earlier; it may be that they
> permit themselves—or are permitted—fewer distractions; it may be that they are
> pushed as fast as possible by their families. In any event, the proportion of Jewish ap-
> plicants among those candidates who might be expected to matriculate has increased
> far beyond the proportion of Jewish applicants to the whole group of applicants.
> Moreover, even in the "young" group, the matriculants, the Jewish boys are younger.
> Thus, for example, the proportion of Jews in the class matriculating in July, 1943, was
> slightly under 10%. By the end of the summer term, 133 of these Freshmen had left
> to enter service; when the class reached its Sophomore year, the proportion of Jews
> had jumped to 23%, and the increase in proportion will continue as long as the class
> remains in college. Realization of this situation has made it necessary for the Board
> of Admissions to adopt standards of selection from this group more severe than in
> the past, in order to prevent it from reaching an undue proportion in the residential
> colleges.[8]

One year later University Secretary Carl Lohmann suggested that the "final"
number of matriculating Jews, as determined by the Chaplain's Office, did not
represent the true extent of Yale's Jewish problem: "A number of Hebrews
record themselves among the Protestants, chiefly as Episcopalians, and some
don't reply at all."[9] In his 1944–45 annual report Noyes noted that

> the Jewish problem . . . continues to call for the utmost care and tact. The propor-
> tion of Jews in the total number of candidates has increased very little, if at all, but
> the proportion of Jews among the candidates who are both scholastically qualified
> for admission and young enough to matriculate has somewhat increased and re-
> mains too large for comfort.[10]

To prevent a class from ending up with too many Jews because of Christian at-
trition, Yale formalized all the remaining informality in its limitation of Jewish
enrollment.

Alumni attitudes were generally in consonance with the restrictive policy.
Some graduates felt that Yale was not doing enough, even now, to limit the Jewish proportion. Seymour's correspondence with a 1906 Yale College graduate
indicated the kind of pressure that the university faced from alumni with such
views. In 1945 the alumnus caustically demanded that Yale increase its Chris-

tian outlook and limit "faculty appointments to native born Christian Americans with a substantial American background and preferably of Yale education."[11] The presidential response on this occasion was sympathetic. Four years later, the 1906 graduate wrote back to the president, requesting that Seymour "reduce and restrict the student body. . . . Draw a line on Jews, foreign-born, communistic, and atheistic alements and revert to the standards of our days with Arthur Twining Hadley."[12] On this occasion the president did not respond. Had the alumnus appreciated Hadley's strong dislike of prejudice, he might have been disappointed. Though long-winded cranks were usually ignored, general alumni feeling—a disciplined form of the graduate's ranting—was heard and respected within the Yale administration.

POSTWAR REACTIONS

As discussed earlier, the conclusion of the Second World War allowed for an efflorescence of American civil rights movements. President Harry Truman established commissions to investigate discrimination in employment and education throughout the United States.[13] At a time when the nation was horrified by the brutal visions of the Nazi death camps and showed great sympathy toward Jewry, the Anti-Defamation League of B'nai B'rith initiated a campaign to crack racial and religious quotas in college admissions.[14] What specifically affected Yale, however, was the tumult occurring at Columbia University in nearby New York City.

War's end had hurriedly led Columbia to remove questions about religion and nationality from its college application form. This action was not enough to mollify New York progressives. By September 1945 Columbia was being threatened with the loss of its tax exemption because of a lawsuit charging discrimination against blacks and Jews. Immediately, Frederick Wiggin—chief of the Wiggin and Dana firm that provided legal counsel for Yale—warned the Yale executives of the possibility of similarly disastrous results in Connecticut.[15]

The legal activity in New York was likely the impetus for the enunciation of a new Yale-wide policy adopted in May 1946. As a regular practice, applicants "of outstanding intellectual capacity" were to be given first preference in admission. For those students scholastically qualified, "but not of the highest intellectual capacity," admission would be granted to those whose personal qualities promised "leadership and effective influence and service in the life of the community after graduation." Finally, the policy stated that although the university wanted a varied student body, quotas for social, racial, and religious groups were explicitly forbidden. This enunciation, however, did not represent the end of racially and religiously biased admissions. The quota *qua* quota was buried, but effectively it was to be resurrected in other guises.[16]

If the threat to Columbia University's finances was not enough to shake off complacency toward discriminatory quotas, public evaluation of discrimination and the need for counteractive laws were. Between 1947 and 1949, four important reports (by President Truman's Commission on Higher Education, the New York State Commission on the Need for a State University, the American Council on Education, and the Connecticut State Inter-Racial Commission) argued that Jewish students experienced greater difficulty in gaining admission to their college of choice than did gentile students. In 1948 a committee of the Association of American Colleges acknowledged with a "troubled conscience," a long history of discriminatory practices against Jews. A national "Conference on Discriminations" in 1949 voted that racial, religious, and ethnic quotas were not compatible with democratic principles. Most northern American colleges and universities consequently felt pressured to drop their twenty-five-year-old application questions pertaining to race and religion. Progressive leaders such as Alvin S. Johnson called for the enforcement of the extant anti-discrimination bills in states like New York, while other individuals rallied to pass such a bill in Connecticut. Yale and its sister private colleges in Connecticut feared public scrutiny of their admissions operations, and they banded together to offer a common opposition to such legislative proposals.[17]

The most strident voice for a Connecticut antidiscrimination bill was heard in the 1949 report of the Connecticut State Inter-Racial Commission. Introducing data obtained from graduates of secondary schools in 1947, Governor Chester Bowles (B.S. 1924) stated that "the record of our private non-denominational colleges in their field of discrimination seems to be a rather dismal one. [The] commission's report prevents us from closing our eyes any longer to how sharp and ugly that discrimination often is." Unambiguously labeled a national problem, discrimination was implicitly linked to Connecticut's private nondenominational colleges—a group that included Yale.[18] Stung by the public charges, Chairman Noyes of admissions examined each of the report's assertions with meticulous effort. In a long critique of the state report, Noyes correctly disputed some of its conclusions by arguing that charges of discrimination, particularly of discrimination against Jews, were based on a statistically small sample. The conclusion offered may have been correct, but the marshaled evidence was not convincing. Beyond the veil of statistics, however,

Noyes's rebuttal evidenced his blindness to his own past actions, as is best seen in his discussion of the application form questions regarding an applicant's religion, birthplace, and maternal maiden name:

> The question about religious affiliation always occurred on Yale blanks; until 1947 no complaint had ever been made. In that year the Board [of Admissions] voted to remove it, but applicants in that year were still using the old form. . . .
>
> This raises the question of how much a college has a right to know about the background of its candidates. The private colleges have always assumed that they had a right to know a good deal, and the notion that such knowledge might be used for discriminatory purposes did not occur to them until it was suggested by the [Connecticut Inter-Racial Commission] Report. During the war, for example, it was necessary for the colleges to report to government authorities on every applicant of foreign birth or parentage; there is no way of knowing when such information will again be required and vital. In any case, to guess at a candidate's religion because of the place of birth of his father or his mother would be a distinctly hazardous proceeding. As for the question about "Mother's maiden name," this was removed at one time from the Yale blanks, and put back on because the answers revealed that some candidates were, on the maternal side, related to families with long Yale traditions, although their fathers were not alumni. The insinuation that all information about a candidate sought by the colleges is for the hidden purpose of discriminatory action is made pretty generally throughout the original Report. . . . To such an insinuation, the only answer that can be given is that it is not true.

Noyes was correct in denying that *all* background information regarding applicants was used for hidden discriminatory action. For a college that gave strong consideration to familial connections, knowledge of maternal maiden name sometimes did provide useful information. Yet the question of maternal maiden name had originally been placed on the application precisely in order to determine the applicant's religio-racial background. (See chapter 3). Noyes was on the mark in stating that place of parental birth was no guarantee for the proper identification of religion.[19] But his statement that the idea of using such information, including the question on religious identity, as a method of discrimination did not occur to admissions officers until the commission report suggested so, flatly contradicted his own previous reports describing admissions policy during the war. Judging from the fervent tone of Noyes's rebuttal to the charges of discrimination, one might suspect that his desire to visualize the admissions process that he managed as one completely free from prejudice blinded him to the inconsistencies in his own behavior.

Noyes was not alone in his criticism of the report's statistical deficiencies.[20]

So many concerned citizens spoke up to demand a new investigation that a follow-up study by the Connecticut Commission on Civil Rights (successor to the Inter-Racial Commission) was begun. Examined on this occasion were the Connecticut public high school graduates of 1949 and 1950. Chaired by Morris Silverman, a prominent Hartford rabbi, this investigative committee included two Christian clergymen among its large membership. Its goal was to determine if a need existed in Connecticut for a "Fair Educational Practice Law," as then existed in New York and Massachusetts.

Protestant applicants were found to have the best overall opportunities for securing higher education. Catholics were found to have "good" opportunities, but were handicapped by a lower average academic achievement and a higher rate of nonenrollment in high school college preparatory courses than Protestants. A substantially lower proportion of Catholics than of other religious groups actually attended college. Though Connecticut Catholics applying in Connecticut did not face discrimination, Connecticut Catholics applying out of state had a lower acceptance rate in private nondenominational colleges than Protestants. Many Catholic students, the study noted, were enrolled in Catholic institutions. When Italian-American students were examined, they were found to fit virtually the same patterns as Catholics. Connecticut blacks were found to have the worst lot in the application process. Of all the religious and racial groups surveyed, blacks were found to rank lowest in level of college preparation, high school rank, college acceptance rate, and college attendance rate. Connecticut Jews were found to have a better academic performance and greater degree of extracurricular participation than any other group studied, despite a lower national acceptance rate than any other group except blacks. The commission noted that Jewish applicants compensated for the higher rejection rate by applying to more colleges than others, so that the actual proportion of Jews attending college was the highest of any group. Connecticut Jews applying in-state were not found to suffer discrimination. The committee concluded that on a statewide basis the Jewish situation was not as bad as previously described. On a national basis discrimination was continuing, but lessening. The situation of black students was alarming, but the most appropriate solution was considered to be one of helping more blacks to complete high school and encouraging more to enter college preparatory courses. The colleges were not deemed at the heart of the black admissions issue. Passage of a Fair Education Act did not seem critical, therefore.[21] Despite a failure to examine how out-of-state applicants fared in the admission process, the public seal of approval was granted to the private nondenominational colleges of Connecticut.

The real story of the impact of admissions policies upon Jews was to some extent peripheral to the above investigations. That saga involved a struggle between conflicting views of the character of Yale College. Was it to be a training ground for the nation's managerial leaders, for its intellectual leaders, or both? As noted in the introduction, in 1948 Dean William Clyde DeVane of Yale College issued his call for action on this question. Appealing for Yale College to have "an intellectual eminence as great as her athletic or her social or her eminence in activity of all sorts," DeVane called for Yale to catch up with Harvard, Columbia, and the University of Chicago and turn itself toward producing more of the intellectual leadership of America. Calling for change at a time when the veterans' presence made such a change imaginable, DeVane saw the first requirement for real changes in the Yale character as needing to emerge from modifications in the policy of the Board of Admissions and in the associated scholarship committee: "There a closer scrutiny of the intellectual and imaginative qualifications of candidates must be made, and scholarships given for real intellectual promise."[22] Such cries, however, had been heard before. In 1948, as in previous years, the university would make a limited response. By the start of the 1948–49 academic year Yale created a new "Committee on Enrollment and Scholarships," with the express purpose of widening the Yale net of recruitment and retaining some of the most promising candidates.[23]

Discrimination in admissions remained, though the mechanisms continued to evolve. Prejudicially motivated restriction of scholarship aid to Jews was dropped. Under the tenure of Edward Noyes as chairman of admissions, Jews were no longer to be singled out and "admitted without aid" as a way of discouraging their matriculation. Restriction of the number of transfer students continued as it had since 1924, but there is no evidence that any racial or religious group continued to be affected particularly by this policy. Scholastic Aptitude Tests (SATs) continued to be required, yet these examinations proved to correlate far more with learning than with religious or psychological profiles. Even the strict Jew-counting that had grown over the war years was abandoned. New methods were employed. The growing practice in which high school admissions officers consulted with Yale admissions officers prior to a student's applying to Yale allowed Yale and the secondary schools to collude in selecting the most desirable candidates to apply to Yale. Unwanted candidates were simply urged to apply elsewhere. The chief means of discrimination, though, was the conscious effort by the Board of Admissions to limit Jewish enrollment. President Seymour's 1944 dictum calling for an effort to "balance" racial and religious groups was recognized by some of the admissions staff of the 1950s.[24]

Jewish applicants felt the pressures of balance in the 1950s because of the stereotypes that some admissions officers held against them. A few of the stereotypes were complimentary. Jewish boys were considered to be bright, hard-working, and successful. Their academic records were considered as "extremely powerful," and those grades were matched by similar SAT scores. To this point, Jews were considered to be ideal Yale students. Beyond this point, they ceased to be idealized. Since the imposition of Limitation of Numbers in 1923, academic achievement had stopped being of paramount importance in Yale admissions. A highly subjective evaluation of personality had also become crucial to admissions. This was where discrimination gathered force, for Yale applicants were not always evaluated by impartial judges. The interviewers, many of them alumni of the period of greatest anti-Jewish social discrimination by Yale undergraduates, often considered Jews as "single-minded" until proven otherwise. Admissions staff justified their restrictive behavior by resurrecting some of the same stereotypes of the Jewish student that they had had as collegiates. The caricatures that had formed of immigrant and first generation Jews of decades earlier were silently imposed by admissions officers on the first and second generation Jewish applicants of the postwar era. Despite Dean DeVane's dreams, concentration on academics was not the optimum use of Yale, some admissions officers felt. Consequently, Jews were disparagingly tagged as "placing performance before everything else" and as "book-grinds." Individual candidates were therefore forced to fight their way out of an ethnic slur. One first-rate Jewish student, for example, possessing "Mediterranian [sic] lips," was admitted because he overcame his interviewer's Jewish stereotype. "There is an air of quiet assurance here," the admissions officer wrote, "nothing pushy, aggressive or self-centered." Bias was most operative in some of the large urban high schools where Jewish applicants tended to be concentrated. Applicants from Stuyvesant High School and the Bronx High School of Science—whose entrance examinations assembled an already concentrated New York Jewry— had especially poor chances of being evaluated as individuals rather than as stereotypes. Recalled one admissions officer: "Many of the boys from the large high schools were much too competitive. They were only bred to live in the dog-eat-dog imaginary world that they thought was real. A significant proportion of these boys were Jewish." With admission officers secondarily interested in scholarship and primarily interested in a "balance and mix" of students with "breadth" of personality and attitude, Jewish students from high schools with large Jewish populations faced a far less than average chance of acceptance. The

10 percent mark around which Jewish undergraduate enrollment hovered was not fortuitous. The informal quota reigned supreme.[25]

AFRICAN-AMERICANS

In the postwar period, the question of Jewish admissions is inseparable from that of black admissions. That Jews were among those on campus most concerned about improving the position of the Yale black was indicative both of the increasing confidence that Jews felt about their own positions at Yale and their commitment to a society with equal opportunities for achievement. From a social perspective, the tapping of Levi Jackson by Skull and Bones had indicated that in at least some of the most prestigious circles blacks had arrived. Yet most striking was the virtual absence of black faces on the campus. University officials emphatically denied prejudice against black applicants. Though the Jewish proportion of students was constantly bursting at the university's seams, Yale consistently fell short of the number of blacks that some of its administrators hoped to admit. The problems were several. As noted above, many black applicants had inadequate secondary schooling to qualify for admission. Their grades and SAT scores tended to be inferior to those of white applicants. Many blacks were also too poor to afford Yale. Though a poor black would have as good a chance as an equally poor white before the scholarship committee, wealth was a factor in accepting students in the years before "need-blind" admissions were adopted. The student from a poor home had to be truly exceptional to gain admission and financial aid. A second-rate black applicant from a poor home thereby faced fewer prospects for admission than his wealthier second-rate white counterpart. And if a black had crossed all previous barriers he still had to face the bias of some admissions committee members who regularly rejected Jews, but had ample venom for blacks and other urban "minorities." Yale's image as an elite, white institution also served to discourage black applicants, many of whom assumed that Yale would not accept them. Convinced that Yale had no interest in blacks, high school officials occasionally shielded fully qualified black students from meeting with Yale admissions officers. Other black students, conscious of the white American's capacity for accepting blacks as third-class citizens, must have hesitated to become one of the mere handful of black undergraduates in each class of one thousand or more. In 1954, which for all these reasons was a typical year, the admissions office accepted eleven black students, while only four chose to matriculate. The Yale student body was not insensitive to the problem. With 87 percent of the undergraduates voting in favor of the proposal, the student Budget Drive (later named the Charities Drive) decided to contribute to a scholarship fund earmarked solely for blacks—this at a time when all other Yale College scholarships were granted without regard to race or creed. Furthermore, in 1951 an informal student-faculty committee (composed of the Reverend Sidney Lovett, professors Maurice Davie, Maynard Mack, Thomas Mendenhall, and Paul Weiss, and five undergraduates) formed to study the problem of black integration. Though Arthur Howe, Jr., the acting chairman of admissions in 1954, would feel constrained about publicly identifying himself "with any group interested in getting particular types of boys into Yale," he privately allied himself with the committee's goals. (In the 1960s, Howe would publicly commence the targeting of blacks for Yale to accept.) Between 1950 and 1952 Dwight Hall, the campus religious action group, scouted major cities where high schools had many blacks enrolled in academic tracks. As a result of this effort, more blacks applied to Yale and the number admitted doubled. But, in retrospect, the combined efforts were feeble. The resulting increase from about four blacks matriculating per year to eight was hardly significant. There would be a decade's hiatus before effective action would occur.[26]

THE ADMISSIONS PROCESS

Those who believe that real changes in Yale admissions were born in the outspoken reign of R. Inslee Clark as dean of admissions (1965–1970) would be mistaken if they ignore the formative years of the 1950s. To understand the changes it is valuable to understand what existed prior to the changes. With this objective in mind, we may trace the route of a Yale application from mailbox to decision.

Once the applicant of the 1950s had sent in his package of essays and data, an interview with a nearby Yale alumnus was scheduled for the applicant if possible. If the particular interviewer was respected by the admissions office, his opinion would later carry great weight in the admissions decision. If the student was from a school with strong ties to Yale, he would have a personal interview with an admissions officer and after the interview would receive an A, B, or C rating informing him of his chances of admission. Once the admissions office received the interviewer's report, the file was abstracted. In the case of children of prominent alumni or national citizens all the particulars might be ignored except for a brief statement describing the applicant's personal connections. All of the individual's records were then placed in a batch with those of other applicants from the same secondary school. These materials were saved until the two-week spring marathon when all decisions were made. At decision time each school was judged separately so that the admissions staff could prepare itself for possible defenses regarding why a lower-ranked candidate was sometimes accepted over a higher-ranked one at a particular school. Students competed for admission, therefore, on a local rather than a national basis. At least two faculty or admissions staff members (to assure consistency, one was always either the director or an assistant director of admissions) then read the file and together decided whether or not to recommend admission. The staff presented their recommendations to the entire admissions committee. This body included the director of admissions, the associate director of admissions, the director of the financial aid office, representatives of the offices of the freshman dean, college dean, and engineering dean (if not the deans themselves), and, in the late 1950s, a few members of the college faculty. A small number of "borderline" applicants were the source of intense debate and consensus building. In close to 90 percent of the decisions, however, the collegial members of the admissions committee acted as a rubber stamp for staff recommendations. Prejudices of interviewers and staff members could therefore pass unchecked. Financial aid offers, which sometimes played a role in the decision of whether or not to admit a student, were given at the same time. The motivation was usually to save money, but sometimes a poor boy was rejected "for his own good." Such a decision was not regular policy, but rather represented a reluctant action of the admissions officers. If a potential financial aid package required a student to spend so many hours working his way through Yale that he would have no time for the Yale extracurricular life, the admissions staff felt that the boy would be much happier at a less expensive state institution. Yet even these "merciful rejections" were delivered inconsistently. Over one hundred financially strapped applicants were annually "admitted without aid." Many of these men chose to attend Yale despite the limited support.[27]

Significant modifications in admissions policy and routine had occurred throughout the long tenure of Chairman Noyes. One important move was to allow the proportion of entering public school graduates to creep upward. Dean Howe promoted this trend. Indeed, his appointments of R. Inslee Clark (1961) and Robert Ramsey (1959)—both public high school graduates—to the admissions staff likely stimulated Yale interest in publicly educated youth. Representing 36 percent of the entering freshmen in 1950, the public school students increased to 56 percent of the entering freshmen in 1964.[28] The impact of such a change arose from the poor relations that Yale and the public schools had once maintained. On one side there were defects in the public schools. When Yale admissions officers would meet with high school principals (at schools that did not have guidance counselors), Yale admissions staff members found themselves to be speaking with men who did not know their students well and were consequently unable to recommend any of their applicants personally. The remaining problems with the relationship originated at Yale. Rather than work to solve the problem of separating the wheat from the chaff among the high school population, Yale had often chosen to ignore the field entirely. Lacking evidence to back up their claims, senior members of the admissions committee would assert that the public schools produced students less qualified for Yale than the private schools. For an unenlightened Yale this was true. For an intellectually stimulating college, however, the opposite was true. As early as 1935, in fact, President Angell had remarked that class standings revealed that "public school graduates, as usual, somewhat outstrip their socially more prominent colleagues from the prep schools." When a junior member of the admissions committee might suggest increasing the recruitment of high school students, his idea would be rebuffed by anti–public school sentiments. A paucity of alumni interviewers was another problem. The one hundred of these men that were spread across the United States in 1948 were hardly enough to recruit qualified high school students. Since one of the senior admissions officers personally interviewed every potential applicant from traditional "feeder" schools— virtually all of which were private schools—personal contact gave independent school students an added edge in the admissions process. Yale's reputation of having limited financial aid available discouraged many a public school applicant as well.[29]

For Jewish public school students, in particular, the Yale quest for diversity also proved problematic. At a high school where there were many excellent Jewish applicants, for example, all of them presenting similar grades and board scores, Yale admissions officers had little means available to gauge who was the best because Yale had not maintained close relations with the school. One admissions officer recalled that some of the "most able students might be denied admission [because of] outright discrimination on the grounds of not being able to discriminate between the kids." The lack of suitable connections with the public schools was sometimes offered, consequently, as an excuse for not accepting students from public schools. Without a personal, trusting relationship with a local guidance counselor (who would reliably separate the desirable from the undesirable), Yale admissions officers were often more reluctant to accept public school students than to accept independent school students. Yale had fewer difficulties learning who were the most intelligent, creative, and personable members of the preparatory school graduating classes. At high schools, where students might appear too similar in the eyes of ignorant or prejudiced admissions officers, where Yale did not make the effort to sort out differences, many a qualified student was rejected.[30]

Much of the early 1950s failure to keep pace with national trends in admissions grew out of a bureaucracy that did not readily respond to President Griswold's vision of the university college. Other leading members of the Yale community spoke for Griswold when they argued in 1951 that Yale was not reaching out to obtain applicants:

> The Board [of Admissions] seems to have inherited from an earlier era the point of view that it is beneath the dignity of a great University to take steps to interest boys in Yale other than to furnish them with literature of doubtful inspirational values. . . . Whatever the situation may have been twenty-five or thirty years ago, today we face well-organized competition for the really top-flight boys not only from those whom we choose to consider our natural rivals, but from other institutions of lesser breed.

Chairman Noyes represented an older generation whose time had passed in America and at Yale. When he modified his stands to accept the views of others at Yale, it was often only with great reluctance. So it was arranged for Donald K. Walker (B.A. 1926) to be appointed manager of the Office of Admissions in 1951. Though Walker's presence helped Yale expand recruiting, Griswold became increasingly aware that Walker did not have a working grip on admissions.[31]

To establish is own authority over admissions, Griswold was forced to act decisively. He first promoted Noyes to become director of Yale's teacher training program. Then, with the intent of widening the applicant pool and involving more people in the admissions process, Griswold invited Arthur Howe, Jr., to serve as guard over the outermost portals of Yale. Howe, who regularly consulted with his president, continued by increasing degrees to demand that prep school graduates present academic credentials as strong as those of the public school graduates. Prep school officers were sometimes astonished by Howe's raising the standards of quality. Donald K. Walker recalled the challenge: "It was hard to convince the [prep school] officials that they didn't have the cream of the crop. And they didn't." Insisting that faculty begin to take a direct role in admissions, Howe also encouraged Griswold to appoint rotating faculty members to serve in limited capacities on the admissions committee. In 1956 Dean Howe provoked outrage among faculty, students, and especially alumni, when his proposal that Yale admit female undergraduates was leaked to the press. Only a quick admission by President Griswold and Dean DeVane that such an event was unlikely to take place in the foreseeable future calmed the agitated members of the Yale community.[32] Nevertheless, the increase in high school graduates and the serious discussion of admitting women signaled that the gatekeepers themselves were moving to permit breaches in Yale's Gothic walls.

THE CALM BEFORE THE STORM

Assessment of the exact degree of religious prejudice in admissions during the 1950s is difficult because such prejudice as existed was often well-veiled. Three decades later, some admissions committee members from this era denied that *any* religious discrimination took place. Others did not recall observing any biases but allowed that religious biases might have operated without their knowledge. Still other participants insisted that racial and religious prejudices were integral components of the admissions committee fabric. It seems likely that what was considered as prejudice by some members was seen as objectively justifiable by others. Since Yale was so near to New York City and its tremendous Jewish population, a large proportion of Yale's Jewish applicants were New Yorkers. As New Yorkers they (and others) were limited by geographical ceilings. Had a New York Jew been considered by the admissions staff as equal to a New York Protestant, the Yale record of the 1950s might have been more honorable. But this was not the case. The most outstanding of Jewish applicants, as always, found easy acceptance, but discrimination against Jews operated when choosing among the less extraordinary candidates. Because some of the admissions committee members apparently possessed strong racial and religious prejudices (one member openly admitted such thoughts), when character was considered as a method of selection, Jewish and black applicants suffered. Admission of Jews, per se, was never discussed openly at committee meetings, because public sympathies were, in principle, opposed to religious discriminations. Recalled one committee member, admission of Jews was "a subject you just didn't talk about." But absence of talk did not stop discriminatory action. Not until the 1960s would a prejudiced staff member be relieved of his duties.[33]

On the occasion of Yale's two hundred fiftieth anniversary in 1951, *Time* magazine looked at the institution and admitted that while Yale had produced many of the nation's leaders, the institution itself was not a leader: "Consciously or unconsciously, Yale had traditionally waited for others to lead, observed their course, then picked the middle road to follow. . . . In the best and truest sense of the world, Yale has stood from its earliest beginnings for conservatism triumphant."[34] In the manner in which it removed racial, religious, and sexual barriers from its admissions process, Yale was to prove consistent in its character with *Time*'s description.

Throughout the 1950s, the pressure for passage of Connecticut Fair Educational Practice Laws lessened. In 1945, 1949, 1953, 1955, and 1957 repeated attempts to enact such a law failed. While Yale continued a subtle, sometimes unconscious, form of racial and religious discrimination, enough other institutions were opening their doors in the 1950s so that each year the perceived need for such a bill declined. University Counsel Frederick H. Wiggin noted in 1957 that even those in favor of Fair Education laws "had little fire and not great enthusiasm as compared with former years." By then, activist concerns centered on the state's private preparatory schools. "All the [bill's] proponents," wrote Wiggin, "agreed expressly or by implication that there is no need for regulation of the present practices of the colleges, which are found to be excellent."[35] In 1959, John Q. Tilson, Jr., also of the Wiggin and Dana law firm, presented University Treasurer Charles S. Gage with the news that "for the first time that I can remember, there are no bills on fair educational practices" being considered by the Connecticut General Assembly.[36]

Yale Jews, however, did not give their college such a pristine bill of health. By decade's end, concerned Jews on the campus felt increasingly disturbed at the way the Jewish proportion of Yale College students hovered suspiciously close to 10 percent year after year,[37] especially since the Second World War had opened admissions to more Jews at many of the nation's best colleges. By 1952 Jewish enrollment at the liberal arts colleges of Harvard and Cornell was approaching 25 percent,[38] but at Yale the informal quota remained. Either the Jewish applicants to Yale were markedly inferior to those at the nation's other top-flight colleges, or the Harvards and Cornells of America had lowered their admissions standards, or Jews were avoiding applying to and matriculating at Yale, or Yale was prejudicially biased in its admissions. The first two of these explanations cannot be substantiated. The third was true to some extent. In the 1950s it was harder to be a religious Jew at Yale than at some of the other great American colleges. (See chapter 11.) Observant Jewish students, therefore, tended to avoid applying to Yale. As for outright bias against Jewish students in admissions, though it was small in magnitude, it was very real. It persisted despite repeated assurance of unbiased admissions policies and the growing conviction within much of the Yale community that any form of racial and religious discrimination was contrary to Yale ideals.[39]

Despite the apparent discrimination, no one dared challenge the existing order. No one, that is, prior to Rabbi Richard J. Israel, who arrived from UCLA in 1959 to direct the B'nai B'rith Hillel Foundation on the Yale campus. His remarkable drive and personality can be seen from the words of William Sloane Coffin, university chaplain. Writing to Provost Kingman Brewster, Jr., in 1962, the Reverend Coffin delivered a stirring accolade: "I am sure you have heard of the outstanding work of Rabbi Israel. Not since the days of Rabbi [Samuel Sandmel, Hillel Director at Yale from 1945 to 1949,] has the Hillel Foundation had such an effective director-counselor, and I have yet to meet his match on any other university campus."[40]

Speaking to members of the admissions committee, Israel learned that a good Jewish applicant was accepted like any other, a bad Jewish applicant rejected like any other, but the marginal Jewish student would never stand a chance, while the marginal non-Jew might be accepted. Others told him of code words used by some of the admissions staff. If those in the know wanted to allude to the fact that an undesirable (often Jewish) applicant was being discussed, yet those officers did not want to appear bigoted in the eyes of the more tolerant members of the admissions committee, a code word might be used to identify the student and thereby reduce his chances of admission.[41]

Driven by concern, Israel quickly approached Dean Howe to discuss the matter. From Israel's point of view, Howe's words about a desire to be unbiased and to protect Yale were doubletalk. Since Jews were overrepresented in the ranks of Phi Beta Kappa members, given their enrollment in the college, the argument went, they were overachievers and consequently not contributing to the social life of the college. Since Jewish boys were said not to contribute to Yale, there was a valid reason to restrain the Jewish proportion of the Yale population—a similar thesis to that offered by administrators of the 1920s. The perceived doubletalk was seen in the two fallacies in the argument. The first was that Jewish students did not contribute to Yale life. Even a cursory glance at Yale classbooks of the 1950s reveals that Jewish students participated in a wide range of extracurricular activities on the campus. And, as secret society barriers slowly dissolved in the 1940s and 1950s, Jewish students came to participate in and lead many of the major organizations on the campus. As for the second fallacy, a policy that discriminated against academically marginal Jews selected much more against Jewish applicants with social interests that were strong enough to harm their academic standing. The admissions officers had effectively created a self-fulfilling prophecy. By design, "the average" Yale Jew was likely to be more disposed to the intellectual offerings of the university than to the social system. And again by design, the "average" Yale non-Jew would be more balanced.[42]

Where Howe and Israel disagreed the most was on the definition of a Jew. Israel recalled that Dean Howe suggested to him that perhaps as many as one-quarter of the students he was admitting were Jewish. Rabbi Israel was sure this was not the case. The two men decided to study the matter and, good-naturedly, wagered five cents on the outcome. Counting the religious preference cards filled out by the class of 1963 (at a time when the number of undergraduates not returning such cards or marking "no preference" for religion was still small), Israel found approximately one hundred twenty Jewish freshmen. In a letter to Dean Howe, Israel concluded, "At the end of our investigation you are going to owe me a nickel. There are not as many Jews at Yale as you suspect."[43] Howe's list of names was longer than Israel's. The difference, Israel felt, was that the dean's list presupposed every student with a German name to be Jewish and considered every student with a Jew lurking somewhere in his family tree to be a Jew.[44] From Howe's point of view, the questions that Israel raised were of interest, but of lesser importance than other concerns. With vocal alumni regularly asserting that Yale was admitting too few athletes or Yale sons, the subject of minority admissions was a minor deity in the pantheon of issues that Yale had to pay homage toward.[45] Matters were at an impasse.

Approaching the issue from another angle, Rabbi Israel turned to William Horowitz (B.A. 1929), local businessman, supporter of the Friends of the B'nai B'rith Hillel Foundation at Yale, and chairman of the Connecticut State Board of Education. Horowitz, a most loyal Yale alumnus and perhaps the most important supporter of Jewish communal life at Yale, had been appointed to his state position by Governor Abraham Ribicoff. Arming himself with Rabbi Israel's statistics, Horowitz asked his Yale College classmate, President Griswold, for permission to meet with him outside of Horowitz's official position. Consequently, on April 5, 1960, Horowitz handed Griswold a letter detailing the number of Jewish students in the freshman classes of Yale College for the years 1951 through 1959 and the entering classes at the Yale School of Medicine for the years 1952 through 1959. (See appendix 5.) Beneath his tables of statistics, Horowitz wrote: "My interpretation of these figures [is] that in both cases there is a quota. In my opinion this is contrary to the spirit of a University and I bring it to your attention for consideration by you."[46] A gauntlet had been politely handed to the Yale president.

Fortunately for the historian, Griswold dictated a memorandum to himself following the cordial meeting with his classmate. Griswold's own words are instructive:

> I . . . spent about half an hour discussing this matter with [Mr. Horowitz] in complete candor. I began by acknowledging that no institution was perfect and that I made no such claim for Yale. I then pointed out the following:
>
> 1. The tremendous improvement in the position of Jews at Yale that had taken place since he and I were undergraduates. I gave many details and illustrations, all of which he recognized; and he agreed without reservation with the general conclusion.
>
> 2. I then said that the numbers listed in his letter were the result of a search for human beings of specific characteristics rather than the result of an application of a predetermined quota for Jews. I told him I based this statement on my confidence in the directors of the [undergraduate and medical] admissions offices. I also observed that the most frequent complaint on this score was that of non-Jewish alumni whose sons were not admitted to Yale and who brought the complaint that we were discriminating in some way or other against them. . . .
>
> I assured Mr. Horowitz that I would call his letter to the attention of both offices of admission and that I would make it my own duty to follow up all such criticism; and further that our aim would continue to be to find students of the proper qualities whether they were Jews or non-Jews.[47]

On April 5, 1960, President Griswold put his integrity on the line and promised that he would make it his own personal "duty" to see that racial and religious factors would not serve as determinants of whether a student had the "proper qualities" for admission.

The next morning Griswold set about to investigate the charges. He personally telephoned Arthur Howe, Jr., dean of admissions, and Hartley Simpson, dean of the graduate school, and arranged for George Vaill, recording secretary of the university, to contact the college's Freshman Year Office and Thomas Forbes, assistant dean of the medical school. Griswold expressed his desire to know how Yale knew who was and was not Jewish and if there really were or were not Jewish quotas at the university. The responses uniformly denied the existence of quota systems.

Dean Simpson insisted that "we do not know the number of Jewish students registered in the Graduate School, and in the [nearly two decades] I have been in office we have never known. Neither the administrative officers nor the faculty have ever evinced the slightest interest in these statistics." Simpson explained that applicants to the graduate school were not asked about religion prior to admission; on registration day, their religious preference was requested, but not required. The preferences, Simpson reported, were sent to all the central university offices. Backing up Simpson's claim, the historical record shows that the Yale Graduate School had reflected the post-Second World War acceptance of Jews in education in its admissions policies. In 1947 Jews had made up 9 percent of the graduate students, in 1953 17 percent, and in 1960 Dean Simpson estimated a 20 percent Jewish enrollment. Simpson had no sense that Jewish students at Yale were clustered in any particular fields of graduate study.[48]

George Vaill reported that the Freshman Office staff had told him that admissions policies toward Jews had been modified years before:

> The marking of Jewish applicants was abandoned long ago. . . . There is nothing on the admissions application form (except possibly the photograph) to indicate whether the candidate is Jewish or Gentile or Coptic Roller. *After the candidate has been accepted,* he receives a card on which he may record his religious . . . preference. The statistics gleaned from these cards form the basis of the Chaplain's lists—but many of the boys fail to return their cards and so are not counted.
>
> The number of candidates qualifying for admission in *all* of the so-called minority groups strike so nearly the same average year after year that the results give the impression that quota systems are used. The same consistency of average probably obtains among *fat boys* and *harelips*—but we have never been accused of discrimination in these categories.[49]

Vaill's position was well-taken. To claim that annual constancies of any group at Yale was evidence of a quota was a form of *post hoc, ergo propter hoc* reasoning. In the case of the consistent Jewish proportion of the 1950s, the conclusion by Horowitz and Israel that some form of limit existed was a correct one. As of April 1960 the evidence supporting that conclusion, however, was insufficient.

Dean Howe's report to President Griswold denied a quota but evidenced the difficulty that he and Rabbi Israel shared in developing a rapport with one another. One problem was that Howe had mistakenly referred to Israel as "Rabbi Goldman." Of more concrete importance was that Howe had come away from his January discussions with a quite different interpretation of events than had Rabbi Israel:

> Pursuant to our conversations this morning, Rabbi Goldman advised me on 11 Jan [1960] that between 109 and 113 entering Freshmen had annually recorded "Jewish" on the religious preference cards filed *after admission* with the Chaplain[']s office, except for the entering Class of '62, which had 143 such registrations. This apparently satisfied him that we do not have a quota, which is of course the fact.[50]

Rabbi Israel, though, was far from satisfied with his conversations with Dean Howe. Was Dean Howe deceiving his president? No. Rabbi Israel and Dean Howe had never learned to communicate with each other. And though Israel was uncertain of Howe's commitment to fairness, Howe was considered by colleagues at Yale to have been above bigotry. Indeed, there had been no formal counting of Jews since the Second World War. Were Jews discriminated against in admissions? Yes. But at this stage for Griswold and Howe, and for Horowitz and Israel, the issue was not bias, but formal quotas.

For Rabbi Israel the discussions were far from over. Equipped with many unsubstantiated rumors, Israel began an inquiry that would ultimately encourage the creation of a more impartial admissions system. Israel detailed his investigation in a November 1960 letter:

> After a year and a half of sniffing and snooping about, tracking down rumors and counting Jewish noses, a somewhat guilt-ridden member of the admissions committee has made a clear unequivocal statement about the undergraduate admissions policy. . . . He has told us that there is a plain and open double standard for Jews and that many candidates otherwise qualified are rejected solely and exclusively on the grounds of their presumed . . . Jewishness.
>
> There is nevertheless no "quota" as such. The administration is . . . unaware of the number of Jewish students in Yale College. They simply have a policy of "conscious self-restraint." That is to say, they automatically turn down a "suitably" large number of Jews. . . .
>
> When I told the dean of admissions last year that the percentage varied from 10% to 12% he found it impossible to believe and asserted that surely there were many more Jews who did not declare themselves. I then went through the religious preference cards of all the Unitarians, Universalists, Congregationalists, Quakers, Christian Scientists and varying types of nonbelievers and thereby produced another five preference cards, all but one appearing to be the children of an intermarriage (as determined by the mother's name). They were only definable as Jews by a kind of Hitlerian definition.
>
> The dean still found the figures unbelievable. . . . It might seem that without knowledge of the number of Jewish students they plan to allow in they are going to be overly cautious. The explanation for this caution is perhaps to be found in Dean Howe's assertion (later echoed by other admissions interviewers) that when Harvard removed its quota it rapidly became 55% Jewish and was well on its way to becoming a Jewish school until the quota was re-established. [Rabbi Maurice Zigmond, Boston Hillel director,] told me that he is certain that the figure never went over 23%. No one believed this either. The myth of the ubiquitous Jew dies hard.[51]

This letter again evidenced the communications gap between Dean Howe and Rabbi Israel. Dean Howe had come away from his spring 1960 discussions with Rabbi Israel convinced that anti-Jewish discrimination was a dead issue, whereas for Israel the issue lived on.

It was approximately November 1960 when Israel turned for assistance to the Reverend William Sloane Coffin, Jr. (B.A. 1949, B.D. 1956), spiritually the most influential man at Yale in the 1960s and one of the more influential progressives in the United States of the 1960s. Coffin, former head of the American Veterans at Yale and a Skull and Bones man, served as the Yale University chaplain and pastor in the Church of Christ in Yale University from 1958 through 1975. In his memoirs Mr. Coffin recalled Rabbi Israel's appeal for assistance:

> After [Rabbi Israel] had sized me up as "a goy for whom there is hope," he came by to report that the number of Jews in Yale College was small. Even Princeton had more. . . . I decided to take up the matter, thoroughly documented by Rabbi Israel, with President Griswold, who seemed reluctant to do much until I told him that "the conscience of Yale" was not about to go to sleep on this one. Then he got angry.[52]

Griswold's anger was understandable, for barely one year before, in April 1960, he had discussed the Jewish admissions issue with Dean Howe, and Dean Howe had assured him that there was no quota. For the dean and the president it was a closed issue. But Coffin, as his autobiography cites, pressed on:

> "Well, what do you want me to do? [Griswold] asked tartly. "It's very simple," I said. . . . "[You] start an investigation to find out why there are so few Jews in Yale College." "Do your own investigating," he said angrily. "I will," I said, "if you'll put it in writing that you want me to." Suddenly he relaxed. He had an infectious grin which he now gave me. "Go to hell, Coffin," he said. Within twenty-four hours I had a letter. . . . Armed with it I soon confirmed what I thought would be the case: anti-semitism at Yale was not overt as once it had been, but there were no Jews on the admissions committee, in the admissions office, and few among the alumni recruiters.[53]

Though Coffin's account implies that Yale admissions policies and procedures changed overnight, the documentary record establishes that this episode in the history of Yale admissions took place over a ten-month period from May 1961 through February 1962. Metaphorically, however, any change taking place within ten months, given the often-inefficient Yale bureaucracy, was equivalent to an overnight change.

Following one of the administrative pathways open to him, Mr. Coffin, together with David M. Byers, associate university chaplain, and Rabbi Israel, approached the University Council alumni "Committee on Religious Life and Study." In front of this body, which was led by Sidney Lovett (the old Bones man who was Coffin's predecessor as chaplain), the three active chaplains detailed the charges of discrimination against Jewish applicants in college admissions. They also expressed concern that Roman Catholic and black applicants were being unfairly treated in the admissions process. From that moment on, it was but a matter of bureaucratic time before changes took place.[54]

The alumni committee's initial response to the charges was a letter to the chairman of the University Council, the Reverend Henry K. Sherrill (B.A. 1911), reiterating the concerns of the university chaplains. Shortly afterword, Mr. Sherrill and Mr. Lovett met with President Griswold to discuss the issue. Griswold then met with Mr. Coffin and Rabbi Israel. As Israel recalled, by this time "the President seemed genuinely horrified at the thought that there might be discrimination at Yale. He offered us carte blanche to investigate any records of the University which could demonstrate the existence of either implicit or explicit quotas." Almost concurrently, Griswold formally conveyed the chaplains' points to Kingman Brewster, Jr., his new provost, and to Dean Howe.[55]

Griswold's style of working with his dean of admissions was to state his own attitudes toward policies, allow the man a free hand in administering those policies, and then defend his dean when that man's judgment was called into question. Regarding admissions, in the summer of 1961 Griswold shared two directives with his provost and dean of admissions:

  1. The policy of Yale in the recruitment of its student body, as in all other respects, is to discover and develop the greatest intellectual, moral, and spiritual potential of its students without regard to race, creed, or color.
  2. Yale is proud of its Protestant Christian tradition. Its policy is to preserve that tradition and at the same time to direct and guide it in such a way as to ensure respect for other faiths, to draw upon their inspiration and to further the interests of their practitioners.[56]

Without equivocation, the president declared that his university valued its heritage but looked toward a future that welcomed all.

In December, thanks to one final set of data compiled by Rabbi Israel, the vehicles of change lodged within the bureaucratic traffic jam broke loose of their restraints. Deciding to match up Yale against its peers, Israel asked the Hillel directors at each of the Ivy League colleges to inform him of the estimated Jewish proportion at their respective institutions. The results for the 1961–62 academic year were varied:

Columbia	45%
Cornell	26%
Univ. of Pennsylvania	25%
Harvard	21%
Brown	18%
Princeton	15%
Dartmouth	15%
Yale	12%

Columbia was located amidst a heavy concentration of Jews in New York City, so it would have been inappropriate to expect that Yale's Jewish population would have matched that of Columbia. But Yale's appearing at the bottom of a list that included even the legendarily prejudiced Princeton seemed to be confirmation of anti-Jewish bias in Yale admissions.[57]

Mr. Lovett turned this datum over to President Griswold and Dean Howe and then discussed its implications with Griswold, Howe, Coffin, and H. Bradford Westerfield, assistant professor of political science and faculty representative to the admissions committee. With all of this water under the bridge, the University Council Committee on Religious Life and Study met in New Haven on December 15 and 16, 1961. In short order

> the Committee voted to request President Griswold to invite the University Chaplains to prepare a confidential and constructive report of their criticisms levelled at the Board of Admissions and present the same to the President and Mr. Howe before February 1st 1962, when the processing of applicants for admissions to the Class of 1966 begins.[58]

By protocol, Griswold then asked Coffin to recommend changes. Coffin proposed diversifying the makeup of the admissions staff to include representatives of more faiths. Griswold and Howe responded favorably to the proposal, though corrective action was not taken immediately.[59]

President Griswold, too, went to work. In consultation with Dean Howe and the law firm of Wiggin and Dana, the president prepared a detail of his undergraduate admissions policy. Little more than a year before his death from cancer, the Yale president came to grips with the embarrassing charges of discrimination that occasionally surfaced in the last years of his administration. Much of what he outlined contained little new in the way of policy directive.

What was the most significant was Griswold's attempt to emphasize his own specific concerns about admissions. Sufficient explicit criteria for choosing between applicants were introduced so that race was not to have any room to operate in the admissions process.[60]

In broad terms Griswold saw two aims for Yale College. The first, he wrote, arose from the historic goal stated in the college charter:

> Namely, the preparation of youth, through instruction in the arts and sciences, "for Publick employment both in Church and Civil State," or as we would define it today, for any and all professions and occupations demanding of those who practice them an enlightened sense of obligation for the general welfare and a corresponding ability to discharge that obligation with competence and distinction.

Griswold saw the second aim of the college as emerging from the university tradition in which Yale College was steadily finding its place:

> Namely, the advancement of liberal learning, and higher learning, as ends in themselves; as the means of a happy life; as the foundation of the learned professions; as standards for the educational system; and as instruments of national welfare and cultural progress.[61]

Employing language more forceful than had been used previously, Griswold placed Yale College solidly within the university model:

> A university is first and foremost an intellectual enterprise, as education, especially higher education, is primarily an intellectual process. Those who take part in the process must be equipped with the intellectual powers equal to its demands at every stage. . . . The first concern of those who administer Yale's undergraduate admissions policy should be for evidence of the ability not only to meet this demand but to excel in meeting it.[62]

Elsewhere in the directive President Griswold renewed Yale's commitment to favoring the applications of alumni children and accepting students of the finest character and moral potential. Though the latter phrase had once been used invidiously to limit the enrollment of Jews and others, on an admissions committee multi-religious and multi-ethnic in composition, the definition of character and moral potential was to be applied in an unbiased manner. The principle of geographic distribution was also reaffirmed as part of Yale's century-old design of patterning itself as a national university.[63] Though many individual Jews (concentrated in the northeast region from which Yale received most its applications) would be affected by this principle, it was not an innately anti-Jewish principle. A geographical policy applied without regard to religion that would help an individual Milwaukee Jew or Duluth Catholic as much as it would hurt a New York atheist or Hoboken Protestant could not appropriately be termed religiously biased.

The president called for Yale to further its democratic ideal of equal opportunity for all qualified students. He envisioned Yale as having the obligation of "removing economic, social, religious or social barriers to the fulfillment of that ideal." Optimistic almost to the point of naiveté, but characteristic of the 1960s, Griswold looked to the day when inter-faith and inter-racial relations among Yale students would be so harmonious that they would not only be source of pride for Yale students but would also serve "as an object lesson for the country."[64]

Squarely, Griswold confronted the position of religion at the university. Though one senior admissions officer, an anecdote records, was still suggesting that Yale should handle its Jewish applicants by publicly declaring that Yale was a Christian institution, Griswold appreciated that Yale, as a whole, had already ceased to be an actively Christian institution. Specifically Christian activities were looked upon as entirely personal and voluntary in nature. A pre-Christmas dinner was still the major feast in the university dining halls, and the practice of Christian ethics was still encouraged, but Christianity was not the only religion openly being expressed on campus. To call the Yale of the post-Second World War era a Christian institution was, as implied by William F. Buckley, Jr.'s *God and Man at Yale,* to make a hollow mockery of Christianity. Repeating the convictions that he had shared with Dean Howe in the summer of 1961, the president expressed his pride in Yale's Christian past but saw the proper locations for the Christian spheres of influence at Yale to be the university's Church of Christ, its associated Protestant ministries, and the Yale Divinity School—which had been created in 1822 as a new haven for the teaching of Protestantism following the 1818 disestablishment of Congregationalism as the Connecticut state religion. Outside of these spheres, Griswold saw Yale as needing to embrace other faiths from within and without Christianity.[65]

Matters were not allowed to rest at this stage. It was the 1960s and Yale students, too, were sensitive to the stench of discrimination that was then considered a poison in the national atmosphere. In October 1962 the *Yale Daily News* entered the discussion by publishing its own inquiry into Yale College admissions patterns. Among its many questions of Dean Howe were a few concerning minority admissions. The dean openly asserted that because of Yale's desire to achieve diversity among its students, it was "absurd to think that color, religion, and so on are not important considerations" in choosing the freshmen.

Careful to avoid an unsubstantiated insinuation of bigotry, the *News* admitted its dissatisfaction with the apparent complacency of the admissions officers: "Some would insist that there is [an] important contradiction—Absence of any quota system and the recurring, constant numbers of Yale students who are, for instance, Jewish. Dean Howe and his assistants do make such denials, though the figures have never been fully explained."[66] On inquiring of admissions officers why more blacks and more lower income bracket students were not arriving at Yale, the paper was told, "They are just not applying."[67] Having raised disturbing questions but leaving them unanswered, the newspaper's investigation ended.

The articles on admissions piqued the interest of Paul Weiss, the first Jew to gain tenure on the Yale College faculty, a Sterling professor of philosophy, and one of the most greatly admired, if controversial, men on the campus. Reading the *News* reports, Weiss sensed an incipient controversy. He brought it to light in a letter to the editor of the *News* in which he accused the admissions office of preferring non-New York Protestants to all other applicants. The philosopher demanded an answer to his critical question: "On what grounds and by what right has anyone the privilege of denying admission to Yale to a student who is qualified but does not have some particular color, creed, or geographical location?"[68] Arthur Howe, who had begun to implement Griswold's new admissions policy, again denied any prejudice on the part of his office:

> There is a significant difference between, on the one hand, an interest in race and religion as factors which may provide insights (what biographer is not interested in them?), and on the other hand, the biased use of such information as specific bases for selection, rejection or the establishment of quotas.
>
> If Mr. Weiss does not think that matters of race and religion are significant for the fullest possible understanding of applicants, I can only register my respectful disagreement.[69]

For Dean Howe, interest in religious and racial background complemented a rejection of bigotry.

Where did the truth lie? In an editorial in the same day's *News*, the editors tried to resolve the issue, one which they admitted was rarely discussed in public at Yale: "We believe that Mr. Weiss is most inaccurate when he implies conscious bigotry on the part of the Admissions Committee. However, we must admit that over the years, Yale has not been a national leader in admitting applicants from certain minority groups." The paper attributed this situation to three causes: Yale's Dink Stover image of snobbery, which discouraged many potential applicants; Yale's failure to recruit minorities vigorously; and finally, "all other things being equal," preference in the admissions process for non-minority applicants. Couched in tactful phrases was a cautious acknowledgment of bigotry. Optimistically, and very correctly, the paper noted that times were changing and that Yale was slowly catching up with them:

> We believe that subtle prejudices are playing an ever-declining role in admissions decisions. One striking piece of evidence for this statement is that this year the percentage of Jewish students in the freshman class has risen significantly. . . .
>
> In short, we believe that Mr. Weiss vastly overstates the case when he implies that blatant bigotry or racial and religious quotas exist today in the admissions process. However, we would also admit that Yale's record in the past on the admission of minority group applicants has not been so clear cut as we would like.

Taking a conciliatory stance, the paper concluded by proposing that "minority group" faculty representatives should be placed on the admissions committee, as that would "certainly silence the cries of discrimination and bigotry."[70] One year earlier Mr. Coffin had made the same suggestion. As of 1964, there was still no Jew or black on the admissions committee.[71]

Despite the public denials, some junior members of the admissions committee were just as concerned as Professor Weiss was about bigotry. R. Inslee Clark (B.A. 1957), an assistant director of undergraduate admissions and freshman scholarships from 1961 through 1965, remembered that when he joined the committee, "anti-Semitism, and anti-black, and anti-Hispanic bias was blatant" among some of the staff. Dean Howe, Clark felt, brooked no such feelings, but some of his staff were not so objective. What made the bigoted feelings so hard to fight was that the prejudice was often cloaked so that the reasons for rejecting a particular applicant were not outwardly objectionable. Additionally, with a number of the staff holding deep prejudices it was difficult for junior men to fight every instance of unfair bias. From a philosophical standpoint, it was not considered "good form" to vote against the recommendations of colleagues. From a practical standpoint, a junior man looking to rise within the Yale ranks had to be careful not to rock the boat to much. When two committee members once questioned why a group of students (with apparently Jewish surnames) from their district of-responsibility had all been voted down after these admissions officers had voted in favor of acceptance, senior members of the committee responded, "Well, we could fill all of Yale with them. But we can't, of course."[72] The young admissions officers did not feel secure enough to pursue the subject.

Who were the admissions staff? From Clark's perspective upon his arrival in 1961, they were a small, lethargic, and content group, having limited interest in discovering talent. All were of a white Anglo-Saxon Protestant background. The office manager had been working for the committee since 1918. Three officers were in their late fifties and sixties. Age and tenure would not have been such an issue had some of them not retained the prejudices of their youth, while losing their youthful energy to find the most qualified students wherever they would be. (Dean Howe later explained that he had appointed a few "grey-beards" to the staff in order to have older alumni on his side to defend the broader recruitment policies that he was instituting for Yale.)[73] There was one full-time faculty member on the committee. The ex-faculty who were involved were men whose research careers had reached unproductive ends.[74] The later retirement and dismissal of some staff members and the subsequent placement of "minority-group members" on the committee would be required before Yale could end its forty-year chapter of sub-rosa religio-racial bias in admissions procedures.

There was one particular factor beyond Dean Howe's control that caused Yale to discriminate against poor students and because of which lower income bracket students were "just not applying" to Yale. The nation's third oldest college, which in its democratic heyday had prided itself on its low expenses and liberal financial aid policies, had become exclusionarily expensive. Financial aid was often restricted to the most outstanding of applicants, and borderline students were regularly rejected for financial reasons alone. Others were admitted without aid, only to pass frenzied undergraduate careers sacrificing all "social growth" time to the need to earn their way through the costly college. The Yale reputation of limited availability of financial aid convinced many a high school senior not to consider New Haven. A "need-blind" admissions policy that would remove financial considerations from the admissions process was required to bring the impoverished into Yale. By 1963 financial aid was promised for all Americans who needed it; wealth was no longer to serve as a crucial factor in the admissions process.[75]

THE DOOB REPORT

Of equal importance to financial aid in changing the character of Yale was a faculty study that came to be nicknamed "the Doob Report." This report arose from the growing feeling among some of the college faculty during the 1950s that the Yale undergraduate program of placing freshmen on the Old Campus under the supervision of a freshman year dean, followed by three years in one of the residential colleges, had become something of an anachronism. With a completely separate social life, the freshman year was serving less as a first year of college than as an extra year of preparatory school.[76] To evaluate the status of the freshman year, President Griswold commissioned a blue-ribbon committee in 1961 that would change the shape of Yale College. Its seven members were William Clyde DeVane, dean of Yale College; G. Evelyn Hutchinson, Sterling Professor of Zoology; John Perry Miller, incoming dean of the Yale Graduate School; Frederick A. Pottle, Sterling Professor of English; Eugene V. Rostow, dean of the Yale Law School; George A. Schrader, Jr., master of Branford College; and as chairman, Leonard W. Doob, psychology professor and former chairman of the Yale College Course of Study Committee. Each man brought to the committee a unique perspective. Since 1948 DeVane had urged the development of the intellectual side of Yale life. The brilliant Hutchinson represented the many Yale scientists who were mistrustful of Yale's emphasis in the twentieth century on the development of humanities departments. The Harvard-educated Miller was able to offer the viewpoint of a director of Yale's division of social sciences. Rostow brought his lifelong commitment to the university as an educational institution. Pottle, a deeply religious Episcopalian and a member of the Yale community since 1920, brought the perspective of one of Yale's best scholars. Schrader offered the understanding gained by a college master who had lived with Yale undergraduates. Doob brought with his intellectual prowess and devotion to Yale a reputation for being willing to fight with Griswold, if necessary.[77] The Freshman Year Committee was a group of heavyweights that could not fail to have a powerful impact upon Yale.

Doob checked with Griswold to learn just what the mandate for his committee was. "Do what you damn please!" the president responded. Doob therefore chose two areas for his committee to examine. One was the freshman year educational program; the other was the policy that led to the selection of those freshmen.[78]

Evaluating the state of Yale, the committee kept in close contact with the president. Griswold's own admissions policy statement of March 1962 reflected the early drafts of the Doob committee's study. The underlying question that motivated the committee's efforts was an echo of the Chaucerian plaint: "How shall the world be served?"[79] Even before Sputnik, some in the Yale community had argued that a Yale admissions policy dedicated to recruiting the "balanced man" was ignoring men of intelligence. Asked the *Yale Daily News* in a 1957 editorial, "Would Dostoievsky or Van Gogh have gained admission to Yale under the current conditions?" In the post-Sputnik years Americans were acutely aware that their educational system, as it had previously functioned, was, in theory, no match for modernity, because, in practice, it was no match for the Soviets. As the Second World War had forced the establishment of meritocracies in some sectors, Sputnik threatened complacency toward inadequate learning. Democracies would have to increase their respect for learning, or risk losing their cherished freedoms. The Doob committee therefore saw a need for increasing the role of formal education in the Yale mission:

> The changes wrought by time, by developments in scholarship, science, and technology, and by the position now occupied by the United States have imposed new responsibilities upon Yale and a few other comparable universities in this country. . . . Yale is no longer an 18th-century academy or a 19th-century college but is a university of the 20th-century in one of the great nations. Under these conditions the task of advancing knowledge and of training future scholars must be emphasized. . . .
>
> We must view the whole educational process as a more mature and serious undertaking not only for those students who will join the learned professions, but also for those who will enter business, industry, or government. For the improvement of our national culture, as well as for the good name of Yale, the students we educate should exemplify and radiate the power and grace of learning. More of the graduates of Yale College, we think, must become professional scholars and teachers. It is incumbent upon Yale and similar institutions consciously to increase the number and proportion of learned men in our society.[80]

In light of the faculty opinion that "Yale is first and foremost an intellectual enterprise," changes recommended in admissions centered on attracting students of intellectual distinction.[81] Suspicious of the admissions office staff, committee members first suggested that Yale College admissions become a part of the administrative structure of Yale College—in order to match the model extant in the rest of Yale's schools. President Griswold, however, warned Doob to permit the president to keep his personal control over the process. Consequently, the committee suggested that the faculty play a more active role in the recruitment and selection of students. Finally, Doob's committee called for the dissolution of the separate Freshman Year program and, almost parenthetically, the admission of women as undergraduates.[82] On April 13, 1962, the Doob report was officially released.[83]

The university college ideal had come of age, and the Doob report demanded that the ideal be upheld. The report effectively called for tremendous changes in the physical and philosophical status of Yale College. From Professor Doob's point of view the most important aspects of the report concerned the dissolution of the Freshman Year program and placing greater emphasis on the intellect in Yale admissions. Because there were strong vested interests among some faculty in preserving the Freshman Year, Doob pressed the faculty to discuss the admission of women. This smokescreen, he hoped, would deflect faculty attention from what he saw as the urgent recommendations of the report. Doob's hopes came to fruition. The energy that was spent in the discussion of Yale's preserving its inviolate maleness left little spirit for fighting over the other important aspects of the report. On May 19, with the endorsement of the faculty and President Griswold, the Yale Corporation approved all measures that the report had recommended for immediate attention. The curriculum was to have a more scholarly emphasis. More intellectually oriented students were to be admitted. The faculty's role on the board of admissions was to be increased. Freshmen would be affiliated with residential colleges from their first days at Yale, and the separate Freshman Year was to become history. The principle of admitting women was accepted, but the lack of financial resources to admit women in more than token numbers without reducing the number of men admitted would delay the actual admission of women until more turbulent times forced the issue.[84] As the Doob report assumed reality, the twentieth-century integration of university ideals into collegiate mores became complete.

By reaching out to the best public high school students of the nation— whom Yale College admissions officers had often missed in recruitment efforts—Yale was earnestly to try and attract the nation's best talent. Some children of multimillionaires, congressmen, and the like continued to be admitted, primarily for the social prestige, political clout, and financial wherewithal they brought to the college. But training future Nobel prize winners and America's intellectual leaders was to be valued as highly as training the nation's social, political, or business leadership long had been. By raising academic standards for admission, by raising intellectual standards within the college, by turning the college into more of what Kingman Brewster later termed a "pressure cooker," Yale hoped that even the children of patricians would be graduated from Yale better prepared to serve and guide the nation.[85]

THE SIXTIES

This is not the place to rehearse the profound changes that the structure of American society experienced in the 1960s. Suffice it to say that the opening of Yale society hardly took place in a vacuum. Americans of the time realized that they were living in an era of unusual opportunity for the inclusion of those whom society had long excluded. In the 1960s, doors that had been opened with some resistance a decade earlier were thrown wide open. With the exception of some socially aberrant clubs that continued to bar groups such as blacks and Jews, the once-universal racial discrimination moved from being unfashionable to being abominable. Even Yale's traditional conservatism would not restrain the university from fighting discrimination in that era. The *Yale Daily News,* once a bastion of campus conservatism, in some years of the 1960s was a great champion of social reforms.[86]

By 1960 the university housing bureau, fighting the widespread denial of New Haven housing to blacks, required that all landlords who listed property with Yale pledge not to discriminate between prospective tenants on the basis of race, creed, color, or national origin. Despite the actions of 572 landlords (a few of whom were Jewish) who removed their properties from the Yale rolls, the university refused to be a party to unfair bias. When a black drama student complained to President Griswold in 1962 that the prejudice of New Haven landlords prevented his finding a local apartment, Griswold, the busy officer, pledged his personal help to resolve the situation.[87]

After the student sit-in movement began in a Greensboro, North Carolina, Woolworth store, students across the nation became aware of their own powers for remolding the society of their parents. Largely, they were honoring the inspiration of the nation's president. Historian Calvin B. T. Lee described the impact on American college life that came from the 1961 inauguration of John F. Kennedy:

> Here was a symbol not only of youthfulness but also of idealism and commitment. . . . When Kennedy introduced the Peace Corps, he was challenging the student generation. When Kennedy spoke of discrimination and racial prejudice, he was speaking to the college generation who wanted to do something about it. When Kennedy spoke the words of his inaugural speech, "Ask not what your country can do for you, ask what you can do for your country," he spoke to the student generation—and they followed him.[88]

In like manner, the Reverend William Sloane Coffin captured the imagination of Yale students and the attention of the nation in 1962. With his battle against bias at Yale already fought, Coffin took his show on the road. As a leading "Freedom Rider," Coffin made himself directly, and Yale indirectly, a symbol of justice in America.[89]

Whatever ambiguities that remained at the beginning of the 1960s in the

Yale attitude toward social justice were wiped away by the vision of the man who led Yale through the 1960s and early 1970s. Kingman Brewster, Jr., provost of the university at the time of President Griswold's death in April 1963, inherited Griswold's place as a spokesman for American education. Cut from the same patrician cloth as previous Yale presidents, Brewster uniquely made some aspects of social justice part of his agenda.

Heir apparent to the presidency at the time of Griswold's death, Brewster (B.A. 1941) had had a distinguished undergraduate record. As an editor of the *News,* he had resigned the Zeta Psi fraternity presidency in order to gain the freedom to criticize the fraternity system. Later named chairman of the *News* and approached to become a member of Skull and Bones, Brewster, who had no personal interest in the trappings of the secret societies, achieved a level of social eliteness even higher than the secret societies when he turned down a place in the most prestigious undergraduate association.[90]

Brewster saw it as his duty as president of one of a few nationally recognized universities to speak out on moral issues that had a pervasive impact upon his community. While President Johnson spoke of the Great Society and President Nixon promised law and order, Brewster spoke of the draft, civil rights, and the government's role in education. Though he hated to provoke the wrath of Yale alumni, Brewster enjoyed the controversies he sometimes helped foster at Yale. A community filled with frank discussion, Brewster thought, would be a better place in which to be educated. He would have his disagreements with the liberal Mr. Coffin, but after each "knock-down, drag-out fight" with the chaplain, Brewster would support Coffin all the more. Importantly, Brewster won the support of the Yale Corporation trustees when he took stands on controversial issues. So it was that when the turmoil of the late 1960s struck the Yale campus, events transpired rather calmly in comparison with elsewhere. Thinking that Brewster had a sincere commitment to justice, knowing that the outspoken Coffin enjoyed the president's trust, even the most radical Yale students of the era could still love Yale. Students revolting against "the Establishment" had little anger toward Yale, for under Brewster's deft leadership, the "Yale Establishment" was, largely, on their side.[91]

Brewster was a firm opponent of religious and racial discrimination. Though he did not approach the public in the way that Ralph Bunche had in 1959, when a Forest Hills tennis club had excluded his son apparently on racial grounds, Brewster made it his personal practice to refuse to participate in social and educational functions at locations that practiced such discrimination. For example, when he learned that the University Club of New York refused to accept blacks, he (and representatives of other institutions) arranged for meetings of the Association of American Universities to be moved out of that facility. This action was not taken in the face of any particular pressure from black groups, Brewster recalled. It was simply a matter of new sensitivities that Yale and other universities were beginning to develop. In late 1965, when a Yale alumni meeting was scheduled for early 1966 in the racially restrictive Duquesne Club of Pittsburgh, a letter of protest followed by alumnus Alexander Lowenthal (B.A. 1920). Brewster supported moving the venue of the meeting as a sign of displeasure with that club's policies and assured Lowenthal that Yale gatherings should be held in places that "are open to all" Yale alumni. During the years that the hotels of Atlanta practiced racial segregation, Brewster refused to travel to that city.[92] While Coffin railed against bigotry, Brewster quietly avoided it outside of Yale and actively worked to remove its influence within Yale.

Recognizing the need for increased government financial support if Yale was to maintain its standing relative to other universities, Brewster increasingly concerned himself with obtaining federal funds and with examining the implications of governmental support of a private university. One obvious corollary was that the Johnson administration in Washington was not about to fund an institution that practiced unfair discrimination. Had there been no other reason to remove bias from Yale except the mercenary reason, it would have been a forceful incentive. When Brewster's 1964 inauguration was preceded by a symposium on the relationship of the university to the federal government, Brewster was acknowledging the tremendous role that federal money had come to play at Yale in the Griswold years. Between 1950 and 1960 the contribution of federal money to the Yale budget had risen from 2 percent of the total to 18 percent. Over the following decade, that proportion would rise to 28 percent,[93] as Brewster convinced his faculty and his trustees that it was necessary to expand and upgrade the university educationally. Even if such an expansion meant the deficit-spending of monies that were still part of fund-raisers' dreams, Brewster was certain that it was unrealistic to expect the government to invest in a second-rate institution.[94] And expand Yale, he did.

One means of expansion was through the admissions office. Shortly after Brewster's inauguration, Dean Howe resigned his Yale position to head the American Field Service. In his stead, Brewster called on A. Rufus Hyatt (B.A. 1918) to serve as the acting dean of admissions. Inaugurating a need-blind admission and an open financial aid policy—following a course set by Dean Howe before he left—Hyatt set about to publicize Yale's new attitude. No longer, the word spread forth from New Haven, would lack of financial backing harm a candidate's chances for admission, his ability to afford college, or his social success at Yale. The dream once envisioned by the bursary system was finally turned into reality. Well-paying on-campus jobs or generous loans would be available to *all* who needed them.[95] Renewal of Yale scholarships had previously required recipients to be in the academic top quarter of their class or, if they were making a substantial contribution to Yale social life, in the top half. In the 1960s, standards were liberalized so that the only requirement for renewal was that one remain a student in good standing.[96] Every Yale student would finally have the opportunity to play a meaningful part in the Yale extracurricular life.

At a crucial juncture in American and Yale history the interim appointment of Hyatt gave Brewster a year in which to ponder carefully over what he expected of Yale admissions and the man who would head it. That eventful year of 1964 saw the passage of the Civil Rights Act that legislated against unfair discrimination by prohibiting federal funding of any academic institution that practiced discrimination on the basis of race, color, or national origin. The man Brewster chose to reshape Yale admissions policies in the light of that act and Yale's reemphasized university college ideals was R. Inslee "Inky" Clark, Jr. (B.A. 1957). A Protestant, born in Brooklyn, raised on Long Island, and a graduate of a public high school, Clark brought an atypical background to the Yale admissions office. His mother had attended Vassar; his father was a self-made businessman who had never attended college. As a Yale College student, Clark had been shocked by the great proportion of "mediocre" students that populated the campus. This memory was to influence his own attitudes toward admissions. Appointed by Dean Howe in 1961 as an assistant director of undergraduate admissions and freshman scholarships, Clark as the junior member was required during his first years on the admissions committee to handle recruiting and interviewing for the two regions of the nation that he was told were the "crummiest": the northwest and the New York City–Long Island districts. The northwest was affectionately tagged as "the boondocks," because there were few Yale alumni to socialize with "and no posh hotels to stay in." The New York City–Long Island territory was considered "the jungle," because it contained so many schools and so many Yale applicants. Clark, a New Yorker at heart, relished the opportunity to be responsible for his native territory. But from his assignment to the northwest and the New York City areas, Clark guessed that his fellow admissions officers were often more interested in the accoutrements of their work than in the recruitment of the best students.

Following Dean Howe's resignation, President Brewster, who knew Clark by name but was not personally close to him, invited the admissions officer to describe his perception of the ideal Yale. To the young Clark, "Yale was a special place," which needed a stronger group of students to inhabit it. As one of a handful of internationally renowned centers of learning with the outstanding faculty, library, laboratories, and support services to back the learning up, Yale, Clark felt, had an obligation to serve the nation by admitting the students who could most benefit from Yale. These were to be "the most able, the most motivated, those with the most potential to succeed." Such thoughts were music to the president's ears. For Brewster, the purpose of Yale was to help students "develop an interest and a capacity for continuous learning and to teach students the enjoyment of intellectual and aesthetic experiences." The students that he saw Yale as ideal for were those with the motivation to make the most of its resources and then put their learning to good use for society. If that talent was not yet applying to Yale, Clark said that he was committed to searching it out. Though in later years Brewster would sometimes regret some of Clark's strident rhetoric, the policies of R. Inslee Clark—Bones man, dean of admissions from 1965 through 1970—earned the full support of his president.[97]

Clark's first act as dean was to redefine the composition of the team entrusted to carry out admissions policy. Responding to the concerns expressed in the Doob Report, President Brewster, in concert with Clark and with Yale College's Dean Georges May, moved to appoint active faculty to serve as recruiters and readers for the admissions office. Other faculty were appointed to an advisory committee that gave them a direct voice in determining the general guidelines of Yale admissions. The faculty thereby obtained a meaningful opportunity with which to wage their campaign for a diversified character within the student body and improved average scholastic ability. With Brewster's permission, Clark substantially replaced the staff working in the admissions office and doubled the staff size to fifteen. In the first of many actions that provoked charges of heresy by some on the campus, Clark hired non-Yale graduates to serve among the Yale graduates on the committee. The insular Yale style was under its last siege. Recognizing that some subtle prejudices were maintained by even the most broad-minded members of the human species, Clark purposely hired a black to be part of the committee. Thereby, Clark felt, a necessary perspective would be part of all committee decisions.[98]

Dean Clark and his team were then ready to work. The larger staff made greater recruiting efforts possible. High schools across the nation that Yale had once ignored, particularly inner-city high schools, received representatives of the Yale College admissions staff. In 1959 Dean Howe had explained that southern high schools with predominantly black populations were often not visited by Yale recruiters, because "you can't make those alumni go to places they don't want to go to." In the Clark era, recruiting was expanded to include previously snubbed locations. Approaching these institutions for the first time, the Yale representatives had been instructed by Clark to apologize for the past and promise that Yale wanted their very best students: "It was our fault [for ignoring you] and we'll prove to you that we're interested by coming back each year." Clark then took the lead in inviting the admissions directors at Harvard and Princeton to drop the "A, B, C" system by which preparatory school applications were given an advantage in college admissions. In that year of 1965 the Princeton admissions director agreed to go along with Clark in this action. From that moment prep school applicants would have to compete for admission to Yale on the same terms as public school graduates. Many a prep school headmaster was saddened by the change in procedure, though most accepted the philosophical rationale behind the action. Vying for places on equal terms, the public school graduates rose from 44 percent of the entering freshmen in 1960 to 58 percent in 1970. According to J. Richardson Dilworth, Corporation fellow, the Civil Rights movement had succeeded in attuning the Yale community to the needs of the republic. Dean Howe recalled Griswold's telling him of being called by President Kennedy to Washington, where Kennedy implored the leaders of the nation's great universities to bring "minorities" into their ranks. The hour was late, but the university leadership had finally become conscious of the inherent contradictions between democracy and exclusivity. Yale had long paid homage to the myth of democracy. It was time to put more substance behind the myth. Some of the clublike nature of the college was to be sacrificed for the national good and for the name of Yale. Believing in an open American society, the university set about to include members of various races in the leadership elite that it was trying to produce. Particular efforts were begun to recruit three of the minority groups that in the 1960s were at the bottom of American society: blacks, Mexican Americans, and Puerto Ricans. The intent was not to lower standards of quality, but to call Yale to the attention of talented students of all backgrounds.[99] Clark expanded a recruitment plan that had tentatively begun under Arthur Howe's leadership. In the 1950s Dean Howe had considered it unethical for a dean of admissions to countenance the recruitment of any one particular type of student. Inspired by Kennedy and Griswold, by the 1961–62 school year Howe had directed Charles McCarthy (B.A. 1960) to begin work on a "talent searching" program. McCarthy's work was admired so much that other Ivy League colleges asked Dean Howe to have

McCarthy expand his recruitment program so that it would advertise the entire league. This scheme was, in effect, the forerunner of what later was to be called affirmative action. Ivy League admissions officers visited high schools with large black populations, especially in the south and in the nation's big cities. Their noble, if patronizing, goal was to recruit applications "from promising students, however limited their backgrounds may be."[100] In 1964 Howe helped organize a summer program that brought talented students from mediocre high schools across the nation to Yale for a disciplined preparatory school atmosphere. According to one administrator of the program, the vast majority of summer "graduates" were eventually accepted at much better colleges than they otherwise might have attended. The changing environment increased the number of black applicants to Yale from 37 in 1960 to 163 in 1968. When women were permitted to apply to enter Yale College in 1969, the number of black applicants increased to 525. Paralleling a nationwide pattern of black entrance to institutions of higher education, the matriculating proportion of Yale that was black increased from approximately 1 percent in 1963 to 9 percent in 1970.[101]

The renewed emphasis upon obtaining talented students and the vigorous attempt to recruit students from schools where Yale had never searched before had a profound effect upon Jewish enrollment in the college. Jews, like blacks, began to apply to Yale in greater numbers. Brewster's emphasis on bringing in actors, artists, and musicians influenced admissions officers to look for more than class presidents, valedictorians, and athletes. The desire to admit racial minority group members also encouraged admissions officers to appreciate nontraditional forms of achievement. Dean Clark recalled the change: "Nobody came to my office screaming for more Jews. It was just a matter of natural selection. When we were picking that first class in 1965, no one counted Jews, but I knew that [the Jewish enrollment] was going up. It had to."[102] Brewster later noted that the place of Jewry at Yale was not a significant issue for him, nor a conscious concern. The dual goals of including minority groups and attracting a diversity of talent forced Yale to accept students it once might have rejected. Catholic and Italian enrollment also apparently increased as Yale recruiters targeted more of the nation's schools. If the college was to accept the highest ranked black at the Bronx High School of Science (for example, let us say that he ranked tenth in his class), then the admissions officers were forced to accept many of the students who had a higher class rank. Had they been rejected, a publicly embarrassing double standard would have been created. The Jewish enrollment consequently came close to doubling in one year, reflecting

Jewish performance and interest in higher education and the fact that by this era the majority of American Jews were no longer poor and were fully Americanized. Although the rise of religious intermarriage and the decrease in Jewish identification make exact quantification difficult, it was estimated that for the following three decades the Jewish undergraduate proportion would remain near the one-quarter level.[103]

The changing pattern of admissions was welcomed by most segments of the Yale community, with the vocal exception of a narrow-minded, small proportion of the Yale alumni. Disappointed by the failure of their progeny to gain admission to Yale College, this group of individuals, searching for convenient excuses to withhold financial support from the university, attacked the admissions policies of Dean Clark and President Brewster. Clark's blunt statements that mediocre children of alumni would have little chance of acceptance further ruffled the feathers of the disgruntled alums. The statistics show, however, that in decreasing the bias that the admissions staff had shown for "legacies," Dean Clark was merely continuing a trend that had been set in motion by Dean Howe and President Griswold in 1962, when the president and the Doob committee began to insist that Yale was preeminently an intellectual enterprise. The class of 1961, 24 percent of which entered as sons of Yale College alumni, was the last to benefit from an overwhelming bias for alumni children. The class of 1966, the first to be admitted under Griswold's 1962 policy directive, had its legacy proportion reduced to 19 percent. The drop in legacy representation that Dean Clark's first class would see was small compared to what already had taken place under Griswold. Nevertheless, the drop was real. Under Dean Clark, children of alumni faced two pressures that they had not previously faced. (It must be realized that these pressures only reduced a bias *in favor* of alumni children; there was no bias *against* alumni children.) First, the increased pool of applicants led to a higher standard for admissions than previous Yale applicants had had to face. Second, Clark arranged that alumni children would only receive "one break" in the admissions process. In competition with applicants of equal caliber, the alumni children would be favored, but alumni sons who did not survive the competition with other applicants were no longer admitted. Some of the wealthier alumni were also upset by the need-blind admissions policy. One university administrator explained the origins of their resentment: "As soon as you say you'll admit people without regard to need, you effectively say that you'll dismiss many traditional Yalies, and take others in their place." For all these reasons the proportion of children of Yale College alumni dropped below 15 percent in Clark's first class (of 1970). The class of

1971 had a 12 percent legacy enrollment—a level which obtained through the class of 1976.[104] Beginning with the class of 1977 (enrolled in 1973), family connections and financial exigencies were again permitted to influence Yale admissions. As a result, the proportion of alumni children was permitted steadily to return by 1980 to the levels standard in the years prior to Griswold's 1962 admissions directive.[105]

Because Dean Howe and President Griswold had acted silently and Dean Clark had moved noisily, at times caustically, some alumni held the Brewster administration fully responsible for their children's own failures to make good. Pierson has noted that the parents of the 1960s were from classes with unusually high proportions of legacies. Consequently, many double-generation Yale families may have been particularly offended by the tighter admissions policies.[106] When Rabbi Israel's successor as Hillel director at Yale, Arnold Jacob Wolf, revealed to the alumni the increased proportion of Jewish undergraduates at Yale in 1973, a hidden trove of anti-Jewish feeling erupted.[107] One typical reaction to the news was published in the pages of the *Yale Alumni Magazine*:

I must admit . . . that I was shocked to learn that the majority of Yale students today are Jewish, insofar as denominations are concerned. I do not know the denomination of Chaplain Coffin but I am quite sure he is not Jewish. If what I am told is true, then it seems reasonable that Coffin should resign and Rabbi Wolf, or his equivalent, be named the Yale Chaplain. The last issue [of the *Yale Alumni Magazine*] spark-plugged letters like the following:

"Dear Dick: In the January issue of *YAM* is an article . . . by the rabbi appointed apparently by the Hillel people and [it] is very well written from the Jewish standpoint. Jewish students at Yale are now in the majority. . . .

"This imbalance is the result achieved by Clark and his extremists who made up the team admitting students to the Freshman Class a few years ago. They turned down scores of sons of Yale men who richly deserved to succeed their fathers and scoured the ghettos of New York and elsewhere to recruit freshmen. That is what has today made Yale a Jewish university. . . .

"I number many fine Jewish gentlemen among my good friends and the only thing I have against their religion is their rabid segregation. I do not know a single Jew who doesn't have a Jewish doctor, a Jewish dentist, a Jewish lawyer, and a Jewish accountant, as well as a Jewish wife. Rabbi Wolf, in his article, openly preaches the Jewish segregation. He states, for example: 'Half the kids who come to see me are inquiring about prospective marriage to a non-Jew and are more or less surprised that I cannot endorse their nuptial plans.' He states that Yom Kippur fills the Law School auditorium beyond its legal capacity, which probably means that every other lawyer graduating from Yale from now on will be Jewish.

"These facts are why . . . I cannot go along with your thoughts that I should help support Yale of today. The place we knew and loved has been wrecked by three men, Brewster, Coffin, and Clark. Let them look to those they have recruited for the money to run Yale today. It saddens me to prophesy that Yale will soon be just another public institution, thanks to the lack of foresight of the Corporation and the wilfulness of three men, who have made Yale a Jewish haven. I write you thusly so you . . . will know why I am today supporting to the best of my ability those colleges which my grandsons have been forced to attend."[108]

The "Jewish denomination," of course, was not a majority. It was a plurality when compared with individual denominations such as Episcopalians, Presbyterians, Methodists, Baptists, and Roman Catholics. There were still far more Christians at Yale than Jews, however. Had the "Jewish denomination" been divided up among Reform, Conservative, and Orthodox Jews, even the supposed plurality would have dissipated. Yet for the substantial minority of bitter Yale alumni with deep-seated prejudices against Jews and other groups such as blacks and Hispanics, the open and democratic Yale of Brewster, Clark, and Coffin was not one that they could support. So the liberal attitudes of Yale's president, chaplain, and chief admissions officer cost the university millions of dollars in lost donations.[109]

In a sequence of events that has been discussed at length elsewhere, the "last" category of discrimination in admissions that Yale would face also came to a head during Dean Clark's tenure. After a pitched emotional battle between students, administrators, and alumni, Yale College opened its doors to women. Accepting the philosophy that the duty of a university college was to educate all of the nation's most talented (at a time when the women's equality movement was taking shape in the nation), the idea of excluding women became unpalatable to most segments of the Yale community. The greatest barrier of discrimination began to be torn down on November 9, 1968, when the Yale Corporation approved a co-educational program to begin with the next academic year.[110]

As women were first counted on a quota system, as athletes were counted to assure respectable teams, as "underprivileged minorities" were counted to ensure certain minimums, as Jews overlapped with all of these groups, as intermarriage and assimilatory trends made Jews harder to identify, as the number of Yale applicants approached the ten thousand per annum mark, as bigots were fired or retired from the admission staff and replaced by a multi-racial and multi-religious group, the idea of keeping track of Jewish enrollment became not just repugnant but preposterous. Religion was no longer an issue. Although the Brewster-Clark changes in admissions proved expensive and served to alienate some alumni, these alterations marked the optimistic quest for excellence and open opportunity that symbolized the university of the 1960s.

1. Judah P. Benjamin, Yale Class of 1829, later Secretary of State of the Confederacy. Manuscripts and Archives, Yale University Library.

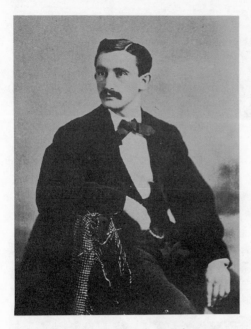

2. Lewis R. Ehrich (B.A. 1869), 1868 photo

3. Sigmund Waterman (Instructor in German, 1844–47)

4. Student room of Lafayette B. Mendel (B.A. 1891)

5. Professor Lafayette B. Mendel (B.A. 1891, Ph.D. 1894) at his desk. Manuscripts and Archives, Yale University Library

6. Dean Milton C. Winternitz

7. Paul Weiss honored in Jan. 1963, photo depicts from left to right, Rev. William Sloane Coffin, Jr. (B.A. 1949, B.D. 1956), Paul Weiss, Martin Gordon (M.D. 1946), Rabbi Richard Israel. Manuscripts and Archives, Yale University Library

RAM'S HORN

PUBLISHED BY THE B'NAI B'RITH HILLEL FOUNDATION AT YALE

Vol. 4, No. 3   NEW HAVEN, CONNECTICUT   FEBRUARY, 1953

JEWISH APPEAL DRIVE BEGINS

MYRON CONOVITZ ELECTED NEW PRESIDENT

by A. Greenberg

On January 12th, 1953 the annual election of officers took place in the Dwight Hall Common Room. The meeting presided over by the out-going president Don Sheff, 1953, saw Myron Conovitz, 1954, elected as the new president for the coming year.

Conovitz has been one of the outstanding members of Hillel for the past few years. His contributions to Hillel have been outstanding. His last formal position in the organization before being elected president was that of forum chairman. In that position Conovitz displayed remarkable talent. His quick thinking and outstanding character helped to make each and every forum an evening well spent. In addition to this trait, Conovitz has been successful in obtaining for the forums the finest speakers available. One has only to look at the group of speakers he has obtained, to understand why the forums have become the most stimulating part of Hillel activities.

MEL PERLMAN ELECTED FIRST VICE-PRESIDENT

The office of first vice-president went to Mel Perleman, 1955. Mel is a relative new-comer to Yale Hillel. He is one of the group of enthusiastic sophomores who have been taking over the reins of the organization from the outgoing officers. Mel, a very active member of Hillel, has as his most important contribution to Hillel, the wonderful Jewish folk dances that he has been conducting after services on Friday night.

(Continued on page 4)

WILL HERBERG
Author of "Judaism and Modern Man"

Noted Author To Address Hillel Forum

by J. Joseph

One of the outstanding highlights on the 1953 Yale Hillel program, and indeed on the Yale campus this Spring term, will be the arrival on the scene of Mr. Will Herberg, dynamic, controversial figure in contemporary Jewish philosophy and theology. Mr. Herberg will be here on Monday, February 23rd, to address a regular Hillel Forum in Dwight Hall Common Room at 8:00 on the topic: "Faith and Life: An Existential Approach to Jewish Religion," and to conduct an informal seminar on his views that afternoon from 4:30 to 6:00 in the same room.

(Continued on page 3)

YALE JEWISH APPEAL DRIVE GETS FULL COOPERATION OF BURSAR'S OFFICE

by A. Tobias

To many Jewish D.P.'s struggling desperately to survive the persecutions inflicted both by nature and men, their transplantation from Europe to Israel must have undoubtedly seemed to them to be the work of a miracle. And this would require no stretch of the imagination either. For the nature of the work carried on by the Joint Distribution Committee can be justly described as life-saving, wherein miracles are most apt to lie.

This year the Hillel Yale Jewish Appeal has been fortunate enough to be placed on the Bursars list. With this privilege all Yale students who are contributing to the drive have a choice. They may either make their donation in cash, or they may have their donation put on their bursar's bill. This is the first year that this has been done, so, now's your chance to contribute to a cause that really needs your help.

The achievements of this agency throughout its existence have been phenominal. Wherever the need has been greatest, the J.D.C. has always been on the job, getting things done swiftly and effectively despite cost and danger. The risks taken by its agents in effecting the escape of Jews stamped by Hitler and his disciples for persecution or extermination would comprise volumes of gripping drama. After the war, with the same dauntless, energetic zeal, the Committee undertook the tremendous task of re-settling and providing for thousands of Jewish D.P.'s in addition to its efforts to secure Israel as the national Jewish homeland. At the same time the status of Jews in the Communist countries continued to grow progressively worse. Rising to meet the emergency, the Com-

(Continued from page 2)

9. William Horowitz (B.A. 1929), Louis Rabinowitz, President A. Whitney Griswold (B.A. 1929, Ph.D. 1933) (Photo ca. 1960). Manuscripts and Archives, Yale University Library

10. Dean Eugene V. Rostow (B.A. 1933, LL.B. 1937)

11. Dean Florence S. Wald (M.N. 1941, M.S. 1956), 1958 photo.
Manuscripts and Archives, Yale University Library

12. Yale Corporation meeting in Woodbridge Hall (Photo ca. 1967)

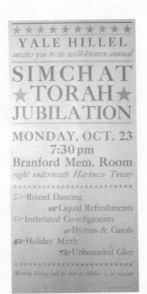

13. Announcement of Simchat Torah Celebration (1978). Reproduced with the permission of David S. Rose (B.A. 1979) and Pierson Press.

14. Yale Seal, from the 1978 Presidential Inauguration
Program of A. Bartlett Giamatti (B.A. 1960, Ph.D. 1964)

15. Rabbi Laurie Rutenberg (1981 photo). Manuscripts and Archives, Yale University Library

16. Rabbi James Ponet (B.A. 1968), photo by Harold Shapiro

17. President Richard C. Levin (M.Ph. 1972, Ph.D. 1974), photo by Michael Marsland

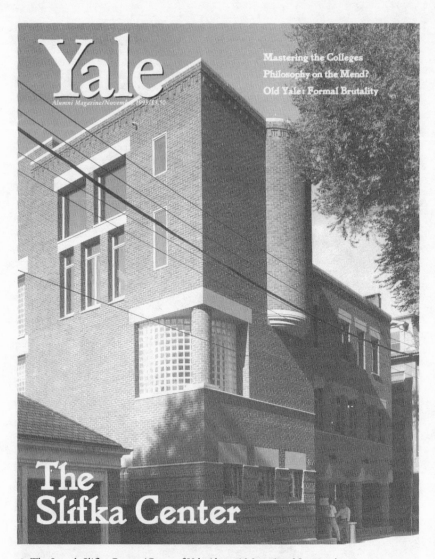

Yale

Alumni Magazine/November 1995/$3.50

Mastering the Colleges
Philosophy on the Mend?
Old Yale: Formal Brutality

The
Slifka Center

18. The Joseph Slifka Center (Cover of Yale Alumni Magazine, Nov. 1995)

Chapter 10 Hillel

With Christian efforts at Yale concentrating in the university ministry and in the divinity school after the Second World War, other segments of university life took on an increasingly secular nature. Evolutionary accommodation allowed for acceptance of an increasing variety of faiths. But, given the diverse religious backgrounds of the Yale students, at no time was the changing status of religion at Yale acceptable to all. From one viewpoint in 1951 William F. Buckley, Jr., a Catholic, argued that Yale had lost its Christian nature. Few professors were conspicuously pro-Christian, he lamented.[1] Conversely, as late as the 1970s, a Jew might look at "Christian Yale" and feel alienated. One Jewish alumnus of the class of 1974 would later recall that there was "something in the architecture of the buildings, the alcoholic oriented socializing, the reserve, that made me realize that I . . . had no place I felt comfortable acknowledging my Jewishness."[2] Another Jew defensively would see the singing of Puritan hymns at university assemblies as an "attempt to deny me what I proudly called my immigrant origins."[3] Many a Protestant in the middle might resort to a "Yale, love it or leave it" argument. Following the publication of Buckley's *God and*

Man at Yale, for example, the Reverend Henry Sloane Coffin (B.A. 1897, M.A. 1900, Fellow of the Yale Corporation 1922–45) was reported to have expressed the ornery conviction that "Yale is a Puritan and Protestant institution by its heritage and [Buckley] should have attended Fordham or some similar institution."[4] To some extent there was legitimacy in Coffin's words. The university had made no secret of its origins or of its religious philosophies and traditions. No one was forced to attend Yale, and a candidate accepted by Yale almost always could have found other similarly respectable universities with more suitable religious characters. There were, as well, other universities with "warmer" atmospheres and less alcohol. If Yale was not Christian enough, or was too Christian for a student, it was partially his own fault for not doing his homework before choosing Yale. Yet part of the complaint of the religiously disgruntled was a natural consequence of Yale's ambiguous removal of its Protestant robes. In the eighteenth century Yale had stood for a specific brand of Congregational Protestant Christianity. The college was open to members of all faiths, but the terms of education were clear: a solid foundation in Christianity for all. In the nineteenth century the terms were no less plain: Members of all faiths were permitted to observe their own religious customs, but the curriculum was prescribed. When Yale College abandoned its mandatory course in Christianity (1890) and mandatory chapel (1925), whatever was left of the formal Christian nature of Yale was allowed to dissolve. By the 1940s Yale was trying simultaneously to mix Christian-spirited traditions with completely secular practices. And because the university tried to straddle both sides of a tension-bound fence, inconsistencies arose and the expectations of members of the campus community became impossible to meet consistently. Not wanting to alienate any constituency unnecessarily and thereby hesitating to publicly enunciate its goals, the university gradually moved toward the position spelled out in President Griswold's policy directive of 1961. (See chapter 9.) The Protestant Yale tradition was to be valued in the Yale Church of Christ and in the divinity school, but the university was to incorporate a multitude of faiths into its patterns.

An inherent irony in the discomfort that some of the Jewish students felt with the university's Christian symbolism was the fact that these Jews had by their practices cast away symbolic traditions that their ancestors had followed for generations and therefore were resentful that Yale was retaining a handful of symbolic traditions of its own.

The attempt to relieve such discomforts and to help Jewish students find renewed meanings in their ancient religion was the essence of the B'nai B'rith

Hillel Foundations that were founded on college campuses across the nation. Like most religious enterprises in America, their record of achievement in the postwar era was mixed. In this chapter the successes and failures of postwar Yale Hillel will be reviewed.

1944–1959

An account has been left of the attitudes of Yale Jewish students during the Second World War in the form of a study undertaken by Rabbi Meyer Greenberg of Hillel in fall, 1944. Greenberg began his study by obtaining an apparently incomplete list of the Jewish college students from the university chaplain's office. To this roster he added a few students who were of Jewish parentage but had registered with the university as having either no religious preference or a non-Jewish religious preference. Those who would not publicly admit that they were "members of the Jewish group" were excluded from the study. Greenberg discovered that Yale's Jews were not representative of America Jewry or of American Jewish university students. Most Yale Jews of 1944 came from upper middle class homes; most American Jews as a whole had not yet reached this class. Yale's Jews ranked higher in intelligence than other Yale students and than Jewish students at most colleges since they had to fulfill especially high academic requirements to gain admission. Most were already second generation Americans. Of those with foreign-born parents, the majority came from East Europe. Their attitudes were not uniform. Almost half thought that being Jewish had a worthwhile effect on their daily lives, while a quarter thought that assimilation into the surrounding peoples was the best solution to the Jewish problem then troubling the world. Many of these latter students, Greenberg noted, actively practiced the assimilation that they preached. In general, though, Greenberg believed that "the students are generally tolerant of religion and do not oppose it for those who wish to observe, but they are lacking in interest personally." Eighty-two percent thought that "every Jewish child should receive an elementary Jewish education." Reform and Conservative Jews made up 74 percent of the Jewish students, and 16 percent came from Orthodox homes. Only 10 percent of the Jewish students indicated no affiliation with a branch of American Judaism—a proportion extremely low in comparison with trends among American Jews of the 1940s. Greenberg consequently suggested that Yale students' coming from a social class where "it is customary to have at least nominal affiliation with some religious group" might have explained this result. Though normative Orthodox, Conservative, and Reform Judaism then saw no place for religious intermarriages, 47 percent of Yale's Jewish students raised no objections to intermarriage. Greenberg's doleful conclusion was that in the future up to half of the Jewish students at Yale would "try to dissociate themselves from Jewish life and participate in as few Jewish activities as social pressure [would] allow."[5]

During the difficult war years, with the minds of most students on the war and on the accelerated curriculum, many of Yale's extracurricular organizations struggled to maintain their ranks. Hillel was no exception. Very few students were interested in Jewish cultural or intellectual activities; only tension-relieving social events such as dances with local girls met with success.[6]

In 1945 Rabbi Samuel Sandmel (Ph.D. 1949) was installed as the new Hillel director. Yale provided him an office with several rooms in the Lawrance Hall basement, and the Hillel organization came alive. A nucleus of some fifteen to twenty involved students organized many programs.[7] Hillel steadily gained respectability, so that on the national organization's twenty-fifth anniversary in 1949 the *Yale Daily News* praised the local group in an editorial entitled "For the Hillel Foundation":

> The extent of Hillel's activities on the campus is impressive. For in addition to providing the Jewish student with religious counsel, the Foundation has sought to indoctrinate him in the ancient culture of his faith, whose significance pervades our civilization.[8]

Much of Hillel's prosperity was attributed to its adult leader:

> We find it impossible to disassociate the present success of the group from the personality of its director, Rabbi Sandmel. His interest in his work, his unrelenting sympathy for individual problems, his enlightened aggressiveness and clairvoyance have made the Hillel group all the more meaningful to Jewish students.[9]

Under Rabbi Sandmel's direction, the accomplishments of Hillel were considerable. In 1948 Hillel at Yale and *Commentary* magazine—edited by Elliot Cohen—sponsored a conference in New Haven on "The Role of the Creative Mind in America." Guest speakers included Nathan Glazer, Oscar Handlin, and Sidney Hook.[10] Of a more continuous nature were the Harvard-Yale Hillel Colloquia that Sandmel and Harvard's Hillel director, Rabbi Harry Essrig, organized in 1947. First held at Yale, the colloquia represented a serious attempt to generate a student conference on the meaning of Judaism. The theme of the first meeting was "Towards an Ideology for American Jews." As part of a revival of Zionist fervor among students, the colloquium discussed the Palestine crisis on the eve of the declaration of the state of Israel in 1948. The conference was expanded in 1950 to include Princeton, and, to meet student demand, women from neighboring colleges such as Wellesley, Vassar, Lesley, Hunter, Smith, and Radcliffe were welcomed in 1951.[11] The popular colloquia continued through 1972. At the behest of the National Hillel Office, Yale Jewish students joined Jewish students across the nation in establishing a campus Jewish Appeal about 1947. This fund-raising organization became a link to virtually every Jewish student on campus as it reached out for a personal financial commitment to Judaism. Many Jewish students who shunned other Jewish commitments would generously support this fund drive. As early as 1951 Rabbi Joseph Gumbiner, Sandmel's successor, would note "that the Jewish Appeal is the only activity which can still command the participation of some of our constituents. There were men on this committee whom I have never seen at any other Hillel activity." "Checkbook Judaism" was strong and the Yale student campaign grew to be among the most successful in the nation.[12]

In many ways the 1950s were a creditable but lackluster time for the Hillel Foundation at Yale. In part this was due to the general student cynicism toward religious activity and involvement. It was not a uniquely Jewish phenomenon, but Hillel was as susceptible as other religious organizations. Under the competent direction of Rabbi Joseph Gumbiner (1949–54) non-credit classes continued as well as the colloquia and the successful Jewish Appeal. The impressive *Ram's Horn* newsletter was printed during Gumbiner's term. Volunteer work was engaged in through occupational therapy at the State Mental Hospital in Middletown, orderly work at the New Haven Hospital, and teaching at the New Haven County Jail. Many Yale students taught classes in local synagogue Sunday schools. Guest lecturers such as Will Herberg and Martin Buber addressed Hillel events, and Friday night services were followed by "Forums" that were often led by local faculty. Professor of the history of religion Erwin Goodenough (a non-Jew) regularly volunteered his time to address the Hillel assemblies. The weekend exodus to nearby women's schools prevented the development of regular social programs, though an occasional Hillel dance was enough to attract the majority of Jewish Yale undergraduates to purchase a Hillel membership.[13] Reflecting the growing interests of Conservative Jews on campus, the Hillel Religious Committee in 1953 abandoned use of the Reform Union Prayer Book in favor of the Conservative Rabbinical Assembly volume.[14] In 1954 the Hillel office, courtesy of Norman S. Buck, dean of freshmen, moved from its "old, damp, dark dungeon deep in Lawrance Hall" to more pleasant quarters adjacent to Chaplain Sidney Lovett's office in Durfee

Hall on the university's Old Campus.[15] Rabbi Ephraim Fischoff (1955–57) had not been a successful administrator and counselor, and the subsequent pressure led the National Hillel Foundation to grant him a leave of absence for the 1957–58 year. These events had capped the decade.[16]

The worthiest Hillel achievement of the 1950s was the formation of a group of alumni who labeled themselves the "Friends of Yale Hillel." It was a curious collection of characters who gathered together to establish a financial support for Jewish life at Yale. In its first years the Friends were a group of townies with few contemporary connections to the university. Some were Jewish alumni of the 1920s and 1930s who possessed good feelings toward their alma mater, but had little sense of enduring personal connection with an institution that they had only half felt a part of in their undergraduate days. Others among the Friends had no formal connection with the university but wanted to enjoy a real, if somewhat vicarious, association with Yale. When the group met early on at Mory's for a planning session, it was the first time for some of the Yale alumni to set foot within its fabled walls. The enterprise grew as President Griswold and other university administrators lent their encouragement to the project. Sydney Bruskin (B.A. 1936) proudly recalled one meeting when University Secretary Carl Lohmann stood up and bade that the Friends sing Yale's traditional song, "Bright College Years." It was an invitation to be part of the Yale spirit that many in attendance had never experienced. Bruskin, whose difficult situation as an undergraduate townie had led him to live at home and walk the few blocks to campus each day, remembered that after hearing Lohmann's words, "All of a sudden I felt a little identity with Yale."[17] Among the group's first actions was to make a contribution to Dwight Hall, in recognition of its long-standing tradition of placing its facilities at Hillel's disposal. The Friends later embarked on a fund drive to buy a home on Edwards Street for the Hillel director. Their record of accomplishment was substantial.[18]

RICHARD J. ISRAEL

The rejuvenation of Jewish activity that Yale experienced in the 1960s was in large part due to the arrival at Yale in 1959 of Richard J. Israel as Hillel rabbi and director. In the previous chapter his effort to purge Yale of unfairly biased admissions was detailed, but this activity was only one facet of a man whose sprightly sense of humor and deep convictions regarding inherent human decencies inspired Jewish life on the Yale campus for a dozen years. Educated at the University of Chicago and Hebrew Union College in Cincinnati, Israel possessed a wide range of cultural, intellectual, and administrative talents that enabled him to prance adroitly from being a civil rights demonstrator to circuit lecturer, from collector of esoterica to adviser and writer for *The Jewish Catalog*, from beekeeper to National Hillel consultant, from provocative teacher to personal counselor.[19]

The house of Yale Jewry that Rabbi Israel found in 1959 was resting on an insecure foundation. Yale had always had its share of "self-hating" Jews who, hoping to be accepted by the nonreligious campus elites, labored to hide their every palpable Jewish connection. What troubled Rabbi Israel, though, was that even "mainstream" Jewish students who participated in campus Jewish life were strangely timid in affirming their faith. The syncretic slogan of Yale Hillel, "It's shoe to be a Jew," pointed out the embarrassing position of self-identifying Jews. "Shoe" had referred to the dusty white buck shoes that connoted eliteness or "coolness" on campus. Unfortunately, by the time that the Jewish students began to use the term, the expression was on its way out of the Yale vocabulary. Though the shoe no longer fit, Hillel wore it.[20]

Three vintage Richard Israel anecdotes richly illustrate the difficulty that Jewish students of his first years often had in coming to grips with their religious identity. The first anecdote concerned a group of "ten exceedingly assimilated" Jewish seniors who were recruited by the Hillel student president to provide formal advice to the Hillel Foundation:

> [The student president] suggested to them that Hillel's reputation on campus was not what it might be and asked them if they would come and give us advice. They had been around. They knew the campus (indeed many of them held responsible student positions,) and if they would give us guidance they could turn Hillel into an up and coming organization on campus.
>
> They came to my home (none of them would ever set foot in Hillel), we served sherry and cookies and then asked them what was wrong with the Jewish community on campus. Everything broke loose . . . Jews were too pushy . . . Jews were too aggressive . . . They didn't dress well . . . They were too intellectual . . . the works!

Difficulty in continuing the traditions of one's Jewish faith was commonplace, Israel recalled:

> At the first [Hillel] student cabinet meeting I attended at Yale I witnessed an argument as to whether it was right and proper for Hillel to expose the non-Jews who attend the talks following services to the [Sabbath candles]. We should put them out or remove them for "they shine in people's eyes and are annoying," [it was stated].
>
> When this important issue was . . . resolved, . . . a heated debate began over the

propriety of following our weekly Friday night discussion with an *Oneg Shabbat,*"
... after all, by having an *Oneg Shabbat* we are forcing our guests to participate in a
Jewish religious ceremony." One student contended that ... many organizations
served punch and cookies after lectures. These refreshments encouraged people to
remain for a period of time after the talk; they would continue discussion among
themselves and ask further questions of the speaker in an informal setting. Thus, this
might be an alternative procedure. There was general consensus that this was an as-
tute comment, and so the cabinet concurred: Instead of an *Oneg Shabbat,* punch and
cookies it would be after each Sabbath discussion. I found myself rubbing my eyes to
be sure that I was not in [the mythical city of Jewish fools called] Chelm, but I sum-
moned up the courage to ask what the difference was between our customary *Oneg
Shabbat* and the punch and cookies idea. The response was clear and immediate: "At
an *Oneg Shabbat* you serve Danish."

Appearances and concern over the image of Jews in the minds of their non-
Jewish neighbors meant far more than any substantive religious issues. The final anecdote centered on the *Sukkah*—the wooden hut that traditional Jews
erect outdoors for eight days during the fall festival of Sukkot. Israel recalled a
discussion held but a few weeks after his arrival at Yale in fall, 1959:

> I asked whether it would not be appropriate to build a *Sukkah* since the holiday
> would shortly be upon us. I was greeted with great uproar and hilarity followed by
> rather patronizing explanations about how such a remark clearly indicated that I
> didn't understand the situation at Yale. With that I thought the better part of discre-
> tion was to let the matter drop.
>
> Two years later, I again asked about building a *Sukkah.* The cabinet thought it was
> a silly sort of notion, but maybe I should be humored, so [we built a *Sukkah* inside]
> the room in which we hold our services. So it remained for the next two years.

In a fortress community where religiously committed Jews felt out of place, the
Judaism that was practiced was done so in a closet.[21]

This was a far cry from the confidently optimistic days when Rabbi Samuel
Sandmel was Hillel director (1945–49). Had the Yale campus turned sour toward Jews? Had the Yale campus's cynical attitude toward religious belief
snuffed out any remaining comfort with Judaism? No. The slow, but progressive, opening of the campus through the 1950s did not promote significant
anti-Jewish feeling. In the late 1950s Yale Hillel suffered from the inner weakness of trying to thrive without an effective leader. During a period when the
Jewish chaplain had provided unsteady guidance, some Jewish students and
faculty developed a particular hostility to Hillel. On a campus whose daily
agenda challenged one to define one's religious values, vulnerable Jewish stu-

dents found it difficult without a strong chaplain teaching and exemplifying the values and meaning of Jewish life. By the time that Israel arrived on campus, with no one of respect having argued otherwise for the few previous years, being a Jew stood for little more than being an employer of outdated slang.[22]

Israel's tenure at Yale was a lively roundelay—each year's verses were different, for he encouraged Jewish expression in many forms, but his actions shared a common refrain. Vis-à-vis the university, he would argue that Yale, if it was sincere about accepting Jewish students, should permit those students who wished to observe their religious traditions to do so free from the worry of being penalized by bureaucratic regulations. Regarding Yale Jewry, students and faculty alike, Israel would help the interested find the teachings of Judaism that applied to the prevailing currents of public opinion. He attempted to make Yale and Yale's Jews more comfortable about observing Judaism on the campus.

To Jewish applicants hesitant about attending a college with a mixed record of welcome toward Jews, Israel would assert that the Yale of the 1960s was a new Yale:

> Administratively I think there is no question but that the university is as friendly as one could possibly hope. Within the student body there are still vestiges of the boys finishing school atmosphere and that means occasional incidents of urbane anti-Semitism. It by no means is a serious problem and many students go through the Yale experience without even finding it.
>
> In any university with a class of a thousand students it would seem to me that a boy can always find all the good friends he can possibly manage. There is no reason for him to love everyone at Yale. If he has any kind of good and substantial reasons for wanting to come to Yale, he should certainly not be discouraged on the grounds of anti-Semitism, overt or implicit.[23]

Cooperating with the Christian chaplains on the campus, Rabbi Israel organized inter-faith groups that maintained a regular lunchtime dialogue. Pioneering one form of town-gown relations, Israel recruited some eighteen Hillel undergraduates as voluntary tutors for the predominantly poor and black students at the nearby Winchester Elementary School. Israel believed this to be the first such organized program to emanate from the Yale campus. When the concerns of students moved from the outward and civil rights oriented time of the early 1960s to the "Me" era of the 1970s, Israel responded to the students' spiritual needs and helped the core members of the student organization become something of a "T" (sensitivity) group. When Humble Oil and Refining and the First National Bank of Chicago, representative firms of industries known for discriminatory hiring practices, first began to recruit Jewish students in the 1970s, Hillel became a conduit for students to learn of such opportunities. In many guises, Israel's Hillel thrived.[24]

The common theme was helping students appreciate their religion. The potential for improvement was great, as Israel noted in a 1963 assessment based on his annual interviews with the majority of Jewish freshmen: "Religion is by and large meaningless to the great majority of Jewish students. Since, however, everyone must have a religion and they have no other religion, then their 'religion' is obviously Judaism." One reason for the lack of interest of one population, Israel noted, was that Jewish students who came to Yale after four years at a preparatory school arrived with virtually all interest in Judaism extinguished by a four-year absence from home and synagogue, and with little more than an eighth-grade Sunday School background to sustain them.[25] Occasionally Israel would be successful in reversing the lack of interest. With the ten aforementioned students who considered Jews too pushy, aggressive, sloppy, intellectual, and so forth, a small miracle occurred:

> At the end of [two one-hour sessions of criticism] it became apparent . . . to them that this much self-hate was rather loathsome. I then asked them if in view of their attitudes they would evaluate an article for me (Koestler's "Judah at the Crossroads") and we would then meet once again. At this meeting, in terms of Koestler's arguments and in view of their own attitudes I played devil's advocate and tried to make a case for their conversion to Christianity. They were quite disturbed. They realized that as peripheral as they considered themselves they did not have the courage to convert or the knowledge to make Judaism anything but an unfortunate accident of birth.
>
> Then for awhile it was even a bit pathetic. They were almost pleading. Did Judaism have any merits? There *must* be a reason for them to remain *Jews*! Could I perhaps teach them? Imperceptibly the character of the group had completely changed. They had no interest in giving Hillel guidance. They wanted guidance themselves. They were more anxious to learn than any group I have ever had.[26]

On other occasions Israel would provoke an unsuspecting freshman into a deep conversation about religion by telling him that he looked Jewish—an unflattering comment to many. The most meaningful Jewish experience for many Yale Jewish students proved to be the Sabbath dinners in the family atmosphere of the rabbi's home. The warmth of one family nourished many a Jewish student away from home in Israel's day.[27]

By the time he left Yale in 1971 to become the regional director for Hillel in the greater Boston area Rabbi Israel had concluded that Yale had become a comfortable place for Jewish students. Quoted by the *Yale Daily News,* he commented:

> The Jewish Yale student of the fifties was far more defensive—sometimes with good reason—about being a Jew on campus. The place felt like a fortress.
>
> Today the atmosphere is far more relaxed. Jews feel as much a part of the university as anyone else.[28]

Individual Jews might later contest Israel's conclusion as Pollyannaish, but the general consensus was that Israel's opinion was true. The reasons for the change were many. On one level, Israel's own work doubtless served as a model for Jewish students to follow. On another level the students of Yale had themselves greatly changed during the 1960s. There were more Jews, and this helped Jews develop a sense of security. There were more public school Jews, who, on the average, brought with them a greater commitment to Judaism than their prep school co-religionists. As we shall see in the next chapter, during the 1960s Yale also moved to accommodate traditional Jewish students. The knowledge that even a visible Jew, whose religious convictions were far stronger than those of the average Yale Jew, was not just tolerated but was welcome on the Yale campus helped those with less commitment find security.[29] The growing presence of blacks, Hispanics, Asian Americans, and other "minority" groups made Jewish students feel less like a "minority" on a campus that valued being a potpourri of America's best. The presence of women, beginning in 1969, also proved to be important in forming a socially more tolerant campus. Through the 1950s there was a dominant culture at Yale, and those raised outside of that culture were expected to meld into it. Some Jews and Catholics had been able to pass as Protestants. But in the 1960s the limits of melding were reached. Barring radical surgery, a woman could not be a man, a black could not be a white; if differences were not respected there would be explosion. At times there was real tension. Most people learned to respect differences, though some refused. But a pluralistic institution in a society that was beginning to respect ethnicity had room for students of every creed, race, and sex.

Kingman Brewster, Jr., recalled the expansion of Yale's spiritual tradition in describing his 1963 baccalaureate address as acting president of the university. Part of his "sermon" was based on a quotation from the ancient Rabbi Hillel that was recorded in *Pirke Avot* [Sayings of the Fathers]: "If I am not for myself, then who will be for me? And if I am only for myself, then what am I?" Unaware of its source, divinity scholars at Yale and Harvard were stumped as to where the "biblical" quotation had originated from, Brewster gleefully recalled. In Brewster's first Baccalaureate a religiously polyvalent tradition began.[30]

For Rabbi Israel the preeminent symbol of decreasing Jewish defensiveness during the 1960s was the *Sukkah,* the religious hut that had almost clandestinely stood in Dwight Hall for some eight days in 1961 and 1962. Israel recalled that when *Sukkot* was approaching in 1963, he didn't even mention the subject, "after all, by this time I was familiar with 'the situation at Yale.'" At a cabinet meeting, Ivan G. Marcus (B.A. 1964) naively asked Israel why the *sukkah* was always built indoors. Other students, Israel wrote in a letter that year, suddenly chimed in . . .

> "Isn't a *Sukkah* supposed to be built outside?" "Of course it should be outside." "What would be a good location?" "What about next to Dwight Chapel near the middle of the Campus?" Within five minutes a site was selected. I sat silent and stunned. The next day the *Sukkah* was built.
>
> It was a rousing success. The boys were terribly proud of it. Cookies were available [inside] throughout the week. A little sign explaining what it was and that everyone was welcome was tacked on to it.
>
> I am sure that there will never again be a discussion of the issue. I can't really explain what happened, but there has been a very dramatic change in the Jewish student's image of himself at Yale, even in the short time that I have been here.

Many nonreligious Jewish students, too, thought of the *Sukkah* as a sign that Yale Jews had finally arrived.[31]

THE WOLF YEARS

The era of Rabbi Arnold Jacob Wolf as director of the Hillel Foundation from 1972 was largely one of quiet, steady growth, and consolidation of the major changes that had taken place in the decade before: an increasing Jewish population and the arrival of women undergraduates. The survival of Israel in the years after the 1973 Yom Kippur War lent a rallying dimension for many Jewish students. A notable change during his tenure was an increase in the number of the Jewish Sabbath services on the campus. The Friday evening services he conducted demanded participation rather than observation. Walking through the Branford College gate whose stonework urged allegiance to God, country, and Yale, students would fill the awe-inspiring Harkness Memorial Room. Under intricately carved wainscoting depicting the first 220 years of Yale history, Wolf's services encouraged worshipers to contemplate their relationship with God, with Yale, and with each other. The Friday night discussions of Bible and human affairs that he led were some of the most creative and mind-opening of all sorts on the campus of that era. As a rabbi, Wolf's puckish charm offered comfort and friendship to numerous undergraduates and graduates and some faculty. Administratively, Wolf saw his professional role not as creating the community that some Jewish students sought but as inspiring and facilitating it. Yale students were a talented bunch, not worthy of infantilization, he thought. If they wanted something to happen, not only could they make it happen, but it was their responsibility to make it happen. Not every student agreed.

The controversial element to Wolf's ministry was predictable from the start of his term. A devotee of the intellectual spirit of the University of Chicago, an iconoclast who was seen by some of the most active members of the Yale Jewish community as following in the tradition of the ancient Jewish prophets railing against the kings of Israel, Wolf often evoked disagreement. He told the members of the innovative Congregation Solel that he left behind in Highland Park, Illinois, that his reasons for going to Yale in 1972 were varied. A primary reason was his wanting to become a more observant Jew than he had been able to be in the context of his previous synagogue. The great challenge of a campus like Yale also tempted him, he informed his congregants:

> American Jews have done less, and more poorly, for their college young than for anyone else supported by their great agencies of the communal weal.
>
> There is something guilty, or self-righteous in me—or maybe a trifle saintly—that makes me relish a deep salary cut and a funny old office bordering on academic slums. . . .
>
> I have found denominationalism repugnant and go with joy into a Jewish community that eschews such divisiveness. I will be a rabbi to the traditional and the humanist, to freaked-out and scholarly Jews. . . .
>
> Now I can . . . share my ideas with people who will disagree with them even more than you have.[32]

As time would prove him in many respects, Wolf was right. The Hillel selection committee had been looking for just such a "Jewish Bill Coffin." They found a man whose ideas regarding Israelis and Palestinians proved a decade ahead of their time and whose newness to Yale prevented him from fully appreciating how far Yale had come in the years before him.

In an era when statistics from the university chaplain's office showed that the most popular religion on campus was "no preference,"[33] Wolf became increasingly concerned about Yale Jews' adopting the emotional restraint of the typical Yale student and the selfishness of the typical American student of the late 1970s. His article in the January 1973 *Yale Alumni Magazine* sounded the alarm that would resound throughout his Yale career. It was less a criticism of Yale than of Yale's Jews:

> The Jewish student at Yale seems, . . . on balance, to be balanced and secure of place. Why then does he also seem so often to be gloomy and repressed? Why does one see so little touching or kissing or laughing? So little political or even personal concern for the cheated of the world? Why are the Kosher meals filled with talk about exams and papers, the Sabbath *Oneg* (party) so grim, or at least so refined? Why was even *Simhat Torah*, when by traditional demand we drink and dance with the scrolls, why was even that day so decorous and serene? Is this phenomenon simply the wholesale incorporation of the Wasp ethos, a typically Jewish attempt to become more *goyish* than the gentiles in those midst we live?[54]

On a campus where enthusiasm for football, a bladderball, or an alcoholic drink was permitted to inspire any form of behavior short of personal violence, Wolf found the relative solemnity of Jewish life to be disturbing. His criticisms of the Jewish faculty at Yale would one day be even more severe. We shall return later to the dramatic events that preceded Wolf leaving Yale in 1980.

FINANCING

In *A Midrash on American Jewish History,* Henry Feingold concisely pointed out the national problem for Jews on the college campus:

> The seductive campus, usually located in an idyllic natural setting, and the watered-down liberal-arts curriculum, with its persuasive universalistic assumption, combined with the heady social atmosphere of a summer camp, is something the demanding Judaic ethos cannot compete against. Many survivalists have come to consider the campus a "disaster area" where the Jewish enterprise loses its youth.[35]

On this point Rabbi Israel and Rabbi Wolf wholeheartedly agreed. One of the causes that both men championed was the need for adequate financing of the Jewish ministry on the Yale campus. A small cause of the "disaster" of Hillel at Yale was the minimal support that had traditionally been contributed to the program by a moribund New Haven Jewish community. The gradual shift of New Haven Jewry from city to suburb in the 1950s and 1960s and a gradual decline in the proportion of local students among the total Yale population may have also sapped further interest by New Haven Jewry in Jewish students at Yale. The growing number of Yale faculty of Jewish origin who exhibited minimal interest in New Haven Jewish communal organizations also exacerbated one aspect of town-gown relations. A larger problem was the failure of Yale's Jewish alumni to support the work of a Jewish ministry at Yale. Devoted Protestants had generously supported the work of the Yale Church of Christ for centuries. In the twentieth century Father Thomas Lawrason Riggs and other Roman Catholic alumni had established a building and endowment to secure the Catholic chaplaincy at the university. Through the 1970s no Jewish angel had blessed Yale Hillel to the same extent. In 1967 Rabbi Israel compared notes with the other religious ministries at Yale and demonstrated the problem:

> There are roughly 1100 Roman Catholics at Yale, who are served by three full-time and five part-time priests. Proportionately, the figures for Protestants are comparable. These figures meet normal professional standards. The group-work profession suggests that a group-worker can be in an effective living relationship with no more than 250 people. . . . I am one man on my campus, with no supplementary [professional] staff, serving 1500 Jewish students. Every morning I must ask myself: What of the other 1250? The unhappy conclusion is, that there is almost nothing to be done for them.[36]

The Yale campus offered many worthy activities that competed with Judaism, but Judaism was not adequately funded to offer any real competition of its own. The record of fund-raising for Yale Hillel was a litany of omissions and mediocre successes. The Friends of Yale Hillel regularly saved the organization from bankruptcy but then proved unable to build a secure permanent program or a place of worship more permanent than borrowed rooms in campus chapels. In the 1950s a fund was announced to honor retiring university chaplain Sidney Lovett, who for decades had been a great supporter of Jewish life at Yale. Though distinguished scholars and writers such as Samuel Sandmel, David Daube, and Isaac Bashevis Singer were imported to Yale as "Lovett Lecturers" for half a decade, the limited funds soon ran out and the Lovett lectureship was forgotten.[37] A mid-1960s drive to raise monies for a Hillel building on the campus enabled the purchase of a new house for the Hillel director, but the effort then lost steam and collapsed. The 1970s were no more productive. The causes of failure were numerous. As Hillel director, Ephraim Fischoff had had little practical grasp of the means to conduct such projects, and Arnold Jacob Wolf had little interest in devoting his ministry to fund-raising. The wealthiest Jewish alumni tended to be either penurious or so ambivalent about their religious identity that they rejected the Hillel organization's ideals completely.[38] Others felt comfortable about being Jews, but, remembering their own distant experiences as undergraduates, feared supporting anything which might renew the old charge of self-segregation. Even the most generous alumni gifts proved small in comparison to the support that other campus ministries received from friends and alumni of their respective faiths. With a limited budget, the best of Hillel directors were forced eventually to search for pastures that were less physically demanding, as Rabbi Israel admitted five years after he left Yale:

> I was . . . never able to provide the support staff which could have bailed me out in a number of areas. . . . The physical shlepping got to be too much. I remember a time when Ben Kahn was National [Hillel] Director, and came to visit me at Yale. . . . I was stuck setting up the chairs again. I asked Ben, "What does Hillel do when the Director gets too old to move the chairs?" Ben's response was, "We get a new Hillel Director," and that's what happened.[39]

If Yale Jewry was destined to be impotent in that era it would not be a result of the oppression of a hostile university. Presidents Griswold and Brewster had been consistently supportive of the Hillel mission.[40] Instead, Yale Jewry suffered from its inability to support its own spiritual weight.

Chapter 11 A Kosher Whiffenpoof: The Religiously Observant Student

Few areas of personal belief and action have spawned such strong feelings as religion has. Within any particular religious tradition, those who are less traditional than their co-religionists risk being thought of as godless, while those who are more ritually observant than a certain standard might be considered fanatics. For Jews, relations between Reform, Conservative, Orthodox, and Ultraorthodox communities have followed this pattern especially. If we leave aside the Ultraorthodox, the practical boundaries separating Reform, Conservative, and Orthodox Jews from their fellow co-religionists, however, have often been quite frail. Because of the difficulty in meaningfully separating the labels, this chapter will concern itself with the "observant" or "traditional" Jewish student within Yale College. In this context, the "observant" student is defined as one who tries to practice the rituals and tenets of Judaism. Where those practices came into conflict with Yale College and how that conflict was (partially) resolved is the concern of this chapter. The scheduling of classes or exams on the Sabbath, availability of kosher food, and acceptance of the highly visible, religiously nonconformist student were the battlegrounds of the conflict. For the sake of perspective the reader must keep in mind that with the exception of the observance of Yom Kippur (which concerned the vast majority of Yale Jews), the "traditional" Jewish population represented less than 4 percent of all the Jewish students in Yale College.[1] The real issues to be considered, therefore, represented the issues of philosophical principle rather than bureaucratic nightmares.

FUNDAMENTALS

The first major question to be raised effectively by traditional students was one of religious courtesy: To what extent should an institution respond to the varying religious needs of its constituents? There was no correct answer to this question. It was simply a matter of the kind of character that the institution wished to have.[2] As long as there is no deception involved (e.g., if it advertises flexibility while maintaining rigidity) then an institution may be as rigid as "the market" permits it to be. The rigid option prevents students with strong nonconformist religious principles from attending an institution. The alternative of accommodating students with deep religious convictions requires more administrative work, especially in terms of providing alternative times for registration or examinations when these happen to occur on a religious holiday. In coming to grips with traditional Jewish students, Yale College was forced to decide whether to opt for rigidity or flexibility. Each had its cost. Rigidity meant that some of the "best" students in the nation could not be part of Yale. The cost of the alternative of flexibility was financial.

The second fundamental question was one of collegial definition: To what extent is a college a "college" when its students do not all participate in communal activities? In its first century the ideal at Yale College was an institution where students would all dine, recline, study, play, and pray together. A common spirit deriving from a common mold was to be gained. More importantly, a powerful and vital sense of community was encouraged by the intense experience of eating, sleeping, learning, sporting, and worshiping as a group. Such a community would not necessarily produce the best scholars, football players, or ministers, but it would be capable of producing a spirit that was valid in its own right. The Yale collegiate ideal, however, was imperfectly realized through most of the college's history. In the earliest years disputes among the Yale trustees left the college physically divided on multiple campuses. The nineteenth-century rise of Episcopalianism, Presbyterianism, and other denominations as viable alternatives to a Connecticut Congregationalism led to Yale's allowing students to attend Sunday worship in the local churches of their choice. "Mandatory daily chapel" continued through 1925, but, as described previously, it was essentially a nonreligious routine. The collegiate ideal was also far from realization in the nineteenth century because of the college's continued inability to provide adequate housing and dining facilities for all of its students. When married students were permitted to enter Yale College, they, too, could not fully participate in college life. But even as Yale College moved to become a "university college" in the Angell administration of 1921–37, it tried to retain its collegiate character. For the first time in over a century the construction of residential colleges in the 1930s brought the college closer to its collegiate ideal in terms of eating and sleeping. By 1950, when 94 percent of the undergraduates were successfully squeezed into college-owned buildings, Yale had largely succeeded in restoring the collegiate ideal in the categories of eating and lodging.[3] Separate kosher dining might threaten this ideal, it would be argued in the 1950s and early 1960s.[4] The tension between university and college, therefore, lay at the heart of the matter: Should a break in the collegiate rigor be allowed for the sake of the university ideal?

Throughout the twentieth century students from traditional homes were in attendance at Yale College. Since customary traditional practice did not include the wearing of a *kippah* (skullcap) outside of the home or sanctuary, a religious Jew was generally not identifiable as such before the 1950s. Prior to then the most traditional Jews were also "invisible" at Yale because they gave up some of their traditions to fulfill Yale regulations. Before coming to Yale many students of Orthodox Jewish background had never written on the Sabbath. The regular pressure of examinations forced those who wished to remain in college to conform to the general pattern. In some cases students were able to convince their instructors to offer oral exams as alternatives to the Saturday tests, but if an instructor was inflexible or if courses demanded writing, religious obligations had to be sacrificed for grades. There were simply no other options, short of leaving Yale. A cut system that prescribed the number of class periods that a student could miss allowed observant Jewish students to miss class for major holidays without penalty. When a sympathetic official occupied the dean's office, then a Jewish student was sometimes permitted greater leeway.[5]

In his study made during the Second World War, Meyer Greenberg found that some 16 percent of Jewish students in the college were products of nominally Orthodox homes. This percentage was extremely low when compared with the nationwide proportion of nominally Orthodox Jews to other Jews. The low proportion was not a result of any known bias against Orthodoxy in the process of admission decision-making.[6] It was caused largely by economics and self-selection. The economic rise of American Jewry had long correlated with departure from the Orthodox branch of Judaism. Consequently, many students from Orthodox homes likely realized that they did not have the financial means to attend Yale. Poor students were also less likely to be accepted for admission. Self-selection also must have operated because of a cognizance that Yale academic requirements and social pressure urging strict conformance to the norm were not conducive to traditional Jewish observance. Joseph H. Gumbiner, Hillel rabbi from 1949 to 1954, bluntly warned observant inquirers that they would have difficulty at Yale if they insisted on their religious beliefs.[7] Parallel messages came from Yale administrators. Edward Noyes, chairman of admissions, suggested to one observant Jewish applicant that he consider whether he was looking for a seat in "the wrong pew" by applying to Yale. Other administrators were more encouraging but explained that it would be up to the individual student to work his way through Yale bureaucratic requirements.[8]

Traditional Jews were not alone in having to find their way through the Yale system. Good Friday was of particular concern to ritually oriented Episcopalian and Roman Catholic students at the college. Because Yale had been founded as a Congregationalist institution Good Friday had received no place on the college calendar. After the Reverend Elmore McKee was installed as university pastor in 1927 the campus Good Friday service had been forced to fit itself into the daily schedule between the classes that the faculty insisted occupy the day—and on at least one occasion it had also to contend with the din of Calcium Light Night that the fraternities insisted fill the evening. The student who wished to miss classes for a service in the university chapel or in a local parish had to suffer the same cuts against his record that the traditional Jewish student would suffer for observing his holy days. When Mr. McKee audaciously informed the *Yale Daily News* in 1930 that he opposed the faculty's refusal to cancel noon hour classes to permit a well-attended Good Friday service, the faculty's wrath descended upon him. In his own defense McKee informed President James Rowland Angell that with a sizable number of Episcopalians and Roman Catholics and others who might observe Good Friday among the students, "there is certainly a considerable portion of our community who would see the appropriateness of such University recognition." McKee was not worried that this would set an undesirable precedent for tolerance:

It has been suggested that if the University observed Good Friday officially, Jewish and other festivals would also have to be recognized. I have assumed that the University felt no hesitancy about stressing a definitely Christian position, and that these other occasions do not require observance.[9]

Though Angell was sympathetic to McKee's request for an hour's break from classes on Good Friday, he hesitated about invoking the "Christian Yale" theme; if "Christian Yale" was taken in its original meaning Judaism was not the only faith that was outside of the Yale tradition. The scythe of intolerance could span a wide path, Angell explained:

> While it is true that Yale has a perfectly explicit Christian origin and tradition, it is equally true, is it not, that the early generations were highly suspicious of anything that looked to them like Episcopal and Catholic ceremonial and that they took little or no notice of the great feast days of the church? This fact has only a remote bearing on the properties of the present issue, but I am disposed to feel that it has some relation to the psychology of the situation.[10]

Angell had astutely appraised the events at hand. Current policies had to be based upon current situations. Blind invocation of past prejudices was a risky business. Yet the realist in Angell was well aware that on a campus that reveled in its past some ghosts were slow to die.

A memorable resurrection of one of these ghosts was stimulated by the Second World War. Knowing that the undergraduate departmental examinations for 1943 coincided with the Yom Kippur day of atonement—the holiest day of the Jewish calendar—Dean Samuel W. Dudley (of the engineering school), Dean Charles H. Warren (of the scientific school), and Dean William C. DeVane (of the college) invoked the war emergency to justify a harsh new policy. Any student who wished to be excused from classes on the Jewish new year holiday of Rosh Hashanah or on Yom Kippur was required to meet with the dean of his school. The basic policy was that, "if possible, excuses shall be granted for . . . Yom Kippur." But the possibilities were quite limited:

> Excuses are to be granted those Jewish students on the other Holy Days only if the student can make a real case to the Dean's Office concerned for his being absent. The assumption is that these excuses will not be lightly given.
>
> In any case, excuses will not be given for any of the Holy Days if an important . . . examination occurs on that date.[11]

Because undergraduate departmental examinations for that year were scheduled on Yom Kippur, all of the Jewish seniors taking those exams were automatically barred from observing the holy day. Several of the religiously minded students grumbled about the deans' action, but, given the exigencies of a hurried wartime educational program, they accepted the deans' cold-hearted attitude without major protest.

After the war, the observant Jewish students would not be so restrained. About 1947 Norman "Steve" Buck, dean of freshman year, circulated a flyer to all of the freshmen who had missed classes on Rosh Hashanah. In an unsympathetic tone, Buck threatened to suspend any student who missed any further classes without a legitimate excuse. For the many Jewish freshmen anticipating the arrival of Yom Kippur, Buck's threat was ominous. It was no less of a portent for the university. A century of limited religious tolerance (only interrupted by wartime pressures) was at risk of being cast away. Not content to suffer, one Jewish student entered Buck's office to appeal the decision. As Richard Sewall, former associate dean of freshmen, recalled, Dean Buck refused the student's request, and he explained that Yale was a Christian college with a consequently Christian calendar. If Jewish students were to attend Yale they would have to conform. Sewall, then a newcomer to his post, soon passed word of the incident to the Reverend Sidney Lovett. The university chaplain suggested that Sewall and he immediately pay a visit to his old friend and Yale class of 1913 classmate Buck. Together, Lovett planned, they would talk some sense into the dean. Lovett, the tolerant pragmatist, argued not for rights but for courtesy. He explained to Buck that the Jewish people had suffered enough in recent years and that it was time for treating them with more sensitivity. In the midst of the discussion, University Secretary Carl Lohmann telephoned with distressing news. Lohmann reported that he had received that day a series of telephone calls (apparently from Director Samuel Sandmel of Hillel and other local rabbis) concerning the college's new Yom Kippur policy. Lohmann asked the freshman dean to explain just what was going on. Buck promptly looked up at Lovett and Sewall and announced "I've changed my mind. I can make mistakes, but I can also change them pretty well." On the day before Yom Kippur, all of the freshmen who had received the previous warning received a handwritten note from Dean Buck withdrawing his threat. A similar intercession with Yale College's Dean William Clyde DeVane by Lovett occurred regarding absence from classes on the much less observed holiday of Sukkot.[12] In this manner, momentary crises were resolved, but the underlying issues remained.

JOSEPH MUSKAT AND THE 1950S

In the way that Yom Kippur posed a problem for most of the Jewish Yale students in 1947, the ordinary Sabbath entailed special arrangements for the most

traditional students every week. Through the 1940s and 1950s the few traditional Jewish students attending Yale usually made individual arrangements
with their professors to avoid taking tests on Saturdays. If an administrator or
individual teacher proved himself unsympathetic to religious requirements,
that was when tensions developed.[13]

The pioneering experience of Joseph Muskat (B.A. 1955) foreshadowed the
difficulties that would face the rare observant student in the 1950s. Born and
raised in Marietta, Ohio, Muskat was admitted to Yale as one of the first group
of Ford Foundation Early Admissions Scholars after having completed his junior year of high school. He entered Yale determined to maintain his religious
practices. Other family members were just as concerned about this matter,
Muskat recalled:

> My father closed his office for two weeks and drove me to New Haven, seeing Uni-
> versity officials and people in the Orthodox community of New Haven, not leaving
> until he was satisfied that I could maintain myself Jewishly. . . . In 1951 we were re-
> questing consideration for practices based upon religious beliefs, not demanding my
> civil rights.

Classes were offered on a Monday–Wednesday–Friday (MWF) and Tuesday–
Thursday–Saturday (TThS) schedule. Though Muskat initially hoped for a
schedule without TThS classes, the freshman dean's office would not oblige
him, thinking that a concentrated schedule would overwhelm the young student. Consequently, Muskat's freshman year schedule had TThS classes in German and chemistry. When he learned that the German class often had Saturday
quizzes (in order to discourage "cutting"), Muskat switched to French. His
chemistry professor excused him from Saturday quizzes. By taking an 8 A.M.
section, young Muskat would sit in on every Saturday's class and then be able to
be in synagogue in time for morning services. In later years he attempted to enroll in courses that met only on MWF or in classes with understanding professors who would allow him to turn in his Saturday homework in advance and
absent himself from the Saturday session. Final examinations scheduled for
Saturdays were more problematic. During Muskat's first three years, exam conflicts were resolved by permitting him to pay a "conflict" exam fee and take the
exam at a different time.[14] But for reasons that are not entirely clear, in 1954 the
college momentarily promulgated a new stone-hearted policy. Lewis M. Wiggin, assistant dean of Yale College, explained in a note to President Griswold's
executive assistant, Catherine Tilson, that "we are not permitting postponement of final examinations for religious reasons on Saturdays." The Executive

Committee of Yale College, Wiggin informed Tilson, was firmly upholding the university regulation stating "all students are required to attend their classroom and other University [exercises] as scheduled."[15] Yale thereby exhibited its true conservatism. Whereas by the 1950s Harvard was already permitting its Sabbath-observing students to postpone Saturday examinations until Saturday night (when tests would be administered by Hillel Foundation-paid proctors), Yale was caught up in bureaucratic rigidity.[16]

Undoubtedly, some of the sudden strictness was a result of a new problem that had cropped up in 1954. Through an oversight on the part of the college dean's office, Rabbi Joseph Gumbiner of Hillel had not learned of the college calendar for 1954–55 until long after it had been irrevocably adopted. The challenge to Jewish students was that college registration had been planned for the September date which happened to be Rosh Hashanah. Since Yale had no provision for such conflicts, a Jewish student who failed to register would be liable to incur financial penalties, while the traditional Jewish student who chose to register would be compromising his traditions. Rabbi Gumbiner therefore called on the university to make reasonable accommodation for the traditional Jewish students. The discussions that followed were cordial, but resulted in strong disagreements between the university chaplains and the college dean's office. In a profoundly ironic message that echoed a twentieth century Yale irony, it was university chaplain Sidney Lovett who called on the university to resolve the conflict that traditional Jews sometimes had with the Yale calendar. At an institution that had been founded by devout Christians, that valued its Protestant Christian tradition as expressed through the University Church of Christ, the foremost spokesman for Christianity on campus was the one calling for understanding toward Jews, while administrators were invoking Christianity to serve their own intolerant needs. In his characteristic conciliatory style, Lovett recommended one course of action to president Griswold:

> Jewish students, because of their non-Christian religious and cultural heritage, find themselves, at times, in a somewhat isolated position, not because of the content and character of the University curriculum, but in a purely temporal conflict between a religious calendar year . . . and the Gregorian measurement of days and years . . . and naturally the basis of the University's timetable of operations. These conflicts are . . . exacerbated by the fact the Jew . . . and his forebears have been and still are subjected [to racial discrimination] by the Gentile majority. Here in the University much has been done, and is being accomplished, to allay this ugly fact and to reduce its dimensions. It seems to the Chaplain that it would be wise for the University officials who establish its annual schedule to consult with the Jewish rabbi, so that the Chris-

tian and the Jewish calendar may be mutually adjusted so as to reduce if not to avoid altogether a situation where the undoubted rights of the University are in conflict with the religious sensibilities of one of its minority groups.[17]

Acting college dean Alfred R. Bellinger accepted Lovett's suggestions, but concluded along with his deans that since the 1954–55 calendar was already determined, the Jewish students would have to live with it. As an "exceptional" gesture, Bellinger allowed that a separate registration session for observant Jewish students would be established for that fall. The only stipulation was that Hillel or the registrants themselves would have to pay a twenty-five dollar fee to cover the costs of the separate procedure.[18] Rabbi Gumbiner agreed that his office would cover the registration fee, but placed himself on record as considering the fee inappropriate. He expressed hope that the university would continue to provide an alternative time for observant students to register if such a conflict ever occurred again.[19] Gumbiner was well aware that Yale administrators could not "be expected to provide for all the minutiae of Jewish observance," but he hoped that when administrative convenience conflicted with religious conviction the latter would be allowed to prevail.[20]

By fall, 1954, President Griswold was ready to rule on the vexing issue. He had discussed the matter extensively with Rabbi Gumbiner and with other Jews and Christians from inside and outside the university. Though individual administrators would rule their duchies as they saw fit, Griswold provided specific guidelines for the deans of the college, the engineering school, and the freshman year:

It is the aim of Yale to avoid discrimination for or against any religious group. . . .
　　The rules and regulations governing Yale, including the academic calendar and schedule of classes, are drawn up with this aim firmly in mind. . . .
　　It is difficult in so diversified a community to maintain such rules . . . without occasional conflicts between the regulations and the special interests of groups or individuals. . . .
　　The possibility of such conflicts is and should continue to be constantly borne in mind by those responsible for drawing up the University's rules and regulations. . . .
　　Conflicts . . . involving serious hardships to individuals are and should continue to be dealt with compassionately on an individual *ad hoc* basis.

The president continued to insist that the twenty classes permitted to be cut per term be used to solve conflicts with religious holidays. Griswold was hesitant to specify flow-charts diagramming how to resolve conflicts, for fear of locking himself and his administrators in to undesirable pathways.[21] Most importantly, Griswold introduced a new word to the Yale bureaucracy: *compassion*. There had been occasional sympathetic administrators long before, there would long afterward be occasional unsympathetic administrators, but from 1954 the "official" university policy was to be on the side of compassion. At about this time the college also decided not to fine students who would not register on a High Holy Day provided they notified the college in advance of the conflict.[22]

Of all the undergraduates that he had contact with, Rabbi Gumbiner recalled only one who kept to a strictly kosher diet in the early 1950s: Joseph Muskat. Gumbiner remembered that when he received Muskat's religious preference card at the start of the fall term in 1951, he saw that Muskat had indicated Orthodox Judaism, with the word "Orthodox" underlined three times in red ink. Gumbiner recalled their first meeting:

> He had two problems: where could he get kosher food in New Haven and could I get his schedule changed since it called for classes on Saturday. I replied that I would do whatever I could, but asked him why, since his academic record was so excellent, he had not gone to a university which provided kosher food and did not hold classes on [the Sabbath], places like Yeshiva or Brandeis University. He drew himself up to his full height and answered in one word: "Prestige."[23]

It is a yet unproven theorem that traditional Jews of the post Second World War era were attracted to Yale in particular for its status. But it seems likely. The quality of a Yale education was high, but it was high elsewhere. The Yale residential colleges did offer an experience that was paralleled only by Harvard College, but the price for a traditional student was great. The Yale name was a mighty one, but, to metaphrase Deuteronomy, man does not live by prestige alone. Kosher food was not easy to come by.

The High Holy Days came once a year. Six days separated every Sabbath. Food, however, was of at least thrice-daily concern. For the Yale student who wanted to keep kosher, it was an even greater concern. During the 1930s the off-campus student who did not have a kitchen could take mealtime refuge at the great *Yeshiva* (religious academy) in New Haven.[24] Some students would maintain a moderate degree of kosher observance by restricting themselves to a vegetarian diet in the university dining halls. Chefs and dining hall managers were usually cooperative in these dietary efforts.[25] The graduate and professional students on campus who wished strictly kosher meals ate in nearby kosher delicatessens and in the homes of New Haven families. Fox's Delicatessen earned a particular reputation for accommodating itself to hungry students.[26]

Joseph Muskat was again something of a pioneer in regard to kosher meals. His interpretation of tradition did not allow him to eat even the vegetarian food that was served in the dining halls, so when he arrived at Yale it appeared that college would be an unusually expensive proposition for him. He would not eat in the dining halls and the university was unwilling to exempt him from paying his board contract. Thanks to the intercession of Rabbi Gumbiner and assistant dean of freshmen Arthur Howe, Jr. (whom Muskat found to be "decent, reasonable, and respectful"), Muskat was permitted a rebate on his board a few weeks after the start of the fall term. The understanding with the university was that he would eat with a family off the campus. On weekdays, however, he ate in his room. This practice violated university regulations, but he was never bothered about it. Many people on campus, in fact, came to respect him because he was serious about fulfilling what he considered to be his religious obligations. For his first years, a window left open in cold weather provided makeshift refrigeration. When sophomore year approached, Muskat tried to move off the campus to simplify his eating arrangements. Financially, the move would prove impossible. The college, which had provided him with scholarship money, threatened to withdraw it unless he remained on campus. So he stayed. During his senior year a neighbor with a digestive disorder received permission to install a small refrigerator in his room. (This was well before the era of the ubiquitous refrigerators that were later permitted.) Muskat was able to enjoy his neighbor's courtesy and have a place to store food.[27]

Through the 1950s Orthodox families in New Haven noted the increasing demands from Yale students for kosher food. Aside from a rare student like Muskat, the demand was primarily from a few students scattered among the graduate and professional schools of the university. To meet the demand adequately, the local Orthodox Young Israel Synagogue, a twenty-five minute walk from the campus, opened a "Kosher Kitchen" for Yale students in the fall of 1959. Generous financial support from synagogue members Herbert Batt, Max Bleich, and Ben Cohen allowed the graduate students to obtain five meat dinners a week at the synagogue. On weekends the graduate students continued to be welcomed into local homes. Undergraduates were not yet a part of the institution.[28]

The Kosher Kitchen could not be an undergraduate institution because so few traditional students were coming to Yale. They were not coming, despite President Griswold's 1954 call for understanding in the Yale bureaucracy, because many a Yale official was so caught up in following rules that he forgot that the rules were designed to help students and not harm them. Minor changes in bureaucratic procedure overwhelmed Yale administrators. Arthur Howe described such a feeling in a 1957 note to Yale College associate dean Richard Carroll: "Having struggled with Joe Muskat, . . . I am fully sympathetic with your difficulties in handling an Orthodox Jewish boy." It went against the grain of some of the Yale administrators to prove flexible when flexibility was called for. Rather than working to accommodate the sincere student with different needs, undergraduate deans made it their policy to "make it perfectly clear to the [student] that he should be prepared to meet his regularly scheduled appointments or else should seek another institution." Few traditional students found solace in words like these.[29]

It would be unfair to place all responsibility for the deans' recalcitrance on the deans themselves. The deans did not have dictatorial powers. The faculty also had a voice in such matters. Through the early 1960s many of Yale's professors (including a few of the Jewish faculty) were often unenthusiastic about writing alternative make-up exams for traditional students. Because Yale students had never proved sufficiently interested in reporting ethical violations of their classmates, there was no Honor System in the college. In order to protect the integrity of the grading system, alternative contents were required for make-up exams. As any competent teacher can testify, the preparation of a good examination requires considerable effort. For the overworked and underpaid faculty *any* reason to prepare an extra exam was an unwelcome reason. Though a persuasive dean could usually twist a professor's arm enough to gain his agreement to prepare an extra examination, the arm-twisting was costly. The bitter professor was left feeling abused and the dean was left frustrated over the great emotional energy that he had spent in achieving his goal.[30]

THE 1960s

The solution to these crises proved again the recurrent theme in twentieth-century Yale history, that one of the best friends of the Jew at Yale was the most sincere Christian. In 1960, that sincere Christian was William Sloane Coffin, successor to the Reverend Lovett. Ending his second year in office, the Reverend Coffin decided to tackle the difficulties facing the traditional Jewish student in Yale College. In an elegantly persuasive May 1960 letter to Norman S. Buck (by then provost of the university), Coffin suggested that Yale not rely on failed sympathies, but rather on a formal policy governing dietary laws and Sabbath examinations:

Protestant, Roman Catholic and most Jewish students find no conflict between institutional requirements at Yale and their own religious observances. For a handful of the more traditional Jewish students, however, dietary laws and occasional Sabbath examinations do present problems.

Of the twenty to thirty undergraduate and graduate students in this category some now take one meal a day at the Young Israel Synagogue. . . . Others who cannot afford the extra two dollars a day either lose weight, eat eggs for four years, keep illegitimate hot plates in their rooms, or even, as is the case with two chemistry students, keep a kosher kitchen in the Chemistry Lab! As the University has no official policy regarding reimbursement on board bills, some have been partly reimbursed; others have received nothing.

The same confusion exists in respect to Sabbath examinations. With no official policy to guide them, students are forced, often with understandable hesitation, to raise the issue, then their teachers, with like hesitation, are forced to deal with it as best they can.

Failure to have a policy on these matters means that the University annually loses a number of outstanding and interesting students who find the provisions elsewhere more encouraging. Many universities, for instance, have a Hillel House with kitchen, while others, such as M.I.T., provide a kosher kitchen. As regards Sabbath examinations, State universities must provide alternate dates, while certain private institutions, such as Harvard, allow the students to hire a proctor who sits with them from the time of the examination until sundown, then himself gives and supervises the examination.

It seems anomalous that the setup at Yale should appeal, for example, to students of strong social inclinations and discourage students of strong and quite legitimate religious inclinations. The argument that Yale is a Protestant institution breaks down at this very point, for surely the interests of Fraternity Row are not as close to the Protestant Church as the interests of Hillel. Furthermore, the argument that all students should eat together in the Colleges three times a day in order to benefit fully from their Yale experience breaks down at the same point when fraternity members are allowed to eat separately.

Fortunately, the situation can be remedied at minimal expense to the university. When consulted, [the director of the dining halls] stated that within the framework of his existing staff he could handle separate meals for Jewish students. The members of Young Israel have agreed to provide all equipment necessary for a kosher kitchen. The small extra cost of the food would be borne by Hillel. Hence the University need only provide the space and establish an official policy of reimbursements.

May I urge also that the University consider the establishment of an official policy regarding the Sabbath examinations, according to which faculty members would be requested to provide alternate dates, and where impossible, to allow students as at Harvard to provide for their own proctor.[30]

Norman Buck was as opposed to such ideas as a provost as he was earlier as dean of freshmen, but he passed Coffin's letter on to the other members of the College Executive Committee for their consideration.[31]

In contrast to the 1950s, however, by 1960 the tide of opinion had already brought the first warm waters of real sympathy to New Haven. Because the data are not yet fully explored, we still do not have a complete understanding of where this tide came from, but two sources are evident. One source was Yale's competition, led by Harvard. Yale College had long prided itself on the qualities that it thought made it superior to Harvard College. Yet putting pride aside, Yale often kept an eye on the example set by chief rival Harvard. Just as for generations of sportsmen the entire athletic season, be it of football, or hockey, or crew, was really only a prelude to The Game, or The Race, in admissions Yale wanted to be just as competitive as Harvard. Therefore, if in the name of good will, excellence, and diversity Harvard had accommodated traditional Jews, that was strong reason for Yale to consider doing the same.[32] The second source of the new current was apparently President Griswold. In 1960 he was ten years into his administration, and issues that should have been settled long before were still proving troubling. On the charge of biased admissions, he thought that the Connecticut Inter-Racial Commission had cleared Yale seven years before. Yet just two months prior to Coffin's letter to Provost Buck, William Horowitz (see chapter 9) had reported strong suspicions of quotas in Yale admissions. Regarding the needs of traditional Jews, six years had passed since he had called for sympathy to reign. Yet in 1960 the Reverend Coffin was informing him that "sympathy" was insufficient. The genie had escaped from its bottle, and Griswold knew that it was time to act again.

By the summer of 1961 President Griswold instructed his new provost, Kingman Brewster, Jr., that Yale policy was for the university to retain its Protestant tradition, yet simultaneously "ensure respect for other faiths . . . and further the interests of their practitioners." When Arthur Howe, Jr., now dean of admissions, conducted a December 1961 investigation into university policy toward Orthodox Jewish students, he noted that "the University is striving to make it possible for Orthodox Jewish boys to attend Yale with as little difficulty as possible." Rebates were to be given for students taking kosher meals outside the dining halls. Makeup exams were to be available outside of the Sabbath hours, and Sabbath classes were to be avoided in scheduling observant students. At first, makeups for Sabbath hour final exams were to be scheduled during periods at the start of the following semester with a conflict fee charged. In 1965 the penalty fee was dropped, and in 1966 Dean Georges May of the college promised not to penalize students who missed classes because of religious convictions.[33] Instructors whose own sympathies would be broadened by the growth in ethnic pluralism in the America of the late 1960s and 1970s were to prove ever more willing to prepare alternative exams that would be offered on a weekday during the exam period. Thus, a student would not be informally penalized by having to spend a vacation studying. Many students (of all faiths) with other legitimate reasons for rearranging examination schedules also took advantage of the new flexibility. The professors had to work harder, but the end result was a more humane institution.

In the aftermath of the Reverend Coffin's discussions with President Griswold and Rabbi Israel the university dining halls implemented a kosher "TV dinner" system to allow undergraduates to eat their kosher meals alongside their classmates. Frozen meals were stored in the freshman Commons; upperclassmen had to hand-carry their meals from Commons to their college. In the first years of the system the diners were required to pay a surcharge for each kosher meal. The growing presence in the 1960s of vegetarians, with their own special dining habits, increased administration appreciation for the desires of kosher students, however, and by the 1970s the fee was dropped. Predictably, the frozen dinners were never able to match the style or variety of the residential college dining hall food (which was widely considered then as among the best institutional food in the nation). But now the student who was sincere about his religious convictions was able to partake fully in the residential college camaraderie.[34]

While all of the administrative discussions were occurring at the start of the 1960s, the Kosher Kitchen (formally called the Young Israel Diners' Club in its first years) was growing. Much of the success in its first years grew out of the developing friendship between Rabbi Israel and Rabbi Aaron Gelman of Young Israel Synagogue. Both agreed that kosher food should be conveniently available to Yale students. Both were willing to work for it. A great step toward convenience occurred in 1962 when Daniel Greer (LL.B. 1964) found an inexpensive Dixwell Avenue apartment at the edge of the Yale campus to house the facility. Approximately a dozen students from throughout the university regularly ate there at the time, so a small apartment sufficed. That fall, freshman Carl Posy became the first undergraduate to purchase a full dining contract at the kitchen. The following year, one-third of the thirteen diners were undergraduates. With an undergraduate presence and the active support of Rabbi Israel, the permanence of the Kosher Kitchen was assured.[35]

By 1964 the kitchen moved into a rented suite at the Hotel Taft, across from

Yale's Old Campus. In 1965 the Friends of Yale Hillel purchased a home for the use of the Hillel rabbi, and the Kosher Kitchen moved into the basement of that residence at 35 High Street—a half-minute walk from the Old Campus.[36]

The change in the official Yale attitude from discouragement to tolerance to welcome toward traditional Jewish students had its impact on traditional students who might otherwise have avoided applying to Yale. The growth of the Kosher Kitchen proved just as important. Of the new breed of traditional Jews to attend Yale in the 1960s, the first was Carl Posy. A graduate of the modern Orthodox Yeshiva of Flatbush, Posy wore his upbringing in the *kippah* (skullcap) that rested upon his head. He was the first Yale collegiate to don the sign of humility before God that many traditional Jews wore on their heads.[37]

Posy recalled that he had applied to the best colleges in the vicinity of New York. Yale College particularly interested him, because of its "seductively alien" atmosphere, its reputation as a center of learning, and its grand old traditions. Skullcap atop his head, Posy traveled to New Haven in 1962 to meet interviewer R. Inslee Clark, Jr.—then the admissions officer for the New York area. In the course of their discussions Posy learned that Yale would be a problematic college for a traditionally minded student. Posy asked Clark about arrangements for kosher food. Never having had to answer that question before, Clark telephoned the Freshman Office for advice and learned that Yale had no kosher facilities. In fact, it had been university policy to discourage anyone who wanted to maintain a kosher diet from attending Yale.[38] (Kosher TV dinners were available, but this was not widely known at the time.) Would a desire to keep kosher be held against him by admissions officers, Posy asked Clark. The admissions officer replied, "Absolutely not, although it's something you might want to hold against us." When admissions time arrived, Posy found that he had been accepted, and with a generous scholarship offer. Selecting an institution that he thought offered adventure by expanding his horizons and challenging his religious position, Posy chose Yale.[39]

His opening weeks were instructive of how Yale was changing with the "unbiased" and intellectually centered admissions policy that President Griswold had enunciated and Dean Howe had initiated in 1962. The Yeshiva student's learning began with his first disappointing evening in college. Wearing his *kippah* to the opening freshman dinner in his residential college, Posy felt uncomfortable and out of place. The meal itself was, for him, unappetizing. Unaware of the availability of kosher TV dinners at university dining halls, Posy limited his consumption to the salad. The after-dinner ceremonies were no more reassuring. When the students sang the Yale alma mater, "Bright College Years," and waved their white napkins in time with the concluding phrase "For God, for country, and for Yale," Posy felt most uncertain. Everyone seemed to know exactly what he was doing. Everyone seemed so much a part of the Yale tradition. This religious New York Jew felt like an alien. Soon afterward, however, Posy became friends with a classmate who had also felt out of place at the opening night dinner. Most striking was that the friend remarked at how Posy had seemed to fit in perfectly there. Within a few days, Posy discovered that many of his fellow classmates had thought that everyone *else* had fit in. No longer were the majority of students from the traditional Yale mold. As Posy put it, "Clearly I was different—but one of the many different things happening at Yale."[40]

A cumbersome bureaucracy challenged Posy in his first attempts to avail himself of the kosher kitchen that had just opened next to the Yale campus in the fall of 1962. Though other students had previously obtained board rebates, though by 1961 it was an official university policy to make it as easy as possible for a Jewish boy to attend Yale, the bureaucracy was still recalcitrant. Upon learning of the TV dinner system, Posy decided that such a plan was far less appealing than the ten freshly cooked meals available on weekdays at the Kosher Kitchen. The dining hall administrator that Posy contacted regarding obtaining a rebate was not willing to grant Posy an exemption. When he turned to Rabbi Israel of Hillel, Posy was offered the suggestion that he settle for TV dinners during his freshman year (when meals were served in the University Commons) and quietly work things out with his college master during his sophomore year (when he would otherwise take meals in his college). For the insistent Posy, delay was not a reasonable option. Rabbi Israel's efforts, which brought the issue to the level of Provost Kingman Brewster's office, proved successful. In a move that Rabbi Israel termed "creative administration," the observance of kosher dietary laws was classified as one of the diseases that potentially qualified one for a meal contract rebate. (Others were diabetes and peptic ulcers.) For the high-ranking administrators who considered philosophical issues of managing a university, this solution affirmed the Griswold principle of religious accommodation. For the lower level bureaucrats whose framework of operation was the enforcement of regulations, it modified the rules so as to fit within a bureaucratic context.[42]

Posy was but the first of a small, but steady, trickle of traditional Jews that began to attend a more tolerant Yale. By the mid-1960s members of the Kosher Kitchen were traveling back to their high schools—with the blessing of the admissions office—to recruit more applicants. The reputation that Yale had once shared with Princeton of being hostile to Jews began to fade into memory.[43]

The experience of Orrin Persky (B.A. 1970) was a prime example of the new Yale. What made his 1960s Yale different from the Yale of previous decades was that now, despite outward appearance of differences of faith, the social doors on campus were open to all who had the congeniality, talent, and drive necessary for success. When Persky left Yale at the end of his sophomore year in 1968, he became what he believed to be the first Yale undergraduate to spend his junior year abroad at the Hebrew University in Jerusalem. In May 1969, while still in Israel, he received a telegram. The celebrated Whiffenpoof songsters, he read, had chosen him to join their company upon his return to Yale. When he arrived in September, Persky had a surprise for his friends among the Whiffs. In Israel he had adopted the trappings and practices of traditional Judaism; he had placed a *kippah* upon his head and did not travel on the Sabbath. Persky intended to maintain that level of observance at Yale and was to become the first traditional Jew to be a Yale Whiffenpoof.[44]

The singing troupe was quite willing to accommodate his needs, more so even than many of the secular Jews that he encountered in Israel:

> The Whiffs were always, first and foremost *gentlemen* songsters and·I was accepted and welcomed as an equal in all matters and as a friend. My acceptance as a Whiff stands out in my mind . . . in contrast to certain experiences as an observant person among non-religious Israelis, where respect for another man's beliefs did not find similar expression.[45]

Had he still been alive, Whitney Griswold would likely have been warmed by this testimonial to the changing Yale. He had dreamed of a Yale where inter-racial and inter-religious relations would serve as a model for national behavior. The Yale of the late 1960s was far from a perfect place in terms of human relations, but it had come a long way.

The Whiffenpoofs were always cooperative and understanding when special arrangements were necessary because of conflicts between Persky's religious obligations and the Whiffenpoof schedule. One example was a weekend that began with a Friday evening concert at the Yale Club of New York City. Following the concert, the group flew to Cleveland for the beginning of their midwestern tour. Since Persky was unwilling to fly on the Sabbath, he sang in the Yale Club concert and remained at the club (walking up and down fourteen flights of stairs) through the end of the Sabbath the next evening. He then flew from the Newark airport to Cleveland wearing his tie and tails beneath his overcoat. Once in Cleveland he took a taxi to the auditorium where the Saturday night Whiffenpoof concert was in progress. In full view of the audience he walked in through the stage door wearing his overcoat and carrying his suitcase. He then shed his coat to reveal his outfit, joined the group, and immediately commenced singing: "No one batted an eyelash. What began as an inconvenience caused by my religious observance ended as a typical piece of Whiffenpoof élan."[46] What one generation would have called an objectionable Jewish peculiarity had become a respectable diversity to a second.

Regarding his public identification as a Jewish Whiffenpoof, Persky received a wide range of comment from the audiences. Some Jewish individuals bitterly reproached him for appearing with a *kippah*—as if he had somehow caused them an embarrassment. Similarly, some of the most critical thoughts on the presence of blatantly observant Jews on campus came from Jews who were insecure about their own position. In the same way that a socially conscious Yale student of the 1910s and 1920s did not want to be "queered" by being seen in association with a Jewish student, many nonreligious Jews of the 1960s would avoid their traditional co-religionist. It was not out of a dislike of the personal characteristics of the religious student, but out of a fear of pointing to anything that might make the typically nonreligious Jew any different from his nonreligious non-Jewish classmate. Other Jews in the Whiffenpoof audiences were proud of Persky's costume and told him so. Of the non-Jews in the audience, few shared their thoughts with him. When Carl Posy had first worn his *kippah* around the Yale campus he had appeared as strange as a Martian to most Yale eyes. Doubtless, many a non-Jew reacted similarly to such an unusual Whiffenpoof as Persky.[47]

On the road Persky felt that he was treated with warm hospitality from the many families that hosted him. As a Whiffenpoof, he was given entrée to the most "exclusive" social circles and enjoyed the rare opportunity to get to know America's upper crust from the inside. Despite his very visible brand of Judaism, Persky felt that every bit of the Yale experience was open to him. There would be real disappointments. Traveling through "Middle America," he became especially conscious of his Judaism making him part of a minority in America. The United States was a nation with a constitutional separation of church and state, but the dominant religion clearly was Christianity. Later, after graduation, to feel part of a majority without giving up his beliefs and to give full meaning to his religious ideals, Persky returned to Israel to settle. But Yale and the Whiffs, he felt, had treated him honorably.[48]

By the end of the 1960s the "castle" called Yale had opened all of its gates and doors to the most visible of male Jews. If the landscape of the national "kingdom" or the decor of the campus "castle" was not to the liking of such a Jew, he was free to exercise his right to be a full participant in a democratic process of change. If he did not want to participate, he would have only himself to blame.

EPILOGUE

The two issues that were raised by the presence of the traditional Jewish student at Yale were those of religious courtesy and collegial character. In principle, courtesy was seen as a prime factor in the making of a true gentleman. At a college such as Yale where the learning of proper codes of personal behavior was so highly valued, the idea of courtesy was central to the institution. The practice of courtesy, however, was another matter, for that required work. In the case of religious courtesy, that involved the cumbersome acts of extra registration periods and makeup examinations. Consequently, when a handful of Jewish students appealed for such courtesy in the 1950s and early 1960s, accommodation was often not granted, or granted only reluctantly. Much of the pressure that was generated to convince the university administrators that religious courtesy should be practiced and not just preached arose from Hillel Foundation rabbis Joseph Gumbiner and Richard Israel. Their messages were amplified by university chaplains Sidney Lovett and William Sloane Coffin. Mr. Coffin, drawing upon the religious bonds between Christianity and Judaism, persuasively argued that the Yale Christian tradition had far more in common with the practices of traditional Jewish students than many of the university's more secular practices. In the fall of 1954, President Griswold called for compassion to rule in the case of religious conflicts with university regulations. Most significant, the notion of flexibility, however, was introduced by President Griswold in the summer of 1961 when he called upon Yale to further the interests of practitioners of faiths outside of Yale's Protestant tradition. When his 1962 admissions policy envisioned a Yale that would serve as a national model for inter-religious relations, Griswold issued the blueprint for a new college and university. The timing of these actions was a consequence of a host of events. Griswold's personal commitment to humanizing Yale lay at the heart of the changes. The launching of Sputnik and the consequent desire to bring a more diverse student body to Yale at the start of the 1960s also played their part in teaching the college the value of courtesy. The commitment and extended efforts of William Sloane Coffin and David M. Byers would also be difficult to overestimate.[49]

Permitting traditional Jewish students to eat outside of the residential college community entailed a loss to the college character of Yale, but the loss ended up to be quite small, and some unexpected benefits were accrued. Although kosher students absented themselves from mealtime in the colleges, they proved to be full participants in the life of the campus. In 1968 the Kosher Kitchen officially became affiliated with the Yale University Dining Halls.[50] Following this agreement, Yale students were assigned to the Kosher Kitchen just as they would be to any residential college dining hall. They were permitted transfer privileges enabling them to eat occasionally in the university dining halls, and other Yale students gained transfer privileges to eat occasionally in the Kosher Kitchen. The college ideal was being imperfectly realized, but the university was gaining. Nonreligious Jews and non-Jews would regularly be found dining with their roommates or friends in the Kosher Kitchen. Yale students of all types began to have yet a new laboratory to learn the beliefs and practices of those with traditions different from their own. As the number of Yale undergraduates increased from four thousand to five thousand between 1965 and 1975 and the residential colleges became grossly overcrowded, the Kosher Kitchen served an important purpose. On a campus where it was not unusual to stand in line for twenty minutes waiting for lunch at Commons or where finding a table for four at dinner could be a formidable challenge during peak hours, the Kosher Kitchen provided an alternative to the crowds.[51]

Though one deficiency in the college ideal was kosher-inspired, the late 1960s also produced other cracks in the collegiate ideal that were even more fundamental. The 33 percent growth in the undergraduate population between 1960 and 1975 (largely caused by budgetary pressures and the acceptance of groups that had previously been avoided in Yale admissions) led to a decline in the percentage of students living in college-owned buildings, from 97 percent to 87.[52] University administrators therefore turned their attention from the more minor issue of kosher dining to the major threat to the collegiate ideal posed by inadequate collegiate housing. Within the dining halls themselves, a growing concern was that white and black students were tending to eat at separate tables.[53] In continuing its move from being college to university college Yale chose to give up some of its homogeneity. But the gain in its universal character, it was hoped, would allow for the respect of different ideas and different peoples to teach more than a purely collegiate setting had ever offered.

Chapter 12 Finding the
Best Doctors

For all the controversy that he evoked, Milton Winternitz had moved Yale from the dark ages of American medicine into modernity. Old-timers still in New Haven fifty years after the Winternitz deanship would fondly reminisce about the man whom they considered to be the strongest leader that the medical school had ever had. Later deans would expand the school further, but, said the old men, the later deans were mere caretakers. Winternitz certainly was the most charismatic leader of Yale medicine. In the seventeen-year "interregnum" that followed his leaving the deanship in 1935, the medical school lost some of its vitality. Dean Stanhope Bayne-Jones (1935–40) weakened the Winternitz commitment to developing the scientific foundations of the art of medicine and restrained the emphatic efforts that had previously been made to link the medical and social sciences. Bayne-Jones was succeeded by Francis Gilman Blake (1940–47) and Cyril N. H. Long (1947–52). Though some of the departments (e.g., pediatrics) retained their preeminence throughout the interregnum, not until the deanship of Vernon Lippard (1952–67) would the Yale School of Medicine once again be a center of progress. The most significant changes during these years were as much a function of New Haven personalities as of outside events. The passage of the Hill-Burton Act in 1946 funded hospital construction across the nation, and the subsequent federal funding of the National Institutes of Health released vast amounts of research dollars. Between 1947 and 1952 the federal government's share of medical research support in America increased from less than one-third to over one-half of the total. With new grants readily available, the Yale School of Medicine became swept up in the vortex of schools striving for the financing that would permit new experiments, new laboratories, new professors, and new hospital beds. The governmental commitment to distributing funds to the nation's best scientists, regardless of personal background, forced medical schools that wished to compete for federal support to place competence and creativity at the top of their list of criteria for selecting faculty. Personality would have to take second place when tenure was being considered. Racial and religious barriers would no longer be permitted to influence decisions. In an unprecedented postwar expansion of American medical science, it was the competition for quality that broke down the discriminatory barriers that had operated especially against Jews, and to some extent against Catholics and women, at the Yale School of Medicine.[1]

THE FACULTY

It is not surprising that the break in anti-Jewish policies regarding the hiring of faculty emerged from the department of psychiatry. Among Jewish physicians in the United States a disproportionately high percentage have long chosen the field of psychiatry. There are several reasons speculated for this choice. The most common one is that Jews have been attracted to psychiatry because of its cerebral and analytical nature. Despite its being a low-paying medical specialty, psychiatry also allowed a physician a great degree of independence. Because so many Jewish doctors chose psychiatry it was natural that from the days of Sigmund Freud through the present day, many outstanding psychiatrists have been Jewish.[2] The 1930 appointment of Eugen Kahn as Sterling Professor of Psychiatry and Mental Hygiene did not represent any philo-Jewish form of behavior but rather a search for the man most qualified to lead a new department of psychiatry at Yale.

A regular commitment to hire the most qualified faculty to senior positions, however, did not commence prior to the 1950s. But the seed for the commitment was planted in 1942, when Kahn's department of psychiatry and mental hygiene appointed Fredrick C. Redlich as an instructor. Redlich, born an Austrian Catholic, yet of Jewish grandparentage, was a 1935 graduate of the medical school at the University of Vienna. Because of the Nazi rise to power he left Europe and emigrated to the United States. Among the pieces of emotional baggage that he transported to the United States was a disdain for prejudice. Plainly aware of what his own fate might have been had he remained in Europe, Redlich was determined to evaluate people on their merits rather than on racial or religious grounds. Protecting his own position, however, he was also careful to conceal the religious strains in his family tree; he left people guessing about his background. Redlich's scientific work was creditable and his political abilities were formidable: in nine years at Yale he would soar from the lowly position of instructor up to full professor and psychiatry department chairman. As his departmental influence gained, he played an increasing role in faculty discussions over hiring. On several occasions, he recalled, there would be departmental debates over the appointment of too many Jews. On occasion a Jewish friend of his within the department would tell him that he feared Yale psychiatry's earning the label of "a Jewish department." When Redlich helped influence the hiring of Lawrence S. Kubie as a lecturer in 1947, the university's director of medical affairs warned Redlich to be careful not to encourage too many Jews. The appointment of Rudolph M. Loewenstein, an honored developer of ego psychology, as a clinical professor of psychiatry elicited the same reaction. As late as 1948, Abraham White (associate professor of physiological chemistry) felt obliged to leave the university (to become full professor and biochemistry department chairman at U.C.L.A.). He had been told by senior Yale faculty that his being Jewish would prevent him from ever gaining a full professorship in New Haven. White eventually became a co-author of one of the most highly respected textbooks in his field. In the name of "balance"—the watchword at Yale—the good were retained and a few of the excellent were lost forever.[3]

Redlich observed the quest for quality originating from both the "grass roots" and the very top levels of the university. At the bottom, by 1950 there were enough low-level faculty who wanted to see Yale improve that they refused to tolerate bias on the part of their fellow professors. At the top there was President A. Whitney Griswold. He encouraged his deans and department chairmen to appoint the most qualified teachers regardless of religion, race, or personal beliefs. Symbolic of this conviction, Redlich recalled hiring a Communist to teach in the psychiatry department in 1954—amidst the McCarthy era witchhunts. When Redlich came under fire for this move, Griswold, no supporter of Communism, came to Redlich's defense and backed up the department chairman.[4]

Within a few months of Redlich's appointment in 1951 as chairman of the psychiatry department, he moved to bring in Theodore Lidz as a full professor of psychiatry. On visiting Yale, Lidz was well aware of the rumors claiming that Yale discriminated against Jews in the hiring process. By fall 1950, for example, of the twenty-four professors on the medical school board of permanent officers, not one was a Jew. Professor Joseph Fruton of biochemistry was the sole Jew among the twenty-seven full professors on the teaching faculty. These numbers alone could not prove discrimination, but they were suspicious. There were simply too many excellent Jewish medical professors in the nation for a school that boasted of its eminence not to have a single Jew among its most senior faculty. The prejudice against hiring of Jews operated to a lesser extent at the lower faculty levels. Since Lidz had not previously advertised his religion but was conscious of the rumors, he was uncertain if the exclusive faculty had themselves been unaware of his background and had appointed him in error. Not wanting to enter under false pretenses, Lidz approached senior administrators to inform them of his Judaism before he would accept the position. As of 1951 the bias against hiring Jewish faculty, Lidz learned, had disappeared. Led by faculty such as Harry S. N. Greene (pathology department chairman 1951–69), Yale medicine was recognizing talent. Greene set a standard by refusing to leave Yale for Johns Hopkins and the nation's most prestigious pathology chair, a position that he thought was rightfully deserved by a Jewish professor already at Johns Hopkins. Other medical school leaders who committed themselves to the quest for talent were Paul Beeson, chairman of the department of medicine from 1952 through 1965, and Vernon Lippard, dean of the medical school over the same period. Lidz was the first of a wave of Jewish medical faculty who would have successful careers at Yale.[5]

THE STUDENTS

At Yale, as at many other of the nation's other medical schools, the effort to restrain the enrollment of certain minorities so that their proportions would partially represent their representation among the American people continued unabated through the Second World War. Throughout the era, the Yale medical school dean kept close personal rein over the process which was not a purely

Jewish quota but rather a conglomeration of "ethnic" quotas. Because of the volume of Jewish applicants, Jews were most greatly limited by the system, though Italians, Catholics, and women also suffered.[6]

Just as the war stimulated the growth of meritocracy in so many aspects of American life, it stimulated the opponents of discrimination in medical schools to speak out. Alvin S. Johnson, guiding light of the New School for Social Research, was one of many after the war to point out the sharp cleavage between the needs of the nation and unfair admissions practices:

> If it is hard for the democrat to tolerate a discriminatory way of life in the colleges, it is impossible for him to tolerate discrimination in the graduate and professional schools. These do not exist for the promotion of a peculiar way of life, but for the training of men and women for the service of the public. The public needs the best physicians, the best engineers and architects, the best research scientists it can get. Any warping of admissions requirements away from the principles of competence is a serious betrayal of the public trust.[7]

To those who would defend the limitation of Jewish medical students because of the supposed character flaws in Jews, Johnson had an original answer:

> It is charged by members of [some] medical faculties that Jews do not make good doctors. They are said to be dominated by commercialism. Jewish doctors, at least some of them, are very alive to the main chance. How about other doctors? The most injurious form of commercialism is the striving for monopoly. What does the exclusion of Jewish students from the medical colleges mean except an effort to monopolize the emoluments of medicine for the Gentile group?[8]

Arguments such as Johnson's did not succeed in pushing an antidiscrimination bill through the Connecticut legislature. The voices of justice, however, did reach some sympathetic ears.

Among the responsive listeners was Fredrick Redlich. When he joined the admissions committee in the mid-1940s, he found evidence of an effective *numerus clausus* that restricted the Jewish enrollment to six or fewer students per year—approximately 10 percent of each class. Most of these students were from wealthy homes; applicants from the Bronx or Brooklyn were generally not accepted because, a priori, they were considered to have poor manners. Redlich, who wondered how the quota could operate so silently, without his knowledge, precisely while he sat on the admissions committee, approached Registrar Kathleen Dasey for enlightenment. Dasey, who had faithfully served as assistant registrar from 1921 to 1923 and since that time as registrar, explained that the reason the same number of Jews regularly entered the medical school was that she kept a separate file for Jewish applicants. She also kept track of how many were being sent letters of acceptance. Given Redlich's own personal background it was no wonder that he asked her how she identified Jewish applicants. That, she explained, was determined from her appraisal of a candidate's last name. On investigation, Redlich discovered that her system was not fully reliable. Some Jews would slip in undetected while other non-Jews might find themselves unfairly excluded from Yale. Redlich was convinced that the system, reliable or not, was an unfair one.

So arose the Yale question: In a "civilized" institution, supposedly above prejudice, how did one confront very real racial and religious biases that were in operation? Redlich turned to a friend for advice. And once again the name of Eugene Rostow entered the story. Rostow, now a full professor of law, suggested that Redlich speak to Milton Winternitz on the issue. Winternitz, after all, was Jewish, had been dean of the medical school for fifteen years, and would best understand the Yale admissions system that he had established. Winternitz was unsympathetic. The ex-dean was not opposed to Jews entering medicine, per se. In the late 1940s he supported the development of the Hadassah Medical School in Jerusalem. His thoughts regarding New Haven, however, were somewhat different. Politically sidelined and embittered by his ouster as dean, Winternitz abruptly dismissed Redlich's protests with his stock answer to charges of discrimination: "Redlich, what are you trying to do? Do you want to make a synagogue out of this place?" When Redlich explained that, having once lived under Nazi rule, he could not accept racial or religious discrimination, Winternitz was unimpressed. So Redlich moved on. Having failed to win the former dean's sympathy, Redlich confronted the problem directly. He approached Donald H. Barron, assistant dean of the school of medicine (1945–48) and chairman of admissions. Again a stone wall. Barron was unhappy that Redlich, then a lowly assistant professor, was trying to rock the boat. Since the ship of Yale medicine wanted to think that it was cruising smoothly, the plaints of a disgruntled crew member were not welcome. A different tack, Redlich realized, was required.[9]

In the meantime, Eugene Rostow as also growing increasingly disenchanted with Yale duplicity and double standards. When in the spring of 1945 Yale representatives testified before the Connecticut Legislature in opposition to anti-discrimination bills, Rostow suspected that the university was not just engaging in offering misleading testimony, but was also abandoning its ideals of serving the nation. He approached University Secretary Carl Lohmann, who told him that Yale opposed the contemplated laws because the punishment they threatened (removal of tax exemptions on the university) did not fit the crime of discrimination. Besides, Lohmann told the law professor, Yale did not practice any forms of discrimination at all. Therefore, such a bill was completely unnecessary. Rostow could not accept Yale's refusal to look at itself.[10]

If the navy captains would not put Yale on an even-keeled course, Rostow would speak directly to their commander-in-chief. In 1931, while an undergraduate, he had fought prejudice in the pages of the *Harkness Hoot;* as a full professor of law in 1945 he thought it more prudent to work through private channels. Acting with discretion but refusing to deviate from his direction, Rostow called on Yale to mend its ways. Two days after Germany surrendered to the Allied forces, one month before Rostow would publish a landmark article condemning the treatment of Japanese Americans during the Second World War, he penned a letter to President Charles Seymour and expressed a determination to fight injustice locally:

> [For some time,] I have meant to take up a question of University policy with you[:] discrimination in our admission practices, and especially the quota system against Jews in the School of Medicine. . . . Yale's record in this respect is not bad, except in one or two particulars, and has been improving—[yet, unlike our testimony before the Legislature,] we are in no position to claim that we are free of the disease. . . .
>
> Our experience with Hitlerism in all its forms has changed the meaning of anti-Semitism and other kinds of group discrimination. They are no longer merely unattractive social sins, but a powerful symbol, a political weapon, a tool of violence. The University should not condone them, nor further their spread, by example or otherwise. It is more important than ever that the University, like other institutions which mold attitudes and opinion, take a bold lead in vindicating its educational principles in ever possible way. . . .
>
> There is another aspect of the question. The war has quickened the process of social change. New men and new classes are demanding equal opportunities. The fair employment practice statues are a profound and, as I believe, a healthy sign of the times. The great private universities, which have so far led in the development of American scholarship and education, must meet the challenges of new social needs and conditions. We are a national trust, and our responsibilities in the field of educational policy are the very heavy obligations of creative, constructive leadership. The policies which govern our action should rest on principle, without equivocation or compromise. And we must realize that in our time the need for trained men is so great, and our national resources of ability and character so limited, that the community can no longer afford the waste of allowing a poor student to displace a good one.
>
> This is an issue of principle and social circumstance, not to be considered on

grounds of risk. Yet the University faces real risks if present practices are continued. Manifestly, such practices will be known. And public criticism at this state will be severe, and damaging both to the University and to other values in the community.

Any such controversy is likely to be especially acute over the medical schools. In the last twenty years, great progress has been made in raising the standard of medical training. But in admissions what our medical schools have all done is to accept the commercial-country-club criteria of the American Medical Association. . . . Unworthy standards have prevailed in the selection of candidates for admission to this restricted circle. Our practice of having a quota, which normally amounts to 10 percent for Jewish students, is a shocking anomaly, unworthy of Yale, or any other American university. To the extent that medical schools pass over applicants of superior professional promise, they attack the standards of medical science and medical care for the community at large. I doubt whether people are going to continue to stand for it. . . .

This is an issue of direct concern to every member of the Yale family. I urge that in this regard, Yale should fully satisfy its own values, and base its admission policy on educational and professional criteria alone. This is the only possible standard for a university which aspires to serve the American community.[11]

At a meeting that followed between Seymour and Rostow, the latter warned again of the great controversy that would brew as America began to demand a meritocratic and less aristocratic leadership. President Seymour, recalled Rostow, assured him that there would be a change.[12]

By 1948, 20 percent of the students entering the medical school were Jewish. Under the direction of Thomas R. Forbes, Jr., the admissions committee moved to become blind to color and religion. This is not to say that Jewish (or other "minority") applicants immediately found themselves having the same chances of admission as "non-minority" applicants. For example, in 1948 a "Hebrew" (as the medical admissions office still referred to Jews) would have a one in fifty chance of entering the medical school, a "Negro" applicant would have a one in forty chance, while the non-Negro non-Hebrew would have a one in twenty chance. In terms of grades, accepted Jews had a 87.2 average and accepted non-Jews had a 85.0 average. The average grades of rejected Jews were greater than those of rejected non-Jews by a similar margin. It was a difference, but not a spectacular one. There were still anti-Jewish and antiblack biases in admissions at many of the nation's better colleges (which acted as feeder schools for the medical schools in a manner similar to the way that prep schools acted for colleges like Yale). The fact alone could account for the difficulty that Jewish and black students faced in Yale medical admissions in 1948.[13]

On the regional scene, Yale medical admissions gave up their racial and religious biases at approximately the same time as other medical schools. By the mid-1950s anti-Jewish discrimination was no longer a realistic charge to be leveled. The changes had come about for many reasons. An important one was the growth of science in postwar America. The explosive increase in scientifically oriented jobs in the postwar era drew many Jews away from medical interests to the more solid sciences. Consequently, some of the pressure on medical schools to accept Jewish applicants declined. The opening of the Albert Einstein Medical College of Yeshiva University, which promised and delivered racially and religiously blind admissions, also helped relieve some of the pressure on other medical schools. The chances of acceptance for all medical school applicants increased through 1960 as the number of applicants to medical schools nationwide declined from four applicants per place in 1948 to less than two in 1960. By then sociologists Nathan Glazer and Daniel Moynihan were able to state that "qualified Jewish students have no problem getting into a medical school." Also significant were the thinkers who began to expose the deception in the "balanced" classes that medical schools like Yale had once claimed to be accepting. One example was Lawrence Bloomgarden's castigation of "balance" in a 1953 issue of *Commentary:*

> It is clearly an argument of convenience, never used to justify expansion of opportunity for minority groups, but only for limitation. It is never said, for example, that Negro medical students should constitute 10 per cent of the total to correspond to the Negro percentage of our population; nor is it ever argued that Jewish executives in banks and insurance companies, two fields in which Jews are poorly represented on the administrative level, should . . . correspond to the Jewish percentage of the population.[14]

When women and blacks gained political power in the 1970s exactly such arguments would be heard, especially in regard to the distribution of government construction contracts to female- or black-owned businesses. Nevertheless, for the 1950s Bloomgarden was correct in his assessment. "Balance" had operated to exclude rather than include. By 1960 the specious need for national balances had yielded to promises of quality.

Through the 1950s there were sub rosa suggestions of anti-Jewish bias in Yale medical admissions. But these seem to have persisted more because of the public relations difficulties of the dean of admissions than because of any real bias. For example, when asked if Yale discriminated on the basis of race or religion, Dean Forbes would sometimes insist that the admissions office had no knowledge of an applicant's religion or race. In the 1950s the application form made no request for race or religion, nor did it ask for a photograph. What undercut this claim, however, was that on other occasions Forbes would point to the list of medical students printed in the school catalogue and state that "the briefest examination of . . . the names of our students . . . would confirm how unfair is the accusation of racial discrimination." Despite his recognized decency, Forbes could not claim blindness to a candidate's ethnic background and simultaneously identify a student's ethnic background on a list in the course catalogue without feeding the fires of suspicion.[15]

EPILOGUE

Although significant liberalization took place in the 1950s, all forms of unfair discrimination did not disappear in that decade. Through the late 1960s women (of all colors and faiths) were admitted under a strict quota. Not until the 1970s and the growth of the women's movement in America did truly sex-blinded principles find their way into the admissions office. Black students, reportedly, were not discriminated against by the medical admissions office in the 1960s, but attempts to increase the number of blacks admitted to Yale in that decade did not easily succeed. From one standpoint, relatively few of the black applicants were academically competitive with their white counterparts. Few were therefore accepted. From a second standpoint, the low acceptance rate led many blacks to avoid wasting an application on Yale and therefore harmed Yale's attempts to increase the enrollment of qualified black applicants.[16]

Though it would not have its full impact until the 1970s, the commitment to quality made in the early 1950s would affect the members of all races, religions, and sexes in the school of medicine.

Chapter 13 Breaking the Barriers: The Faculty, Corporation, and Administration

Prior to the Second World War, Yale Jewish faculty existed in an intellectual and social demimonde. In the spiritual heart of Yale, in the college, one could occasionally find an insignificant Jewish instructor or assistant professor, but never a senior faculty member. In the graduate school an outstanding man like a Lafayette B. Mendel might shine, if he was sufficiently brilliant. Departments such as English were notorious for excluding Jews.

In the eighteenth and nineteenth centuries these restrictive policies were fully in keeping with the religious character of Yale. Though the appointment of a Jewish professor then might have been a meaningful gesture to the ideals of knowledge and inquiry, those ideals were not widely held at Yale in its early years of existence. Outstanding minds were sometimes passed over in favor of those whose creeds were compatible with Yale. Its first priority was the preservation of its Congregationalist Protestant Christian collegiate way of life. That men like Ezra Stiles, Benjamin Silliman, and Nathan Smith happened to possess some of the most brilliant intellects of their times was the college's good fortune. With such goals the exclusion of Jews and other worshipers of unacceptable gods was a natural consequence.

The late nineteenth- and early twentieth-century Yale, however, retained its religious prejudices even when its religious core had virtually dissolved. The formal creation of Yale University in 1887 represented the first major crack in the core, when expansion of formerly collegiate departments into graduate and professional schools left no room for religious or collegiate requirements. Had the school of medicine perhaps chosen to stress faith healing, religion might still have held its powerful place, but this was not the course that Yale medical leaders chose. The commitment to graduate study as a path to national enlightenment theoretically left no room for personal biases: The purpose of a graduate school was simply to train the finest scholars. In the college itself, the declining religious interest of the students led to the abandonment of the last formal religious requirements in 1925. Yale College forsook true commitment to a religious character of any sort. Still, the desire for a collegiate homogeneity survived. Because Jewish faculty did not fit this model of homogeneity, their acceptance into the college and university was not complete.

The Japanese thunderbolt that struck Pearl Harbor in 1941 sent shock waves through Yale. A nation at war needed its best minds to combat the threats from Asia and Europe. As a result, many of the university's best faculty were called away from New Haven to serve U.S. intelligence organizations such as the Office for Strategic Services. Meanwhile, battalions of soldiers were stationed at Yale for a military training that the depleted faculty was ill-equipped to handle. The fighting in the Far East required that soldiers gain familiarity with obscure languages that had not been part of the regular Yale curriculum. A solid grounding in Greek and Latin made one an educated man, but an ability to communicate with natives of Burma or the Philippine Islands might allow one to live. If the best available instructor for Yale was a Jew, so be it. For the sake of national duty, past prejudices would be held in abeyance. It was no coincidence, therefore, that in 1942 Isidore Dyen was placed on the Yale College faculty as an instructor in Malayan languages. The next year he was promoted to the level of assistant professor. No Jewish member of the college faculty before him had ever achieved a senior position. When he was appointed an associate professor in 1948, he was transferred to the graduate school faculty. Following the merger of the college and graduate faculties some two decades later, Dyen was to serve both schools. In February 1943 Bernard Bloch was brought to the Yale Graduate School to teach Japanese as an assistant professor of linguistics.

He would rise to become chairman of the department of Indic and Far Eastern languages and literature in 1952.[1]

In the department of history the trailblazers were Rollin Osterweis and Robert Lopez. As Osterweis recalled, prejudices in that department evanesced when the war left it short-handed. Desperate for faculty, the historians appointed Osterweis as a full instructor in 1943 despite his not having yet submitted his dissertation. Well aware of Osterweis's religious background and Yale's past record, department chairman Leonard W. Labaree explained to him that if he did well, he would be eligible for tenure on the college faculty. In later years Osterweis would achieve prominence as director of the college's debating and public speaking program, and, in 1968, he would become a full professor of history and oratory.[2] Lopez, son of the Italian playwright Sabatino Lopez and a student of medieval economic history, was appointed to the history department college faculty as an assistant professor in 1946. When Lopez was brought to Yale, he was told that he was coming in a time of crisis; he was to replace three professors who had either retired or died. A Sephardic Jewish refugee from Mussolini's Italy (by way of Wisconsin), Lopez informed the appointments committee of his religious background. Knowing something of Yale's past, he did not want to enter under false pretenses. Lopez would eventually rise to become a Sterling Professor of History.[3]

The first fair employment practices law prohibiting racial and religious biases in selecting employees was enacted in New York state in 1945. Connecticut passed its version of the law in 1947. State laws such as these reflected public sentiment, but were not always immediately effective.[4] In the university setting, where subjective factors often played a legitimate role in hiring faculty, such laws could only hold the force of moral suasion, not the power of coercion.

Throughout the university, some of these moral forces did take hold. Even the imposing English department, exclusive and anti-Jewish like its counterparts at Harvard and Princeton, could not go unaffected by the meritocratic impulses of the world war. It had already come under attack by the undergraduate intelligentsia of the 1930s when the pages of the *Harkness Hoot* and the drawing rooms of the Elizabethan Club became wellsprings of publicized criticism. The students badgered a department that they claimed offered more show than substance. Indeed, it is possible that a part of the department's fear about hiring competent Jewish faculty was that it would be hiring people who would challenge its real weaknesses. At the start of the world war, when the name of Lionel Trilling was recommended for appointment at an interdepartmental meeting, Professor Chauncey Brewster Tinker summarily vetoed the idea because of Trilling's Jewish background. After the war, as the department came to accept the undergraduate view that its courses sorely lacked intellectual vigor, its policies changed. Also significant was the retirement in 1945 of Tinker: No longer was his voice on the faculty so influential. Another cause for the change came from a philosophical standpoint. There were Jewish graduate students in the department whose work was of the very highest caliber. Richard Ellmann received his Ph.D. in 1947 and Charles Feidelson (B.A. 1938) received his the following year. The idea that two of Yale's very best students should be denied a place at Yale seemed incongruous with the standards of excellence that the college hoped to maintain. It had prided itself on being the best in the nation. To exclude men like Ellmann and Feidelson would risk Yale's losing its preeminence. When Feidelson was appointed an instructor in the department in 1947, he became the first known Jew to hold a teaching position in English at Yale. No fanfare attended the appointment because there was no longer a Jewish issue. Quality would out. By 1959 he was a full professor. Had Feidelson listened to his Yale undergraduate professors, he would not have embarked on the quixotic enterprise. But through his own efforts and a world-shaking war, he defeated a windmill.[5]

Pioneers on the science faculty of the college included botanist Arthur Galston and chemist Harry H. Wasserman. In 1946 Galston, discoverer of a chemical that promoted plant growth, became an instructor on the college faculty. Though his unhappiness with being what he called "low man on the totem pole" of academe led him to leave the university after only one year, his Judaism did not adversely affect his appointment. He represented excellence, and the postwar botany faculty was committed to that goal. For Wasserman, who was told by many in 1948 that he was unwise to accept an appointment as instructor at Yale College (because of its reputed lack of hospitality toward Jews), his move to New Haven was the start of a successful career. He proved to be one of the most popular science professors in the college. With a warm lecturing style and creative use of wit and the chalkboard, Wasserman made organic chemistry a pleasure for thousands of pre-medical students.[6]

THE WEISS APPOINTMENT

All the changes in the Yale attitude toward the hiring of faculty crystallized in the appointment of philosopher Paul Weiss as full professor in Yale College in 1946. When the college and university appointed him, he became the first Jew to hold the rank of full professor, complete with tenure and the other trappings of senior rank. At that time Yale took a step from which there could be no turning back. Other Jews had received tenure before. Most prominent were Winternitz in the medical school, Mendel in the medical, scientific, and graduate schools, and Sapir in the graduate school. Mendel and Sapir were far better known, however, for being academic gewgaws, ornaments to a great university, than for being central to the institution. By inviting Weiss to the college faculty in 1946, the academic center of Yale opened its doors to give a Jew a chance to share in the responsibility for determining the nature of Yale as well as its prestige.

The particulars of the great Yale change began in 1945 when Brand Blanshard arrived in New Haven to assume the acting chairmanship of the philosophy department. A sudden illness dampened his arrival, forcing him to take a one semester leave of absence. To cover his withdrawal, Blanshard arranged for Paul Weiss, chairman of the Bryn Mawr College philosophy department, to assume his teaching responsibilities for the term. Filmer S. C. Northrop, professor of philosophy and master of Silliman College, took a liking to the new visiting professor of philosophy and invited Weiss to join the fellowship of Northrop's residential college. As Weiss's first Yale semester passed and as Blanshard regained his health, it came time to decide Weiss's fate. Opinions were mixed. The students clamored for him to be permitted to stay. His fellow philosophers welcomed his presence. The rest of the college faculty, however, was not so taken by the prospect of having Weiss on a permanent basis. Some were aghast at the idea of his appointment. Weiss was a product of the poverty of New York City's Lower East Side. He had been a student of Morris R. Cohen's at the City College of New York. He was also a Jew.[7]

From an intellectual standpoint, Weiss's credentials were spectacular, as attested to by his letters of recommendation. Harvard's great philosopher Alfred North Whitehead called his former pupil Weiss a "first-class" teacher. Former Harvard and Yale professor of philosophy William Ernest Hocking recognized Weiss's "incisive mental power, stimulating quality as a teacher, [and] cogent writing on the great themes of metaphysics." Harvard chairman of philosophy Clarence I. Lewis called Weiss one of the best American philosophical thinkers of his generation. University of Chicago acting philosophy chairman Charner Perry placed Weiss "in the very small group [of] American teachers of philosophy [of his generation] who are doing original, sound and important work." The only deeply felt criticism of intellect came from the religiously minded former Yale trustee Henry Sloane Coffin, who felt that Weiss knew too little about the Christian basis for ethics. For the expanding department of philosophy at Yale, the consensus was that Weiss would have been a plum.

The question of personality was where the real conflict of opinion occurred. In this sphere of decision-making, racial stereotypes were sometimes allowed to cloud rational thought. Those who knew Weiss well were full of praise. The Silliman College fellowship lauded this philosopher who enlivened their company with his brilliance and congeniality. Alfred North Whitehead called Weiss "a close friend" of almost two decades. Harvard philosophy chairman Lewis was effusive in his acclaim:

> In point of personality and character, I have the highest admiration and liking for him. His steadiness, integrity, frankness and balance make him the kind of loyal and effective co-worker with whom one is glad to be associated.

Along with his praise, William Ernest Hocking also had a vague uneasiness. Hocking doubted that Weiss had the "breadth of beam for a position in which a sympathetic rapport with the whole extent of our culture is as necessary as argumentative skill." Hocking was uncertain as to whether Weiss would be able to command the "intuitive regard" of the Yale students. Others on the faculty, who knew him only from a distance, considered him a caricature of the all-knowing and pushy Jew. Their underlying hesitation was best expressed in the qualified endorsement of Weiss by Charles W. Hendel—titular head of the philosophy department, who at the time of the deliberations was still giving service to the United States War Department in the aftermath of the war. Hendel had kept Weiss in mind since Whitehead had recommended the metaphysicist to him several years earlier. In one paragraph, Hendel, a Princetonian by education, summarized the attitudes of a generation:

> I have the very highest opinion of his intellectual qualities, of his philosophical powers, vision, acumen, etc., and of his teaching abilities. . . . But there is a possible liability which we must frankly face. It is not that he is a Jew. But it has to do with the deficiencies that Jewish people labor under apart from racial prejudice. It is a likely lack of social discretion. I say "likely" only because I have heard from Professor Blanshard himself reports previously of his manners, so to speak, in assemblies of people, philosophical gatherings which can forgive things that others will not tolerate. It is so difficult for men who like Weiss have been brought out of the lowliest social conditions to know how to behave in a society of genuine equality where it is not necessary to assert oneself. I wonder whether there is any trace of bravado, intellectual bravado, in him where he might feel himself called upon to champion some cause for intellectual freedom. Something like that has been reported to

me. . . . Yale is too great an institution to be deterred by slight things from acquiring the services of a really great scholar. I believe that Weiss has these qualities—that he might go beyond any one of us who are choosing him for this . . . appointment. It is always possible that when a man finds a great environment he shows *only* his own greatness and power. This is what I hope. So I welcome more than I can say the experiment with Weiss.[8]

As long as a Jew could not have been a "gentleman," he could not have been part of a society of gentleman scholars. With Paul Weiss, however, the college faculty was ready to break the shackles of its prejudiced past.

However much modern sensibility pierces through the rationalizations of men like Hendel, they honestly thought they were above bigotry. Their biases were not purely anti-Jewish. A great deal of the prejudice was an upper class desire to exclude men they thought deficient in social refinement. To the extent that they could, the faculty were "objectively" evaluating that subjective quality called personality. But it was in their subjective evaluations that biases came through. Some Jewish academics had become iconoclastic as a result of their exclusion from some of the most respected halls of academe. There is no doubt that there were offensive Jews in 1940s America, just as there were offensive members of every other ethnic and establishment group. There is no doubt that the social manner of the nation's upper classes differed from its lower classes and that academic and economic climbing of the American ladder of opportunity proceeded faster than the acquisition of social graces. But prejudices operated where individuals were judged on the basis of the stereotype of the ethnic or social group to which they belonged. Until 1946 even the most genteel of Jews was unwelcome in the highest Yale circles. In the case of Weiss, who was at times abrasive or critical of perceived mediocrity, a Whitehead or a Lewis who judged on the basis of personal knowledge would call the Jewish philosopher a friend or a loyal and effective co-worker. A Hendel, who was not personally acquainted with the man he was judging, would create a cloud of suspicion regarding Weiss's social background, rather than completely deferring personal judgment until he got to know the man.

Yet Hendel's words also heralded the onset of modernity. By war's end Yale was ready to commit itself (if hesitantly) to the quest for quality. Hendel wrote Seymour that he did not want "to miss any opportunity to observe [Weiss] in his new post and in all his relationships, as early as possible and as long as possible." But the essential conclusion was that Yale was willing to open its doors somewhat. The Second World War had convinced the university powers that for Yale best to serve its country it had to risk some of its societal nature for the sake of talent. In later decades the college and university would often continue to choose what one Yale economics professor called "comfortable people" who would not overly disturb a sense of complacency. French scholar Henri Peyre, chairman of the departments of French and Romance languages between 1939 and 1964, had no hesitation about recruiting faculty whose personalities would be compatible with others in his department. Intradepartmental feuding, he considered, was the plague of many a university and he was determined to avoid that curse in his dominion. Yet, as Peyre built one of the outstanding French departments in the nation, he had no hesitation about judging people on their own merits. One of his most significant appointments was that of Erich Auerbach as professor of French and Romance philology in 1950. Personality would continue to count, but it would come second, and it would be judged on the basis of the individual, not stereotypes.[9]

To break through the stereotypes, Brand Blanshard, the recuperating acting head of Yale philosophy, wrote to Grace de Laguna, retired professor of philosophy at Bryn Mawr. In explicit terms, Blanshard asked for a thorough analysis of Weiss's personality and abilities:

> Would you be good enough to lay reserves and proprieties on the shelf for a little while and tell me just what kind of fish we have got in Paul Weiss? We are all sure of one thing: he is no minnow. But whether he is authentic Leviathan (as he appears to believe profoundly) or one of those strange irridescent creatures that inhabit the depths and are likely to burst through their own inner pressure if landed we don't feel sure.
>
> Yale has a program of expansion afoot in philosophy. When we asked Paul to come, it was of course immediately because my own place had to be filled for a term while I was carpentered into shape. But it is inevitable that our thought should turn to him as a possible man for permanent tenure. And here we are not sure of our ground. As you know, I think, I both like and admire him. And yet he constantly says and does things that so completely disregard what most of us regard as the minor proprieties that one doesn't quite know what to make of him. If he did come to Yale, his field and mine would overlap: all would be well if neither of us were the sort of person who pushed, encroached, or competed; but if either of us failed in such things, it might mean a deal of the sort of heartburning that no department ought to have. He *seems* to me a fundamentally sweet-tempered fellow. But I have had rumors of his fluttering the administrative dovecotes at Bryn Mawr by his extreme individualism, and I can't think of anyone but you—who have worked with him so intimately and so long—from whom I could reasonably expect to get the truth about these. It is not, I hope, that I attach undue importance to externals. It is rather that a university like Yale is in a position to command people who are *both* intellectually

first-rate *and* personable all the way through, and that an inquiry into Weiss's personal quality is inevitable.

I know I am asking you a question that may be hard to answer with confidence or definiteness; but I think so much of your objectivity of mind that if you can give something of an answer, I shall be most grateful. . . .[10]

Professor de Laguna did not disappoint her questioner. In a detailed exposition she separated Weiss's quirks from his qualities. With critical honesty, she was full of praise:

The truth about Paul is not simple. The problem you are now meeting is the same one I faced when it was a question of bringing him here to Bryn Mawr, although at that time I had to guess at the sheer intellectual ability which has since become manifest. I was well aware then that one could not expect him to respect such proprieties as you mention, and that there would be difficulties in living and working with one at once so dynamic and impetuous and so little regardful of conventions and even of amenities. But I decided then—and . . . would make the same decision again today—that the value of his intellectual stimulus to the department and to the College was worth the cost. . . .

Of his philosophical ability there is no need for me to speak. [You] have had ample [opportunity] to judge that for yourself. And you doubtless have a pretty good idea of what a stimulating teacher he is and of the enthusiasm for work he inspires in his students. . . .

Miss [Katharine E. McBride, president of Bryn Mawr,] has before this talked to me very freely about her attitude toward Paul, and I think you will be glad to know about that. She feels that while he may sometimes cause trouble, it is not likely to be serious, and certainly not too much to pay in return for the positive contribution he makes to the College. She thinks Bryn Mawr—and any institution—needs to have some persons like him to act as gad flies, persons with such vitality who will be stimulating and provocative. . . . She told me on a recent occasion when there seemed a chance of his leaving that [she] would be sorry to have him go. This seems to me the more significant as she does not have, I believe, as much respect for his intellectual ability as you and I probably both have. I am not at all sure he is the leviathan he believes himself to be, but I think he is a pretty good sized fish. He needs and deserves a bigger sea to swim and disport himself in than our little pond here.

In a later paragraph, the Bryn Mawr philosopher homed in on the issue that Blanshard's letter had delicately skirted:

Personally I should like to see Yale take him, not so much for his sake or for yours in the department, since it will be you who suffer the disadvantage, but because it would be such a fine thing for conservative anti-Semitic Yale to take to its bosom such a Jewish semite as Paul.[11]

This response left Blanshard (who was new to Yale himself) convinced that he was making the right move in supporting the permanent appointment of Weiss.[12] Even if Weiss was a formidable individualist, a man of outstanding intellect who was liked and admired by his colleagues belonged on the faculty. The gentility of Yale might be challenged by a nonconformist like Weiss. Yet even those who were sometimes surprised by his social lapses were inspired by his entire character. If the Yale College faculty would accept Weiss, some degree of refinement might be lost, but tolerance of diversity and a sincere respect for learning might emerge as equally important values at Yale.

So the Weiss appointment was brought before the senior Yale College faculty for their consideration. Many of them were well aware that Yale's anti-Jewish reputation was spreading across the nation. The acceptance that other faculties were beginning to make of Jews was seen in marked contrast to citadel Yale. Harvard College was a noteworthy example of new-found acceptance. A Harvard committee in 1939 had already stated that:

> Conscious or unconscious anti-Semitism would be a betrayal of the best traditions of the University. . . . It would run counter to our cherished national tradition of fair play and equal opportunity. Finally, it would deprive America's oldest university of the opportunity to set a high standard for its sister institutions in this and other countries.[13]

At Yale, neither race nor religion was ever publicly mentioned in the ensuing discussions regarding Weiss, but the college professors were conscious that they were discussing the appointment of what was to be the first Jewish full professor ever to serve in their ranks.

The debate was vigorous. President Charles Seymour was supportive of the appointment, but, recognizing the decision as resting with the college faculty, he maintained a low profile throughout. The voices from the past of emeritus philosophy professors Charles Bakewell and Wilmon Sheldon were known to have been in opposition. The divinity school gave its blessing through the Reverend Robert L. Calhoun, Pitkin Professor of Historical Theology. Acting philosophy chairman Filmer Northrop presented the case for Weiss on behalf of his department. A report that Weiss had been Whitehead's ablest student at Harvard was noted as justifying his intellectual qualifications. A stirring letter from former dean of Bryn Mawr College Helen Taft Manning, whose name carried great weight at Yale, attested to the high caliber of Weiss's teaching. The conflicting opinions regarding his personality were not easily resolved. As the final decision was about to be made, Provost Edgar S. Furniss termed the discussion about Weiss the fairest and most objective evaluation to date of any proposed faculty member. In the end the faculty decided that Weiss's abilities were too much to pass up and that they had enough self-confidence to defend themselves against any charge that Weiss might make. Even those who jeered at his idiosyncrasies bowed to his talent. In 1946 the senior faculty of Yale College voted to start a new page of history and invite a Jew to join their midst.[14]

For Jews connected with the college the presence of Paul Weiss changed the atmosphere of Yale almost overnight. For the first time, Jewish students at Yale had a hero and a role model who did not downplay his Judaism. Weiss entered into this position because he was comfortable with his background and was brave enough to make an issue of it, if necessary. When President Seymour in 1946 strongly affirmed that Yale was a Christian university, Weiss, who saw the university in a different light, was ready to argue with the president. As a first response to Seymour, Eugene Rostow organized a meeting between Weiss, Rostow, associate professor of history A. Whitney Griswold, and Sterling Professor of Law Harry Shulman. After discussing the nature of Yale the four men chose Shulman, a diplomatic fellow with much experience as a union negotiator, to talk with President Seymour without creating any unnecessary rancor. Shulman returned from his conference with Seymour and reported that Seymour would explain himself more fully in forthcoming addresses. In future addresses he would also emphasize the Judaic tradition from which the Christian founding spirit of Yale derived. During Weiss's first year on the campus, he delivered a speech to interested students on the topic of "What It Means to Be a Jew." The enlightenment gained from the talk astonished many a Christian and Jewish Yale student. Immediately, "being Jewish" at Yale became much more open than it had been. Weiss instilled a religious pride among many of the students. By the time that the *Yale Daily News* of 1956 called him "one of the most highly respected members of the Yale faculty," it had long been clear that the Weiss experiment was a success.[15]

The impact of that assay was felt through the university, particularly in the college. In a steady and continuous progression that would last over the following two decades, Jews would be welcomed into all of the ranks of the college faculty. Though casting off their prejudicial shackles, some departments moved less quickly than others. There was often a question as to whether more than just a token representative of excellence should be taken. The ever outspoken Paul Weiss recalled years later that once the exclusive barriers were lifted, barriers of "balance" sometimes remained:

If, for example, we had a mathematics department which had two Hungarian faculty who were absolute geniuses and a third absolute genius Hungarian came along, he couldn't be appointed since then the department would have three Hungarians. This policy, [for many years], applied to Jews, Catholics, and blacks, but never WASPs.

"Minorities" were often viewed for their minority status as well as their capabilities. Nevertheless, as talent secured its preeminence over personality in the appointment process, and as both qualities took greater precedence over racial and religious background, the college faculty gave up some of its societal nature. With more undergraduates plunging into occasional graduate school courses in the 1950s, artificial distinctions between the college and graduate faculties blurred. In the 1959–60 academic year the Yale Graduate School and College Faculty Appointments Committees were merged and in the following decade both faculty bodies were entirely merged into a gargantuan whole. Theoretically, among the arts and sciences divisions of the university there would be single standards of faculty hiring. The competition with the great state universities that Yale and the other Ivy League institutions faced at the start of the 1960s for faculty and prestige was so great that E. Digby Baltzell was able to proclaim in 1963 that "no faculty at any leading university can afford to be anti-Semitic in its hiring policies." The large concentration of Jewish faculty that Yale developed in the 1960s was typical of the nation's ranking universities, as some of the most dedicated teachers and scholars of the era were Jewish.[16] The academic position of Jewish faculty became secure enough that when Richard Bernstein, a Jew in the philosophy department who was Weiss's successor as editor of the *Review of Metaphysics,* was denied tenure in 1965 and many critical questions were raised regarding Yale's policies on tenure, there was no "Jewish issue." When a 1972 report by a faculty study group led by Robert A. Dahl concluded that Yale College had an obligation to try to attract more minority groups and women to the faculty, it was clear that for Jewish males, at least, there was no longer even a suspicion of bias in hiring.[17]

RELIGIOUS IDENTITY

Despite the concerns that some professors had about the presence of Jewish faculty at Yale, the religious identification of the vast majority of Jewish faculty at Yale was always marginal. From the mid-1940s through the late 1960s the only senior Jewish faculty member to display a consistent interest in Jewish life or affairs was Paul Weiss. During his first years at Yale Weiss would participate in public debates on religious issues with professors such as theologian Robert Calhoun. These discussions encouraged both Christian and Jewish students at the university to find increased meaning in their religious traditions. But Weiss's outspokenness and confidence were not mirrored in the other Jews who joined him on the faculty. Weiss became "Yale's Jew," while most of the other Jewish faculty deliberately remained unidentified.[18]

In this respect, Yale Jewish faculty members were not unlike their counterparts across the nation. Some had changed their names to conceal their identity and to improve their chances for employment. Even when a "foreign" name was no longer a hindrance to promotion, some Jewish professors were still resentful of the Jewish stain that had once impeded their career. A 1969 Carnegie Commission study showed that while 32 percent of U.S. faculty with a Protestant religious background and 25 percent of faculty with a Catholic religious background considered themselves indifferent or opposed to religion, for Jews that proportion was 67 percent. When faculty at "high quality universities" were examined, the respective proportions were 48, 39, and 72 percent. Given such national trends, the Yale pattern was not unique. Though publicly identified Christian faculty at Yale provided a strong counterexample to hidden Jewish faculty, the Yale Jewish professors were but an extreme example of a national phenomenon.[19]

The Jewish faculty first showed signs of interest in their religion during the 1959–60 school year, when assistant professor of philosophy Richard Bernstein, history instructor Jerome Cohen, and English instructor Geoffrey Hartman organized a faculty association in coordination with the Hillel office. These three men, whom Rabbi Israel called, "Young Turks in their willingness to affirm Judaism," had felt that at an institution like Yale, there was a distinct need for an intellectual outlet for faculty Jewish life. Their spiritual and sentimental outlets required complements. Consequently they formed a group to meet occasionally and discuss matters of historical and contemporary Jewish interest.[20]

With the encouragement of Rabbi Richard Israel of Hillel, increasing numbers of Jewish faculty joined the students of the 1960s in asserting their religious presence at Yale; they established an independent Sunday School and a charitable Faculty Jewish Appeal. Law professor Abraham S. Goldstein served as the first chairman of the appeal, and Alexander Bickel, another law professor, followed him. The outbreak of the Six-Day War in 1967 stirred dormant ethnic interest among an even larger group of Yale Jewish faculty.[21]

ADMINISTRATORS

The Second World War also stimulated a diversification in the ranks of Yale administrators. This was evidenced in 1953 when the Yale Law School faced a decision regarding the appointment of a new dean. In 1939 Harry Shulman had been denied the post because of his Jewish background. The appointment had then gone to Ashbel G. Gulliver. In 1946 Gulliver was succeeded by Wesley A. Sturges, who that year was the most popular candidate among the law faculty. In 1953 Shulman received a second opportunity for consideration. On that occasion he was again the favorite candidate of the law school alumni. Only one of the many letters of recommendation made any reference to his religious background. In that missive, Arthur Corbin, the William K. Townsend Professor Emeritus of Law at Yale, argued that unfair prejudices should not be permitted to compete with reality:

> Certain supposed objections to Harry's appointment should be disregarded. He is a Harvard man, of high standing and good repute. He is a Yale man now. He is a Jew, and was law clerk to Justice Brandeis. His associates know that he has none of the supposed disagreeable characteristics that anti-Semites like to dwell upon. His character and personality are sufficient rebuttal. He can be depended upon to give a fair and unbiased administration and one that all Yale men will respect.[22]

What made the accolades particularly significant was that they came during a time when President Griswold was under great pressure from alumni and McCarthyites to "straighten out" the law school. Some of this sentiment came from the heart of the Yale Corporation. Consequently, when President Griswold presented his nomination of Shulman for the Corporation's consideration, a great dispute broke out. Underlying the discussion was a concern as to whether Shulman was a man who could limit Communistic tendencies that might develop within the school. Judaism had not previously been discussed openly, but, according to Mary Griswold, the president's widow, the fight to appoint Shulman occurred "entirely because of the Jewish issue." President Griswold, who fought to the end for his man Shulman, would later write of the Corporation meeting as having been a "bruiser." Mrs. Griswold recalled her husband's reporting to her that he had felt compelled to tell the Corporation flatly, "Either you have Harry or you don't have me!" An enthusiastic six-page endorsement by former secretary of state and absent Corporation fellow Dean Acheson (B.A. 1915) played a major role in finally convincing the trustees to accept Shulman. Corporation Fellow Wilmarth S. Lewis (B.A. 1918) sent Shulman a warm letter of congratulations following the decisive vote:

In my sixteen years on the Corporation I have never heard such enviable statements made by so many people whose good opinion one would hope to have as were made on your behalf. If it is characteristic of our frightened time that your appointment should have caused excessive discussion, I think it is also a heartening sign of the healthiness of present-day Yale that you now have what you should have had years ago.

Shulman's sudden death in March 1955 prevented him from setting his stamp upon the school, but the coincidental fact that four of the law faculty who followed him in that post were Jewish (Eugene V. Rostow, Louis H. Pollak, Abraham S. Goldstein, and Harry H. Wellington) was indicative that the "present-day Yale" to which Lewis referred was willing to look for its leadership in previously overlooked ranks. Other Jewish deans at the university would include Robert Brustein (1966–79) in the drama school and Robert W. Berliner (1973–84) in the school of medicine and Sidney Altman (1985–89) and Donald Kagan (1989–92) in the college.[23]

From his hospital bed in 1963 President Griswold asked Georges May, professor of French, to succeed William Clyde DeVane as dean of Yale College. Though a few faculty unhappily whispered that May was Jewish, Griswold was convinced that the college needed new blood to lead it and that May was the best man for the position. Born to Jewish parents, May did not call himself a Jew but was open about his background. The new blood that he represented was not just religious or racial, but psychological as well. By appointing May as the first non-Yale graduate to serve as dean of Yale College, Griswold made it plain that Yale was looking to new molds for sources of vigorous leadership. The 1970 appointment by Kingman Brewster, Jr., of Abraham S. Goldstein (not just a Jew, but a product of New York's Lower East Side and the once-derided City College of New York) as law dean further demonstrated the pluralistic university that Yale had become.[24]

When a 1966 study revealed that, compared to the percentage of Jewish students in nonsectarian colleges and universities in America, Jews were underrepresented in administrative positions, the once-forbidden microcosm of the establishment at Yale was ahead of the nation. For example, although the first Jewish residential college master was not appointed until that year, other Jews had previously turned down offers of the mastership. Henry Chauncey's cochairperson of the committee to implement coeducation was Elga Wasserman, a Jewish woman. If some Jewish faculty found research and teaching more stimulating than administrative chores, leading them to decline such positions, their nonparticipation in administration by the 1960s was a matter of personal choice, not of prejudice.[25]

THE YALE CORPORATION

R. Inslee Clark, Jr., former dean of admissions, recalled a story that he traced back to the mid-1960s. One weekend, when the Corporation was in session, he was invited to give a personal report directly to the Corporation on Yale admissions policy. Because normal protocol called for his annual report to reach the Corporation through the channels of President Brewster's office, this invitation was clearly an unusual event. Dean Clark addressed the Corporation on the changing trends in his admissions policy. Following the presentation, one Corporation member who had "hemmed and hawed" throughout the report attacked Clark's modern ideas: "Let me get down to basics. You're admitting an entirely different kind of class than we're used to. You're admitting them for a different purpose than training leaders." Clark responded that the America of the 1960s was different from what it once had been and that more national leaders would be coming from more groups, including women. The Corporation fellow was unsympathetic: "You're talking about Jews and public school graduates as leaders. Look around you at this table. These are America's leaders. There are no Jews here. There are no public school graduates here."[26] Although the Yale Corporation minutes do not record the above exchange, the essentials behind Clark's story were quite real. As late as fall, 1964, the Yale Corporation was an essentially homogeneous group. Of the fourteen Corporation fellows listed in the university catalogue for 1964, only two were graduates of public high schools. The group was solidly white, male, and Protestant. Given that the successor fellows (elected by the Corporation itself) had usually been recruited directly from the secret society brotherhoods, and that those brotherhoods had routinely excluded Jews prior to the 1960s, the absence of a Jew on the Corporation did not represent any greater degree of bigotry than had been expressed in earlier decades. But the fact that never had Yale had a Catholic corporation fellow—and Catholics had regularly found places among the secret societies and did number a sizable proportion of Yale alumni—seemed to indicate the self-replicatory nature of Yale power. Until the Griswold administration, those in power had always recruited replacements in their own racial, religious, and economic images. Such a procedure was understandable to a point. It was always easier to trust what one was familiar with. Yet the unwillingness to trust reflected a desire to exclude. The fact that a Corporation fellow could proclaim that Jews and public school graduates had no place among America's leadership and the fact that women and blacks and Hispanics were in a similar position evidenced the narrow-minded underpinnings of Yale elitism.[27]

Not until the homogeneous matrix of the Yale Corporation could be broken could the university publicly demonstrate that it could accept multifarious definitions of quality, excellence, and leadership. When Abraham A. Ribicoff became governor of Connecticut in 1955, the university bylaws made him an ex officio member of the Yale Corporation. In practical terms, however, the Connecticut governor had little influence on the Corporation and his Yale activities consisted chiefly of ceremonial appearances. Supreme Court Justice Felix Frankfurter, known for his almost desperate desire to be a part of the nation's social as well as political elite, had hoped that the Yale Corporation successor fellows would choose him to serve as a successor fellow in 1956. Had he been chosen, he would have been the first Jewish full member of the Corporation. More importantly, he would also have been the first person without an earned Yale degree to serve on the Corporation in two centuries. For Jew or gentile, the Corporation was unwilling to yield its Yale ties.

The man who broke the corporation mold was William Horowitz (B.A. 1929). An industrious man from Kansas City, who had worked his way through college as a Hebrew teacher and a dishwasher, Horowitz had become a bank president by 1949. In later years he would devote his charitable time to Yale, the Hillel Foundation at Yale, the Yale-New Haven Hospital, the NAACP, and the Connecticut State Board of Education. Building on these interests, he decided in 1964 to try for a position on the Yale Corporation. It was not an easy task. One had either to be appointed by the Corporation itself to a successor trusteeship or else to be elected in an alumni "beauty contest" to a six-year term. As of 1964 the successor trustees had routinely reproduced themselves; the idea of a Jew or a Catholic or a woman or a black ever becoming a successor trustee was still a vision in the minds of dreamers. The election process for alumni fellows was democratic but had oligarchic overtones. One alumni fellow would annually be elected from a slate of candidates prepared by a select alumni committee. A democratic loophole allowed any alumnus who could collect two hundred fifty Yale signatures to earn an equal place on the ballot. Never had anyone been elected by such a procedure. Though he succeeded in having his name added to the 1964 ballot by petition, Horowitz lost in the subsequent election to John V. Lindsay (B.A. 1944, LL.B. 1948), future mayor of New York City. In 1965 Horowitz employed the same mechanism to run again. With the support of many Jewish and non-Jewish alumni who thought that "it was about time that the Yale Corporation had someone with a name like Horowitz on it," the genial banker broke a tradition. Under the leadership of Kingman Brewster, Yale's first non-Protestant trustee was followed by women and blacks as successor and alumni fellows. Within a decade the corporate body that had once defined national leadership in almost uniform terms provided visible testimony that the American establishment was welcoming and recruiting the most talented members of both sexes and of different races and religions into its centers of power.[28]

THE ROSOVSKY OFFER

For those who were reluctant to accept the notion that the establishment was incorporating previously excluded groups, the 1970s at Yale conclusively proved the change. One symbol was the time in 1977 when Henry Rosovsky, a publicly identifying Jew, born in Poland, was offered the university presidency.

The offer was especially remarkable because few Jews had previously served as American university presidents. The first to do so was Ephraim M. Epstein, a convert to Christianity, who became the founding president of the University of South Dakota in 1882. Paul Klapper became the first professing Jew to head a public college when he was appointed president of Queen's College in 1937. In 1948 Abram L. Sachar became the first president of Brandeis University and was the first Jew to lead a major American university. The 1967 appointment of Edward H. Levi, a rabbi's son, as president of the University of Chicago symbolized the acceptance of Jews into the mainstream of the national intelligentsia. By 1971, Jews had served as presidents at the Ivy League universities of Pennsylvania and Dartmouth. Because Dartmouth had been founded as an academy for Christian missionaries, it set the precedent for a potential Jewish president at an institution with Christian origins.[29]

The general consensus that Yale was obligated to have a "Christian" president died during the years that A. Whitney Griswold was president (1950–63). Kingman Brewster recalled that at the time of Griswold's death in 1963 there had been concern among some quarters of the university community that Brewster, provost, acting president, and heir apparent, had no formal church affiliation, nor had he ever been baptized. Aside from supplying the grist for a few short-lived gossip mills, his religious background apparently played no part in the deliberations over his selection to succeed Griswold. When Provost Hanna Gray became acting president after Brewster's retirement in 1977, there was no public attention paid to her religious background, despite the fact that her mother, though not her father, was Jewish. She did not claim any public identification with Judaism and no one in the university community publicly held that background against her.[30]

Henry Rosovsky was born in Danzig (Gdansk) in 1927. After escaping with his family from the Nazis, the young Rosovsky emigrated to the United States in 1940. By 1949 he was graduated from the College of William and Mary—the second of the nation's three oldest colleges (Harvard, 1636; William and Mary, 1693; Yale, 1701). He then went north to Harvard to study for a doctorate in economics. When he was offered a teaching position at the University of California at Berkeley, he moved west. From California his Yale connection began.

When the aggressive student activism on the Berkeley campus of the mid-1960s left him feeling uncomfortable, he looked for a position back on the east coast, where he thought (mistakenly) that he would find a more peaceful atmosphere. John Perry Miller, professor of economics and dean of the Yale Graduate School, tried to convince him to become part of the Yale faculty. Had Harvard not stepped in and invited him to return to his graduate alma mater, he would have transferred his allegiances to Yale. But, already in 1965, his sense of institutional loyalty pulled him to Cambridge; he bypassed Yale's offer. When the Yale economics department some years later invited him again to teach in New Haven, his answer was still negative.

Appointed dean of the Harvard Faculty of Arts and Sciences in 1973, Rosovsky became nationally known in education as he began to reform the Harvard educational system. Articles in newspapers such as *The New York Times* regularly trumpeted the "core curriculum" that he was trying to steer through the Harvard bureaucracy. He was, therefore, a natural candidate when the University of Chicago set about choosing its new president in 1977. Despite indications to Chicago board members that his availability was highly unlikely, Rosovsky was offered the presidency of that institution in October 1977. It was a tempting and flattering opportunity. The University of Chicago, occupying a unique place in American education, Rosovsky felt, had been a more influential pioneer of modern educational reforms than either his beloved Harvard or rival Yale. At the time, he thought that it would be the best job offer he would ever receive. His having no previous Chicago connection and his religious background were evidently not issues. Nevertheless, his duty to Harvard prevented him from accepting the position at the time. He had three pieces of unfinished business in Cambridge that he felt obliged to complete: a reform of Harvard undergraduate education, a reform of the Harvard Graduate School, and a fund-raising effort to provide for faculty salaries. Chicago had to look elsewhere for its president.

Rosovsky's first inkling that Yale was considering him for its top post came at about the same time as the Chicago offer, when he saw his name listed among a large group of candidates in a national newsmagazine. He did not believe the report because his only previous contact with a Yale trustee had been a discussion with Harvard law professor Lance Liebman regarding which Harvard faculty might be considered potential Yale leaders. When senior Yale Corporation fellow J. Richardson Dilworth telephoned Rosovsky late in October to inform him that he was high on the Yale candidate list, he was extremely surprised. When he was told soon afterward that he was one of the three final candidates, he explained that his accepting the position would be extremely unlikely. The selection committee responded by asking him if they could keep his name on their list, and if he would meet with the full corporation in Washington.

Though in later years he would ask himself if he should have removed his name from the list at that point, Rosovsky did not think it wise at the time. He felt a genuine excitement about being considered for the post. Though Chicago had been the outstanding center of intellectual leadership, he considered Yale to be a national treasure. He did not feel capable of considering the leadership of an institution like Yale in an abstract sense. President Derek Bok of Harvard feared losing his able dean but encouraged him to have a formal interview. Rosovsky's wife, Nitza, encouraged him to meet the Corporation. She was eager to spend more time with her husband through the activities that the Yale presidency would provide. Finally, Rosovsky became convinced that to avoid a meeting with the Yale Corporation would have been an enormous discourtesy: "Certain bodies are sufficiently august that when they invite you to meet them, you are obligated to meet them." The Yale Corporation was one of those bodies.

In the course of the interview, Rosovsky brought up his Jewish background and asked if that would be an issue. He was immediately assured that his Judaism was not problematic at all. One Corporation fellow did ask if Rosovsky's level of Sabbath observance would prevent him from giving speeches on Saturdays. The Harvard dean replied that he had no qualms about speaking on Saturdays. Regarding his Judaism, he explained that he had never embarrassed Harvard because of his religion, but he was an "open, committed, and active American Jew." The Yale Corporation was satisfied. Following the interview, a delegation from the trustees came to his home outside Boston and formally offered him the presidency of Yale.

For the Yale fellows, Rosovsky's Jewishness and his close association with Harvard were never seen as negative factors. They had canvassed the world in search of the man who they thought would best serve Yale. Rosovsky, a charming and extraordinary leader, with many innovative ideas for education, fit that description. From the start of their consideration of him, however, they also realized that he might reject their offer.

For Rosovsky, the week that he took to decide the proposition was a "terrible" week of evaluation. Embarrassing leaks to the news media regarding the offer further increased the pressure on the dean. President Bok implored his dean to support him at Harvard. In the meantime, the Yale Corporation fellows did their best to sell Rosovsky on the new job. One well-meaning trustee told Mrs. Rosovsky that her husband owed it to his "humble heritage" to accept the Yale offer. Though Rosovsky was quite proud of his heritage and did not find it so "humble," he was torn between Harvard and Yale.

He had to weigh the merits of the competing alternatives. Reasons to stay at Harvard were Bok's need of his assistance, Rosovsky's strong loyalty to Harvard, and his as-yet-unfinished agenda as dean: "I never wanted to leave Harvard in a way that I wouldn't be able to return with my head held up high. I didn't want to run out in the middle." A reason to leave Harvard was that despite what he liked to believe about himself, he was only a human being, and was therefore replaceable. A quotation hung above his desk proclaimed that "the cemeteries are full of irreplaceable people." A strong reason not to go to Yale was the great financial difficulty that Yale was experiencing in 1977. Even subdivisions of the university that should have been self-sufficient were accumulating large deficits. For an outsider who did not know the politics and intricacies of Yale well, it might take years to learn how it functioned. Part of a Harvard tradition that valued institutional loyalty, Rosovsky was uncertain as to how he would fit in at a place such as Yale with equally commanding traditions. But there were also strong reasons to accept the Yale offer. Leading a national treasure out of its economic morass would almost be a patriotic act. Whatever prestige he had as Harvard dean would be magnified by taking the Yale position. His wife wanted to move to a new setting. And as a Jew, if he were to take the position, it would be a significant milestone. In all ways, it would be an exciting challenge.

In the end, two factors weighed most heavily on Rosovsky. One was his dedication to Harvard. He could not leave there with a major commitment uncompleted. Equally important, however, was his opinion that the best academic administrators were those who had developed a strong sense of loyalty to their particular institutions. He was therefore concerned about being an outsider at Yale. Every Yale person that he had been connected with had treated him like a gentleman, yet

> I felt I represented bitter medicine to them. They made the choice, but I felt I didn't fit their image. I wasn't a graduate. I was a Jew. In style and appearance I wasn't their kind of guy. I never saw myself in the mold of the other university presidents and U.S. senators whose names I saw in the lists of candidates that appeared in the media.

Not a student of educational history, Rosovsky was unaware that fifty years earlier, James Rowland Angell, in Yale terms also an outsider, had been invited to assume the Yale presidency and had, in fact, become one of Yale's most highly regarded presidents. On that occasion, the Corporation offer had been immediately followed by a personal visit to Angell from retiring president Arthur Twining Hadley. Hadley had strongly urged Angell to accept the position. The next day Hadley wrote to reassure Angell that he would have the full support of the Yale alumni and Yale administrators. In 1977 the Yale Corporation would give its complete encouragement to Rosovsky, but the support of the past administration was absent. Acting president Hanna Gray had once entertained hopes for the Yale presidency herself. Though she was going to become the president of the University of Chicago, it could hardly be expected for her enthusiastically to cheer her rival. Former president Kingman Brewster, Jr., was busy as United States ambassador to Great Britain. He was also in no position to deliver a resounding vote of confidence from the conservative Yale alumni who had been alienated by his liberalizing moves. Rosovsky feared entering as a seven million dollar budget cutter, who would be blamed for administering the economic belt-tightening that Yale would have to withstand to survive. Summing up the considerations, Rosovsky did not accept the Yale offer.[31]

When Henry Rosovsky rejected the Yale presidency the Yale Corporation immediately turned to A. Bartlett Giamatti, John Hay Whitney Professor of English. In doing so, they echoed the Yale commitment to searching out the most qualified candidate regardless of ethnic background.[32] Though Giamatti (B.A. 1960, Ph.D. 1964) was a Yale man throughout—his father was an alumnus and he himself was a member of Scroll and Key—his partial Italian parentage, in a previous generation, might have made him an unfairly excluded outsider. In a new world, he was welcome not just to participate, but to lead.

Chapter 14 The Club

At Yale, social qualities defined success almost as much as talent. The two hung in a precarious balance that shifted according to the tenor of an era. The dominance of the social gave way to respect for merit in the course of the Second World War. But in the orchestra of Yale, the social side continued to play a strong second fiddle. As in the debate over the Weiss appointment, personality was a crucial factor, even when talent was recognized.

For faculty in a socially stratified community, exclusion from the city's club life (the Graduate Club and the Lawn Club, for example) had a double impact. On a mundane level, excluded faculty had fewer options than their included counterparts when it came to their social entertainment. On a more significant level the social obstacles meant, for some, exclusion from some of the dominant parts of the university community. For some, it meant a painful loneliness. For others, it meant the embarrassment of participating in and sometimes presiding at functions on premises where one knew that one's membership was unwanted. Though he sometimes appeared to like being left out, Paul Weiss, too, learned that he was a social outcast in his early years when he could find no one at Yale willing to sponsor him for membership in either the Graduate or Lawn Club. When he asked his department chairman Charles W. Hendel how to go about joining the Graduate organization, Hendel told him not to bother with attempting such a proposition, since Weiss would not like the club anyway. Others saw it as unimportant examples of adults playing children's games. Florence S. Wald (M.N. 1940), a Jewish woman who served as Nursing School dean in the 1960s and later pioneered the American hospice movement, recalled her and her fellow deans' amusement that she had to enter the Graduate Club through its kitchen stairway rather than through the front door for President Brewster's monthly Yale Dean's lunches because she was a woman. In a pre–"women's liberation" era, no one, including her, felt angry about the arrangement.[1]

The consequence of the exclusive clubs' being so much a part of university life was not that those good people who were excluded were denied advancement. Rather, it was more difficult for them to advance, since, by being excluded from some of the social playgrounds of the adult community, Jewish and other stereotypically undesirable faculty were denied an opportunity to earn the personal currency of social trust that, as in the business world, so often permitted personal influence.[2]

TOWN

In the club world, as in the academic world, the exclusionary social curtain began to unravel soon after the Second World War. Emphatically pulling at its threads was University Chaplain Sidney Lovett. In concert with several friends who were members of the Graduate Club, Lovett organized a drive to stop the policy of "blackballing" prospective Jewish members. Always the diplomat, Lovett refrained from accusing anyone of blatant anti-Jewish feeling, but rather warned the membership of the dangers of ignoring "the common humanity of all of us." President Hadley had expressed similar thoughts decades earlier, but Lovett would not rest with mere verbal expression. Choosing a man who held both town and gown dear to his heart, and who, as the first Jewish president of the Yale Club of New Haven, would be impossible to blackball without generating scandal anew, Lovett arranged for Rollin Osterweis (B.A. 1930, M.A. 1943, Ph.D. 1946) to be nominated for membership. Soon afterward, Osterweis received an unsolicited offer to become a member of the Graduate Club. For the young historian, it was as much an ultimatum as an invitation. One friend of his within the club warned him that if he turned down the election, no Jew would gain admission for many years to come. If, however, he accepted, then the prospects would be improved for the eventual welcoming of more Jews. Osterweis accepted, and in 1950 he formally became a member. The next Jew to follow was Colonel Richard Gimbel (B.A. 1920), professor of air science and tactics for the Yale ROTC. Gimbel, member of the famous department store family, had his membership application accepted without debate in 1952. Following Gimbel by five years, law school dean Eugene Rostow was accepted by the club. By the 1960s racially and religiously exclusive policies had eased greatly. The always exclusive Lawn Club of New Haven also modified its policies to admit a small proportion of members of previously unwanted groups through the 1950s and 1960s. By virtue of his deanship and his high-society wife, Milton Winternitz had been a Lawn Club member in previous decades. By 1959 the Eugene Rostows were accepted into the Lawn Club, and, by 1964, they would be joined by the Robert Arnsteins. Just as the welcome given to non-WASPs in the Kennedy White House opened up the stratified Washington social structure of the 1960s, the friendships that President Kingman Brewster maintained with members of racial and religious groups other than his own had a strong impact on expanding the horizons of Yale society of that decade.[3]

FACULTY

There was another dimension to the university's interaction with club life as well. Just as the undergraduates had their senior societies to stimulate their loyalty to Yale, their personal growth, their intellectual development, and their egos, similar institutions flourished among the Yale faculty. More mature than their undergraduate counterparts, the adult societies were simpler organizations that occasionally met for dinner and high-minded discussion. Shunning ostentatious pylons, closed tombs, and sophomoric ritual, the faculty societies offered their members some of the most intelligent conversation in New Haven and the reassuring knowledge that they were part of a select group of "insiders." One of these exclusive groups was known as "The Dissenters." Another that thrived in New Haven simply called itself "The Club."[4]

The second oldest social organization in the Yale community, preceded only by Skull and Bones, The Club apparently came into existence in 1838. Because of the unusual longevity that membership in The Club seemed to confer upon its members, it acquired the nickname of "The Old Men's Club." Although its first membership roster included leading members of the city of New Haven, The Club came to be solely a concern of members of the Yale community. Its members received lifetime appointments to the organization and participated as long as their health and their interest continued. The approximately twenty-five people who made up The Club represented the social and intellectual elite of the entire university. John Ferguson Weir (dean of the Yale School of the Fine Arts from 1869 through 1913) deemed it "the best area in the community for studying varieties of mind."[5]

The Yale presidential term of Jeremiah Day (1817–46), during which The Club was founded, had been an extraordinary time for the growth of organizations across the nation and at Yale College. At the student level, the first Greek letter junior fraternities of Alpha Delta Phi and Psi Upsilon sprang forth on the campus as did *The Yale Literary Magazine* and *The Yale Banner.* On a scholarly level Benjamin Silliman became the founding editor of the *American Journal of Science.*[6] Challenges offered to the status of secret associations were also important to the context of the era. Following the apparent murder of a New York bricklayer who had divulged the secrets of his masonic lodge, a national Anti-Masonic party arose in 1826 to combat secret societies. The movement grew so strong that it succeeded in electing at least two state governors and, in 1831, it nominated presidential candidates who drew thousands of Northern votes away from Henry Clay. The national nominating convention that the Anti-Masonics first developed became the model for the country's major political parties. The spread of the antisecrecy movement led to ideological attacks on the secret ritual of the honorary Phi Beta Kappa fraternity at Harvard and, eventually, Yale. As a counterreaction to the stripping of secrecy from Phi Beta Kappa, it seems, a group of fifteen undergraduates from the Yale class of 1833 founded the secret Skull and Bones society. Within a decade every class at Yale had at least one secret society. And in 1838, it is believed, The Club was organized.[7]

Its six founders were all New Haven residents. Two taught in Yale College: professor of sacred literature Josiah Willard Gibbs (B.A. 1809, M.A. 1812) and professor of the Greek language and literature Theodore Dwight Woolsey (B.A. 1820, M.A. 1823). Two were local ministers. The fifth was a local lawyer. And the sixth was a local physician. Early members included William H. Russell (B.A. 1833, M.A. 1836, M.D. 1838, founder of Skull and Bones) and William L. Kingsley (B.A. 1843, founder of Scroll and Key). By 1873 The Club drew its membership entirely from the university community. Since club memberships were offered only to those who had already established themselves within the Yale community, the organization did not offer its members artificial stepping stones to renown. They were all talented and unique men. On the one hundred and twenty-fifth anniversary of its founding, Club historian Alexander M. Witherspoon (B.A. 1918, M.A. 1921, Ph.D. 1923) described the select group that had made up The Club:

> The 160 or so men whose names have been on the roster of the Club have all ren-
> dered faithful and honorable service in their day and generation, and many of them
> have been distinguished in public and professional life. In the various learned pro-
> fessions, as teachers, scholars, and editors, as presidents of universities, and in the
> public roles of Governor, Ambassador, Chief Justice of the State and nation, and
> President of the United States, they have played their part.[8]

Certainly not every influential member of the Yale community had been invited to join The Club, nor did everyone who was invited choose to participate
in the private body, but if there were "insiders" and "outsiders" at Yale, this
group was certainly a group of "insiders."

So it was in 1947 that when Henri Peyre, Sterling Professor of French and
chairman of the French department, pressed his colleagues to elect a Jewish
thirty-four-year-old full professor of law named Eugene Rostow to their fellowship, he was calling for a fundamental reassessment of the de facto Yale Social Register. Pushing for Rostow, Peyre triggered the reaction that would melt
down the protective barrier surrounding the very core of Yale society. Influenced by the French legal tradition of looking at Jews as full citizens in society,
Peyre, a long-time advocate of merit, prodded his colleagues to accept a clearly
remarkable man like Rostow. His earning a full professorship by age thirty-one
was no ordinary achievement. During the Second World War, he had served as
an adviser to the State Department. He was never afraid to argue his ideas, but,
as had been recognized during his undergraduate years, he was also a man of
character.

There was a Jewish issue. Rostow was not religiously observant, yet he was
Jewishly conscious. As an undergraduate and as a professor he had urged that
Yale maintain "single standard educational values" in its admissions procedures. The decision over how to vote on Rostow was a difficult one. His youth
might have been an issue. Only one thirty-four-year-old had ever previously
been inducted into "The Old Men's Club" and that was Charles Seymour, who
had entered in 1919 and by 1947 was the president of Yale.[9] Prejudice was also a
critical factor. Never had there been a Jew in The Club. Fringe hate groups like
the Ku Klux Klan had their particular prejudices against groups such as Jews,
Catholics, and blacks. And in different eras nativist associations had directed
their wrath at particular groups such as Native Americans and the Chinese. But

"mainstream" American social bigotry had generally not operated with a Nazi-like hatred against specific races. Its reservoir of prejudice could supply disdain for many an ethnic group in America. If Jews were disproportionately the victims of social discrimination, it was because their energy had enabled them intellectually and economically to rise faster than many other groups of outsiders. If a Jew were admitted to the select group of insiders, then it would only be a matter of time before other outsiders, such as blacks and women, for example, would also be admitted.

For some of The Club members, such as Chauncey Brewster Tinker, Sterling Professor Emeritus of English Literature, the idea of a Jew among their company was repulsive. But in the postwar era, rationalizations about the unfitness of Jews for an English department, for a college, or for a social company lost their appeal to most people. In 1947 The Club members voted to invite Eugene Rostow to join their midst.[10]

The Club that Rostow joined provided more than conviviality. The lectures that the members presented to each other and the discussions that followed touched on a wide variety of subjects that excited the intellect. Topics ranged from a consideration of "Darwin's *Origin of Species*" in 1860, to "Pre-Frontal Lobotomy" in 1947. Current events were also a popular topic. In 1856 Club members heard a lecture on "Slavery: How Should it be Treated by Literary Men?" and a century later they heard a physics expert explain what would happen "If a Hydrogen Bomb Drops on New York." Within a few weeks of journalist Walter Lippmann's 1938 renewal of an old proposal that refugees from Nazism be settled in Africa, Club members heard an address on that subject. Other subjects arose from the expertise and interests of the membership.[11]

Given the Yale penchant for being interested in Yale, it was not unusual that Yale was a frequent topic on the agenda. In 1864 the members heard a talk on the "Education of the Medical Profession." In 1888 they considered the "Study of Bible in College." In 1916 "The Silent Revolution in the Yale Corporation" was evaluated. Club members are quick, though, to point out that it never tried to act outside its own bounds. Because some two of every three Club members (through 1963) were past, present, or future holders of administrative positions within the university, the bounds of The Club, however, were wide. The Club historian described those limits in the following terms:

> The Club has never aimed at action or influence outside itself, but has sought simply to provide social pleasure and intellectual intercourse. But in the very nature of the case its members informally make decisions unrelated to it but certainly not unrelated to the University, as they chat informally before and after dinner.

The Club was not omnipotent. The decisions of its individual members were not automatically university policy. Numerous key administrators were not Club members. Since Corporation fellows were usually not Club members their important voices were not heard at Club meetings. And during the terms of A. Whitney Griswold and Kingman Brewster, Jr., when the two presidents chose not to join The Club, any decision that required presidential input had to be made through other lines of communication.

Still, the future of Yale was intimately tied to The Club. In 1851 the men asked each other, "How Shall Our Services on Sunday be Conducted, and Religious Instruction on Week Days?" and a century later (while the Doob committee was simultaneously preparing its Yale-changing report) The Club heard Henri Peyre speak on "The Search for Excellence and Leadership in American Education." Themes that the university had no courage to discuss in public could confidentially come to the fore in that company. One example occurred after December 12, 1923, the date that President James Rowland Angell sent letters to his chief administrators asking whether the university's Limitation of Numbers admissions policy should be extended beyond the freshman year and medical school, where it then existed. Club members were able to discuss privately the major impact of the limitation outside of restricting the entire Yale enrollment. At The Club meeting of December 19, 1923, hosted by Charles Seymour (Sterling Professor of History and future Yale president), members participated in a discussion and talk led by Frederick Scheetz Jones, the dean of Yale College. The subject of the evening was not a general consideration of Limitation of Numbers. In the intimacy of their society, the "Limitation of the Number of Jewish Students" could specifically be discussed. The words uttered on that occasion, as on every other meeting of The Club, did not leave the room in which they were spoken. If the consequent events are a reliable reflection of the conversations of that December, then the elect faculty concluded that there was no need then for a Yale limitation of Jews or of total numbers to extend beyond the two academic divisions where it already existed. But that is purely a matter of conjecture.[12]

EPILOGUE

Spurred by men such as Henri Peyre and Sidney Lovett who committed themselves in the era after World War Two to fighting people's inability to recognize "the common humanity" of all persons, centers of social power in the Yale and New Haven communities began to open their doors to Jews and other "outsider" groups. The changes took place neither overnight nor universally. The admission of Rollin Osterweis to the Graduate Club, of the Rostows to the Lawn Club, or of Rostow to The Club did not make these exclusive clubs suddenly plebeian. The Graduate Club retained its exclusivity until the 1960s and the Lawn Club and The Club never gave up theirs. Nonetheless, they all had begun to give up their racial and religious prejudices by the 1950s, allowing members of formerly outcast groups to join them. In later decades The Club, reflecting the evolving composition of the Yale faculty, invited women to take their place among the men. In 1980 Cornell graduate Robert Evans became the first Jew to be elected a president of the former bastion of town and gown bigotry called the Graduate Club.[13]

The entrance of outsiders into the social life of the university elite was of more than academic interest. Because of the informal influence that the social world exerted in helping many of those who wielded power analyze their policies and formulate their future plans, the transformation of social outsiders into insiders was essential in giving outsiders a meaningful voice in university affairs. Sociologist E. Digby Baltzell had argued in 1964 that it was only this transformation that could allow for the dissolution of anti-Jewish feeling:

> The sociological fact of caste . . . fosters anti-Semitic attitudes, which stereotype the Jew as an outsider. . . . As long as the Jew remains an outsider, the stereotype will be reinforced. For anti-Semitism is, contrary to conventional common sense, not overcome through friendship or pleasant relations with Jews. Rather, it is only overcome, in the long run, when Jews are seen in the role of *insiders*—when one's close associates are Jews, some of whom will then become friends while others will be heartily disliked. In other words, until the caste line as a sociological fact is de-institutionalized, as it were, no amount of individual contact or developing friendships between Jews and gentiles will counteract the dehumanizing stereotype.[14]

A similar case could be made for other traditionally excluded groups as well. The acceptance of Jews into the social world, therefore, constituted a stage in the shift of Yale power from a narrowly defined elite to a meritocratic oligarchy.

Part Four **Epilogue**

Chapter 15 Coda—1980
and Beyond

Only the most prescient of science fiction writers could have anticipated how different the world of 2000 is from that of 1980. Even predicting the outcome of 1980 at year's beginning would have been futile. President Jimmy Carter could not have anticipated that his uncertain handling of the nascent hostage crisis in Iran would cost him the White House and that Ronald Reagan's promise of "morning in America" would offer an antidote to national malaise. In a year when Mount St. Helens would suddenly erupt in Washington state, few could have imagined that an event of similar drama was to be part of that year in the Yale-Jewish relationship as well.

Some of the pressure leading to explosion had been building since the year before. Limited by a lackluster economy and a struggling fund-raising Campaign for Yale, one of President Giamatti's first challenges in 1978 had been to rein in the university's deficit spending left over from the Brewster years. Giamatti quickly appointed former Law School Dean Abraham S. Goldstein to serve as his provost and chief academic officer in wielding the ax of inevitable budget cuts and controls. Unfortunately, the partnership would not last. As Henry

Rosovsky had anticipated in turning down the Yale presidency in 1977, no institutional leader would win a popularity contest in this climate. The *Yale Daily News* was also determined to make its mark by exposing waste in the tight financial climate. In a venomous set of articles on Yale financial management that began in April 1979, the *News* published an exposé entitled: "DeLaney Kiphuth: Odd Jobs under Fancy Title," in which the paper argued that the "Special Adviser to the President on Athletics" did little to justify his Yale salary. It made for gripping copy, but in the still relatively small community that was Yale, the attack was cruel and unfair. Smelling scandal in an era of supposed financial restraint, within two weeks the paper turned its attention to Goldstein and detailed a litany of charges of seemingly wasteful expenditures in renovating the university-owned home that Provost and Mrs. Goldstein were set to occupy. When Goldstein saw that no public questioning concerned similar expenditures on renovating the university-owned home provided to the President, and when Goldstein perceived that his boss was avoiding defending him, Goldstein resigned his administrative post and resumed his Yale Law School professorship.

The historical record and subsequent interviews with all the leading principals suggest that Goldstein's resignation came about largely because of the failed personal relationship between Goldstein and Giamatti. Neither man was particularly known for compromise. Giamatti, whose simultaneous mark of character and tragic flaw was his great difficulty in separating his persona from his person, could not find a way to work with Goldstein. There is no evidence, however, that the Jewish identity of Goldstein played any role in their break.[1]

Unfortunately, the controversial resignation of the first Jew to reach high office at Yale took place at the same time that documentary evidence began to surface revealing anti-Jewish feeling and action at Yale earlier in the century. Just a few years before, the Nixon tapes had stripped the nation of illusions about the nature of leadership, even of democratically elected power. The letters found in the Yale archives would have similar repercussions in New Haven. "Smoking gun" documents with such raw emotion were simply unknown to the public at Yale or elsewhere in what previously had been the rarefied world of American academe. For those who were becoming privy to the Yale historical record in 1980, the temples of higher learning and Yale, in particular, could never again be seen in the same light. An innocent, romantic view lay shattered. The 1979 resignation of the Jewish provost thereby carried a confusing message to some Jews on the campus. Was the scandal merely office politics? Was it evidence of administrative corruption? Or, to use Watergate terminology, was the

Jewish "tax-collector" being made a scapegoat of budget-cutting tensions and being hung out to twist in the wind? No public data were available then to address such speculations.[2] Among those considering such implications was Rabbi Arnold Jacob Wolf.

Meanwhile, Wolf had decided that the time had come for him to leave Yale. He had accomplished almost all that he thought he could, and the "grim pre-professionalism" that Kingman Brewster had criticized at Yale earlier in the decade wore on him. By and large, Wolf felt that the newer students in 1980 lacked the political fervor that for him was the breath of life. He told a reporter: "The freshmen and sophomores are extremely attractive and charming, but they're . . . preoccupied with personal needs, and they're unimaginative about larger ethical issues."[3] In his characteristic way, such a provocative statement about his own flock challenged those dedicated students who did volunteer on behalf of the underprivileged or who did pursue political agendas that went far beyond themselves. But in publicly scolding the vast majority of Yale students of all backgrounds, he was on target.

He was also increasingly disenchanted with Yale. Working out of a cramped, dismal, basement office, Wolf felt that a respect for the Jewish religious tradition should have earned the Hillel office more dignified surroundings. Wolf saw Yale's accommodations as half-measures when full ones were called for. Moreover, in the spring of 1980, the Baccalaureate service of Commencement weekend—the most religious remaining component of collegiate ceremony— was broadened to include for the first time a priest and a rabbi alongside the Protestant minister in its proceedings. Rather than fully appreciating the historic significance of the move, Wolf allowed himself to be galled by a callous Yale College dean who accused Wolf of "Balkanizing" the ancient ceremony. Early in the Giamatti years (1978–86), when a selection committee had met to appoint a new associate chaplain for the university, a further evolutionary step had been taken. At that committee's first meeting it decided to consider non-Protestant as well as Protestant applicants. Wolf, however, was disturbed that no Jew had been placed on the search committee until he complained.[4]

He was also feeling that the most important peer relationships he had striven for at Yale had failed. Wolf had not connected with President Giamatti and his administration in the way he would have hoped. He was especially unhappy with a Jewish faculty that displayed little interest in Jewish life. This displeasure had grown from the cold reception that he had encountered upon his arrival in New Haven in 1972. In private conservation, Wolf recalled that early on, a Jewish faculty couple stopped by his home to visit. On that occasion Wolf asked the couple why he seemed to be so isolated from so many Yale Jewish faculty. The professor's wife suggested to Wolf that he host a party in his own honor and introduce himself by inviting Jewish faculty. Wolf thought this amazing. Normal standards of hospitality dictated that established members of a community invite a newcomer, especially an incoming leader, to a welcoming reception. But in New Haven tables were turned. Hurt by being ignored, Wolf, unlike his predecessor Rabbi Israel, never proved eager to play middleman to the Yale Jewish faculty. Without anyone stepping in to bridge the faculty–rabbi gap and neither Wolf nor the faculty sufficiently motivated to seek rapprochement on their own, an atmosphere of noninterest therefore grew from both sides.[5] By the fall of 1980, Wolf had given up hope on all fronts at Yale and was ready to move on.

He did not leave quietly. A man who could be playful, wise, and loving, Wolf also loved to tweak "the Establishment." On September 19, 1980 he gave his final *Kol Nidre* sermon to a packed congregation in Yale's Battell Chapel on the holiest night of the Jewish calendar. Wolf spent the first moments of that sermon reading a selection from the 1920s-era correspondence of Yale deans criticizing Jews. He suggested that the prior behavior had residual importance, in particular stating that Yale of 1980 had apparent difficulty in welcoming Jewish styles and persons, as well as other minorities into intimate circles of influence and power. He cited the seemingly shabby way that Abraham Goldstein had been treated by the press and by his fellow administrators during the events that had led to his resignation a year before. Wolf then lashed out (for the bulk of his sermon) at his primary unhappiness with the Yale community: a Jewish faculty that he felt had little demonstrable interest in Jewish life.

The issues that Wolf raised were complex. Yale in that era could be a very lonely place for anyone whose upbringing, values, or patterns of behavior did not place them in the mainstream. Graciela Trilla (B.A. 1979) would later recall her isolation as a Latino student who felt a severe lack of "support, advice, attention, empowerment, leadership, mentoring, role modeling, counseling, and sense of community at Yale for minorities."[6] Even in an era when discrimination against minorities at Yale would have been unthinkable, the alienation of being a minority was very real for those whose personal insecurities might have inhibited their involvement with the majority culture or for those whose value systems might have conflicted with certain aspects of the majority culture. The difficulties faced by minorities seeking security within the majority culture were not unique to Yale or to universities.

The *Yale Daily News* coverage following Wolf's sermon provided a powerful example of the ability of a newspaper to skew the news. A sermon that focused on challenging Jews to return to their roots was publicized as being all about Yale as a hostile place toward Jewish identity. Controversy quickly spread to the pages of the local and national press. For his own part, Wolf was slow to correct some of the erroneous impressions that had first been published. Some Jewish faculty were deeply offended by what they read of the sermon in the newspapers. Some of the publicly identified Jewish faculty, however, were quite supportive of Wolf's contentions regarding their fellow teachers.[7] The provocative sermon and the publicity that followed were far from the "good form" valued in the Yale ethos. Yet the frustration that Wolf voiced reflected a wound that could no longer be left to fester. Despite the evoked pain, the past could not be rewritten. Issues of ethnicity and racial identity and Yale's mixed legacy would have to be confronted. For Yale to grow it would have to make peace with its past and go out of its way to build a demonstrably more inclusive future for outsiders of all sorts.

HEALING THE WOUNDS

Yale administrators were determined the next year to demonstrate that it was proud of its diverse community and that they would not tolerate challenges to that ideal. For Giamatti, Wolf's charges against the university were initially rejected, but clearly heard, and clearly taken as personal charges against Giamatti. He would do all he could to demonstrate that Yale was no longer a place where conformity was required or where suppression of personal identity was the ticket to success. Well beyond Wolf's sermon, undoubtedly, the increased sensitivity that emanated from the Yale administration was reflective of the diversity of backgrounds of its most influential members, who included Protestants, Catholics, and Jews, and descendants of English, German, Irish, Italian, and Russian immigrants. In an act of healing, President Giamatti chose Rabbi Laurie Rutenberg in May 1981 to serve as the new assistant university chaplain.[8] Later the same year, reminding the Yale community of the university's commitment to equal opportunity in education and employment and the creation of a racially integrated community, another significant step was taken. Five "human relations counselors," of varied races, religions, and sexes were appointed to offer counseling and to investigate charges of racial or sexual harassment or unlawful discrimination on the basis of race, religion, color, sex, national origin, age, or handicap. These counselors did not have the power to change prejudices of the mind, but the formal grievance programs that they administered were engaged to redress actions of prejudice.[9] Further, the forceful standards and discussion concerning discrimination may have urged thinking members of the Yale community to reconsider their own residual biases. Certainly, this openness encouraged many new expressions of personal identity. Though the guidelines did not then specifically include sexual orientation, they had a similar impact on homosexuals. Writer David Leavitt (B.A. 1983) would later recall that at Yale in this era, "being gay was not only socially acceptable, it was trendy."[10]

Some also attributed the accelerated enhancement of a Judaic studies program at Yale that year to the fallout from Goldstein's resignation and Wolf's sermon. Giamatti declared that a Judaic studies program was a demonstration that Yale was committed to being "what it says and much of America thinks it is as a university."[11] So Giamatti further salved a wound. He also committed Yale to support fund-raising by the Jewish community so that it could have a spiritual space of its own—as Protestants and Catholics had long enjoyed as a result of their own efforts. By the time the first edition of this book was published and endorsed by Giamatti in early 1986, he was confident that doors were fully open at Yale for Jews, as Jews, and that the process of discussing nonmeritocratic exclusion was irrevocably opening doors for people of all backgrounds at Yale with the talent and drive to succeed. He took pride in his stance and was proud for Yale. Such confidence was justified.[12]

Within the Jewish community, members began to address their own establishment of boundaries. Rabbi Bernard Och served a six-month term as acting Hillel foundation director and quickly confronted the Jewish religious denominations with their own self-imposed isolation. For centuries worldwide, Friday night dinners had been the quintessential meal of the week in Jewish families. Of those Yale Jewish undergraduates who observed some communal form of the Sabbath, Orthodox students ate their Friday night meals in the basement Kosher Kitchen on Crown Street, Conservative students ate with classmates in their own residential colleges, and Reform students (the "Chavurah") migrated as a group from one residential college fellows' lounge to another—all eating in different spaces at different times. Och wondered what kind of a community could Yale's Sabbath-marking Jews create if they could not bring themselves to dine at the same table once a week. To the credit of such student leaders as Scott Cantor (B.A. 1981), Jordan Lurie (B.A. 1984), Deena Cohen (B.A. 1984), and others, they recognized Och's wisdom at once and put denominational differences aside in order to share a weekly meal. In the broader Jewish world outside, where tensions between different Jewish denominations sometimes ran high, the communal experience at Yale was a refreshing contrast. This simple move was a key factor in leading many of these Jewish students to feel part of a common entity.[13]

Healing steps also took place in the process of trying to find a permanent replacement for Rabbi Wolf. Again with Rabbi Och's encouragement, Orthodox, Conservative, and Reform students joined together in serving on the search committee led by law professor Robert Cover. The Orthodox involvement was particularly meaningful because Orthodox students previously had little connection with Yale Hillel. The committee's choice of Rabbi James Ponet (B.A. 1968) came easily. In the committee's eyes Ponet, who possessed an almost electric energy and charisma, seemed certain to generate positive responses from students.[14] His being a Yale graduate was similarly important. Wolf felt he was an outsider; the committee's hope was that Ponet would more easily feel at home. More importantly, the hope was that Ponet's Yale allegiance would facilitate the necessary commitment to create a secure presence for a Jewish organization at Yale. His own life story allowed him to connect with students and faculty of all degrees of religious persuasion. Born in a Reform Jewish family as James Podnetsky, he changed his name so that he would arrive at Yale College in 1964 as Jim Ponet. At Yale he had first distanced himself from Judaism, later recalling that "if there were other Jewish students in Timothy Dwight College, I had nothing to do with them. The fact that they were Jewish made them too familiar to deal with." Nonetheless, he found religion while in college and after graduating from Yale attended rabbinical school. With his wife and partner, Elana Ponet, he became the glue that helped Yale Jews become a community rather than being just a collection of individuals. Often sacrificing their private space and time, the two Ponets opened their Hillel-owned townhouse at 35 High Street to students, alumni, faculty, and townspeople week after week, year after year. Ponet's devotion to students, faculty, and alumni and his commitment to the Yale campus (despite years of discouragement in fund-raising and bureaucratic battles) would pay off in the later development of a Yale home for Jewish life. The eventual construction of a formal building would be a concrete extension of what was already beginning to exist in spirit.[15]

BUILDING A CENTER

Recalling their own sense of isolation as undergraduates, some older Jewish alumni from the 1920s and 1930s feared that building a Jewish center on campus would lead to self-segregation. Rabbi Ponet would successfully counter this charge and earn financial support from Jewish alumni by repeatedly and successfully demonstrating that segregation of Jews would not be an issue, because Jewish students already took full part in Yale life. From year to year, for example, one might find a Jewish student with a skullcap walking out of Scroll and Key, another without skullcap as coxswain of the crew, a Jewish student as publisher or editor of the *News,* and yet another coordinating the Big Brother/Big Sister volunteer program in the New Haven community. The building of a center, Ponet argued, would allow the students the same dignity and fulfillment on the spiritual side of their lives as in other aspects of their lives. Reinforcing their religiosity would reinforce their commitment to serving the world at large. A novel and major function of the building would also be to share Jewish life with the rest of the university.[16]

Ponet could also argue that Jewish faculty had begun to emerge, and he enlisted their support. It had once been the case at Yale, Princeton, and other elite universities that "someone who had wanted to be considered an intellectual would have been reluctant to express any personal interest in religion."[17] Ponet found increasing numbers of individual faculty who would involve themselves with Jewish life alongside their scholarly interests.

Ponet wisely complemented his own strengths with those of Donald J. Cohen (M.D. 1966), director of the Yale Child Study Center and professor of psychiatry. As chair of the Friends of Yale Hillel at the beginning of the 1990s, Cohen brought unstoppable optimism and organization to the effort to build a Jewish building on campus. His willingness to identify publicly as a Jew emboldened other Jewish faculty to feel more comfortable in expressing their own identification. His psychological understanding would also prove beneficial. He had learned the psychotherapist's art of containing the anxiety of interpersonal processes within himself and would use that skill to prevent inevitable challenges from dooming success. While he absorbed recurrent doubts that would arise, his Hillel board would remain focused on success and not just be "a complaint that we don't have a building." Cohen also brought a useful psychological awareness of human motivations that proved critical in overcoming the many bureaucratic obstacles that would crop up in gaining approval from the university for Hillel to occupy a space on the main campus. "Everyone has dark motives within them, but in the end, everyone wants to do the right thing and be part of something good," Cohen recognized. He relentlessly promoted the idea to Jew and non-Jew alike that permitting the Jewish community to raise the funds and build its own space at Yale *was* the right thing to do, *was* an inevitable aspect of modern American life and, most importantly, would be good for the university. Cohen's successful navigation through Yale bureaucracy was aided by the warm support of Yale President Benno C. Schmidt, Jr., Yale Vice President Michael Finnerty, and Presidential Adviser Henry Broude.[18]

By 1990 any notion that Jews were not active and fully accepted players in university life not only would have been absurd, but also would have been decades-old history. Major donors to the general funds of the university by then included such Jews as Frederick Rose (B.E. 1944), the Cullman family, and Richard Rosenfeld (B.A. 1963). Rose himself had been excluded as a Jew from the fraternities and senior societies as an undergraduate, but he had loved Yale enough that he would later serve as founding chairman of its alumni association and include, among many other gifts, a donation to the university of the former DKE fraternity building that would serve as home of the Alumni House.[19] In 1989 Sidney Altman had completed a term as dean of Yale College and won a Nobel Prize in chemistry for his work describing catalytic properties of ribonucleic acid. As an active member of the Hillel Board, and chair in 1994, Altman was a visible symbol of someone who was engaged in Jewish life, who was a full, active, and forceful contributor to Yale University life, and who was a valued contributor to the world. In this environment, it was only natural that Yale would recognize such commitment to the university and facilitate the Jewish community's attempts to construct its own home on campus.

The absence of such a facility at Yale was a growing anomaly, of which Jewish students and alumni had become acutely aware. Harvard, Princeton, and many other leading universities had centers of one sort or another for Jewish life by this time. The hope of assuring survival of Jewish life in America was another critical motivation. For example, Eugene Rostow advocated such a building in 1991 when he noted that "more and more American Jews are drifting away from their moorings and ceasing to be Jews, either in the religious or moral sense."[20] Senator Joseph I. Lieberman thought the building would facilitate Jewish observance and full engagement in Yale life. Rostow and Lieberman served as national honorary co-chairs for the effort. Annual panels at alumni reunion weekends from 1991 through 1995 allowed Jewish alumni to reflect on the limits and genuine accomplishments of the past and form a consensus to erect a building on behalf of the Jewish community. Following his participation in the first such panel in 1991, Alan Slifka (B.A. 1951) became engaged in the process that would lead to dedicating the Joseph Slifka Center for Jewish Life as a memorial to his father. Other donors were won over by the determination of development officer Robin Golden (B.A. 1979) or became loyal to the effort through Ponet's critical persistence with the quest, year after year, living his devotion to the community.[21]

Ground-breaking for the Slifka Center occurred on Wall Street near the middle of the campus on May 30, 1993, and its doors opened the following year.[22] The building was designed by Harold Roth (M.Arch. 1967). The award-winning facility was intentionally open and welcoming to attract all through its doors, was understated so as not to risk charges of ostentatiousness or profligate spending, and had limited overt religious symbolism that would make it overly sectarian. But there were Hebrew letters on the entrance column, Jewish texts and religious items on display throughout, and a kosher kitchen at its core. On the Sabbath as well as other times its public spaces became chapels.

Its earliest years succeeded beyond its founders' dreams. Ponet kept his promise that the building would both support Jewish identification and support the sharing of Judaism with the larger Yale community. Hundreds of students, Jewish and a good number non-Jewish, would flock to the Friday night Sabbath dinners to take part in the festive atmosphere. The lunchtime food was so satisfying and available in such quantity that for a time the men's lightweight crew took their regular lunchtime meals there! The meeting space nurtured Jewish interests of students and faculty and provided a boost to New Haven Jewry and volunteerism in general at Yale.

As the year 2000 ended, the Hillel Foundation at Yale formally took on the name of the building that sheltered it. Guided by the cooperative work of Ponet, Orthodox Rabbi Michael Whitman, the newly-honored Sterling Professor of Child Psychiatry Donald Cohen, Eric I. Beller (J.D. 1978), Dr. Bernard Lytton, and others, the kosher kitchen housed within the building legally became a corporate part of the Slifka Center as well. Simultaneously, and in recognition of all that Yale itself had achieved, Judge Howard M. Holtzmann (B.A. 1942, J.D. 1947) promised an endowment to the university to support the Jewish chaplaincy.

THE APPOINTMENT OF LEVIN

The appointment of economist and Dean of the Graduate School Richard C. Levin (Ph.D. 1974) as Yale President in 1993 was almost anticlimactic from a Jewish perspective. It is too soon to be able to make more than the most cursory and likely myopic historical judgments about the Levin era, a time of prosperity for Yale and unprecedented wealth for America, during which these pages were written. By the time of his appointment, Jews had already served as presidents at several other Ivy League universities and there was little sense of dramatic change occurring.[23] Levin noted that his being Jewish showed Yale to be the meritocracy it should be. In office he would affirm his Jewish background in a modest, sincere, and authentic way. A Jew's occupying the Yale presidency in 1993 may also have been less momentous than it might once have been because the job of being a university president, and for that matter the Yale president, no longer carried the same stature or national moral force that it once had. Whereas A. Whitney Griswold and Kingman Brewster, Jr., had graced the cover of *Time* magazine in their day, and A. Bartlett Giamatti's profile could be found in the *New York Times Magazine,* those days were over. Already by the 1980s, university presidencies nationwide were losing some of their prestige as leaders became more like cogs, albeit chief cogs, in institutions that were acting more like corporations and less like cohesive communities.[24] No university president commanded a bully pulpit any longer, and if Levin or any contemporary had tried to claim such a podium, it is unclear how many people would really have listened.[25]

Levin, nonetheless, set his own mark of distinction. A Stanford graduate, Levin brought a California-tempered openness and geniality to develop a new example for leadership style at Yale. His rhetoric may not have reached the heights of historian Griswold, lawyer Brewster, or literary master Giamatti, but his actions had eloquence of their own. Inspired by the ethos of social justice taught in his Reform Jewish upbringing, Levin firmly steered the university to take increasing and substantial interest in improving the economic and social conditions of New Haven—whose economic survival became increasingly dependent upon the university as the large industries of the town collapsed.[26]

Chapter 16 Conclusions

Acceptance of Jews into the Yale community represented neither the first nor the last stage in the long history of nonmeritocratic discrimination at Yale and in America. In Yale's early years, a student was ranked by the college administration throughout his undergraduate career. This assignment of position was largely based on the wealth and social status of the student's family. According to historian Brooks Mather Kelley, the ratings had far more impact than a mere *Social Register:* "Once the class members were . . . ranked, a student took that place in everything he did: his seat in class, chapel, commons, and all else was fixed by it. . . . He had to act out his ranking every day of his college life." An early scrimmage between the forces of established privilege and earned merit was won by merit when the Yale Corporation, reacting to student discontent, voted in 1766 to discard the imposed elitism.[1] As religious tolerance increased in the following century and religion became less central to Yale, non-Congregationalist Protestant males and later non-Protestant Christian males came to be welcomed in the various corners of the university community. In the middle of the twentieth century, Jewish and, later, black men, too, began to find their respective niches. At their heels came women of all racial and religious backgrounds in the 1970s. At the start of the Brewster administration (1963–77), the commitment that the university made to providing adequate financial aid to every candidate accepted guaranteed that all Yale students would have the opportunity to participate in campus social life.

The acceptance of previously excluded groups into the community did not, by any means, mark the absolute end of discriminatory patterns. On the road to that far-off destination there were many detours. In the late 1960s Henry Chauncey, Jr., special assistant to President Brewster, was asked to spend a year studying the university to learn how to make undergraduate co-education work at Yale. Speaking to many members of the community, Chauncey came away convinced that Yale was still permeated with bias against Catholics, Jews, and women. Most of those he met did not exhibit such prejudices, but real biases existed in enough employees and faculty, Chauncey felt, as to make a difference: "There was clear discrimination in attitude. I'm sure there was discrimination in activity."[2] In the late 1960s and 1970s, some black students, motivated by fears of being considered as tokens, talked of creating all-black entryways in Yale's residential colleges. In one such college, black student leaders insisted to the college master that if he intended to invite any of that college's black students to a social function, he should plan to invite all of that college's black students or none at all.[3] In the late 1970s some of Yale's earliest women graduates filed a class action lawsuit charging some of their male professors with sexual harassment. Though the lawsuit was unsuccessful, it raised troublesome issues of remaining discrimination. In the early 1980s some undergraduates fought quiet battles to counter discrimination against homosexuals.[4] The Elihu Club and Manuscript senior societies had tapped women undergraduates as soon as was possible after female undergraduates were admitted in 1969. Some other societies moved much more slowly. Scroll and Key tapped women as of 1989, and battling alumni resistance, the Skull and Bones undergraduates selected their first women members in 1991.[5]

Signs of advance were continuously in evidence even among those long graduated from the campus. Of Jewish alumni from the 1920s and 1930s, many of whom were social outsiders as undergraduates, many told stories of returning to their thirtieth and fortieth and fiftieth class reunions and discovering that old caste lines had been broken down by the liberalizing influences in the nation.[6] Rather than signaling the end of discrimination, increased sensitivities toward previously excluded groups served as markers along a highway indicating that progress was being made.[7]

THE CASUALTIES OF IGNORANCE

At Yale, as elsewhere, ignorance bred mistrust. Some alumni were wont to bare their chests and detail laundry lists of undergraduate associations that excluded Jews, particularly during the 1910s, 1920s, and 1930s. Yet their recollections did not uniformly jibe with the published classbooks from those years: Some undergraduate organizations were not as *judenrein* as rumor had it. That is not to minimize the real anti-Jewish prejudice that did exist, particularly in the secret societies and in the fraternities. These organizations were critical organizations in Yale life, yet they certainly were not all of Yale life. Some of the non-Jews who attempted to justify the anti-Jewish feeling that existed in parts of the campus explained that their Jewish classmates had lesser ethical standards than their Christian counterparts. Yet their recollections did not uniformly correlate with those of their classmates or the documentary record. They had learned of the inferior styles of Jews from general talk at home and on the campus.

At the faculty level, issues of prejudice were no less complex. There was clear prejudice on the basis of religious background in the early twentieth century at a time when Protestant Christianity had already grown peripheral to campus life. A prominent history professor was said to have been proud in the 1950s that no Catholics were in his department, since their allegiances to papal authority undermined their capacity to search unhesitatingly for truth. Jewish faculty of utmost character such as Lafayette B. Mendel or Edward Sapir saw their role in Yale life limited by their Jewish background. Steering Jewish students away from academic careers was a recurrent theme, particularly before the Second World War. Questioning of character on account of Jewish background was a reality, as noted in the ultimately successful permanent appointment of Paul Weiss. Yet, if we look at the record without sentiment or apologetics, we must also acknowledge that some Jewish scholars, a Milton Winternitz or a Morris Cohen for example, like their Protestant counterparts, were not always gentlemen, and could, at times, be bullies. Though their genuine accomplishments may very well have been aided by the twin capacity to intimidate *and* enchant that bullies who are leaders sometimes possess,[8] the proposition that the ends justify the means remains dubious. Since being a Jew or a Catholic or another minority does not define character, where prejudice muddied thinking was when ignorance allowed group membership to be used as a method to assess character.

Unfortunately, the barriers that grew out of ignorance fed upon each other. Many Jews came to the campus expecting to find prejudice and universal exclusion. By looking hard enough, without considering their own capacities for bias, they found prejudice. Fully convinced that their Judaism was an impediment, some gave up the attempt to make a sports team, for example, when a situation seemed bleak, but not yet hopeless. And some Christian students refused any more than the minimal necessary contact with their Jewish classmates because of their own ingrained, unsubstantiated prejudices. By looking hard enough for deficiencies among Jews, without looking at deficiencies within themselves, they found inferior Jews.

The most pervasive form of prejudice at Yale was largely applied on the basis of social class. In many ways it was a failure of the imagination, a complacency with contemporary norms that could not conceive of social advances. In the days when nativism thrived on campus, many of the most prominent of Yale undergraduates had no inner dislike or hatred toward Jews or blacks or the poor or townies; they simply had a profound lack of interest in the lower class groups. This form of prejudice simply and instinctually led many of the campus upper class to ignore the lower class because, as one elite undergraduate of the 1930s put it, "we thought they had nothing to offer." Similarly, most of the men who until the 1960s directed women away from positions of leadership and responsibility had no hatred or dislike of women; to them, the idea of women as leaders was simply inconceivable. In essence this same callousness underlay the barriers that handicapped people found throughout the nation until the 1970s. When architects and city planners designed sidewalks lacking easements to the street and buildings with high steps that lacked entrance ramps, few of them had any deep-seated prejudice against people in wheelchairs. But the narrow confines of tradition had previously instructed these molders of society that handicapped people could not manage for themselves. In many generations and in many forms the benign failure to imagine the potential of others proved as virulently exclusive as any form of blatant bigotry.[9]

A "beleaguered elite minority" syndrome (often indicative of justified insecurity) became part of the consciousness of many students to have gone through Yale. Some Jews often looked at a campus led by non-Jews who excluded. Some white Anglo-Saxon Protestants were concerned about the rising numbers of ethnics. Some Catholics felt that Jews and Protestants racing for success had kept them behind. Some New Englanders feared hordes of New Yorkers. Some midwesterners felt out of place among stuffy easterners. Some religious devotees saw themselves as loners surrounded by pagans. Some nonbelievers saw themselves in a world dominated by the faithful. Some intellectuals saw themselves surrounded by Philistines. Some socialites felt hard-pressed to compete with bookworms. Despite the multiplicity of definitions, had a Venn diagram been drawn to symbolize all the categories into which people placed themselves the areas of overlap would have been great.

Yale, by counting some categories and ignoring others, artificially exaggerated the influence of some of its minority components and hid that of others. While the principle of "balance" was used to limit Jews to 10 percent of the undergraduates (more than three times their proportion of the national population) only a few on campus bothered to notice the great degree of underrepresentation of blacks—or, for that matter, the greater overrepresentation of Episcopalians and Presbyterians, who in 1950 represented 40 percent of the undergraduate population as compared to a national representation of under 7 percent.[10] When Jews and blacks had no advocates among the admissions officers there was no one to argue that the sword of "balance" could cut in two directions. Still, advocacy alone was not enough. In the medical school, where Abraham White, for example, had argued against quota systems, a lone voice could not overcome the dominant bigotry. In the final analysis, the actions of admissions committees, no matter who their members, were largely a function of the policies established by senior university administrators and the men who led those committees. Because of their explicit or implicit support, bias reigned over one epoch in Yale history.

In later years, when white Jews and Catholics had won their place alongside white Protestants, other minority groups would take up the cry for balance, suggesting that changes be made to compensate for the Jewish overrepresentation in educational fields and the Presbyterian and Episcopalian domination of big business and national politics. At times these cries were calls for new quota systems, masquerading in the guise of equal opportunity.[11] Basic questions regarding the nature of democracy continued to be ignored on campus. Did a particular group achieve its success honestly and fairly? Did a "minority" choose to spend its energies in pursuing success in an area of societal enterprise? To what extent were other "minorities" discriminated against in the process of one group's rise? For Jews, Episcopalians, and Presbyterians, essential questions concerning their particular successes often went unasked and unanswered: Did these three groups achieve success because of their wealth? Or did they become wealthy because they valued the "Protestant Work Ethic?" more than other segments of society? Does the Jewish tradition of marrying Jews allow for the retention of wealth and power that the intermarriage of other groups dilutes? Can the same be said of Episcopalians and Presbyterians? Is there a significantly higher rate of intermarriage within the groups of Jews, Episcopalians, and Presbyterians than between any one of these groups and a fourth religious group? To what extent might the lower birthrates among these groups preserve concentrations of wealth and power or permit children greater degrees of valuable parental guidance? To what extent do non-Episcopalians, non-Presbyterians, or non-Jews feel that they must identify with or marry into one of these religious groups to achieve status within the American educational, political, social, and business establishment? And the fundamental question of a democracy, "Is the result a product of the forces of coercion or free will?" went unasked.

THE DILEMMA OF THE ELITE JEW

The absence of Jews from any particular organization did not necessarily mean that the organization had an anti-Jewish bias. Some of the most talented members of every majority or minority group, sensing an unfair or improper social structure, have always chosen to march to the beat of a different drummer than the majority. Waldo Frank (B.A.–M.A. 1911) was a classic example:

> The regular pattern was to be popular, to make a team and one's letter or an editorship, to join a fraternity and to be tapped on tap-day of junior year for one of the secret societies. Any of these goals was hard for a Jew to achieve at Yale, although not impossible. I was too proud to try. From the start I elected to be of the minority who chose *not* to run for the *right* goals.[12]

Rather than fight and win a difficult battle against discrimination, so gaining respect in the eyes of the discriminators, many minority group members chose to compete in arenas where equal opportunity rather than discrimination prevailed. Others refused to be token members of prejudiced groups. They preferred instead to restrict their affiliations to organizations that did not harbor *any* resistance toward members of their minority.[13]

Some of the Yale Jews (particularly those of East European origin whose parents were immigrants) were reluctant to join an elite that would not tolerate less elite Jews. Though Christians who joined "exclusive" organizations left many of their fellow Christians behind among the huddled masses, for Jews close to their traditions there was a hesitance to do the same to their fellow Jews. What complicated the decisions for many a Jew who was conscious of his tradition, though not necessarily religiously observant, was the fundamental dilemma facing the historically conscious Jew. Since Jewish tradition taught that every Jew was to view himself as having been *both* a slave in ancient Egypt and present when the Lord delivered the Law at Mount Sinai, the Jew was caught between the contrasts of his tradition. On one hand, he had been designated to receive God's word. Yet, on the other hand, he was obliged to remember the bitterness and denigration of slavery. As was annually recounted at the Passover Seder, ultimate lowliness was imposed upon the awareness of supreme eliteness. This eternal dialectic faced every historically conscious Jew considering joining the most elite organizations. Because joining a club meant, to some extent, turning one's back on those left behind, one could not be part of both the elite and the common folk at the same time. For the Jew whose religion and culture impressed upon him the commandments of remembering the tears of slavery, clothing the poor, feeding the hungry, caring for the widow and orphan, doing justly to the stranger, over-indulgence in exclusiveness carried the risk of abandonment of his historical ideals.

In general, however, the tempting fruits of the tree of American educational opportunity, particularly in the post-Second World War period, have weaned American Jews away from their traditions. Demographer Sidney Goldstein in 1971 noted the success that colleges nationally seemed to have in diverting Jewish students away from their past:

> Jews with higher education may have . . . higher . . . rates of intermarriage and . . . alienation from the Jewish community. This involves not only the possible impact of physical separation from home and the weakening parental control on dating and courtship patterns, but also the general "liberalization" a college education may have on the religious values and Jewish identity of the individual. It would be ironic if the very strong positive value that Jews traditionally have placed on education and that now manifests itself in the very high proportion of Jewish youths attending college may eventually be an important factor in the general weakening of the individual's ties to the Jewish community.[14]

Yet is seems unfair to blame Yale and American educational institutions for being too attractive. From the Mosaic days of the ancient Israelites longing for the fleshpots of Egypt to the Herodian times of Greco-Roman emulation to the America of the late twentieth century, the life-styles of non-Jews have often proved attractive to Jews. Though most eighteen- to twenty-one-year-olds are impressionable, and often clumsily learning the ways of the world, they do not have blank slates for brains. Most are quite capable of independent thought and analysis. To explain a person's decision on how closely to affiliate himself with Judaism solely on the basis of the attractiveness of gentile society removes responsibility from the individual making the decision. Such an explanation also fails to consider any possible unattractiveness in Judaism. It also ignores the fact that most American Jews expect their children to make adult decisions concerning the value of their religion with only an elementary school level of religious knowledge upon which to base their thinking. If there was an irony for American Jews it was that their historical penchant had primarily been directed toward a religious education. In America the religious component of that learned commitment foundered.

CLUB, COLLEGE, AND UNIVERSITY

That American definitions of the words "club" and "college" overlapped is far more than a matter of semantic coincidence. *The American Heritage Dictionary of the English Language* offers "a group of people organized for a common purpose, especially a group that meets regularly," among its definitions of "club." Under the listing "college," in addition to more educationally oriented explanations, one may find "a company or assemblage; especially a body of persons having a common purpose or common duties."[15] The overlapping definitions in American usage allowed for ambiguity. One of the crucial questions that Yale faced in the twentieth century was whether it was foremost a college or a club.

The conflict between club and college on a university campus was, of course, not unique to Yale. Princeton, perhaps, had a greater reputation for its clannish ways. Woodrow Wilson, president of Princeton from 1902 to 1910, based his widely approved preceptorial system on the choice of men who were "companionable and clubbable. . . . If their qualities as gentlemen and as scholars conflict, the former will win them the place." The founding president of Johns Hopkins University, Daniel Coit Gilman (B.A. 1852), thought that a professor "should be cultivated in manners & at his ease in the social relations" that a university was obligated to maintain. At the University of Chicago, President Robert Maynard Hutchins (former dean of the Yale Law School) told his faculty after the Second World War that "as long as we are a university, and not a club, we cannot invoke racial distinctions as a basis for the selection of our students." If a club atmosphere prevailed on campuses where racial, religious, and sexual background a priori determined whether one was or was not of the "right" character, then Jews and other groups that suffered discrimination were caught between the conflicting ideals of the club, college, and university.[16]

When America became a nation of joiners in the late nineteenth century, society returned to a mode of assessing status less on the basis of individual capability and personality and more on belonging to the proper associations. Social clubs such as the Knickerbocker, Union, Racquet, and University Club in New York, the Philadelphia Club in that city, and the Graduate Club of New Haven, which had once welcomed "elite" Jews (some of these clubs had Jews among their founders) began regular practices of exclusion. (Elite German Jews reacted by forming equally exclusive clubs—New Haven had its own Harmonie Club.) Colleges such as Yale simultaneously became links in the national chain of associations that were the honored breeding ground for the "right people." With the rise of a wealthy class at Yale in this era, clubbiness took over where collegiality left off.[17]

Writing of the Yale of the late nineteenth and early twentieth centuries, historian George Pierson described the homogeneous nature of the college:

> Yale conformed. There was no doubt about it. . . . At Yale individualism was not encouraged. Campus sentiment was against it, and traditions stood in the way. . . . Originality of ideas was suspect and, outside of a tolerated range, eccentricity of dress or conduct was frowned upon.[18]

The Yale "religion" of uniformity had little room for believers of different "faiths," and less space for "heathens" who maintained their independence. By and large, the students and faculty were a happy, though similar group. One 1904 Yale graduate who went on to serve on the Yale Corporation remarked decades after his graduation that Yale had grown to be a better university than it ever was before, yet, upon referring to his undergraduate years, he said, almost wistfully, "We had a wonderful club."[19]

Given the club model, where diversity was unwanted, where over-indulgence in book-learning was suspect, where participation in the standard forms of campus social life was everything, where building the pillars of the social prestige that would launch one's success in a prejudiced world was the goal, the informal schemes of limitation that restricted Jewish enrollment were justifiable. For the community that Yale was trying to be, the acceptance of students who did not fit into the Yale model offered a mortal threat to the communal spirit. One might guess that the Yale College administrators, who knowingly accepted a student population of which 10 percent would be commuters (a large proportion of whom were Jewish, but many of whom were members of other faiths and ethnicities), thought themselves generous and noble. For the sake of lip service to the university ideal, they were willing to commit one in ten of their short supplied spaces to groups who, largely for reasons of economic circumstances, racio-religious prejudice, and differing educational values, could not or would not become part of the all-important community that Yale

College was trying to foster. Still, many of the influential Yale administrators of the 1920s and 1930s were not such exalted and dispassionate men. For these men and for their successors in the next generation, human individuality was submerged in stereotype.

The choice that Yale had to make was between being an academic community and being a communal academy. In the first model the college would devote itself to increasing the bounds of human understanding, but its first goal would be the building of a communal spirit. In the second model the communal nature would be essential, but the intellectual quality would come first. Without sacrificing most of its trappings of clubbiness, twentieth-century Yale chose the latter model, the university college. For the sake of its historical ideals, for national service, and for the desire to retain a national prestige that was slipping away to its less stodgy competitors, Yale shifted its priorities. Older faculty and administrators sometimes grumbled that the Jewish proportions at Yale had increased to maintain that prestige, but in their hearts they were also quite pleased that the Yale they loved remained in the top ranks of world universities and that they were part of that unimpeachable meritocractic elite themselves.

INSIDERS AND OUTSIDERS

Writing in *The American Historical Review,* R. Laurence Moore persuasively argued that

> the lines between historical insiders and outsiders may seem so hopelessly muddled in subjective perceptions that American historians ought simply to drop any suggestion of those categories in constructing narrative. . . . [Yet] we should not . . . reduce the narrative uses of insider and outsider categories but, instead, allow our narratives the chance to heighten rather than conceal the ambiguities.[20]

Moore's concerns fit the Yale paradigm well. The distinction between insider and outsider at Yale, in its various schools, teams, organizations, and clubs, has not always been a clear one. To some extent every newcomer to the campus felt somewhat alienated. Yale grew to be such a large institution, with so many unique traditions belonging to so many parts of it, that no one person, even given a lifetime, could hope to appreciate them all. And many of the traditions were so in-bred that depending on where one stood when viewing the tradition, insiders in one circle could feel like outsiders in another and outsiders to a circle appear as insiders. Because of the loyalties that the institution tried to build to its components there was, nevertheless, a definite consciousness of belonging to whatever parts of Yale one did belong to. This consciousness of belonging was reinforced by exclusionary and limiting policies, many of which were completely justifiable (e.g., grades for Phi Beta Kappa membership, physical ability for election to the varsity tennis teams). Since the great football player was rarely the great scholar, since the great scholar was rarely the best of artists, and since the best of artists was rarely the greatest of football players, even the insiders of some circles were outsiders in others.

Only two types of organizations at Yale successfully cut through the ranks of insiders. To a limited extent the fraternities attempted to bring the most prestigious men of the college and scientific school classes together. To a much greater degree the secret societies succeeded. With the added fact that some university administrators regularly took part in fraternity and society ritual and educational programs, and the fact that in some generations in some societies university officials attempted to redirect campus thought using their old boy network as a conduit for influence, or tried to learn of undergraduate opinion through the voices of the society members, the societies moreso functioned as associations of insiders. They were part of the elite that controlled campus organizations and, depending on the contemporary makeup of the university administration, they were intimately linked to the administrative authority on campus.[21]

The reactions to outsiderism on the campus were many. In general, when a group felt excluded from campus insiders they formed a rival group. Secret societies and fraternities alike sprang up when groups of individuals felt that they deserved insiderhood. Undergraduates Steven Vincent Benét (B.A. 1919) and John F. Carter (B.A. 1919) wrote one poem to poke fun at the Eli's need to belong to an elite crowd:

Do you want to be successful?
  Form a club!
Are your chances quite distressful?
  Form a club!
Never mind the common friendships
  that no politician has!
Seek the really righteous rounders
  and the athletes of the class!
And you'll get your heart's desiring—
  and the rest will get the raz!
  Form a club![22]

From the ashes of failure, for example, rose the society phoenixes of Scroll and Key, Wolf's Head, and Elihu Club.[23]

At Yale, as elsewhere, prejudice bred prejudice. Consequently, when insiders kept others as outsiders solely on the basis of race, religion, and sex, the outsiders reacted by forming their own exclusive and prejudicial organizations that further divided the campus community into enclaves. Pi Lambda Phi, the nonsectarian fraternity formed at Yale in 1895, was Yale's and the nation's first nonsectarian fraternity. But for reasons unknown it failed. In the 1910s and 1920s some Jews reacted to discrimination against them in the fraternities by forming their own discriminatory organizations. In doing so, they effectively granted legitimacy to the discriminatory practices of the Christian societies.

Perhaps the greatest consequence of the belonging that took place on the Yale campus was the indifference and callousness that was shown to those who did not belong and the lack of self-worth engendered in those who knew that they could not belong. The minds of many generations of students and faculty were so consumed by the events and people within their circles that they had little interest in the concerns of those outside the circles. Indeed, for most groups of insiders the affairs of those on the outside are of limited interest. But for those on the outside, keenly aware that there was a powerful inside that was forbidden to them, a resentment developed. Suspicions of insensitivity and callousness therefore arose. The provocative questions centered on fair representation. Could a group of "haves" fairly think of the "have-nots" in the absence of "have-nots?" Could insiders imagine the dignity of outsiders in the absence of outsiders? Could outsiders accepted as insiders remember that they were once outsiders?

Because Yale insiders, for a time, failed to consider outsiders of certain religious, racial, and sexual "persuasions," and because they failed to bring them in to their circles, they left a legacy of exclusion. Even when the barriers came down, the insider/outsider elitist consciousness remained. Only when the descendants of such groups as Mayflower Puritans and East European Jews and African-American slaves proved able to remember their less exalted pasts and show consideration to "outsiders" could democracy be a meaningful expression.

LIMITATION OF NUMBERS—LIMITATION OF TRUTH

Humankind has long bound itself in secret societies of religious or political nature. Private religious and political cults date back to the beginning of civilization. For scholars, who emerged from a historical background that restricted the sharing of truth to members of a fellowship, a pattern of having the most stimulating of learning experiences take place in restricted settings took hold. The biblical book of Proverbs had taught that "a wise man is strong," and Francis Bacon had elaborated that "Knowledge is power." For scholars as for politicians, the judicious retention of knowledge-power in some cases and the distribution of it in others was a key to superiority and prestige. Even after the creation of universities, designed to spread the treasures of understanding, clubs and secret societies retained their privileged positions within the scholarly communities. Among Jews, "Ahavat Shalom"—a secret society made up of the leading Sephardic rabbis and mystics of Jerusalem—was in existence by 1754. This fraternal order had secret rules prescribing codes of pious living, prayer, fasting, charity, and care of fellow members in time of trouble. In Western tradition, "The Club" of London, (founded in 1764), played a large role in that city's intellectual life. In the United States similar societies that thrived for decades were the "Wednesday Evening Club" of Boston (founded in 1777) and the "Social Club" of Concord, Massachusetts (founded in 1782).[24]

Following in the spirit that held that the most advanced knowledge was only worth learning if it could be learned in limited company, the first undergraduate intellectual societies originated at Yale. "Linonia" (1753–1872) and "Brothers in Unity" (1768–1872) were the models for a college and a nation. Highly intellectual, these societies drew the interest and support of their members in a way that classroom routine could not, as Oscar and Mary Handlin noted in *The American College and American Culture:* "Their debates, libraries and publications were often more effective modes of study than the formal academic exercises; and their ability to exclude some students gave gratifying recognition of the distinction of those admitted." At a time of limited financing for the college the private societies accumulated libraries that provided for their members the books that their college could not. Between the years of 1819 and 1853 the two societies, along with the younger Calliope society, were sympathetic enough to make sure that everyone in the college had an opportunity to become a part of one of the associations. The growth of the senior faculty societies in the nineteenth century steadily increased the role of the private society in Yale education. By the 1890s an important part of graduate school education took place in numerous clubs devoted to subjects such as classics, political science, philosophy, Bible, comparative religion, modern languages, English, and engineering. In the twentieth century even the humble red blood corpuscle would have a club devoted to it. Of all these associations, some were publicized, some were discreet, some were for all interested in a field, some were only for the chosen.[28]

For those who hoped to gain prestige outside their private circles, all the knowledge that they gained in their associations could not risk lying fallow. Deanships, Nobel prizes, national elective office, the honors of the world did not go to the selfish. Often the various clubs served as testing grounds for the ideas that their creators hoped to offer to the public.

Unsettled, however, was the essential conflict between the ideal of the university and the privacy of the discussions within the clubs that many agreed provided its most valuable forum for education. James Rowland Angell, the Yale University president (1921–37) who gave substance to the university name in New Haven, once spoke on the university ideal that conflicted with the nature of society:

> The University is dedicated to the discovery, protection, and dissemination of truth. As such it has been subject to attack since time immemorial from every agency that fears new truth and arrogates to itself the exclusive possession of particular areas of truth. In one generation this attack has come from organized religion, in another from vested business interests, and in yet another from political forces that cannot, or will not, brook the light of disinterested investigation and discussion.[26]

The standards of universal inquiry that the university demanded of other areas of society, however, did not always apply to its own components. William Clyde DeVane (dean of Yale College, 1938–63) had strongly argued that the acts of the University were public acts and its policies had to be public policies.[27] But in one era in the case of Jews at Yale open consideration of the goals and purposes of the college and university were suppressed.

For Jews largely, and for other racial, religious, and sexual minorities partially, open investigation and discussion was, at times suppressed. In the 1910s some undergraduates who were too much "gentlemen" to admit publicly their racial prejudices voted secret rulings denying "recognition" to their Jewish classmates. In the 1920s some university administrators publicly trumpeted Limitation of Numbers but privately fretted about methods for limiting the numbers of Jews. Faculties, which in the early twentieth century might have taught the nation to judge a person by his own qualities rather than by his background, themselves succumbed to the prejudices that swept society at large.

The United States Constitution permits private organizations to be exclusive, to restrict their membership to certain races, creeds, sexes, and social classes. But when institutions, particularly academic institutions, claimed that they were acting otherwise, all the while silently "sawing wood," they violated the national trust. Writing in 1931 on "The Jew's Position," Eugene V. Rostow, perhaps the first Jew who "made it" at Yale, decried the double standard that the academic community had come to represent:

> Little faith is possible in the most thoroughly cultivated group in American society, if that group is capable of the moral cowardice, the intellectual stultification, of conscious anti-Semitism. At this level, more than at any other, hypocrisy and surrender to indefensible emotionalism become shocking and indescribably revolting. The failure of the intellectuals is the most miserable of all failures, because it deprives the onlooker of the sorry consolation of hope.
>
> The mere possibility of the existence in democratic America, and especially in the universities, of a series of universal hypocrisies on such a scale will provoke the social historian of another age to Gibbonesque moral fury. While a realistic defense of Jewish segregation might be offered, on the basis of a melancholy resignation to unalterable fact, no such proposal has ever been officially advanced. Authorities prefer a pretense of idealism to the forthrightness of a denial of an uncomfortable democracy, a dubious shadow of nobility to the honesty of consistent illiberalism. These policies, wherever they exist, represent a betrayal of precisely those ideals which have historically formed the most vital and inspiring elements in American tradition. Anti-Semitism . . . represents a secret prostitution on the one principle which universities assert to be inviolable, the axiom, namely, that before all else, the University is a center of education and that no vitality in education can exist in an atmosphere of pious deceit and hypocritical profession of faith.[28]

The failure of the intellectuals was not particular to Yale, for what happened in New Haven happened in many other American cities. In Nazi Germany the failure was far more tragic. Nor was the failure limited to gentiles. Some Jews proved to be as anti-Jewish or as steeped in stereotypes or as complacent as their non-Jewish neighbors. The extent of the failure was widespread.

Nonetheless, from the perspective of completing the third century of Yale's existence, a viewer of the broad expanse of history will see much good in this story. From a narrowly sectarian and classbound small "Collegiate School" in 1701, Yale College and University steadily grew into an institution of international dimension and open opportunity—most of the while striving for encouragement of talent and remaining faithful to its ancient charter to prepare students for service in "church and civil state." A profound commitment to scholarship and to using that learning for public good has been a deserved source of pride and achievement for centuries. The limits now to opportunities are not a person's religion, color, wealth, gender, sexual orientation, or origin, but rather his or her own individual capacity and drive to take advantage of the wealth the University community offered and to give back to the University and society that wealth. Isolated occurrences of intolerance may still arise, but they are surely anomalous counter examples to all the University's significant efforts at inclusivity.

But what does democracy mean? Despite the uplifting spirit with which the American democracy was founded, the cold reality of our world is that people are not created equally nor are they raised equally. Yet birthrights do not separate democracy from other forms of governance, argued Sterling Professor Emeritus of Philosophy Brand Blanshard in his essay on "Democracy and Distinction in American Education":

> My arm may be feeble and my brain equally so, but still I am a person, with my own aspirations and my own capacity for suffering, and when the privileges of society are distributed, . . . I have an equal right with anyone else to have my needs and aims considered. The story is told that Sir James Barrie was walking an Edinburgh street one winter's day in a mood of abstraction and almost bumped into a stranger who, by quickly stepping aside, avoided a collision. When Barrie turned round apologetically, the stranger was standing and looking at him reproachfully. "God made me too," he said. The stranger turned out to be Robert Louis Stevenson, and the encounter began a lifelong friendship. But what interests me at the moment is that that remark is the ultimate reply of the democrat to anyone who would push him around. I may be queer and soiled and seedy, but here I am, a living soul like you, with hopes and pains as real as yours. "God made me too."[29]

The essential meaning of democracy, he wrote, is equality of consideration.

For an institution such as Yale, wishing to educate and train those who would shape that democracy, unvarnished self-examination is critical amidst celebration and lends credence to that commemoration. The tangible goal of learning and scholarship is that in thoughtfully considering our past and present, we will create a more virtuous future. Almost two millennia ago, Talmudic scholars had pondered, "If a flame among the cedars fall, what avails the lichen on the wall?"[30] In the twentieth century, Dean William Clyde DeVane of Yale College applied the same principle, giving timeliness to Geoffrey Chaucers' "If gold rusts, what shall iron do?"[31] The university ideal is all about asking hard questions and all about shining light on spaces where Truth struggles to emerge from ambiguity. When those hard questions can be asked and are addressed, then the dark moments of times gone by can be seen as a difficult chapter in the past, but only as a chapter in a story filled with progress and promise. To the extent that history is a tale of human relationships, fulfillment of that promise lies in the hands of every new generation of leaders.

Appendix One The Yale Seal

The two mysterious words at the center of the Yale seal, אורים ותמים, appear eight times in the Hebrew Bible. They are found in Exodus 28:30, Leviticus 8:8, Numbers 27:21, Deuteronomy 33:8, I Samuel 14:41, I Samuel 28:6, Ezra 2:63, and Nehemiah 7:65. Jewish sources have traditionally defined *Urim* and *Thummim* as a set of gems on the breastplate of the Israelite high priest Aaron. These jewels served as an oracle while the ancient Israelites traveled through the Sinai desert. Richard Israel had proposed that the designers of Yale's seal had selected these stones to symbolize the prophetic mission of the college during the days when many of its graduates were expected to enter the ministry. He has also pointed out that the reference to the *Urim* and *Thummim* appears in the middle verse of some editions of Hebrew Pentateuchs. Had Yale's Puritan founders been aware of this reference, it would seem likely that the Hebrew words were largely placed to indicate that the volume on the seal was a Bible.[1]

Though early Yale leaders such as James Pierpont, Elisha Williams, and Thomas Clap had divine aspirations for their college, though they saw themselves as the American successors to the ancient Israelites, though they studied portions of the Hebrew Bible, it is not obvious why a group of ardently Christian ministers would have drawn directly from patently Jewish sources for the visible emblem of Yale.

The *Historical Register of Yale University* suggests that the Latin words for light and truth were first chosen for the seal and that the Hebrew was then added to complement the Latin sentiment.[2] A problem with this explanation is that the Hebrew words occupied a position of prominence at the center of the seal, with the Latin wrapped around the periphery. If the Hebrew was secondary to the Latin, why was the strange language placed in the primary position? Moreover, this explanation fails to give credit to the deliberation that marked the actions of many of Yale's first mentors. If Yale's public seal—a symbol that would eventually be impressed on the face of every diploma, grace numerous university buildings, and adorn countless collections of memorabilia—had a Hebrew inscription at its center, it was likely to have been carefully planned.

The first record of a seal for Yale appears in the minutes of the Yale College trustees' meeting of October 17, 1722. On that date the board voted to petition the colonial General Assembly to grant them a seal. Two of the trustees, the Reverend Timothy Woodbridge and the Reverend Eliphalet Adams, were designated to apply to the Assembly for the insignia. Before the month was over, the assemblymen acceded to the simple request and granted Yale's trustees not only a seal, but also the right to form it as they desired.[3]

THE HARVARD EXAMPLE

On several occasions in the history of the college, Yale drew upon the experience of its elder sister in Cambridge. In designing its seal, it followed a pattern set by Harvard. Therefore, a brief summary of the history of the Harvard seal, as extensively researched by Samuel Eliot Morison, is instructive for the Yale record. The Harvard *Veritas* and Yale אורים ותמים seals shared the motif of an inscription spread across one or several volumes. This theme of a book or books, open or closed, with or without inscriptions, had its precedents outside North America. Among the earliest examples were the arms of the universities of Oxford and Cambridge; of Trinity College, Cambridge; and Trinity College, Dublin; of all four Scottish universities; of the College of the Sorbonne in Paris; and of the oldest university in the Americas, that of San Marcos in Lima, Peru. The first mention of Harvard's symbol is found in the records of the Harvard Overseers from December 27, 1643, which give a sketch of three open books centered on a coat of arms, *VE RI TAS* syllabically inscribed upon them.[4] Morison believed that the word *Veritas* meant "divine truth" to Harvard's Overseers.[5] Lest the Harvard partisan quickly assume that Yale usurped Harvard's motto, adding a touch of *Lux* to it, it must be pointed out that Harvard quickly forgot the 1643 sketch. *Veritas* would not achieve position as the centerpiece of the Harvard seal until 1843 and it would not secure that place until 1885.[6]

Following the 1643 meeting, Harvard employed at least three seals, one of which had striking similarities to that used later in New Haven. The most famous of these early seals featured a stylized shield exhibiting three blank books, the lowest of which was separated from the upper two by a chevron. Surrounding the shield on three sides were the words *CHRISTO ET ECCLESIAE*. Harvard then stood for Christ and for church. Encircling the coat of arms was the inscription *SIGILLVM: ACADEMIA: HARVARDINA: IN: NOV: ANG:*. This seal, cut by John Coney in 1693, was used irregularly beginning in 1701 and regularly after 1779.[7] Another seal, cut for Harvard in 1650, had at its center a squared shield with three blank books; a chevron again separated the lower one from the upper two. The motto on the upper borders of this shield was *IN CHRISTI GLORIAM*. The inscription encircling the arms read *SIGILL: COL: HARVARD: CANTAB: NOV: ANGL: 1650:*. Though there is no evidence of this seal's use before 1707 and no diploma has been found with the seal used previous to 1752, this seal likely inspired an extremely similar one at Yale.[8]

THE YALE SIGILLUM

Despite the General Assembly's 1722 bestowal upon Yale College of the right to use a seal, there is no proof that it was used before 1736. Prior diplomas did not mention the seal. Beginning that year, the diplomas stated that the college's "*sigillum*" was affixed to them. At the same time three parallel slashes (about two centimeters wide) began to be cut in the sheepskins. A ribbon was placed through them and a wax seal was impressed on the ribbon. The now-worn and cracked wax seal found on the diploma of Benjamin Woodbridge (B.A. 1740) dates from Rector Thomas Clap's first Commencement. Except for condition, that seal appears to have been identical to the next surviving seal (diploma of Ezra Stiles, M.A. 1749), with the still-employed Latin and Hebrew inscriptions clearly stamped on brown-red wax.[9] Under Clap the seal was used regularly. Such use was confirmed in Clap's new charter for Yale College, which was approved by the Connecticut Assembly on May 9, 1745. On that day the state assembly and governor officially created a college corporation and president, and ordered

> that the said President and Fellows and their Successors shall and may hereafter have a common Seal to serve and use for all Causes, Matters, and Affairs of them and their Successors and the same Seal to alter, break, and make new as they shall think fit.[10]

The Corporation was apparently satisfied with the die already cast and shortly afterwards

> Voted and Ordered that the Public Seal heretofore used in this College be . . . Established to be the Seal of this Corporation: And that the President be Keeper of the Seal with the Power to Affix it upon all proper Instruments as Occasion may require.[11]

The Yale seal was quite similar to Harvard's 1650 edition. The encircling border read, "*SIGILL: COL: YALEN: NOV: PORT: NOV: ANGL:*:.*" With a change of name and city and a decoration substituted for the Harvard year 1650, the borders were identical. Inside the official ring three Latin words again surrounded a squared shield. Where Harvard wrote: "*IN CHRISTI GLORIAM,*" Yale inscribed, "*LUX ET VERITAS.*" Within the shield, where Harvard had three blank books and a chevron, Yale placed one large book with two Delphic words.

THE HEBREW WORDS

An approach to understanding the Hebrew is to use the texts available to Yale scholars during the college's earliest years. Many of these volumes are contained in the "1742 Yale Library," which preserves the shelving of the tomes at the time of their first cataloguing. Among those books is a 1578 edition of the commonly used Genevan Bible which explained that

Urim signifieth light and Thummim perfection: declaring that the stones of the brestplate were most cleare, and of perfect beautie: by Urim also is ment knowledge & Thummim holiness, shewing what vertues are required in the Priests.[12]

If the early Yale graduates left the college both holy and knowledgeable, Yale's leaders would have been quite pleased. A 1609 edition of the *Biblia Hebraica,* translating the original Hebrew into the more accessible Latin, explained the Hebrew words as meaning "*Illuminationes & Perfectiones.*"[13] The *Dictionarium hebraicum novum,* published in 1564, explained that the *Urim* and *Thummim* meant "*luces & perfectioes.*"[14] A parallel explanation was given by Joseph Exon's 1633 reference work entitled *A Plaine and Familiar Explication (by way of Paraphrase) Of All the Hard Texts of the whole Divine Scripture.* In that volume Exon stated that the Hebrew words were "two secret signes of knowledge and holiness . . . which signified light and perfection."[15]

Unfortunately, the 1742 Yale Library is a poor reflection of the theological character of education at Yale. As historian Richard Warch pointed out, the 1742 Library, containing a wide spectrum of authors, was far more broad-minded than the curricular fare.[16] Therefore the above explanations remain, by themselves, unsettling. That Yale was long dedicated to producing men of knowledge and character ("holinesse") is unquestioned. In that sense the *Urim* and *Thummim* were appropriate for the Yale mission. Placing these words in the original Hebrew testified both to their biblical origins and tied Yale to the ancient Israelites, whose position Yale theologians saw themselves as imitating. But the 1742 Library does not tie these words particularly to Yale.

Morison suggested an answer that more satisfyingly explains both the *Urim* and *Thummim* of Yale and the three mottoes used by Harvard. In an intriguing argument, he noted that the expressions "*Veritas,*" "*In Christi Gloriam,*" "*Christo et Ecclesiae,*" and "*Urim V' Thummim*" were all discussed in the works of William Ames, spiritual father of the New England churches. The divine truth of "*Veritas*" as part of Ames's *Philosophemata.* "*Christo et Ecclesiae*" was the motto of the University of Franeker in Friesland, where Ames had taught. He had used the Franeker motto as the textual basis for his inaugural address as rector of that university in 1626. He had used the *Urim* and *Thummim* as the text for his inaugural address as professor of theology at Franeker in 1622. There, Morison reported, Ames concluded that *Urim* meant "*inflammationes & illuminationes*" and *Thummim* meant "*perfectiones & simplicitates.*" Morison thought these connections between Ames, Harvard, and Yale to be more than mere coincidence:

When we reflect that William Ames was revered at Harvard above any other theologian; that his *Philosophemata* was a part of the Harvard curriculum; that his widow came early to New England, bringing two sons who were in College in 1643; that his portrait is probably the oldest owned by [Harvard]; and that his books were also used at Yale, where he was no less revered than at Harvard; the hypothesis is not wholly fanciful or far-fetched that Ames inspired [Harvard's] mottoes, and the Yale motto as well.[17]

The early Yale curriculum, indeed, included recitations from Ames's *Medulla Theologiae* on Saturday mornings and the rectors sometimes incorporated Ames's *Cases of Conscience* into their sermons. Until the American Revolution Ames's interpretation of Reformed theology was a backbone of Yale religious training.[18] Morison's conjecture is therefore an attractive one.

Yet the answer for Harvard may not be the solution for Yale. For Ames's lecture on *Urim* and *Thummim* was not integral to the Yale curriculum in the way that the *Philosophemata* was to Harvard. That the college rectors knew of Ames's lectures is likely. But there is nothing more than tenuous speculation to tie Ames's *Urim* and *Thummim* to Yale.

Another perhaps more creditable source for the Hebrew is a book by Johannes Wollebius entitled *Compendium Theologiae Christianae.* This book, not a part of the 1742 Library, was vital to Yale because of the ethics and theology that were of primary concern to its founders. When the Collegiate School first opened its doors in November 1701 its founders selected the texts for these courses. Within a decade the trustees added Wollebius's work to their list and reserved Friday afternoons for its study, so beginning the long preparation for the Christian Sabbath. This text, written by the professor of Old Testament theology at Basel a century earlier, received extensive use because it portrayed "an over-all picture of the accepted 'Orthodox' understanding of the Reformed faith."[19] Offering the same methodological approach as Ames's *Medulla,* Richard Warch wrote: "Wollebius's treatise was the simpler, less burdened by biblical proof-texts, and [it] probably served as an introduction to divinity for Yale undergraduates." Like mother's milk, Wollebius's teachings were the sustenance of a Yale education. Along with Ames's works, Wollebius's book was of such importance, Samuel Johnson (B.A. 1714, M.A. 1717) noted sarcastically, that it was "considered with equal if not greater veneration than the Bible itself."[20]

Where better to search for a link between Yale and a mysterious biblical reference than in the the basic theology text of the college? The purpose of Professor Wollebius's text was explained on the title page of the 1660 translation from the original Latin:

> The Abridgment of Christian Divinitie [as it is called in English, is] So exactly and Methodically compiled, that it leads us, as it were by the hand To the Reading of the Holy Scriptures, Ordering of Common-Places. Understanding of Controversies. Clearing of some Cases of Conscience.[21]

With regard to the Hebrew words, the original Latin was direct: "*Urim & Thummim, h.e. lumina & perfectiones, Christum designabant, Verbum & Interpretem Patris, Lucem & Perfectionem nostram.*"[22] The 1660 translation was faithful: "Vrim and Thummim, that is, light and perfection, did signify Christ the Word and Interpreter of the Father, our light and perfection."[23] Harvard's motto celebrated the glory of Christ. Yale did no less, for the core of a Yale education in those long-past days was religious appreciation. The 1726 College laws, for example, ordered that

> Every student shall exercise himself in Reading Holy Scriptures by himself every day [that] ye word of Christ may Dwell in Him ritchly and [that] he may be filled with ye knowledge of ye will of God all wisdom and spirituall understanding.
>
> Every student shall consider ye main end of his study to wit to know God in Jesus Christ and answerably to lead a Godly sober life.[24]

In his introduction to the college library catalogue, Rector Thomas Clap instructed his flock in the Yale educational priorities: "Above all have an Eye to the great End of all your Studies, which is to obtain the Clearest Conceptions of Divine Things and to lead you to a Saving Knowledge of GOD in his son JESUS CHRIST."[25] No oracle provided a clearer conception of divine things than that on the breastplate of the ancient Israelite high priest. For the early Puritans that oracle was Jesus. Theological historian George H. Williams noted that even secular spheres of knowledge were considered as protected from fallacy when they were dedicated to Christ. Yale College's leaders had a clear conception of what Yale represented. Their seal proclaimed it.[26]

TIMOTHY CUTLER'S APOSTASY

The *Urim* and *Thummim* seal may have had religio-political overtones as well. For the date on which the trustees first applied for a seal, October 17, 1722, was no random one in the college history. Meeting in New Haven, the trustees must have had more important things on their minds than a trivial insignia. On that date the college was caught in the midst of the greatest scandal in its history. Its rector, Timothy Cutler, several ministers from nearby towns, and tutor Daniel Browne had just publicly challenged the Presbyterial ordination of virtually every minister in New England. Cutler and his associates had attacked the foundations of New England society. Brooks M. Kelley compared their earth-shaking Anglican-leaning declaration to an "unthinkable" modern scenario:

> No exact parallel can suggest the shock this statement must have given its auditors, but it was something like what might be expected if the current president and faculty of Yale and the leading citizens of several towns around New Haven were all to announce suddenly that some had decided and others were close to deciding that Russian communism was superior to the American economic and political system.

On October 17, 1722 the college trustees dismissed Cutler and reasserted their beliefs in what Yale symbolized. Anglicanism and Arminianism (the theological doctrine that New Englanders often associated with Anglicanism) were intolerable heresies. On that occasion the Yale trustees imposed a confession of faith to be required of Yale office-holders.[27] Wollebius's book, with the anti-Arminian stance that it took, would therefore have been an especially fitting source for the Yale motto.[28] In this context the request for a seal in 1722 had far more than decorative significance; it was likely a declaration of Yale ideals.

PERFECTIONES VERSUS VERITAS

If we return to the Latin *Lux et Veritas* a remaining question is of how the more common translation of *Thummim* as *Perfectiones* was changed to *Veritas*. It is not a definitive explanation, but there was a precedent in the Vulgate edition of the Bible, where *Thummim* was translated as *Veritas*.[29] It is also possible that *Lux et Veritas* meant even more. Timothy Cutler's apostasy was not the only source of religious turmoil in Yale's first decades. By 1735, under the stimulus of Jonathan Edwards, the first manifestations of the Great Awakening were rocking the Connecticut Valley. Within six years the Awakening hit New Haven in full force and theological battle between "New Lights" and "Old Lights" raged. The "New Lights" attacked the established order by questioning the value of education outside of understanding

Christ. Many "Old Lights" thought religious knowledge was central to an education, but hardly sufficient for one. This latter opinion was the prevailing philosophy at Yale. Despite the strongly felt winds of religious disarray, the college tried to stand firm.[30] Mathematics and metaphysics, insisted Yale's leaders, had to go hand in hand with theology and ethics. By choosing to translate "אורים ותמים" as "*Lux et Veritas*," perhaps, Yale insisted that its college offered the essentials of proper learning: the "light" of a liberal education and the "truth" of an old New England religious tradition.

NOTES TO APPENDIX 1

The best studies of Yale's beginnings are Richard Warch, *School of the Prophets* (1973) and George Wilson Pierson, *The Founding of Yale* (1988). Brooks Mather Kelley, *Yale: A History* (1974), covers the era from a more general perspective. The early Yale Corporation records are easily accessible in Franklin B. Dexter, *Documentary History of Yale University* (1916), and in the Yale Archives. Dexter's *Biographical Sketches of the Graduates of Yale College with Annals of the College History, Volume I* (1885) is also valuable for understanding Yale's foundation era.

The diploma collection in the Yale Archives is much more complete for Yale's early years than Harvard's collection is for Harvard. Beginning with the first degree that Yale awarded (an M.A. to Nathaniel Chauncey in 1702), diplomas from throughout Yale history are fairly well represented, very well organized, and exceedingly well preserved. I have not been able to find any evidence of use of a Yale seal predating its appearance on the diploma in either the treasurer's files or the very limited presidential papers from this era.

The "1742 Yale Library" provides an illuminating glimpse into the library of early Yale. This collection is available in the Beinecke Rare Book and Manuscript Library at Yale. A separate card catalogue for the collection allows easy access to its contents. Thomas Clap, *A Catalogue of the Library of Yale College in New Haven* (1743), was the first printed listing of the Yale library holdings. Many of President Clap's personal manuscripts, which might have definitively interpreted the seal, did not survive the British invasion of New Haven during the Revolutionary War. John C. Schwab, "The Yale College Curriculum," *Educational Review* (June 1901), provides a succinct overview of the first two centuries of Yale education. A microfilm copy of William Ames's lecture on *Urim* and *Thummim* may be found in the Sterling Library microtext room and a number of copies of Johannes Wollebius, *Compendium Theologiae Christianae* (1661), in Latin and English are available in the Yale libraries.

1. My limited search of the Hebrew bibles in the 1742 Yale Library did not find one with a notation of Leviticus 8:8 being at the middle of the Pentateuch. Richard J. Israel, "The Yale Seal," *Yale Alumni Magazine* 30 (February 1967): 4–6; "Urim and Thummim," *The Jewish Encyclopedia* (1906 ed.), vol. 12, pp. 384–86. *Mikraot Gdolot—Vayikra* (New York: Pardes Publishing House, Inc., 1951, p. Tet-Zayin, side 2.

2. *Historical Register of Yale University 1951–1968* (New Haven: Yale University, 1969), p. 11.

3. Dexter wrote of the earliest evidenced use of the seal being in 1738. Based on information that was available seventy years after Dexter, the earliest use could be traced back to 1736. Franklin B. Dexter, *Documentary*, pp. 231, 234–35. *The Public Records of the Colony*

of *Connecticut, Volume 6,* ed. by Charles J. Hoadly (Hartford: Press of Case, Lockwood & Brainard, 1872), pp. 328, 340; "Connecticut Archives, Volume I," Microfilm Reel 15, p. 205, Connecticut State Archives.

4. Samuel Eliot Morison, "Harvard Seals and Arms," *The Harvard Graduates' Magazine* 42 (Sep. 1933): 1–2, 8; Samuel Eliot Morison, *The Founding of Harvard College* (Cambridge, Mass.: Harvard University Press, 1935), p. 329.

5. Morison, *Three,* p. 25.

6. While he was preparing his *History of Harvard University* (1840), President Josiah Quincy of Harvard came across the original *Veritas* sketch. Delighted to find this symbol of his belief in the true function of a university, Quincy had it placed on a banner for the Harvard bicentennial celebration in 1836 and the Harvard corporation approved its becoming the university motto in an ugly design in 1843. Edward Everett, Quincy's successor, took office in 1846 and set about reversing several of Quincy's actions. Among Everett's acts was returning Harvard to the motto of "*Christo et Ecclesiae,*" which had previously dominated Cantabrigian history. Following a poetic campaign first led by Oliver Wendell Holmes and later taken up by other Harvard alumni, the motto *VE RI TAS,* distributed over three books in a more appealing fashion than in 1843, was chosen as the Harvard seal in 1885. Its form remained virtually unchanged through the following century. Morison, *The Harvard Graduates' Magazine,* pp. 9–12; Morison, *Three Centuries,* pp. 267–68, 279, 362; Mason Hammond, "A Harvard Armory," *Harvard Library Bulletin* 29 (July 1981): 263.

7. If the inscription on the original 1693 seal was "*SIGILLUM: ACADEMIAE: HARVARDINAE: IN: NOV: ANG:,*" as Morison claims, then the final E's of the second and third words did not surface with sufficient clarity on the Harvard diplomas that I examined. See Morison, *The Harvard Graduates' Magazine,* p. 5; Samuel Eliot Morrison, *Harvard College in the Seventeenth Century* (Cambridge, Mass.: Harvard University Press, 1936), p. 11.

8. Morison, *The Harvard Graduates' Magazine,* pp. 3–4; Morison, *Founding College,* p. 330; Morison, *Harvard Century,* p. 11; George H. Williams, *Wilderness and Paradise in Christian Thought* (New York: Harper & Brothers, 1962), pp. 201–10.

9. The diplomas of Daniel Gardiner (B.A. 1736) and Daniel Lothrop (M.A. 1736) are the earliest in the Yale collection with the cut marks for a ribbon and mention of "*Sigillum Collegii Yalensis.*" That of Ephraim Strong (B.A. 1737) has no cut marks and no mention of a seal. The cuts and Latin references to the college seal reappear on the 1740 diploma of Benjamin Woodbridge (B.A.). As of November 2000, the diploma of Woodbridge contains the earliest surviving seal in the Yale collection, with a (blue) ribbon still running through the document and a seal of brownish-red wax. The lettering has been worn down. Fittingly, the oldest surviving *legible* seal is that impressed on wax attached to the master's degreee diploma of Ezra Stiles (M.A. 1749). Its Hebrew and Latin texts and its design are virtually identical to the Yale Seal in use 250 years later.

10. Minutes of the Yale Corporation, Yale College Register I, YRG 1-A, HM4S, Reel 2, p. 69.

11. Ibid., p. 73.

12. See the commentary on Exodus 28:30 in the Bible of Christopher Barker (1578), pp. 4, 34, 1742 Yale Library.

13. *Biblia Hebraica,* ed. by Benedicti Arias (1609), pp. 71, 90, 1742 Yale Library. This volume is known to have been part of the Yale collection since 1714.

14. J. Förster, *Dictionarium hebraicum novum* (Basilae, 1564), p. 907, 1742 Yale Library.

15. Joseph Exon, *A Plaine and Familiar Explication (by way of Paraphrase) Of All the Hard Texts of the whole Divine Scripture* (London: M. Flesher, 1633), pp. 56, 63, 1742 Yale Library.

16. Because at early Yale Hebrew is almost synonymous with Ezra Stiles, one might inquire whether he was involved with placing the Hebrew upon the seal. Though possible, this is unlikely. As a young child in 1736 he could not have been responsible for the Yale seal. By the time he became a Yale tutor in 1749 the Hebrew-containing seal was already in regular use. His own knowledge of Hebrew was still rudimentary at this time as well. Perhaps the best evidence of the role that Stiles did not play is his own hesitating speculations on the meaning of the Hebrew words in his *Literary Diary.* Warch, p. 239; Ezra Stiles, "Memoir concerning my learning Hebrew," May 12, 1768, Miscellaneous Volume 4, Roll 16, Item 451, BRBML; Ezra Stiles, *Literary Diary of Ezra Stiles,* Microfilm Reel 1, Roll 8, pp. 89–91, BRBML.

17. Morison, *The Harvard Graduates' Magazine,* pp. 8–9; Morison, *Founding College,* pp. 330–32; William Ames, "*Oratio inauguralis Franquera habita, Anno 1622, Maij 7 cum theologiae professionem auspicaretur,*" in *Disceptatio Scholastica de circulo Pontificio,* contained in *Rescriptio Scholastica & brevis,* vol. 2 (Leyden, 1633), pp. 77–92; *Dictionary of National Biography,* vol. 1, ed. by Leslie Stephen (New York: Macmillan & Co., 1885), pp. 355–57.

18. Warch, pp. 36, 193, 235.

19. Wollebius's book was already part of the Harvard curriculum by the end of the seventeenth century. Ibid., pp. 193, 235; Kelley, p. 42; *Reformed Dogmatics,* ed. by John W. Beardslee III (New York: Oxford University Press, 1965), p. 11.

20. Ames and Wollebius were both studied at Yale until after the American Revolution. Wollebius's work dominated the theological texts used at Yale in the second quarter of the eighteenth century. Warch, pp. 36, 234; Gabriel, p. 22; Samuel Johnson, "Autobiography," in *Samuel Johnson, President of King's College,* vol. 1, ed. by Herbert Schneider and Carol Schneider (New York: Columbia University Press, 1929), p. 6; John C. Schwab, "The Yale College Curriculum," *Educational Review* (June 1901), YMAL; *Laws of Yale College 1745,* p. 7, YMAL; *Laws of Yale College 1772,* p. 9, YMAL.

21. Although Wollebius's text was at the core of the early Yale curriculum, Thomas Clap did not list the book among the 1742 library collection. A possible explanation may be that the book was a personal possession of the college rector and therefore not part of the college library. Thomas Clap, *A Catalogue of the library of Yale College in New Haven* (New London: L. Groen, 1743); Wollebius, *Abridgment,* title page; Theodore D. Woolsey, "The Course of Instruction in Yale College," in *Yale College,* vol, 2, ed. by William L. Kingsley (New York: Henry Holt & Company, 1879), pp. 496–98.

22. Johannes Wollebius, *Compendium Theologiae Christianae* (Oxford, 1661), p. 68.

23. The complete description of *Urim* and *Thummim* by Wollebius is part of a section describing the meaning of ancient Israelite ceremonial law:

> The chief ornaments were the Ephod, or cloak and Breast-plate fastened to the cloak: On the Ephod were the names of the twelve Tribes engraven upon precious stones; on the breast-plate were Urim and Thummim; from whence the Church received Oracles; The Cloak then represented the Church; Vrim and Thummim, that is, light and perfection, did signify Christ the Word and Interpreter of the Father, our light and perfection; the Ephod represented Christ, as he performed the things that concerned us; the Breast-plate shewed him, as he performed the things concerning God.

The modern translation of Wollebius's text incorrectly translates the word "*perfectionem*" as "truth." Wollebius, *Abridgment,* pp. 99–100. See Beardslee, pp. 80–81.

24. "Orders and Appointments to the Observed in ye Collegiate School in Connecticut," transcribed in 1726, reproduced in Franklin B. Dexter, *Biographical Sketches of the Graduates of Yale College with Annals of the College History, October, 1701–May 1745* (New York: Henry Holt & Company, 1885), p. 347.

25. The King's College (later Columbia College) seal, which was prepared by Samuel Johnson and adopted in 1755, paralleled Yale's godly theme. At the top of the New York seal was a blazing sun with the Tetragrammaton (the Hebrew letters for the sacred name of God) placed in the middle of the sun. Elsewhere on the seal were the Hebrew words אורי אל ("God is my light") printed on a small banner, alluding to Psalms 27:1. The motto for that seal was *IN LUMINE TUO VIDEBIMUS LUMEN* ("In thy light shall we see light"), taken from Psalms 36:10. The original seal of Dartmouth College contained a radiant triangle with אל שדי ("Almighty God") inscribed over it. Clap, "To the Students of Yale College," *Library Catalogue; A History of Columbia University 1754–1904* (New York: Columbia University Press, 1904), p. 19.

26. Williams, p. 150.

27. Brooks Mather Kelley, *Yale: A History* (New Haven: Yale University Press, 1974), pp. 31–34, 39, 49; Clap, *History of Yale,* p. 32.

28. Warch, p. 236.

29. The Vulgate Bible was a fourth-century Latin translation of the Bible from a Greek translation (the Septuagint) of the Hebrew original. For *Veritas* as a translation of *Thummim* see the translations of Exodus 28:30 and Leviticus 8:8 in *Biblia Sacra,* vol. 1 (Stuttgart: Württembergische Bibelanstalt, 1969), pp. 116, 144.

30. For a discussion of the Great Awakening as it affected Yale, see Roland H. Bainton, *Yale and the Ministry* (New York: Harper & Brothers, 1957), pp. 1–36. The biography of Thomas Clap by Clifford K. Shipton describes the Yale minister's role in the religious controversies of his day. Kelley, pp. 50–55; Clifford K. Shipton, *Sibley's Harvard Graduates,* vol. 7 (Boston: Massachusetts Historical Society, 1945), pp. 27–49.

Appendix Two Connecticut
and United States Populations

Year	Ct Jews	Ct Populations	U.S. Jews	U.S. Population	Ct % Jews	U.S. %Jews
1790		238,000	1,500	3,929,000		.04
1800		251,000	2,500	5,308,000		.05
1810		262,000		7,240,000		.04
1818			3,000			
1820		275,000		9,638,000		.05
1826			6,000			
1830		298,000		12,870,000		.07
1840		310,000	15,000	17,070,000		.09
1848			50,000			
1850		371,000		23,190,000		.3
1860		460,000	150,000	31,440,000		.5
1870		537,000		39,820,000		.5
1877	1,490		226,000			
1880		623,000	280,000	50,160,000	.4	.6
1888			400,000			
1890		746,000		62,950,000	.6	.8
1897			938,000			
1900		908,000		75,990,000	.8	.16

continued

Year	Ct Jews	Ct Populations	U.S. Jews	U.S. Population	Ct % Jews	U.S. %Jews
1905	8,500					
1907			1,777,000			
1910		1,110,000		91,970,000	3.0	2.5
1917	66,900		3,389,000			
1920		1,380,000		105,700,000	5.4	3.4
1927	91,500		4,228,000			
1930		1,610,000		122,800,000	5.7	3.6
1937	94,100		4,771,000			
1940		1,710,000		131,700,000	5.6	3.7
1950		2,010,000	5,000,000	150,700,000	4.9	3.3
1960		2,540,000	5,531,000	179,300,000	4.0	3.1
1968	104,000		5,869,000			
1969	105,000					
1970			3,030,000	203,200,000	3.4	2.9
1971	103,730					
1980		3,110,000	5,920,000	226,500,000	3.2	2.6
1990		3,290,000		248,800,000	3.0	2.4
1997	101,000		6,041,000			

Sources: The U.S. Jewish population for 1790 is taken from Ira Rosenswaike, "An Estimate and Analysis of the Jewish Population of the United States in 1790," *Publication of the American Jewish Historical Society* 50 (1960); 34. U.S. Jewish populations for 1818–48, 1888–1950, and 1960–68 are taken from *American Jewish Year Book* 1971, ed. by Morris Fine and Milton Himmelfarb (New York: The American Jewish Committee, *1971*), p. 11. U.S. Jewish populations for 1800 and 1860–80 and the Connecticut Jewish population for 1968 are taken from "United States of America," *Encyclopedia Judaica* (1972 ed.), vol. 15, pp. 1594–96, 1606, 1635–37. U.S. Jewish population for 1980 is taken from Abraham J. Karp, "Haven and Home" (New York: Schocken Books, 1985). Jewish populations for 1997 are taken from *American Jewish Year Book 1999,* ed. by David Singer (New York: The American Jewish Committee, 1999). Total U.S. populations and Connecticut populations for 1980 and 1990 are taken from United States Census Bureau, *Statistical Abstract of the United States: 1998,* pp. 8, 28. Connecticut Jewish populations for 1877, 1905–37, and 1969 are taken from "Connecticut," *Encyclopedia Judaica* (1972 ed.), vol. 5, pp. 897–99. The 1971 Connecticut Jewish population is taken from *Newsweek* 77 (Mar. 1, 1971), p. 58. Total Connecticut populations through 1970 are taken from United States Department of Commerce, *1970 Census of Population* (Washington, D.C., 1973), p. 8-7. Percentages were calculated by interpolating between known population levels.

Appendix Three "Church Members" at Yale College, 1873–1904

Class	Yr Admitted	Number of Church Members	Number of Jewish Church Members	Total Enrollment	% Enrolled in Jewish Church
1873	1869	75	0	114	0
1874	1870	62	0	124	0
1875	1871	46	0	98	0
1876	1872	78	3	127	2.4
1877	1873	68	0	120	0
1878	1874	70	2	133	1.5
1879	1875	63	1	138	0.7
1880	1876	63	0	122	0
1881	1877	105*	2	130	1.5
1882	1878	55	0	122	0
1883	1879	85	1	154	0.6
1884	1880	84	7	152	4.6
1885	1881	72	1	127	0.8
1886	1882	67	0	139	0
1887	1883	81	0	150	0

continued

Class	Yr Admitted	Number of Church Members	Number of Jewish Church Members	Total Enrollment	% Enrolled in Jewish Church
1888	1884	65	0	125	0
1889	1885	62	0	124	0
1890	1886	80	0	146	0
1891	1887	95	0	186	0
1892	1888	123	1	182	0.5
1893	1889	111	0	185	0
1894	1890	164	1	239	0.4
1895	1891	141	0	249	0
1896	1892	178	0	278	0
1897	1893	186	0	275	0
1898	1894	192	4	301	1.3
1899	1895	215	4	298	0.3
1900	1896	206	4	321	1.2
1901	1897	152	3	254	1.1
1902	1898	193	2	292	0.7
1903	1899	210	3	316	0.9
1904	1900	181	8	288	2.8
Total		3628†	44	6009	0.7

SOURCES: This table was adapted from appendix D(1) in *Two Centuries of Christian Activity at Yale*, et. by James B. Reynolds, Samuel H. Fisher, and Henry B. Wright (New York: G. P. Putnam's Sons, 1901). Church memberships for the classes of 1873 through 1898 were determined from senior class statistics. The same data for the classes of 1899 through 1904 were taken from freshman year registration records. The number of students listed under total enrollment represents the number of students who were graduated with the indicated class, as recorded in Pierson, *Numbers*, pp. 23, 25. The discrepancy between the number of students enrolled and the number of Jewish church members listed in this table as opposed to figures in the following appendixes as a result of the differing criteria used in arriving at the figures. *This figure includes those students who expressed a religious preference but were not necessarily "church members." Fifty-six members of that class reported that they were "church members" as seniors.

†Memberships by denomination for these classes were: Congregational–1205; Episcopal–948; Presbyterian–755; Baptist–214; Methodist–214; Roman Catholic– 130; Jewish– 44; Reformed–35; Lutheran–17; Disciples (Christian)–17; Unitarian–12; other churches–65.

Appendix Four Sheffield Scientific School Enrollment, 1873–1921

Class	Yr Admitted	Number of Jews	Total Enrollment	% Jewish	Average
1876S	1873	1	48	2.1	
1910S	1907	24	405	5.9	1910S–11S
1911S	1908	24	426	5.6	5.1%
1912S	1909	14	384	3.6	
1915S	1912	24	434	5.5	1915S–16S
1916S	1913	24	399	6.0	5.8%
1921S–22S	1918	67	556	12.1	1921S–25S
1923S	1919	29	324	9.0	11.1%
1924S	1920	24	254	9.4	
1925S	1921	33	244	13.5	

SOURCES: Figures for the class of 1876 are derived from *1876 Sheffield Scientific School Statistics,* pp. 8–9. For the class of 1925 the figures are derived from the "Report on Jews, 1922," Folder 71, box 6, FSJ. The remainder of the table is derived from Russell H. Chittenden to James R. Angell, Jan. 26, 1922, Box 91, "Jewish Problem" Folder, JRA.

Appendix Five Enrollment at Yale College (and Sheffield Scientific School Where Indicated), 1902–1969

Class	Yr Admitted	Number of Jews	Total Enrollment	% Jewish	Average
1902	1898	7	294	2.4	1902–04
1903	1899	6	299	2.0	2.1%
1904	1900	5	285	1.8	
1905	1901	11	288	3.8	
1906	1902	11	303	3.6	
1907	1903	9	337	2.7	1905–10
1908	1904	14	344	4.0	3.4%
1909	1905	8	321	2.5	
1910	1906	11	311	3.5	
1911	1907	23	345	6.7	
1912	1908	18	322	5.6	
1913	1909	12	308	3.9	
1914	1910	17	339	5.0	1911–19
1915	1911	27	348	7.8	6.0%
1916	1912	21	390	5.4	
1917	1913	22	394	5.6	
1918	1914	26	392	6.6	

continued

Class	Yr Admitted	Number of Jews	Total Enrollment	% Jewish	Average
1919	1915	28	400	7.0	
1920	1916	32	387	8.3	
1921	1917	28	310	9.0	
1922	1918	25	390	6.4	1920–26
1923	1919	38	466	8.2	9.7%
1924	1920	32	356	9.0	
1925	1921	71	534	13.3	
1926*	1922	95	878	10.8	
1927*	1923	115	863	13.3	
1928*	1924	88	880	10.0	
1929*	1925	97	864	11.2	1927–33
1930*	1926	106	881	12.0	11.6%
1931*	1927	108	884	12.2	
1932*	1928	90	894	10.1	
1933*	1929	106	834	12.7	
1934*	1930	70	850	8.2	
1935*	1931	70	850	8.2	
1936*	1932	103	884	11.7	
1937*	1933	84	838	10.0	
1938*	1934	68	781	8.7	
1939	1935	109	878	12.4	1934–45
1940	1936	94	846	11.1	9.8%
1941	1937	96	859	11.2	
1942	1938	68	850	8.0	
1943	1939	80	836	9.6	
1944	1940	74	868	8.5	
1945	1941	99	981	10.1	
1945W†	1942	127	1266	10.0	
1946	1943	83	665	12.5	
1947	1944	62	650	9.5	1945W–51
1948	1945	65	583	11.1	9.2%
1949	1945	37	561	6.6	
1950	1946	123	1713	7.2	
1951	1947	102	1082	9.4	
1952	1948	139	1163	12.0	
1953	1949	140	1108	12.6	
1954	1950	105	1050	10.0	
1955	1951	111	1168	9.5	
1956	1952	133	1015	13.1	1952–61
1957	1953	119	1032	11.5	11.3%

continued

Class	Yr Admitted	Number of Jews	Total Enrollment	% Jewish	Average
1958	1954	108	1002	10.8	
1959	1955	122	1007	12.1	
1960	1956	109	1031	10.6	
1961	1957	109	1004	10.9	
1962	1958	143	1007	14.2	
1963	1959	117	1031	11.3	1962–65
1964	1960	118	1014	11.4	11.8%
1965	1961	104	1020	10.1	
1966	1962	172	1075	16.0	1966–69
1967–69	1963–65	489	3035	16.1	16.1%

SOURCES: Statistics for class size and Jewish enrollment for the classes of 1902 through 1904 are from Alfred K. Merritt to Robert N. Corwin, Apr. 11, 1922, "Jewish Problem" folder, box 91, JRA. Statistics for the classes of 1906 through 1910 are estimated on the basis of surname and descriptive biographies from the class histories for those years. For the remaining classes through 1926 the figures are based on the "Report on Jews, 1922," Folder 17, Box 6, FSJ. Dean Jones's criteria were surname, parental birthplace, and his personal knowledge of the students. Jewish enrollments for the classes of 1927 through 1936 are based on the records of the Board of Admissions, sent as a table from Robert N. Corwin to James R. Angell, Oct. 19, 1932, "Board of Admissions" folder, "Board of Admissions" box, JRA. Criteria for these figures were surname, parental birthplace, and admissions interviews. Incoming freshmen who identifies themselves as Jewish on religious preference cards sent to the Yale Religious Ministry are recorded for the classes of 1937 through 1956. These figures are duplicated for some years in an untitled page in Folder 1195, Box 240, Series III, OS and Carl Lohmann to Mr. Spivak, Sep. 11, 1945, Folder 1194, Box 240, Series III, OS. The statistics for the classes of 1957through 1963 are taken from HFSH. Figures for the classes of 1964 through 1966 were provided to the author by Arnold Jacob Wolf. The figures for the classes of 1967 thorugh 1969 were derived from the figures for the class of 1966 and "Annual Jewish Student Census," Oct. 22, 1965, Folder 1966-35, BBHFY. The criteria used for the classes of 1957 through 1969 include religious preference cards, Hillel membership lists, and personal knowledge of the students by the Hillel staff. All remaining statistics for class sizes are based on figures in the university catalogues and class histories. There are no known reliable counts of such statistics in the classes since 1969.

*The figures for these classes represent the students admitted to the combined Freshman Year Program that preceded entrance to Yale College and the Sheffield Scientific School.

†The class of 1945W was admitted in spring 1942 for an accelerated educational program as part of the war effort. Regular admissions and enrollment procedures were not resumed until after the war.

Appendix Six Background of Jewish Students Yale College Classes of 1911–1926

	Yale College Class of 19–																
	11	12	13	14	15	16	17	18	19	20	21	22	23	24	25	26	Total
Residence																	
New Haven	3	1	4	3	9	6	6	6	18	12	18	9	20	9	27	27	178
Hartford	1	4	3	3	2	1	1	2	2	0	1	3	2	2	11	8	46
Bridgeport	0	1	0	1	4	2	2	0	0	0	1	2	2	0	3	1	19
Elsewhere in Conn.	5	2	0	2	0	2	0	6	2	4	4	3	6	8	4	8	56
N.Y. State	3	6	1	5	8	7	6	4	3	6	2	5	4	8	10	22	100
Ohio	4	0	0	0	1	1	0	3	1	1	0	1	0	0	2	5	19
Illinois	1	1	1	1	1	0	0	1	0	0	0	0	1	2	1	7	17
Pennsylva.	0	0	1	0	1	1	0	0	1	3	0	1	0	0	3	1	12
New Jersey	1	0	0	0	1	0	1	0	0	1	1	1	1	0	1	2	10
Elsewhere in U.S.A.	5	3	2	2	0	1	6	4	1	5	1	0	2	3	9	14	58
Total	23	18	12	17	27	21	22	26	28	32	28	25	38	32	71	95	515

continued

	Yale College Class of 19–												
	11	12	13	14	15	16	17	18	19	20	21	22	Total
Birthplace													
U.S.A.	21	14	10	15	24	19	21	22	20	23	20	17	226
Russia or Poland	2	3	2	2	3	1	1	2	8	5	2	8	39
Elsewhere or unknown	0	1	0	0	0	1	0	2	0	3	6	0	13

	Yale College Class of 19–												
	11	12	13	14	15	16	17	18	19	20	21	22	Total
Father's Birthplace													
U.S.A.	11	5	3	4	10	6	10	3	6	6	4	3	71
Russia or Poland	4	8	7	6	14	9	10	11	21	15	17	18	140
Germany	8	4	2	5	1	1	1	5	0	5	1	0	33
Austria-Hungary	0	1	0	1	2	5	1	6	1	1	1	4	23
Elsewhere or unknown	0	0	0	1	0	0	0	1	0	4	5	0	11
Schooling													
Public Schl	13	9	8	14	17	14	12	18	23	23	24	22	197
Private Schl	10	9	4	3	10	6	10	8	5	8	4	3	80
Unclear	0	0	0	0	0	1	0	0	0	0	0	0	1
Total	23	18	12	17	27	21	22	26	28	31	28	25	278

SOURCES: Data on residence were adapted from "Geographical Distribution of Jews," Folder 71, Box 6, FSJ. All other data were adapted from notes prepared by College Dean Frederick S. Jones, Folder 71, Box 6, FSJ.

Appendix Seven Enrollment in the Yale Graduate and Professional Schools

Year	Total Enrollment	Number of Jews	% of Jews
1900–01*	304	0	0
1924–25*	370	38	10.3
1926–27*	671	29	4.3
1939–40*	765	40	5.2
1947–48	2385	192	8.1
1948–49	2330	279	12.0
1949–50	2484	320	12.9
1950–51	2474	429	17.3
1951–52	2633	476	18.1
1952–53	2797	543	19.4
1953–54	3293	553	16.8
1954–55	3220	562	17.5
1955–56	3265	467	14.3
1956–57	3536	589	16.7
1957–58	3483	592	17.0

Sources: Figures for 1900–01 were taken from appendix D(2), *Two Centuries*. The number and percentage of Jews for that year refer only to those students who identified themselves as members of the "Jewish Church." Figures for 1924– 25 were taken from tables found in teh "Jewish Problem" folder, Box 91, JRA. Figures for 1926–27 were from Wilbur Cross to Henry

Graves, Jan. 20, 1927, "Reports of the Committtee on Educational Policy," Yale Corporation Minutes, Secretary's Cleaning Vault No. 23, pp. 170f, g, YMAL. In that year Jewish graduate students were found in the departments of bacteriology (1), chemistry (5), clinical medicine (1), education (1), English (5), psychology (3), physics (1), physiological chemistry (4), Romance languages (2), Semitics (4), and zoology (2). Figures for 1939–40 are from a note dated Mar. 26, 1945, Folder 1194, Box 240, Series III, OS. Data for the remaining years are from either the "Report of the Chaplain" or the "Report of the Church of Christ" in *Yale Reports to the President,* YMAL. The chaplain's figures were based on religious preference cards returned by the students to the Yale Religious Ministry.

*Figures for these years refer only to the Yale Graduate School.

Appendix Eight Full Professors

on the Yale Faculties,

1900–1970

The identity of the Yale College faculty from 1930 through 1960 was taken from lists prepared by Katherine Hauschild, former executive secretary to the Yale College faculty, and shared with me by George Pierson. The 1970 count of Yale College and Graduate School faculties was made with the assistance of lists supplied by Candace Bryce, executive assistant to the dean of the Yale Graduate School. Because of an antecedent merger, by 1970 the two faculties were almost identical. Universitywide totals do not equal the sum of individual school numbers because many of the faculty had appointments in more than one school.

Identification of Jewish faculty members was done with the assistance of Annabelle Cahn, Richard Israel, Rollin Osterweis, Barbara Potter, and Edgar Siskin. Because the methodology was not perfect, the figures are an approximation of the hiring record of Jewish faculty. All counts or Jewish faculty of fifteen of above should be viewed as having a 10 percent margin of error. for those figures below fifteen a possible miscount by one should be assumed.

The 1920 figure for Yale College faculty includes full professors from the separate "Freshman Year" faculty. Beginning in 1930 in the college, graduate school, medical school, forestry school, and 1940 in the engineering school, the figures refer to full professors on the individual school's board of permanent officers. To varying degrees the board of permanent officers of each school shared policy-making decisions with the deans of the schools. The 1930 Sheffield figures represent undergraduate faculty science professors who were not on the Yale College faculty. These numbers provide only a rough approximation of the actual Sheffield faculty. The 1940 Sheffield figures represent undergraduate faculty science professors who

Year		UNI	COL	SH	GRD	MD	DV	LA	AR	MU	FO	NU	DR	EN
1900	Total	84	37	17	58	10	7	8	2	2	2			
	Jewish	0	0	0	0	0	0	0	0	0	0			
1910	Total	93	34	22	76	12	6	10	1	2	3			
	Jewish	1	0	1	1	0	0	0	0	0	0			
1920	Total	117	34	26	24	11	10	9	3	2	6			
	Jewish	3	0	1	1	2	0	1	0	0	0			
1930	Total	158	36	32	42	22	8	10	5	2	7	2		
	Jewish	4	0	1	1	3	0	1	0	0	0	0		
1940	Total	167	36	16	81	22	13	16	5	2	7	1		7
	Jewish	7	0	0	2	2	0	3	0	0	0	0		0
1950	Total	204	65		62	24	13	14	9	6	4	1		13
	Jewish	9	1		5	0	0	3	0	1	0	0		0
1960	Total	260	95		79	33	13	29	5	5	5	2	6	19
	Jewish	28	6		8	6	0	7	0	0	0	0	1	1
1970	Total	468	306		315	95	18	34	12	10	10	3	4	
	Jewish	103	57		59	27	0	12	2	2	2	1	2	

Key to Appendix 8:

UNI	Total Yale University	LA	Law School
COL	Yale College	AR	School of Art (and Architecture in 1968)
	(Board of Permanent Officers as of 1930)	MU	School of Music
SH	Sheffield Scientific School	FO	School of Forestry (BPO as of 1930)
GRD	Graduate School (BPO as of 1930)	NU	School of Nursing
MD	School of Medicine (BPO as of 1930)	DR	School of Drama
DV	Divinity School	EN	School of Engineering (BPO)

NOTE: This table lists full professors on the regular faculty of the indicated schools, as noted in the Yale University catalogue and the individual school catalogue for the appropriate years. The table excludes all lower-ranking members of the faculty as well as temporary and part-time appointments (e.g., assistant, associate, visiting, clinical, and adjunct professors). When someone in one of these excluded categories was listed among that school's board of permanent officers (BPO), then that faculty member was included in this table. Blank spaces represent years during which the indicated schools did not exist.

were on neither the college nor the engineering school faculties; they only approximate the actual scientific school faculty. The "Total" figure for the graduate school listing for 1950 is taken from the 1948 catalogue; the "Jewish" figure under that listing does refer to 1950. The figures listed for the music school for 1960 are taken from the 1961 catalogue. The figures listed for the art and architecture school for 1970 are actually from the 1968 catalogue. The figures listed for the music school for 1970 are from the 1971 catalogue.

Because of the growth in the overall university faculty and the increasing difficulty of identifying Jewish faculty with any surety, numbers are not estimated for the years 1980 and 1990. The general impression on the campus was that Jewish faculty proportion in these years was not significantly different from that of 1970.

Appendix Nine A Chronology
of Judaic Studies at Yale

1701[?]–	*Hebrew language is a regular part of the college curriculum, with emphasis upon reading the Hebrew Psalms and some translation of the Hebrew Bible into Greek.
1778	*Ezra Stiles becomes president of the college and teaches a mandatory Hebrew course for freshmen.
1781	*Former Yale trustee the Reverend Richard Salter promises to donate his two hundred acre estate to Yale College for the "purpose of cultivating, encouraging, and promoting the study of the Hebrew language and other Oriental languages." *President Stiles delivers "An Oration Upon the Hebrew Literature" at Yale's first public commencement exercises following the Revolutionary War: He praises the study of the great rabbinical scholars from earlier centuries.
1787	*Upon the death of the Reverend Salter, his estate becomes Yale property.
1790	*Reacting to student resentment, President Stiles consents to designate Hebrew as an elective in the college curriculum.
1798–1803	*Paid with income from the Salter estate, Ebenezer Grant Marsh (B.A. 1795, M.A. 1798) serves as "Instructor in Hebrew."
1805–17	*James Luce Kingsley (B.A. 1799, M.A. 1802) serves as "Professor of the Hebrew, Greek, and Latin Languages and of Ecclesiastical History." At the end of this period the fields of Hebrew and ecclesiastical history are dropped from the title.

1866	*George Edward Day (B.A. 1833, M.A. 1836) becomes "Professor of the Hebrew Language and Literature and Biblical Theology."
1869	*Samuel Holmes endows the "Holmes Professorship of the Hebrew Language and Literature"—one of the nation's first endowed chairs in Judaica. Assigned to the theological department (later to become the divinity school), the faculty member who holds the chair is required, by terms of the gift, to "hold and be in substantial agreement with the Evangelical system of Faith held by the Congregational Churches of Connecticut."
1870–91	*George Edward Day serves as "Holmes Professor of the Hebrew Language and Literature and Biblical Theology."
1909–10	*Aided by President Arthur T. Hadley, Eugene H. Lehman (B.A. 1902, M.A. 1909) unsuccessfully solicits funds for a Yale professorship of Judaica.
1910–13	*With the encouragement of Charles F. Kent, Woolsey Professor of biblical literature, and Arthur T. Hadley, president of the university, Eugene H. Lehman serves as a part-time "instructor in Jewish Literature" on the Yale College faculty. Lehman teaches a survey course on the "History and Literature of the Jewish People" between the years 70 and 1492. Unable to complete his work on a doctoral thesis, Lehman leaves the university.
1915	*Mrs. Selah Merrill, wife of the U.S. consul in Jerusalem, presents the university with her husband's fourteen hundred volume collection of the works of Flavius Josephus.
	*Impressed by the Hebrew words upon the Yale seal and the interest that Ezra Stiles had shown in Jews and Judaism, George Alexander Kohut donates most of his father's five thousand volume Judaica library to form the nucleus of the Alexander Kohut Memorial Collection. Over the next two decades Kohut gives the remainder of the library, a memorial publication fund to support the production of books on Semitic and oriental studies, a Semitics fellowship for post-graduate students, and an endowment to preserve and expand the Kohut collection.
1923	*Erwin R. Goodenough, scholar of hellenistic and Palestinian Judaism, begins a thirty-nine-year career at the university with an appointment as a history instructor.
1924–1925	*Rabbi Hyman G. Enelow of New York's Temple Emanu-El suggests that one of his congregants wants to donate a chair to Yale in the field of Jewish history and literature. The faculty, administration, and Corporation cheer the idea. The congregant backs out when he discovers just how much ($175,000) an endowed chair costs. Enelow's mediation succeeds in convincing Lucius N. Littauer to endow a chair in Hebrew literature and philosophy at Harvard. Harry Wolfson becomes the first incumbent.
1932	*Julian J. Obermann begins a twenty-four-year career at Yale with an appointment as a visiting professor of Semitic languages.
1944	*Snubbed by a Harvard official, Louis M. Rabinowitz, a leading American corset manufacturer, approaches Yale with an offer of prize money for ac-

complishments in Judaic Studies. At the suggestion of acting librarian James T. Babb (Ph.B. 1924), Rabinowitz accepts the idea of employing people and he establishes the "Yale Judaica Series" to translate major Hebrew texts into English.

*To fulfill Yiddish writer Sholem Asch's desire that the spirit of Judaism be "represented in the general temples of knowledge in . . . America . . . our permanent home," Rabinowitz acquires Asch's collection of art and literature for the university library.

1955   *The American Jewish Congress presents the Stephen Wise Award to the university in recognition for its publication of the Judaica series.

1958   *Judah Goldin arrives at Yale as "Professor of Jewish Studies" on the college faculty. Goldin becomes a member of the department of religion.

1963   *The Department of Religion changes its title to Department of Religious Studies to reflect, according to the Reverend Julian N. Hartt (Ph.D. 1940), departmental chairman, that its purpose was not "to serve religious interests per se," but rather to serve "an irreversible commitment to knowledge."

1965   *Jacob Joel Finkelstein, former student of Albrecht Goetze, is appointed William M. Laffan Professor of Assyriology and Babylonian Literature. His career is ended by his death in 1974.

1974   *Concerned over an apparent increase in the influence of divinity school issues over department of religious studies activities, Judah Goldin resigns from the Yale faculty.

1975   *Provost Hanna H. Gray appoints Wayne A. Meeks (Ph.D. 1965), professor of religious studies, to chair a committee to develop goals for a Judaic Studies fund drive.

1976–78   *Poor performance of the three hundred seventy million dollar "Campaign for Yale" fund-raising drive leads to postponement of Judaic Studies plans.

1978   *A. Bartlett Giamatti becomes president and Abraham Goldstein becomes provost of the university.

1979   *Abraham S. Goldstein resigns as provost. He is succeeded by Georges May, who appoints a "University Committee on Judaic Studies," with William W. Hallo as chairman.

1980   *Report of Hallo committee calls for Judaic Studies major and fund-raising drive.

*Yale College commences offering a major in Judaic Studies. Hillel Levine, associate professor of religious studies and sociology, is appointed director of undergraduate studies for the major.

1981   *Associate Professor Hillel Levine takes a leave of absence, from which he chooses not to return.

*Seven million dollar fund drive for endowment in Judaic Studies commences. Chairmen are Geoffrey Hartman and William Horowitz.

1982   *James Kugel (B.A. 1967), associate professor of religious studies, authority on biblical poetry, accepts tenured position offered by Harvard University.

*Elie Wiesel speaks at inauguration of Yale Video Archive for Holocaust Studies, developed by Geoffrey Hartman.

1983   *Historian David Ruderman appointed professor of religious studies, with a mandate to develop the Judaic Studies program. Frederick P. Rose (B.E. 1944) endows the professorship.

*The Jacob and Hilda Blaustein Foundation establishes a chair in Hebrew Language and Literature, which Benjamin Harshav will later fill.

1984   *Lucy G. Moses, Yale School of Music philanthropist, and widow of Henry L. Moses (B.A. 1900), endows a professorship of Judaic Studies, which Paula Hyman will occupy.

*Robert F. (E.B.A. 1941) and Patricia Ross Weis endow an associate professorship in classical Jewish studies.

*Mark Taper establishes a chair in Judaic Studies, which Steven D. Fraade will occupy first as associate, then as full professor.

1994   *Ivan G. Marcus (B.A. 1964) succeeds David Ruderman as the Frederick P. Rose Professor of Jewish History.

The definitive book on the subject of Judaica in American colleges and universities is by Paul Ritterband and Harold S. Wechsler, *Jewish Learning in American Universities,* Bloomington: Indiana University Press, 1994. It provides important background regarding the slow start of Judaic studies at Yale as compared with some of its peers.

The Yale history is detailed in three public relations pieces: Ivan G. Marcus, "Bringing Judaica to the Liberal Arts," *Yale Alumni Magazine and Journal* (Nov. 1981); William W. Hallo and Wayne A. Meeks, "A Proposal for Judaic Studies at Yale," Yale University, Office of University Development, May 1980; and Judy Wurtzel, "The Third Foundation: Judaic Studies at Yale," *Yale Daily News Magazine* (Oct. 5, 1982).

On the contributions of George Alexander Kohut to Yale Judaic studies, see Leon Nemoy, "The Alexander Kohut Memorial Collection of Judaica," *The Yale University Library Gazette* (Oct. 1927); Leon Nemoy, "George Alexander Kohut," *The Yale University Library Gazette* (Jan. 1935); Carl H. Kraeling, "Yale's Collection of Judaica," *The Yale University Library Gazette* (Apr. 1939); *The Alexander Kohut Memorial Foundation, A Review of Activities 1915–1972* (1973); and Arthur A. Chiel, "The Kohut Judaica Collection at Yale," in *Jews in New Haven* (1978). On Kohut's reasons for supporting Yale, see his letter to Henry Hurwitz, Jan. 27, 1916, Folder 5, Box 27, Henry Hurwitz Menorah Association Memorial Collection, AJA.

On Louis M. Rabinowitz, see Julian Obermann to Charles Seymour, June 1, 1945, "Report to the President"; Charles Seymour to James Babb, July 24, 1944; and James Babb to Edgar S. Furniss, July 19, 1944—all in Folder 839, Box 98, Series I, CS. Also see Folder 543, Box 56, Series I, Records of the Provost Acc. 1/16/81, YRG 3-A, YMAL. The history of the Sholem Asch collection is summarized in the pages of *The Yale University Library Gazette* of 1939–50. Also see Sholem Asch, "A Word about My Collection of Jewish Books," in *Catalogue of Hebrew and Yiddish Manuscripts and Books from the Library of Sholem Asch,* compiled by Leon Nemoy (New Haven: Yale University Library, 1945), pp. vii–xviii.

For assistance in the preparation of this chronology I am grateful to the following people: Steven Fraade, A. Bartlett Giamatti, Judah Goldin, Abraham S. Goldstein, William W. Hallo, Geoffrey Hartman, Miriam Horowitz, William Horowitz, Richard Israel, Hillel Levine, Ivan G. Marcus, Wayne A. Meeks, Leon Nemoy, Samuel Sandmel, Harold Wechsler, Paul Weiss, John A. Wilkinson, and Arnold Jacob Wolf.

Notes

INTRODUCTION

1. Franklin B. Dexter, ed., *Documentary History of Yale University* (New Haven: Yale University Press, 1916), pp. 20–23; Brooks Mather Kelley, *Yale: A History* (New Haven: Yale University Press, 1974), p. 6.

2. George W. Pierson, *Yale: A Short History* (New Haven: Office of the Secretary, Yale University, 1979), p. 92.

3. E. Digby Baltzell, *The Protestant Establishment* (New York: Random House, 1964), p. 347; George W. Pierson, *The Education of American Leaders* (New York: Frederick A. Praeger, Publishers, 1969).

4. William Clyde De Vane, "Report of the Dean of Yale College," *Reports to the President of Yale University, 1947–1948,* pp. 4–6.

5. Pierson, *Short History,* p. 9.

CHAPTER ONE: THE BEGINNINGS

The religious history of early Yale is best described in Richard Warch, *School of the Prophets, Yale College, 1701–1740* (1973). Warch provides an outstanding, well-referenced work with critical evaluation of his many sources. Connecticut history for the seventeenth and eighteenth centuries is entertainingly and comprehensively presented in the companion volumes of Albert E. Van Dusen, *Puritans*

Against the Wilderness (1975) and David M. Roth and Freeman Meyer, *From Revolution to Constitution* (1975).

1. There are but a few stray references in historical records of this era to the presence of Jews in Connecticut. The earliest is found in an entry in the General Court of Hartford from Nov. 9, 1659, recording one "David the Jew" who was arrested for illegal peddling. "Connecticut," *Encyclopaedia Judaica* (1972 ed.), vol. 5, p. 897; "United States of America," *Encyclopaedia Judaica* (1972 ed.), vol. 15, pp. 1586–87; Arthur A. Chiel, "Looking Back," *The Connecticut Jewish Ledger* (Feb. 22, 1973); Jacob R. Marcus, *The Colonial American Jew 1492–1776* (Detroit: Wayne State University Press, 1970), pp. 312–14, 423–26.

2. Albert E. Van Dusen, *Puritans Against the Wilderness,* Series in Connecticut History, ed. by David M. Roth (Chester, Conn.: The Pequot Press, 1975), p. 41; David M. Roth and Freeman Meyer, *From Revolution to Constitution,* Series in Connecticut History, ed. by David M. Roth (Chester, Conn.: The Pequot Press, 1975), pp. 49–50, 68; Henry L. Feingold, *A Midrash on American Jewish History* (Albany, N.Y.: State University of New York, 1982), p. 6; Rollin G. Osterweis, *Three Centuries of New Haven, 1638–1938* (New Haven: Yale University Press, 1953), pp. 212–13; Arthur A. Chiel, "Looking Back," *The Connecticut Jewish Ledger* (Apr. 5, 1973); Bernard Postal and Lionel Koppman, *American Jewish Landmarks, Volume 1* (New York: Fleet Press Corporation, 1977), pp. 34–35.

3. Ralph Henry Gabriel, *Religion and Learning at Yale* (New Haven: Yale University Press, 1958), pp. 26–27; Thomas Clap, *The Religious Constitution of Colleges, Especially of Yale College* (New London, 1754), pp. 12–13; Thomas Clap, *The Annals or History of Yale College* (New Haven: John Hotchkiss & B. Macon, 1766), p. 63; Samuel Eliot Morison, *Three Centuries of Harvard 1636–1936* (Cambridge, Mass.: Belknap-Harvard University Press, 1965), p. 88; Simeon E. Baldwin, "The Ecclesiastical Constitution of Yale College," in *Papers of the New Haven Colony Historical Society, Volume 3* (New Haven: New Haven Colony Historical Society, 1882), p. 416; Kelley, p. 65.

4. Richard Warch, *School of the Prophets, Yale College, 1701–1740* (New Haven: Yale University Press, 1973), p. 169; Clap, *History of Yale,* p. 65.

5. Kelley, p. 63; Johannes Wollebius, *The Abridgment of Christian Divinitie,* translated by Alexander Ross (London: Joseph Nevill, 1660), pp. 24, 231; Feingold, p. 11.

6. Franklin Bowditch Dexter, *On Some Social Distinctions at Harvard and Yale Before the Revolution* (Worcester, Mass.: Press of Charles Hamilton, 1894); Franklin Bowditch Dexter, *Biographical Sketches of the Graduates of Yale College with Annals of the College History, May, 1763–July, 1778* (New York: Henry Holt & Company, 1903), p. 263; Reuben Holden, *Profiles and Portraits of Yale University Presidents* (Freeport, Me.: The Bond Wheelwright Company, 1968), p. 41; Warch, p. 256.

7. As of 2000, the name of Thankfull Pinto was still listed inside the Center Church among the names of those buried inside the church crypt. The tombstones of Thankfull and Abigail Pinto still stand along the north wall of New Haven's Grove Street Cemetery.

Partial View of the Pinto Family Tree, with Approximate Ages Indicated for the Year 1772

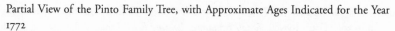

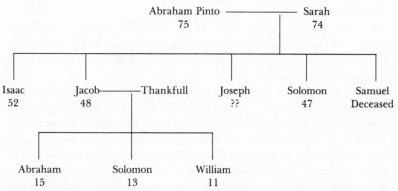

Ezra Stiles wrote that "the first real Jews" did not settle in New Haven until 1772. He did not include the "two Jew Brothers Pintos who renounced Judaism & all Religion" in the category of real Jews. It is unclear, however, whether the brothers that Stiles referred to were Jacob Pinto and one of his four brothers or else one of the three sons of Jacob and Thankfull Pinto. The ages of Jacob and his brothers Isaac and Solomon, at the time of Stiles's 1772 writing, were forty-eight, fifty-two, and forty-seven, respectively. Jacob's brother Samuel had died in 1764 at the age of thirty-seven. The ages of Jacob's sons Abraham, Solomon, and William in 1772 were fifteen, thirteen, and eleven. Because the renouncement of an adult would likely have been respected more than that of a child, it seems probable that the brothers that Stiles was referring to were two of the adult Pintos, rather than the three sons who attended Yale. Malcolm H. Stern, *First American Jewish Families: Six Hundred Genealogies, 1654–1977* (New York: American Jewish Archives, 1978), p. 251; Ezra Stiles, *Itineraries, Volume 3*, Reel 1, p. 218, BRBML; Osterweis, *Three*, p. 90; Arthur A. Chiel, "Looking Back," *The Connecticut Jewish Ledger* (Nov. 16, 1972); Dexter, *1763–1778*, pp. 700–01; Jacob R. Marcus, *Colonial*, p. 425; Malcolm H. Stern, "The Function of Genealogy in American Jewish History," in *Essays in American Jewish History* (Cincinnati: American Jewish Archives, 1958), pp. 69–97.

8. Roth and Meyer, p. 79; Holden, *Profiles and Portraits*, p. 45; Arthur A. Chiel, "Stiles and the Jews: A Study in Ambivalence," in *Jews in New Haven, Volume 3*, ed. by Barry E. Herman and Werner S. Hirsch (New Haven: Jewish Historical Society of New Haven, 1981), pp. 128, 130; Gabriel, p. 46.

9. Kelley, pp. 124–30.

10. Barnett A. Elzas, *The Jews of South Carolina* (Philadelphia: J. B. Lippincott Co., 1905), p. 99; Franklin Bowditch Dexter, *Biographical Sketches of the Graduates of Yale College with Annals of the College History, 1805–1816* (New Haven: The Tuttle, Morehouse & Taylor Press, 1912), p. 279; Joseph R. Rosenbloom, *A Biographical Dictionary of Early American Jews* (Lexington: University of Kentucky Press, 1960), p. 160; Malcolm H. Stern, *First*, p. 271.

11. *Catalogue of the Officers and Students in Yale College, Nov., 1826* (New Haven: Yale College, 1826), p. 25.

12. Robert D. Meade, *Judah P. Benjamin* (New York: Oxford University Press, 1943), pp. 1–30; Martin Rywell, *Judah Benjamin, Unsung Rebel Prince* (Asheville, N.C.: The Stephens Press, 1948), pp. 7–8; Elzas, pp. 163, 185.

13. *Vol. 1, Book of Averages, Classes of 1817–1841,* Hist. MSS, Misc. Film 69, YMAL; Simeon North to Mr. Brayton, Jan. 30, [1828], photostat in MS Vault W, BRBML, original in the Judah P. Benjamin Papers, Library of Congress; "Judah P. Benjamin's Guardian," *The New York Times* (Feb. 26, 1883), p. 3.

14. *Minutes of the Brothers in Unity,* Box I, Folder 3, Brothers in Unity Records, YMAL; *1825 Membership List,* Brothers in Unity Records, YMAL; Rollin G. Osterweis, *Judah P. Benjamin* (New York: G. P. Putnam's Sons, 1933), pp. 30–37; Anson Phelps Stokes, *Memorials of Eminent Yale Men, Volume 2* (New Haven: Yale University Press, 1914), p. 263; Kelley, p. 222; Gabriel, p. 88; William L. Kingsley, "An Eye-Witness's Account," in Maynard Mack, *A History of Scroll and Key* ([New Haven]: Scroll and Key Society, 1978), p. 10; Simeon North to Mr. Brayton, Jan. 30, [1828], photostat in MS Vault W, BRBML, original in the Judah P. Benjamin Papers, Library of Congress.

15. Benjamin has been charged by various historians with a number of crimes that may have led to his departure from Yale. Beyond the rude behavior that he apparently exhibited upon his departure, none of the charges are supportable with the evidence currently available. Dan A. Oren, "Why Did Judah P. Benjamin Leave Yale?" *A Jewish Journal at Yale,* 2 (Fall 1984), pp. 13–17; Judah P. Benjamin to Jeremiah Day, Jan. 14, 1828, Folder 10, Box 61, Day Family Papers, MS Group 175, YMAL; Judah P. Benjamin to James Bayard, Mar. 19, 1861, quoted by Pierce Butler in *Judah P. Benjamin* (Philadelphia: George W. Jacobs & Co., 1906), p. 29; Kelley, p. 168. Simeon North to Mr. Brayton, Jan. 30, [1828], MS Vault W, BRBML, original in the Judah P. Benjamin Papers, Library of Congress; *Faculty Records 1817–1851,* YRG 9-I, YMAL; Judah P. Benjamin to Samuel Stone, Nov. 15, 1827, Judah P. Benjamin Papers, Library of Congress; "Judah P. Benjamin's Guardian," *The New York Times,* Feb. 26, 1883, p. 3.

16. Benjamin's bad debts at Yale were posthumously made good in 1925 by an admiring lawyer who provided a twenty-thousand dollar fund in Benjamin's name to use for the purchase of law books and to subsidize the publication of works by members of the Yale Law Faculty. *Minutes of the Meetings of the Yale Corporation,* Feb. 14, 1925; "Benjamin, Judah Philip," *Encyclopaedia Judaica* (1972 ed.), vol. 4, p. 528; Bertram Wallace Korn, *Eventful Years and Experiences* (Cincinnati: The American Jewish Archives, 1954), p. 93.

17. Ezra Stiles, *Itineraries, Volume 3,* Reel 1, Roll 6, pp. 218–19, BRBML.

18. Nathan Glazer, *American Judaism* (Chicago: University of Chicago Press, 1972), p. 23; Shmuel Ettinger, "The Modern Period," in *A History of the Jewish People,* ed. by H. H. Ben-Sasson (Cambridge, Mass.: Harvard University Press, 1976), p. 791; Feingold, p. 28.

19. John Higham, *Send These to Me* (New York: Atheneum, 1975), pp. 140–43; John Higham, *Strangers in the Land* (New Brunswick, N.J.: Rutgers University Press, 1955), p. 94; Oscar Handlin, *Race and Nationality in American Life* (Boston: Little, Brown, & Co., 1948), p. 35; Baltzell, *Protestant,* pp. 56, 73.

20. In his history of Catholicism at Yale, Peter C. Alegi noted that the first Yale student with a "visibly" Catholic name was Carlos Ferdinand Ribeiro, of the class of 1838. Peter C. Alegi, "A History of Catholicism at Yale to 1943," departmental essay in American Studies, 1956, made available to the author by the St. Thomas More House at Yale. New

Haven Jews looked favorably upon the presence of Yale College in town because of the reputation that it brought New Haven as a source of knowledge. See Edward Engel, "Lehrer," *Die Deborah* 8 (Oct. 31, 1862): 68; "New Haven, Conn.," *Die Deborah* 9 (Nov. 6, 1863): 75. Postal and Koppman, p. 32; "Carrying the war into Africa," *The Columbian Register* (May 13, 1843), p. 2; Charles Reznikoff, "New Haven: The Jewish Community, a Portrait Sketch," *Commentary* 4 (Nov. 1947): 468–69.

21. *Historical Register of Yale University, 1701–1937* (New Haven: Yale University, 1939), p. 532; Rollin Osterweis, Interview, Dec. 12, 1976; Arthur A. Chiel, "Looking Back," *The Connecticut Jewish Ledger* (Apr. 20, 1972; Nov. 16, 1972).

22. Kelley, pp. 147–48, 496; Pierson, *Short History,* p. 20; Guido Kisch, "Two American Jewish Pioneers of New Haven," *Historia Judaica* 4 (Apr. 1942): 19–20.

23. "News Items," *The Occident* 3 (Jan. 1846): 526; "News Items," *The Occident* 3 (Feb. 1846): 572; Arthur A. Chiel, "Looking Back," *The Connecticut Jewish Ledger* (Jan. 11, 1973); Edward Grusd, *B'nai B'rith: The Story of a Covenant* (New York: Appleton-Century, 1966), pp. 55–57.

24. Henry Jacob Labatt to Rev. I. Leeser, Dec. 1, 1849, Folder 449, Box 12, MS Group 1258, YMAL: *Statistics of the Class of 1852,* p. 66; *Twenty-Five Year History of the Class of 1852, Yale College,* p. 84; *Thirty Year History of the Class of 1852, Yale College; Thirty-Five Year History of the Class of 1852,* pp. 26–27; *Yale University Obituary Record of 1901* (New Haven: Yale University, 1901), p. 51; *Record of the Tenth Reunion of the Yale Class of 1852,* p. 57; Kelley, p. 211.

25. W. H. W., "Discipline of College Life," *The Yale Literary Magazine* 23 (Dec. 1857): 98.

26. Higham, *Send,* p. 141.

27. *Yale University Obituary Record 1926–1927* (New Haven: Yale University, 1927), p. 29; Kelley, pp. 227–28.

28. Arthur A. Chiel, "Looking Back," *The Connecticut Jewish Ledger* (Sep. 9, 1976, Sep. 16, 1976, Sep. 23, 1976, Sep. 30, 1976); Lewis Ehrich, *Diary of Lewis Ehrich* (March 19, 1868); Jonathan D. Sarna, "A Jewish Student in Nineteenth Century America: The Diary of Lewis Ehrich — Yale '69," in *Jews in New Haven,* ed. by Jonathan D. Sarna (New Haven: Jewish Historical Society of New Haven, 1978), pp. 70–71.

29. Ehrich's experiences contradict one historian's assertion that because of Yale College laws regarding religion, "no conscientious Jew or agnostic could" have been a student at Yale in this period. Laurence R. Veysey, *The Emergence of the American University* (Chicago: University of Chicago Press, 1965), p. 34; Lewis Ehrich, *Diary of Lewis Ehrich* (Feb. 22, 1868; Oct. 14, 1868); Arthur A. Chiel, "Looking Back," *The Connecticut Jewish Ledger* (Sep. 9, 1976); Kelley, p. 209.

30. "Association of Literary Societies," *The Occident* 24 (Oct. 1866): 334–35.

31. Pierson, *Short History,* p. 47; Lewis Ehrich, *Diary of Lewis Ehrich* (June 25, 1868); Kelley, p. 226; Gabriel, p. 130.

32. J. Wechsler, "New Haven," *The American Israelite* 23 (Dec. 11, 1874): 5; J. Wechsler, "New Haven," *The American Israelite* 26 (Feb. 4, 1876): 5.

33. Baldwin, p. 435.

34. Hood was not a member of a senior society. Lyman Bagg, *Four Years at Yale* (New York: Henry Holt & Company, 1871), pp. 611–12, 614; *Historical Register 1701–1937,* p. 21; Louis Hood, "The Ancient and Modern Jew," *The Yale Literary Magazine* 43 (June 1878):

413–18; *Three Year History Yale College Class of 1878*, p. 58; *Statistics of the Class of 1878 Yale College*, pp. 11, 17–18. For a Yale Christian's perspective on Jewish history, see "The Jew," *The Yale Literary Magazine* 12 (Aug. 1847): 419–22.

35. *Jewish Record* (July 5, 1878), contained in the *Scrapbooks of Mrs. Adolph Asher*, JHSNH.

CHAPTER TWO: INCREASING BIASES

An outstanding portrayal of Jewish and Catholic participation in American college life is Stephen Steinberg, *The Academic Melting Pot* (1974). The earlier works of E. Digby Baltzell, *The Protestant Establishment* (1964) and Ernest Earnest, *Academic Procession* (1953) are also invaluable for an understanding of the national picture. Broad in scope, accurate in character, but limited by the reliability of its sources is Norman Hapgood, "Jews and College Life," *Harper's Weekly*, Jan. 15, 1916.

The unparalleled portrayal of collegiate life in this period is George Wilson Pierson, *Yale College: An Educational History* (1952). Pierson's work is valuable both for its overt content and for the wealth of its bibliographical sources. The college and scientific school classbooks provide reliable pictures of student temperament in various eras. What the students of each generation valued (e.g., ancestry, sports, socializing, or Yale itself) is clearly apparent in the biographical and general sketches. The largest collection of these classbooks is in the Yale University Manuscripts and Archives Library. The classic fictional portrait of Yale College and its social life is Owen Johnson, *Stover at Yale* (1911, 1968). There will long be a debate in interpreting *Stover* as to where to draw the line between fact and fiction. In drawing from fiction to illustrate history there is always the danger of art becoming larger than life. To some, the depiction of campus life in *Stover at Yale* was exaggerated for literary purposes but was based on an underlying reality. Scroll and Key historian Maynard Mack, in contrast, condemned Johnson's work as a gross misinterpretation of societies at Yale. Yet, without a doubt, the societies were influential, sometimes more in the minds of those outside the societies than of those inside. But many students did read Johnson's work and did see it as the Yale code of life. For those students who believed in *Stover*, fiction became reality.

The life of New Haven Jewry may best be appreciated from the seven volumes published by the New Haven Jewish Historical Society as *Jews in New Haven* (1978 through 1997). Arthur A. Chiel's column "Looking Back," which appeared weekly in *The Connecticut Jewish Ledger*, contains a plethora of scattered facts and reminiscences of Jewish life in the city.

1. "United States of America," *Encyclopaedia Judaica* (1972 ed.), vol. 15, p. 1607; Stephen Birmingham, "*Our Crowd*" (New York: Harper & Row, Publishers, 1967), pp. 147–48.

2. Higham, *Send*, pp. 144–46.

3. *Yale News* (Feb. 8, 1878), p. 3; *Yale News* (Feb. 14, 1878), p. 3; *Yale News* (Mar. 13, 1878), pp. 1–2. On the A. E. Rosenberg tailoring clan, see Loomis Havemeyer, *Out of Yale's Past* ([New Haven?, 1960?]), pp. 84–86. Local Jews who read of the *News*'s remarks were offended by the insulting references. See "Letter to the Editor," *The New Haven Union*, from a clipping in the *Scrapbooks of Mrs. Adolph Asher*, p. 33, JHSNH. At other periods in campus life, the Yale community looked upon these neighbors with greater benevolence. In 1892 *The New Haven Evening Register* reported that several "have established their reputations as being trustworthy, and . . . have obtained permits from the faculty to

go on the campus and hunt for second-hand apparel." Some local Jewish clothes dealers became such an intimate part of campus life that they developed a remarkable reputation for predicting the outcome of fraternity and society elections. The Rosenberg and Press families often won the friendship as well as the business of Yale students by bailing them out of jail on the occasions when the New Haven police arrested them. "The Old Clothes Buyer," *The New Haven Evening Register* (Feb. 10, 1892), p. 1; Havemeyer, *Out,* pp. 84–86; "'Wolf of Wall Street' Victim of Pneumonia," *Yale Daily News* (May 2, 1935), p. 1; Paul Moore, Jr., "A Touch of Laughter," in *My Harvard, My Yale,* ed. by Diana Dubois (New York: Random House, 1982), p. 201.

4. Stephen Steinberg, "How Jewish Quotas Began," *Commentary* 52 (Sep. 1971): 72; Irving Howe, *World of Our Fathers* (New York: Harcourt Brace Jovanovich, 1976), pp. 5–6; Louis Greenberg, *The Jews in Russia, Volume 2,* ed. by Mark Wischnitzer (New Haven: Yale University Press, 1951), pp. 73–74.

5. *Statistics of the Jews of the United States* (Philadelphia: Union of American Hebrew Congregations, 1880), p. 8; "New Haven," *Encyclopaedia Judaica* (1972 ed.), vol. 12, p. 1025; Reznikoff, pp. 465–77; J. B. G., *The American Israelite* 28 (Jan. 6, 1882): 221; *B'nai Jacob One Hundred Years* (Woodbridge, Conn.: Congregation B'nai Jacob, 1982), p. 2.

6. Higham, *Send,* p. 152; Stephen Steinberg, *The Academic Melting Pot* (New York: McGraw-Hill Book Company, 1974), pp. 77, 80–81; Thomas Kessner, *The Golden Door, The Urban Life in America Series,* ed. by Richard C. Wade (New York: Oxford University Press, 1977), p. 42.

7. Robert H. Wiebe, *The Search for Order, 1877–1920* (New York: Hill and Wang, 1967), p. 110; Oscar Handlin and Mary Handlin, "Religious Intolerance," in *Immigration as a Factor in American History,* ed. by Oscar Handlin (Englewood Cliffs, N.J.: Prentice-Hall, Inc., 1959), p. 178.

8. Higham, *Send,* p. 154.

9. Membership in Phi Beta Kappa had usually been based on academic excellence. The fraternity first began to decline in the 1840s, but lived on for another three decades. Kelley, pp. 223, 303; George Wilson Pierson, *Yale College: An Educational History* (New Haven: Yale University Press, 1952), pp. 100–01.

10. Baltzell, *Protestant,* pp. 129–30; Ernest Earnest, *Academic Procession* (Indianapolis: Bobbs-Merrill Co., 1953), p. 222; Veysey, p. 235; Edwin E. Slosson, *Great American Universities* (Chicago: University of Chicago Press, 1910), p. 47.

11. George Santayana, "A Glimpse of Yale," *The Harvard Monthly* 15 (Dec. 1892): 95.

12. Earnest, p. 219; Pierson, *Yale College,* pp. 240–41.

13. *1904 Yale College Classbook,* p. 180.

14. Baltzell, *Protestant,* p. 130; Henry Seidel Canby, *Alma Mater: The Gothic Age of the American College* (New York: Farrar & Rinehart, Inc., 1936), p. 129.

15. Baltzell, *Protestant,* p. 110.

16. Wiebe, p. 111.

17. Baltzell, *Protestant,* pp. 61, 113, 138.

18. Wealthy students occasionally suffered the jeers of their poorer classmates, though by Tap Day the well-off had the last laugh in society elections. In 1850 tuition had been $39. By 1914 it had reached $160. These fees were similar to those of Harvard and Columbia. State institutions like Wisconsin undercut private college fees when they demanded lit-

tle or no tuition of in-state residents. John R. Thelin, *The Cultivation of Ivy* (Cambridge, Mass.: Schenkman Publishing Co., 1976), p. 59; Pierson, *Short History*, p. 59; Edward J. Power, *Catholic Higher Education in America* (New York: Appleton-Century Crofts, 1972), pp. 188, 283.

19. Living quarters provided the greatest differences between economic classes at the turn of the century. Many of the poor students lived in the university's Pierson Hall, erected in 1896. Since friendships formed best among people who lived together, Dean Frederick S. Jones of Yale College worked to convince many low and high income students to live in the same buildings beginning in 1914. In 1917 Pierson Hall was razed to allow construction of the Memorial Quadrangle on the same site. Kelley, p. 309; "Dormitories and Democracy," *Yale Alumni Weekly* 15 (Dec. 6, 1905): 184; Ralph H. Gabriel, Interview, Dec. 7, 1982; Reuben A. Holden, *Yale: A Pictorial History* (New Haven: Yale University Press, 1967), p. 3; Maynard Mack, *A History of Scroll and Key* ([New Haven?], Scroll and Key Society, 1978), pp. 147, 169, 180–81.

20. Pierson, *Yale College*, p. 25.

21. Ibid., pp. 3–4, 7.

22. Though a secret senior society in America first appeared at Yale in the 1830s, the model was followed outside of New Haven. Similar societies were formed at Columbia, Wesleyan, and the University of Michigan during the first two decades of the twentieth century. Calvin B. T. Lee, *The Campus Scene: 1900–1970* (New York: David McKay Co., Inc., 1970), p. 5.

23. Harry S. Lewis, "Unknown Undergraduates," *The Yale Literary Magazine* 71 (June 1906): 338; Pierson, *Yale College*, p. 42; Norman Winestine, Interview, Mar. 20, 1983.

24. Mack, p. 169.

25. The pyramidal social system effectively functioned contrary to current definitions of democracy—in spite of Yale's claims to being a "democracy" of talent. Earnest, p. 233. Kingman Brewster, Jr., "Introduction," in *Stover at Yale*, by Owen Johnson (New York: The Macmillan Co., 1968), p. vi.

26. *Stover at Yale* originally appeared in *McClure's Magazine* in 1911. Owen Johnson, *Stover at Yale* (New York: The Macmillan Co., 1968), p. 21; Kelley, p. 310.

27. Kelley, p. 310.

28. J. P. G., "New Haven," *The American Israelite* 31 (July 25, 1884): p. 5.

29. "Shylock, Initiation Play, Class of 1891 to Class of 1892," May 23, 1890, copies in the Delta Kappa Epsilon Records, YMAL, and in the *Scrapbook of Harvey Cushing*, Yale History of Medicine Library. Cushing (B.A. 1891) had been an active member in the Yale DKE chapter. *1891 Yale College Classbook*, p. 135.

30. *1891 Yale College Classbook*, pp. 33, 100; *1895 Yale College Classbook*, p. 53; Pierson, *Yale College*, p. 730.

31. Fisher later became a rabbi and Levy became a partner in the New York City law firm of Chadbourne, Stanchfield, and Levy. Fisher was not the first Yale graduate to enter the rabbinate. The first known Yale graduate to enter that career path was Wolff Willner (B.A. 1885, M.A. 1887). Willner was exceptionally proficient at languages and had a command of English, Hebrew, Syriac, Aramaic, Samaritan, Anglo-Saxon, Sanskrit, French, German, Latin, and Greek. He became a Conservative rabbi. *1885 Yale College Classbook*, p. 73; *Yale University Obituary Record 1932–1933* (New Haven: Yale University, 1933), p. 55.

A local sectarian secret society was the "Knights of Jerusalem." Founded by six young Jewish "townies" in 1871, KOJ was an imitation of the exciting society activity that local Jewish boys observed on the Yale campus. For a few decades KOJ dominated the New Haven Jewish young men's scene. Complete with its own motto, initiation ceremony, secret handshake, and membership pin, KOJ was established for the "pursuance of exercise of a high literary character, and for the purpose of perpetuating friendship and brotherly love, as well as adhering to the laws of our forefathers in Jerusalem." Debates and orations were the major bill of fare of this fraternal society that admitted any Jewish New Haven student between the ages of seventeen and twenty-one. See Arthur A. Chiel, "Looking Back," *The Connecticut Jewish Ledger* (Feb. 8, 1973, Dec. 20, 1973, Dec. 27, 1973, Jan. 3, 1974, Jan. 10, 1974, Jan. 17, 1974); Arthur A. Chiel, Interview, Dec. 9, 1976. "Fraternities, Jewish," *Universal Jewish Encyclopaedia* (1969 ed.), vol. 4, p. 423; "Pledge Manual" of Pi Lambda Phi, pp. 13–15, accompanying George A. Beck to author, July 28, 1983; Steven J. Mason, "The Jewish Fraternity as a Jewish Socializing Agency," thesis for ordination (Cincinnati: Hebrew Union College, 1976), pp. 1, 20; *The Tripod* (Spring 1962), p. i, Pi Lambda Phi Fraternity File, AJA: *1897 Yale College Classbook,* p. 37; *Twenty-Five Year History Class of 1897 Yale College,* pp. 146–47; *Twenty-Five Year History Class of 1898 Yale College,* 157.

32. "Pledge Manual" of Pi Lambda Phi, p. 16, accompanying Beck to author; Beck to author.

33. "Would Not Meet a Colored Debater," *The New York Times* (May 13, 1892), p. 1.

34. Frederick S. Jones to Lawrence Mason, Dec. 6, 1915, Lawrence Mason to Frederick S. Jones, Dec. 11, 1915, Anson Phelps Stokes to Frederick S. Jones, Jan. 6, 1916, all in "Faculty" folder, Box 3, FSJ.

35. My understanding of Lieutenant Totten was aided by Mary-Kathleen O'Connell, "British Israelites: The Chosen People in the Nineteenth Century." A copy of this unpublished 1977 essay was shared with me by Sydney Ahlstrom. On Totten see his journal, *Our Race: Its Origin and Its Destiny,* published from 1890 through 1915. The interpretation of Mother Goose poetry may be found in "Mother Goose for Grown Folk," on pp. 227–30 of the March 20, 1891 (Series I) issue of the journal. *The New York Times,* then published by George Jones, was surprised that a great university like Yale permitted such "curious and novel" doctrines as promulgated by Totten to be taught in its classes. The Yale Corporation, O'Connell noted in her essay, thought that Totten's eccentricities did not sufficiently interfere with his teaching to warrant pressing the War Department for his removal. See "A Clergyman Insane. He is a Graduate of Yale and one of Lieut. Toten's [*sic*] Disciples," *The New York Times* (June 26, 1891), p. 1; "No Rest for Totten," *The New York Times* (Mar. 13, 1892), p. 4; "Lieut. Totten's Vagaries," *The New York Times* (Mar. 30, 1892), p. 1; Thomas F. Gossett, *Race: The History of an Idea in America* (New York: Schocken Books, 1963), pp. 191–92. On the military instruction at Yale in this era see Russell H. Chittenden, *History of the Sheffield Scientific School* (New Haven: Yale University Press, 1928), p. 508.

36. The classification of Jewish student types was partially suggested by Norman Winestine and is consistent with my examination of class records. Norman Winestine, Interview, Apr. 21, 1981.

37. Frederick S. Jones, "Report on Jews, 1922," Folder 71, Box 6, FSJ.

38. J. P. G., "New Haven," *The American Israelite* 31 (July 25, 1884), p. 5.

39. Abraham S. Alderman, "A Literary Approach to Life in the New Haven Ghetto," in *Jews in New Haven, Volume 2*, ed. by Barry E. Herman (New Haven: Jewish Historical Society of New Haven, 1979), p. 141. Also see Oscar Handlin, *The Uprooted* (Boston: Little, Brown & Co., 1951), pp. 146–64.

40. Ettinger, pp. 770, 779, 786; Steinberg, *Melting Pot*, pp. 83–84; S. M. Melamed, "The Academic Boycott," *The Reflex* 1 (Dec. 1927): 8.

41. Abraham S. Alderman, p. 142.

42. Louis Sachs, quoted by Arthur A. Chiel, in "Looking Back," *The Connecticut Jewish Ledger* (Oct. 11, 1973); Louis Sachs, Interview, Oct. 5, 1978; William Echikson, "From Oak Street to Yale and Beyond," *Yale Alumni Magazine & Journal* 45 (Nov. 1981): 29–33. The personal experiences of Sachs, as described by Echikson, are reliable accounts. The remainder of the Echikson article must not be taken as the gospel truth.

43. Sachs, Interview, Oct. 5, 1978; Abraham S. Alderman, Interview, Nov. 8, 1982.

44. J. Carlisle Peet, "Of Discourse," *The Yale Literary Magazine* 79 (May 1914): 336.

45. For several years the school occupied quarters adjacent to the campus. In 1916 it opened in Milford as The Milford School, a preparatory academy. Elliot Cohen, Max Lerner, Morris Sweetkind, and Jacob Warshaw all taught there at one time or another. The tutoring school in New Haven specialized in pre-examination "cram" sessions and was not a "paper mill." It lasted until approximately 1940. *1907 Sheffield Scientific School Classbook, Volume 2*, p. 173; *1908 Sheffield Scientific School Classbook*, p. 249; *Thirty Year History, Class of 1908 Sheffield Scientific School*, p. 346; Alderman, Interview; Robert Rosenbaum, Interview, June 1, 1983.

46. Johnson, p. 199.

47. According to literary biographer Paul Carter, Frank grew somewhat resentful of his classmates for their immature attitudes. Carter suggests that this resentment may have emerged from the college publications' continual rejection of Frank's essays (which later won awards from the faculty). Frank's own recollections of his Yale years show little evidence of bitterness. He felt that his status as a Jew at Yale made social advancement difficult, but not impossible. When Frank was graduated from Yale in 1911 he left with the honorary title of "Fellow of the University"—an accolade bestowed upon him through the efforts of William Lyon Phelps, professor of English. His manuscript "The Spirit of Modern French Letters" was accepted by the Yale University Press in 1912. It was never published, however, as he withdrew the work after a change of convictions regarding his thesis.

    The great literary critic Paul Rosenfeld (B.A. 1912) attended the college at the same time as Frank. Rosenfeld became an editor of *The Yale Literary Magazine* during his senior year. Paul J. Carter, *Waldo Frank* (New York: Twayne Publishers, Inc., 1967), pp. 7, 15, 24–25; Waldo Frank, in *Memoirs of Waldo Frank*, ed. by Alan Trachtenberg (Amherst: The University of Massachusetts Press, 1973), p. 37; Jerome Mellquist, "Seraph from Mt. Morris Park," in *Paul Rosenfeld: Voyager in the Arts*, ed. by Jerome Mellquist and Lucie Wiese (New York: Farrar, Straus & Giroux, 1948, 1977), p. xvii.

48. Harry Sinclair Lewis, "Editor's Table," *The Yale Literary Magazine* 71 (Apr. 1906): 287.

49. Sachs, Interview, Oct. 5, 1978.

50. Ibid.

51. J. P. G., "New Haven, Conn., *The American Israelite* 28 (Feb. 17, 1882): 266.

52. A typical opinion of the Yale student was recorded in the *1891 Yale College Classbook:* "Ninety-one's most prominent characteristic is considered to be class feeling and love for Yale" (p. 113).

Alderman's undergraduate articles appeared in both *The Yale Literary Magazine* and *The Yale Sheffield Monthly.* Some dealt with Jewish themes. Alderman's brother Abraham reported that Joseph's English teacher Henry Seidel Canby (founder of the *Saturday Review of Literature*) encouraged Joseph to consider a career in writing. Joseph entered graduate school in English at Yale but abandoned his studies when offered a rewarding position at the Rosenbaums' school in Milford. Joseph Alderman, "Khesdeb's Quest," *The Yale Literary Magazine* 80 (Dec. 1914): 124–33; Joseph Alderman, "The Still Small Voice," *The Yale Literary Magazine* 79 (May 1914): 369–75; "Editorial," *The Yale Sheffield Monthly* 21 (Apr. 1915): 360; *1915 Sheffield Scientific School Classbook,* pp. 44, 405; Alderman, Interview.

53. Joseph S. Alderman, "Yale Life of the New Haven Student," in *1915 Sheffield Scientific Classbook,* p. 365.

54. Alderman, Interview; Joseph S. Alderman, *1915 Sheffield Classbook,* pp. 365–66.

55. Ibid., pp. 366–69.

56. Eugene H. Lehman, quoted in *Twenty-Fifth Anniversary Volume, Class of 1902 Yale College,* pp. 329–33.

57. Mark Singer, "God and Mentsch at Yale," *Moment* 1 (July–Aug. 1975): 28; Arthur A. Chiel, "Looking Back," *The Connecticut Jewish Ledger* (Dec. 15, 1977); Robert A. Caro, *The Powerbroker, Robert Moses and the Fall of New York* (New York: Alfred A. Knopf, 1974), pp. 39–42; *1905 Yale College Classbook,* p. 136; Jean Baer, *The Self-Chosen* (New York: Arbor House, 1982), p. 39; Sachs, Interview, Oct. 1978; Winestine, Interview, Apr. 21, 1981.

58. Gabriel, Interview.

59. Kelley, p. 388; Gabriel, Interview; Sachs, Interview, Oct. 5, 1978.

60. Robert Nelson Corwin, "Report on Athletics, 1916," "Board of Control" Folder, Box 1, Robert Nelson Corwin Papers, YMAL.

61. Winestine, Interview, Apr. 21, 1981. For a similar description of Jewish interest in athletics at Harvard see Alfred A. Benesch, "The Jew at Harvard," *The New Era* 4 (Feb. 1904): 56–60.

62. "Current Topics," *The New Era* 5 (Aug. 1875): 523.

63. Moses quarreled with legendary Yale football coach Walter Camp over the coach's reluctance to share money with the less established sports at Yale. Caro, pp. 38–42. Another successful Jewish athlete from this era was St. Petersburg-born Max David Kirjassof (B.A. 1910), who received a "Y" for his efforts on the university track squads. He was also a member of the Yale Hebraic Club. *1910 Yale College Classbook,* p. 213. Marcia Graham Synnott, *The Half-Opened Door* (Westport, Conn.: Greenwood Press, 1979), p. 255.

64. These percentages were calculated from the figures on fraternity memberships in Norman Hapgood, "Jews and College Life," *Harper's Weekly* 62 (Jan. 15, 1916): 53, combined with my own statistics on Jewish and total enrollments at Yale. Catholic students did far better than Jews at entering the upper echelons of Yale society. In Marcia Graham Synnott's count for 1912 there were three known Catholics in Alpha Delta Phi, nine in Delta

Kappa Epsilon, four in Zeta Psi, and none in Psi Upsilon and Beta Theta Pi. There were two known Catholics apiece in Skull and Bones, Scroll and Key, Wolf's Head, and Elihu Club that year. Synnott, *Door*, p. 132.

65. The black student fraternity of Alpha Phi Alpha, founded at Cornell University in 1906, had its Yale chapter established in 1909. The reasons behind the formation of the chapter at this time await further elaboration. It is likely, though, that the few Yale black students of this era had slim chances of entrance to the snobbish fraternities. The alienation that some of the townie Jewish students felt led to the formation of the Achevah club at Yale. Meeting once a week for social and musical purposes, the club was founded in 1908, reorganized in 1912 and thereon continued as an alumni club with semiannual meetings. Estelle G. Heil, "Achevah Offered Camaraderie to Yale University's Jews," *The Connecticut Jewish Ledger* (May 24, 1984), p. 2; *1908 Yale College Classbook*, p. 289; *1913 Yale College Classbook*, p. 212; Chrisellen Kolb, "Yale Fraternity Rushes New Members," *Yale Daily News* (Apr. 19, 1983), p. 1; Allen B. Ballard, *The Education of Black Folk* (New York: Harper & Row, Publishers, 1973), p. 55; Gabriel, Interview; Estelle Heil (interviewed in University Towers, New Haven), Apr. 26, 1983; Sachs, Interview, Oct. 5, 1978.

66. In 1916 Norman Hapgood reported (on the basis of third-hand knowledge) that one Jew, a few years earlier, had been accepted by a senior society, "not only because he was captain of a varsity team, but because he was a gentleman who measured up to its stamp." My examination of the names of senior society members from several years prior to Hapgood's article has failed to uncover any evidence that this statement has any factual basis. To the best of my knowledge, no Jew entered a senior society before 1937. Hapgood, *Harper's Weekly*, p. 53; Pierson, *Yale College*, p. 20.

67. The Elihu Club's program of intellectual stimulation for its members included debates on topics of current interest. The debate regarding Jews was held in 1911, apparently. Thirteen voted in the affirmative and none voted for the negative side of the resolution. *Minutes of the Twenty-Sixth General Meeting of the Elihu Club, New Haven, Conn., Nov. 18, 1911*, p. 3; Baltzell, *Protestant*, p. 120.

CHAPTER THREE: THE LIMITATION OF NUMBERS

A comprehensive history of selective college admission in America is Harold Wechsler, *The Qualified Student* (1977). It focuses on the University of Michigan, Columbia University, the University of Chicago, and the City University of New York. Wechsler successfully integrates his case-examinations into the broad frame of American educational history. Also worth consulting is Stephen Steinberg, "How Jewish Quotas Began," *Commentary* (Sep. 1971), and the follow-up correspondence between Wechsler and Steinberg in *Commentary* (Jan. 1972). Crucial to students of Yale, Harvard, and Princeton history is Marcia Graham Synnott, *The Half-Opened Door* (1979), which meticulously compares the unique, but parallel, discriminatory actions in the "Big Three" colleges in the 1920s. My own work owes much to Synnott's efforts.

1. Steinberg, *Commentary*, p. 69; Pierson, *Yale College*, pp. 327–28, 404.

2. Frederick S. Jones, quoted in Kelley, p. 346.

3. Kelley, p. 346; Harold Wechsler, *The Qualified Student* (New York: John Wiley & Sons, 1977), p. 103.

4. Kelley, pp. 346–47; Pierson, *Yale College,* pp. 484, 510–12; George Wilson Pierson, *Yale: The University College, 1921–1937* (New Haven: Yale University Press, 1955), pp. 31, 36, 43, 46; Pierson, *Short History,* p. 67; Wechsler, pp. 124–25.

5. For a discussion of the founding of Yeshiva College (1927–28), see Deborah Dash Moore, *At Home in America* (New York: Columbia University Press, 1981), pp. 177–99; Ettinger, pp. 861–62; Kessner, p. 97; Steinberg, *Melting Pot,* p. 10; James Angell to Conrad Hoffman, Dec. 7, 1933, "Jewish Problem" folder, Box 91, JRA.

6. Though by 1982 they were completely absorbed by the growth of Chinatown, the upper Pell Street and Baxter Street regions of New York City's Lower East Side, Columbia University history professor James P. Shenton has informed me, had once been occupied primarily by German Jews. Ettinger, pp. 980–82; Steinberg, *Commentary,* p. 75; Heywood Broun and George Britt, *Christians Only* (New York: The Vanguard Press, 1931), pp. 15, 73–74.

7. The Italian population of New Haven rose from 7 percent of the inhabitants in 1900 to over 25 percent in 1930. Because only a small percentage of Italian children graduated from high school, the number of New Haven Italians interested in college was small and an "Italian problem" did not develop at Yale. Synnott, *Door,* pp. 131–32; *American Jewish Year Book 5692,* ed. by Harry Schneiderman (Philadelphia: Jewish Publication Society of America, 1927), p. 276; Anson Phelps Stokes, quoted in "University Menorah Addresses," *The Menorah Journal* 1 (Dec. 1915): 321.

8. Pierson, *University College,* pp. 143–44.

9. Synnott, *Door,* p. 139; Minott Osborn to James R. Angell, Nov. 17, 1921, Folder 1324, Box 127, JRA.

10. Russell Chittenden to James R. Angell, Jan. 26, 1922, "Jewish Problem" folder, Box 91, JRA.

11. Alfred K. Merritt to Robert Corwin, April 11, 1922, "Jewish Problem" folder, Box 91, JRA. A copy is also in the Folder 71, Box 6, FSJ.

12. Robert Corwin to Frederick Jones, May 3, 1922, "Jews" folder, Box 6, FSJ.

13. Frederick Jones to Robert Corwin, May 6, 1922, "Jews" folder, Box 6, FSJ.

14. Pierson, *University College,* p. 193.

15. Roswell Angier to Robert Corwin, May 9, 1922, Freshman Office Records, 1920–21/1921–22, Box 1, Folder A.1.10, Admissions Committee, quoted by Marcia Synnott in *A Social History of Admissions Policies at Harvard, Yale, and Princeton, 1900–1930* (Ann Arbor, Mich.: University Microfilms, 1974), p. 512; Synnott, *Door,* p. 141.

16. [Robert Corwin], "Memorandum on the Problems Arising from the Increase in the Enrollment of Students of Jewish Birth in the University," May 12, 1922, "Jewish Problem" folder, Box 91, JRA.

17. Ibid.

18. [Robert Corwin], "Memorandum on Jewish Problem," [May 1922], "Jewish Problem" folder, Box 91, JRA.

19. Minutes of the Committee on Educational Policy, May 12, 1922, *Reports of the Committee on Educational Policy to the Yale Corporation, 1919–1929,* p. 97.

20. On cheating and honor system violations at Yale, see Russell Chittenden to Robert Corwin, May 23, 1922, Abraham Schaefer to James R. Angell, April 11, 1929, Clarence Mendell to James R. Angell, Apr. 13, 1929, James R. Angell to Abraham Schaefer, Apr. 16,

1929, all in "Jewish Problem" folder, Box 91, JRA. Also see Pierson, *University College,* pp. 150, 348, and Clarence W. Mendell, "Yale College," *Reports Made to the President and Fellows, 1931–1932,* pp. 35–36. Robert Corwin, "Memorandum on Jewish Representation in Yale," May 26, 1922, "Jewish Problem" folder, Box 91, JRA.

21. Baltzell, *Protestant,* p. 210; Ettinger, p. 982; Barbara Miller Solomon, *Ancestors and Immigrants* (Cambridge, Mass.: Harvard University Press, 1956), p. 123; Synnott, *Door,* p. 19.

22. Pronouncements like this led American Jews to regard these tests by 1931 as "the banner and symbol of exclusion." Broun and Britt, p. 75; Alfred L. Ripley to James R. Angell, June 3, 1922, "Jewish Problem" folder, Box 91, JRA; Benjamin Ginzburg, "May Jews Go to College?" *The American Hebrew* 111 (June 16, 1922): 130.

23. Julian Morgenstern, "American Judaism Faces the Future," *The American Hebrew* 111 (Sep. 22, 1922): 447.

24. Walter Lippmann made a similar statement that year before the Harvard University investigation committee. Michael R. Marrus, "The Theory and Practice of Anti-Semitism," *Commentary* 74 (Aug. 1982): 41; Quotation from "The Flavor of Harvard," *The American Hebrew* 111 (Aug. 25, 1922): 351.

25. A. Lawrence Lowell to A. A. Benesch, quoted in "Harvard President Explains University's Position," *The American Hebrew* 111 (June 23, 1922): 162.

26. "The Harvard Policy of 'Limitation,'" *The American Hebrew* 111 (Sep. 29, 1922): 529; Feingold, p. 130.

27. "The Jews and the Colleges," *The American Hebrew* 111 (June 9, 1922): 109.

28. Ralph P. Boas, "Who Shall Go to College?" *The Atlantic Monthly* (Oct. 1922): 446.

29. "A. F. of L. to Investigate Harvard Stand on Jews," *The American Hebrew* 111 (June 30, 1922): 176.

30. "Governor Orders Inquiry at Harvard," *The American Hebrew* 111 (June 9, 1922): 128.

31. "The Shot Heard Round the World," *The American Hebrew* 112 (Apr. 20, 1923): 745; "Harvard Vindicates the American Spirit," *The American Hebrew* 112 (Apr. 13, 1923): 714; Ettinger, pp. 885, 956.

32. Statistics from 1924 indicate that although Jews throughout Yale's schools received a total monetary grant in rough proportion to their population, approximately 50 percent of all Jewish scholarship and loan applications were approved, in contrast to a 75 percent approval rate for non-Jews. See Frederick Jones to Robert Corwin, May 6, 1922, "Jews" folder, Box 6, FSJ and 1924–25 Scholarship Statistics in "Jewish Problem" folder, Box 91, JRA.

33. Roswell Angier to Robert Corwin, May 9, 1922, according to Synnott, *Door,* pp. 141, 268.

34. [Robert Corwin], "Memorandum on Jewish Problem," [May 1922], "Jewish Problem" folder, Box 91, JRA.

35. [Robert Corwin], "Memorandum on the Problems Arising from the Increase in the Enrollment of Students of Jewish Birth in the University," May 12, 1922, "Jewish Problem" folder, Box 91, JRA.

36. James R. Angell to Harry Garfield, June 5, 1922, Folder 1193, Box 116, JRA.

37. Frederick S. Jones, "Report on Jews, 1922," Folder 71, Box 6, FSJ.

38. James R. Angell to Frederick Jones, Oct. 5, 1922, James R. Angell to Roswell Angier, Oct.

5, 1922, James R. Angell to Wilbur Cross, Oct. 5, 1922, Frederick Jones to James R. Angell, Oct. 9, 1922, Roswell Angier to James R. Angell, Oct. 10, 1922, Wilbur Cross to James R. Angell, Oct. 7, 1922, all in Folder 1324, Box 127, JRA.

39. "Limitation of Numbers," Freshman Office Records, HGS 6, b-3, c-4, Box 3, "Committee on Limitation of Numbers 1922" folder, p. 1, also in Folder 1324, Box 127, JRA. This paper begins, "It is difficult. . . ."

40. Separate paper filed in the same way as that mentioned in n. 39. The paper referenced here includes handwritten titles (apparently penned by Corwin), and it begins: "The Corporation should. . . ." A duplicate copy is also in Folder 1324, Box 127, JRA.

41. Ibid.

42. Frederick Jones to W. D. Washburn, Apr. 13, 1914, "Temperance and Prohibition" folder, Box 8, Series III, FSJ.

43. Separate paper filed in the same way as that mentioned above in n. 39. The paper referenced here includes handwritten titles (apparently penned by Corwin), and it begins: "The Corporation should. . . ." A duplicate copy is also in Folder 1324, Box 127, JRA.

44. Ibid.; also see *Minutes of the Yale Corporation,* Dec. 12, 1925, Film 49, Reel 8.

45. David T. Langrock, former owner of the land upon which the university's Sterling Memorial Library was built, claimed that he agreed to sell the plot to the university for one dollar on the condition that Yale not discriminate against Jews in its admissions policies. He believed that the Yale Corporation held a formal meeting at which they voted that there would be no particular restriction of Jews as part of Yale admissions policies. David T. Langrock, Interview, by Harvey Ladin, Oct. 27, 1962. I have not been able to confirm the particulars of what Langrock described. *Minutes of the Yale Corporation,* Feb. 10, 1923; Reel: 1923–31.

46. Robert Corwin to James R. Angell, Feb. 29, 1924, "Jewish Problem" folder, Box 91, JRA.

47. James R. Angell to Robert Corwin, Mar. 8, 1924, "Jewish Problem" folder, Box 91, JRA.

48. Minutes of the Board of Admissions, June 10, 1924, Folder 26, Box 2, JRA.

49. Frederick S. Jones, "Report on Jews, 1922," Box 6, FSJ.

50. Jerome Karabel, "Status-Group Struggle, Organizational Interests, and the Limits of Institutional Autonomy. The Transformation of Harvard, Yale, and Princeton, 1918–1940," *Theory and Society* 13 (Jan. 1984): 15, 17. Minutes of the Board of Admissions, Feb. 16, 1925, Folder 26, Box 2, JRA.

51. Robert Corwin to James R. Angell, Feb. 10, 1933, accompanied by table entitled "Yale Fathers," Oct. 17, 1932, "Board of Admissions" folder, Box 2, JRA.

52. These examinations, which for some years had been administered experimentally to each freshman class, grew out of the Army Alpha Tests of the First World War. Following the development of experimental psychology, the aptitude tests allowed for major savings of time and effort in evaluating "native ability and promise." Corwin had once been chairman of the CEEB. Minutes of the Board of Admissions, Jan. 18, 1926, Folder 26, Box 2, JRA; Pierson, *University College,* pp. 145, 484, 493.

53. On the basis of poor data about *Russians* taking the army tests, Brigham concluded that the average Jew was less intelligent than the average non-Jew. Because the standard deviation among Jews was greater than that of any other ethnic group, concluded Brigham, there were a good number of exceptionally talented Jews. Carl C. Brigham, *A Study of*

American Intelligence (Princeton, N.J.: Princeton University Press, 1923), p. 190; Wechsler, p. 160.

54. "Limitation of Numbers," Freshman Office Records, HGS 6, b-3, c-4, Box 3, "Committee on Limitation of Numbers 1922" folder, p. 1, also in Folder 1324, Box 127, JRA. This paper begins, "It is difficult. . . ." "The Harvard Policy of 'Limitation,'" *The American Hebrew* III (Sep. 29, 1922): 529.

55. Robert Corwin to James R. Angell, Jan. 7, 1930, "Board of Admissions" folder, "Admissions" box, JRA.

56. Robert Corwin to James R. Angell, Oct. 17, 1930, "Board of Admissions" folder, "Admissions" box, JRA.

57. "Applicants Submit Photographs," *Yale Daily News* (Mar. 29, 1926), p. 2; "An Ellis Island for Yale," *Yale Daily News* (Mar. 30, 1926), p. 2.

58. "Applicants Submit Photographs," *Yale Daily News* (Mar. 29, 1926), p. 2; "An Ellis Island for Yale," *Yale Daily News* (Mar. 30, 1926), p. 2.

59. Eugene V. Rostow, "The Jew's Position," *Harkness Hoot* 2 (Nov. 23, 1931): 51–52.

60. James L. Leeper, Jr., to [Theodore S. Watson], [May, 1927], Folder 1852, Box 301, Series III, Records of the Treasurer, YRG 5-B, YMAL.

61. [Thomas Wells Farnam] to Theodore S. Watson, May 19, 1927, Folder 1852, Box 301, Series III, Records of the Treasurer, YRG 5-B, YMAL.

62. The influence of Jews in New Haven politics of this era was not entirely coincidental. According to one account, the only U.S. cities that ranked higher than New Haven in the proportion of Jews among their populace were New York and Atlantic City. Samuel Koening, *Immigrant Settlements in Connecticut: Their Growth and Characteristics* (Hartford: Connecticut State Department of Education, 1938), p. 32; Robert Corwin to Francis Parsons, Oct. 1, 1929, "Board of Admissions" folder, "Admissions" box, JRA.

63. *Minutes of the Yale Corporation,* Oct. 12, 1929, Film 49, Reel 8.

64. Wilbur Cross to Henry Graves, Jan. 20, 1927, in *Report of the Committee on Educational Policy,* Yale Corporation Minutes, Secretary's Cleaning Vault No. 23, pp. 170f–70g. Also see the correspondence between James R. Angell and his deans from December 1924, Folder 1324, Box 127, JRA and James R. Angell to Ray Lyman Wilbur, June 30, 1927, Folder 1870, Box 175, JRA.

65. Robert Corwin to James R. Angell, Apr. 28, 1932, Folder 20, Box 2, JRA.

66. Charles Warren to James R. Angell, Apr. 29, 1932, Folder 20, Box 2, JRA.

67. James R. Angell to Robert Corwin, Apr. 29, 1932, Folder 20, Box 2, JRA.

68. Robert Corwin to Members of the Board of Admissions, May 20, 1932, Folder 20, Box 2, JRA.

69. Robert Corwin to James R. Angell, July 26, 1932, "Board of Admissions" folder, "Admissions" box, JRA.

70. Alan Valentine to James R. Angell, Jan. 9, 1934, "Board of Admissions" folder, Box 1, JRA.

71. Pierson, *University College,* pp. 175, 181.

72. Kelley, pp. 385, 392.

73. James R. Angell to N. H. Batchelder, May 1, 1930, Folder 2119, Box 194, JRA. Thomas Winternitz kindly permitted me to identify his name in the context of this quotation.

74. James R. Angell to Percy Walden, Jan. 2, 1936, "Board of Admissions" folder, "Admissions" box, JRA.

75. James R. Angell to Conrad Hoffmann, Jr., Dec. 7, 1933, "Jewish Problem" folder, Box 91, JRA.

76. James R. Angell to Alan Valentine, Mar. 9, 1934, "Board of Admissions" folder 10, Box 1, JRA.

77. See "Alumni University Day 1934, 1935" folder, "Alumni" box, JRA; Robert N. Corwin to James R. Angell, Jan. 3, 1933, and accompanying table, Oct. 19, 1932, "Board of Admissions" folder, "Admissions" box, JRA.

78. Angell was not alone in enjoying this form of humor. Henri Peyre recalled that strong anti-Jewish feelings existed among the Yale faculty members of the early 1930s. When Peyre tried to discuss the prejudices he observed with his colleagues, he could find no one who seemed to care. Many anti-Jewish jokes, one of which was quite similar to Angell's Armenian reference, circulated among the faculty at this time. One such "joke," as Peyre remembered it, concerned the problem of too many Jews entering Yale College: "If there are Jews who want to go to college, let them go to Harvard. Let Hitler be Harvard's president. He'll take care of them." Henri Peyre, Interview, Oct. 26, 1982; James R. Angell to Robert Corwin, Jan. 6, 1933, "Board of Admissions" folder, "Admissions" box, JRA.

79. Karabel, *Theory and Society*, pp. 14–15, 17; Steinberg, *Commentary*, p. 73.

80. For details on age restrictions in undergraduate admissions, see George Wilson Pierson, *A Yale Book of Numbers* (New Haven: Yale University, 1983), pp. 106, 116. Jerome Karabel persuasively argued that institutions such as Yale were "so tied . . . to the outlook and interests of the Protestant upper class that they readily volunteered for service on behalf of its interests and eagerly embraced its fundamental goals." In my opinion, the fact that Yale (and others) felt compelled to cloak their actions in semantics and silence suggests that they were not completely at ease in embracing racism to the extent that was occurring in the most exclusive of Protestant upper class circles. At Yale, the deliberation that preceded the implementation of the "Limitation" is less evidence of eagerness than of an administration wrestling with itself over its fundamental goals. See Karabel, *Theory and Society*, p. 29.

CHAPTER FOUR: MIXED MESSAGES

A penetrating analysis of the evolution of tensions between American society and Jews is Lewis S. Gannett, "Is America Anti-Semitic?," *The Nation* (Mar. 21, 1923). The landmark work by Heywood Broun and George Britt, *Christians Only* (1931), explicitly details the breadth and depth of anti-Jewish feeling in America during the 1920s. A much later expansion of this theme is E. Digby Baltzell, *The Protestant Establishment* (1964). A fascinating refutation of the concept of Jewish self-segregation, strikingly revealing of how defensive the Jewish position on campus was, is "Who's Who in the Colleges," *The American Hebrew* (Dec. 1, 1922).

A popular account of national collegiate life between the World Wars, both well-researched and easy reading, is Calvin B. T. Lee, *The Campus Scene: 1900–1970* (1970). The outstanding written portrait of collegiate life at Yale in this era is George Wilson Pierson, *Yale: The University College 1921–1937* (1955). Two chapters in Diana Dubois, *My Harvard, My Yale* (1982), merit special attention: "My Native Country" by Thomas Bergin and "A Touch of Laughter" by Paul Moore, Jr. The former is a sensitive, though perhaps understated, account of the alienation that some Yale students felt, told by an "underprivileged" undergraduate who became a Sterling professor at Yale. The latter is also a sympathetic account of Yale, presented by a successful undergraduate who became a successor fellow of the Yale Corporation. The John Leggett novel, *Who Took the Gold Away* (1969), in no wise comparable in scope or purpose to the classic *Stover at Yale*, provides clear views of a few stereotypical Yale undergraduates of the late 1930s. The status of Yale Jews is touched upon tangentially when Leggett's hero, Pierce Jay, displays an ability, on occasion, to be anti-Jewish and simultaneously to claim, in full honesty, that some of his friends were Jews. Marcia Graham Synnott, *The Half-Opened Door* (1979), provides invaluable aid for any study of discrimination at Yale in this era. John Whitehead's brief, unpublished essay, "The Jewish Fraternity at Yale College" assisted my study of that episode in Yale history. A detailed, nonjudgmental account of the senior societies appears in Loomis Havemeyer, " *Go to Your Room*" (1960).

1. Higham, *Strangers,* p. 196; Handlin, *Uprooted,* p. 279.
2. Solomon, p. 201; Robert A. Divine, *American Immigration Policy, 1924–1952* (New Haven: Yale University Press, 1957), pp. 11–13; Laura Fermi, *Illustrious Immigrants* (Chicago: University of Chicago Press, 1971), pp. 22–23; Baltzell, *Protestant,* p. 37; Higham, *Strangers,* p. 184; Herbert F. Janick, Jr., *A Diverse People,* Series in Connecticut History, ed. by David M. Roth (Chester, Conn.: The Pequot Press, 1975), pp. 2, 34.
3. Ettinger, pp. 980, 982; Robert Singerman, "The American Career of the *Protocols of the Elders of Zion,*" *American Jewish History* 71 (Sep. 1981): 45–78; Janick, *Diverse,* pp. 35–36.
4. Lewis S. Gannett, "Is America Anti-Semitic?" *The Nation* 116 (Mar. 21, 1923): 330.
5. Ibid., pp. 330–31.
6. John Leggett, *Who Took the Gold Away* (New York: Random House, 1969), pp. 3–4; Fred Hirschhorn, Jr., Interview, Dec. 19, 1982; Max Lerner, Interview, Dec. 28, 1982; Louis Weinstein, Interview, June 4, 1981.
7. Charles Feidelson, Interview, Oct. 24, 1978; Pierson, *University College,* pp. 107–08, 222; Thomas Bergin, "My Native Country," in *My Harvard, My Yale,* ed. by Diana Dubois (New York: Random House, 1982), p. 162; J. Richardson Dilworth, Interview, Feb. 24, 1983; William Horowitz, Interview, Nov. 19, 1982; Harold Feldman, Interview, 1978; John M. Schiff, Interview, Feb. 1, 1983; John S. Ellsworth, Interview, Dec. 6, 1983.
8. "Yale Property Holdings Set at Thirty Millions," *Yale Daily News* (Jan. 1, 1926), p. 1.
9. Maynard Mack, Interview, Dec. 7, 1982; quotation from Pierson, *University College,* p. 72.
10. Sydney Bruskin, Interview, Dec. 16, 1982; Vernon Lippard, Interview, Dec. 2, 1982; Thomas Bergin, Interview, Jan. 25, 1983; Hirschhorn, Interview; Leon Harris, *Merchant Princes,* pp. 81–82; *1920 Yale College Classbook,* pp. 188–89.
11. Baltzell, *Protestant,* p. 210.
12. Bruskin, Interview; *Minutes of the Committee on Educational Policy of the Yale Corporation,* Apr. 27, 1932, p. 327d, YRG 4-A-15, YMAL.

13. Lerner, Interview.

14. Bruskin, Interview.

15. Lerner, Interview.

16. Alderman, Interview; Holden, *Pictorial,* pp. 73–75; Lerner, Interview; Langrock, Interview.

17. Holden, *Pictorial,* pp. 135, 138. See [Robert N. Corwin], "Memorandum of the Problems Arising from the Increase in the Enrollment of Students of Jewish Birth in the University," May 12, 1922, "Jewish Problem" folder, Box 91, JRA; Bruskin, Interview; Jacob Cooperman, Interview, Oct. 21, 1978; Maurice Fleischman, Interview, Apr. 7, 1983; Morris Sweetkind, Interview, Oct. 14, 1982; Loomis Havemeyer, *Sheff Days and Ways* (New Haven: Yale University, 1958), p. 13.

18. Power, pp. 7, 62, 198, 373; Wechsler, p. 134; Steinberg, *Melting Pot,* pp. 33–55; Richard Hofstadter, *Anti-intellectualism in American Life* (New York: Alfred A. Knopf, Inc., 1966), pp. 136–41. For a treatment of Catholic anti-intellectualism as a myth of sorts, see Stephen Steinberg, *The Ethnic Myth* (New York: Atheneum, 1981), pp. 138–50.

19. The Yale College class of 1904, for example, was 2.8 percent Jewish and 6.1 percent Catholic at a time when Jews represented less than 2 percent and Catholics about 12 percent of the United States population. In 1934–35 the freshman class was 8.7 percent Jewish and 13 percent Catholic at a time when Jews represented close to 4 percent and Catholics about 16 percent of the United States population. Reynolds, Fisher, and Wright, appendix D(1); *The World Almanac and Encyclopedia 1904* (New York: The Press Publishing Co., 1904), pp. 177, 328; *The World Almanac and Book of Facts for 1934* (New York: The New York World Telegram, 1934), p. 389; Gannett, p. 331; Untitled page with figures, Folder 1195, Box 240, OS.

20. Oscar Handlin and Mary F. Handlin, *The American College and American Culture* (Berkeley, Cal.: The Carnegie Commission on Higher Education, 1970), p. 66.

21. In 1927 there were no identified Catholics in Bones or Keys, one in Wolf's Head, and two in Elihu. In the fraternities that year the division was ADP–2, DKE–1, ZPsi–2, PsiU–0, BTP–2, ASP–5, and ChiPsi–2. Synnott, *Door,* pp. 130–32; Handlin and Handlin, *College and Culture,* p. 66.

22. Riggs was the first chaplain to Catholic students at Yale. Alegi, pp. 31, 40, 75a, 86; Lippard, Interview; Mack, Interview.

23. Herbert Janick, "Catholicism and Culture: The American Experience of Thomas Lawrason Riggs, 1888–1943," *The Catholic Historical Review* 68 (July 1982): 451–68; Synnott, *Door,* p. 131; Bergin, Interview; Henri Peyre to author, Dec. 16, 1983.

24. Robert A. Warner noted that for many years, "in the Negro community, Yale employment carried an aura of prestige." Student waiters and white maids began to substitute for blacks around 1923. Robert Austin Warner, *New Haven Negroes: A Social History* (New Haven: Yale University Press, 1940), pp. 176, 185, 246–47, 254; Ballard, p. 53; James R. Angell to A. B. Crawford, May 3, 1926, "Bureau of Appointments" folder, Box 11, JRA.

25. Amherst graduate Harold Wade, Jr., suggested that one explanation for the relative success of his alma mater in producing successful black alumni lay within the exclusive, white social atmosphere of Yale. Harold Wade, Jr., *Black Men of Amherst* (Amherst, Mass.: Amherst College Press, 1976), pp. 95–97; Synnott, *Door,* pp. 133–35.

26. Mack, Interview.

27. Richard D. Kuslan, "Education of a Noted Reformer," *Yale Alumni Magazine and Journal* 47 (Oct. 1983), pp. 52–53; Kate Sandweiss, "Not Just a Matter of Luck," *Yale Alumni Magazine and Journal* 47 (Oct. 1983): 57. For a record of the 626 Chinese nationals known to have been students or faculty at Yale between 1854 and 1953, see "China Institute of America," compiled by Nelson I. Wu, 1954, YMAL.

28. Sixty-six institutions were surveyed. The eighteen with "pronounced" anti-Jewish feeling were Adelphi, Armour Institute, Case School of Applied Sciences, Cincinnati, Columbia, Cornell, Johns Hopkins, Illinois, Kansas, McGill, Minnesota, Northwestern, Ohio State, Penn State, Texas, Virginia, Washington, and Yale. Princeton, not in the survey, likely belonged with the above group. Harvard was ranked as having "moderate" anti-Jewish feeling. Broun and Britt, pp. 89–92.

29. Sidney Lovett also observed these phenomena. He recalled having urged Jewish students to take pride in their surnames. Bergin, Interview; Sidney Lovett, Interview, Oct. 19, 1978; Irving Krall, Interview, June 15, 1983; Alexander Lowenthal to author, July 12, 1983; Philip Sapir, Interview, 1978.

30. Higham, *Send,* pp. 153–54.

31. Hirschhorn, Interview; Richard C. Carroll, Interview, Apr. 30, 1981.

32. The Mory's Association roster for 1928 lists several Jews as members. *The Mory's Association, Inc.* (New Haven, 1928), p. 8; Irving Drabkin, Interview, Mar. 6, 1983; Krall, Interview; Lerner, Interview; Sweetkind, Interview.

33. Bergin, Interview; Dilworth, Interview.

34. Norman Hapgood had reported in 1916 "of a Jew, who though leading the competition, was cut off from a college periodical because of his race." Hapgood, *Harper's Weekly,* p. 53; Carlos French Stoddard, Jr., Interview, Nov. 5, 1982.

35. Arthur Saltzstein, Interview, Mar. 23, 1980; Drabkin, Interview.

36. Ellmann had a stunning graduate and postgraduate career. In 1947 he received a Yale Ph.D. and the John Addison Porter Prize for the outstanding work by a Yale student. He became a Yale professor of English in 1968. *The Elizabethan Club of Yale University* (1921); *Historical Register of Yale University, 1951–1968* (New Haven: Yale University, 1969), pp. 80, 98; Pierson, *University College,* pp. 310–11, 359; *1928 Yale College Classbook,* pp. 236–37; *1930 Yale College Classbook,* p. 448; Feidelson, Interview; Rollin Osterweis, Interview, May 12, 1980; Winestine, Interview, Apr. 21, 1981.

37. Fleischman, Interview; Samuel D. Kushlan, Interview, Mar. 18, 1983.

38. See Steinberg, *Melting Pot,* p. 19, for a fine discussion on stereotypes. Richard C. Cabot, *Social Service and the Art of Healing* (New York: Dodd, Mead & Co., 1931), pp. 4–7.

39. Alderman, Interview.

40. Frederick S. Jones, "Report on Jews," [Fall, 1922?], Folder 71, Box 6, Series III, FSJ. See the page entitled, "Social Life."

41. Mary D. McLean, "Jews in Athletics," *The New Era* 5 (Aug. 1904): 273–78; Arthur A. Chiel, "Looking Back," *The Connecticut Jewish Ledger* (Mar. 30, 1972, June 8, 1972, Mar. 7, 1974).

42. The Atlas Club went out of existence in 1931, when other Jewish institutions took over training the local boys. Arthur A. Chiel, "Looking Back," *The Connecticut Jewish Ledger* (Nov. 14, 1972, Mar. 7, 1974).

43. For an account of how Weiner was first rejected by the Yale basketball coach, who later reversed his decision, see "Weiner, Joseph," *Encyclopedia of Jews in Sports* (1965 ed.), pp. 97–98. In 1915 Weiner was part of a team that led the Intercollegiate League of Yale, Cornell, Columbia, Princeton, Pennsylvania, and Dartmouth with an 8–2 record. *Yale Banner and Pot-Pourri for 1914–1915, Vol. 7*, p. 259.

44. Quotation from Elias Lieberman, "Yale Athletics and Jewish Athletes," *The American Hebrew* III (June 30, 1922): 174; "Upheaval in Yale Sports Reaches Head," *Chicago Daily Tribune* (June 17, 1922), p. 9.

45. "Exposé of Yale's System of Athletics Proves Only Subject of Great Ridicule," *The New Haven Evening Register* (June 17, 1922), p. 1.

46. James R. Angell, quoted in Lieberman, *The American Hebrew*, p. 178.

47. Joseph Fogarty, quoted by Stanley Garvey in "Joseph and His Brethren," *The [New Haven] Evening Register* (Mar. 11, 1923), p. 3.

48. Garvey, *The [New Haven] Evening Register*, p. 3.

49. James R. Angell to John Cooper, Mar. 17, 1923, "Athletics General" folder, Box 17, JRA.

50. Reznikoff, *Commentary*, p. 477; Max Glick, Interview, Aug. 27, 1984; Krall, Interview.

51. Reznikoff, *Commentary*, p. 477.

52. Broun and Britt, p. 66; Krall, Interview; Mack, Interview.

53. Pierson, *University College*, p. 210; Lippard, Interview.

54. Leggett, p. 118.

55. Lowenthal to author.

56. See the articles from *The New Haven Evening Register* and *Yale Daily News* from Dec. 15, 1921, in *Scrapbooks of the Zunder Family, Volume 3*, JHSNH. Bryson Thompson to Frederick S. Jones, Apr. 6, 1933, "Fraternities" folder, Box 4, Series II, FSJ; Krall, Interview; Kushlan, Interview.

57. Kingman Brewster, Jr., Interview, May 5, 1981.

58. Hapgood, *Harper's Weekly*, p. 54; Steinberg, *Melting Pot*, p. 17; John Whitehead, "The Jewish Fraternity at Yale College," [1976], an unpublished manuscript kindly shared with the author by Mr. Whitehead; Brewster, Interview; Carroll, Interview; Lippard, Interview; Mack, Interview; Rollin Osterweis, Interview, Dec. 12, 1976.

59. Jospe, p. 135; Zeta Beta Tau Fraternity, Inc., *A Manual for Zeta Beta Tau* (1927), pp. 9, 14–15, 117–18; "Fraternity and Sorority," *Encyclopaedia Britannica* (1973 ed.), vol. 9, p. 816; "Fraternities, Jewish," *Universal Jewish Encyclopedia* (1969 ed.), vol. 4, p. 423; Goren, Arthur A., "Jews" in *Harvard Encyclopedia of American Ethnic Groups*, ed. by Stephan Thernstrom (Cambridge, Mass.: Harvard University Press, 1980), pp. 571–98.

60. "Minutes of the Committee on the Protection of the Yale Name," Dec. 14, 1916, Folder 98, Box 61, Series VI, Acc. 1978 Jul., YRG 4-A-15, OS.

61. "Minutes of the Committee on the Protection of the Yale Name," Oct. 22, 1917, Folder 98, Box 61, Series VI, Acc. 1978 Jul., YRG 4-A-15, OS.

62. Tau Epsilon Phi was founded as a nonsectarian society, but attracted only Jewish members during its Yale years. Alpha Mu Sigma was founded at Yale as a predominantly law school fraternity, but by 1930 it was dominated by undergraduates. Three of Yale's varsity basketball team members that year were Alpha Mu Sigma members, including team captain Eddie Horwitz (B.A. 1931). For a record of a somewhat parallel set of events at Syra-

cuse University, see Harvey Strum, "Louis Marshall and Anti-Semitism at Syracuse University," *American Jewish Archives* 35 (Apr. 1983): 7; "Iota," *The Mirror* 1 (Dec. 25, 1922): 7; "Iota, Yale University," *The Shield* 1 (Oct. 1930): 14–15; "Jewish Fraternities and Sororities," *The Jewish Tribune* (June 5, 1925), pp. 6–7, 16; *Zeta Beta Tau, The First Twenty-Five Years,* ed. by Clarence Weil (New York: Zeta Beta Tau, 1923), pp. 124–26; *Baird's Manual of American College Fraternities,* ed. by John Robson (Menasha, Wis.: George Banta Co., 1963), p. 216; Mason, pp. 26–29; "Minutes of the Committee on the Protection of the Yale Name," Jan. 23, 1920, Folder 98, Box 61, Series VI, Acc. 1978 Jul., YRG 4-A-15, OS; "Report to the University Council by Special Committee Appointed to Investigate Position of Pi Lambda Phi Fraternity for Official Recognition by the University Authorities," Apr. 12, 1923, "Fraternities" folder, Box 4, Series II, FSJ; Frederick S. Jones to F. M. Adler, Oct. 22, 1923, "Fraternities" folder, Box 4, Series II, FSJ; "Report of the Committee on University Fraternities," [1923?], "Fraternities" folder, Box 4, Series II, FSJ; Lowenthal to author.

63. Max Lerner, who was not a legacy, waited until his senior year to join Phi Alpha after giving up on finding a space in one of the Christian fraternities. Rappaport later changed his name to Barry Wood and achieved prominence as a producer for NBC. Whitehead, "The Jewish Fraternity at Yale College"; Milton Baker, Interview, Jan. 17, 1982; Feidelson, Interview; Feldman, Interview; Lerner, Interview; Osterweis Interviews, Dec. 12, 1976, May 12, 1980; Rollin Osterweis, Interview, Jan. 4, 1982; Theodor Rittenberg, Interview, Sep. 18, 1979.

64. Synnott has recorded that Schiff had considered joining the Zeta Beta Tau chapter at Yale, though his father Mortimer L. Schiff had hoped he would join his own fraternity of Beta Theta Pi. (The father had attended Amherst College.) If Synnott's account is correct, it does not jibe with Schiff's own recollections in 1983. Baer, p. 41; *1925 Yale College Classbook,* pp. 280–81; Feidelson, Interview; Schiff, Interview.

65. *1942 Yale College Classbook,* pp. 69, 461; Hirschhorn, Interview.

66. Loomis Havemeyer, *"Go to Your Room"* ([New Haven?]: Yale University, 1960), pp. 66–67, 71; Pierson, *University College,* p. 4; Brewster, Interview.

67. In his mention of the secret societies, Jones reported that one Jew had been a member of the Elihu Club. On reviewing the detailed charts of Yale Jews that Jones had compiled, I was unable to find "Elihu Club" listed in the "Societies" column for any individual student. Next to the name of Louis Weiss (B.A. 1915), however, Jones had recorded "Eliz. Club" in script handwriting under the "Societies" column. My suspicion is that in noting the one "exception" to the absence of Jews from the societies, Jones misread Weiss's membership in the Elizabethan Club and, instead, read Elihu Club. Frederick S. Jones, "Report on Jews," [Fall, 1922?], Folder 71, Box 6, Series III, FSJ.

68. See the *1929 Yale College Classbook,* for example, regarding society memberships. Bergin, p. 162; Giamatti, *Scroll and Key,* pp. 15, 55.

69. Hessberg was not the first Yale Jew on the university football team, though he was the first Jewish "star" on the squad. Rollin Osterweis, "Who was Yale's first Jewish Football Star?" an unpublished manuscript, JNSNH; Reznikoff, p. 477; Dilworth, Interview; Albert Hessberg II, Interview, Feb. 25, 1980; Hirschhorn, Interview.

70. Pierson, *University College,* pp. 609–10; Rostow, *Harkness Hoot,* p. 45; Mack, Interview; Eugene V. Rostow, Interview, Nov. 14, 1978.

71. Pierson, *University College*, pp. 56–60, 139, 151, 261–62.

72. Max Lerner reported that he worked on the *Pest* as its second editor, though he did not meet Rothko until years after both had left Yale. In 1969 Yale would award Rothko with an honorary degree of Doctor of Fine Arts. Handlin and Handlin, *College and Culture*, p. 67; Pierson, *University College*, p. 140; Lee Seldes, *The Legacy of Mark Rothko* (New York: Holt, Rinehart & Winston, 1978), pp. 12–14, 91; *The Yale Saturday Evening Pest* 1 (Feb. 17, 1923): 1; Lerner, Interview.

73. Pierson, *University College*, pp. 286–314.

74. Ibid., pp. 138, 215.

75. Ibid., pp. 248, 418; the percentages were derived from the table "Percentage of Undergraduates Housed in University Dormitories, 1920–21 to 1946–47," kindly supplied to me by George Pierson. Also see *Committee on Educational Policy of the Yale Corporation, Minutes of,* Apr. 27, 1932, pp. 327d–327h.

76. Pierson, *University College*, pp. 420–21; Thomas G. Bergin, *Yale's Residential Colleges: The First Fifty Years* (New Haven: Yale University, 1983), pp. 32–34; *Committee on Educational Policy of the Yale Corporation, Minutes of,* June 8, 1932, p. 327a and Apr. 7, 1933, p. 356; Memo of George Vaill, April 1960, Folder 215, Box 24, AWG; George D. Vaill, Interview, Dec. 13, 1976.

77. Of the 154 "neophytes" in the fraternities that year, none had an average greater than 90 and thirty were on general academic warning. Havemeyer, *"Go to Your Room,"* p. 28; Clarence Mendell to Chairman of Interfraternity Council, Nov. 28, 1928, "Yale College" folder, Box 38, JRA.

78. Dates of dissolution of the Jewish fraternities were: Phi Alpha–1925, Tau Epsilon Phi–1929, Alpha Mu Sigma–ca. 1933, Pi Lambda Phi–1932, Zeta Beta Tau–1933, and Sigma Alpha Mu–1934. That three of these fraternities closed their doors prior to the opening of the colleges indicates the underlying weakness of their support. *Baird's Manual,* p. 216; Pierson, *University College*, pp. 134, 311–13; Havemeyer, *"Go to Your Room,"* p. 24; Glick, Interview.

79. Gannett, p. 332.

80. Handlin, *Race*, p. 177.

81. Rostow, Interview, Nov. 14, 1978.

82. Bergin, *My Yale*, p. 163.

83. Ellsworth, Interview.

CHAPTER FIVE RELIGIOUS SPIRIT

Glimmers of understanding as to the student attitude toward religion in early twentieth-century Yale may be obtained from George Wilson Pierson's two-volume history of Yale from 1871 through 1937. *Uncle Sid of Yale*, ed. by William A. Wiedersheim (1981) less a work of history than a labor of love, is a collection of essays that recaptures, to the extent that words can do so, the spirit of Sidney Lovett. The early years of Yale's religiously oriented Jewish clubs and societies may be traced through the pages of *The Menorah Movement* (1914) and the early volumes of *The Menorah Journal*. Deborah Dash Moore, *B'nai B'rith and the Challenge of Ethnic Leadership* (1981), is a lucid and penetrating history of the Jewish fraternal order. Moore devotes a number of pages to the early years of the B'nai B'rith Hillel Foundations.

1. Kelley, pp. 145, 211.
2. Pierson, *Yale College,* pp. 85, 97; Pierson, *University College,* p. 76; *Historical Register 1701–1937,* pp. 25, 37; Arthur Hadley to H. S. Pritchett, May 5, 1906, Box 109, p. 700, ATH; *Yale Corporation, Minutes of the Meetings of,* Apr. 23, 1906.
3. *Yale Corporation, Minutes of the Meetings of,* Jan. 20, 1919.
4. J. P. G., *The American Israelite* 28 (Jan. 6, 1882): 221.
5. For an example of the strict requirements governing absence from courses, see *Minutes of the Yale College Freshman Governing Board, 1920–1953,* Sep. 21, 1920, p. 15, YRG 12-C, YMAL; Sachs, Interview, Oct. 5, 1978.
6. Pierson, *Yale College,* pp. 155, 157.
7. Sachs, Interview, Oct. 5, 1978; Alderman, Interview.
8. Robert A. Taft biographer James T. Patterson suggested that Taft's Judeophilia was largely based upon his associations with Rabbi Abba Hillel Silver of Cleveland. That Taft was a member of the Hebraic Club at Yale indicates that his Jewish interests went back at least to his collegiate days. James T. Patterson, *Mr. Republican: A biography of Robert A. Taft* (Boston: Houghton Mifflin Co., 1972), pp. 280–82. Descriptions of the activities of members of the Hebraic Club were obtained by cross-checking their names from the membership roster with their autobiographical sketches in their classbooks. Many members on the Hebraic Club roster did not list the club as an activity in their classbooks. A philosophical predecessor to the Yale Hebraic Club was the Yale Divinity School Hebrew Club. In existence as early as 1881, the club co-sponsored a banquet with the university's Semitic Club in 1891. The banquet program listed fifty-six members between the two clubs; no apparently Jewish names were listed. There is no evidence of there having been any formal linkage between the Hebrew Club and the Hebraic Club. Both the 1891 banquet program and a minor 1881 publication of the Hebrew Club are available through the Yale archives. "Constitution and List of Members, Yale Hebraic Club," ca. Fall, 1907, YMAL; Eugene H. Lehman to Arthur T. Hadley, Oct. 19, 1908, Folder 1029, Box 53, Series I, ATH; *The Menorah Movement* (Ann Arbor, Mich.: The Intercollegiate Menorah Association, 1914), pp. 136–37; Elliot E. Cohen to A. Whitney Griswold, Oct. 31, 1951, Folder 1025, Box 132, AWG.
9. Baer, p. 131; *1908 Yale College Classbook,* p. 289; *1913 Yale College Classbook,* p. 212; Winestine, Interview, Apr. 21, 1981.
10. Winestine, Interviews, Apr. 21, 1981, May 20, 1981; *The Menorah Movement,* p. 136; "Dr. Magnes in New Haven," *The American Hebrew* 91 (June 7, 1912): 168.
11. Henry Hurwitz, "The Menorah Movement," *The Menorah Journal* 1 (Jan. 1915): 55.
12. Steven W. Siegel, *Archival Resources,* Jewish Immigrants of the Nazi Period in the USA Series, ed. by Herbert A. Strauss (New York: K. G. Saur, 1978), p. 61; Deborah Dash Moore, *B'nai B'rith and the Challenge of Ethnic Leadership* (Albany: State University of New York Press, 1981), p. 137; Jospe, p. 135.
13. Arthur T. Hadley, "Before the Yale Menorah Society, October 14, 1914," *The Menorah Journal* 1 (Jan. 1915): 45–46; "University Menorah Addresses," *The Menorah Journal* 1

(Dec. 1915): 321; *The Menorah Movement*, p. 137; Winestine, Interviews, April 21, 1981, May 20, 1981.

14. *The Menorah Movement*, p. 136; Winestine, Interview, April 21, 1981.

15. In the wake of the national "Newman Movement," the Yale Catholic Club was orga-nized about 1916 by English instructor Courtland Van Winkle. Alegi, pp. 27, 64. See Folder 5, Box 27, Henry Hurwitz Menorah Association Memorial Collection, AJA. *The Menorah Movement*, pp. 136–37; R. Horchow, "Yale University," *The Menorah Journal* 1 (Jan. 1915): 69; *The Yale Banner and Pot-Pourri 1914–1915*, p. 414; "First Meetings," *The Menorah Journal* 2 (Dec. 1916): 325; Sachs, Interview, Oct. 5, 1978.

16. Benjamin Levinson, "Yale University," *The Menorah Journal* 3 (Feb. 1917): 59–60, *1917 Yale College Classbook*, p. 224.

17. *1918 Yale College Classbook*, pp. 105–06; *History of the Class of 1918, Volume 2*, p. 65; Alan Wald, "The Menorah Group Moves Left," *Jewish Social Studies* 37 (Summer–Fall 1976): 289–320; "Menorah Prize Competitions," *The Menorah Journal* 2 (Dec. 1916): 323; Elliot E. Cohen, "The Promise of the American Synagogue," *The Menorah Journal* 4 (Oct. 1918 and Dec. 1918): 278–286, 368–374; Winestine, Interviews, Apr. 21, 1981, May 20, 1981.

18. "University Menorah Addresses," *The Menorah Journal* 1 (Dec. 1915): 321.

19. Jenna Weissman Joselit, "Without Ghettoism: A History of the Intercollegiate Menorah Association 1906–1930," *American Jewish Archives* 30 (Nov. 1978): 147–51; Lowenthal to author; Winestine, Interviews, Apr. 21, 1981, May 20, 1981.

20. *Minutes of the Committee on the Protection of the Yale Name*, Dec. 2, 1919, Folder 98, Box 61, Series VI, Acc. 1978, Jul., YRG 4-A-15, OS.

21. Kelley, pp. 209–10; Roth and Meyer, pp. 49–50, 68.

22. Hapgood, p. 54; Pierson, *University College*, p. 84; Alderman, Interview; Lerner, Inter-view; Sachs, Interview, Oct. 5, 1978; Elmore McKee to author, July 20, 1980.

23. Stoddard, Interview.

24. Charles Smith to Frederick S. Jones, Mar. 25, 1925, Folder 91, Box 8, FSJ. In a response to the complaint (which may be found in the same folder), Jones admitted that there were problems with student behavior in chapel but thought the correspondent's description to be an exaggeration.

25. The *Yale Daily News* for October and November 1925 give evidence of the brilliance and the fair-minded approach of the *News* board of that year in handling the chapel issue. Kelley, p. 387; Pierson, *University College*, pp. 84–93; Yale University News Statement, Mar. 11, 1926, "Chapel (Sunday)" folder, "Chapel" box, JRA; *Minutes of the Yale College Freshman Faculty, 1923–1950*, Apr. 9, 1926, p. 13, YRG 12-C, YMAL.

26. Paul Moore, Jr., p. 202; *Committee on Educational Policy of the Yale Corporation, Minutes of*, Dec. 13, 1935, p. 435; Hirschhorn, Interview; Charlotte Horton, Interview, Dec. 3, 1982.

27. Quotation about Lovett and Yale, by A. Bartlett Giamatti, in *Uncle Sid of Yale*, ed. by William A. Wiedersheim (New Haven: Yale Alumni Fund, 1981); Rollin G. Osterweis, "Mishkan Israel—Since 1940," in *Jews in New Haven, Volume 3*, ed. by Barry E. Herman and Werner S. Hirsch (New Haven: Jewish Historical Society of New Haven, 1981), p. 98; Deborah Dash Moore, pp. 138, 142; Sidney Lovett to James R. Angell, Apr. 21, 1933, "Chapel" folder, "Chapel" box, JRA.

28. Sidney Lovett to James R. Angell, May 25, 1936, "Chapel" folder, Box 33, JRA.
29. James R. Angell to Sidney Lovett, May 28, 1936, "Chapel" folder, Box 33, JRA.
30. Isaac Rabinowitz, Interview, Nov. 18, 1979.
31. Edgar Siskin, Interview, Aug. 7, 1981.
32. Lovett, Interview; Maurice Zigmond, Interview, May 18, 1979.
33. Rabinowitz, Interview, Nov. 18, 1979; Horton, Interview.
34. Siskin, Interview; Zigmond, Interview, May 18, 1979.
35. *Proceedings of the Union of American Hebrew Congregations, Sixty-First Annual Report* (Union of American Hebrew Congregations, 1935), p. 85.
36. *Proceedings of the Union of American Hebrew Congregations, Sixty-Second Annual Report* (Union of American Hebrew Congregations, 1936), p. 92; Irving Goleman to James R. Angell, Nov. 21, 1934, "Jewish Problem" folder, Box 91, JRA; *1938 Yale College Classbook*, pp. 257, 412; Felix Zweig, Interview, Nov. 13, 1978.
37. Fay Goleman, Interview, Oct. 13, 1982.
38. Zigmond, Interview, May 18, 1979; Siskin, Interview.
39. Zigmond, Interview, May 18, 1979; Horton, Interview.
40. Siskin, Interview.
41. *Proceedings of the Union of American Hebrew Congregations, Sixty-Fourth Annual Report* (Union of American Hebrew Congregations, 1938), p. 102; *Proceedings of the Union of American Hebrew Congregations, Sixty-Third Annual Report* (Union of American Hebrew Congregations, 1937), p. 117; Abraham J. Karp, *To Give Life* (New York: Schocken Books, 1981), pp. 125–31; *1937 Yale College Classbook*, p. 470; *1938 Yale College Classbook*, pp. 264, 357–58; Stephen J. Whitfield, "From Publick Occurrences to Pseudo-Events: Journalists and Their Critics," *American Jewish History* 72 (Sep. 1982): 54; Edgar Siskin to author, Dec. 2, 1980; Sam Weintraub, Jr., Interview, Apr. 20, 1983; Arthur Berliss, Interview, Jan. 3, 2000.
42. Richard J. Israel, "Jews at Yale," an unpublished manuscript, revised 1980, kindly provided to the author by Rabbi Israel.
43. Maurice Zigmond, "1939–40 Annual Report of Counselor to Jewish Students," an unpublished manuscript, HFSH.
44. Joseph Gumbiner, Interview, Nov. 27, 1979.
45. Zigmond, "1939–40"; Alegi, p. 58.
46. Zigmond, "1939–40."
47. Maurice Zigmond, "The Jewish Office at Yale: Some Reminiscences," an unpublished manuscript written in 1962, HFSH; Jospe, pp. 139–40; Deborah Dash Moore, pp. 137–51.

CHAPTER SIX THE FACULTY

The primary documents on which most of this chapter was based are the decanal papers of Frederick S. Jones and the presidential papers of Arthur T. Hadley, James R. Angell, and Charles Seymour. All are contained in the Yale University Manuscripts and Archives Library. Relevant documents are scattered throughout the archival collection.

1. Pierson, *University College,* pp. 29, 268–69.

2. Ettinger, pp. 807–08.

3. Pierson, *University College,* p. 730; A. McGehee Harvey, *Science at the Bedside* (Baltimore: The Johns Hopkins University Press, 1981), pp. 33, 48.

4. Harvey, p. 48.

5. Early Jewish professors in America included Isaac Nordheimer (appointed in 1835 as professor of Arabic and Oriental languages at New York University), James J. Sylvester (appointed in 1841 as professor of mathematics at the University of Virginia and appointed in 1876 as professor at the Johns Hopkins University), Felix Adler (appointed in 1874 as professor of Hebrew and Oriental literature at Cornell University and appointed in 1902 as professor of social ethics at Columbia University), Edwin Seligman (appointed in 1888 as professor of political economy and finance at Columbia University), Morris Loeb (appointed in 1891 as professor of chemistry at New York University), and Charles Gross (appointed in 1901 as professor of history at Harvard University). Lewis S. Feuer, "The Stages in the Social History of Jewish Professors in American Colleges and Universities," *American Jewish History* 71 (June 1982): 432–42; Harvey, p. 48; "Dr. Mendel Dies; Nutrition Expert," *The New York Times* (Dec. 10, 1935), p. 25; Russell H. Chittenden, *Biographical Memoir of Lafayette B. Mendel* (Washington, D.C.: National Academy of Sciences, 1937); *Yale University Obituary Record of 1935* (New Haven: Yale University, 1936), pp. 50–53; *Historical Register 1701–1937,* p. 387; *1891 Yale College Classbook,* pp. 33, 100; Harry Zimmerman, Interview, June 2, 1981.

6. Siskin, Interview; Siskin to author, Dec. 2, 1980; Regina Bear, Interview, Nov. 10, 1980; Arthur Ross, Interview, Nov. 19, 1980; Alfred Gilman, Interview, Dec. 17, 1980.

7. Ettinger, p. 845; Bear, Interview.

8. Siskin to author, Dec. 2, 1980; Edgar Siskin to author, Feb. 18, 1983.

9. Synnott, *Door,* p. 129.

10. Arthur T. Hadley to Otto T. Bannard, Apr. 19, 1918, Book 32, p. 729, ATH; Arthur T. Hadley to George Parmly Day, Apr. 24, 1918, Book 32, p. 748, ATH.

11. Synnott suggests that Mendel's presence may have been merely a matter of administrative expediency. My impression is that if Mendel's appointment to the library committee was the product of considerable thought on Hadley's part, how much more so would an appointment to the important board of admissions have been carefully thought out. Synnott, *Door,* p. 129.

12. Robert Corwin, "Report of the Chairman of the Board of Admissions," in *Reports to the President of Yale University, 1930–1931,* p. 5.

13. Mendel was known for the many women who were graduate students in his laboratory—at a time when few women were encouraged to pursue graduate work. Margaret W. Rossiter, *Women Scientists in America: Struggles and Strategies to 1940* (Baltimore: The Johns Hopkins University Press, 1982), pp. 37, 152–53, 184–85, 200. Robert Corwin to Francis Parsons, Oct. 1, 1929, "Board of Admissions" folder, "Admissions" box, JRA.

14. *Yale Alumni Weekly* 41 (Feb. 12, 1932), p. 381; "Dr. L. B. Mendel Succumbs at 63," *Yale Daily News* (Dec. 10, 1935), p. 1; "Rites for Dr. Mendel Will Be Held Today," *The New York Times* (Dec. 11, 1935), p. 24; Siskin to author, Dec. 2, 1980.

15. "University Menorah Addresses," *The Menorah Journal* 1 (Dec. 1915): 321.

16. The *American Jewish Year Book 1917–18*, p. 406, lists Yale and the University of Chicago as the two colleges in the nation in which Yiddish was taught. My reading of the Yale College course catalogue from that time fails to confirm that Yiddish was a regular course in the college. Perhaps instructor in Russian Max Mandell (1907–24) may have been supplementing his income with some Yiddish instruction on the side. *Twenty-Five Year History Class of 1902 Yale College*, pp. 329–33; Eugene H. Lehman to Arthur T. Hadley, June 11, 1908, Oct. 19, 1908, June 17, 1909, Jan. 22, 1910, and Arthur T. Hadley to Adolf Lewisohn, Mar. 10, 1910, all in Folder 1029, Box 53, Series I, ATH; Arthur T. Hadley to Eugene H. Lehman, June 12, 1908, Box 113, Series II, ATH; Arthur T. Hadley to Eugene H. Lehman, June 18, 1909, Box 114, Series II, ATH.

17. It is not apparent why Schiff would have turned Yale down. The year 1909 was well before the era in which Yale held a less than sterling image in some Jewish circles. Perhaps Lehman's status within Yale was not great enough to command Schiff's interest. Eugene H. Lehman to Arthur T. Hadley, July 20, 1909, Sep. 20, 1909, both in Folder 1029, Box 53, Series I, ATH; Arthur T. Hadley to Eugene H. Lehman, Aug. 6, 1909, Sep. 29, 1909, both in Box 114, Series II, ATH.

18. For Lehman's teaching record see the Yale College Course Catalogue for the 1910–13 school years. *Twenty-Five Year History Class of 1902 Yale College*, pp. 329–33; *Historical Register 1701–1937*, p. 355; Eugene H. Lehman to Arthur T. Hadley, Feb. 14, 1910, Apr. 5, 1910, Dec. 2, 1913, Jan. 2, 1914, all in Folder 1029, Box 53, Series I, ATH; Arthur T. Hadley to Eugene H. Lehman, Feb. 4, 1910, Mar. 4, 1910, Box 115, Series II, ATH.

19. *Historical Register 1701–1937*, p. 552; *Yale University Obituary Record 1913–1914*, pp. 691–92; Gertrude Mandell, Interview, Nov. 12, 1982.

20. Frederick S. Jones to James R. Angell, Nov. 21, 1922, "Faculty" folder, Box 3, FSJ.

21. Frederick S. Jones to James R. Angell, Nov. 14, 1922, "Faculty" folder, Box 3, FSJ.

22. The new world realities created by the Second World War would stimulate interest in Sovietology at Yale. Assistant professor of Slavic languages George L. Trager (a Jew) taught Russian during the 1942–43 academic year. Alexander Vasiliev was appointed assistant in Russian in 1945. In 1946 William Cornyn (M.A. 1942, Ph.D. 1944) was appointed assistant professor of the Russian language. *Historical Register of Yale University 1937–1951* (New Haven: Yale University, 1952), p. 299; *Historical Register 1951–1968*, pp. 228, 744, 841; Frederick S. Jones to Max Mandell, Feb. 28, 1924, "Faculty" folder, Box 3, FSJ; Isidore Dyen, Interview, Oct. 25, 1983.

23. Melamed, *The Reflex*, p. 3.

24. There was a price for not considering personality as a factor, Henri Peyre argued: feuding among faculty. Peyre prided himself for many years at Yale as French department chairman by hiring faculty that he felt would be compatible and form a harmonious group. Some of his most outstanding appointees, he believed, were Jews. Peyre, Interview; Ballard, p. 44.

25. In his history of Yale Catholics, Alegi identified Albert G. Feuillerat (Sterling Professor of French 1929–43) as the first full professor in the college. In fact, Feuillerat was on the Yale Graduate School faculty, *not* the Yale College faculty. Alegi, p. 29; *Historical Register 1937–1951*, p. 149; Yale College Faculty Lists 1930–31, 1940–41, prepared by Katherine

Hauschild and shared with the author by George Pierson; Peyre to author; Jacob Cooperman, Interview.

26. From 1932 until 1937 Mitchell Levensohn (B.A. 1928, Ph.D. 1931), a Jew, was instructor in classics on the college faculty. Other early twentieth-century Jewish Yale teachers, otherwise unmentioned, included Isidore Troostwyk, instructor in violin from 1894 to 1923, his son Leo, instructor in violoncello during 1916–17, Julian J. Obermann, visiting professor of Semitic languages as of 1932, and Hortense Powdermaker, assistant professor of anthropology and sociology from 1934 through 1937. *1928 Yale College Classbook*, pp. 293–94. *Historical Register 1701–1937*, pp. 355, 378, 413, 516; Jacob R. Marcus, *The American Jewish Woman, 1654–1980* (Cincinnati: American Jewish Archives, 1981), pp. 173–74; Walter Camp and Lewis Sheldon Welch, *Yale: Her Campus, Class-Rooms, and Athletics* (Boston: L. C. Page & Company, 1899), pp. 286–87; Rostow, *Harkness Hoot*, p. 45. Faculty lists of Yale College were prepared by Katherine Hauschild and shared with the author by George Pierson. Siskin to author, Dec. 2, 1980.

27. Richard Sewall, professor emeritus of English, recalled a colleague telling a Jewish graduate student not to even consider teaching at Yale, since Jewish faculty were not wanted. Pierson, *University College*, p. 187; Pierson, *Numbers*, p. 285; Leonard Doob, Interview, Nov. 11, 1982; Bergin, Interview; Richard Sewall, Interview, Oct. 17, 1978; Sweetkind, Interview.

28. Harold Harrison (B.S. 1928, M.D. 1931) remembered that he had considered attending graduate school in chemistry. He then approached a young member of the chemistry faculty for advice. The professor told him that if he entered the Yale Graduate School, he would be an "embarrassment" to the chemistry department. His record was strong enough that Yale would have had to accept him, but he would be impossible to place in a job after he received his degree. Many chemical companies would not hire Jews, and Yale, the professor stated, would definitely bar him because of his Judaism. Harrison, therefore, chose to pursue medicine. Harold E. Harrison, Interview, Dec. 12, 1983; Lerner, Interview.

29. Sidney Hook, *Out of Step: An Unquiet Life in the Twentieth Century* (New York: Harper and Row, 1987), pp. 210–12; Feidelson, Interview.

30. Sweetkind, Interview.

31. George Pierson to Arthur Galston, Jan. 26, 1971. This letter was shared with the author by Arthur Galston, and is quoted from with the permission of George Pierson.

32. As an example of the cultural divide. Maynard Mack recalled, one "very able" Jewish graduate student in the department wrote a dissertation on the devil in medieval literature. The first draft of the student's dissertation, containing insights into Christianity that she had found exciting, was elementary to the Christian audience reading it. A later draft of the dissertation was accepted. Mack, Interview; Feidelson, Interview.

33. Sewall, Interview, Oct. 17, 1978.

34. Cohen's overall feelings about Yale were positive. In later years he became a good friend of Dean William Clyde DeVane of Yale College and often spoke before the B'nai B'rith Hillel Foundation at Yale. See *The Menorah Journal* 4 (Oct. 1918): 278. Elinor Grumet, "Elliot Cohen: The Vocation of a Literary Mentor," in *Studies in the American Jewish Experience*, ed. by Jacob R. Marcus and Abraham J. Peck (Cincinnati: American Jewish Archives, 1981), pp. 9, 11–12, 22, 24; Wald, *Jewish Social Studies*, pp. 289–320; Howe,

p. 412; *Forty Year History Class of 1918 Yale College,* p. 65; Thomas E. Cohen, Interview, Feb. 22, 1983.

35. Harold Stein (B.A. 1922, Ph.D. 1932), author of *Studies in Spenser's Complaints* (London: Oxford University Press, 1934), reportedly was not hired by the Yale English department because of his religion. Stein later attributed his failure to obtain a permanent university post in America to the Depression. For a vision of Zunder's life through newspaper clippings and the like, see the scrapbooks of the Zunder family, particularly volume 3, in the New Haven Jewish Historical Society Archives. Mary Griswold, Interview, Oct. 19, 1983; Sweetkind, Interview; *Fifteen Year History Class of 1932 Yale College,* pp. 196–97.

36. Hook, *Out of Step,* p. 211.

37. Feuer, *American Jewish History,* p. 450.

38. Whitfield, *American Jewish History,* pp. 66–67.

39. Filmer Northrop, Interview, Oct. 12, 1980.

40. Sewall, Interview, Oct. 17, 1978.

41. Morris R. Cohen to Felix Frankfurter, Feb. 4, 1936, quoted in Leonora Cohen Rosenfield, *Portrait of a Philosopher: Morris R. Cohen* (New York: Harcourt, Brace & World, Inc., 1962), p. 273.

42. Albert Einstein, in contrast, thought Princeton to be inhospitable toward Jews. In 1948 he wrote, "Die Universität Princeton ist übrigens besonders antisemitisch." As for Yale's attitudes and its stature, one may note that Yale's English department, then among the nation's most anti-Jewish, suffered no loss of national ranking as best. A 1982 study of American English professors by the National Academy of Sciences showed that the Yale English department, which then numbered several Jews among its faculty, still retained its preeminence. A copy of the Einstein letter was made available to me by Susan Schleger. Also see Jack Gourman, *The Gourman Report* (Los Angeles: National Education Standards, 1980), p. 25; Kelley, p. 416.

43. "Cassirer, Ernst," *Encyclopaedia Judaica* (1971 ed.), vol. 5, pp. 232–33; "Cohen, Gustave," *Encyclopaedia Judaica* (1972 ed.), vol. 5, p. 670; *American Jewish Biographies* (New York: Lakeville Press, 1982), p. 95; "Loewenstein, Karl," *Encyclopaedia Judaica* (1972 ed.), vol. 11, p. 451; Fermi, pp. 74–76; Peter Gay, "Weimar Culture," in *Perspectives in American History, Volume 2,* ed. by Donald Fleming and Bernard Bailyn (Cambridge, Mass.: Charles Warren Center for Studies in American History, 1968), p. 44; *Historical Register 1937–1951,* p. 115; Kelley, p. 396; Haim Genizi, "American Interfaith Cooperation on Behalf of Refugees from Nazism, 1933–1945," *American Jewish History* 70 (Mar. 1981): 352; Nathan Reingold, "Refugee Mathematicians in the United States of America, 1933–1941: Reception and Reaction," *Annals of Science* 38 (1981): 320; J. Kirk Sale, "The New School at Middle Age," *Change* 1 (Jul.–Aug. 1969): 37–38; Siegel, p. 6; James R. Angell to Chairmen of Departments, June 24, 1933, "James R. Angell (2)" folder, Box 1, 1910–20, YRG 27-A-5-9, YMAL; James R. Angell to Alexander Brin, Dec. 28, 1934, "Jewish Problem" folder, Box 91, JRA; "The Emergency Committee in Aid of Displaced German Scholars," 1934 report, p. 8, 1935 report, p. 9, 1936 report, p. 12, all in Folder 905, Box 90, JRA; Peyre, Interview; Peyre to author; Doris Wolfers, Interview, Dec. 15, 1982.

44. Melvin I. Urofsky, *A Voice that Spoke for Justice* (Albany: State University of New York Press, 1982), p. 234; Siegel, p. 211; Horowitz, Interview, Dec. 7, 1976.

45. "Jerome N(ew) Frank," *Current Biography, 1941* (New York: The H. H. Wilson Co., 1941), p. 301; Jerome Frank to Charles Clark, Mar. 12, 1931, and Charles Clark to Jerome Frank, Mar. 26, 1931, Folder 41, Box 2, Jerome Frank Papers, YMAL.

46. Max Lerner recalled that Dean Hutchins had invited him to become a junior law professor, although this offer was withdrawn when Hutchins left Yale to become president of the University of Chicago. Lerner, Interview; Abraham Goldstein, "A Law School Memoir," *Yale Alumni Magazine and Journal* 15 (Feb. 1977): 39; Broun and Britt, pp. 163–64; *Historical Register 1937–1951*, p. 153; Goren, p. 590; Eugene Rostow to Carl Lohmann, [ca. 1945], Folder 1194, Box 240, Series III, OS; Rostow, Interview.

47. Siskin to author, Dec. 2, 1980; Abraham S. Goldstein, Interview, Jan. 31, 1979; "Harry Shulman," *Yale Law Report* 1 (1955): 6–9.

48. See Arthur L. Corbin to Charles Seymour, Nov. 9, 1939, and accompanying letters, Folder 803, Box 93, CS; Record off Faculty vote, appended to Arthur L. Corbin to Charles Seymour, Jan. 11, 1940, Folder 803, Box 93, CS.

49. Baltzell, *Protestant*, pp. 247–48; Goren, p. 591; Dov Fisch, "The Libel Trial of Robert Edward Edmondson: 1936–1938," *American Jewish History* 71 (Sep. 1981): 79–102; Genizi, p. 349.

50. See letters accompanying Arthur L. Corbin to Charles Seymour, Nov. 9, 1939, and notes of Charles Seymour's meeting with Justice William O. Douglas, Nov. 8, 1939, both in Folder 803, Box 93, CS.

51. Kelley, pp. 240–41; Charles Seymour to Harry Shulman, Feb. 9, 1940, Folder 803, Box 93, CS.

52. Figures were determined from The Graduate Club catalogues of 1901 through 1938 in concert with the *Historical Register of Yale University, 1701–1937* and *1937–1951*. Clinical professors, non-emeritus ex-faculty, and future faculty, administrators, and fellows were not counted as being Yale faculty, administrators, or corporation fellows. Had they been counted, the affiliation between the Graduate Club and Yale would have appeared even greater. "Nonresident" members of the club had severely restricted rights of club use and therefore were not considered in this counting. Identification of Jewish members of the Graduate Club was done with the assistance of Rollin Osterweis. *The Graduates Club 1963* (New Haven: Tuttle, Morehouse, and Taylor Press, 1963), p. 2.

53. Wilbur L. Cross, quoted in the "History of the Graduates Club," *The Graduates Club 1938* (New Haven: Tuttle, Morehouse, & Taylor Press, 1938), pp. 23–24.

54. *The Graduates Club 1903* (New Haven: Tuttle, Morehouse, & Taylor Press, 1903), pp. 23–24; Camp and Welch, pp. 115–16.

55. George Parmly Day, "The Early Years," in *The Graduates Club 1963* (New Haven: Tuttle, Morehouse, & Taylor Press, 1963), pp. 25–27; Holden, *Pictorial*, p. 185.

56. The Graduate Club's ornate insignia may be found on the cover of the club catalogues. See *The Graduates Club 1901* and *The Graduates Club 1963*, for example.

57. David L. Daggett, "The Years of Peace," in *The Graduates Club 1963* (New Haven: Tuttle, Morehouse, & Taylor Press, 1963), pp. 28–29.

58. *The Graduates Club 1901* (New Haven: Tuttle, Morehouse, & Taylor Press, 1901), pp. 12–13.

59. Arthur T. Hadley to Committee on Admissions, Mar. 5, 1918, Box 129, ATH.

60. Mary Cheever, Interview, Oct. 11, 1981.

61. Arthur T. Hadley to Frederick B. Luquiens, Nov. 25, 1920, Box 133, Part 2, ATH; Frederick B. Luquiens to Arthur T. Hadley, Nov. 30, 1920, Folder 1063, Box 55, ATH.

62. Rollin G. Osterweis, Interview, Dec. 12, 1976.

63. Holden, *Profiles and Portraits*, p. 111.

64. Helen Swick Perry, *Psychiatrist of America, The Life of Harry Stack Sullivan* (Cambridge, Mass.: The Belknap Press of Harvard University, 1982), pp. 354, 374, 378–79; Feuer, *American Jewish History*, p. 443; David G. Mandelbaum, in *Selected Writings of Edward Sapir*, ed. by David G. Mandelbaum (Los Angeles: University of California Press, 1949), p. ix.

65. The Yiddish scholar Max Weinreich was one of his students in the seminar, and was greatly influenced by the course. Mandelbaum in Sapir, pp. ix–x. Mary Rouse, Interview, Sep. 30, 1980; David G. Mandelbaum, Interview, Oct. 21, 1982; Lucy S. Dawidowicz, "Max Weinreich (1894–1969): The Scholarship of Yiddish," in *American Jewish Year Book 1969*, ed. by Morris Fine and Milton Himmelfarb (New York: The American Jewish Committee, 1969), p. 65; John Dollard to Sydney Walker, Jul. 15, 1940, Folder 600, Max Weinreich Papers, YIVO Institute, New York, N.Y.

66. Many of the personal descriptions of Sapir are based on the recollections of Rabbi Edgar Siskin. Siskin became friendly with Sapir shortly after the former was admitted as a graduate student in anthropology. "Edward Sapir," *Jewish Social Studies* 1 (Apr. 1939): 142; Morris R. Cohen, "Publisher's Foreword," *Jewish Social Studies* 1 (Jan. 1939): 3–4; Mandelbaum in Sapir, pp. ix–x; Perry, p. 243; Gabriel, Interview; Mandelbaum, Interview, Oct. 21, 1982; Mary Rouse, Interview; Siskin to author, Dec. 2, 1980, Feb. 18, 1983.

67. Lipset and Ladd, p. 90; Osterweis, Interview, Dec. 12, 1976.

68. David Mandelbaum suggested that Sapir's candidacy was not helped by his sponsor's being a "tactless" and "difficult to deal with" member of the graduate school faculty. Ira V. Hiscock, Interview, Nov. 19, 1982; Mandelbaum, Interview, Oct. 21, 1982; Cornelius Osgood, Interview, Sep. 29, 1980.

69. Club enrollment dropped significantly during the 1930s; later official histories attribute this decline solely to the financial difficulties many members faced because of the Depression. Gabriel also notes the opening of the residential colleges, which stole their faculty fellows from the club. *The Graduates Club 1930* (New Haven: Tuttle, Morehouse, & Taylor Press, 1930), pp. 4, 28; Francis Coulter, "In the Twentieth Century," in *The Graduates Club 1963*, p. 32; Leonard Doob, Interview, Oct. 28, 1983; Dyen, Interview; Gabriel, Interview; Hiscock, Interview; Siskin to author, Dec. 2, 1980.

70. Edward Sapir to James R. Angell, Sep. 18, 1931, Folder 1790, Box 170, JRA.

71. Edgar Siskin to author, Feb. 18, 1983.

72. Perry, p. 366.

73. Sapir, Interview.

74. *Yale University Catalogue 1937–1938*, pp. 59–64.

75. Sapir brought two Jews to the graduate school faculty: anthropologists George Herzog and Leslie Spier. Perry, pp. 370–75; Irving Rouse, Interview, Sep. 18, 1980; Siskin to author, Dec. 2, 1980.

76. In time, Murdock established himself as a leading American anthropologist. He left Yale in 1960 to become chairman of the anthropology department at the University of Pittsburgh. Siskin to author, Dec. 2, 1980; *Historical Register 1951–1968,* p. 546.
77. David G. Mandelbaum, Interview, Oct. 5, 1982.
78. Siskin to author, Dec. 2, 1980.
79. Melamed, *The Reflex,* p. 4.
80. Peyre, Interview.

CHAPTER SEVEN THE SCHOOL OF MEDICINE

A researcher studying the position of Jews at individual American medical schools of the 1930s will want to consult the Morris S. Lazaron Papers at the American Jewish Archives in Cincinnati. Operating on the premise that "too many of our Jewish students are going into medicine," Rabbi Lazaron solicited data from medical deans and hospital program directors throughout the country. Many of the 44 medical school deans and 421 hospital officials that responded made extremely frank statements. Essential to consult, too, for the Yale story, are the medical school records, Dean Milton Winternitz's papers, and the presidential papers of James R. Angell and Charles Seymour, all in the university archives. A helpful secondary source is Jacob A. Goldberg, "Jews in the Medical Profession—A National Survey," *Jewish Social Studies* (July 1939), which provides many statistics and presents an important sociological survey of attitudes of the era.

1. Lenn Evan Goodman, *Rambam* (New York: Viking Press, 1976), p. 15; "Moses Maimonides," *Encyclopaedia Judaica* (1972 ed.), vol. 11, pp. 758, 778–79.
2. The model for behavior is found in Genesis 18:1, where the Lord appeared to Abraham following his circumcision. Pliskin states that in Sotah 14a of the Talmud, the rabbis taught that God appeared to Abraham because he was in great pain following his operation. Since man's duty is to emulate God, the rabbis required people to visit the sick. In Aruch Hashulchan, the commentary on Yorah Daiah 335:1 of the Shulchan Aruch states that visiting the sick is one of the most important of commandments. Zelig Pliskin, *Love Your Neighbor* (Jerusalem: Yeshiva Aish HaTorah, 1977), p. 52, Also see Mark Zborowski and Elizabeth Herzog, *Life Is with People* (New York: International Universities Press, Inc., 1952), p. 355; Kessner, p. 88; and "Medicine," *Encyclopaedia Judaica* (1972 ed.) vol. 11, p. 1178.
3. For a twentieth-century example of prejudicial barriers leading a Jewish student to shift from a natural science to a medical career, see n. 28 of chapter 6. Pliskin notes that in Sefer Hayashor, chapter thirteen, it is written that if one does his part to aid a sick person and alleviate his suffering it is considered as if he had saved his life. The Maimonidean principle may be found in his Mishnah Torah, Sanhedrin 12:3. The ancient rabbis were well acquainted with charlatan physicians, healers who only had time for the rich, and doctors who attributed successes to their own power rather than to divine succor. The ideal physician in rabbinic eyes was competent, humble, and helpful to all classes of people. For a fine collection of rabbinic thoughts on doctors, see chapter two of Harry

402 Notes to Pages 146–150

Friedenwald, *The Jews and Medicine* (Baltimore: The Johns Hopkins University Press, 1944). Lewis S. Feuer, *The Scientific Intellectual* (New York: Basic Books, Inc., 1963), p. 310; Pliskin, p. 52.

4. Harvey Ladin (conversation at the Westville Synagogue, New Haven), Apr. 30, 1980.

5. "Nathan Smith," in *Dictionary of American Biography,* quoted by Kelley, p. 132.

6. Whitfield J. Bell, Jr., "The Medical Institution of Yale College, 1810–1885," *Yale Journal of Biology and Medicine* 33 (Dec. 1960): 171; Camp and Welch, pp. 264–70, 414–17; Holden, *Pictorial,* pp. 85–91; Kelley, pp. 202, 218, 255.

7. One of the events that played a significant role in integrating science into medicine occurred when the Sheffield Scientific School initiated a course entitled "Studies Preparatory to Medical Sciences" in 1869. Medical historian A. M. Harvey believed that this was probably the first course of its kind in the nation. Harvey, p. 31.

8. Abraham Flexner, *Medical Education in the United States and Canada* (Buffalo, N.Y.: The Heritage Press, 1973), pp. 199–200.

9. Harvey, p. 301; Robert P. Hudson, "Abraham Flexner in Perspective: American Medical Education 1865–1910," in *Sickness and Health in America,* ed. by Judith Walzer Leavitt and Ronald L. Numbers (Madison: University of Wisconsin Press, 1978), p. 109.

10. When Flexner and Winternitz would reminisce and try to define who was the most responsible for the improvement at Yale, both agreed that Ullman (along with the two of them and the General Education Board) played a pivotal role. In Flexner's memoirs, the medical reformer recalled that President Hadley, ever the opponent of discrimination, realized that for new medical facilities to be built at Yale, financial support would have to come from Yale alumni and the New Haven townspeople. Hadley wanted Flexner, a Jew, to make sure that Ullman (who was not a Yale graduate, and whose closest friend was a Roman Catholic) would realize that Hadley's approaching the colonel was not out of a desire to have the Jews or Catholics alone contribute to a Protestant institution, but rather out of a desire for Ullman to contribute his fair share to an institution which would be of direct benefit to the entire New Haven community. Flexner quotes Hadley as writing that "we are anxious to avoid anything that might be attributed to racial and religious prejudice." Judging by the favorable results, everything worked well and without incident. Abraham Flexner, *I Remember* (New York: Simon & Schuster, 1940), pp. 258–261; Abraham Flexner, *Abraham Flexner: An Autobiography* (New York: Simon & Schuster, 1960), pp. 162–64; "Notable Citizens Extoll Col. Ullman," *The New Haven Register* (Jan. 28, 1930), pp. 1, 6; Osterweis, *Three,* pp. 255, 419; Isaac Ullman, quoted by Judith A. Schiff in "Colonel Isaac Ullman: Philanthropist, Politician, and Patriot," in *Jews in New Haven, Volume 2,* ed. by Barry E. Herman (New Haven: Jewish Historical Society of New Haven, 1979), pp. 36–37; Abraham Flexner to Milton Winternitz, Feb. 24, 1947, and Milton Winternitz to Abraham Flexner, Dec. 14, 1948, Box 15, Abraham Flexner Papers, Library of Congress; Zimmerman, Interview.

11. Harvey, p. 292; Holden, *Pictorial,* p. 235.

12. Kelley, pp. 353–54; J. Morris Slemans to Milton C. Winternitz, Mar. 24, 1917, Milton C. Winternitz to J. Morris Slemans, Mar. 29, 1917, George Blumer to Milton C. Winternitz, Apr. 28, 1917, all in Binder 1, Box 2, Milton C. Winternitz Papers; Milton C. Winternitz to Simon Flexner, Mar. 15, 1937, "William Henry Welch, M.D." folder, Box 5,

Milton C. Winternitz Papers. See A. Clifford Barger, Reinier Beeuwkes III, Lewis L. Lainey, and Kenneth J. Silverman, "Hypothesis: Vasa Vasorum and Neovascularization of Human Coronary Arteries," *New England Journal of Medicine* 310 (Jan. 19, 1984): 175–77.

13. Harvard's first Jewish dean was not chosen until 1971. Lipset and Ladd, p. 92; "Dean Winternitz," *The Yale Scientific Magazine* 7 (Autumn 1932): 15.

14. *Committee on Education Policy of the Yale Corporation, Minutes of,* Nov. 9, 1934, p. 397; Flexner, *Remember,* pp. 258–61; Pierson, *Numbers,* p. 548.

15. William Welch, as recounted by Harvey, p. 292.

16. Ibid.; Holden, *Pictorial,* pp. 235–39.

17. Harvey, p. 292; Pierson, *Short History,* p. 71; Sharon Austin Mulgrew, "Autonomy Vs. Integration, The History of the Relocation of the Yale Psychiatric Institute," M.P.H. essay for the Department of Epidemiology and Public Health, Yale University, 1977, p. 4.

18. Zimmerman, Interview.

19. James Rowland Angell, "Dr. Winternitz as Dean of the School of Medicine," *Yale Journal of Biology and Medicine* 22 (July 1950): 469–70.

20. David A. Dolowitz to author, Mar. 4, 1983; Gilman, Interview; Louis Goodman to author, May 12, 1981; Lippard, Interview; Joe Milici, Interview, Nov. 6, 1981; Max Taffel, Interview, Nov. 5, 1982; Zimmerman, Interview.

21. *The Yale Scientific Magazine,* p. 25.

22. Taffel, Interview.

23. Zimmerman, Interview.

24. According to Zimmerman, there was an occasional student who would not put up with abuse. One student, after being told by Winternitz to obtain a physician's excuse for coming late to a pathology class, responded by dumping a roll of toilet paper on Winternitz's podium during a lecture. A Jewish boy who had tired of the dean's insults one day responded by making fun of the dean to his face. Winternitz walked out. In general, though, the students were thoroughly intimidated. Harrison, Interview; Taffel, Interview; Herman Yannet, Interview, Dec. 16, 1982; Zimmerman, Interview.

25. Taffel, Interview.

26. Ibid.

27. Osterweis, Interview, Dec. 12, 1976; William Welch Winternitz, Interview, Oct. 5, 1981.

28. Thomas Winternitz, Interview.

29. Cheever, Interview, Oct. 11, 1981.

30. Zimmerman, Interview; Gilman, Interview.

31. Kathryn M. Yochelson to author, Feb. 6, 1986; David A. Dolowitz to author, Oct. 21, 1987; Alan A. Rozen, Interview, Oct. 26, 1987.

32. Milton C. Winternitz to Abraham Flexner, Feb. 5, 1950, Box 15, Abraham Flexner Papers, Library of Congress.

33. Zimmerman reported that in private conversation with him, Winternitz would acknowledge the poor East European immigrant background that the two men shared. In public, however, he maintained a solid front. Milton C. Winternitz to Henry Gildersleeve Jarvis, Dec. 9, 1925, "J General Correspondence" folder, Box 3, YRG 22-A-5-9, YMAL; Gilman, Interview; Zimmerman, Interview.

34. Cheever, Interview, Oct. 11, 1981.

35. Mary Cheever, Interview, Dec. 8, 1982; William Welch Winternitz, Interview, Dec. 12, 1982.

36. See clipping from *Waterbury Herald* (Apr. 10, 1932), in Binder 1, Box 2, Milton C. Winternitz Papers.

37. "Ovid in Ossining," *Time* 83 (Mar. 27, 1964), p. 70; Sigmund Freud, *The Standard Edition of the Complete Psychological Works of Sigmund Freud, Volume 8, Jokes and Their Relation to the Unconscious,* ed. by James Strachey (London: The Hogarth Press, 1960), p. 33.

38. *Who's Who in America 1920–1921* (Chicago: A. N. Marquis & Company, 1920), p. 3121.

39. Loeb's class also had two black members. *1897 Yale Medical School Yearbook,* p. 21.

40. *1905 Yale Medical School Yearbook,* pp. 31, 35.

41. Abram Hessman was vice-president of the class of 1908. Abraham Smernoff was secretary of the class of 1909. *1908 Yale Medical School Yearbook,* p. 26; *1909 Yale Medical School Yearbook,* p. 37. In addition to the yearbooks listed in the previous two notes, also see those for 1904 and 1910. These yearbooks are kept in the Yale University Archives Library and in the Yale History of Medicine Library. Camp and Welch, p. 209.

42. PDE owned a chapter house in which some of its members lived. The house was sold by the Second World War. The fraternity gradually declined in level of activity and disbanded during the 1950s. Dolowitz to author, Mar. 4, 1983; Sidney S. Feuerstein, Interview, Mar. 7, 1983; Harrison, Interview; Kushlan, Interview; Maxwell Lear to author, May 31, 1977; Yannet, Interview; Harry Zimmerman to author, Mar. 3, 1983.

43. Mary Roth Walsh, *Doctors Wanted: No Women Need Apply* (New Haven: Yale University Press, 1977), p. 209; Susan J. Baserga, "The early years of coeducation at the Yale University School of Medicine," *The Yale Journal of Biology & Medicine* 53 (May–June 1980): 181–90.

44. William G. Turnbull to Morris S. Lazaron, Feb. 10, 1934, Folder 1, Box 38, Morris S. Lazaron Papers, AJA.

45. John J. Mullowney to A. D. Bevan, Feb. 22, 1936, Folder 14, Box 37, Morris S. Lazaron Papers, AJA.

46. Jacob A. Goldberg, "Jews in the Medical Profession—A National Survey," *Jewish Social Studies* 1 (July 1939): 335.

47. William Pepper to Morris S. Lazaron, Jan. 30, 1934, Folder 15, Box 37, Morris S. Lazaron Papers, AJA.

48. Fred C. Zappffe to Morris S. Lazaron, Nov. 19, 1935, Folder 14, Box 37, Morris S. Lazaron Papers, AJA.

49. Alfred Shapiro, "Racial Discrimination in Medicine," *Jewish Social Studies* 10 (Apr. 1948): 103; Wechsler, *Qualified,* pp. 169–71.

50. Milton C. Winternitz, "Medical Education at Yale University," *Yale Alumni Weekly* 41 (Jan. 29, 1932): 347; *Committee on Educational Policy of the Yale Corporation, Minutes of,* Nov. 9, 1934, p. 397; James R. Angell to deans, Dec. 12, 1923, Folder 1324, Box 127, JRA.

51. Leonard Dinnerstein, "Anti-Semitism Exposed and Attacked, 1945–1950," *American Jewish History* 71 (Sep. 1981): 139; Goldberg, *Jewish Social Studies,* p. 331. See table prepared by American Jewish Congress, cited by A. S. Johnson in his article "Discrimina-

tion in Education," marked "for Survey," [1947], Folder 205, Box 12, Series III, Alvin S. Johnson Papers.

52. *The Yale Scientific Magazine*, p. 16.

53. Cheever, Interview, Oct. 11, 1981; Kushlan, Interview; Zimmerman, Interview.

54. *The Yale Scientific Magazine*, p. 19.

55. Goodman to author, May 12, 1981; Krall, Interview; Yannet, Interview.

56. Goodman to author, May 12, 1981.

57. Lippard, Interview.

58. A psychohistorian might guess that Winternitz switched the names of Jewish students as a way of acting out his own inner desires to change his religious group background. Vernon Lippard recalled that Irish and Jewish surnames were most susceptible to manipulation by Winternitz. Lippard, Interview; Harrison, Interview; Weinstein, Interview; Zimmerman, Interview.

59. Goodman to author, May 12, 1981; Taffel, Interview; Yannet, Interview; Zimmerman, Interview.

60. On one occasion the committee was reviewing the application of a boy with curly dark hair and a relatively dark complexion. The boy had a good record, but the dean was not impressed. According to Zimmerman, Winternitz told the assembled committee: "His name is Jewish, but he looks like a nigger to me. There's nothing worse for this medical school than a black Jew." Winternitz then threw the application in the trash. One committee member, associate professor of physiological chemistry Arthur Henry Smith, became furious with Winternitz and stormed out of the room. The rest of the committee was far too terrified to challenge the man who had created their jobs. At a later date, the committee accepted the "black" Jew, despite Winternitz's bravado. The dean did not reverse his committee's decision and the student entered Yale. Years later the student would become a prominent American physician and would help raise large sums for the medical school. John S. Nicholas to Milton C. Winternitz, Jan. 17, 1935, "Applicants, 1935–38" folder, Box 2, 23 page box run, YRG-27-A-5-9, YMAL, Dolowitz to author, Mar. 4, 1983; Zimmerman, Interview.

61. The percentage of New York medical applicants who were Jewish was the highest of any state in the nation. Pennsylvania, Maryland, and Connecticut followed, in that order. Lawrence Bloomgarden, "Medical School Quotas and National Health," *Commentary* 15 (Jan. 1953): 30–31; F. A. Moss to Morris S. Lazaron, Mar. 17, 1934, Folder 1, Box 38, Morris S. Lazaron Papers, AJA.

62. Prior to the Second World War, the Yale School of Nursing excluded blacks to "protect" patients who did not want to be treated by black nurses. Synnott, *Door,* p. 210. A. R. Larrain to Morris S. Lazaron, Mar. 7, 1934, Folder 16, Box 37, Morris S. Lazaron Papers, AJA. Also see other letters to Morris S. Lazaron in Folders 15–16, Box 37, Morris S. Lazaron Papers, AJA.

63. Bernard Postal to Milton C. Winternitz, Dec. 4, 1934, and Milton C. Winternitz to Bernard Postal, Dec. 8, 1934 and accompanying drafts, all in YRG-27-1-5, YMAL.

64. *The Yale Scientific Magazine*, p. 16.

65. Ibid.

66. Taffel, Interview; Zimmerman, Interview.

406   Notes to Pages 161–163

67. Arthur J. Viseltear shared this thought with me.

68. The establishment of a department of social work within the New Haven Hospital had been greeted unenthusiastically by the medical school's clinical departments. *Committee on Educational Policy of the Yale Corporation, Minutes of,* Nov. 9, 1934, pp. 399–400.

69. The dean was quite bitter as a result of the turn of events. For a time he threatened to destroy the medical school. This was only talk, however, and not action. The medical school was, after all, a monument to himself. As he subsequently saw the medical school decline in quality, intellectual curiosity, and social concern, Winternitz withdrew from local activities. His New Haven time was spent in the Elba of his second-floor Brady Hall office. He retained some influence by controlling the funds of the Jane Coffin Childs Fund for cancer research. A traditional medical school story has it that upon his retirement in 1950 Winter became a touch intoxicated at a party given in his honor in the school's stately Beaumont Room. After climbing onto someone's shoulders, the dean carved the initials "M.W." into the wood panel above the entrance to the room. His final signature on the character of the Yale School of Medicine was still visible as of 2000. *Committee on Educational Policy of the Yale Corporation, Minutes of,* Nov. 9, 1934, p. 401, Jan. 11, 1935, p. 411; Minutes of the Prudential Committee of the Yale School of Medicine, Nov. 21, 1934, p. 4, "Prudential Committee 1934–35" folder, Box 25, YRG 27-A-5-9; Minutes of the Yale School of Medicine, Board of Permanent Officers, Dec. 12, 1934, Dec. 19, 1934, accompanying Harold S. Burr to Stanhope Bayne-Jones, Sep. 9, 1935, "BPO 1934–35" folder, Box 25, YRG 27-A-5-9; Milton C. Winternitz, note of Apr. 11, 1935, "James R. Angell (2)" folder, Box 1, YRG 27-A-5-9; Goodman to author, May 12, 1981; Hiscock, Interview; Lippard, Interview; Winternitz, Interview, Oct. 5, 1981; Zimmerman, Interview.

70. Frank Kingdon, "Discrimination in Medical Colleges," *The American Mercury* 61 (Oct. 1945): 392–98; Shapiro, *Jewish Social Studies,* p. 103; "Applicants for Admission," Jan. 18, 1936, "Admissions, Committee on, 1935–36" folder, Box 6, 23 paige box run, YRG 27-A-5-9, YMAL.

71. White had been a post-doctoral fellow in Lafayette B. Mendel's laboratory. Goodman to author, May 12, 1981; Edna White, Interview, Nov. 23, 1980.

72. See the record of Edwin R. Weinerman, May 1938, in the correspondence between Stanhope Bayne-Jones, Charles Seymour, and David T. Weinerman, in "We" folder, "War to Wi" box, CS.

73. Tragic irony was to become a theme in this man's life. Following his earning his M.D. from Georgetown in 1942, Harvard would grant him a master's degree in public health in 1948. In 1962 a very different Yale than he had previously known would invite him back as an associate professor of medicine and public health. In 1965 he was promoted to full professor. In 1970 he and his wife boarded a Swissair jet in Zurich, as he progressed to his next stop on a three-nation study of health care delivery. Soon after take-off an onboard explosion caused the Israel-bound plane to crash. An Arab terrorist organization was linked to the crash, which killed everyone aboard. "Explosion and Crash Kill 47 on Israel-Bound Swiss Jet," *The New York Times* (Feb. 22, 1970), pp. 1, 3; "Yale Medical Professor, Wife Perish in Crash," *The New Haven Register* (Feb. 22, 1970), p. 2A; "Swiss Suspect Link in 2 Air Explosions," *The New York Times* (Feb. 28, 1970), p. 3; "Swiss Crash

Clue Found in Wreckage," *The New York Times* (Mar. 4, 1970), p. 7. Also see *The Yale Journal of Biology and Medicine* 64 (Aug. 1971).

74. Parallel ratios between Jews and non-Jews prevailed at Cornell Medical School. Bloomgarden, "Medical School," *Commentary,* p. 32; Stanhope Bayne-Jones, *Report of the Dean of the School of Medicine of Yale University 1938–39,* pp. 26–27.

75. On Kahn, see Mulgrew. *Minutes of the Prudential Committee, Yale School of Medicine,* Dec. 16, 1933, Jan. 6, 1934; Gilman, Interview; Zimmerman, Interview.

76. The timing of Angell's remarks was important, because they were made in a boom-time. Recessionary periods always make it more difficult for foreigners to compete in an already tight job market. Such pressures were not yet operating when the Kahn offer was made. *Committee on Educational Policy of the Yale Corporation, Minutes of,* Oct. 11, 1929, p. 223.

77. Melamed, *The Reflex,* p. 3.

78. T. Swann Harding, "Another Jew Without Money," *The Atlantic Monthly* 148 (Aug. 1931): 166–70.

79. James R. Angell to Milton C. Winternitz and Lafayette B. Mendel, Aug. 6, 1931, Lafayette B. Mendel to James R. Angell, Aug. 12, 1931, James R. Angell to Frank P. Underhill, Aug. 15, 1931, Frank P. Underhill to James R. Angell, Aug. 20, 1931, Ellery Sedgewick to James R. Angell, Aug. 31, 1931, all in "Appointment Bureau As" folder, Box 16, JRA.

80. Arthur J. Viseltear, "C.-E. A. Winslow and the Early Years of Public Health at Yale, 1919–1925," *The Yale Journal of Biology and Medicine* 55 (March / April 1982): 139.

81. George Parmly Day to Charles-E. A. Winslow, May 17, 1938, and C.-E. A. Winslow to George P. Day, May 20, 1938, both in Yale's C.-E. A. Winslow Papers, I/9/212, made available to me by Arthur J. Viseltear; Interview, an anonymous physician.

82. In retrospect, Weinstein was glad that he left Yale. The frustration that he felt as a result of the anti-Jewish feeling in New Haven led him to change career interests from academic immunology to medicine. He enrolled in the Boston University School of Medicine for a medical degree. He eventually became a professor of medicine at the Harvard Medical School. Weinstein, Interview; Harrison, Interview.

83. Max Danzis, "The Jew in Medicine," *The American Hebrew and Jewish Tribune* 134 (Mar. 23, 1934): 391.

84. Harrison, Interview.

CHAPTER EIGHT EVOLVING MERITOCRACY

The national perspective on changing attitudes regarding racial and religious minorities in post-Second World War America may be gained from two insightful works by E. Digby Baltzell: *The Protestant Establishment* (1964) and "The Protestant Establishment Revisited," *The American Scholar* (Autumn 1976). Calvin B. T. Lee, *The Campus Scene: 1900–1970* (1970) summarizes the impact of social trends on campus life in this era.

On the postwar specifics at Yale, Brooks Mather Kelley, *Yale: A History* (1974) once again provides a flavor of the depth of change on the campus. Thomas Bergin, "My Native Country," *My Harvard, My Yale,* ed. by Diana Dubois (1982), presents a residential college master's eye view of Yale collegiate life. To some extent Bergin downplays the role of the fraternities in the social world of the 1950s, diminishing the function they served as a gathering place for many of the college's most socially ambitious students.

Loomis Havemeyer, *"Go to Your Room"* (1960) dwells on the history of the secret societies. Of all Yale's secret senior societies, Scroll and Key has allowed the most light to be shed on its history. Without compromising the society's secret traditions, a penetrating examination of the society's composition after the Second World War is provided in A. Bartlett Giamatti, *History of Scroll and Key* (1978). Norman Oder prepared two fine reviews of the history of the senior societies for "Senior Societies," *Yale Daily News* (Apr. 13–14, 1982).

With specific regard to the class structure and the position of Jews in postwar Yale, special attention is worth directing toward Anthony Astrachan, "Class Notes," *My Harvard, My Yale* (1982). The "Yale Hillel Foundation Papers" at the American Jewish Historical Society in Waltham, Mass. also merit consultation. Richard Israel's article "Jews at Yale" (1980) was of great import in the preparation of this chapter.

1. The proportion of European Jewry that perished is based on my own evaluation of figures in Ettinger, p. 1031. Also see Ettinger, pp. 1037–58.

2. E. Digby Baltzell, "The Protestant Establishment Revisited," *The American Scholar* 45 (Autumn 1976): 505–06.

3. Early in his administration, Griswold reimposed the dress code for undergraduates at mealtime. Daniel Catlin, Jr., *Liberal Education at Yale, The Yale College Course of Study 1945–1978* (Washington, D.C.: The University Press of America, 1982), p. 28; Kelley, pp. 396–97; Pierson, *Short History,* p. 79; Synott, *Door,* p. 211; Bergin, *Residential,* pp. 68–69; Bergin, Interview; Lionel Kestenbaum, Interview, May 12, 1983; Harold J. Morowitz, Interview, Apr. 28, 1983.

4. Warren saw the needless rivalry between the "Ac" and "Sheff" faculties as an equally important reason for merging the two undergraduate schools. Report of Charles H. Warren, accompanying note of Charles Seymour, Aug. 3, 1943, Folder 591, Box 68, Series I, CS.

5. David D. Henry, *Challenges Past, Challenges Present* (San Francisco: Jossey-Bass Publishers, 1975), pp. 57, 60; Holden, *Profiles and Portraits,* p. 124; Kelley, pp. 403–05, 448, 540.

6. Dinnerstein, *American Jewish History,* p. 145; Benjamin R. Epstein and Arnold Foster, "Barriers in Higher Education," in *Barriers: Patterns of Discrimination Against Jews* (New York: Friendly House Publishers, 1958), p. 66; Henry, p. 63; *Fortune* quotation from Kelley, p. 410. Also see Louis Krapin, "The Decline of Fraternity Bias," in *Barriers: Patters of Discrimination Against Jews,* p. 80.

7. Giamatti, *Scroll and Key,* p. 21.

8. Thomas Cohen (B.A. 1957) recalled spending one of his first hours at Yale learning the Yale ways from his freshman counselor. At the very end, the counselor told him, "One thing you don't have to worry about here is anti-Semitism." Until that point he had not been worried. Only the mention of the subject alarmed him. Thomas E. Cohen, Interview; Sewall, Interview, Oct. 17, 1978.

9. In his history of Scroll and Key A. Bartlett Giamatti notes that the society offered election to a black for the first time in its history in 1948, though the first black did not join

until 1968. If the 1948 black was Levi Jackson (B.A. 1950), the tapping was likely in 1949 and not 1948. Giamatti also notes that the Scroll and Key membership lists of the 1950s indicate names clearly identifiable as Irish, Jewish, and Greek. Astrachan noted that the mass media had hailed Levi Jackson as the first black to make a senior society, though a black from the class of 1899 had been a member of Skull and Bones. My own review of the class of 1899 Bones roster and the pictures of Bones men in the *1899 Yale College Classbook* fails to support Astrachan's assertion. Anthony Astrachan, "Class Notes," in *My Harvard, My Yale,* pp. 214–15. The Levi Jackson quotation appears in Baltzell, *Protestant,* p. 279. Giamatti, *Scroll and Key,* pp. 4–5; Norman Oder, "Senior Societies," *Yale Daily News* (Apr. 14, 1982), p. 4; *1950 Yale College Classbook,* p. 302; Bergin, Interview; William S. Coffin, Jr., Interview, Jan. 10, 1983; Victor H. Frank, Jr., Interview, Jan. 11, 2000; Levi Jackson, Interview, Jan. 11, 2000.

10. When Trillin's *News* questioned "whether the interests of American Jews really lie with overall American interests," campus Jews felt secure enough to unleash a week's worth of letters critically responding to the editorial. Yale was not alone in its difficulties in opening up its societies to more "types" of students. Princetonians, for example, were openly resistant to expanding their club system to include high school graduates from the New York–New Jersey metropolitan area. In time, many Jewish students would come to assume leadership positions on the *News.* It must also be recognized that the social prestige of the *News* severely declined over this era. By the 1970s the *News* could no longer boast that election to its board represented one of the highest honors on campus. Becoming its publisher or its editor-in-chief, however, still brought one great status. "Dr. Weiss' Address," *Yale Daily News* (Oct. 2, 1956), p. 2; Earnest, p. 338; *1957 Yale College Classbook,* p. 498; *1962 Yale College Classbook,* p. 388; *Historical Register 1951–1968,* p. 98; Lance Liebman, Interview, Mar. 3, 1978.

11. Lehrman had also been a member of the then "selective" Fence Club at Yale. As for Newberger, he considered it a "singular honor" that Lehrman was assigned as the Wolf's Head alumnus who contacted him before Tap Night and encouraged him to join Wolf's Head. Israel, "Jews at Yale"; Baltzell, *Protestant,* p. 348; *1958 Yale College Classbook,* p. 355; *1960 Yale College Classbook,* p. 455; Henry Chauncey, Jr., Interview, Dec. 3, 1982; Eli Newberger, Interview, Oct. 10, 1980.

12. Norman Oder, "Senior Societies," *Yale Daily News* (Apr. 13, 1982), p. 2; Pierson, *University College,* p. 671; "Summary: Senior Society Elections, May 1956," Folder 2102, Box 226, AWG.

13. Bergin, *My Yale,* p. 165; Havemeyer, *"Go to Your Room,"* p. 70; Norman Oder, "Senior Societies," *Yale Daily News* (Apr. 14, 1982), p. 1.

14. Emile Godchaux (B.A. 1896) was an early Jewish member of Corbey Court. *Catalogue of the Legal Fraternity of Phi Delta Phi,* ed. by George A. Katzenberger (Ann Arbor, Mich.: The Inland Press, 1897), p. 287; *1943 Yale College Classbook,* p. 427; *1944 Yale College Classbook,* p. 399; Camp and Welch, p. 208; "Morgenthau," *Encyclopaedia Judaica* (1972 ed.), vol. 12, pp. 321–22; Dilworth, Interview; Goldstein, Interview, Jan. 31, 1979; Lowenthal to author; William Lee Frost to author, March 12, 1986.

15. For an account of similar rooming policies at Syracuse University in the 1920s and 1930s, see Strum, *American Jewish Archives,* pp. 8–9. Astrachan, p. 212.

16. Samuel Sandmel, Interview, Oct. 19, 1978. Also see memo entitled "G.D.V.," April 1960, Folder 215, Box 24, AWG.

17. Donald K. Walker, Interview, Dec. 13, 1982. On blacks at Yale, see Scott Fletcher, "Separatism or Support? 15 Years at the Afro-Am Center," *The New Journal* 16 (Apr. 20, 1984): 25–31.

18. In the early 1960s, when a Jewish undergraduate complained to Dean William Clyde DeVane of Yale College about a dance to be held at the historically exclusive New Haven Lawn Club, Dean DeVane thought little of the matter until Chaplin William Sloane Coffin backed the student up. Coffin, Interview; Walker, Interview.

19. Lee, p. 99; "The Steady Hand," *Time* 57 (June 11, 1951): 75; Kelley, p. 433; Jacob Weisberg, "Cavett Will Return to Yale to Give Class Day Address," *Yale Daily News* (Commencement 1984), p. 8; Chauncey, Interview; Liebman, Interview.

20. Chauncey, Interview.

21. The national veterans movement to press for lowering of racial fraternity barriers took force when a national fraternity forced its Amherst chapter to expel a black member. Dinnerstein, *American Jewish History,* p. 147; Lee, p. 100; "The Negro at Yale," *Yale Daily News* (Apr. 8, 1959), p. 2; Whitehead, "The Jewish Fraternity"; Richard C. Carroll to A. Whitney Griswold, July 12, 1962, Folder 202, Box 21, AWG; Liebman, Interview.

22. Kelley, p. 448; Bergin, Interview; Chauncey, Interview; John A. Wilkinson, Interview, Sep. 16, 1982.

23. Griswold, Interview; Stoddard, Interview.

24. A. Whitney Griswold, as quoted by the *New Haven Journal-Courier,* Apr. 9, 1953, filed in the "Yale Hillel Foundation" folder, AJHS.

25. Holden, *Profiles and Portraits,* pp. 138, 173; Louis Finkelstein to A. Whitney Griswold, Mar. 19, 1957, Folder 1583, Box 174, AWG.

26. Kelley, p. 448; Chauncey, Interview; John A. Wilkinson, Interview, Apr. 21, 1983.

27. Holden, *Profiles and Portraits,* pp. 131–32; A. Whitney Griswold to Robert B. Fiske, Nov. 22, 1957, Folder 2102, Box 222, AWG.

28. A. Bartlett Giamatti, Interview, Apr. 14, 1983; Wilkinson, Interview, Apr. 21, 1983.

29. Bergin, *My Yale,* p. 167.

30. Norman Oder, "Senior Societies," *Yale Daily News* (Apr. 13, 1982), p. 2; Wilkinson, Interview, Apr. 21, 1983; William Zinsser, Interview, Oct. 20, 1978.

31. In 1970 the average sum of initiation fee, annual dues, and annual social fee for the five Yale associations was $522. "Fraternities: The Benign Irrelevancy," *1969 Yale Banner,* pp. 242–47; Neil Bermel, "Yale Fraternities: A Dwindling Breed," *Yale Daily News* (May 5, 1983), p. 10; "IFC/Cost Sheet," Box I, Fence Club Records, YRG 40-A-8, YMAL; Giamatti, Interview, Apr. 14, 1983.

32. Oder, "Senior Societies," *Yale Daily News* (Apr. 14, 1982), p. 4; Giamatti, Interview, Apr. 14, 1983; Wilkinson, Interview, Apr. 21, 1983.

33. Joseph H. Gumbiner, "Annual Report on the Activities of the Yale Hillel Foundation," ca. 1950, p. 3, Folder 1954-1, BBHFY; Kezerian, Interview, Jan. 21, 1986; Richard D. Schwartz, Interview, Oct. 9, 1980; Robert L. Weinberg, Interview, Oct. 22, 1983; Edwin L. Wolff, Interview, Jan. 10, 2000.

CHAPTER NINE UNDERGRADUATE ADMISSIONS

Because the change in patterns of collegiate admissions is so recent, there are limited published discussions of this subject. Preliminary summaries of this change appear in Marcia Graham Synnott, *The Half-Opened Door* (1979), and Harold Wechsler, *The Qualified Student* (1977). Laurence Bloomgarden, "Our Changing Elite Colleges," *Commentary* (Feb. 1960) appraises Ivy League admissions policies at their moment of flux with respect to Jews. The student of Connecticut education will find many statistics regarding "minority" and religious group acceptances at Connecticut colleges in the postwar era in the studies conducted by Henry G. Stetler. The most competent effort was his *New Study of College Admissions Practices with Respect to Race, Religion and National Origin* (1953). Statistics regarding the affinity of Jewish Americans for learning may be found in Seymour Martin Lipset and Everett Carll Ladd, Jr., "Jewish Academics in the United States: Their Achievements, Culture, and Politics," *American Jewish Year Book 1971* (1971).

Two published sources comment on the end of the "Jewish quota" at Yale College. The autobiography of William Sloane Coffin, Jr., *Once to Every Man* (1978), provides a revealing glimpse into the personality of this remarkable activist and aptly characterizes other players in the historical drama. Mark Singer, "God and Mentsch [*sic*] at Yale," *Moment* (July–Aug. 1975), touching on the work of Dean R. Inslee Clark, Jr., provides background flavor to the story. Richard Israel's unpublished sketch "Jews at Yale," kindly made available to me by Rabbi Israel, proved valuable in understanding his perspective throughout the admissions controversy.

Changing attitudes in the admission of blacks are discussed in Orde Coombs, "The Necessity of Excellence: Making It at Yale," *Change, The Magazine of Higher Learning* (June 1973). Another perspective on the higher education of blacks in America is Allen B. Ballard, *The Education of Black Folk* (1973).

A general appreciation of national changes in educational policy from 1941 through 1970 may be grasped from Calvin B. T. Lee's popular history, *The Campus Scene: 1900–1970* (1970), and John R. Thelin, *The Cultivation of Ivy* (1976).

Yale curricular changes from 1945 through 1978 are detailed in Daniel Catlin, Jr., *Liberal Education at Yale, The Yale College Course of Study 1945–1978* (1982). The "Doob Report" is reproduced in its entirety in Leonard W. Doob et al., "The Education of First Year Students in Yale College," *Yale Alumni Magazine* (June 1962). An official evaluation of Yale College one decade later is Robert A. Dahl et al., *Report of the Study Group on Yale College* (1972). Essential to any future study of the first 275 years of Yale history is the wealth of statistics and interpretations in George W. Pierson, *A Yale Book of Numbers* (1983).

The publicly known work of the Griswold administration is discussed briefly in "The Steady Hand," *Time,* June 11, 1951, authoritatively in Brooks Mather Kelley, *Yale, A History* (1974), and illustratively in Reuben Holden, *Profiles and Portraits of Yale University Presidents* (1968). Holden briefly mentions the first years of the Brewster administration as well. The Yale College admissions process is described extensively in Katharine T. Kinkead, "The Brightest Ever," *The New Yorker* (Sep. 10, 1960).

Although the final analysis of some of the events discussed in this chapter remains to be written, many of the important primary records are available for examination. The following proved especially helpful in this study: the Charles Seymour Presidential papers, the A. Whitney Griswold Presidential papers, and the Office of the Secretary Papers. Of particular interest in the presidential collections are the annual reports to the president by university administrators. Also useful are the tables and records in Folders 1194–95, Box 240. Series III, in the Office of the Secretary Papers.

1. Edward S. Noyes, "Memorandum to the President and Provost," Dec. 13, 1941, "Subcommittee on Methods of Admissions" folder, "Board of Admissions, Misc." box, CS.

2. Thelin, pp. 53–54.

3. Peyre, Interview.

4. Anecdotally, the 1946 graduating class at the Taft School had twenty-nine students applying to Yale as their "first choice" college. Of these students, twenty-seven Christians were accepted by Yale and two Jews were not. The headmaster apologized to John Hammerslough, one of the Jewish boys, following notification of the decisions: "This is a terrible thing. Nothing like this has happened before!" The Jewish applicants saw nothing unusual about the exclusion. Two years later the Jewish "head-monitor" (ranking the highest in prestige at Taft) was rejected by Yale and reportedly was offered the same apology by the headmaster. John Hammerslough, Interview, Feb. 13, 1979; Meyer Greenberg, "The Jewish Student at Yale: His Attitude Toward Judaism," *YIVO Annual of Jewish Social Science* 1 (1946): 230.

5. Leonard Shiman to Charles Seymour, June 23, 1944, "Shem" folder, "Schu through Sherill" box, CS.

6. Charles Seymour to Leonard Shiman, July 7, 1944, "Shem" folder, "Schu through Sherrill" box, CS.

7. Edward Noyes to Charles Seymour, July 10, 1944, "Shem" folder, "Schu through Sherrill" box, CS.

8. Edward S. Noyes, "Report of the Board of Admissions," *Yale Reports to the President, 1943–44,* p. 4.

9. Carl Lohmann, to F. H. Wiggin, Mar. 24, 1945, Folder 1194, Box 240, Series III, OS.

10. Edward S. Noyes, "Report of the Board of Admissions," *Yale Reports to the President, 1944–45,* p. 3.

11. Paul Sheehan to Charles Seymour, Aug. 3, 1945, "130 Sh" folder, "Schu through Sherill" box, CS.

12. Paul V. Sheehan to Charles Seymour, Feb. 14, 1949, "130 Sh" folder, "Schu through Sherrill" box, CS.

13. Dinnerstein, *American Jewish History,* pp. 142–43.

14. Anti-Defamation League of B'nai B'rith, *Purpose and Program* (New York, 1983), p. 17; Rostow, Interview, Nov. 14, 1978.

15. Harold Wechsler, p. 195; Frederick Wiggin to Carl Lohman, Sep. 12, 1945, Folder 1194, Box 240, Series III, OS.

16. The 1946 policies were echoed in Noyes's 1948 report to the Yale Corporation Committee on Educational Policy. See p. 727 of that committee's minutes for Apr. 16, 1948. "Policy on Admissions," May 20, 1945, Folder 41, Box 6, AWG.

17. In 1949 President Seymour allied himself with the presidents of Trinity College, Wesleyan University, and the Connecticut College for Women to deny quotas or racial restrictions at their institutions. Yale opposition to the Fair Educational Practices legislation was conducted (sometimes in concert with the other Connecticut institutions) through 1959. *Discriminations in College Admissions*, ed. by Francis J. Brown (Washington, D.C.: American Council on Education, 1950), p. 5; Laurence Bloomgarden, "Our Changing Elite Colleges," *Commentary* 29 (Feb. 1960): 152; Synnott, *Door*, p. 178; Harold Wechsler, p. 201. On Alvin S. Johnson see the drafts of his essays from 1947 entitled, "Discrimination in Education," Folder 205, Box 12, Series III, Manuscript Group 615, Alvin S. Johnson Papers, YMAL. Yale University News Release, Apr. 27, 1959, Folder 1195, Box 240, and Series III, OS; Folder 611, Box 63, Series III, AWG.

18. Chester Bowles, "Statement," in *College Admissions Practices with Respect to Race, Religion and National Origin of Connecticut High School Graduates*, ed. by Henry G. Stetler (Hartford: Connecticut State Inter-Racial Commission, 1949), p. 5.

19. Fifty-two percent of all Russian immigrants to the United States between 1881 and 1910, for example, were not Jews. Samuel Joseph, *Jewish Immigration to the United States 1881–1910*, cited by Alice Goldstein in "The Coordinated Use of Data Sources in Research on the Demographic Characteristics and Behavior of Jewish Immigrants to the United States," *American Jewish History* 72 (Mar. 1983): 298; Edward S. Noyes, "Summary of an Extended Criticism of the Report Issued through the Connecticut Inter-Racial Commission," May 9, 1949, p. 16, Folder 605, Box 63, AWG.

20. "Inter-Racial Group Defends College Study," *New Haven Register* (May 1, 1949), p. 4.

21. The commission made no attempt to discern among the individual Connecticut institutions. Consequently, if one college discriminated against a particular group while another favored that subpopulation, the survey would not have found evidence of discrimination. Or if the consequence of discrimination against a subgroup was that most of that subgroup applied elsewhere, little evidence of discrimination would have emerged from the study. Of all the surveyed "high ranking" applicants to four-year private nondenominational institutions in Connecticut, 80 percent gained admission, regardless of race, religion, or national origin. Similar "overall" non-discrimination" toward Connecticut applicants prevailed among lower ranking students. Where discrimination still thrived, the report noted, was among Connecticut applicants to out-of-state institutions. Out of state, Connecticut Protestants had an 80 percent acceptance rate, Connecticut Catholics had a 70 percent acceptance rate, and Connecticut Jews had a 63 percent acceptance rate. Henry G. Stetler, *New Study of College Admissions Practices with Respect to Race, Religion, and National Origin* (Hartford: Connecticut Commission on Civil Rights, 1953), pp. 28–30, 38, 52, 54–56.

22. William Clyde DeVane, "Report of the Dean of Yale College," *Yale Reports to the President, 1947–1948*, pp. 4–5.

23. Walker, Interview.

24. Denying the existence of formal quotas, Donald Walker would later insist: "I could swear on the Bible; we never had quotas for anything. We didn't want to know numbers." Walker, Interview; Carroll, Interview; Edward Noyes, "Report of the Board of Admissions," *Reports to the President of Yale University, 1947–1948*.

25. The 1982 recollections of Donald K. Walker were representative of one school of thought among the admissions officers: "Take your big city high schools, like Bronx High School of Science and Stuyvesant High School. They have a high percentage of Jews. Now these Jews are good students and get relatively higher test scores than the non-Jews. [We turned down the Jewish boys] because some Jewish kids were not interested in contributing to Yale. They were interested only in getting what Yale had to offer: grades and a way to get into graduate school. They were only wanting to move ahead. This is a little characteristic of Jewish kids, and a fairly common thing in the New York Jewish boys. . . . [So at places like Bronx High School and Stuyvesant, I would sit down with the guidance counselor and pick out the good ones.] They'd know what I was looking for." Katharine T. Kinkead, "The Brightest Ever," *The New Yorker* 36 (Sep. 10, 1960): 143; Walker, Interview; Arthur Howe, Jr., Interviews, Oct. 21, 1983, May 9, 1984; quotations from the interview of A—S—, as recorded by an assistant director of admissions office, a copy of which was in the "Jews at Yale" folder provided to the author by Richard J. Israel. Minutes of the Yale Corporation Committee on Educational Policy, Apr. 16, 1948, p. 728; Pierson, *University College*, p. 475; Carroll, Interview.

26. Eugene H. Kohn to Sally Eaton, Apr. 21, 1948, Folder 1194, Box 240, Series III, OS. See Arthur Howe, Jr. to Mrs. Catherine J. Tilson, June 1, 1954, and other papers within Folder 854, Box 94, AWG. Astrachan, p. 214; *Ram's Horn* 3 (Dec. 1951): 3; Chauncey, Interview; Howe, Interviews, Oct. 21, 1983, May 9, 1984; Walker, Interview.

27. As Henry Chauncey put it, "No Yale president was ever so unrealistic as to believe that there were not institutional reasons for admitting certain people." For this reason the college admissions office operated largely independent of the Yale College Dean's office (despite the attempts of various Yale College deans to win greater influence over the process). The central administration feared that if the faculty commandeered the admissions process, they would admit students for academic reasons alone. As a reflection of the wishes of the university trustees, the president had personal control over admissions by appointing the dean of admissions. Admissions committee members had a summary of each candidate's application package at hand for reference should they have ever wanted to examine a student's record in the course of deliberations. Kinkead, *The New Yorker*, pp. 142, 146; Chauncey, Interview; Brewster, Interview; R. Inslee Clark, Jr., Interview, May 6, 1981; Walker, Interview.

28. Pierson, *University College*, p. 671; Pierson, *Numbers*, pp. 96–98; Howe, Interview, May 9, 1984.

29. Harold Wade reported that the first of the "prestige" schools whose dean of admissions visited public schools for recruitment was Amherst. According to Wade, Ivy League recruiters avoided public schools in order to avoid encouraging the application of Jews. Financial barriers to admission naturally affected high school students the most. Less than 20 percent of the high school students accepted at Yale in the 1950s were men who could pay their own way. As Donald K. Walker put it, "The only way that Yale was getting the cream of high school kids was by buying them." A tenfold increase in alumni interviewers between 1948 and 1960 served at one level to increase contacts with the public schools. Wade, p. 80; James R. Angell to Norman S. Buck, Jan. 14, 1935, "Yale College" folder, Box 38, JRA; Ralph C. Burr, Interview, Nov. 29, 1983; Howe, Interview, Oct. 21, 1983; Walker, Interview.

30. Clark, Interview; Howe, Interview, Oct. 21, 1983; Walker, Interview.

31. The quotation is taken from a report outlining the turmoil within Yale admissions at the start of the 1950s. The date of the report is Feb. 21, 1951, and it accompanies a letter from Norman S. Buck, dean of freshman year, to Professor Noyes, Records of the Provost, Acc. Jan. 16, 1981, Series I, Box 1, YRG 3-A, YMAL; Howe, Interview, May 29, 1984.

32. At a Yale College faculty meeting Howe had proposed the admission of women as a means of improving the academic standing of Yale. Behind the closed doors Dean De-Vane supported the proposal because he thought that women would set higher academic standards, that many outstanding students would only attend co-educational schools, and that the absence of women led the Yale community to disintegrate on weekends, while students traveled to women's colleges for dates. Allan S. Katz, "Women at Yale Proposed by Dean of Admissions Howe," *Yale Daily News* (Sep. 28, 1956), p. 1; Paul Botts, "Past Elis Dreaded Co-ed," *Yale Daily News* (Jan. 27, 1983), p. 5; Bergin, *Residential,* p. 100; Folder 48, Box 7, AWG, Howe, Interview, Oct. 21, 1983; Walker, Interview.

33. The issue of anti-Catholic discrimination in admissions involves one of the most poorly defined aspects of historical prejudices at Yale. Though some admission officers insisted that some members of the admissions committee of the 1950s discriminated against Catholics, other admissions officers who admitted bearing anti-Jewish stereotypes firmly denied anti-Catholic prejudices. Perhaps different members of the admissions committee had different bents to their prejudices. Donald Walker pointed out that applicants from Catholic schools that did not want their students to attend nondenominational Yale sometimes hindered the application efforts of their students. One Catholic school, for example, refused to allow an admissions officer to solicit applications and interview applicants on its premises. Another refused to send its students' transcripts to Yale. Yale admissions officers also suspected that many of the teacher recommendations for boys from Catholic schools deliberately downplayed the positive qualities of the students. In contrast, admissions committee member W. Jack Cunningham recalled that applicants from Catholic parochial schools faced a stiffer than average challenge in the application process because their schools were then not considered to be of top quality, and because some of the school day had been devoted to religion, rather than to more "proper" academic fields. Some Yale Catholics suspected that some form of Catholic quota existed at Yale in this time. William F. Buckley, Jr. recalled one occasion in this era when the law firm Wiggin and Dana asked him to testify at the Connecticut State Legislature against a proposed Fair Education Practices Bill. Frederick Wiggin of the law firm assured Buckley that Yale had no quotas. Buckley mentioned this to the Catholic chaplain at Yale, who told him that "it was an extraordinary coincidence" that exactly the same percentage of undergraduates were Catholics year after year. William F. Buckley, Jr., to author, May 24, 1983; Burr, Interview; Chauncey, Interview; W. Jack Cunningham, Interview, Dec. 13, 1983; Lawrence M. Noble, Jr., Interview, Mar. 29, 1984; Walker, Interview.

34. "The Steady Hand," *Time* 57 (June 11, 1951): 75–76.

35. Frederick H. Wiggin to A. Whitney Griswold, Feb. 20, 1957, Folder 611, Box 63, AWG.

36. John Q. Tilson, Jr. to Charles S. Gage, Feb. 11, 1959, copy in Folder 611, Box 63, AWG.

37. Gumbiner, Interview.

38. Seymour Lipset and David Riesman, *Education and Politics at Harvard* (New York: Mc-Graw-Hill, 1975), p. 179.
39. For an example of the pride that some members of the Yale family had in what they thought were Yale's "non-discriminatory" policies see the letter of S. E. Gleason to the *Yale Daily News* in which he repeats official university statements that Yale did not practice racial or religious discrimination in admissions. Gleason argued that Yale's official statement corresponded with the true spirit of Yale. S. E. Gleason, "Harvard and Yale Deny Discrimination in Admissions," *Yale Daily News* (Jan. 7, 1960), p. 2.
40. William Sloane Coffin to Kingman Brewster, Jr., Oct. 26, 1962, copy in Folder 1965-33, BBHFY.
41. Israel, "Jews at Yale"; Wilkinson, Interview, Sept. 16, 1982.
42. Richard J. Israel, Interview, Nov. 19, 1978; Israel, "Jews at Yale."
43. For example, in Fall 1960, of 3875 undergraduates, only 316 had indicated no religion, or had not answered at all. See the table in Folder 41, Box 6, AWG. Richard Israel to Arthur Howe, Jan. 12, 1960, Folder I-117, BBHFY; Israel, "Jews at Yale."
44. Israel, "Jews at Yale"; Howe, Interview, May 9, 1984.
45. Howe, Interview, Nov. 22, 1983.
46. William Horowitz to A. Whitney Griswold, Apr. 5, 1960, Folder 44, AWG; Israel to author, Oct. 31, 1983.
47. Memorandum of A. Whitney Griswold, Apr. 5, 1960, Folder 44, Box 6, AWG.
48. Synnott, *Door,* pp. 214–17; Hartley Simpson to A. W. Griswold, Apr. 6, 1960, Folder 44, Box 6, AWG.
49. Religious preferences were taken from the cards that entering freshmen completed for the university chaplain's office. The religion was then placed onto a student's permanent Yale record. This procedure continued until Dean Georges May suggested that this practice be discontinued shortly after his appointment in 1963. "G.D.V. consulted . . . ," Apr. 1960, Folder 215, Box 24, AWG; A. Whitney Griswold, "4/6/60 Jews," Folder 215, Box 24, AWG; Israel to author, Oct. 31, 1983.
50. Arthur Howe, Jr., to A. Whitney Griswold, Apr. 6, 1960, Folder 44, Box 6, AWG.
51. If one examines the written sources on which these paragraphs are based, it becomes evident that the recollections of Mr. Coffin and Rabbi Israel, though agreeing with each other and with other manuscript sources on the fact of certain events and meetings, do not always agree on the specific timing. The chronology I present here is heavily based on the manuscript evidence, although I have attempted to bring in the memories of the two chaplains where they most logically seemed to fit in. Richard Israel to Benjamin M. Kahn, Nov. 23, 1960. A copy of this letter was provided to me by Arnold Jacob Wolf.
52. William Sloane Coffin, Jr., *Once to Every Man* (New York: Atheneum, 1978), pp. 137–38; Lee, p. 134.
53. Israel's letter detailed both his feeling for Coffin and one approach that Coffin first suggested to solve the issue:

> The University Chaplain, Bill Coffin, whose aid in this matter has been invaluable and of whom I cannot speak too highly tells me that many of the people in the administration to whom he has spoken admit that Jewish students pose a problem for

them (though until now we had not had it spelled out so specifically) and that they feel they have a dragon by the tail. They are disturbed, but don't know what to do about it.

Coffin now feels that it would be advisable to ask the corporation for a quota of 20%, pointing out how far Yale is behind other schools in the nation. . . . His position is that if we don't state a quota we are going to have one anyway of half the size.

Coffin, pp. 137–38; Richard Israel to Benjamin M. Kahn, Nov. 23, 1960. A copy of this letter was provided to me by Arnold Jacob Wolf.

54. Sidney Lovett, "Report of the Committee on Religious Life and Study," Jan. 19, 1962, Folder 41, Box 6, AWG; Israel to author, Oct. 31, 1983.
55. Sidney Lovett, "Report of the Committee on Religious Life and Study," Jan. 19, 1962, Folder 41, Box 6, AWG; Israel, "Jews at Yale."
56. Arthur Howe, Jr., to A. Whitney Griswold, July 31, 1961, Folder 41, Box 6, AWG. Also see the two policy statements attached to Howe's letter.
57. Nathan Glazer and Daniel Moynihan, *Beyond the Melting Pot* (Cambridge, Mass.: The MIT Press, 1970), p. 157; Richard Israel to Sidney Lovett, Nov. 27, 1961. Copies of this letter were provided to me by William Horowitz and Arnold Jacob Wolf. Also see Sidney Lovett to A. Whitney Griswold, Dec. 11, 1961, Folder 41, Box 6, AWG.
58. Synnott, *Door*, p. xix; Sidney Lovett, "Report of the Committee on Religious Life and Study," Jan. 19, 1962, Folder 41, Box 6, AWG.
59. Coffin, pp. 137–38.
60. The Griswold admissions policy reached its final form with the copy dated 3/9/62. Six weeks before he died President Griswold reviewed the policy one last time. See the draft marked by "E.S." as sent to Griswold on March 6, 1963. All references in the following five footnotes are to the draft dated 3/9/62. "Undergraduate Admissions Policy," Folder 42, Box 6, AWG.
61. "Undergraduate Admissions Policy," p. 1.
62. Ibid., pp. 1–2.
63. Ibid., pp. 2, 6–7.
64. Ibid., p. 3.
65. William F. Buckley, Jr., *God and Man at Yale* (Chicago: Henry Regnery Co., 1951); Thelin, p. 60; "Undergraduate Admissions Policy," pp. 5–6; HFSH; Israel to author, Oct. 31, 1983.
66. "Admissions," *Yale Daily News* (Oct. 30, 1962), p. 1.
67. "Admissions," *Yale Daily News* (Oct. 31, 1962), p. 1.
68. Paul Weiss, "Letter to the Editor," *Yale Daily News* (Nov. 2, 1962), p. 2.
69. Arthur Howe, "Letter to the Editor," *Yale Daily News* (Nov. 2, 1962), p. 2.
70. "Editorial," *Yale Daily News* (Nov. 2, 1962), p. 2.
71. Wilkinson, Interview, Sep. 16, 1982.
72. Clark, Interview; Wilkinson, Interview, Sep. 16, 1982.
73. Clark, Interview; Howe, Interview, May 9, 1984.
74. Cunningham, Interview.
75. Brewster, Interview; Chauncey, Interview; Clark, Interview; Noble, Interview; Wilkinson, Interview, Apr. 21, 1983.

76. Georges May, Interview, Apr. 26, 1983; Kingman Brewster, Jr., to author, Aug. 15, 1983.

77. Catlin, p. 167; Kelley, p. 451; William Clyde DeVane, "Report of the Dean of Yale College," *Reports to the President of Yale University, 1947–1948,* p. 5; Doob, Interview, Nov. 11, 1982. In the late 1930s Pottle had saved a German Jewish family from the Nazi menace by signing a financial affidavit allowing them to immigrate to the U.S. Edgar Siskin to author, Mar. 18, 1988.

78. Doob, Interview, Nov. 11, 1982.

79. For example see Geoffrey Chaucer, "The General Prologue," to *The Canterbury Tales* in *Chaucer's Poetry,* ed. E. T. Donaldson (New York: The Ronald Press Company, 1975), p. 11, line 187.

80. Leonard W. Doob, William C. DeVane, G. Evelyn Hutchinson, John Perry Miller, Frederick A. Pottle, Eugene V. Rostow, George A. Schrader, Jr., "The Education of First Year Students in Yale College," *Yale Alumni Magazine* 25 (June 1962): 9, "Admissions: III," *Yale Daily News* (Sep. 23, 1957), p. 2; Ellsworth, Interview.

81. Doob recalled Hutchinson's complaint that Yale admissions procedures were biased against students at the Bronx High School of Science. R. Inslee Clark, Jr., recalled that engineers and scientists on the faculty would protest that Yale admissions officers, tending to favor "class-presidents over horn-rimmed laboratory experts," discriminated against scientists. According to Clark, that charge was true in the early 1960s. Clark also recalled the faculty expressing to him the conviction that there were many bright people out in the world, but not at Yale. These faculty thought that the Yale students then admitted were often "nice and decent, but not brilliant or special." Howe, in contrast, never had this impression as dean. He recalled that many faculty felt that a substantial number of Yale undergraduates were actually better students than many of the students in the Graduate School. Doob et al., p. 11; Clark, Interview; Doob, Interview, Nov. 11, 1982; Howe, Interview, May 9, 1984.

82. Doob et al., pp. 8–13; Doob, Interview, Oct. 28, 1983.

83. *Historical Register, 1951–1968,* p. 9.

84. The Yale alumni were similarly distracted by the report's call for the admission of women. While Yale graduates were fulminating over the women and over the award of an honorary degree to President John F. Kennedy, Yale moved to carry out the report's major recommendations. Catlin, p. 172; Holden, *Profiles and Portraits,* p. 135; Kelley, p. 453; Doob et al., p. 9; Chauncey, Interview; Doob, Interview, Nov. 11, 1982.

85. Brewster, Interview; Gustav Ranis, Interview, Apr. 2, 1981.

86. The 1964 *News* Board, for example, chaired by Joseph Lieberman, a practicing Jew, was known as one interested in social justice. Jefferson Morley and Marcy Ressler, "1960–1970," in *100: A History of the Yale Daily News,* ed. by J. Harris (New Haven: OCD Foundation, 1978), p. 59; "The Ambiguities of Public Morality," *Yale Daily News* (Oct. 6, 1959), p. 2.

87. See Folder 133, Box 124, AWG—especially see the copy of the "pledge card," "The Housing Bureau," p. 22, and the letter from Robert E. Shelton to A. Whitney Griswold of Sep. 4, 1962, and Griswold's reply of Sep. 20, 1962.

88. Lee, pp. 110–11.

89. See, for example, *Kingman Brewster, Remembrances* (New Haven: Yale University, 1977).

90. After Brewster turned down Skull and Bones, he organized the "Phoenix Club," as an "underground" senior society that regularly met without a building or ritual. Brewster asked his Jewish classmate Robert Arnstein to be a member. In 1967 Brewster would appoint Arnstein's sister Margaret Arnstein to serve as dean of Yale's nursing school. Holden, *Profiles and Portraits,* p. 147; Chauncey, Interview; Robert Arnstein, Interview, April 10, 1987.

91. See John Taft, *Mayday at Yale* (Boulder, Col.: Westview Press, 1976); Brewster, Interview; Coffin, Interview; Dilworth, Interview.

92. "A Study of Religious Discrimination in Social Clubs," *Rights* 4 (Jan. 1962), reprinted in *Race, Class, and Power,* ed. by Raymond W. Mack (New York: American Book Company, 1963), p. 95; Brewster, Interview; Stephen Kezerian, Interview, Oct. 1977. Correspondence between Brewster and Alexander Lowenthal, Nov. 29, 1965 to Dec. 3, 1965, provided to me by Mr. Lowenthal.

93. Holden, *Profiles and Portraits,* p. 148; Pierson, *Numbers,* p. 614.

94. Pierson, *Numbers,* p. 618; Brewster, Interview; Dilworth, Interview.

95. Brewster, Interview; Clark, Interview; Howe, Interview, May 9, 1984.

96. Burr, Interview.

97. Brewster, Interview; Clark, Interview.

98. Brewster, Interview; Clark, Interview.

99. Pierson, *Numbers,* pp. 98–99; Herschel E. Post, Jr., "The 'Well Rounded' Myth," *Yale Daily News* (Nov. 23, 1959), pp. 1, 5; Thelin, p. 45; Brewster, Interview; Clark, Interview; Dilworth, Interview; Howe, Interview, Oct. 21, 1983.

100. Arthur Howe, Jr., "Report of the Dean of Admissions and Student Appointments to the President and Fellows of Yale University, 1961–1962," Folder 202, Box 21, AWG; Howe, Interviews, Oct. 21, 1983, May 9, 1984.

101. Ballard, p. 59; Orde Coombs, "The Necessity of Excellence: Making it at Yale," *Change, The Magazine of Higher Learning* 5 (June 1973): 52; Synnott, *Door,* pp. 208, 211; Table from Fall 1961, Folder 41, Box 6, AWG; Clark, Interview; Ellsworth, Interview; Howe, Interview, Nov. 22, 1983; Noble, Interview.

102. Dean Clark recalled that the expansion of Yale recruiting primarily stimulated applications of Jews and blacks. The question that committee members guessed at regarding the new applicants was: "Would they survive the competition?" The credentials of the group were as good as or better than those offered by many of Yale's traditional applicants. R. Inslee Clark, quoted by Mark Singer in "God and Mentsch at Yale," *Moment* (July–Aug. 1975): 28; John Mauceri, "An Explosion of Music All Over Yale," *Yale Alumni Magazine* 40 (June 1977): 24; Israel, "Jews at Yale"; Burr, Interview; Clark, Interview; Noble, Interview.

103. In 1970 Lipset and Ladd found that 80 percent of college-age Jews were enrolled in higher education, as opposed to 40 percent of the American college population as a whole. Jewish students were found to be concentrated in institutions with higher academic standards. Seymour Martin Lipset and Everett Carll Ladd, Jr., "Jewish Academics in the United States: Their Achievements, Culture, and Politics," in *American Jewish Year Book, 1971,* vol. 72, ed. by Morris Fine and Milton Himmelfarb (Philadelphia: The Jewish Publication Society of America, 1971), p. 99; Wilkinson, Interview, Sep. 16, 1982.

104. Pierson, *Numbers,* p. 88; Brewster, Interview; Carroll, Interview; Chauncey, Interview; Clark, Interview; Walker, Interview.
105. Margaret Corvini, "Admissions Office Accepts More Yale Alumni Children," *Yale Daily News* (Oct. 3, 1980), pp. 1, 3.
106. Pierson, *Numbers,* p. 86.
107. Arnold Jacob Wolf, "Jewish Experience Is Vividly Present at Yale," *Yale Alumni Magazine* 36 (Jan. 1973); Zinsser, Interview.
108. "Class of 1912S Notes," *Yale Alumni Magazine* 36 (Apr. 1973): 43.
109. Corvini, pp. 1, 13.
110. Robert A. Dahl, William Kessen, Jonathan D. Spence, Horace D. Taft, Elga Wasserman, *Report of the Study Group on Yale College 1972* (New Haven: Yale University, 1972), p. 47; *Historical Register, 1951–1968,* p. 10; Holden, *Profiles and Portraits,* p. 63; Janet Lever and Pepper Schwartz, *Women at Yale, Liberating a College Campus* (Indianapolis: The Bobbs-Merrill Company, Inc., 1971); Pierson, *Short History,* p. 62; David Lee Saurer, "Women at Yale"—a comprehensive collection of primary and secondary source material, Yale Miscellaneous Manuscripts S, Group 1258, Box 18.

CHAPTER TEN: HILLEL

A well-thought-out analysis of religion and the Yale curriculum from 1945 to 1949 is William F. Buckley, Jr., *God and Man at Yale* (1951). Buckley discusses the controversies that his book engendered in "God and Man at Yale: Twenty-Five Years Later," published in his *A Hymnal* (1978). Meyer Greenberg provides a sociological appraisal of the Jewish student at Yale during the Second World War in "The Jewish Student at Yale: His Attitude Toward Judaism," *YIVO Annual of Jewish Social Science* (1946). Two detailed personal examinations by Hillel rabbis are Richard J. Israel, "The Rabbi on Campus," *Judaism: A Quarterly Journal of Jewish Life and Thought* (Spring 1967), and Arnold Jacob Wolf, "Jewish Experience Is Vividly Present at Yale," *Yale Alumni Magazine* (Jan. 1973). The writing of this chapter was greatly aided by the unpublished paper of Maurice L. Zigmond, "The Jewish Office at Yale—Some Reminiscences" (1962), made available to me by Susi Hauser. Also helpful was Richard J. Israel, "Jews at Yale" (1980), which Rabbi Israel provided to me. An excellent discussion of Jewish life on the national campuses appears in Alfred Jospe, "Jewish College Students in the United States," *American Jewish Year Book* (1964). Printed publications of Hillel at Yale with the titles of *Hillel Hello, Hilleli,* and *Ram's Horn,* kept in the Yale Manuscripts and Archives Library, document Hillel history from the time of its founding through 1953. The pertinent primary source collections used were the Hillel Files that Susi Hauser kindly shared with me and the Yale Hillel papers at the American Jewish Historical Society and at the Hillel Foundation at Yale.

1. Buckley, *God,* pp. 12–13.
2. Jonathan Rose to Arnold Jacob Wolf, "Letter," *Hillel Newsletter,* Oct. 1979. For a sense of how the imposing architecture at Harvard intimidated some women there, see Vivian Gornick, "Why Radcliffe Women are Afraid of Success," *The New York Times Magazine* (Jan. 14, 1973), p. 58.

3. Anna Rosen, "Attic Envy," *A Jewish Journal at Yale* (Summer 1983), p. 36; Bob Lamm, "Christian God and Jewish Man at Yale," *Response* 8 (Fall 1974), pp. 7–16.

4. William F. Buckley, Jr., "God and Man at Yale: Twenty-Five Years Later," in *A Hymnal* (New York: G. P. Putnam's Sons, 1978), p. 426.

5. Greenberg, pp. 218, 221–22, 227, 229, 231, 233.

6. Zigmond, "Office"; Israel, "Jews at Yale"; Bernard I. Spinrad and Mark W. Neitlich, "The Horns of the Dilemma," *Hilleli* (Nov. 1944).

7. Zigmond, "Office"; Sandmel, Interview.

8. "For the Hillel Foundation," *Yale Daily News* (Feb. 12, 1949), p. 2.

9. Ibid.

10. "Yale" folder, Box 20, B'nai B'rith Hillel Collection, AJHS.

11. Zigmond, "Office"; *Ram's Horn* 1 (Mar. 1950); *Ram's Horn* 2 (Mar. 1951), p. 1. Both issues of the *Ram's Horn,* as well as another pertinent undated article by Charles Kroloff, are contained in HFSH. Ivan Marcus, Interview, Jan. 10, 1983.

12. Beginning with the 1952–53 school year, Yale students were permitted to charge their Yale Jewish Appeal donations to their Yale bursar's bill account. With that method of donation the appeal was able to raise over $2,700 by 1954. Following pressure from the United Palestinian Appeal in the years of 1969 and 1970, the Yale Jewish Appeal's bursar privileges were terminated. By 1981 the Yale students succeeded in raising $14,000 for the appeal. In 1954 dollars this was $4,300. The 1954 dollar value was estimated from "Average Annual Purchasing Power of the Dollar," *The World Almanac and Book of Facts 1983* (New York: Newspaper Enterprise Association, Inc., 1981), p. 69; Jospe, p. 142; David Meter and George Singer, "Letter to the Editor," *Yale Daily News* (Feb. 12, 1969), p. 2; David Meter and George Singer, "Letter to the Editor," *Yale Daily News* (Feb. 13, 1969), p. 2; Zachary T. Paris and Thomas F. Handel, "YJA Replies," *Yale Daily News* (Feb. 18, 1969), p. 2; Daniel Freedman, "United Arab Appeal at Yale," Fall 1969?, Folder 1969–62, BBHFY; "Yale Bursar Misuses His Position to Aid the Israeli Military Establishment," HFSH; Joseph Gumbiner, "Annual Report on the Activities of the Yale Hillel Foundation," 1951, Folder 1954-1, BBHFY; Joseph Gumbiner to Arthur J. Lelyveld, May 12, 1953, Folder 1954-1, BBHFY; Joseph Gumbiner to Arthur J. Lelyveld, May 20, 1954, Folder 1954-1, BBHFY; William Horowitz to Friends of Yale Hillel, Oct. 5, 1953, "Yale" folder, Box 20, B'nai B'rith Hillel Collection, AJHS; *Ram's Horn* 1 (Mar. 1950): 4; Report of Paul Freedman, 1952-53, HFSH; Arthur Tobias, "Jewish Appeal Drive Begins," *Ram's Horn* 4 (Feb. 1953): 1; Sandmel, Interview; Dassi Wolf to author, Feb. 24, 1983.

13. Ephraim Fischoff, "The Jewish Student at Yale," *Yale Alumni Magazine* 21 (Dec. 1957): 16–17; "Yale" folder, Box 20, B'nai B'rith Hillel Collection, AJHS; Gumbiner, Interview; *Ram's Horn* 4 (Feb. 1953); Richard Israel to Erwin Goodenough, Oct. 26, 1961, Folder I-130, BBHFY; Joseph Gumbiner to Arthur J. Lelyveld, May 12, 1953, Folder 1954-1, BBHFY; "Hillel Dance Huge Success," *Ram's Horn* 5 (Apr. 1954); Zigmond, "Office"; Richard Israel to Benjamin Kahn, May 1961?, Folder 1962-13, BBHFY.

14. Reform liturgy remained in hibernation on the Yale campus until occasional Reform services resumed in the mid-1960s. A regular Reform prayer group did not emerge until an initiative led by Lisa Stone (B.A. 1978), Lisa Brachman (B.A. 1979), and Pierson College Dean Rachel Wizner produced a "Creative Reform Shabbaton" in fall 1977. As the given

names attest, women had begun to play a dynamic role in Yale Jewish life of the 1970s. See Robert Hess's article in HFSH. Israel to author, [Oct. 31, 1983].

15. Joseph H. Gumbiner to Arthur J. Lelyveld, May 20, 1954, Folder 1954-1, BBHFY; *Hillel Newsletter* 1 (Nov. 22, 1954), "Yale" folder, Box 20, B'nai B'rith Hillel Collection, AJHS.

16. Judah J. Shapiro to Harvey M. Applebaum, May 7, 1958, Folder 1958-4, BBHFY; Sidney Lovett, "Report of Church of Christ in Yale University," *Yale Reports to the President, 1957–1958;* Alfred Jospe to Richard Israel, Apr. 7, 1959, a copy of which was made available to me by Richard J. Israel.

17. Bruskin, Interview; Drabkin, Interview; William Horowitz, Interview, Oct. 29, 1978.

18. Letters of William Horowitz, May 3, 1951, May 15, 1951, "Yale" folder, Box 20, B'nai B'rith Hillel Collection, AJHS; "Service of Dedication," "Yale" folder, Box 20, B'nai B'rith Hillel Collection, AJHS; Joseph Gumbiner to Alfred Jospe, May 25, 1951, Folder 1954-1, BBHFY; Joseph Gumbiner, "Annual Report on the Activities of the Yale Hillel Foundation," Folder 1954-1, BBHFY; Krall, Interview.

19. For a record of Israel's arrest alongside other clergymen in a 1962 Albany, Georgia, civil rights disturbance, see "Act of Belief," *Time* 80 (Sep. 7, 1962): 45.

20. Israel, "Jews at Yale."

21. Richard M. Pfeffer to "the Chairman of the *News,*" Nov. 20, 1957, copy in Folder Q-105, BBHFY; Richard Israel to Alfred Jospe, Jan. 10, 1961, Folder 1962-13, BBHFY; Richard Israel to Saul Goldberg, Nov. 22, 1963, Folder 1964-26, BBHFY; Marcus, Interview.

22. Alfred Jospe to Richard Israel, Apr. 7, 1959, a copy of which was made available to me by Richard Israel.

23. Richard Israel to Allan Rodgers, Apr. 7, 1965, Folder 1965-32, BBHFY.

24. "Voluntary, After-School 'Clubs' Promote Learning," *New Haven Register* (May 22, 1960), p. 28; Monroe E. Price, "Undergraduate Yale," *Yale Alumni Magazine* 23 (May 1960): 25; Richard Israel to Alfred Jospe, Jan. 9, 1962, Folder 1962-13, BBHFY; Harold Bufferd, "Report of Hillel Chairman for Connecticut 1961–1962," Folder 1963-18, BBHFY; Richard J. Israel to Samuel Z. Fishman, Jan. 30, 1968, Folder 1968-52, BBHFY; Malcolm C. Webber to Richard Israel, Nov. 10, 1970, Folder 1970-65, BBHFY; Ethan Kra, Interview, Jan. 10, 1983.

25. Richard Israel to Eli Karetny, Mar. 12, 1963, Folder M-138, BBHFY; Richard Israel to Sylvin Wolf, May 3, 1962, Folder Z-134, BBHFY.

26. Richard Israel to Alfred Jospe, Jan. 10, 1961, Folder 1962-13, BBHFY.

27. Israel, Interview, Nov. 19, 1978; Marcus, Interview.

28. Albert Shamash, "Rabbi Resigns After 13 Years," *Yale Daily News* (Oct. 22, 1971), p. 1.

29. The "general consensus" that I note is largely based on my impressions from my undergraduate Yale years (1975–79) and the impressions of many students that I have informally conversed with over the ensuing years. Israel, "Jews at Yale."

30. A later sign of the evolution of Yale tradition toward embracing other faiths was the 1973 decision to refer to the "Christmas" recess as a "Winter" recess in the Graduate School Catalogues. The vacation still took place over December 25, but the name reflected the more ecumenical approach. Brewster, Interview.

31. Richard Israel to Saul Goldberg, Nov. 22, 1963, Folder 1964-26, BBHFY; Israel, "Jews at Yale"; Ivan G. Marcus to author, Feb. 10, 2000; Richard Israel, Interview, Feb. 11, 2000.

32. Marc Margolius, "Hillel Offers Wide Variety of Services to Yale Jews," *Yale Daily News*

(Apr. 8, 1975), p. 1; Charlie Homer, "Rabbis Knock 'Bluish' Values, Traditions," *Yale Daily News* (Apr. 11, 1975), pp. 1, 5; Arnold Jacob Wolf, quoted in "Rabbi Wolf going to Yale," Folder 7, Box 13, Edgar Siskin Papers, AJA.

33. Charlie Homer, "Palestine Issue Polarizes Jews," *Yale Daily News* (Apr. 10, 1975), pp. 1, 4; Arnold Jacob Wolf, cited by Sarah Peck in "Should Yale University Support Religious Institutions on Campus?" Sep. 5, 1976, p. 10—an unpublished essay shared with the author by Arnold Jacob Wolf.

34. On the occasion of a *Simhat Torah* celebration during one of Wolf's first years at Yale, he led his dancing congregation through the Branford College Fellows' Lounge, where Master William Zinsser was entertaining a group of "conservative and stuffy old men" who had been alienated from Branford during the period of student activism in the 1960s. Zinsser recalled that the fellows' meeting had just begun when he heard the noise of banging drums and "weird, crazy chanting" that sounded like a carnival. Into the fellows' lounge a "raggle-taggle gypsy crowd ringing bells" entered brazenly. As the line tapered off into women and children, it seemed like it would never end. Some of the older fellows were shocked by the impudent but friendly-spirited action of the crowd and these fellows stormed out. As the fellows left, one woman in the procession was shoved and physically kicked out of the lounge. With a figurative egg splattered on the faces of the enthusiastic crowd and the acidulous fellows, the procession left the lounge and the fellows resumed their meeting. The criticism that followed from many of the committed members of the Yale Jewish community convinced Wolf to make all future Jewish activities less disturbingly public. Zinsser, meanwhile, appreciated the variety that the procession had brought to the routine meeting. Wolf, *Yale Alumni Magazine,* p. 14. Drabkin, Interview; Susi Hauser, Interview, Oct. 16, 1978; Arnold Jacob Wolf, Interview, Oct. 25, 1978; Zinsser, Interview.

35. Feingold, p. 222.

36. Regarding the proportionate decline in Connecticut representation, in 1919–20, Connecticut led the nation by providing 37 percent of Yale's students. By 1975–76 the state had dropped behind New York to second place, providing 14 percent of Yale students. Pierson, *Numbers,* p. 73; Holden, *Pictorial,* "Chronological List of Buildings," p. 5; Richard J. Israel, "The Rabbi on Campus," *Judaism: A Quarterly Journal of Jewish Life and Thought* 16 (Spring 1967): 188; Goldstein, Interview, Jan. 31, 1979.

37. The first six Lovett Lecturers were Samuel Sandmel, Nahum Glatzer, Maurice Samuel, David Daube, Abraham Kaplan, and Isaac Bashevis Singer. Wiedersheim, p. 29; "Testimonial Honoring Reverend Sidney Lovett," "Yale" Folder, Box 20, B'nai B'rith Hillel Collection, AJHS; Yale University News Bureau Releases of Mar. 2, 1959 and Apr. 29, 1962, Folder 1126, Box 123, AWG; Folder 1962-13, BBHFY; Richard Israel to Saul Goldberg, May 19, 1964, Folder 1964-26, BBHFY; Richard Israel to Zalman Schachter, Feb. 17, 1966—a copy of this letter was shared with me by Richard Israel.

38. "To be worthy of the traditions of a great university," Yeg 8, H5, +1, YMAL; Sidney Lovett to Ephraim Fischoff, Feb. 16, 1956, Folder 1955-90, BBHFY; Bruskin, Interview; Hirschhorn, Interview; Horowitz, Interview, Oct. 29, 1978.

39. Richard J. Israel, "Why I Chose Hillel," May 9, 1976, Richard J. Israel Nearprints File, AJA. Israel's immediate successor as acting Hillel director was Susi Wugmeister, one of the first women to direct a Hillel Foundation.

40. "The Hillel Foundation is an important part of Yale life. It has the University's complete support, thanks and confidence and deserves yours," wrote Kingman Brewster, Jr., in "To be worthy . . ."—see note 38 above.

CHAPTER ELEVEN A KOSHER WHIFFENPOOF

The primary sources on which this chapter was most heavily based were the Griswold Presidential Papers in the Yale Archives and the records in the office of the B'nai B'rith Hillel Foundation at Yale. Both provide understandably different perspectives on the issue of religious observance in the post-Second World War era. The papers of Dean Richard C. Carroll provide insight into the day-to-day workings of the Yale College bureaucracy. Of crucial import to the study of the Young Israel House at Yale is the "History" file on the premises of the Kosher Kitchen.

1. In 1965 it was estimated that 4 percent of American Jews were "Sabbath observers." This percentage closely correlated with the proportions at Yale as of the late 1960s. Charles S. Leibman, "Orthodoxy in American Jewish Life," *American Jewish Year Book 1965,* ed. by Morris Fine and Milton Himmelfarb (New York: The American Jewish Committee, 1965), p. 36.

2. Although many institutions were far more accommodating to traditional Jewish students than Yale, there were also less accommodating institutions. One notable instance of the latter type was Stanford University in the mid-1960s. A Yale professor, incidentally, played a major role in encouraging religious accommodation at Stanford when the Reverend B. Davie Napier (B.D. 1939, Ph.D. 1944), gave up the Holmes Professorship of Old Testament Criticism and Interpretation at Yale and the mastership of Calhoun College in 1966 to become the dean of the chapel at Stanford. See *The Stanford Daily* of Feb. 18, Feb. 21, May 6, May 11, May 20, 1966, and Charles Familant to Richard Israel, Apr. 4, 1966, Folder 1966-37, BBHFY. I am indebted to Lawrence S. Hurwitz for sharing with me his oral history tape of "The Stanford Minyon."

3. Pierson, *Numbers,* p. 128.

4. Israel, Interview, Nov. 19, 1978.

5. Synnott notes that Harvard's President Lowell purposely objected to special treatment for observant Jewish students as this would indicate a "recognition of the Jewish religion by Harvard University." For the 1909 attitude of Columbia University regarding Saturday entrance exams see Wechsler, pp. 144–45. Synnott, *Door,* p. 46; Kestenbaum, Interview; Louis Sachs, Interview, Oct. 23, 1980.

6. Greenberg, p. 223; Walker, Interview.

7. Gumbiner, Interview; Joseph H. Gumbiner to Murray Rockowitz, Oct. 20, 1954, Folder 1126, Box 123, AWG.

8. Kestenbaum, Interview.

9. Elmore M. McKee to James R. Angell, Apr. 21, 1930, "Chapel" Folder, "Chapel" Box, JRA. On "Calcium Light Night" see Pierson, *University College,* pp. 72–73, 131, 132, 134.

10. James R. Angell to Elmore M. McKee, Apr. 23, 1930, "Chapel" Folder, "Chapel" Box, JRA.

11. "Agreement of the Undergraduate Deans' Concerning Jewish Holy Days," Sep. 23, 1943, Folder 51, Box 3, Series I, Yale College, Office of the Dean Papers, YRG 9-A-5, YMAL; Kestenbaum, Interview.

12. Kestenbaum, Interview; Sandmel, Interview; Richard Sewall, Interview, Jan. 24, 1982.

13. Kestenbaum, Interview; Joseph Muskat to author, [May 17, 1983].

14. Muskat to author; Joseph H. Gumbiner to author, Feb. 21, 1983.

15. Lewis M. Wiggin to Catherine Tilson, May 10, 1943, Folder 1127, Box 123, AWG.

16. Muskat to author.

17. Sidney Lovett, "Report of the Chaplain," *Yale Reports to the President, 1953–54,* p. 6, YMAL.

18. Alfred R. Bellinger to Joseph H. Gumbiner, May 24, 1954, Folder 1127, Box 123, AWG.

19. Alfred R. Bellinger to A. Whitney Griswold, May 25, 1954, Folder 1127, Box 123, AWG.

20. Joseph H. Gumbiner to Alfred R. Bellinger, May 26, 1954, Folder 1127, Box 123, AWG.

21. The week before Griswold's policy statement Dean DeVane had prepared a statement of principle that he admitted "may sound cold and unsympathetic (and bare)" but the dean promised that he would "take care of special individual cases and not offend the religious consciences of genuine believers in any creed." Griswold adopted some of DeVane's language but breathed some warmth into it. A. Whitney Griswold to William C. DeVane, Walter J. Wohlenberg, and Harold B. Whiteman, Oct. 20, 1954, Folder 1127, Box 123, AWG; William C. DeVane to A. Whitney Griswold, Oct. 13, 1954, Folder 1127, Box 123, AWG; Joseph H. Gumbiner to Murray Rockowitz, Oct. 20, 1954, Folder 1126, Box 123, AWG; William Horowitz, Interview, Jan. 28, 1979.

22. Richard Israel, Flyer to Students, [Sep., 1964?], Folder 1965-33, BBHFY; Horowitz, Interview, Jan. 28, 1979.

23. Gumbiner to author.

24. Rabinowitz, Interview, Nov. 18, 1979.

25. When the University Dining Hall, "Commons," opened in 1901, diners were regularly charged $3.25 per week for vegetarian meals and $1.50 extra per week for optional meat supplements. By Gumbiner's time, the Yale Dining Halls were already making matzahs available for Passover. Students trying to determine if the foods prepared by the dining halls contained pork or shellfish had to wait until 1980 for such a listing. Loomis Havemeyer, *Eating at Yale 1701–1965* (New Haven: Yale University, 1965), pp. 20–21. See letter of Joseph H. Gumbiner to Students, Jan. 25, 1954, "Yale" Folder, "B'nai B'rith Hillel Foundation" Collection, AJHS; Gumbiner to author; Ephraim Fischoff to Barry Augenbraun, Sep. 27, 1955, Folder 1955-87, BBHFY; Joseph Gumbiner to Murray Rockowitz, Oct. 20, 1954, Folder 1126, Box 123, AWG; Kestenbaum, Interview; Ethan Kra, Interview; Monroe Price, Interview, Apr. 20, 1983; Arnold Jacob Wolf, Interview, Sep. 28, 1980.

26. David Schimmel to Allan Arfa, Apr. 1, 1959, Folder B-108, BBHFY; On the desire for a food rebate by residents of the Harkness Dormitory on the medical school campus, see Thomas R. Forbes to Stanley H. Davis, Jr., Nov. 24, 1964, Folder 1965-33, BBHFY; Robert Harris to Myron Tavin, Aug. 11, 1982, made available to me by Judah Shechter; Philip Felig, Interview, May 7, 1980.

27. Muskat to author; Gumbiner to author.

28. Madeline F. Berman to Allan D. Arfa, May 22, 1959; Folder B-108, BBHFY; "Young Israel House at Yale," undated photocopy, YIHY; Aaron Gelman, Interview, June 13, 1983; Elijah Gold, Interview, Nov. 25, 1980; Daniel Greer, Interview, Nov. 21, 1982; Ethan Kra, Interview.

29. Arthur Howe, Jr., to Richard C. Carroll, Jan. 19, 1957, Folder 1, Box 1, Richard C. Carroll Papers; Muskat to author.

30. William S. Coffin to Norman S. Buck, May 19, 1960, Folder 918, Box 101, AWG.

31. Norman S. Buck to Members of the Executive Committee, May 31, 1960, Folder 918, Box 101, AWG.

32. Coffin, Interview.

33. Resistance to Saturday classes was offered throughout the university. Students of all faiths disliked the Saturday courses and tried, when possible, to arrange schedules with as few Saturday courses as possible. Faculty resented being cheated out of a full weekend. Through the 1960s fewer and fewer students elected Saturday courses, and fewer were offered. Some of the last to remain were pre-medical science courses. On occasion a Jewish pre-medical student would try to avoid a Saturday requirement and be met with skepticism by one of the nonreligious Jewish scientists teaching in the college! By 1971 there were no courses that were formally scheduled on either Saturday or Sunday. See the Yale College catalogues for timing of course offerings. See the two policy statements of A. Whitney Griswold attached to the letter from Arthur Howe, Jr., to A. Whitney Griswold, July 31, 1961, Folder 41, Box 6, AWG; Arthur Howe Jr., "Memorandum Concerning Orthodox Jewish Boys," Dec. 21, 1961, Richard Israel to William S. Cofffin, Jr., Feb. 1, 1962, Harold B. Whiteman, Jr. to William C. DeVane, Richard C. Carroll, Samuel Graybill, Arthur Howe, Jr., William Coffin, Richard Israel, Apr. 24, 1962, all in HFSH; Richard C. Carroll to The Residential College Deans, Apr. 21, 1965, Folder 1965-33, BBHFY; Richard Israel to Georges May, June 6, 1966, Georges May to Richard Israel, June 15, 1966, both made available to me by Arnold Jacob Wolf; Wilkinson, Interview, Apr. 21, 1983.

34. Beginning in 1981 the Yale University Dining Halls began providing an all-kosher meal in Commons for the benefit of students who wished to break their Yom Kippur fast. Richard Israel to Morris Goldfarb, Apr. 18, 1961, Folder 1961-10, BBHFY; Arthur Howe, Jr., "Memorandum Concerning Orthodox Jewish Boys," Dec. 21, 1961, HFSH; See the correspondence in Folder 1962-12, BBHFY, Coffin, Interview; Israel, Interview, Nov. 19, 1978; Israel to author, [Oct. 31, 1983?]; Marcus, Interview.

35. "Young Israel House opens at Yale U.," HFSH; Benjamin Kahn to Richard Israel, June 26, 1962, Folder 1963-19, BBHFY; Gelman, Interview; Daniel Greer, Interview, Oct. 15, 1980; Carl Posy, Interview, Dec. 22, 1980; Israel to author, [Oct. 31, 1983?].

36. The politics of the founding and growth of the Kosher Kitchen is a story in itself. When it was decided to move the facility to 35 High Street, the national Young Israel Association suggested naming it "The Hillel-Young Israel Dining Room." The traditional students, however, did not want to be affiliated with the political machinations of the national association. Half of the kitchen members came from Conservative homes and therefore were also reluctant to affiliate with the national Orthodox body. The students preferred affiliation with the *local* Young Israel Synagogue. Nevertheless, on Sep. 5, 1965, the "Kosher Dining Club" was chartered by the National Council of Young Israel. With

an Orthodox association governing the religious standards, there would be no legitimate grounds for questioning the kosher status of the food served. The kitchen was required to pay a monthly rental to the Hillel Foundation for use of the basement space. As late as 1968 its status was vague enough that Rabbi Israel noted that the Hillel Foundation called it "the Hillel Kosher Kitchen" and Young Israel called it "the Young Israel Kosher Kitchen and no one wants to push to clarify the matter." When Rabbi and Mrs. Arnold Jacob Wolf moved into the home in 1972, Mrs. Wolf became quite concerned over the fire safety of the basement facility. This engendered an ultimatum demanding that the kitchen either limit its membership by fall 1973 to forty students from throughout the university, or else find new quarters. The university made space available in the basement of the old Yale Hope Mission on Crown Street, some two blocks from the Old Campus. The same dining area that had provided food and spiritual support to hungry souls years earlier was renovated to fill the hungry mouths of students with religiously contented souls. The cost of renovation was paid for by monies collected from the kosher diners of previous years and from private donations. Benjamin M. Kahn to Harry Kaplan, Mar. 29, 1965, Folder 1965-32, BBHFY; Richard Israel to Benjamin Kahn, Apr. 29, 1965, Folder 1965-32, BBHFY; Charter of "The Young Israel House at Yale,"; Richard J. Israel to William J. Gordon, May 29, 1968, Folder 1968-52, BBHFY; David A. Kra, Adean Zapinsky, and Paulette Asher to George D. Langdon, [Mar.?], 1973, YIHY; Friends of the Yale Hillel Foundation, "1973-74 Facilities," Spring, 1973?, YIHY; David Kra to Interested Parties, Apr. 9, 1973, YIHY; David Kra to Martin Gant, Aug. 7, 1973, YIHY; David A. Kra to Mrs. Herman Alpert, Sep. 12, 1973, YIHY; Stanley W. Schlessel to Hillel J. Chiel, May 2, 1974, YIHY; Greer, Interview, Oct. 15, 1980; Israel, Interview, Nov. 19, 1978; David Kra, Interview, Jan. 10, 1983; Ethan Kra, Interview; Posy, Interview.
37. Posy, Interview; Marcus, Interview; Israel to author, [Oct. 31, 1983?].
38. Clark, Interview.
39. Posy, Interview.
40. Ibid.
41. Arthur Howe, Jr., "Memorandum Concerning Orthodox Jewish Boys," Dec. 21, 1961, HFSH.
42. Greer, Interview; Israel, Interview, Nov. 19, 1978; Posy, Interview.
43. Posy, Interview. Princeton would later convert one of its eating clubs to serve kosher food on an equal basis with the other eating clubs on its campus.
44. Orrin Persky to author, Mar. 28, 1983; Posy, Interview; Stephen G. Wald (B.A. 1975) thought that he became the first observant Jew in Skull and Bones. Stephen G. Wald, Interview, Aug. 20, 1991.
45. Persky to author.
46. Ibid.
47. Ibid.; Posy, Interview; Lamm, p. 15.
48. Persky to author.
49. Israel to author, [Oct. 31, 1983?].
50. Richard Israel to Richard C. Carroll, Feb. 16, 1965, Folder 1965-33, BBHFY; Posy, Interview.

51. Jonathan Kaufman, "Kosher Kitchen: 'Eat, Eat and Enjoy,'" *Yale Daily News* (Apr. 9, 1975), pp. 1, 3.

52. Pierson, *Numbers,* p. 128.

53. Crocker Coulson, "Islands in the Mainstream," *The Yale Daily News Magazine* (Apr. 1984), pp. 18–19, 25.

CHAPTER TWELVE FINDING THE BEST DOCTORS

Two excellent discussions of the national changes in medical school admissions in the 1950s are Harold Braverman, "Medical School Quotas," in *Barriers: Patterns of Discrimination Against Jews,* ed. by Nathan C. Belth (1978), and Lawrence Bloomgarden, "Medical School Quotas and National Health," *Commentary* (Jan. 1953). The Bloomgarden article focuses on discrimination at New York medical schools. Primary information on the facts and figures of Yale medical admissions in the 1940s is available in Folder 1195, Box 240, Series III, Office of the Secretary Papers, YMAL, and in the Medical School Records, YMAL.

1. A major step in the expansion of Yale medicine during Dean Lippard's term was the inclusion of the West Haven Veterans Administration Hospital under the Yale hospital umbrella. The addition of staff positions at the VA hospital and the 880 added patient beds permitted Yale to expand greatly both its population of medical faculty and students. Kelley, pp. 413–15, 445; *The National Institutes of Health Almanac 1968* (Bethesda, Md.: Office of Information, N.I.H., 1968), p. 79. See the Minutes of the Yale Corporation Committee on Educational Policy, Jan. 10, 1936, pp. 440–41, YMAL, for the thoughts of Dean Bayne-Jones; Daniel X. Freedman to author, Sep. 12, 1983; Lippard, Interview; Robert M. Lowman, Interview, Mar. 7, 1983; Frederick C. Redlich, Interview, May 30, 1983.

2. See "Psychiatry," *Encyclopaedia Judaica,* 1972 ed., vol. 13, pp. 1335–41.

3. "Loewenstein, Rudolph Maurice," *Encyclopaedia Judaica,* 1972 ed., vol. 11, p. 451; Claude A. Villee, Jr., "Book Review," *New England Journal of Medicine* 309 (July 28, 1983): 247–48; *Who's Who in America 1974–1975, Volume 2* (Chicago: Marquis Who's Who, Inc., 1974), pp. 3277–78; Freedman to author; Gilman, Interview; Redlich, Interview; Fredrick C. Redlich (lecture at Grace Building, Yale University, New Haven), Oct. 5, 1983; White, Interview.

4. Redlich, Interview.

5. In an example of reverse discrimination, Milton Senn, a non-Jew, recalled that as chairman of the pediatrics department (1951–64) he occasionally favored the hiring of Jewish faculty as a reaction to the discrimination that he felt he had often suffered at the hands of others who had suspected him of being Jewish for one reason or another! Robert W. Berliner, Interview, Nov. 14, 1978; Freedman to author; Theodore Lidz, Interviews, Dec. 3, 1976, Dec. 1, 1982; Redlich, Interview; Milton J. E. Senn, Interview, June 8, 1983.

6. At Cornell Medical School, for example, Jews, women, and older applicants were the particular victims of admissions committee prejudices. Alvin S. Johnson, "Discrimination in Education," Folder 205, Box 12, Series III, Alvin S. Johnson Papers, YMAL; Senn, Interview; Zimmerman, Interview.

7. Alvin S. Johnson, "Discrimination in Education," Folder 205, Box 12, Series III, Alvin S. Johnson Papers, YMAL.

8. Ibid.

9. Milton C. Winternitz, "Science and the World of Tomorrow," Binder 5, Box 2, Milton C. Winternitz Papers, YMAL; Redlich, Interview.

10. Eugene V. Rostow to Charles Seymour, May 9, 1945, Folder 807, Box 94, CS; Rostow, Interview, Nov. 14, 1978.

11. *American Jewish*, p. 363; Eugene V. Rostow, "The Japanese American Cases—A Disaster," *The Yale Law Journal* 54 (June 1945): 489–533; Eugene V. Rostow to Charles Seymour, May 9, 1945, Folder 807, Box 94, CS.

12. Eugene V. Rostow to Charles Seymour and accompanying envelope, May 17, 1945, Folder 807, Box 94, CS; Rostow, Interview, Nov. 14, 1978.

13. The figures for 1948 are taken from a survey carried out at the request of the university secretary's office when it was trying to ascertain the presence or absence of biased admissions in the medical school. The psychology of medical admissions officers can be seen in the way that applicants were classified into "minority" groups. Forty percent were "Hebrews," 35 percent were "other U.S.," 8 percent were "Italians," and 2 percent were "negroes." For some comparable figures from Cornell Medical School from 1946 see Wechsler, p. 209; "Medical School 1948–49," Folder 1195, Box 240, Series III, OS; Redlich, Interview.

14. Former Yale associate professor of pathology Harry Zimmerman was the founding director of the medical college at Yeshiva University. Glazer and Moynihan, pp. 156–57; Harold Braverman, "Medical School Quotas," in *Barriers: Patterns of Discrimination Against Jews*, ed. by Nathan O. Belth (New York: Friendly House Publishers, 1958), pp. 74–77; Bloomgarden, "Medical School," *Commentary*, pp. 32–33; Zimmerman, Interview.

15. Thomas R. Forbes to Carl Lohmann, Nov. 3, 1950, Folder 1195, Box 240, Series III, OS; J. Woodruff Ewell to Thomas Forbes, Oct. 29, 1958, Folder 1385, Box 152, AWG; Thomas Forbes to J. Woodruff Ewell, Nov. 7, 1958, Folder 1385, Box 152, AWG; A. Whitney Griswold, [memo to himself?], "4/6/60 Jews," Apr. 6, 1960, Folder 215, Box 24, AWG; Freedman to author; Lippard, Interview.

16. E. Richard Weinerman, fittingly (see page 163), was a leader in the drive to increase the number of black students in the school of medicine. Leslie A. Falk, "E. Richard Weinerman, M.D., M.P.H.," *The Yale Journal of Biology and Medicine* 44 (Aug. 1971): 3–23; Walsh, p. 243; Redlich, Interview; Redlich, Lecture.

CHAPTER THIRTEEN BREAKING THE BARRIERS

The complete story of how anti-Jewish feeling in America was countered and of how it largely dissolved in the aftermath of the Second World War is yet to be written. A brief but important account that portrays the national turn is Leonard Dinnerstein, "Anti-Semitism Exposed and Attacked, 1945–1950," *American Jewish History* (Sep. 1981). Focusing directly on the changing position of Jewish faculty is Lewis S. Feuer, "The Stages in the Social History of Jewish Professors in American Colleges and Universities," *American Jewish History* (June

1982). A personal memoir of anti-Jewish feeling, especially at Columbia University, appears in Sidney Hook, *Out of Step: An Unquiet Life in the Twentieth Century* (1987). A standard reference is "The Intellectual Migration: Europe and America, 1930–60," *Perspectives in American History,* vol. 2, ed. by Donald Fleming and Bernard Bailyn (1968).

A comprehensive assessment of American Jewish faculty is Seymour Martin Lipset and Everett Carll Ladd, Jr., "Jewish Academics in the United States: Their Achievements, Culture, and Politics," in *American Jewish Year Book 1971,* ed. by Morris Fine and Milton Himmelfarb (1971). A gold mine of statistical information on faculty distribution, attitudes, and religious beliefs for Protestants, Catholics, and Jews is Stephen Steinberg, *The Academic Melting Pot* (1974). The outstanding general portrayal of the opening of the "establishment" to new minorities is E. Digby Baltzell, *The Protestant Establishment* (1964). Also worth consulting is his follow-up article "The Protestant Establishment Revisited," *The American Scholar* (Autumn 1979).

The Charles Seymour and A. Whitney Griswold Papers in the Yale University Archives provide valuable primary source material for the study of postwar Yale.

1. Prior to his college appointment, Dyen had already worked as a research fellow at Yale for three years. During the 1940s Yale's leading linguistic light was also a Jew: Leonard Bloomfield. Sterling Professor of Linguistics from 1940 to 1949, Bloomfield had an appointment to the graduate school faculty and was best known for guiding the development of American descriptive linguistics. Edgar S. Siskin was the first rabbi to teach on the Yale faculty. He was appointed as a lecturer (with the rank of assistant professor) in anthropology for the 1947–48 school year. Siskin, at age twenty-one, had been the youngest student ever to be ordained by the Hebrew Union College. See the various materials in Folder 12, Box 13, of the Edgar S. Siskin Papers, AJA. *Historical Register, 1937–1951,* p. 100; *Historical Register, 1951–1968,* pp. 160, 271; Reznikoff, *Commentary,* p. 477; "Bloomfield, Leonard," *Encyclopaedia Judaica* (1972 ed.), vol. 4, p. 1173; Yale College General Faculty Minutes, June 4, 1942, p. 673, Box 1, YRG 9-1, YMAL; Dyen, Interview; Rollin Osterweis, Interview, Feb. 13, 1979; Yale College Faculty Lists 1940–50, prepared by Katherine Hauschild and shared with me by George Pierson.

2. Osterweis was academically most noted for his history of New Haven. As a recognition of his atypical interest in New Haven, Osterweis was chosen to serve as one of the seven proprietors who "owned" the New Haven Green on behalf of the townspeople. A former president of the Zeta Beta Tau fraternity at Yale, he was exceptionally proud of his Judaism, his Yale ties, and his appointment to the Yale College faculty. Oddly enough, his obituary in the *Yale Alumni Magazine and Journal* made no mention of his religion. His funeral was held at Congregation Mishkan Israel, where President A. Bartlett Giamatti delivered a eulogy. The service for this Yale loyalist ended with the entire assembly rising to sing "Bright College Years." Gabriel, Interview; Osterweis, Interview, Dec. 12, 1976; Rollin G. Osterweis, Interview, Jan. 28, 1981; "Rollin G. Osterweis Dies at 74; a 'Townie' and a Full Professor," *Yale Alumni Magazine and Journal* 45 (May 1982), p. 17 and "Class notes," pp. Cn5–Cn6 in the same issue; "Professor Osterweis Dies Sunday at Age 74," *Yale Daily News* (Mar. 3, 1982), p. 6; Rollin Osterweis file, JHSNH. On required qualifi-

cations for instructors during the Second World War, see "Rules Governing Appointment and Tenure," Nov. 1941, Folder 588, Box 68, Series I, CS.

3. Robert S. Lopez, Interview, Dec. 6, 1976; Roland Bainton, Interview, Dec. 3, 1982; "Lopez, Robert Sabatino," *Encyclopaedia Judaica* (1972 ed.), vol. 11, p. 489; 1946–47 Yale College Faculty List prepared by Katherine Hauschild and shared with me by George Pierson.

4. Dinnerstein, *American Jewish History,* p. 138; Janick, *Diverse,* p. 82.

5. Baltzell recorded that no Jew had ever had tenure in an English department at Harvard, Yale, or Princeton prior to the Second World War. Feidelson was the valedictorian of the 1938 Yale College class. Pierson, *Numbers,* p. 333; Baltzell, *Protestant,* p. 212; Peyre, Interview; Feidelson, Interview; Pierson, *University College,* pp. 305–11.

6. Arthur W. Galston, Interview, Oct. 25, 1978; "General Faculty in Yale College, 1946–47," prepared by Katherine Hauschild and shared with me by George Pierson; Elga F. Wasserman, Interview, Jan. 26, 1983; Harry H. Wasserman, *Conversation,* Apr. 17, 1978.

7. Rosenfield, p. 97; Brand Blanshard, Interview, Oct. 8, 1980; Northrop, Interview; Peyre, Interview; Paul Weiss, Interview, Oct. 27, 1978.

8. At some universities a rationale commonly used for discriminating against Jewish faculty was that Jews were "intellectual middlemen, not original inventors." The many counterexamples provided by the work of men such as Einstein, Bohr, Freud, and Boas were used by defenders of equal opportunity like Alvin S. Johnson to defeat this myth. See Alvin S. Johnson, "Discrimination in Education," 1947, Folder 205, Box 12, Series III, Alvin S. Johnson Papers, YMAL; Alvin Johnson, *Pioneer's Progress: An Autobiography,* cited by Feuer in *American Jewish History,* p. 461; Henry Sloane Coffin to Charles Seymour, Dec. 31, 1945; Charles Hendel to Charles Seymour, Oct. 2, 1945; William Ernest Hocking to Filmer S. C. Nothrop, Jan. 9, 1946; C. I. Lewis to Filmer S. C. Northrop, Jan. 11, 1946; Charner Perry to Filmer S. C. Northrop, Jan. 10, 1946; Alfred North Whitehead to Filmer S. C. Northrop, Jan. 5, 1946. The above letters are all contained in Folder 1077, Box 127, CS; Blanshard, Interview; Northrop, Interview; Peyre, Interview; Weiss, Interview, Oct. 27, 1978; Paul Weiss to author, Oct. 15, 1980.

9. Auerbach considered his position at Yale as "almost ideal." Peyre also prided himself on having brought Alvis L. Tinnin (M.A. 1954, Ph.D. 1961), a black, to the French department as a graduate student. Harry Levin, "Two *Romanisten* in America: Spitzer and Auerbach," in *Perspectives in American History,* ed. by Donald Fleming and Bernard Bailyn (Cambridge, Mass.: Charles Warren Center for Studies in American History, 1968), vol. 2, pp. 464–68; Charles Hendel to Charles Seymour, Oct. 2, 1945, Folder 1077, Box 127, CS; Bergin, Interview; Peyre, Interview; Gustav Ranis, Interview.

10. Brand Blanshard to Grace de Laguna, Dec. 7, 1945, from the Archives of the Bryn Mawr College Library, through the courtesy of Bob Castiglione.

11. Grace de Laguna to Brand Blanshard, Dec. 11, 1945, from the Archives of the Bryn Mawr College Library, through the courtesy of Bob Castiglione.

12. Brand Blanshard to Grace de Laguna, Jan. 18, 1946, from the Archives of the Bryn Mawr College Library, through the courtesy of Bob Castiglione.

13. *Report of Some Problems of Personnel in the Faculty of the Arts and Sciences,* prepared by a

special committee, appointed by the Harvard president, Cambridge, 1939, pp. 150–53, cited in "Jews on University Faculties," *Contemporary Jewish Record* 2 (May–June 1939): 86–87.

14. Blanshard, Interview; Robert L. Calhoun, Interview, May 18, 1980; Northrop, Interview; Peyre, Interview; Weiss, Interview, Oct. 27, 1978; Paul Weiss to author, Oct. 15, 1980.

15. Weiss's address on Judaism was largely paralleled in Paul Weiss, "The True, the Good, and the Jew," *Commentary* 2 (Oct. 1946): 310–16; Weiss, Interviews, Oct. 27, 1978, Oct. 20, 1983; Paul Weiss to author, May 21, 1981; Kestenbaum, Interview; Sewall, Interview, Oct. 17, 1978; "Dr. Weiss' Address," *Yale Daily News* (Oct. 2, 1956), p. 2.

16. Two departments that had anti-Jewish reputations in the years after the Second World War were the history of art department and the sociology department. The former department brought in a string of Jews as visiting professors but was slow to make permanent appointments. The latter department's larger problem, however, was not anti-Jewish feeling, but a difficulty in justifying its place at Yale. Historian Brooks Mather Kelley termed the department: "a constant problem." Determined action was required in 1961 in order for the university administration to bring the department up to Yale standards. In an unusual move for the university, Provost Kingman Brewster appointed that year an ad hoc committee to evaluate the department. The reviewers included Brewster, Dean John Perry Miller of the Graduate School, Dean Eugene V. Rostow of the Law School, Harvard sociologist Fred Bales, and several other nationally recognized leaders in the field of sociology. The evaluation resulted in a stronger department and a greater commitment by the university to support the department. The first known Jew to receive tenure in the Yale sociology department was Rosabeth Kanter, who received that appointment in the late 1970s. Catlin, p. 171; Kelley, p. 378; Pierson, *Short History,* p. 30; May, Interview; "Is the Ivy League Still the Best?" *Newsweek* 64 (Nov. 23, 1964): 65; Baltzell, *Protestant,* pp. 336–37; Lipset and Ladd, pp. 92–95; Steinberg, *Melting Pot,* p. 67; August de B. Hollingshead, "Report to the President by the Chairman of the Department of Sociology," July 6, 1962, Folder 207, Box 22, AWG; Brewster, Interview; Doob, Interview; Ellsworth, Interview; Kai Erikson, Interview, Oct. 14, 1982; Goldstein, Interview, Jan. 31, 1979; Helen Lane, Interview; Oct. 30, 1978; Hillel Levine, Interview, May 12, 1981; Seymour Martin Lipset, Interview, Apr. 12, 1981; Leon Lipson, Conversation, Mar. 31, 1979; May, Interview; Sidney W. Mintz, Interview, Sep. 9, 1980; Omar K. Moore, Interview, Apr. 16, 1981; Conversations with George Pierson; Posy, Interview; Rachel Ranis, Interview, Apr. 30, 1981; Redlich, Interview; James Rosenbaum, Interview, Jan. 31, 1983; Schwartz, Interview; Elga Wasserman, Interview; Jerome H. Skolnick, Interview, Apr. 2, 1981; Jerome K. Myers, Interview, Oct. 26, 1983; Paul Weiss, Interview, Sep. 29, 1980.

17. Dahl et al., *Report on Yale College,* p. 36; Kelley, p. 416; Morley and Ressler, p. 59; Pierson, *Numbers,* pp. 356, 359; Paul E. Steiger, "Publish or Perish," *Yale Alumni Magazine* 28 (Apr. 1965): 12–19; Richard Bernstein, Interview, Feb. 25, 1983; Paul Weiss, Interview, Sep. 29, 1980; Paul Weiss to author, Nov. 24, 1978.

18. Bruskin, Interview; Goldstein, Interview, Jan. 31, 1979; Gumbiner, Interview, Nov. 27, 1979; Israel, Interview, Nov. 19, 1978; Paul Weiss to author, Oct. 15, 1980.

19. Henry Rosovsky, "From Periphery to Center," *Moment* 5 (June 1980): 24; Steinberg, *Melting Pot,* pp. 135, 141; Lipset and Ladd, p. 108.

20. Richard J. Israel to Friends, Dec. 14, 1960, Folder 1964-26, BBHFY; Bernstein, Interview; Geoffrey Hartman, Interview, Oct. 20, 1982; Israel, Interview, Nov. 19, 1978.

21. Susi Wugmeister, "A 'Yeshiva' for Non-Believers," *Education in Judaism* 15 (May–June 1968); Felig, Interview; Goldstein, Interview, Jan. 31, 1978; Hauser, Interview, Oct. 16, 1978.

22. Ashbel G. Gulliver to Charles Seymour, Apr. 25, 1946, Folder 804, Box 93, CS; Sidney Davidson to A. Whitney Griswold, Nov. 5, 1953, Folder 1237, Box 136, AWG; Arthur Corbin to A. Whitney Griswold, Dec. 7, 1953, Folder 1237, Box 136, AWG.

23. After the meeting, Griswold wrote to Acheson of the challenges he had faced in the discussion: "The meeting was a bruiser. Your letter was a great help. I am, Sir, slightly disfigured but still in the ring." David Lauter, "Abraham Goldstein: Paperboy to Provost," *Yale Daily News* (Mar. 6, 1978), p. 1; Dean Acheson to A. Whitney Griswold, Dec. 18, 1953, Folder 1237, Box 136, AWG; Minutes of the Yale Corporation, Jan. 9, 1954; p. 17, Folder 661, Box 71, AWG; Lefty Lewis to Harry Shulman, Jan. 12, 1954; Folder 54, Box 2, Series I, Group No. 239, Harry Shulman Papers, YMAL; A. Whitney Griswold to Dean Acheson, Jan. 13, 1954, Folder 174, Box 14, Series I, Group No. 1087, Dean Acheson Papers, YMAL; Edmund M. Mortan to Harry Shulman, Mar. 15, 1954, Folder 71, Box 3, Series I, Group No. 239, Harry Shulman Papers, YMAL; Griswold, Interview; Stephen Kezerian, Interview, Oct. 1977; Weiss, Interview, Oct. 27, 1978.

24. Norman Oder, "Senior Societies," *Yale Daily News* (Apr. 13, 1982), p. 2; Goldstein, Interview, Jan. 31, 1979; May, Interview; Osterweis, Interview, Jan. 28, 1981; Peyre, Interview; Elga Wasserman, Interview.

25. Henry Broude served as presidential confidant and *éminence grise* in the administrations of Kingman Brewster, Jr., and A. Bartlett Giamatti. Eugene V. Rostow was the first Jew to accept an appointment as a Yale master. He was to begin serving in Trumbull College in 1966, but President Lyndon Johnson's calling him to serve in the state department preempted his mastership. Rostow's replacement at Trumbull, law professor Ronald Dworkin, was also a Jew. Arnold Band, "Jewish Studies in American Liberal-Arts Colleges and Universities," in *American Jewish Year Book 1966,* ed. by Morris Fine and Milton Himmelfarb (Philadelphia: The Jewish Publication Society of America, 1966), p. 7; Richard J. Israel to Richard Rubenstein, Feb. 28, 1966, Folder 1966-37, BBHFY; Boris I. Bittker, Jack R. Cooper, Victor Erlich, Joseph Goldstein, Nathan Jacobson, Arthur A. Leff, Herbert E. Scarf, Albert J. Solnit, Harry H. Wasserman, "Letter to the Editor," *Yale Daily News* (Sep. 29, 1980), p. 3; Brewster, Interview; Carroll, Interview; Judah Goldin, Interview, Feb. 24, 1983; Lane, Interview; Mintz, Interview; Elga Wasserman, Interview.

26. Clark, Interview.

27. The first Catholic was elected to the Harvard Corporation in 1920. The minutes of the Yale Corporation and the Corporation Committee-of-the-Whole for the years 1964 through 1967 apparently make no mention of any meeting between the corporate fellows and Dean Clark. Based on other background material that Dean Clark supplied me with in connection with this anecdote my best guess is that the exchange occurred at

some point during the first several months of 1965. I am grateful to Sharyn Wilson, associate university secretary, for her efforts to determine the date of this anecdote in the restricted pages of the Corporation minutes. Baltzell, *Protestant*, p. 338; Sharyn Wilson to John A. Wilkinson, June 7, 1983, accompanying John A. Wilkinson to author, June 9, 1983; *Yale University Catalogue 1964–1965*, p. 11; May, Interview.

28. The first Jew elected as a successor fellow of the Corporation was Lance Liebman, the young former chairman of the *Yale Daily News*, captain of the debate team, member of Elihu Club, and Harvard Law School assistant professor. He was elected by the corporation in 1971 along with Hanna H. Gray, who was the first female successor fellow of the Corporation. Elected by the alumni that year was Marian Wright Edelman, a black woman who was the first black and the first woman to be elected an alumni fellow of the Corporation.

The first known Catholic serving as a fellow on the Yale Corporation was José A. Cabranes, appointed in 1987. The earlier presence of many other "minority" groups on the board and the presence of Catholics among the faculty and administrators of the 1960s and 1970s made the Catholic absence more of an anomaly than evidence of bigotry during these decades. Though an anti-Catholic bias might have played a role in the defeat of William F. Buckley, Jr., when he tried to run for the Yale Corporation, his controversiality played a greater role.

On Jewish trustees at Columbia University see Harold Wechsler, pp. 136–38; On Louis Marshall's impact as a Jewish trustee at Syracuse University see Harvey Strum, "Louis Marshall and Anti-Semitism at Syracuse University," *American Jewish Archives* 35 (Apr. 1983): 1–12. Horowitz was a strong supporter of meritocratic admissions policies. *Historical Register 1951–1968*, p. 619; H. N. Hirsch, *The Enigma of Felix Frankfurter* (New York: Basic Books, Inc., 1981), p. 23; Felix Frankfurter to Wilmarth S. Lewis, Oct. 5, 1956, and Lefty Lewis to Felix Frankfurter, Oct. 8, 1956, both in the Wilmarth S. Lewis Library and made available to me by William Horowitz; "Trustee of Yale Breaks Tradition," *The New York Times* (June 21, 1965), p. 31; M. A. Farber, "Buckley 'Interferes,'" *The New York Times* (Oct. 29, 1967), p. B9; "Our April Salute: William Horowitz," *The New Haven Register* (Apr. 30, 1973), p. 22; Brewster, Interview; Chauncey, Interview; Clark, Interview; Doob, Interview; Horowitz, Interviews, Dec. 7, 1976, Jan. 28, 1979, Nov. 19, 1982, Sep. 25, 1987; Cabranes, Interview, Feb. 22, 2000.

29. "The American Jew Today," *Newsweek* 77 (Mar. 1, 1971): 58; "Sachar, Abram Leon," *Encyclopaedia Judaica* (1972 ed.), vol. 14, pp. 590–91; David G. Dalin, "A History of Brandeis University," *Midstream* 25 (June/July 1979): 98; "Levi, Edward H.," *Encyclopaedia Judaica* (1972 ed.), vol. 11, p. 79; Baer, p. 244.

30. Brewster, Interview; Chauncey, Interview.

31. *Who's Who in America, 1980–1981* (Chicago, Ill.: Marquis Who's Who, Inc., 1980), vol. 2, p. 2834; Baer, pp. 246–57; "Hunt for Successors to Brewster Draws More Rivals to Yale," *The New York Times* (Nov. 29, 1977), p. 23; "Harvard Dean Considered For Presidency of Yale," *The New York Times* (Dec. 7, 1977), p. IV:16; "Rosovsky Declines Offer to Head Yale," *The New York Times* (Dec. 15, 1977), p. II:13; Jonathan Kaufman, "Rosovsky Refuses Yale Presidency," *Yale Daily News* (Dec. 15, 1977), p. 1; "Yale Faces Budget Cuts," *The New York Times* (Dec. 15, 1977), p. II:13; Pierson, *Yale College*, p. 541; "The Presiden-

tial Search," *Yale Alumni Magazine and Journal* 41 (Sep. 1977): 5; Chauncey, Interview; Dilworth, Interview; Goldstein, Interview, Dec. 1, 1982; Liebman, Interview. Rosovsky kept a written record of his feelings regarding the Yale and Chicago offers during 1977, and I am grateful to him for sharing portions of that journal with me. Henry Rosovsky, Interview, Dec. 29, 1982; Henry Rosovsky to author, Aug. 22, 1983.

32. "Yale Resumes Presidency Search After Rejection by Harvard Dean," *The New York Times* (Dec. 16, 1977), p. II:4; Jonathan Kaufman, "Yale Search Focuses on Giamatti," *Yale Daily News* (Dec. 19, 1977), p. 1; Dilworth, Interview.

CHAPTER FOURTEEN: THE CLUB

Past membership lists for the various clubs discussed in this chapter are available at the Yale University Library. A complete history of the first century and a quarter of The Club is Alexander M. Witherspoon, *The Club: 1838–1963* (1964). Some of this chapter is based on interviews with individuals whose names must remain confidential. Virtually all of the material considered in this chapter is documented in the publicly available sources that are noted below.

1. Peyre to author; Max Taffel, Interview, Nov. 5, 1982; Elga Wasserman, Interview; Florence Wald, Interview.

2. Robert Brustein, *Making Scenes* (New York: Random House, 1981), pp. 16–17; Richard L. Zweigenhaft and G. William Domhoff, *Jews in the Protestant Establishment* (New York: Praeger Publishers, 1982), p. 48; Weiss, Interview, Oct. 27, 1978.

3. Some members of the Yale faculty who were able to join some of New Haven's socially exclusive enclaves chose not to be part of those organizations until their policies liberalized. Regarding exclusion of Jews, blacks, and Asians from downtown men's clubs nationally, see Stephen L. Slavin and Mary A. Pradt, *The Einstein Syndrome* (Washington, D.C.: University Press of America, 1982), pp. 40–43; *The Graduates Club 1963* (New Haven: Tuttle, Morehouse, & Taylor Press, 1963), pp. 37, 40–41; Robert A. Dahl, *Who Governs?* (New Haven: Yale University Press, 1961), p. 235; Warner, p. 183; "Membership of the New Haven Lawn Club Association," July 1, 1959, p. 14; Membership roster of the Lawn Club of New Haven for 1964; Lovett, Interview; May, Interview; Osterweis, Interview, Dec. 12, 1976; Elga R. Wasserman, Interview; Wilkinson, Interview, Sep. 16, 1982.

4. John Ferguson Weir, "Memories of a Yale Professor," *Yale University Library Gazette* 32 (Jan. 1958): 93–98. See Box 22, Series II, Group 2, James R. Angell Personal Papers, YMAL and Folder 648, Box 62, JRA; Dyen, Interview.

5. Wiedersheim, pp. 27–28; Alexander M. Witherspoon, *The Club: 1838–1963* (New Haven: The Club, 1964), pp. 17, 26; Weir, *Yale University Library Gazette*, p. 93.

6. Handlin and Handlin, *College and Culture*, pp. 39–40; Holden, *Profiles and Portraits*, pp. 3, 66; Pierson, *University College*, p. 129.

7. Pierson, *University College*, p. 129; "Antimasonic Party," *Encyclopaedia Britannica* (1973 ed.), vol. 2, p. 69; Camp and Welch, pp. 204, 207; Kelley, p. 224; Mack, p. 8; Witherspoon, p. 7.

8. *Catalogue CSP 1842–1979,* p. 396; Mack, p. 8; *Russell Trust Association Catalogue May, 1898;* Kelley, p. 224; Witherspoon, pp. 27, 49.

9. Witherspoon, pp. 26, 55; Eugene Rostow to Carl Lohmann, [ca. 1945], Folder 1194, Box 240, Series III, OS; Peyre, Interview.

10. Witherspoon, p. 55; Peyre, Interview.

11. Witherspoon, pp. 57, 59, 95, 99, 104. On Lippmann see Whitfield, *American Jewish History,* p. 61, and "We Are Wanderers," *Time* 32 (Dec. 5, 1938): 18.

12. Witherspoon, pp. 28, 48, 60, 61, 73, 86, 89, 106. Russell H. Chittenden, "The Club," Oct. 12, 1938, Folder 38, Box 2, Manuscript Group 611, Russell H. Chittenden Papers, YMAL. See letters of James R. Angell to his deans, Dec. 12, 1923, Folder 1324, Box 127, JRA.

13. Robert Evans, Interview, Sep. 15, 1980.

14. Baltzell, *Protestant,* p. 325.

CHAPTER FIFTEEN CODA—1980 AND BEYOND

In writing this chapter, I made liberal use of the newspapers of the era and made extensive interviews with many of the key players that occupied the stage. In reviewing the events of 1980, I also drew upon a journal that I kept for some of that year. Lenny Picker's unpublished "The State of the Hillel: An Informal Assessment" written July 1981 and Scott Cantor's unpublished "Yale Chavurah: A History" written in 1983 were also very helpful in reconstructing this era.

1. Some of the pertinent *News* articles regarding the resignation of Provost Goldstein are Andy Perkins, "DeLaney Kiphuth: Odd Jobs under Fancy Title," *Yale Daily News* (Apr. 13, 1979), p. 1; Stanley E. Flink, "Letter to the Editor," *Yale Daily News* (Apr. 20, 1979), p. 2; Mrs. Whitney Griswold, "Letter to the Editor," *Yale Daily News* (Apr. 20, 1979), p. 2; Edmund Morgan, "Letter to the Editor," *Yale Daily News* (May 10, 1979), p. 2; Andy Perkins, "Provost's Home Gets $67,000," *Yale Daily News* (Apr. 23, 1979), p. 1; Abraham Goldstein, "Resignation Letter," *Yale Daily News* (May 2, 1979), p. 1; Yale Law Faculty, "Letter to the Editor," *Yale Daily News* (May 10, 1979), p. 2; Abraham Goldstein, "Letter to the Editor," *Yale Daily News* (Sep. 24, 1980), p. 2; A. Bartlett Giamatti, "Letter to the Editor," *Yale Daily News* (Sep. 24, 1980), p. 2; Georges May to author, Oct. 6, 1980; Chauncey, Interview; A. Bartlett Giamatti, Interview, Feb. 16, 1983; Abraham S. Goldstein, Interview, Dec. 1, 1982; Horace Taft to author, December 1980; Wilkinson, Interview, Sep. 16, 1982. The perspective on Giamatti's persona was provided by Gaddis Smith in his fall 1998 DeVane Series lectures on the twentieth century history of Yale.

2. Then a first-year medical student, the author presented details of his research in progress at a Hillel-sponsored lecture on Jan. 25, 1980 and shared some of the correspondence detailed in chapter 3 with Rabbi Wolf. Dan A. Oren, "An Overview of the History of Jews at Yale," *Hillel Newsletter* (February 1980), pp. 1b, 2; and report of Arnold Jacob Wolf to the New Haven Jewish Federation (Feb. 15, 1980), both in the files of the author.

3. Joanne Lipman, "Rabbi Arnold Wolf," *Yale Daily News* (Sep. 23, 1980), pp. 1, 6.

4. Howard Shapiro, "Wolf Warns Students of Yale's Insensitivity," *Yale Daily News* (Dec. 5, 1980), p. 6; Howard Shapiro, "Chaplain Selection Underway," *Yale Daily News* (Jan. 26, 1981), p. 1.

5. Arnold Jacob Wolf, Interview, Sep. 28, 1980; Howard I. Gralla, Interview, Feb. 14, 2000.

6. Graciella Trilla, quoted in "Class of 1979 Notes," *Yale Alumni Magazine* 63 (February 2000): 84.

7. The initial *News* article on the sermon—at which the author was present—was Mark Schmitt, "Yale Callous to Jews, Wolf Says in Sermon," *Yale Daily News* (Sep. 22, 1980), pp. 1, 4. For a critical response by two Jewish professors, see John Hollander and Harold Bloom, "Letter to the Editor," *Yale Daily News* (Sep. 23, 1980), p. 2. More reliable descriptions of the sermon than the initial *News* account appear in Wolfgang Saxon, "Departing Chaplain Accuses Yale of 'Callousness' on Needs of Jews," *New York Times* (Sep. 24, 1980), p. 2; Joshua Gutoff, "Letter to the Editor," *Yale Daily News* (Sep. 25, 1980), p. 2; and Sam Fleischacker and Sherry Glied, "Letter to the Editor," *Yale Daily News* (Sep. 25, 1980), p. 2. Wolf entered his own criticism of the reporting in Arnold Jacob Wolf, "Letter to the Editor," *Yale Daily News* (Sep. 22, 1980), p. 3 and in "On Being a Jew at Yale," *Yale Daily News* (Sep. 29, 1980), p. 3. Alvin Berkun, Conversation, Dec. 11, 1980; William W. Hallo, Interview, Nov. 2, 1982; Hartman, Interview; Gustav Ranis, Interview; Arnold Jacob Wolf, Interview, Sep. 28, 1980.

8. To emphasize the deliberate, ground-breaking nature of Rutenberg's appointment and its meaning to the university, it was very important to Giamatti that the permanent historical record credit him with the decision to hire Rutenberg. Ruth Marcus, "Yale Rabbi's Legacy of Controversy," *New York Times* (Oct. 19, 1980), p. CN1; "Rutenberg Named Assistant Chaplain," *Newsletter of the University Chaplain's Office* (May 1981), p. 1; John Vannorsdall, "Pastor's Column," *Newsletter of the University Chaplain's Office* (May 1981), p. 1; Dilworth, Interview; A. Bartlett Giamatti, Interview, Jan. 26, 1983.

9. A. Bartlett Giamatti, "Statement by The President," *University Grievance Procedures and Yale Policies on Affirmative Action and Non-discrimination, Supplement to the Yale Weekly Bulletin and Calendar* (Sep. 17, 1981), p. 1; Giamatti, Interview, Feb. 16, 1983; Krall, Interview; Wilkinson, Interview, Sep. 16, 1982.

10. David Leavitt, "The Way I Live Now," *New York Times Magazine* (July 9, 1989): 29.

11. A. Bartlett Giamatti, "Address to the New England Regional Board, Anti-Defamation League of B'nai B'rith, Boston, Mass., Nov. 7, 1982," shared with the author by President Giamatti; James Ponet, "An Open Letter to Rabbi Arnold Wolf," *Sh'ma* 21 (May 3, 1991): 102–103.

12. On publication of the first edition of this book, see William W. Hallo, "Letter to the Editor," *Yale Alumni Magazine* 53 (December 1989): 3 and Dirk Johnson, "Yale's Limit on Jewish Enrollment Lasted Until Early 1960s, Book Says," *New York Times* (Mar. 4, 1986), pp. B1, B5. Confronting the tensions documented in this book afforded a catharsis for the university itself as well as a chance to celebrate Yale's overall record. A videotape of the reception hosted by Giamatti in the university's President's Room on April 6, 1986, in honor of the book publication provides further insight into the described process. After Giamatti's sudden death in 1989, Rabbi Ponet would write: "The Jews of Yale and America have lost a true friend, a President who successfully secured the future of Judaic Stud-

ies at Yale, a colleague who was deeply engaged by the rhetoric of the Jewish tradition." James Ponet, "Giamatti on Rabbi Tarphon," *National Jewish Post and Opinion* (Sep. 13, 1989): N8. A. Bartlett Giamatti, Conversation, Apr. 6, 1986.

13. Scott Cantor, unpublished 1983 manuscript: "Yale Chavurah: A History."

14. Stephen Neuwirth, "Hillel Chooses Yale Graduate as New Director, Jewish Chaplain," *Yale Daily News* (May 1, 1981), p. 5.

15. Sara Heitler, "Blueprints of a Life: The Story of Jim Ponet," *Urim v'Tumim* (Winter 1992): 6–7; Letter of James Ponet to author, Jan. 1989.

16. Letter from Sam Weintraub, Jr. to James Ponet, Sep. 19, 1983; letter from James Ponet to Sam Weintraub, Jr., Sep. 28, 1983, both shared by James Ponet.

17. Edward Feld, "Jewish Professors Coming Home," *Sh'ma* 21 (Jan. 11, 1991): 33–34.

18. Donald J. Cohen, Interview, Dec. 20, 1999.

19. Given DKE's history and Rose's Jewish background, he took a special pleasure in purchasing the DKE building for the benefit of all of Yale. Letter from Frederick P. Rose to author, Mar. 6, 1986; Frederick P. Rose, Interview, May 14, 1986.

20. Letter from Eugene Rostow to James Ponet, Apr. 8, 1991, shared by James Ponet.

21. "Yale Hillel House Campaign," 1991 brochure; Cohen, Interview, Dec. 20, 1999.

22. The presence of Yale President Howard Lamar and Yale President-Designate Richard Levin at the ground-breaking was heartwarming and surrealistic for Jews in attendance who saw their presence as a sign of full "arrival" in the Yale world. Levin's leading the Hebrew "Shehecheyanu" prayer at the ceremony and later singing a Hebrew song "Hiney Ma Tov" (how good and pleasant it is) at the dedication meal after the ceremony had a similarly symbolic meaning. See Bruce Fellman, "A Home of One's Own," *Yale Alumni Magazine* 59 (November 1995): 32–39. Roth had been drafting plans for such a space for almost three decades.

23. Carolyn J. Mooney, "New Yale Head Is Both Traditional and Ground-Breaking Choice," *Chronicle of Higher Education* 39 (Apr. 28, 1993): A15–A16; Jennifer Kaylin, "The New Man Takes Command," *Yale Alumni Magazine* 56 (Summer 1993): 32–37.

24. William E. Geist, "The Outspoken President of Yale," *New York Times Magazine* (Mar. 6, 1983): 42–56; Mary Jordan, "Wanted: Presidents for U.S. Universities," *Washington Post* (June 15, 1992), pp. A4–A5; Donald J. Cohen, Interview, Jan. 3, 2000.

25. Some missed the bully pulpit at Yale. In 1998 Levin would be criticized by one young historian for a tendency to appear more as a "chief financial officer" than as a leader in the world of ideas. Garry Reeder, "A Challenge to President Richard Levin," *Yale Daily News* (Nov. 9, 1998), p. 8.

26. Levin correctly noted that Kingman Brewster, Jr., had similar interests in social justice that derived from Brewster's own very different personal background. Richard C. Levin, Interview, July 25, 2000. In 1997 the Levin administration had to confront a Jewish issue that reached the pages of the national press. A handful of ultra-Orthodox Jewish undergraduates (the "Yale Four") charged the university with unlawfully requiring them to live on campus during their freshman and sophomore years. Their position put them at odds with many. Yale College officials were frustrated, since they were trying to adapt their policies to accommodate the stated religious needs within the confines of dormitory life. Other observant Orthodox students at Yale felt that these students were implying that

their own Jewish practices were not authentic. Even Rabbi Michael Whitman, a peaceable Orthodox rabbi skilled at building bridges between different groups of people—and hired by the Hillel Foundation to support the traditional Jewish community at Yale—was left unable to serve in his hoped for role as mediator due to the four students' unwillingness to negotiate with him. The college based its arguments on its view of residential life as a key to the identity of a Yale College education, and keeping freshman and sophomores on campus allowed Yale to play some role *in loco parentis*. Yale undermined its own arguments in this respect, however, by repeated misjudgments of student enrollment in the 1970s through 1990s. Frequently, students who wished to live in the residential colleges found themselves forced to live off-campus or in ad hoc spaces. Meanwhile, the university demanded that these four students conform with the rules.

Ostensibly, the sexual behavior and dress code in the dormitories posed a threat to these students and drew attention to several meritorious questions: Does the ideal Yale College education require students to have common dormitory experiences? Does a College that demands a common residential experience have an equal obligation to make sure that in fact it has enough rooms available to assure that experience for all who do want it? Did the sexual activity in the dormitories of the late twentieth century create an environment that vigorously challenged those who were uncomfortable with the behavior? The answers to such questions are not simple. Defining and then wrestling with sexual mores is a challenge faced by virtually every human and culture on Earth. The questions raised by these Jewish students are not uniquely Jewish questions and might well have resonated with students of all sorts throughout the college, thereby serving as a focal point for intelligent discussion between an institution and its constituents. The students failed to realize that the essence of a successful relationship, whether it is between individuals or between individuals and an institution, is the art of resolving inevitable differences and the determination to do so. With no persistent effort that might lead to mutual growth and respect, the students broke off their discussion with Yale and transferred the matter into Federal Court, where their case was dismissed.

See, for example, extensive initial discussion of the issues in William Glaberson, "Orthodox Jews Defy Yale's Housing Rules, Spurring a Moral Debate," *New York Times* (Sep. 7, 1997), p. 45; Elisha Dov Hack, "College Life vs. My Moral Code," *New York Times* (Sep. 9, 1997), p. A27; and several replies to that article in "Dormitory Life is Essential to a Yale Education," *New York Times* (Sep. 11, 1997), p. A30; Marilyn Henry, "God and Sex at Yale," *Jerusalem Post Magazine* (Nov. 7, 1997), pp. 8–9; Betty Trachtenberg, Interview, Jan. 5, 2000; Jen Richler, "When There's No Home Away From Home," *Yale Herald* (Apr. 9, 1999), pp. 1, 7.

CHAPTER SIXTEEN: CONCLUSIONS

A thoughtful essay that considers the conflicts between democratic principles and the need for higher education to focus on the talented is Brand Blanshard, "Democracy and Distinction in American Education," in *On the Meaning of the University*, ed. by Sterling M. McMurrin (1976). Updating E. Digby Baltzell's *The Protestant Establishment* is an important collection of studies by Richard L. Zweigenhaft and G. William Domhoff entitled *Jews in the Protestant Establishment* (1982). Examining representative sections of the Protestant (really Episcopalian and Presbyterian) establishment, the two authors consider the attitudes and backgrounds of the Jews who are accepted by the establishment, the changes in the establishment that result from the acceptance, and the limits of the acceptance. Stephen Steinberg, *The Ethnic Myth* (1981), is an excellent dissection of the ethnic factors that did and did not play a role in the rise or lack of social movement of minorities. A similarly skillful dissection is R. Laurence Moore, "Insiders and Outsiders in American Historical Narrative and American History," *The American Historical Review* (Apr. 1982).

1. Kelley, pp. 78–98.
2. Chauncey, Interview.
3. Coffin, Interview.
4. "Class Action Suit Alleges Sexual Harrassment," *Yale Alumni Magazine and Journal* 41 (Sep. 1977): 8; David Bokman and Brad Berenson, "The Party of the Right," *The New Journal* 16 (Dec. 9, 1983): 27; Interview with a residential college master.
5. Peggy Edersheim, "Wolf's Head Votes Not to Tap Women," *Yale Daily News* (Jan. 18, 1984), p. 1. Nancy Marx Better, "Another Vote on Girls In an Old-Boy World," *The New York Times* (May 12, 1991), p. F23. In the 1990s fraternities again became popular for some students in Yale life, as drinking laws stifled alcohol consumption in the residential colleges. Two fraternities were for Jewish men, one for African-American men, and one for African-American women. In 1997 Oliver Ben Karp and Lubavitch Rabbi Shmully Hecht founded the Chai Society in order to create a salon atmosphere that would attract elite Jewish and non-Jewish undergraduate and graduate students on campus. By 2000 they had successfully enrolled a full membership and owned three buildings on Crown Street and were supporting several start-up businesses that they hoped would boost the New Haven economy. Paul Bass, "Ben & Shmully Talk," *New Haven Advocate* (Feb. 3, 2000), pp. 12–15.
6. A sign of the growing acceptance of American Jews in the 1960s was the high proportion of Jews that began to marry non-Jews. Some of these marriages included members of the most elite Jewish and Protestant establishment families. Fred Massarik and Alvin Chenkin, "United States National Jewish Population Study: A First Report," in *American Jewish Year Book 1973,* ed. by Morris Fine and Milton Himmelfarb (New York: The American Jewish Committee, 1973), p. 295; Ruby Jo Reeves Kennedy, "Single or Triple Melting Pot? Intermarriage in New Haven, 1870–1950," *American Journal of Sociology* 57 (July 1952): 56–59; Baltzell, *The American Scholar,* p. 513; Ruth Marcus, *The New York Times,* p. CN1; Howard Shapiro, "Chaplain Selection Underway," *Yale Daily News* (Jan. 26, 1981), p. 1; "Rutenberg Named Assistant Chaplain," *Newsletter of the University Chaplain's Office* (May 1981), p. 1; John Vannorsdall, "Pastor's Column," *Newsletter of the University Chaplain's Office* (May 1981), p. 1; Dilworth, Interview; A. Bartlett Giamatti, Interview, Jan. 26, 1983; Stoddard, Interview.
7. A prime example of the continuing need for social discrimination came in April 1978 when one wealthy undergraduate invited an exclusive quarter of other Yale undergraduates to a $40,000 party planned for a Saturday night in the University Commons. Only the widespread negative public attention (including advance reports on the national

television newscasts) that the event garnered resulted in the hurried cancellation of the extravaganza. A *Yale Daily News* editorial called the cancellation "a victory of sensitivity to those who couldn't dream of affording or attending such an affair." "Monte Carlo Comes to Commons," *Yale Daily News* (Apr. 6, 1978), p. 1; "Campus Alive with Colorful Party Markers," *Yale Daily News* (Apr. 10, 1978), p. 1; Jefferson Morley, "Party Cancellation Shocks Community," *Yale Daily News* (Apr. 10, 1978), p. 1; "Drawing the Line," *Yale Daily News* (Apr. 10, 1978), p. 2.

8. See, for example, Philip C. Rodkin, Thomas W. Farmer, Ruth Pearl, and Richard Van Acker, "Heterogeneity of Popular Boys: Antisocial and Prosocial Configurations," *Developmental Psychology* 36 (Jan. 2000), pp. 10–14.

9. For a fictional summary of attitudes toward "outsiders," see Owen Johnson, p. 150. Chip Cowell and Malcolm Russell, "Handicapped Suffer from Poorly Designed Buildings," *Yale Daily News* (Apr. 28, 1976), p. 7.

10. Yale percentages calculated from Synnott, *Door*, pp. 214–17.

11. Robert Rodriguez, "Letter to the Editor," *Yale Daily News* (Sep. 29, 1980), p. 3; Charles G. Burck, "A Group Profile of the Fortune 500 Chief Executive," *Fortune*, 93 (May 1976), p. 175; Zweigenhaft and Domhoff, p. 20; Albert M. Shulman, *The Religious Heritage of America* (San Diego: A. S. Barnes & Company, Inc., 1981), p. 295.

12. Frank, p. 39.

13. A study of corporate directors of East European Jewish background noted that they were unanimously uninterested in being the only Jewish member of a gentile social club. Zweigenhaft and Domhoff, pp. 54–55; Dolowitz to author; Goldstein, Interview, Jan. 31, 1979; Kushlan, Interview.

14. Sidney Goldstein, "American Jewry 1970: A Demographic Profile," *American Jewish Year Book 1971*, ed. by Morris Fine and Milton Himmelfarb (New York: The American Jewish Committee, 1971), pp. 67–68.

15. *The American Heritage Dictionary of the English Language*, ed. by William Morris (Boston: Houghton Mifflin Company, 1970), pp. 254, 261.

16. An "outsider's" view of the Yale residential college fellowships as being stuffy men's clubs appears in Vivian Gornick, "A Woman among the Ivy Fellows," *The Nation* (Nov. 18, 1978), pp. 544–48; Woodrow Wilson, quoted by Arthur S. Link, *Wilson: The Road to the White House*, in Baltzell, *The Protestant Establishment*, p. 14; Robert M. Hutchins, quoted by Wechsler, p. 236; Daniel Coit Gilman, quoted by Veysey, p. 163.

17. Baer, p. 319; Baltzell, *Protestant*, pp. 61, 113, 138; Birmingham, pp. 131, 239, 345; Arthur A. Chiel, "Looking Back," *The Connecticut Jewish Ledger* (June 29, 1972, Oct. 12, 1972, Nov. 22, 1972); Lee Stock Hershman, Interview, May 16, 1983.

18. Pierson, *Yale College*, pp. 8, 18–19.

19. Stoddard, Interview.

20. R. Laurence Moore, "Insiders and Outsiders in American Historical Narrative and American History," *The American Historical Review* 87 (Apr. 1982): 407–08.

21. Pierson, *Yale College*, p. 26; Pierson, *University College*, p. 130; May, Interview.

22. Steven V. Benét and J. F. Carter, quoted in Pierson, *Yale College*, p. 367.

23. Mack, p. 147.

24. "Fraternal Orders," *Universal Jewish Encyclopedia* (1969 ed.), vol. 4, p. 420.

25. Handlin and Handlin, *College and Culture,* p. 39; Kelley, pp. 107–08, 284–85; Gabriel, p. 22; Pierson, *University College,* 128–29.
26. Havemeyer, *Eating,* pp. 24–25; James Rowland Angell, quoted by Reuben Holden in *Profiles and Portraits,* pp. 116–17.
27. Pierson, *University College,* p. xi.
28. Rostow, *Harkness Hoot,* p. 57.
29. Brand Blanshard, "Democracy and Distinction in American Education," in *On the Meaning of the University,* ed. by Sterling M. McMurrin (Salt Lake City: University of Utah Press, 1976), pp. 30–31.
30. *The Babylonian Talmud, Mo'ed Katan, Vol. 4,* ed. by Isidore Epstein, trans. by Dayan H. M. Lazarus (London: The Soncino Press, 1938), p. 160.
31. William Clyde DeVane, "Report of the Dean of Yale College," *Reports to the President of Yale University, 1947–48,* pp. 4–6.

Bibliography

INTERVIEWS

Following many of the names below is a brief indication of the interviewee's rela
tions to Yale University or to one of the characters or subjects discussed in the text.
Where a title is given it refers to the status of that person at the time of the interview. Some of the interviews were conducted by telephone.

Alderman, Abraham S. (B.A. 1923), Nov. 8, 1982.

Allen, Charles, Jr., Mar. 22, 1981.

Anonymous (B.A. 1937), Nov. 4, 1982.

Arnstein, Robert (B.A. 1941, Clinical Professor of Psychiatry), Dec. 1976, Apr. 10,
1987.

Bainton, Roland H. (B.D. 1917, Ph.D. 1921, Faculty 1920–62, Titus Street Professor Emeritus of Ecclesiastical History), Dec. 3, 1982.

Baker, Milton (B.A. 1929), Jan. 17, 1982, Oct. 29, 1982.

Bear, Regina (Friend of Lafayette B. Mendel), Nov. 10, 1980, Jan. 4, 1983.

Bergin, Thomas G. (B.A. 1925, Ph.D. 1929, Faculty 1925–30, 1948–73, Sterling
Professor Emeritus of Romance Languages), Jan. 25, 1983.

Berkun, Alvin (Synagogue Rabbi), Dec. 11, 1980.

Berliner, Robert (B.S. 1935, Administrator since 1974, Dean of the School of
Medicine), Nov. 17, 1978.

Berliss, Arthur (B.A. 1936), Jan. 3, 2000.

Bernstein, Richard (M.A. 1955, Ph.D. 1958, Faculty 1956–66, Former Associate Professor of Philosophy), Feb. 25, 1983.

Blanshard, Brand (Faculty 1945–61, Sterling Professor Emeritus of Philosophy), Oct. 8, 1980.

Brewster, Kingman, Jr. (B.A. 1941, Administration 1960–77, Former President), May 5, 1981.

Bruskin, Sydney (B.A. 1936), Dec. 16, 1982.

Burr, Ralph C. (B.A. 1944, M.A. 1946, Ph.D. 1954, Administration since 1952), Nov. 29, 1983.

Cabranes, José A. (J.D. 1965, General Counsel 1975–80), Feb. 22, 2000.

Calhoun, Robert L. (B.D. 1918, M.A. 1919, Ph.D. 1923, Faculty 1920–65, Sterling Professor Emeritus of Historical Theology), May 18, 1980.

Carroll, Richard C. (B.A. 1932, Administration 1936–68, Former Associate Dean of Yale College), Apr. 30, 1981.

Chauncey, Henry, Jr. (B.A. 1957, Administration 1957–79, Former Secretary), Dec. 3, 1982.

Cheever, Mary (Daughter of Milton Winternitz), Oct. 11, 1981, Dec. 8, 1982.

Chiel, Arthur A. (Synagogue Rabbi), Dec. 9, 1976.

Clark, R. Inslee, Jr. (B.A. 1957, Administration 1961–70, Former Dean of Undergraduate Admissions and Student Appointments), May 6, 1981.

Coffin, William S., Jr. (B.A. 1949, B.D. 1956, Religious Ministry 1954–75, Former Chaplain), Jan. 10, 1983.

Cohen, Donald J. (M.D. 1966, Faculty since 1972, Sterling Professor of Child Psychiatry, Director of the Yale Child Study Center), Dec. 20, 1999, Jan. 3, 2000, Nov. 13, 2000.

Cohen, Sylvia (Wife of Elliot Cohen), Feb. 22, 1983.

Cohen, Thomas E. (B.A. 1957, Son of Elliot Cohen), Feb. 22, 1983.

Cooperman, Jacob (B.S. 1934), Oct. 21, 1978, Sep. 15, 1980.

Cooperman, Nonnie (Assistant Registrar of the Department of Political Science and Former Secretary to the Registrar of the Law School), Oct. 21, 1978.

Cunningham, W. Jack (Faculty since 1946, Professor of Electrical Engineering), Dec. 18, 1983.

DeSilver, Harrison (B.A. 1937), Dec. 21, 1982.

Dilworth, J. Richardson (B.A. 1938, LL.B. 1942, Corporation Fellow since 1959), Feb. 24, 1983.

Doob, Leonard W. (Faculty 1934–77, Sterling Professor Emeritus of Psychology), Nov. 11, 1982, Oct. 28, 1983.

Drabkin, Irving (B.A. 1941, Former President of the Friends of the B'nai B'rith Hillel Foundation at Yale), Mar. 6, 1983.

Dyen, Isidore (Faculty since 1942, Professor of Comparative Linguistics and Austronesian Languages), Oct. 25, 1983.

Ellsworth, John S. (B.A. 1929, M.A. 1946, Ph.D. 1947, Faculty 1946–56, Administration 1956–70), Dec. 6, 1983.

Evans, Robert (President of the Graduate Club of New Haven), Sep. 15, 1980.

Feidelson, Charles (B.A. 1938, M.A. 1941, Ph.D. 1948, Faculty since 1947, Bodman Professor of English Literature), Oct. 24, 1978.

Feldman, Harold (B.A. 1939), 1978.

Felig, Philip (M.D. 1961, Faculty 1966–67 and since 1969, C. N. H. Long Professor of Internal Medicine), May 7, 1980.

Feuerstein, Sidney S. (M.D. 1945), Mar. 7, 1983.

Fleischman, Maurice (Class of 1931), Apr. 7, 1983.

Frank, Victor H., Jr. (B.A. 1950), Jan. 11, 2000.

Gabriel, Ralph H. (B.A. 1913, M.A. 1915, Ph.D. 1919, Faculty 1915–58, Sterling Professor Emeritus of History), Dec. 7, 1982.

Galston, Arthur W. (Faculty 1946–47 and since 1955, Eaton Professor of Botany and Professor of Forestry), Oct. 25, 1978.

Galton, Barry (B.A. 1954), Feb. 20, 1979.

Gelman, Aaron (Rabbi at the Young Israel Synagogue of New Haven 1956–65), June 13, 1983.

Giamatti, A. Bartlett (B.A. 1960, Ph.D. 1964, Faculty 1966–78, Administration since 1978, President of the University), Jan. 26, 1983, Feb. 16, 1983, Apr. 14, 1983, Apr. 6, 1986.

Gilman, Alfred (B.S. 1928, Ph.D. 1931, Faculty 1935–43, 1973–84, Lecturer in Pharmacology), Dec. 17, 1980.

Glick, Max (B.A. 1933), July 5, 1984.

Gold, Elijah (Ph.D. 1963), Nov. 25, 1980.

Goldin, Judah (Faculty 1958–74, Former Professor of Classical Judaica), Oct. 5, 1980, Feb. 24, 1983.

Goldstein, Abraham S. (LL.B. 1949, Faculty 1956–70, 1975–78, and since 1979, Administration 1970–75, 1978–79, Sterling Professor of Law, Former Provost, and Former Dean of the Law School), Jan. 31, 1979, Dec. 1, 1982.

Goleman, Fay (Former Social Secretary to Mrs. James R. Angell), Oct. 13, 1982.

Gralla, Howard I. (M.F.A. 1975), Feb. 14, 2000.

Greer, Daniel (LL.B. 1964), Oct. 15, 1980, Nov. 21, 1982.

Griswold, Mary (Widow of President A. Whitney Griswold), Oct. 19, 1983.

Gumbiner, Joseph (Hillel 1949–54), Nov. 27, 1979.

Hallo, William W. (Faculty since 1962, William M. Laffan Professor of Assyriology and Babylonian Literature), Nov. 2, 1982.

Hammerslough, John, Feb. 13, 1979.

Harrison, Harold E. (B.S. 1928, M.D. 1931, Faculty 1934–38), Dec. 12, 1983.

Hartman, Geoffrey (Ph.D. 1953, Faculty 1955–62, and since 1967, Professor of English and Comparative Literature), Oct. 20, 1982.

Harvey, A. McGehee, Dec. 9, 1982.

Hauser, Susi (Wugmeister) (Assistant Dean of Yale College and Former Hillel Administrator), Oct. 16, 1978, July 14, 2000.

Heil, Estelle (Daughter of George Goldman, M.D. 1910), Apr. 26, 1983.

Hershman, Lee Stock (Daughter of Bane Stock), May 16, 1983.

Hessberg, Albert, II (B.A. 1938), Feb. 25, 1980.

Hirsch, Pauline Band (B.N. 1935), Oct. 5, 1982.

Hirschhorn, Fred, Jr. (B.A. 1942), Dec. 19, 1982.

Hiscock, Ira V. (M.P.H. 1921, Faculty 1920–60, Anna M. R. Lauder Professor Emeritus of Public Health), Nov. 19, 1982, Dec. 9, 1982.

Horowitz, Miriam (Wife of William Horowitz), May 15, 1984.

Horowitz, William (B.A. 1929, Corporation Fellow 1965–71), Dec. 7, 1976, Oct. 29, 1978, Jan. 28, 1979, May 3, 1980, Nov. 19, 1982, Apr. 24, 1983, Sep. 25, 1987.

Horton, Charlotte (Religious Ministry 1929–73, Former Secretary to the Chaplain), Dec. 3, 1982.

Howe, Arthur, Jr. (B.A. 1947, Administration 1951–64), Oct. 21, 1983, Nov. 22, 1983, May 9, 1984.

Israel, Richard J. (Hillel 1959–71, Former Jewish Chaplain), Nov. 19, 1978, Sep. 29, 1980, Oct. 28, 1980, Feb. 11, 2000.

Jackson, Levi (B.A. 1950), Jan. 11, 2000.

Kashgarian, Michael (Professor of Pathology), "William Henry Welch, Milton Winternitz, and the Yale Department of Pathology," a lecture delivered before the Beaumont Medical Club at the Yale Medical Historical Library, New Haven, Jan. 16, 1981.

Kestenbaum, Lionel (B.A. 1948), May 12, 1983.

Kezerian, Stephen (University News Bureau since 1948, Director of the News Bureau), Oct. 1977.

Kra, David (B.S. 1974), Jan. 10, 1983.

Kra, Ethan (B.A.-M.A. 1969, M.Phil. 1973, Ph.D. 1974), Jan. 10, 1983.

Krall, Irving (B.A. 1930), June 15, 1983.

Kushlan, Samuel D. (B.S. 1932, M.D. 1935, Clinical Faculty since 1939, Clinical Professor of Internal Medicine), Mar. 18, 1983.

Ladin, Harvey (Curator of the Jewish Historical Society of New Haven), Apr. 30, 1980.

Lane, Helen (New Haven author), Oct. 30, 1978.

Langrock, David T. (New Haven Tailor), a tape-recorded interview by Harvey Ladin, Oct. 27, 1962, available through the courtesy of Mr. Ladin.

Lazarus, Frederick (B.A. 1934), Nov. 16, 1983.

Lerner, Max (B.A. 1923), Dec. 28, 1982.

Levin, Richard C. (Ph.D. 1974, Faculty 1974–92, Administration since 1992, Professor of Economics, Former Dean of the Graduate School, President of the University), July 25, 2000.

Levine, Hillel (Faculty 1974–82, Associate Professor of Religious Studies and Sociology), Dec. 14, 1980, May 12, 1981.

Lidz, Theodore (Faculty 1951–78, Sterling Professor of Psychiatry), Dec. 3, 1976, Dec. 1, 1982.

Liebman, Lance M. (B.A. 1962, Corporation Fellow 1971–83), Mar. 3, 1978.

Lippard, Vernon (B.S. 1926, M.D. 1929, Administration 1952–67, Former Dean of the School of Medicine), Dec. 2, 1982.

Lipset, Seymour M. (Faculty 1960–61), Apr. 12, 1981.

Lipson, Leon (Faculty since 1956, Henry R. Luce Professor of Jurisprudence), Mar. 31, 1979.

Lopez, Robert (Faculty 1946–81, Sterling Professor of History), Dec. 6, 1976.

Lovett, A. Sidney (B.A. 1913, Religious Ministry 1932–58, Woolsey Professor Emeritus of Biblical Literature and Former Chaplain of the University), Oct. 19, 1978.

Lowman, Robert M. (Clinical Faculty 1943–56, Faculty 1956–83, Professor of Radiology), Mar. 7, 1983.

Mack, Maynard (B.A. 1932, Ph.D. 1936, Faculty 1936–78, Sterling Professor Emeritus of English), Dec. 7, 1982.

Mandelbaum, David G. (Ph.D. 1936, Student of Edward Sapir), Oct. 5, 1982, Oct. 21, 1982.

Mandell, Gertrude (Daughter of Max Mandell), Nov. 12, 1982.

Marcus, Ivan G. (B.A. 1964), Jan. 10, 1983.

McDougal, Myres (J.S.D. 1931, Faculty since 1934, Sterling Professor Emeritus of Law), Apr. 5, 1992.

May, Georges (Faculty 1945–63, 1971–79, and since 1981, Administration 1963–71, 1979–81, Sterling Professor of French, Former Dean of Yale College, and Former Provost of the University), Apr. 26, 1983.

Meeks, Wayne A. (Ph.D. 1965, Religious Ministry 1965–67, Faculty since 1969, Professor of Religious Studies), Apr. 2, 1981.

Milici, Joseph (Barber for Yale-New Haven Hospital since 1941), Nov. 6, 1981.

Mintz, Sidney (Faculty 1951–74, Former Professor of Anthropology), Sep. 9, 1980.

Moore, Omar K. (Faculty 1954–63, Former Associate Professor of Sociology), Apr. 16, 1981.

Morowitz, Harold J. (B.S. 1947, M.S. 1950, Ph.D. 1951, Faculty since 1955, Professor of Molecular Biophysics), Apr. 28, 1983.

Myers, Jerome K. (M.A. 1947, Ph.D. 1950, Faculty since 1948, Professor of Sociology), Oct. 20, 1982, Oct. 26, 1983.

Newberger, Eli (B.A. 1962, M.D. 1966), Oct. 10, 1980.

Noble, Lawrence M., Jr. (B.A. 1953, Administration 1962–81), Mar. 29, 1984.

Northrop, Filmer S. C. (M.A. 1919, Faculty 1923–62, Sterling Professor Emeritus of Philosophy and Law), Oct. 12, 1980.

Och, Bernard (Hillel Director 1981), June 18, 1982.

Osgood, Cornelius (Faculty 1930–73, Professor Emeritus of Anthropology and Honorary Curator of the Peabody Museum of Natural History), Sep. 29, 1980.

Osterweis, Rollin G. (B.A. 1930, M.A. 1943, Ph.D. 1946, Faculty 1943–44, 1945–46, 1950–76, Professor Emeritus of History and Oratory and Former Director of Debate and Public Speaking and the Political Union), Dec. 12, 1976, Feb. 13, 1979, May 12, 1980, Jan. 28, 1981, Jan. 4, 1982.

Peyre, Henri M. (Faculty 1928–33, 1939–69, Sterling Professor Emeritus of French), Oct. 26, 1982.

Pierson, George W. (B.A. 1926, Ph.D. 1933, Faculty 1926–27, 1929–30, 1933–73, Larned Professor Emeritus of History and Historian of the University), interviewed on many occasions, 1980–83.

Posy, Carl (B.A. 1966, Ph.D. 1971), Dec. 22, 1980.

Press, Paul (President of J. Press, Inc.), Nov. 9, 1982.

Price, Monroe E. (B.A. 1960, LL.B. 1964), Apr. 20, 1983.

Rabinowitz, Isaac (Ph.D. 1932, Hillel 1933–34), Nov. 18, 1979, Nov. 23, 1979.

Ranis, Gustav (M.A. 1953, Ph.D. 1956, Faculty since 1956, Professor of Economics), Apr. 2, 1981.

Ranis, Rachel (Former Graduate Student in Yale Sociology Department), Apr. 30, 1981.

Redlich, Fredrick C. (Faculty 1942–67, Administration 1967–72, Former Dean of the School of Medicine), May 30, 1983, and lecture at Grace Building, Yale University, New Haven, Oct. 5, 1983.

Rittenberg, Theodor (B.A. 1931), Sep. 18, 1979.

Rose, Frederick P. (B.E. 1944, Yale Corporation), May 14, 1986.

Rosenbaum, James (B.A. 1966, Faculty 1973–79, Former Associate Professor of Sociology), Jan. 31, 1983.

Rosenbaum, Robert (B.A. 1936, Son of Joseph Rosenbaum), June 1, 1983.

Rosovsky, Henry, Dec. 29, 1982.

Ross, Arthur M., Jr. (B.S. 1934, Ph.D. 1939, Administration since 1965, Secretary to the Science Advisory Committee), Nov. 19, 1980.

Rostow, Eügene V. (B.A. 1933, LL.B. 1937, Faculty 1938–83, Sterling Professor of Law and Public Affairs), Apr. 4, 1977, Nov. 14, 1978.

Rouse, Irving (B.S. 1934, Ph.D. 1938, Faculty since 1939, Charles J. MacCurdy Professor of Anthropology), Sep. 18, 1980.

Rouse, Mary (Ph.D. 1945, Student and Secretary of Edward Sapir), Sep. 30, 1980.

Rozen, Alan A. (B.A. 1933, M.D. 1937), Interview, Oct. 26, 1987.

Sachs, Louis (B.A. 1914, LL.B. 1917), Oct. 5, 1978, Oct. 23, 1980.

Saltzstein, Arthur (B.A. 1942), Mar. 23, 1980.

Sandmel, Samuel (Ph.D. 1949, Hillel 1945–49), Oct. 19, 1978.

Sapir, Philip (B.A. 1938), Fall 1978.

Schiff, John M. (B.A. 1925), Feb. 1, 1983.

Schwartz, Richard D. (B.A. 1947, Ph.D. 1952, Faculty 1952–61; Former Assistant Professor of Sociology and Law), Oct. 9, 1980.

Senn, Milton J. E. (Faculty 1948–70, Sterling Professor Emeritus of Pediatrics and Psychiatry in the Child Study Center), June 8, 1983.

Sewall, Richard B. (Ph.D. 1933, Faculty 1934–76, Professor Emeritus of English), Oct. 17, 1978, Jan. 24, 1982.

Siskin, Edgar E. (Ph.D. 1941, Faculty 1947–48, Former Rabbi of Temple Mishkan Israel and Former Lecturer in Anthropology), Aug. 7, 1981.

Skolnick, Jerome H. (M.A. 1953, Ph.D. 1957, Faculty 1956–62, Former Assistant Professor of Sociology and Law), Apr. 2, 1981, Dec. 15, 1982.

Stoddard, Carlos F., Jr. (B.A. 1926, Administration 1948–73), Nov. 5, 1982.

Sweetkind, Morris (Ph.B. 1920, M.A. 1923), Oct. 14, 1982.

Taffel, Max (M.D. 1931, Faculty 1936–39, 1941–42, 1945–50, Clinical Faculty 1939–41, and since 1950, Clinical Professor of Surgery), Nov. 5, 1982.

Trachtenberg, Betty (Administration since 1988), Jan. 5, 2000.

Vaill, George D. (B.A. 1935, Administration 1937–76, Retired Associate Secretary of the University), Dec. 13, 1976.

Wald, Florence (Schorske) (M.N. 1941, M.S. 1956, Faculty 1957–1971, Former Dean of the Nursing School), Dec. 20, 1999.

Wald, Stephen G. (B.A. 1975), Aug. 20, 1991.

Walker, Donald K. (B.A. 1926, Administration 1948–60, Former Associate Director of the Office of Admissions and Freshman Scholarships), Dec. 13, 1982.

Wasserman, Elga R. (Administration 1962–73, Former Assistant Dean of the Graduate School), Jan. 26, 1983.

Wasserman, Harry H. (Faculty since 1948, Professor of Chemistry), Apr. 17, 1978.

Weinberg, Robert L. (B.A. 1953, LL.B. 1958), Oct. 22, 1983.

Weiner, Joseph (Ph.B. 1916), Jan. 6, 1981.

Weinstein, Louis (B.S. 1928, M.S. 1930, Ph.D. 1931, Faculty 1937–39, Former Instructor in Immunology), June 4, 1981.

Weintraub, Sam, Jr. (B.S. 1936), Apr. 20, 1983.

Weiss, Paul (Faculty 1945–68, Sterling Professor Emeritus of Philosophy), Oct. 15, 1978, Oct. 27, 1978, Sep. 29, 1980.

White, Edna (Wife of Abraham White), Nov. 23, 1980.

White, Julius (Brother of Abraham White), Dec. 17, 1980.

Wilkinson, John A. (B.A. 1960, M.A.T. 1963, Administration 1961–74, and, since 1978, Secretary of the University), Sep. 16, 1982, Apr. 21, 1983.

Winestine, Norman (B.A. 1914), Apr. 21, 1981, May 20, 1981, Mar. 20, 1983.

Winternitz, Thomas (Son of Milton Winternitz), Apr. 1, 1985.

Winternitz, William W. (Son of Milton Winternitz), Oct. 5, 1981, Dec. 12, 1982.

Wizner, Rachel (Administration 1975–80, Dean of Pierson College), Fall 1978.

Wolf, Arnold Jacob (Hillel 1972–80), Oct. 25, 1978, Sep. 28, 1980.

Wolfers, Doris (Widow of Arnold Wolfers), Dec. 15, 1982.

Wolff, Edwin L. (B.A. 1950), Jan. 10, 2000.

Yannet, Herman (M.D. 1929, Faculty 1931–40, Clinical Faculty 1940–72, Clinical Professor Emeritus of Pediatrics), Dec. 16, 1982.

Zigmond, Maurice (Ph.D. 1941, Hillel 1935–43, 1957–59), May 18, 1979, Sep. 15, 1980.

Zimmerman, Harry M. (B.S. 1924, M.D. 1927, Faculty 1928–43, Former Associate Professor of Pathology), June 2, 1981.

Zinsser, William (Alumni Magazine 1970–80, Master of Branford College and Lecturer in English), Oct. 20, 1978.

Zunder, Brendon (Son of Theodore Zunder), Dec. 27, 1982.

Zweig, Felix (B.E. 1938, Ph.D. 1941, Faculty since 1941, Professor of Engineering and Applied Science), Nov. 13, 1978.

LETTERS AND E-MAILS

Banner, James M., Jr. (B.A. 1957), Jan. 6, 1984.

Beck, George A. (Executive Director of Pi Lambda Phi Fraternity), July 28, 1983.

Brewster, Kingman, Jr. (B.A. 1941, President of Yale University 1963–77), Aug. 15, 1983.

Buckley, William F., Jr. (B.A. 1950), Nov. 15, 1978, May 24, 1983.

Dolowitz, David A. (M.D. 1937), Mar. 4, 1983, Oct. 21, 1987.

Fischoff, Ephraim (Hillel 1955–57), Dec. 2, 1979.

Freedman, Daniel X. (M.D. 1951, Faculty 1955–66, Former Professor of Psychiatry), Sep. 12, 1983.

Frost, William Lee (LL.B. 1951), Mar. 12, 1986.

Goodman, Louis S. (M.D. 1932, Faculty 1935–43), May 12, 1981, Feb. 2, 1983.

Gumbiner, Joseph (Hillel 1949–54), Feb. 21, 1983.

Israel, Richard J. [Oct. 31, 1983].

Krensky, Rosemary (Great-granddaughter of Sigmund Waterman), Dec. 9, 1976.

Lear, Maxwell (M.D. 1911, M.S. 1923, Faculty 1922–24, Clinical Faculty 1924–36), May 15, 1977, May 31, 1977.

Lowenthal, Alexander (B.A. 1920, LL.B. 1921), July 12, 1983.

Marcus, Ivan G. (B.A. 1964, Faculty since 1994, Frederick P. Rose Professor of Jewish History), Feb. 10, 2000.

McKee, Elmore M. (B.A. 1919, B.D. 1921, Religious Ministry 1927–30, Former Chaplain), July 20, 1980.

May, Georges, Oct. 6, 1980.

Mintz, Sidney, Oct. 10, 1980.

Muskat, Joseph (B.A. 1955) [May 17, 1983].

Nemoy, Leon (M.A. 1926, Ph.D. 1929, Library 1923–66, Editor Yale Judaica Series), Nov. 26, 1978.

Osterweis, Rollin G., April 30, 1977.

Persky, Orrin (B.A. 1970), Mar. 28, 1983.

Peyre, Henri M., Dec. 16, 1983.

Ponet, James (B.A. 1968, Hillel Director since 1981), Jan. 1989.

Rose, Frederick E. (B.E. 1944), Mar. 6, 1986.

Rosovsky, Henry, Aug. 22, 1983.

Rostow, Walt W. (B.A. 1936, Ph.D. 1940), Nov. 20, 1978.

Siskin, Edgar, Dec. 2, 1980, Feb. 18, 1983.

Taft, Horace (B.A. 1949, Faculty 1956–71, 1979–83, Administration 1971–79, Professor of Physics and Former Dean of Yale College) [Dec., 1980].

Weinstein, Louis (B.S. 1928, M.S. 1930, Ph.D. 1931), Apr. 27, 1983.

Weiss, Paul, Nov. 24, 1978, Oct. 15, 1980, May 21, 1981.

Williams, George H., Dec. 2, 1982.

Wolf, Dassi, Feb. 24, 1983.

PRIMARY SOURCES

The majority of the primary sources used are from the collections of the Yale Manuscripts and Archives Library (YMAL). Some of these collections as well as the other archives that were consulted are listed below with the abbreviations used for them in the notes. Where unspecified in the notes, primary sources are available in the Yale University Archives.

Following the abbreviations is a list of the major collections that were extensively examined. Listing below, however, does not imply review of every document in the following collections. Virtually all of the collections below are available for scholarly examination.

AJA	American Jewish Archives, Cincinnati, Ohio
AJHS	American Jewish Historical Society, Waltham, Massachusetts
ATH	Arthur Twining Hadley Presidential Papers
AWG	Alfred Whitney Griswold Presidential Papers
BBHFY	B'nai B'rith Hillel Foundation at Yale Papers
BRBML	Beinecke Rare Book and Manuscript Library, Yale University

CS   Charles Seymour Presidential papers
FSJ   Frederick Sheetz Jones Decanal Papers
HFSH   Hillel File of Susi (Wugmeister) Hauser, made available to the author
JHSNH   Jewish Historical Society of New Haven
JRA   James Rowland Angell Presidential Papers
OS   Office of the Secretary Papers
YIHY   Young Israel House at Yale, New Haven

Acheson, Dean, Papers, MS Group 1087, YMAL.

Angell, James Rowland, Presidential Papers, YRG 2-A-14, YMAL.

Angell, James Rowland, Personal Papers, YMAL.

B'nai B'rith Hillel Foundation at Yale Papers, Bingham Hall, Yale University, New Haven.

Carroll, Richard C., Dean of Undergraduate Affairs Papers, YMAL.

Committee on Educational Policy of the Yale Corporation, Minutes of 1919–49, Yale University Records of the Secretary, YRG 4-A-15, Add. July 1978, YMAL.

Corwin, Robert Nelson, Chairman of the Yale Athletic Association Papers, YMAL.

Flexner, Abraham, Papers, Library of Congress Manuscript Collection.

Griswold, Alfred Whitney, Presidential Papers, YRG 2-A-16, YMAL.

Hadley, Arthur Twining, Presidential Papers, YRG 2-A-13, YMAL.

Hallo, William W., and Meeks, Wayne A., "A Proposal for Judaic Studies at Yale," May 1980.

Hillel Files of Susi Hauser, A collection of primary material and copies of primary source material compiled by Richard J. Israel and Susi Hauser, and shared with the author by Susi Hauser.

Hurwitz, Lawrence S., "The Stanford Minyon," an oral tape recollection of Stanford University policies regarding religious worship in the 1960s, shared with the author by Lawrence S. Hurwitz.

Johnson, Alvin S., Papers, MS Group 615, YMAL.

Jones, Frederick S., Decanal papers, YRG 9-A-2, YMAL.

Laws of Yale College, 1721–1772, YMAL.

Medical School Board of Permanent Officers, Minutes of, 1920–50, Yale Medical School Deans' Files, Box 25, YMAL.

Medical School Records, YRG 27-A, YMAL.

Mendel, Lafayette B., Papers, MS Group 1146, YMAL.

Pierson, George W., Collection, YMAL.

Reports to the President of Yale University, YMAL.

Saurer, David Lee, "Women at Yale," Yale Miscellaneous Manuscripts S, Group No. 1258, YMAL.

Secretary, Office of the, Papers, YRG 4-A, YMAL.

Seymour, Charles, Presidential Papers, YRG 2-A-15, YMAL.

"Shylock," Initiation Play, Class of 1891 to Class of 1892, May 23, 1890, Delta Kappa Epsilon Records, YMAL.

Stiles, Ezra, *Itineraries,* BRBML.

Stiles, Ezra, *Literary Diary,* BRBML.

Stiles, Ezra, *Miscellaneous Volumes,* BRBML.

Troostwyk, Isidor, Scrapbooks, copies lent to the author by Werner Hirsch.

University Committee on Judaic Studies, Minutes of 1979–81, lent to the author by William W. Hallo.

Winternitz, Milton C., Papers, YMAL.

Yale Corporation, Minutes of the Meetings of, 1701–1933, YMAL.

Yale Hillel Foundation Papers, AJHS.

Young Israel House at Yale History File, YIHY.

Zigmond, Maurice, "1939–40 annual report of the Counselor to Jewish Students," HFSH.

SECONDARY SOURCES

Daily newspaper articles are not referenced in the list below, but are referenced in the endnotes.

Acts of the General Assembly of Connecticut with Other Permanent Documents. New Haven: The Tuttle, Morehouse & Taylor Co., 1871, 1878, 1889, 1901.

"Admissions: III." *Yale Daily News.* Sep. 23, 1957, p. 2.

"A. F. of L. to Investigate Harvard Stand on Jews." *The American Hebrew* III (June 30, 1922): 176.

Alderman, Abraham S. "A Literary Approach to Life in the New Haven Ghetto." In *Jews in New Haven, Vol. 2.* Ed. by Barry E. Herman, pp. 140–49. New Haven: Jewish Historical Society of New Haven, 1979.

Alderman, Joseph. "Khesdeb's Quest." *The Yale Literary Magazine* 80 (Dec. 1914): 124–33.

———. "The Still Small Voice." *The Yale Literary Magazine* 79 (May 1914): 369–75.

———. "Yale Life of the New Haven Student." In *1915 Sheffield Scientific School Class Book.* 1915, pp. 365–69.

Alegi, Peter C. "A History of Catholicism at Yale to 1943." Departmental essay in American studies, 1956, available through the St. Thomas More House at Yale, New Haven, Conn.

The Alexander Kohut Memorial Foundation, A Review of Activities 1915–1972. New York: American Academy for Jewish Research, 1973.

Allen, Charles R., Jr. "The Strange Case of V. D. Samarin." *Jewish Currents* 30 (May 1976): 4–13, 30–33.

"The Ambiguities of Public Morality." *Yale Daily News.* Oct. 6, 1959, p. 2.

"The American Jew Today." *Newsweek* 77 (Mar. 1, 1971): 56–64.

American Jewish Biographies. New York: Lakeville Press, 1982.

Ames, William. *"Oratio Inauguralis, Franequere habita, Anno 1622, Maij 7.* In *Rescriptio Scholastica & brevis* (Volume 2: *Disceptatio Scholastica de circulo Pontificio),* pp. 77–92. Leyden, 1633.

Andersen, Ruth O. M. *From Yankee to American.* Series in Connecticut History, ed. by David M. Roth. Chester, Conn.: The Pequot Press, 1975.

Angell, James Rowland. "Dr. Winternitz as Dean of the School of Medicine." *Yale Journal of Biology and Medicine* 22 (July 1950): 469–70.

Anti-Defamation League of B'nai B'rith. *Purpose and Program.* New York, 1983.

Antonovsky, Aaron. "Aspects of New Haven Jewry." In *YIVO Annual of Jewish Social Science, Volume 10,* pp. 128–40. New York: YIVO Institute for Jewish Research, 1955.

Appel, John J. "Jews in American Caricature: 1820–1914." *American Jewish History* 71 (Sep. 1981): 103–33.

Arias, Benedicti, ed. *Biblia Hebraica.* 1609.

Asch, Sholem. "A Word about My Collection of Jewish Books." In *Catalogue of Hebrew and Yiddish Manuscripts and Books from the Library of Sholem Asch.* Compiled by Leon Nemoy. New Haven: Yale University Library, 1945.

"Association of Literary Societies." *The Occident* 24 (Oct. 1866): 334–35.

Astrachan, Anthony. "Class Notes." In *My Harvard, My Yale.* Ed. by Diana Dubois, pp. 210–21. New York: Random House, 1982.

Baer, Jean. *The Self-Chosen.* New York: Arbor House, 1982.

Bagg, Lyman. *Four Years at Yale.* New York: Henry Holt & Company, 1871.

Bainton, Roland H. *Yale and the Ministry.* New York: Harper & Brothers, 1957.

Baird's Manual of American College Fraternities. Ed. by John Robson. Menasha, Wis.: George Banta, Co., 1963.

Baldwin, Simeon E. "The Ecclesiastical Constitution of Yale College." In *Papers of the New Haven Colony Historical Society, Volume 3.* New Haven: New Haven Colony Historical Society, 1882.

Ballard, Allen B. *The Education of Black Folk.* New York: Harper & Row, Publishers, 1973.

Baltzell, E. Digby. *The Protestant Establishment.* New York: Random House, 1964.

———. "The Protestant Establishment Revisited." *The American Scholar* 45 (Autumn 1976): 499–518.

Band, Arnold. "Jewish Studies in American Liberal Arts Colleges and Universities." *American Jewish Year Book 1966.* Ed. by Morris Fine and Milton Himmelfarb, pp. 3–26. Philadelphia: The Jewish Publication Society of America, 1966.

Baserga, Susan J. "The Early Years of Coeducation at the Yale University of Medicine." *The Yale Journal of Biology & Medicine* 53 (May–June 1980): 181–90.

Bass, Paul. "Ben & Shmully Talk." *New Haven Advocate* (Feb. 3, 2000): 12–15.

Beardslee, John W., ed. *Reformed Dogmatics.* New York: Oxford University Press, 1965.

Belden, Ezekiel Porter. *Sketches of Yale College with Numerous Anecdotes.* New York: Saxton & Miles, 1843.

Bell, Whitfield, Jr. "The Medical Institution of Yale College, 1810–1885." *Yale Journal of Biology and Medicine* 33 (Dec. 1960): 169–83.

Benesch, Alfred A. "The Jew at Harvard." *The New Era* 4 (Feb. 1904): 56–60.

Bergin, Thomas G. "My Native Country." In *My Harvard, My Yale.* Ed. by Diana Dubois, pp. 160–69. New York: Random House, 1982.

———. *Yale's Residential Colleges; the First Fifty Years.* New Haven: Yale University, 1983.

Birmingham, Stephen, *"Our Crowd."* New York: Harper & Row, Publishers, 1967.

Blanshard, Brand. "Democracy and Distinction in American Education." In *On the Meaning of the University.* Ed. by Sterling M. McMurrin, pp. 29–49. Salt Lake City, Utah: University of Utah Press, 1976.

Bloomgarden, Lawrence. "Medical School Quotas and National Health." *Commentary* 15 (Jan. 1953): 29–37.

———. "Our Changing Elite Colleges." *Commentary* 29 (Feb. 1960): 150–54.

B'nai Jacob One Hundred Years. Woodbridge, Conn.: Congregation B'nai Jacob, 1982.

Boas, Ralph P. "Who Shall Go to College?" *The Atlantic Monthly* 130 (Oct. 1922): 441–48.

Braverman, Harold. "Medical School Quotas." In *Barriers: Patterns of Discrimination Against Jews.* Ed. by Nathan C. Belth, pp. 74–77. New York: Friendly House Publishers, 1958.

Brewster, Kingman, Jr. "Introduction." To *Stover at Yale,* by Owen Johnson, pp. v–vii. New York: The Macmillan Co., 1968.

Brigham, Carl C. *A Study of American Intelligence.* Princeton, N.J.: Princeton University Press, 1923.

Broun, Heywood, and Britt, George. *Christians Only.* New York: The Vanguard Press, 1931.

Brustein, Robert. *Making Scenes.* New York: Random House, 1981.

Buckley, William F., Jr. *God and Man at Yale.* Chicago: Henry Regnery Co., 1951.

———. "God and Man at Yale: Twenty-Five Years Later." In *A Hymnal.* Ed. by William F. Buckley, Jr., pp. 415–47. New York: G. P. Putnam's Sons, 1978.

Buckley, Christopher. "A Keening of Weenies." In *My Harvard, My Yale.* Ed. by Diana DuBois, pp. 260–77. New York: Random House, 1982.

Butler, Pierce. *Judah P. Benjamin.* Philadelphia: George W. Jacobs & Co., 1906.

Cabot, Richard C. *Social Science and the Art of Healing.* New York: Dodd, Mead, & Co., 1931.

Camp, Walter, and Welch, Lewis Sheldon. *Yale: Her Campus, Class-Rooms, and Athletics.* Boston: L. C. Page & Co., 1899.

Canby, Henry Seidel. *Alma Mater: The Gothic Age of the American College.* New York: Farrar & Rinehart, Inc., 1936.

Caro, Robert A. *The Powerbroker, Robert Moses and the Fall of New York.* New York: Alfred A. Knopf, 1974.

Carter, Paul J. *Waldo Frank.* New York: Twayne Publishers, Inc., 1967.

Catalogue of the Legal Fraternity of Phi Delta Phi. Ed. by George A. Katzenberger. Ann Arbor, Mich.: The Inland Press, 1897.

Catlin, Daniel, Jr. *Liberal Education at Yale, The Yale College Course of Study 1945–1978.* Washington, D.C.: University Press of America, 1982.

Chiel, Arthur A. "Ezra Stiles—The Education of An Hebraician." *American Jewish Historical Quarterly* 60 (Mar. 1971): 235–41.

———. "The Kohut Judaica Collection at Yale." In *Jews in New Haven.* Ed. by Jonathan D. Sarna, pp. 80–94. New Haven: Jewish Historical Society of New Haven, 1978.

———. "Looking Back." *The Connecticut Jewish Ledger.* 1972–83.

———. "The Mystery of the Rabbi's Lost Portrait." *Jewish Digest* 28 (Nov. 1982): 45–49.

———. "Stiles and the Jews: A Study in Ambivalence." In *Jews in New Haven, Volume 3.* Ed. by Barry E. Herman and Werner S. Hirsch, pp. 118–34. New Haven: Jewish Historical Society of New Haven, Inc., 1981.

Chittenden, Russell H. *Biographical Memoir of Lafayette Benedict Mendel.* Washington, D.C.: National Academy of Sciences, 1937.

———. *History of the Sheffield Scientific School.* New Haven: Yale University Press, 1928.

Clap, Thomas. *The Annals or History of Yale College.* New Haven: John Hotchkiss & B. Mecom, 1766.

———. *A Catalogue of the Library of Yale College in New Haven.* New London, Conn.: L. Groen, 1743.

————. *The Religious Constitution of Colleges, Especially of Yale College*. New London, Conn., 1754.

Class Histories of Yale College, Sheffield Scientific School, and the Yale School of Medicine.

"Class of 1912S Notes." *Yale Alumni Magazine* 36 (Apr. 1973): 43.

"Class of 1979 Notes." *Yale Alumni Magazine* 63 (Feb. 2000): 84.

Coffin, William Sloane, Jr. *Once to Every Man*. New York: Atheneum, 1978.

Cohen, Elliot E. "The Promise of the American Synagogue." *The Menorah Journal* 4 (Oct. 1918): 278–86 and (Dec. 1918): 368–74.

Cohen, Morris R. *A Dreamer's Journey*. Glencoe, Ill.: The Free Press, 1949.

————. "Publisher's Forword." *Jewish Social Studies* 1 (Jan. 1939): 3–4.

Cohen, Steven Martin. *Patterns of Interethnic Marriage and Friendship in the United States*. Ann Arbor, Mich.: Xerox University Microfilms, 1974.

Coombs, Orde. "The Necessity of Excellence: Making It at Yale." *Change* 5 (June 1973): 49–54.

"Current Topics." *The New Era* 5 (Aug. 1875): 523–24.

Dahl, Robert A. *Who Governs?* New Haven: Yale University Press, 1961.

Dahl, Robert A.; Kessen, William; Spence, Jonathan D.; Taft, Horace D.; and Wasserman, Elga. *Report of the Study Group on Yale College 1972*. New Haven: Yale University, 1972.

Dalin, David G. "A History of Brandeis University." *Midstream* 25 (June/July 1979): 98.

Danzis, Max. "The Jew in Medicine." *The American Hebrew and Jewish Tribune* 134 (Mar. 23, 1934): 372, 391, 401, and (Mar. 30, 1934): 414.

Dawidowicz, Lucy S. "Max Weinreich (1894–1969): The Scholarship of Yiddish." In *American Jewish Year Book 1969*. Ed. by Morris Fine and Milton Himmelfarb, pp. 59–68. New York: The American Jewish Committee, 1969.

"Dean Winternitz." *The Yale Scientific Magazine* 7 (Autumn 1932): 15–16, 19, 25.

Dexter, Franklin Bowditch. *Biographical Sketches of the Graduates of Yale College with Annals of the College History October, 1701–May, 1745*. New York: Henry Holt & Co., 1885.

————. *Biographical Sketches of the Graduates of Yale College with Annals of the College History, May, 1745–May, 1763*. New York: Henry Holt & Co., 1896.

————. *Biographical Sketches of the Graduates of Yale College with Annals of the College History, May, 1763–July, 1778*. New York: Henry Holt & Co., 1903.

————. *Biographical Sketches of the Graduates of Yale College with Annals of the College History, July, 1778–June, 1792*. New York: Henry Holt & Co., 1907.

————. *Biographical Sketches of the Graduates of Yale College with Annals of the College History, June, 1792–September, 1805*. New York: Henry Holt & Co., 1911.

————. *Biographical Sketches of the Graduates of Yale College with Annals of the College History, 1805–1816*. New Haven: The Tuttle, Morehouse & Taylor Press, 1912.

————. *On Some Social Distinctions at Harvard and Yale Before the Revolution*. Worcester, Mass.: Press of Charles Hamilton, 1894.

Dexter, Franklin Bowditch, ed. *Documentary History of Yale University*. New Haven: Yale University Press, 1916.

Dinnerstein, Leonard. "Anti-Semitism Exposed and Attacked, 1945–1950." *American Jewish History* 71 (Sep. 1981): 134–49.

Discriminations in College Admissions. Ed. by Francis J. Brown. Washington, D.C.: American Council on Education, 1950.

Divine, Robert A. *American Immigration Policy, 1924–1952.* New Haven: Yale University Press, 1957.

Doob, Leonard W.; DeVane, William C.; Hutchinson, G. Evelyn; Miller, John Perry; Pottle, Frederick A., Rostow, Eugene V., and Schrader, George A., Jr. "The Education of First Year Students in Yale College." *Yale Alumni Magazine* 25 (June 1962): 8–13.

"Dormitories and Democracy." *Yale Alumni Weekly* 15 (Dec. 6, 1905): 184.

"Dr. Magnes in New Haven." *The American Hebrew,* 91 (June 7, 1912): 168.

Earnest, Ernest. *Academic Procession.* Indianapolis: Bobbs-Merrill Co., 1953.

Echikson, William. "From Oak Street to Yale and Beyond." *Yale Alumni Magazine and Journal* 45 (Nov. 1981): 29–33.

"Editorial." *The American Hebrew* 112 (Sep. 29, 1922): 529.

"Editorial." *The Yale Sheffield Monthly* 21 (Apr. 1915): 360.

"Edward Sapir." *Jewish Social Studies* 1 (Apr. 1939): 142.

Elzas, Barnett A. *The Jews of South Carolina.* Philadelphia: J. B. Lippincott Co., 1905.

Encyclopaedia Judaica. 1972 ed.

Engel, Edward. "Lehrer." *Die Deborah* 8 (Oct. 31, 1862): 68.

Epstein, Benjamin R., and Foster, Arnold. "Barriers in Higher Education." In *Barriers: Patterns of Discrimination Against Jews.* Ed. by Nathan C. Belth, pp. 60–73. New York: Friendly House Publishers, 1958.

Ettinger, Shmuel. "The Modern Period." In *A History of the Jewish People.* Ed. by H. H. Ben-Sasson, pp. 727–1096. Cambridge, Mass.: Harvard University Press, 1976.

Exon, Joseph. *A Plaine and Familiar Explication (by way of Paraphrase) Of All the Hard Texts of the whole Divine Scripture.* London: M. Flesher, 1633.

Falk, Leslie A. "E. Richard Weinerman, M.D., M.P.H." *The Yale Journal of Biology and Medicine* 44 (Aug. 1971): 3–23.

Feingold, Henry L. *A Midrash on American Jewish History.* Albany: State University of New York, 1982.

Feld, Edward. "Jewish Professors Coming Home." *Sh'ma* 21 (Jan. 11, 1991): 33–34.

Fellman, Bruce. "A Home of One's Own." *Yale Alumni Magazine* 59 (Nov. 1995): 32–39.

Fermi, Laura. *Illustrious Immigrants.* Chicago: University of Chicago Press, 1971.

Feuer, Lewis S. *The Scientific Intellectual.* New York: Basic Books, Inc., 1963.

———. "The Stages in the Social History of Jewish Professors in American Colleges and Universities." *American Jewish History* 71 (June 1982): 432–65.

"First Meetings." *The Menorah Journal* 2 (Dec. 1916): 325.

Fisch, Dov. "The Libel Trial of Robert Edward Edmondson: 1936–1938." *American Jewish History* 71 (Sep. 1981): 79–102.

Fischoff, Ephraim. "The Jewish Student at Yale." *Yale Alumni Magazine* 21 (Dec. 1957): 15–17.

"The Flavor of Harvard." *The American Hebrew* 111 (Aug. 25, 1922): 351.

Fletcher, Scott. "Separatism or Support? 15 Years at the Afro-Am Center." *The New Journal* 16 (Apr. 20, 1984): 25–31.

Flexner, Abraham. *Abraham Flexner: An Autobiography.* New York: Simon & Schuster, 1960.

———. *I Remember.* New York: Simon and Schuster, 1940.

————. *Medical Education in the United States and Canada.* Buffalo, N.Y.: The Heritage Press, 1973, pp. 199–200. Reprint of 1910 original report.

Förster, J. *Dictionarium hebraicum novum.* Basilae, 1564.

Frank, Waldo. *Memoirs of Waldo Frank.* Ed. by Alan Trachtenberg. Amherst: The University of Massachusetts Press, 1973.

"Fraternities: The Benign Irrelevancy." *1969 Yale Banner,* pp. 242–47. 1969.

"Fraternities, Jewish." *Universal Jewish Encyclopedia,* vol. 4, p. 423. 1962.

Friedenwald, Harry. *The Jews and Medicine.* Baltimore: The Johns Hopkins Press, 1944.

Furniss, Edgar S. *The Graduate School of Yale.* New Haven: The Yale Graduate School, 1965.

Gabriel, Ralph Henry. *Religion and Learning at Yale.* New Haven: Yale University Press, 1958.

Gannett, Lewis S. "Is America Anti-Semitic?" *The Nation* 116 (Mar. 21, 1923): 330–32.

Gay, Peter. "Weimar Culture." In *Perspectives in American History, Volume 2.* Ed. by Donald Fleming and Bernard Bailyn. Cambridge, Mass.: Charles Warren Center for Studies in American History, 1968.

Genizi, Haim. "American Interfaith Cooperation on Behalf of Refugees from Nazism, 1933–1945." *American Jewish History* 70 (Mar. 1981): 347–61.

Giamatti, A. Bartlett. "Address to the New England Regional Board, Anti-Defamation League of B'nai B'rith, Boston, Massachusetts, Nov. 7, 1982." A copy of which was shared with the author by A. Bartlett Giamatti.

————. *History of Scroll and Key.* [New Haven]: Scroll and Key Society, 1978.

————. "Statement by the President." *University Grievance Procedures and Yale Policies on Affirmative Action and Non-Discrimination, Supplement to the Yale Weekly Bulletin and Calendar.* Sep. 17, 1981.

Ginzburg, Benjamin. "May Jews Go to College?" *The American Hebrew* 111 (June 16, 1922): 130.

Glazer, Nathan. *American Judaism.* Chicago: University of Chicago Press, 1972.

Glazer, Nathan, and Moynihan, Daniel Patrick. *Beyond the Melting Pot.* Cambridge, Mass.: The MIT Press, 1963, 1970.

Goldberg, Jacob A. "Jews in the Medical Profession—A National Survey." *Jewish Social Studies* 1 (July 1939): 327–36.

Goldstein, Abraham. "A Law School Memoir." *Yale Alumni Magazine and Journal* 15 (Feb. 1977): 38–39.

Goldstein, Alice. "The Coordinated Use of Data Sources in Research on the Demographic Characteristics and Behavior of Jewish Immigrants to the United States." *American Jewish History* 72 (Mar. 1983): 293–308.

Goldstein, Sidney. "American Jewry, 1970: A Demographic Profile." In *American Jewish Year Book, 1971.* Ed. by Morris Fine and Milton Himmelfarb, pp. 3–38. New York: The American Jewish Committee, 1971.

Goodman, Lenn Evan. *Rambam.* New York: Viking Press, 1976.

Gorelick, Sherry. *City College and the Jewish Poor.* New Brunswick, N.J.: Rutgers University Press, 1981.

Goren, Arthur A. "Jews." In *Harvard Encyclopedia of American Ethnic Groups.* Ed. by Stephan Thernstrom, pp. 571–99. Cambridge, Mass.: Harvard University Press, 1980.

Gornick, Vivian. "A Woman among the Ivy Fellows." *The Nation* 227 (Nov. 18, 1978): 544–48.

Gossett, Thomas F. *Race: The History of an Idea in America.* New York, Schocken Books, 1963.

Gourman, Jack. *The Gourman Report.* Northridge, Cal.: National Education Standards, Inc., 1980.

"Governor Orders Inquiry at Harvard." *The American Hebrew* 111 (June 9, 1922): 128.

The Graduates Club. New Haven: Tuttle, Morehouse, & Taylor Press, 1901, 1903, 1906, 1909, 1911, 1913, 1915, 1919, 1921, 1925, 1930, 1938, 1963, 1967.

Greenberg, Louis. *The Jews in Russia, Volume 2.* Ed. by Mark Wischnitzer. New Haven: Yale University Press, 1951.

Greenberg, Meyer. "The Jewish Student at Yale: His Attitude Toward Judaism." *YIVO Annual of Jewish Social Science* 1 (1946): 217–30.

Grumet, Elinor. "Elliot Cohen: The Vocation of a Literary Mentor." *Studies in the American Jewish Experience, Volume 1.* Ed. by Jacob R. Marcus and Abraham J. Peck, pp. 8–25. Cincinnati: American Jewish Archives, 1981.

Grusd, Edward. *B'nai B'rith: The Story of a Covenant.* New York: Appleton-Century, 1966.

Hadley, Arthur T. "Before the Yale Menorah Society, October 14, 1914." *The Menorah Journal* 1 (Jan. 1915): 45–46.

Hammond, Mason. "A Harvard Armory, Part I." *Harvard Library Bulletin* 29 (July 1981): 261–83.

Handlin, Oscar. "American Views of the Jew at the Opening of the Twentieth Century." *Publications of the American Jewish Historical Society* 40 (June 1951): 323–44.

——. *Race and Nationality in American Life.* Boston: Little, Brown & Company, 1948.

——. *The Uprooted.* Boston: Little, Brown & Company, 1951.

Handlin, Oscar, and Handlin, Mary F. *The American College and American Culture.* Berkeley, Calif.: The Carnegie Commission on Higher Education, 1970.

——. "Religious Intolerance." In *Immigration as a Factor in American History.* Ed. by Oscar Handlin. Englewood Cliffs, N.J.: Prentice-Hall, Inc., 1959.

Hapgood, Norman. "Jews and College Life." *Harper's Weekly* 62 (Jan. 15, 1916): 53–55.

Harding, T. Swann. "Another Jew Without Money." *The Atlantic Monthly* 148 (Aug. 1931): 166–70.

Harris, Leon. *Merchant Princes.* New York: Harper & Row, Publishers, 1979.

"Harry Shulman." *Yale Law Report* 1 (1955): 6–9.

"The Harvard Policy of 'Limitation.'" *The American Hebrew* 111 (Sep. 29, 1922): 529.

"Harvard President Explains University's Position." *The American Hebrew* 111 (June 23, 1922): 162.

"Harvard to Take a Year for Its Investigation." *The American Hebrew* 111 (June 30, 1922): 176.

"Harvard Vindicates the American Spirit." *The American Hebrew* 112 (Apr. 13, 1923): 714.

Harvey, A. McGehee. *Science at the Bedside.* Baltimore: The Johns Hopkins University Press, 1981.

Havemeyer, Loomis. *Eating at Yale 1701–1965.* New Haven: Yale University, 1965.

——. *"Go to Your Room."* [New Haven]: Yale University, 1960.

——. *Out of Yale's Past.* [New Haven, 1960?].

———. *Sheff Days and Ways.* New Haven, 1958.

Heil, Estelle G. "Achevah Offered Camaraderie to Yale University's Jews." *The Connecticut Jewish Ledger.* May 24, 1984, p. 2.

Heitler, Sara. "Blueprints of a Life: The Story of Jim Ponet." *Urim v'Tumim* 7 (Winter 1992): 6–7.

Henry, David D. *Challenges Past, Challenges Present.* San Francisco: Jossey-Bass Publishers, 1975.

Higham, John. *Send These to Me.* New York: Atheneum, 1975.

———. *Strangers in the Land.* New Brunswick, N.J.: Rutgers University Press, 1955.

Hirsch, H. N. *The Enigma of Felix Frankfurter.* New York: Basic Books, Inc., 1981.

Historical Register of Yale University, 1701–1937. New Haven: Yale University, 1939.

Historical Register of Yale University, 1937–1951. New Haven: Yale University, 1952.

Historical Register of Yale University, 1951–1968. New Haven: Yale University, 1969.

A History of Columbia University 1754–1904. New York: The Columbia University Press, 1904.

Hoadly, Charles J., ed. *The Public Records of the Colony of Connecticut, Volume 6.* Hartford: Press of Case, Lockwood & Brainard, 1872.

Hofstadter, Richard. *Anti-intellectualism in American Life.* New York: Alfred A. Knopf, Inc., 1966.

Holden, Reuben. *Profiles and Portraits of Yale University Presidents.* Freeport, Me.: The Bond Wheelwright Co., 1968.

———. *Yale: A Pictorial History.* New Haven: Yale University Press, 1967.

Hood, Louis. "The Ancient and Modern Jew." *The Yale Literary Magazine* 43 (June 1878): 413–18.

Hook, Sidney. *Out of Step: An Unquiet Life in the 20th Century.* New York: Harper & Row, 1987.

Horchow, R. "Yale University." *The Menorah Journal* 1 (Jan. 1915): 69.

Howe, Irving. *World of Our Fathers.* New York: Harcourt Brace Jovanovich, 1976.

Hudson, Robert P. "Abraham Flexner in Perspective: American Medical Education 1865–1910." In *Sickness and Health in America.* Ed. by Judith Walzer Leavitt and Ronald L. Numbers, pp. 105–15. Madison, Wis.: University of Wisconsin Press, 1978.

Huehner, Leon. "Jews in the Legal and Medical Professions in America Prior to 1800." *Publications of the American Jewish Historical Society* 22 (1914): 147–65.

———. "The Jews of New England (Other than Rhode Island) Prior to 1800." *Publications of the American Jewish Historical Society* 11 (1903): 75–99.

Hurwitz, Henry. "The Menorah Movement." *The Menorah Journal* 1 (Jan. 1915): 50–55.

"Inside Yale." *Yale Weekly Bulletin and Calendar.* Oct. 20–27, 1980, p. 3.

"Iota." *The Mirror* 1 (Dec. 25, 1922): 7.

"IOTA Yale University." *The Shield* 1 (Oct. 1930): 14–15.

"Is the Ivy League Still the Best?" *Newsweek* 64 (Nov. 23, 1964): 65–70.

Israel, Richard J. "Jews at Yale." An unpublished manuscript, revised 1980, shared with the author by Richard J. Israel.

———. "The Rabbi on Campus." *Judaism: A Quarterly Journal of Jewish Life and Thought* 16 (Spring 1967): 188.

————. "The Yale Seal." *Yale Alumni Magazine* 30 (Feb. 1967): 4–6.

Janick, Herbert F., Jr. *A Diverse People*. Series in Connecticut History, ed. by David M. Roth. Chester, Conn.: The Pequot Press, 1975.

————. "Catholicism and Culture: The American Experience of Thomas Lawrason Riggs, 1888–1943." *The Catholic Historical Review* 68 (July 1982): 451–68.

"The Jew." *The Yale Literary Magazine* 12 (Aug. 1847): 419–22.

"Jewish Fraternities and Sororities." *The Jewish Tribune*. June 5, 1925, pp. 6–7, 16.

"The Jews and the Colleges." *The American Hebrew* III (June 9, 1922): 109.

"Jews on University Faculties." *Contemporary Jewish Record* 2 (May–June 1939): 86–87.

Johnson, Owen. *Stover at Yale*. New York: The Macmillan Company, 1912, 1968.

Johnson, Samuel. "Autobiography." In *Samuel Johnson, President of King's College, Volume 1*. Ed. by Herbert Schneider and Carol Schneider, pp. 5–6. New York: Columbia University Press, 1929.

Joselit, Jenna Weissman. "Without Ghettoism: A History of the Intercollegiate Menorah Association, 1906–1930." *American Jewish Archives* 30 (Nov. 1978): 133–54.

Jospe, Alfred. "Jewish College Students in the United States." In *American Jewish Year Book, 1964*. Ed. by Morris Fine and Milton Himmelfarb, pp. 131–45. Philadelphia: The Jewish Publication Society of America, 1964.

J. P. G. *The American Israelite* 38 (Jan. 6, 1882): 221.

————. "New Haven." *The American Israelite* 31 (July 25, 1884): 5.

————. "New Haven, Conn." *The American Israelite* 28 (Feb. 17, 1882): 266.

Kalman, Laura. *Legal Realism at Yale, 1927–1960*. Chapel Hill, N.C.: University of North Carolina Press, 1986.

Karabel, Jerome. "Status-Group Struggle, Organizational Interests, and the Limits of Institutional Autonomy. The Transformation of Harvard, Yale, and Princeton, 1918–1940." *Theory and Society* 13 (Jan. 1984): 1–40.

Karp, Abraham J. *To Give Life*. New York: Schocken Books, 1981.

Kaylin, Jennifer. "The New Man Takes Command." *Yale Alumni Magazine* 56 (Summer 1993): 32–37.

Kelley, Brooks Mather. *Yale: A History*. New Haven: Yale University Press, 1974.

Kennedy, Ruby Jo Reeves. "Single or Triple Melting Pot? Intermarriage in New Haven, 1870–1950." *American Journal of Sociology* 57 (July 1952): 56–59.

Kessner, Thomas. *The Golden Door*. The Urban Life in America Series, ed. by Richard C. Wade. New York: Oxford University Press, 1977.

Kingdon, Frank. "Discrimination in Medical Colleges." *The American Mercury* 61 (Oct. 1945): 391–99.

Kingman Brewster, Remembrances. New Haven: Yale University, 1997.

Kinkead, Katharine T. "The Brightest Ever." *The New Yorker* 36 (Sep. 10, 1960): 132–81.

Kisch, Guido. "Two American Jewish Pioneers of New Haven." *Historia Judaica* 4 (Apr. 1942): 16–37.

Koenig, Samuel. *Immigrant Settlements in Connecticut: Their Growth and Characteristics*. Hartford: Connecticut State Department of Education, 1938.

Kohut, George Alexander. *Ezra Stiles and the Jews*. New York: Philip Cowen, 1902.

Korn, Bertram Wallace. *Eventful Years and Experiences*. Cincinnati: The American Jewish Archives, 1954.

Kosman, Josh, and Leaf, Louise. "The Early Years." In *100: A History of the Yale Daily News*, p. 6. New Haven: OCD Foundation, 1978.

Kraeling, Carl H. "Yale's Collection of Judaica." *The Yale University Library Gazette* 13 (Apr. 1939): 85–94.

Krapin, Louis. "The Decline of Fraternity Bias." In *Barriers: Patterns of Discrimination Against Jews*. Ed. by Nathan C. Belth, pp. 78–88. New York: Friendly House Publishers, 1958.

Kriger, Lewis H. "Jewish Varsity Athletes." *The Menorah Journal* 2 (Oct. 1916): 262–63.

Kuslan, Richard D. "Education of a Noted Reformer." *Yale Alumni Magazine and Journal* 47 (Oct. 1983): 52–55.

Lamm, Robert. "Christian God and Jewish Man at Yale." *Response* 8 (Fall 1974): 7–16.

Lee, Calvin B. T. *The Campus Scene: 1900–1970*. New York: David McKay Co., Inc., 1970.

Leggett, John. *Who Took the Gold Away*. New York: Random House, 1969.

Lever, Janet, and Schwartz, Pepper. *Women at Yale, Liberating a College Campus*. Indianapolis: The Bobbs-Merrill Company, Inc., 1971.

Levin, Harry. "Two *Romanisten* in America: Spitzer and Auerbach." In *Perspectives in American History, Volume 2*. Ed. by Donald Fleming and Bernard Bailyn, pp. 464–69. Cambridge, Mass.: Charles Warren Center for Studies in American History, 1968.

Levinson, Benjamin. "Yale University." *The Menorah Journal* 3 (Feb. 1917): 59–60.

Lewis, Harry Sinclair. "Editor's Table." *The Yale Literary Magazine* 71 (Apr. 1906): 287–88.

———. "Unknown Undergraduates." *The Yale Literary Magazine* 71 (June 1906): 335–38.

Lieberman, Elias. "Yale Athletics and Jewish Athletes." *The American Hebrew* 111 (June 30, 1922): 174, 178.

Lipset, Seymour Martin, and Ladd, Everett Carll, Jr. "Jewish Academics in the United States: Their Achievements, Culture, and Politics." In *American Jewish Year Book, 1971*. Ed. by Morris Fine and Milton Himmelfarb, pp. 89–128. Philadelphia: The Jewish Publication Society of America, 1971.

Lipset, Seymour Martin, and Riesman, David. *Education and Politics at Harvard*. New York: McGraw-Hill, 1975.

"Louis Sachs Dies at 88." *The New Haven Jewish Ledger*. May 20, 1982, p. 1.

Mack, Maynard. *A History of Scroll and Key*. [New Haven]: Scroll and Key Society, 1978.

Marcus, Ivan G. "Bringing Judaica to the Liberal Arts." *Yale Alumni Magazine and Journal* 45 (Nov. 1981): 25–28.

Marcus, Jacob R. *The American Jewish Woman, 1654–1980*. Cincinnati: American Jewish Archives, 1981.

———. *The Colonial American Jew, 1492–1976*. Detroit: Wayne State University Press, 1970.

Marrus, Michael R. "The Theory and Practice of Anti-Semitism." *Commentary* 74 (Aug. 1982): 41.

Mason, Steven J. "The Jewish Fraternity as a Jewish Socializing Agency." Thesis for ordination, Hebrew Union College, Cincinnati, 1976, AJA.

Mauceri, John. "An Explosion of Music All Over Yale." *Yale Alumni Magazine* 40 (June 1977): 24–25.

McLean, Mary D. "Jews in Athletics." *The New Era* 5 (1904): 273–78.

Meade, Robert Douthat. *Judah P. Benjamin.* New York: Oxford University Press, 1948.

Melamed, S. M. "The Academic Boycott." *The Reflex* 1 (Dec. 1927): 3–8.

The Menorah Movement. Ann Arbor, Mich.: The Intercollegiate Menorah Association, 1914.

"Menorah Prize Competitions." *The Menorah Journal* 2 (Dec. 1916): 323.

Mooney, Carolyn J. "New Yale Head Is Both Traditional and Ground-breaking Choice." *The Chronicle of Higher Education* 39 (Apr. 28, 1993): A15–A16.

Moore, Deborah Dash. *B'nai B'rith and the Challenge of Ethnic Leadership.* Albany: State University of New York Press, 1981.

Moore, Paul, Jr. "A Touch of Laughter." In *My Harvard, My Yale.* Ed. by Diana Dubois, pp. 196–208. New York: Random House, 1982.

Moore, R. Laurence. "Insiders and Outsiders in American Historical Narrative and American History." *The American Historical Review* 87 (Apr. 1982): 390–413.

Morgan, Edmund S. *The Gentle Puritan: A Life of Ezra Stiles, 1727–95.* New Haven: Yale University Press, 1962.

Morgenstern, Julian. "American Judaism Faces the Future." *The American Hebrew* 111 (Sep. 22, 1922): 447, 498–99, 502, 510.

Morison, Samuel Eliot. *The Founding of Harvard College.* Cambridge, Mass.: Harvard University Press, 1935.

———. *Harvard College in the Seventeenth Century.* Cambridge, Mass.: Harvard University Press, 1936.

———. "Harvard Seals and Arms." *The Harvard Graduates' Magazine* 42 (Sep. 1933): 1–15.

———. *Three Centuries of Harvard 1636–1936.* Cambridge, Mass.: Belknap-Harvard University Press, 1965.

Morley, Jefferson, and Ressler, Marcy. "1960–1970." In *100: A History of the Yale Daily News,* p. 59. New Haven: OCD Foundation, 1978.

The Mory's Association, Inc. New Haven: The Mory's Association, Inc., 1928.

Mulgrew, Sharon Austin. "Autonomy Vs. Integration, The History of the Relocation of the Yale Psychiatric Institute." M.P.H. essay for the Department of Epidemiology and Public Health, Yale University, 1977.

Nemoy, Leon. "The Alexander Kohut Memorial Collection of Judaica." *The Yale University Library Gazette* 2 (Oct. 1927): 17–25.

———. "George Alexander Kohut." *The Yale University Library Gazette* 9 (Jan. 1935): 96–98.

"New Haven, Conn." *Die Deborah* 9 (Nov. 6, 1863): 75.

"News Items." *The Occident* 3 (Jan. 1846): 526.

"News Items." *The Occident* 3 (Feb. 1846): 572.

Noyes, Edward S. "Selecting Him." In *Seventy-five: A Study of a Generation in Transition.* New Haven: Yale Daily News, 1953.

O'Connell, Mary-Kathleen. "British Israelites: The Chosen People in the Nineteenth century." An unpublished essay, dated April 29, 1977, lent to the author by Sydney Ahlstrom.

Oren, Dan A. "Why Did Judah P. Benjamin Leave Yale?" *A Jewish Journal at Yale* 2 (Fall 1984): 13–17.

Osterweis, Rollin G. "Mishkan Israel 1840–1940." *The Congregation Mishkan Israel Bulletin,* Dec. 10, 1971.

———. "Mishkan Israel—Since 1940." In *Jews in New Haven, Volume 3.* Ed. by Barry E. Herman and Werner S. Hirsch, pp. 98–100. New Haven: Jewish Historical Society of New Haven, 1981.

———. *Judah P. Benjamin.* New York: G. P. Putnam's Sons, 1933.

———. *Three Centuries of New Haven, 1638–1938.* New Haven: Yale University Press, 1953.

———. "Who Was Yale's First Jewish Football Star?" JHSNH.

"Ovid in Ossining." *Time* 83 (Mar. 27, 1964): 70.

Peck, Sarah. "Should Yale University Support Religious Institutions on Campus?" Sept. 5, 1976, manuscript shared with the author by Arnold Jacob Wolf.

Peet, J. Carlisle. "Of Discourse." *The Yale Literary Magazine* 79 (May 1914): 335–38.

Perry, Helen Swick. *Psychiatrist of America, The Life of Harry Stack Sullivan.* Cambridge, Mass.: The Belknap Press of Harvard University, 1982.

Pierson, George W. *The Education of American Leaders.* New York: Frederick A. Praeger, Publishers, 1969.

———. *The Founding of Yale: The Legend of the Forty Folios.* New Haven: Yale University Press, 1988.

———. *A Yale Book of Numbers.* New Haven: Yale University, 1983.

———. *Yale College: An Educational History, 1871–1921.* New Haven: Yale University Press, 1952.

———. *Yale: A Short History.* New Haven: Office of the Secretary, Yale University, 1979.

———. *Yale: The University College, 1921–1937.* New Haven: Yale University Press, 1955.

Pliskin, Zelig. *Love Your Neighbor.* Jerusalem: Yeshiva Aish HaTorah, 1977.

Ponet, James. "Giamatti on Rabbi Tarphon." *The National Jewish Post and Opinion* (Sep. 13, 1989): N8.

Postal, Bernard, and Koppman, Lionel. *American Jewish Landmarks, Volume 1.* New York: Fleet Press Corporation, 1977.

Power, Edward J. *Catholic Higher Education in America.* New York: Appleton-Century Crofts, 1972.

"The Presidential Search." *Yale Alumni Magazine and Journal* 41 (Sep. 1977): 5.

Price, Monroe E. "Undergraduate Yale." *Yale Alumni Magazine* 23 (May 1960): 25.

Proceedings of the Union of American Hebrew Congregations. Union of American Hebrew Congregations, 1935, 1936, 1937, 1938, 1941.

Ram's Horn. 1950–54, HFSH, YMAL.

Reingold, Nathan. "Refugee Mathematicians in the United States of America, 1933–1941: Reception and Reaction." *Annals of Science* 38 (1981): 313–38.

Reynolds, James B.; Fisher, Samuel H.; and Wright, Henry E., eds. *Two Centuries of Christian Activity at Yale.* New York: G. P. Putnam's Sons, 1901.

Reznikoff, Charles. "New Haven: The Jewish Community, A Portrait Sketch." *Commentary* 4 (Nov. 1947): 465–77.

Richler, Jen. "When There's No Home Away From Home." *The Yale Herald* (Apr. 9, 1999): 1, 7.

Ritterband, Paul, and Wechsler, Harold S. *Jewish Learning in American Universities.* Bloomington: Indiana University Press, 1994.

Rose, Louise Blecher. "The Secret Life of Sarah Lawrence." *Commentary* 75 (May 1983): 52–56.

Rosen, Anna. "Attic Envy." *A Jewish Journal at Yale*. Summer 1983, pp. 34–37.

Rosenbloom, Joseph R. *A Biographical Dictionary of Early American Jews*. Lexington: University of Kentucky Press, 1960.

Rosenfield, Leonora Cohen. *Portrait of a Philosopher: Morris R. Cohen*. New York: Harcourt, Brace & World, Inc., 1962.

Rosovsky, Henry. "Then and Now: The Jewish Experience at Harvard." *Moment* 5 (June 1980): 20–28. Also published as "From Periphery to Center." *Harvard Magazine* 82 (Nov./ Dec. 1979): 81–82, 89–91.

Rossiter, Margaret W. *Women Scientists in America: Struggles and Strategies to 1940*. Baltimore: The Johns Hopkins University Press, 1982.

Rostow, Eugene V. "The Japanese American Cases—A Disaster." *The Yale Law Journal* 54 (June 1945): 489–533.

———. "The Jew's Position." *Harkness Hoot* 2 (Nov. 23, 1931): 45–59.

Roth, David M., and Meyer, Freeman. *From Revolution to Constitution*. Series in Connecticut History, ed. by David M. Roth. Chester, Conn.: The Pequot Press, 1975.

"Rutenberg Named Assistant Chaplain." *Newsletter of the University Chaplain's Office*. May 1981, p. 1.

Rywell, Martin. *Judah Benjamin, Unsung Rebel Prince*. Asheville, N.C.: The Stephens Press, 1948.

Sale, J. Kirk. "The New School at Middle Age." *Change* 1 (Jul.–Aug. 1969): 37–45.

Sandweiss, Kate. "Not Just a Matter of Luck." *Yale Alumni Magazine and Journal* 47 (Oct. 1983): 56–59.

Santayana, George. "A Glimpse of Yale." *The Harvard Monthly* 15 (Dec. 1982): 89–97.

Sapir, Edward. *Selected Writings of Edward Sapir*. Ed. by David G. Mandelbaum. Berkeley: University of California Press, 1949.

Sarna, Jonathan D. "A Jewish Student in Nineteenth Century America: The Diary of Louis Ehrich—Yale '69." In *Jews in New Haven*. Ed. by Jonathan D. Sarna, pp. 70–79. New Haven: Jewish Historical Society of New Haven, 1978.

———. "Jews in New Haven: A Preliminary Bibliography." In *Jews in New Haven*. Ed. by Jonathan D. Sarna, pp. 133–37. New Haven: Jewish Historical Society of New Haven, 1978.

Schiff, Judith A. "Colonel Isaac Ullman: Philanthropist, Politician, and Patriot." In *Jews in New Haven, Volume 2*. Ed. by Barry E. Herman, pp. 32–40. New Haven: Jewish Historical Society of New Haven, 1979.

Schwab, John C. "The Yale College Curriculum." *Educational Review*. June 1901. YMAL.

Seldes, Lee. *The Legacy of Mark Rothko*. New York: Holt, Rinehart & Winston, 1978.

Shapiro, Alfred. "Racial Discrimination in Medicine." *Jewish Social Studies* 10 (Apr. 1948): 103.

"The Shot Heard Round the World." *The American Hebrew* 112 (Apr. 20, 1923): 745.

Shulman, Albert M. *The Religious Heritage of America*. San Diego: A. S. Barnes & Co., Inc., 1981.

Siegel, Steven W. *Archival Resources*. Jewish Immigrants of the Nazi Period in the USA Series, ed. by Herbert A. Strauss. New York: K. G. Saur, 1978.

Singer, Mark. "God and Mentsch [*sic*] at Yale." *Moment* 1 (July–Aug. 1975): 27–31.

Singerman, Robert. "The American Career of the *Protocols of the Elders of Zion.*" *American Jewish History* 71 (Sep. 1981): 48–78.

Slavin, Stephen L., and Pradt, Mary A. *The Einstein Syndrome.* Washington, D.C.: University Press of America, 1982.

Slosson, Edwin E. *Great American Universities.* New York: Macmillan, 1910.

Snyder, Charles. "Why Leave Harvard to Go to Yale." Mar. 21, 1978. An unpublished manuscript made available to the author by Arthur J. Viseltear.

Solomon, Barbara Miller. *Ancestors and Immigrants.* Cambridge, Mass.: Harvard University Press, 1956.

Spinrad, Bernard I., and Neitlich, Mark W. "The Horns of the Dilemma." *Hilleli.* Nov. 1944.

———. "An Uphill Struggle." *Hilleli.* Nov. 1944.

Spodick, Edward F. "The History of Congregation Mishkan Israel." An unpublished manuscript, JHSNH.

"The Steady Hand." *Time* 57 (June 11, 1951): 74–82.

Steiger, Paul E. "Publish or Perish." *Yale Alumni Magazine* 28 (Apr. 1965): 12–19.

Steinberg, Stephen. *The Academic Melting Pot.* New York: McGraw-Hill Book Co., 1974.

———. *The Ethnic Myth.* New York: Atheneum, 1981.

———. "How Jewish Quotas Began." *Commentary* 52 (Sep. 1971): 67–76.

Stern, Malcolm H. *First American Jewish Families: Six Hundred Genealogies, 1654–1977.* New York: American Jewish Archives, 1978.

———. "The Function of Genealogy in American Jewish History." In *Essays in American Jewish History.* Cincinnati: American Jewish Archives, 1958.

Stetler, Henry G. *College Admissions Practices With Respect to Race, Religion and National Origin of Connecticut High School Graduates.* Hartford: Connecticut State Inter-Racial Commission, 1949.

———. *New Study of College Admissions Practices With Respect to Race, Religion and National Origin.* Hartford: Connecticut Commission on Civil Rights, 1953.

Stokes, Anson Phelps. *Memorials of Eminent Yale Men.* New Haven: Yale University Press, 1914.

Strum, Harvey. "Louis Marshall and Anti-Semitism at Syracuse University.' *American Jewish Archives* 35 (Apr. 1983): 1–12.

"A Study of Religious Discrimination in Social Clubs." In *Race, Class, and Power.* Ed. by Raymond W. Mack, pp. 95–102. New York: American Book Company, 1963.

Synnott, Marcia Graham. *The Half-Opened Door.* Westport, Conn.: Greenwood Press, 1979.

———. "*The Half-Opened Door.* Researching Admissions Discrimination at Harvard, Yale, and Princeton." *American Archivist* 45 (Spring 1982): 175–82.

———. *A Social History of Admissions Policies at Harvard, Yale, and Princeton, 1900–1930.* Ann Arbor, Mich.: University Microfilms, 1974.

Taft, John. *Mayday at Yale.* Boulder, Colo.: Westview Press, 1976.

Thelin, John R. *The Cultivation of Ivy.* Cambridge, Mass.: Schenkman Publishing Co., 1976.

Tremellius, ed. *Testament Veteris Biblia Sacra.* Geneva, 1590.

"University Menorah Addresses." *The Menorah Journal* 1 (Dec. 1915): 321.

Urofsky, Melvin J. *A Voice That Spoke for Justice.* Albany, N.Y.: State University of New York Press, 1982.

Van Dusen, Albert E. *Puritans Against the Wilderness.* Series in Connecticut History, ed. by David M. Roth. Chester, Conn.: The Pequot Press, 1975.

Vannorsdall, John. "Pastor's Column." *Newsletter of the University Chaplain's Office.* May 1981, p. 1.

Veysey, Laurence R. *The Emergence of the American University.* Chicago: University of Chicago Press, 1965.

Villee, Claude A., Jr. "Book Review." *New England Journal of Medicine* 309 (July 28, 1983): 247–48.

Viseltear, Arthur J. "C.-E. A. Winslow and the Early Years of Public Health at Yale, 1919–1925." *The Yale Journal of Biology and Medicine* 55 (Mar. / Apr. 1982): 137–151.

Wade, Harold Jr. *Black Men of Amherst.* Amherst, Mass.: Amherst College Press, 1976.

Wald, Alan. "The Menorah Group Moves Left." *Jewish Social Studies* 37 (Summer–Fall 1976): 289–320.

Walsh, Mary Roth. *Doctors Wanted: No Women Need Apply.* New Haven: Yale University Press, 1977.

Warch, Richard. *School of the Prophets, Yale College, 1701–1740.* New Haven: Yale University Press, 1973.

Warner, Robert Austin. *New Haven Negroes: A Social History.* New Haven: Yale University Press, 1940.

Wechsler, Harold. *The Qualified Student.* New York: John Wiley & Sons, 1977.

Wechsler, Judah. "New Haven." *The American Israelite* 26 (Feb. 1876): 5.

W. H. W. "Discipline of College Life." *The Yale Literary Magazine* 23 (Dec. 1857): 98.

Weil, Clarence, ed. *Zeta Beta Tau, The First Twenty-Five Years.* New York: Zeta Beta Tau Fraternity, 1923.

Weir, John Ferguson. "Memories of a Yale Professor." *Yale University Library Gazette* 32 (Jan. 1958): 93–98.

Weisberg, Jacob. "Cavett Will Return to Yale to Give Class Day Address." *Yale Daily News.* Commencement, 1984, pp. 8, 19.

Whitehead, John S. "The Jewish Fraternity at Yale College." [1976?], an unpublished manuscript shared with the author by John Whitehead.

———. *The Separation of College and State.* New Haven: Yale University Press, 1973.

Whitfield, Stephen J. "From Publick Occurrences to Pseudo-Events: Journalists and Their Critics." *American Jewish History* 72 (Sep. 1982): 52–81.

"Who's Who in the Colleges." *The American Hebrew* 112 (Dec. 1, 1922): 63, 116–21, 125, 132–33.

Wiebe, Robert H. *The Search for Order, 1877–1920.* New York: Hill & Wang, 1967.

Williams, George H. *Wilderness and Paradise in Christian Thought.* New York: Harper & Brothers, 1962.

Winternitz, Milton C. "Medical Education at Yale University." *Yale Alumni Weekly* 41 (Jan. 29, 1932): 345–47.

Witherspoon, Alexander M. *The Club: 1838–1963.* New Haven: The members of The Club, 1964.

Wolf, Arnold Jacob. "Jewish Experience Is Vividly Present at Yale." *Yale Alumni Magazine* 36 (Jan. 1973): 14.

Wollebius, Johannes. *The Abridgment of Christian Divinitie.* A translation by Alexander Ross of *Compendium Theologiae Christianae.* London: Joseph Nevill, 1660.

———. *Compendium Theologiae Christianae.* Oxford, 1661.

Woolsey, Theodore D. "The Course of Instruction in Yale College." In *Yale College.* Ed. by William L. Kingsley, pp. 495–502. New York: Henry Holt & Co., 1879.

Wugmeister, Susi. "A 'Yeshivah' for Non-Believers." *Education in Judaism* 15 (May–June 1968).

Yale Banner. New Haven: Yale Banner Publications.

The Yale Saturday Evening Pest 1 (Feb. 17, 1923).

Yale University Catalogue. New Haven: Yale University.

Yale University Obituary Record. New Haven: Yale University, 1901, 1914, 1916, 1927, 1933, 1935, 1936, 1939.

Zborowski, Mark, and Herzog, Elizabeth. *Life Is with People.* New York: International Universities Press, Inc., 1952.

Zeta Beta Tau Fraternity, Inc. *A Manual for Zeta Beta Tau.* 1927.

Zigmond, Maurice L. "The Jewish Office at Yale—Some Reminiscences." 1962, HFSH.

Zweigenhaft, Richard L., and Domhoff, G. William. *Jews in the Protestant Establishment.* New York: Praeger Publishers, 1982.

Index

Acheson, Dean, 291, 433
Adams, Eliphalet, 340
Adler, Felix, 395
Adler, Fred, 139–40
Admissions, School of Medicine, 156–60, 306, 429
Admissions, Undergraduate: financial need, 24, 65, 216, 222–23; Latin requirement, 41; staff, 42, 196, 216; process, 42, 65, 193, 198–200; Limitation of Numbers, 45, 55–60, 64–65, 68, 157, 173, 306, 335; alumni children, 59, 212, 227–28; minorities, 60, 197, 205, 214–15, 225–27, 276; and religion, 60–61, 123–24, 190, 196, 205, 210, 214–15, 383, 415, 417; and personality, 196; academic achievement, 196, 198–200, 219; geographic distribution, 212–13; women, 276, 418. *See also* Board of Admissions
African-Americans: 21, 107, 241, 322, 387,

431; in Law School, 29; undergraduate admissions and financial aid, 77, 197–98, 210, 214–15, 225, 276, 419; on faculty, 127, 289; in medical schools, 156–57, 159, 162, 276, 405, 429; in senior societies, 174, 197, 408–09; housing arrangements, 178, 220, 323; in Connecticut, 194; in American society, 225; in New Haven, 239; in dining halls, 267; on Yale Corporation, 294, 434; form Alpha Phi Alpha, 379–80; employees, 387; excluded from School of Nursing, 406
Alderman, Abraham, 36, 74, 83, 130
Alderman, Joseph S., 35–37, 75, 378–79
Altman, Sidney, 292, 319
Alumni, 136, 323; and admissions, 41–42, 59, 200, 212, 227–28, 418; and Brewster administration, 228; non-support of Jewish ministry, 245; on Yale Corporation, 294

Connecticut: 294; laws regarding religion, 3–4, 11; Jews, 31, 44, 53, 194, 371; source of Yale undergraduates, 63–64, 423; Agricultural Experiment Station, 122; Inter-Racial Commission, 192–94, 260, 413; Commission on Civil Rights, 194; Legislature considers antidiscrimination bills, 203, 272, 273, 280, 415; Board of Education, 205, 294; General Assembly, 340, 341

Conservative Jews, 233, 235, 316, 426

Cook, Albert Stanburrough, 129

Corbey Court, 176–77, 409

Corbin, Arthur, 291

Cornyn, William, 396

Corwin, Robert Nelson: on Jewish enrollment, 45–46, 47–48, 49, 53, 55–56, 58, 59–60, 62–63, 64–65, 67; retirement, 65; on "Negro question," 77; praises Lafayette B. Mendel, 124

Coughlin, Charles E., 67, 135

Counselorship to Jewish students, 115–18

Cover, Robert M., 317

Cox, Oscar S., 136

Cross, Wilbur L., 45, 55, 64, 137

Cullman Family, 319

Cunningham, W. Jack, 415

Curriculum, 30, 103, 104, 148, 279, 342

Cushing, Harvey, 148, 151

Cutler, Timothy, 344

Daggett, David L., 138

Daggett, Naphtali, 5

Dahl, Robert A., 289

Dasey, Kathleen, 272

Daube, David, 245, 423

Davie, Maurice, 198

Davis, Jefferson, 9

Day, George Edward, 364

Day, George P., 89

Day, Jeremiah, 8–9, 111, 303

de Laguna, Grace, 285–86

Debate teams, 84

"Deep Thinkers," 137–38

Depression, 59, 64, 100, 187, 398

DeVane, William Clyde: 292, 337, 397, 410; calls for intellectual emphasis, xxii–xxiii, 195; on admission of women, 202, 415; on Freshman Year committee, 217; on absences for religious holidays, 251, 252, 425; on public nature of Yale, 335

Dilworth, J. Richardson, 80, 176, 225, 297

Dining, 87, 155, 176, 256–60, 261, 267, 408, 425–27. *See also* Commons Dining Hall and Kosher dining

Diplomas, 341, 346

Divinity School, 84, 103, 213, 287, 364, 365, 392

Dolowitz, David, 153

Doob, Leonard W., 217, 418

"Doob Committee," 216–19, 224, 306, 418

Dormitories, 24–25, 37, 56, 376, 425

Douglas, William O., 136

Drabkin, Irving, 79

Drama School, 292

Dress code, 408

Drugs, 184

DuBois, W. E. B., 77

Dudley, Samuel W., 251

Durfee Hall, 235–36

"Dusty Bucks," 178–79

Dwight Hall: 47, 107; supports "townies," 35, 74, 75–76; YMCA adjunct, 106, 117; encourages blacks to apply to Yale, 198; accommodates Jewish activities, 117, 236, 242

Dwight, Timothy: appoints Benjamin Silliman, 6–7, 164; rejects faculty, 103–04, 147; dislikes foreigners for faculty, 120, 134

Dworkin, Ronald, 433

Dyen, Isidore, 279, 430

East European Jews: 21, 70, 139, 233, 403; upbringing, 30; versus German Jews, 31; play basketball, 84; joining elite groups, 327

401–07, 428–29; Albany, 150;
Meharry, 156; Association of American,
157; Chicago, 160; Albert Einstein, 276;
Boston University, 407; Cornell, 407,
428

Meeks, Wayne A., 365

Mendel, Lafayette B.: ancestry, 28; faculty
member, 121–24, 164, 165, 324, 395;
Graduate Club member, 138, 139, 142

Mendell, Clarence W., 61, 99, 114, 138

Mendenhall, Thomas, 198

Merrill, Mrs. Selah, 364

Merriman, Daniel, 180

Merritt, Alfred K., 45

Meyer, Eugene Isaac, 28

Meyer, Eugene, 3d, 117

Milford Academy, 33, 378, 379

Miller, John Perry, 217, 296, 432

Mishkan Israel, Temple, 11, 107, 113, 117,
123, 430

Morgan, Edmund M., 135

Morgenthau, Henry, Jr., 176

Morgenthau, Robert, Jr., 176–77

Mory's Association, 79, 138, 181, 236, 388

Moses, Robert, 38, 39, 379

Mullowney, John J., 156

Murdock, George Peter, 143–44

Muskat, Joseph, 252–53, 256–58

Myers, Nathan C., 14

NAACP, 294

Napier, B. Davie, 424

Nathan, Frederick, 176–77

National Council of Christians and Jews,
114, 159

National Institutes of Health, 269

Native Americans, 11

Nazism, 100, 142, 191, 270, 418

Nettleton, George H., 83

New Haven: 105, 106, 139; town-gown relations, 35–37, 59, 67–68, 74, 104, 149,
239, 321; Jewish community, 9–10, 31–
33, 118, 244; clothes-dealers, 20, 72,
374–75; East European Jews, 21, 32;

Jewish students, 31, 37, 44, 56, 67–68,
74, 84–85, 111, 380; streets, 32–33, 34,
37, 154; Jewish population, 53; political
strength of Jews, 63, 384; synagogues,
11, 107, 115, 117, 123, 430; landlords,
220; clubs, 300–02, 330; Italians, 381

New Haven High School, 54, 95

New Haven Hospital, 148–49, 150, 235,
294, 406

"New Lights," 344

New School for Social Research, 134, 272

New York City, 84, 196, 202, 223, 294, 414

New York State, 31, 44, 159, 188, 191–92,
280

Newberger, Eli, 175, 409

Nordheimer, Isaac, 395

North, Simeon, 8

Northrop, Filmer S. C., 132, 282, 287

Noyes, Edward S.: 187, 201; on bias in admissions, 192–93, 195; increases public
high school representation in college,
199; discourages traditional Jewish observance, 250

Nursing, School of, 405

Obermann, Julian J., 364, 397

Och, Bernard, 316, 317

Old-boy network, 27

Old Campus, 74, 76, 115, 216, 235–36

Old Clothes men, 20, 374–75

"Old Lights," 344

Orchestra, 84

Oren, Dan A., 436, 437

Orthodox Jews, 84, 233, 249–50, 253, 316,
317, 438–89. *See also* Traditional Jews

Osborne, Thomas Burr, 122

Osterweis, Rollin, 91, 101, 280, 301–02,
307, 430

"Outsiders," 331–33

Palestine, 21, 110, 234–35, 243

Palmer, Arthur H., 109

Parsons, Francis, 62

Passover, 328, 425–26